IRM DIRECTORY OF STATISTICS OF INTERNATIONAL INVESTMENT AND PRODUCTION

IRM DIRECTORY OF STATISTICS OF INTERNATIONAL INVESTMENT AND PRODUCTION

John Dunning and John Cantwell

Institute for Research and Information on Multinationals

with the assistance of
Paz E. Tolentino and Faith Province

M
MACMILLAN
REFERENCE
BOOKS

Published by MACMILLAN PUBLISHERS LTD
(Journals Division) 1987
Distributed by Globe Book Services Ltd
Brunel Road, Houndmills
Basingstoke, Hants RG21 2XS, England

British Library Cataloguing in Publication Data

Dunning, John H.
IRM Directory of statistics of international
investment & production.
1. Investment, Foreign—Statistics
I. Title
332. 6'73' 021 HG 4538

ISBN 0-333-40435-1

Printed in Great Britain

TABLE OF CONTENTS

ACKNOWLEDGEMENTS

This volume would not have been possible in its present form but for the help and support of numerous friends in the academic community, and official contacts of theirs and ours all over the world. A great many of the individual country entries compiled in Section A have travelled back and forth between us and our correspondents, and they have been substantially improved as a result of their comments and suggestions. In some cases this has led us to use entirely new sources or publications, in preference to those that we had originally found. Indeed, in a few notable instances – Italy and Portugal especially come to mind – the research on which our colleagues in the country in question were themselves directly engaged provided us with new information.

Firstly, however, we must thank colleagues and students at Reading who have given us assistance at one time or another. Jeremy Clegg (now in Bath), Paul Walker (now in Portsmouth), Joanne Hilton, Paula dos Santos (studying in Reading while on leave from Lisbon) and Gaby Engel have all contributed to our efforts, helping us to search and process new data. In the later stages Joanne Hilton performed the invaluable task of proof reading and copy editing much of Section A. The original typesetting of tables was done by Debbie Blessett in the College of Estate Management at Reading, while the corrected proofs and comparative tables and text were prepared by Pat Rathgay and her colleagues at Technical Typing Services in Wokingham.

Some of our correspondents deserve particular mention for their lengthy and detailed responses to our earliest efforts. Julien Savary, of the University of Social Sciences in Toulouse gave us extensive comments which helped us to improve the tables for France. We have incorporated his suggested alterations and additional sources. In the case of the Portuguese entry, we are indebted to Vitor Simoes of the Foreign Investment Institute in Lisbon. Not only did he provide us with constructive remarks on every table in the entry, but he also supplied us with supplementary statistical information which enabled us to eliminate various gaps. Juan José Durán Herrera of the Autonomous University of Madrid made important contributions which have helped us to extend the coverage of our data on Spain. He sent us a series of revised and updated statistics, and again helped us to plug a number of gaps with new information. The Italian entry, as well, could not have been properly compiled without regular discussions with our friends in that country. Gianfranco Viesti and Giovanni Balcet of the Institute of Social Research in Milan provided us with a range of new data, and helped us to resolve some of the discrepancies in the official data. The results of their own research (carried out with Fabrizio Onida) was instrumental in some of our calculations. The work of Francesca Sanna Randaccio and Nicola Acocella at the University of Rome also proved helpful in this respect.

It is difficult to do full justice to all the many others who have helped and encouraged us at various stages of our work. We list many of them below, but undoubtedly we have missed some who perhaps gave us useful hints at conferences or other meetings, or put us in touch with contacts of their own. We would like to express our gratitude to all the following, who have pointed us in the direction of new sources, or directly provided additional information; we have grouped them according to the country whose data they were kind enough to assist us with.

Argentina: Eduardo White of CEDREI (Centre for the Study of International Economic Relations).

Australia: Tom Parry of the University of New South Wales; D Scoullar of the Foreign Investment Division of the ABS (Australian Bureau of Statistics); M J Sattler, Director of Information Services at the ABS; and F G H Pooley, First Assistant Secretary at the Australian Treasury.

Austria: Kanitz Coreth, Werner Fiala and colleagues of the Austrian National Bank.

Belgium: Daniel Van Den Bulcke of the Economische Hogeschool Limburg; A Nyssens, Economist, and W Brumagne, Chief of Statistics at the National Bank of Belgium.

Brazil: Reinaldo Goncalves of UNCTAD in Geneva.

Canada: A E Safarian of the University of Toronto; Alan Rugman of Dalhousie University; and John McVey, Christie Richards, and Athos Sani at Statistics Canada.

Chile: Fernando Albavera and Eugeno Lahera of the United Nations Unit in Santiago.

Denmark: Andreas Wildt, Head of the Balance of Payments Section at Denmarks Statistik; Christian Estrup of M & A International; and Kurt Pederson of the Arhus School of Business Administration, Economics and Modern Languages.

Finland: Seija Kulkki of the Foreign Finance Department at the Bank of Finland; and Reijo Luostarinen, Director of the FIBO (Finland's International Business Operations) Research Project at the Helsinki School of Economics.

France: Julien Savary of the University of Toulouse 1; Charles Albert Michalet of the University of Paris X; and Dominique de Laubier of CEPII (Centre for International Research and Information).

W. Germany: Helmut Kruger of the Deutsche Bundesbank; and Paulgeorg Juhl of Fachhochschule Offenburg.

Greece: Nicos Nanopoulos of the World Bank.

India: Sanyaya Lall of the Institute of Economics and Statistics at Oxford; and V N Channa of the Indian Investment Centre.

Ireland: Dermot McAleese of the University of Dublin; Michael O'Sullivan of University College, Cork; and Paul Turpin, Secretary of the National Economic and Social Council.

Italy: Gianfranco Viesti and Giovanni Balcet of the IRS (Institute of Social Research) in Milan; Francesca Sanna Randaccio and Nicola Acocella of the University of Rome; Guido Rey of ISTAT (The Central Institute of Statistics); and Massimo Roccas and Carlo Santini of the Bank of Italy.

Jamaica: Omri Evans of Paul Chen-Young and Associates.

Japan: Terutomo Ozawa of Colorado State University; Toshikazu Nakase of Osaka Industrial University; and Y Tanzawa of JETRO (Japan Trade Centre).

Kenya: N A Rweyemamu of the Commonwealth Secretariat.

S. Korea: Bohn-Young Koo of the Korea Development Institute; and Eul Park of the World Bank.

Morocco: Zoubair Hakam, currently studying at the University of Reading.

Netherlands: Henry de Jong of the University of Amsterdam; Mivan Nieuwkerk and various officials at the Bank of the Netherlands.

New Zealand: The Director of the Investment Unit at the Department of Trade and Industry; and the Secretary of the Overseas Investment Commission.

Nigeria: James Landi of the University of Jos.

Norway: Liv Bjornland of Statistik Santralbyra; Egil Gunnery of Norges Bank; and Ivar Bredesen of Finnmark Distriktshogskole.

Portugal: Vitor Simoes of the IIE (Foreign Investment Institute).

Philippines: Glory Chanco and Meynardo Orbeta of the Board of Investments; and A Z Tiangco of the Central Bank of the Philippines.

Singapore: Pang Eng Fong of the University of Singapore; the Chief Statistician at the Department of Statistics; and Madhev Kadambi, Ph.D. candidate at the University of Reading.

Spain: Juan José Durán Herrera and Maria Paloma Sánchez Muñoz of the Autonomous University of Madrid.

Sweden: Birgitta Swedenborg of the Economic-Secretariat; and Gunilla Lundholm of Statistics Sweden.

Switzerland: Kuno Hamisegger and Silvio Borner of the University of Basel.

Taiwan: Chi Schive of the National Taiwan University.

Thailand: Chaiyawat Wibulswasdi of the Bank of Thailand; and Somjate Archaviboonyobone, former student at the University of Reading.

Trinidad and Tobago: Trevor Farrell of the University of the West Indies.

Turkey: Asim Erdilek of Cape Western Reserve University; and Ibrahim Cakir of the Foreign Investment Department of the State Planning Organisation.

USA: R David Belli and George Kruer of the Bureau of Economic Analysis in the Department of Commerce; Allan Lenz of the International Trade Administration in the Department of Commerce; and Philip Lincoln of the Office of Investment Affairs in the Department of State.

Yugoslavia: Marjan Svetlicic of the Research Centre for Cooperation with developing countries.

Africa (general): Vincent Cable of the Commonwealth Secretariat, B W Mutharika of the United Nations ECA/UNCTC Joint Unit on TNCs in Addis Ababa; and Raphael Kaplinsky of the University of Sussex.

Asia (general): Friedrich von Kirchbach of the United Nations ECAP/UNCTC Joint Unit on TNCs in Bangkok.

Latin America (general): Jan Knakal and Fernando Albavera of the United Nations ECLA/UNCTC Joint Unit on TNCs in Santiago; and Eduardo White of CEDREI in Buenos Aires.

Finally, we would like to thank Geoffrey Hamilton, Georges Sandeau, Sue Mitchell and Anthony McCall of the IRM, and Andy Williams and David Clutterbuck of Macmillan Reference Books, who have helped and encouraged us throughout the various different stages of our project. None of those that we have mentioned are responsible for any errors or omissions that remain. With this qualification, we are quite happy to acknowledge that the preparation of this book has been a genuinely cooperative effort.

PREFACE

It is one of the curious aspects of the huge upsurge of interest in the theme of multinational companies which took place in the late sixties and seventies that no centralized data-gathering body was set up to measure foreign direct investment flows between countries. This lack of a data-base resource is perhaps more surprising when it is considered that this interest in the role of these companies stimulated the creation of a large number of international bodies to undertake research on the multinational company. Special bodies were established within such international organizations as the Organization of Economic Cooperation and Development (OECD) and the International Labour Office (ILO) and, most notably, the United Nations Commission on Transnational Corporations (UNCTC) to study the impact of these companies. The results of this impressive activity have been huge amounts of valuable research in an area which had been almost untreated in previous decades. Yet, despite this activity, no statistical unit underpinning this research work was created.

There are several reasons why such a body was not created to compile statistics on the flows of the foreign direct investment between countries. Firstly, as the authors of this volume indicate in their Introduction, the task of compiling such a data base is extremely difficult. For example countries use different methods to measure foreign direct investment flows, making the task of gathering and comparing such statistics almost impossible. Another factor which certainly did not assist such a research task in these international organizations was the failure to reach agreement on what constitutes foreign direct investment and indeed the definition of a multinational corporation. It is worth mentioning that the failure to agree on a definition of a multinational company has halted progress at the UN on the formulation of a code of conduct for international companies. Despite having been begun over ten years ago, negotiations have not resolved this stumbling block. The Western delegations argue that the socialist countries of Eastern Europe and the Soviet Union have their own multinational companies, while the latter maintain that their commercial activities abroad have to be seen in the context of foreign aid and cooperation and not foreign direct investment. It is inevitable that international bodies like the UNCTC are beset with spillovers from East-West conflicts and it is perhaps remarkable that in spite of such political disputes the research output of the UNCTC has been extremely impressive. But how can an international body easily prepare a data base of statistics if there is no agreement at the political level on what constitutes foreign direct investment and whether some countries should be treated as being the origin of foreign direct investment or not?

Where the UNCTC and OECD have published data on foreign direct investment there have been drawbacks. On occasion, they have made available estimates of the total stocks and flows of international investment for many different countries (as has the International Monetary Fund in the case of flows). However, the UNCTC and OECD do not explain how their estimates of foreign capital stocks have been obtained, and how they relate to the original home and host country sources. It is often far from clear in the original sources which figure is appropriate and, in cases where only partial information is provided, some reworking of data is required. To have greater confidence in a comparative study it is necessary to be able to trace back the derivation of the estimates for each individual country. It is noteworthy that in this book it is possible to do just that, and this distinguishes it from the earlier efforts of the international organisations. At the other extreme, the OECD has also published data which simply reproduces original sources with no attempt to establish a proper basis of comparison between countries. Until now, those who want statistics on foreign direct investment have been confronted with a choice between, on the one hand, broad comparisons whose relationship to more detailed sources is unclear and which give little guide as to the geographical and industrial distribution of the investment of individual countries and, on the other, a variety of particular country sources which cannot be readily compared or used in comparative statistical analysis.

Given the absence of a statistical source which publishes data on foreign direct investment in a large number of countries in a systematic and comparable way the IRM was delighted to encharge one of the world's leading experts on the theme of multinational companies, Professor John Dunning, and his colleague Dr. John Cantwell, with the task of trying, in some measure, to fill this gap.

Despite the fact that the controversy over the multinationals has greatly decreased in the last few years, there is still a pressing need for reliable data on intra-country flows of foreign direct investment. To take one example, many countries are spending large sums of money to attract inward investment. They are thus anxious not only to discover whether or not their efforts have been successful but also if they have been successful in relation to rival countries and their own package of investment incentives. If their rivals are shown to be successful then countries may feel that the amount of incentives they offer to foreign firms need to be increased; and, if it is shown that their competitors are lagging so far behind as to be offering no significant challenge, then countries may reason that their incentives to firms could be reduced.

Even if the international controversy over the role of multinational companies has subsided to some extent it still remains salient in specific situations, none more so than in South Africa. How dependent is the South African economy on foreign direct investment? Is she more or less dependent than comparable countries like Sweden or Austria? What would happen to the economy if foreign companies disinvested? Questions like these are being daily posed but the absence of authoritative statistical sources means that many of them remain unanswered.

The authors are not suggesting that this volume will provide all the data needed to answer such questions; much of the responsibility for this lies with national statistical agencies improving their coverage and governments agreeing on definitions. But their painstaking work represents, nonetheless, the current 'state of the art' and is a major contribution which the IRM warmly applauds and commends to as wide a readership as possible. In particular, this Directory should become an essential reference book for researchers in universities working in the area of international business and management as well as government departments specializing in this field. Finally, the businessman, working more intensely in what is now becoming known as the "global economy", will find this book of great interest as a guide to overall investment movements.

Geoffrey Hamilton
IRM, Geneva
August 1986

INTRODUCTION

1 Objective of the Directory

This directory represents the first attempt to obtain, assemble and publish data on the International direct investment position of a large number of countries, in a systematic and comparable way. While we would not claim to have captured all the available information for each of the 80 countries, we do believe that the directory is unique, both for its degree of comprehensiveness and for its method of presenting the statistics.

The Directory collects together in a common format for the first time evidence drawn from a wide variety of sources. It includes some data that has not been previously published elsewhere. The reader will be able to make comparisons between countries, and to assess the importance of international investment for any particular country. Until now, no other study has attempted to calculate and bring together as many different indicators of multinational activity, for such a large number of countries.

The task of seeking out, interpreting and classifying the data has been a daunting one. In doing so, we have been assisted by a large number of individuals, and particularly government officials and academic economists in the countries surveyed in this volume. Some of these, to whom we owe a particular debt, are listed under Acknowledgements below; but there are others who in a variety of ways have contributed to our work to whom we would also extend our appreciation.

2 Origin of the Project

We began our project three years ago in the belief there was need for a directory which brought together and summarised the main features of the international direct investment position of countries. Previously in our own researches we found the absence of such information inhibiting, and we know this opinion is shared by our academic colleagues, governments international agencies and indeed the investing firms themselves.

In 1981, John Stopford and John Dunning put together a directory on the world's leading multinationals enterprises (MNEs)[1]; this was a pioneering attempt to give some details of the background growth activities, and geographical involvement performance of the 500 or so largest industrial MNEs.

The present authors saw the need for a companion volume giving details of the extent and significance of both inward and outward direct investment in the leading economies of the world.

3 Coverage of this volume

In our search for data, we quickly discovered that the quantity and quality varied enormously between countries. This is clearly demonstrated in this present volume where, for some countries, e.g. US, UK, Canada, Japan and Korea, there is extensive macro-type information on investment of their own companies outside their national boundaries and on that of foreign MNEs in their midst; but for others e.g. most African countries, the data are extremely sparse. Initially, we had anticipated presenting data on about 50 developed and developing countries. However, as our work progressed, an increasing number of countries — and particularly those in Asia and the Pacific — began collecting and publishing statistics, and our coverage steadily rose; and by the end of 1985 stood at 80. We decided then this should be our cut-off point, although

---

1 *The World Directory of Multinational Enterprises* Macmillan 1981. A second edition of this volume edited by John Stopford was published in 1983. An interpretative volume written by John Stopford and John Dunning — *Multinationals: Global Performance and Trends* was published in 1983.

we acknowledge that there are several countries omitted from this volume, which publish *some* statistics or qualitative data on their international investment position. It is to be hoped in later editions that these omissions might be rectified.

We estimate that the 80 countries contained in this volume account for at least 99% of the outward direct investment of companies throughout the world and between 96% and 98% of the inward direct investment stake. To this extent, our coverage is very comprehensive. However, several countries – particularly developing countries, but including one or two important developed countries, e.g. Switzerland, provide little or no geographical or industrial breakdown of the capital stake or investment; and for this reason, and because of differences in the categorisation of industries, it is difficult to be so complete in our assessment of the international significance of particular sectors.

4 Structure of the volume

The tables set out in the following pages follow a standard pattern. They begin with a one page description of the main features of the international investment position of the country in question, the policies adopted towards inward and outward capital flows[1] and the main sources of statistical data. Table A1 then sets out a statistical summary of the international investment position of the country for 1984 or the latest date for which data are available; and also new investment flows over the preceding 5 year period. The next two Tables *viz.* A2 – A3 set out in some detail the changing inward and outward direct capital stake and investment flow position since the early 1970s. Where possible, the relative significance of direct as compared to portfolio capital stake is shown in Table A2; while Table A3 distinguishes between reinvested profits and new capital flows in the financing of new investment.

These Tables are followed by others (Tables A4 – A7) which present the geographical and industrial structure of both the inward and outward direct investment stake for the early 1970s and the latest data. Again the format is standardised as far as possible; and in some cases this has meant a slight reclassification of the data provided by national authorities. The user who wants to compare the industrial distribution of outward or inward investment in different countries can do so conveniently by using Tables A4 and A6.

Tables A8 and A9 are important tables in that they try and pinpoint indices of the significance of international direct investment to the country in question, including, for several entries, the proportion of the domestic assets, output or employment in individual sectors that are accounted for by affiliates of foreign MNEs or the foreign affiliates of domestic MNEs.

Table A10 sets out such data as are available on the structure of ownership of inward and outward direct investment. Table A11 presents some information on royalty and other receipts, but only a few countries separate those paid to or received from the affiliates of MNEs. The final table in Section A (A12) gives some details about the leading MNEs investing in the country and of domestic MNEs producing abroad. This allows the reader to check on some of the leading companies that are responsible for the investment position described in the earlier tables.

The tables in Section B present some cross country comparisons of data set out in Section A. These entries will be of considerable interest to those wishing to identify geographical similarities between the level and structure and significance of international direct investment and related statistics.

---

1 Information of which has been drawn from various sources but particularly the US Department of Commerce's (International Trade Administration) four volume study *Investment Climate in Foreign Countries* Washington, 1985.

5 Sources of data

Another key feature of the Directory is that it helps to direct the user to more detailed sources for each country that can be followed up if required. The primary sources of data contained in this volume are identified in the individual country entries. Mostly, however, these are twofold — firstly data collected by departments or ministries of individual governments or agencies of governments, for example Central Banks; secondly by private (often academic) enquiries.

The secondary sources are mainly international institutions and particularly those specialising in international economic statistics. Of these special mention should be made of the *International Monetary Fund* (IMF), which since the late 1960s has regularly published statistics on inward and outward direct investment flows; the *United Nations Centre on Transnational Corporations* (UNCTC) which is perhaps the main data gathering agency on the activities of MNEs throughout the world; the *International Labour Office* (ILO) which has produced several extremely valuable surveys on the employment effects of MNEs in both developed and developing countries; and the *Organisation of Economic Cooperation and Development* (OECD) which collects and publishes data on the international investment position of its member countries, and particularly on the investment flows from such countries to the developing world.

We have used some of the estimates of these institutions (and particularly the OECD and UNCTC) for the foreign capital stake in developing countries in the 1970s, but the greater part of the more recent information contained in this volume is that provided (and in some cases specially provided) by the governments of the countries in question or by independent surveys.

It is important to emphasise that we have used the sources of the country named in each entry, rather than that of home countries in the case of inward investment and host countries in the case of outward investment. Often due to differences in definitions, coverage and timing of reporting data provided on a particular investment (say US investment in the German chemicals industry) by source and recipient country may diverge a great deal. Because of this, we have chosen to use only one of these sources; the exception is where no data are available (usually on the geographical or industrial structure of inward investment) in which case we have resorted to presenting data published by the other (in this case the investing country).[1] All of the data contained in this volume should be interpreted with a good deal of caution. The reader is first asked to study the notes on definitions set out at the end of (most) of the countries. It is the bugbear of the statistical interpreter that rarely do countries adopt the same criteria for defining foreign direct investment (e.g. what percentage of equity stake translates a portfolio to a direct investment) let alone the methods for collecting the data and the classification of it.

We have not attempted to reconcile the data set out in this volume. The main difficulty is that most statistics on foreign direct investment stake reflect book values rather than replacement cost values; and although in some countries, for example the US, many MNEs adopt replacement cost accounting, this is still rarely reflected in aggregate statistics. This means that inflation and exchange rate movements present problems when making cross-country comparisons.

Methods of calculating depreciation allowances also vary noticeably across countries. Similarly methods of calculating the labour force are more comprehensive in developed than in most developing countries, and particularly those with a substantial non-market sector. In research elsewhere we have begun to try and come to terms with such problems, but to have done so here would have distracted from our efforts to assemble for the first time such a wide variety of data.

Nevertheless, in spite of these interpretative difficulties, we believe that the data set out in this volume will be of very real value to those interested in knowing more about structure, growth and significance of international direct investment and the activities of MNEs in the world economy.

---

1 We have used such home country data particularly in the case of the African countries.

Abbreviations Used in the Tables:

eg	for example
ie	that is
EEC	European Economic Community
FDI	Foreign Direct Investment
IMF	International Monetary Fund
MNE	Multinational Enterprise
N.S.A.	Not Separately Available
N.A.	Not Available
neg.	negligible
OECD	Organization for Economic Cooperation and Development
UK	United Kingdom
UN	United Nations
UNCTC	United Nations Centre on Transnational Corporations
USA	United States of America
USSR	Union of Soviet Socialist Republics
W. Germany	West Germany

Currency Abbreviations:

Australia Dollar	A $
Austria Schilling	A Sch
Barbados Dollar	B $
Belgium Franc	BF
Botswana Pula	Pula
Brazil Cruzeiro	Cr
Canada Dollar	C $
Colombia Peso	C P
Congo Franc	C Fr
Denmark Krone	D Kr
Ecuador Sucre	Sucre
Egypt Pound	E £
Fiji Dollar	F $
Finland Mark	F M
France Franc	F Fr
West Germany Deutsche Mark	DM
Ghana Cedi	Cedi
Guyana Dollar	G $
Hong Kong Dollar	HK $
Hungary Forint	Ft
India Rupee	I Rup
Ireland Pound	Ir £
Italy Lire	Lire
Ivory Coast Franc	IC Fr
Jamaica Dollar	J $
Kenya Shilling	K Sh
Liberia Dollar	L $
Libya Dinar	L Din
Malaysia Dollar	M $
Morocco Dirham	M Dir
Netherlands Guilder	N Fl
New Zealand Dollar	NZ $
Nigeria Naira	₦
Norway Krone	Kr
Papua New Guinea Kina	K
Philippines Peso	P ₱
Portugal Escudo	Esc
Sierra Leone Leone	Le
Singapore Dollar	S $
South Africa Rand	Rand
Spain Peseta	Pta
Sri Lanka Rupee	S Rup
Sweden Krona	S Kr
Switzerland Franc	S Fr
Thailand Baht	Baht
Trinidad & Tobago Dollar	TT $
Turkey Lira	T Lira
United Kingdom Pound Sterling	£
United States Dollar	US $
Venezuela Bolivar	Bol
Yugoslavia Dinar	Y Din
Zimbabwe Dollar	Z $

Part A
Country Tables

DEVELOPED AREAS

EUROPE: EEC

BELGIUM

The foreign investment policies of Belgium have been dominated by the need for a smaller economic power to adjust to membership of the European Economic Community and by the desire for substantial growth in the industrial sector with special emphasis on regional development in the Walloon south. In the 1960s, foreign investment expanded rapidly particularly in the Flemish north. This is partly a reflection of the accessibility of Belgium to other EEC countries and of the generous tax concessions introduced in the Economic Expansion Acts of 1959 and 1970 designed primarily to promote growth. The stock of inward direct investment in Belgium has been estimated at US $ 9.6 billion dollars in 1978 which is approximately twice as high as the stock of Belgian outward direct investment. As a proportion of gross fixed capital formation, the flow of direct investment varied between 5 and 8.5% from 1967 onwards. An estimated 38% of employment in Belgian manufacturing was in foreign-owned firms in 1978 compared with 18% in 1968.

Few controls apply to inward direct investment. The transfer of direct investment funds through the free exchange market is automatically approved once an application has been made to a designated bank. However, if the direct investor prefers that funds be transferred through the official exchange market rather than the free exchange market, authorisation by the Exchange Institute is necessary. Furthermore, the Finance Ministry must approve public offers to buy the shares of publicly-listed Belgian companies, particularly when such offers are made by firms whose headquarters are outside the EEC.

From 1965 to 1967 the flow of Belgian direct investment abroad represented 1.7% of the total Western European flow of direct investments. This proportion has increased significantly to 3% and 5.5% during the period 1974-76 and 1977-79. As a proportion of gross capital formation, Belgian direct investment abroad varied around 1% in the period before 1970 and has reached 2.5% during the 1970s.

Belgian policy towards outward direct investment has been one of encouragement especially since the beginning of the seventies. First, the public investment company 'Société Belge d'Investissement international' (SBI) has made possible the subscription to the equity capital of Belgian subsidiaries established abroad and the granting of loans by the Belgian capital market at the prevailing rate of interest and for five to ten years maturity. Secondly, the government authorities allowed the Office National du Ducroire (OND) to insure against political and catastrophical risks. Finally, in July 1981, the Belgian Office of Development Cooperation created a development cooperation fund called Fonds de Cooperation au Dévelopment which allows Belgian bilateral assistance to be used as loans to, or shareholdings in Belgian firms established in developing countries. However, this latter instrument is restricted to semi-public or public enterprises in developing countries and to national or regional developmental banks.

MAIN SOURCES OF DATA:

A **Official**

1 **Bulletin de la Banque Nationale de Belgique:** provides information on the flows of both outward and inward direct investment.

2 Ministere des Affaires Economiques: publishes *'Investissements Etrangers en Belgique'* indicating the industrial and geographical distribution of the stock of inward direct investment as from 1959.

B Private

1 F Haex and D Van Den Bulcke, 'Belgische Multinationale Ondernemingen', Diepenbeek: LEHOC-VWOL, 1979.

2 L Sleuwaegen and D Van Den Bulcke, 'Multinational Enterprises and Industrial Market Structure in Belgium: A Statistical Decomposition Analysis', Leuven: KUL-CES, 1983.

3 J Stopford and J H Dunning, *Multinationals: Company Performance and Global Trends,* London: Macmillan, 1983.

4 Trends Top 5000: publishes annual information on the largest companies in Belgium.

5 D Van Den Bulcke, 'Multinationale Ondernemingen in de Belgische Economie', Ghent: Serug, 1978 and Chapter on 'Belgium' in J H Dunning, *Multinational Enterprises, Economic Structure and International Competitiveness,* London: John Wiley, 1985.

Table A1

SUMMARY OF THE COUNTRY'S INTERNATIONAL INVESTMENT POSITION

		Inward Investment	Outward Investment
1	Number of foreign affiliates in host country, and of foreign affiliates of home country firms at the end of 1975[1]	1,121	609[2]
2	Number of foreign firms with direct investments in host country, and home country firms with direct foreign affiliates at the end of 1975	967	96
3	Total foreign direct capital stock at book value as a percentage of GNP at factor cost in 1982	11.83	5.53
4	Flow of foreign direct investment in the five year period 1978-82 (BF bn)	226.5	43.6
5	Employment in foreign affiliates or abroad, 1975	331,444	182,379
6	Output of foreign affiliates or abroad	*N.A.*	*N.A.*

Source:

D Van Den Bulcke, *Multinationale Ondernemingen in de Belgische Economie,* Ghent: SERUG, 1978 paper; F Haex and D Van Den Bulcke, *Belgische Multinationale Ondernemingen,* Diepenbeck:VWOL, 1979 paper; Banque Nationale de Belgique, *Bulletin,* various issues.

NOTES TO TABLE A1

1 Represents total number of foreign affiliates in manufacturing only.

2 The total number of foreign affiliates of home country firms including holding, banking and engineering firms is 1,026.

Table A2

PRIVATE FOREIGN CAPITAL STOCK, 1970 - 83
(BF bn)

	Inward Investment			Outward Investment		
	Portfolio	*Direct*[1]	*Total*	*Portfolio*	*Direct*[2]	*Total*
Book value of capital stock						
1978	Not Available	276.5	Not Available	Not Available	155.5	Not Available
1979		306.0[2]			214.3	
1980		348.5			217.5	
1981		398.7			219.5	
1982		462.2			216.0	
1983		505.5			234.3	

Source:

Stopford and Dunning, *Multinationals: Company Performance and Global Trends,* Table 1.2 for outward investment in selected years; D Van Den Bulcke, 'Belgium', chapter in J H Dunning, *Multinational Enterprises, Economic Structure and International Competitiveness,* London: John Wiley, 1985.

NOTES TO TABLE A2

1 From 1979, figures estimated by adding cumulative investment flows to the stock figure of 1978.

2 Figure for 1979 obtained by calculating the change in foreign capital stock in 1978-79 and 1979-80 as proportional to the distribution of investment flows between 1978 and 1980. From 1981, figures estimated by adding cumulative investment flows to the stock figure of 1980.

Table A3

FLOW OF FOREIGN DIRECT INVESTMENT, 1970-83
(BF bn)[1]

	Inward Investment			Outward Investment		
	Reinvested Profits	*Other*	*Total*	*Reinvested Profits*	*Other*	*Total*
1970	*Not Separately Available*		15.9	*Not Separately Available*		7.8
1971			21.8			8.8
1972			17.7			6.5
1973			27.5			6.7
1974			41.8			14.5
1975			33.9			5.5
1976			30.6			11.3
1977			40.0			12.7
1978			40.8			11.4
1979			29.5			32.8
1980			42.5			1.8
1981			50.2			1.1
1982			63.5			-3.5
1983			43.3			18.3

Source:

Banque Nationale de Belgique, *Bulletin,* various issues.

NOTES TO TABLE A3

1 Excluding reinvested profits.

Table A4

SECTORAL DISTRIBUTION OF FOREIGN DIRECT CAPITAL STOCK, 1968-81 (BF bn)[1]

	Inward Investment			Outward Investment		
	Primary	*Secondary*	*Tertiary*	*Primary*	*Secondary*	*Tertiary*
1968		72.65	7.56			
1973		130.60	17.14			
1975	*Not*	160.13	21.79			
1977	*Separately*	174.60	27.07		*Not Available*	
1979	*Available*	189.55	34.98			
1980		192.11	38.15			
1981		197.57	41.27			

Source:
Ministere des Affaires Economiques, *Investissements Estrangers en Belgique,* various issues.

NOTES TO TABLE A4

1 Figure represents cumulative flow figures based on planned new investments reported to the Ministere des Affaires Economiques from 1959. The figures do not include reinvested profits and subsequent investments.

Table A5

GEOGRAPHICAL DISTRIBUTION OF FOREIGN DIRECT CAPITAL STOCK, 1968-81 (BF bn)[1]

	Inward Investment[2]			Outward Investment		
	Developed Countries	*Other Countries*	*Total*	*Developed Countries*	*Developing Countries*	*Total*
1968	70.45	9.76	80.21			
1973	123.60	24.15	147.75			
1975	155.13	26.79	181.92			
1977	171.61	30.07	201.68		*Not Available*	
1979	188.89	35.64	224.53			
1980	198.86	31.40	230.26			
1981	201.48	37.36	238.84			

Source:
Ministere des Affaires Economiques, *Investissements Etrangers en Belgique,* various issues.

NOTES TO TABLE A5

1 Figure represents cumulative flow of figures based on planned new investments reported to the Ministere des Affaires Economiques from 1959. The figures do not include reinvested profits and subsequent investments.

2 Figure for developed countries represent planned investment by the USA, Germany, France, Italy, Netherlands, UK, Denmark, Ireland and Japan. Figures for other countries represent the rest, which include all developing countries.

INDUSTRIAL DISTRIBUTION OF FOREIGN DIRECT CAPITAL STOCK, 1970 - 81 (BF bn)[1]

	Inward Investment		Outward Investment
	1958-70	*1959-81*	
Primary			*Not Available*
Agriculture	*Not Available*	*Not Available*	
Mining & quarrying			
Oil			
Secondary	102.635	197.570	
Food & drink	33.924	81.396	
Chemicals & allied[2]			
Metals	32.767	61.514	
Mechanical engineering			
Electrical equipment			
Motor vehicles			
Other transportation equipment			
Textiles & clothing	6.066	10.374	
Paper & allied	4.471	5.525	
Rubber[2]	*N.S.A.*	*N.S.A.*	
Stone, clay & glass[3]	*N.S.A.*	*N.S.A.*	
Coal & petroleum products	21.426	22.451	
Other manufacturing[3]	3.981	16.310	
Tertiary	11.131	41.268	
Construction	*N.A.*	*N.A.*	
Transport & communications			
Distributive trade	3.924	16.026	
Property	*N.A.*	*N.A.*	
Banking & finance	*N.A.*	*N.A.*	
Other services[4]	7.207	25.242	
TOTAL	113.766	238.838	

Source:
Ministere des Affaires Economiques, *Investissements Etrangers en Belgique,* various issues.

NOTES TO TABLE A6

1 Figure represents cumulative flow figures based on planned new investments reported to the Ministere des Affaires Economiques from 1959. The figures do not include reinvested profits and subsequent investments.

2 Rubber products are included under chemicals & allied.

3 Stone, clay and glass are included under other manufacturing.

4 Figure includes various services, ie, hotels and restaurants, real estate transport, consultation, publicity, editions, insurance, banks and financial institutions and others.

Table A6

INDUSTRIAL DISTRIBUTION OF FOREIGN DIRECT CAPITAL STOCK, 1970 - 1981 (BF billion)[1]

	Inward Investment		Outward Investment
	1959-70	*1959-81*	
Primary			
Agriculture			
Mining & quarrying	*N.A.*	*N.A.*	
Oil			
Secondary	102.635	197.570	
Food & drink			
Chemicals & allied	33.924	81.396	
Metals	32.767	61.514	*No*
Textiles & clothing	6.066	10.374	
Paper & allied	4.471	5.525	*data*
Rubber			
Stone, clay & glass			*available*
Coal & petroleum products	21.426	22.451	
Other manufacturing	3.981	16.310	
Tertiary	11.131	41.268	
Construction			
Transport & communications	*N.S.A.*	*N.S.A.*	
Distributive trade	3.924	16.026	
Property	*N.S.A.*	*N.S.A.*	
Banking & finance	*N.S.A.*	*N.S.A.*	
Other services[2]	7.207	25.242	
TOTAL	113.766	238.838	

Source:
Ministere des Affaires Economiques, *Investissements Etrangers en Belgique,* various issues.

NOTES TO TABLE A6

1 Figure represents cumulative flow figures based on planned new investments reported to the Ministere des Affaires Economiques from 1959. The figures do not include reinvested profits and subsequent investments.

2 Figure includes various services, ie, hotels and restaurants, real estate transport, consultation, publicity, editions, insurance, banks and financial institutions and others.

Table A7

LEADING SOURCE AND RECIPIENT COUNTRIES, 1970 - 81 (BF bn)[1]

	Inward Investment		Outward Investment
	1959-70	*1959-81*	
DEVELOPED AREAS[2]	96.758	201.476	
Europe			
EEC of which:			
Denmark	–	0.162	
France	7.117	24.770	
W. Germany	15.558	27.857	
Ireland	–	0.007	*Not*
Italy	0.253	3.605	*Available*
Netherlands	7.747	24.601	
UK	–	8.518	
North America of which			
USA	65.157	105.293	
Developed countries of which:			
Japan	0.926	6.664	
OTHER COUNTRIES	17.008	37.362	
TOTAL	113.766	238.838	

Source:
Ministere des Affaires Economiques, *Investissements Etrangers en Belgique.*

NOTES TO TABLE A7

1 Figure represents cumulative flow figures based on planned new investments reported to the Ministere des Affaires Economiques from 1959. The figures do not include reinvested profits and subsequent investments.

2 Only those countries listed below.

Table A7

LEADING SOURCE AND RECIPIENT COUNTRIES, 1970 - 1981 (BF billion)[1]

	Inward Investment		Outward Investment
	1959-70	*1959-81*	
DEVELOPED AREAS[2]	96.758	201.476	
Europe			
EEC of which:			
Denmark	–	0.162	
France	7.117	24.770	
W. Germany	15.558	27.857	*No*
Ireland	–	0.007	*data*
Italy	0.253	3.605	
Netherlands	7.747	24.601	*available*
United Kingdom		8.518	
North America of which:			
United States	65.157	105.293	
Developed countries of which:			
Japan	0.926	6,664	
OTHER COUNTRIES	17.008	37,362	
TOTAL	113,766	238.838	

Source:

Ministere des Affaires Economiques, *Investissements Etrangers en Belgique.*

NOTES TO TABLE A7

1 Figure represents cumulative flow figures based on planned new investments reported to the Ministere des Affaires Economiques from 1959. The figures do not include reinvested profits and subsequent investments.

2 Only those countries listed below.

Table A8

INDICATORS OF THE SIGNIFICANCE OF INWARD FOREIGN DIRECT INVESTMENT OR THE ACTIVITIES OF FOREIGN-BASED COMPANIES TO THE NATIONAL ECONOMY, 1975 - 82

1	Direct capital stock of foreign affiliates at book value in 1982 as a proportion of:		
	a GNP at factor cost		11.83
	b population (in BF per head)		46,903.55
2	Employment in foreign affiliates in 1975 as a percentage of all employment		
	a in all industry		18[1]
	b in manufacturing		33
3	Output of foreign affiliates in 1975 as a percentage of all companies' output[2]		
	a in secondary (ie, manufacturing) industry		44
4	Exports[3] of foreign affiliates in 1975 as a percentage of all manufacturing exports		43.6
5	Percentage share of sales and employment accounted for by foreign affiliates in selected sectors, 1975		
		Sales	*Employment*
	Primary Goods Sector		
	Mining & quarrying	3.1	*N.A.*
	Oil	77.7	*N.A.*
	Manufacturing Sector		
	Food & drink[4]	22.5	22
	Chemicals & allied	55.8	57
	Metals	16.1	36
	Mechanical engineering	57.7	23
	Electrical equipment	87.3	74
	Motor vehicles	54.7	} 68
	Other transportation equipment	17.0	}
	Textiles & clothing	11.3[5]	13
	Paper & allied	30.4	19[6]
	Rubber	59.8	62
	Stone, glass & clay	21.0	28
	Timber & furniture	1.3	*N.A.*
	Other manufacturing	2.6	18

Source:

L Sleuwaegen and D Van Den Bulcke, *Multinational Enterprises and Industrial Market Structure in Belgium: A Statistical Decomposition Analysis,* Leuven: KUL-CES paper, 1983; D Van Bulcke, *Multinationale Ondernemingen in de Belgische Economie,* Ghent:Serug, 1978; J Carlsburghe, in D Van Den Bulcke, 'Buitenlandse industriale bedrujuen in Vilaanderen, Nallonie in Brussel: Un actualisening', G.E.R.V. bouchten, no 19, 1978.

NOTES TO TABLE A8

1 Figure is for the year 1968.

2 Figure represents sales.

3 Manufacturing only.

4 Figure includes tobacco.

5 Figure is for textiles alone. For footwear and clothing, the figure is 17.3%.

6 Timber and furniture are included under Paper and allied.

Table A9

INDICATORS OF THE SIGNIFICANCE OF OUTWARD FOREIGN DIRECT INVESTMENT OR THE ACTIVITIES OF HOME-BASED COMPANIES ABROAD FOR THE NATIONAL ECONOMY, 1975 - 82

1	Foreign capital stock of home-based firms at book value in 1982 as a proportion of:	
	a GNP at factor cost	5.53
	b population (in BF per head)	21,928.90
2	Employment in foreign affiliates in 1975 as a percentage of domestic employment in manufacturing	16.5
3	Employment of foreign affiliates of home-based firms as a percentage of that in selected domestic sectors, 1975	
		Employment
	Manufacturing Sector	
	Food & drink	12.5[1]
	Chemicals & allied	86.8[2]
	Metals	13.0
	Mechanical engineering	
	Electrical equipment	
	Motor vehicles	
	Other transportation equipment	
	Textiles & clothing	1.7
	Paper & allied	2.5[3]
	Stone, glass & clay	5.5
	Timber & furniture	*N.S.A.*[3]

Note: the value 13.0 is bracketed across Metals, Mechanical engineering, Electrical equipment, Motor vehicles and Other transportation equipment.

Source:

Bulletin de Banque Nationale de Belgique; F Haex and D Van Den Bulcke, *Belgische Multinationale Ondernemingen,* Diepenbeck: VWOL, 1979 paper.

NOTES TO TABLE A9

1 Includes tobacco.

2 Includes petroleum.

3 Timber and furniture are included under paper and allied

Table A10

DISTRIBUTION OF FOREIGN SUBSIDIARIES AND ASSOCIATES AND FOREIGN CAPITAL STOCK BY PERCENTAGE OWNERSHIP OF PARENT COMPANIES, 1976

	Inward Investment		Outward Investment	
	Number of Affiliates	*Value of Capital Stock*	*Number of Affiliates*[1]	*Value of Capital Stock*
100% owned subsidiaries	684	*Not Available*	170	*Not Available*
50-99.9% owned subsidiarie^c and associates	223		98	
Less than 50% owned subsidiaries and associates	58		85	
TOTAL	965	2,329.1	353	146.5

Source:
D Van Den Bulcke, *Multinationale Ondernemingen en de Belgische Economie,* Ghent:SERUG, 1978; F Haex and D Van Den Bulcke, *Belgische Multinationale Ondernemingen,* Diepenbeck:VWOL, 1979.

NOTES TO TABLE A10 IRG NOTES TO TABLE A10

Based on a sample of 353 foreign subsidiaries in manufacturing from a total population of 609.

Table A11

ROYALTY RECEIPTS AND PAYMENTS, 1975-82 (BF bn)

	Payments			Receipts		
	To Affiliates	*To Non-affiliates*	*Total*	*From Affiliates*	*From Non-affiliates*	*Total*
1975	*Not Separately Available*		6,608.9	*Not Separately Available*		3,572.4
1976			7,532.3			4,011.3
1977			8,829.7			4,686.9
1978			9,029.0			4,534.2
1979			10,265.5			5,113.8
1980			13,282.9			5,404.5
1981			15,849.4			6,961.5
1982			19,117.9			8,676.2

Source:

Banque Nationale de Belgique, *Bulletin,* various issues.

Table A12

LEADING FOREIGN AND DOMESTIC MULTINATIONAL COMPANIES, 1982

A Leading Foreign Multinational Companies in the country

	Name	*Home Country*	*Sector*	*Belgian Turnover (BF m)*
1	Esso	USA	Petroleum	153,375
2	NAFTA	USSR	Petroleum	140,753
3	British Petroleum	UK	Petrochemicals	79,652
4	Belgian Shell	UK/Netherlands	Petroleum	53,786
5	General Motors	USA	Motor vehicles	53,345
6	Chevron Oil Belgium	USA	Petroleum	52,212
7	BASF Antwerpen	Germany	Petrochemicals	36,554
8	Afga-Gevaert	Germany	Chemicals	35,073
9	BPR	USA	Petroleum	31,184
10	Texaco Belgium	USA	Petroleum	30,061
11	International Corn Co	USA	Food products	26,967
12	Volkswagen Bruxelles	W. Germany	Motor vehicles	26,697
13	MAKRO	Netherlands	Retailing	25,833
14	Renault Industrie	France	Motor vehicles	25,803
15	Monsanto Europe	USA	Petrochemicals	25,353
16	Gulf Oil Belgium	USA	Petroleum	24,500
17	Petrochim	USA/Belgium	Petrochemicals	21,663
18	IBM	USA	Computers	21,043
19	Bell Telephone Mfg	USA	Electronics	20,857
20	Volvo Europa Truck	Sweden	Motor vehicles	20,150
21	Caterpillar Belgium	USA	Heavy machinery	19,278
22	Ford Motor Co	USA	Motor vehicles	18,260
23	Philips Industrie	Netherlands	Electronics	17,831
24	Calpam Belgium	Netherlands	Petroleum	16,316
25	Siemens	Switzerland	Electronics	14,476

Table A12 (cont'd)

LEADING FOREIGN AND DOMESTIC MULTINATIONAL COMPANIES, 1982

B Leading Domestic Companies with Multinational interests

Name	*Sector*	*Global Sales (BF m)*
GB INNO BM	Retailing	108,218
INTERCOM	Electricity	81,125
Cockerill-Sambre	Steel	63,200
Metallurgie Hoboken-Ove pelt	Non-ferrous metals	46,574
Fina	Petroleum	45,414
Delhaize de Leeuw	Retailing	43,805
Sabena	Air transport	33,234
CMB	Transport	24,968
Fabrique Nationale	Electrical machinery	22,845
Frere Bourgeois Commerciale	Steel	22,004
Bekaert	Steel	20,016
Belgische Olie Maatschappij	Petroleum	15,930
D'Ieteren	Trade in motor vehicles	15,568
Colruyt	Retailing	15,218
Vander Elst Freres	Tobacco	15,102
Synatom	Engineering	14,843
Wagons-Lits	Tourism	14,702
ACEC International	Electronics	14,417
UCB	Chemicals	13,885
Carbochimique	Chemicals	13,558
Rosseel ETS	Petroleum	12,936
Forges de Clabecq	Steel	12,281
Cobelfret	Transport	12,244
Glaverbel	Glass	11,242
PRB	Chemicals	9,770

Source:
Trends Top 5000 1984 Magazine.

BELGIUM DEFINITIONS

Foreign direct investment implies the control and long term involvement of non-residents in the management of a firm located in Belgium. A minimum participation of 10% in the equity capital stake is the arbritary threshold used in the definition of foreign direct investment.

Foreign direct investment data as obtained from balance of payments statistics of the *Banque Nationale de Belgique* is a financial concept, representing only the flows of capital from abroad used to finance direct investments in Belgium. Such statistics therefore do not include capital that may be raised in whole or in part from the domestic capital market or indeed of other means of obtaining control. Moreover, such statistics do not include reinvested profits but do include loans extended by the parent company to their Belgian affiliates. Furthermore, direct investment data from the balance of payments statistics do not give a sectoral breakdown as between manufacturing and trade and services.

Foreign direct investment as obtained from the *Ministére des Affaires Economiques* relate only to the initial investments by non-residents and do not relate in any way to subsequent investments that may be made. Such registers specifically refer to both the value of planned investments in fixed assets during the initial stage of the investment programme if foreign direct investment is a greenfield investment which may be wholly or partly owned by non-residents and the purchasing value of capital stocks if foreign direct investment is in the form of a total or partial takeover of an existing domestic firm. The registers do not distinguish between foreign control established through the creation of new assets or foreign control established through the acquisition of existing assets. In the case of greenfield investment, the total capital formation made by non-residents is taken into account even though part of the capital may be raised locally and in the case of takeovers, only the purchasing value of the equity capital stake acquired by non-residents is included and not the total value of the equity which is brought under foreign control.

Thus the foreign investment data referring to greenfield investment registered with the Ministére des Affaires Economiques have the distinct advantage of recording the total amount of capital investments in contrast to foreign investment data recorded in the balance of payments which only record that part of capital investment which is brought in from abroad. The two main disadvantages of the Ministére des Affaires Economiques data are: first, subsequent investments by non-residents are not included, and second, declared planned investment may be inflated to get more public aid.

The Ministére des Affaires Economiques and the National Institute of Statistics (NIS) publishes data on realised foreign investment in manufacturing industry. However, even though their data refer to realised rather than planned investment, such data suffer from a high degree of aggregation in both the sectoral and geographical distribution. Moreover, because of regional splitting of the Belgian administration, the 1982 issue of this joint publication is deemed to be the last one.

Source:
Banque Nationale de Belgique, *Bulletin;* Ministére des Affaires Economiques, *Investissements Etrangers en Belgique.*

DENMARK

Information about Danish foreign direct investment is essentially limited to inward investment with information on flows and permits for outward investment. No capital stock figures are officially published, so we have tried to estimate the cumulative position by adding flows or permitted investments over the period 1974-83. The accumulation of permits (Tables A5 and A7) give figures approximately double the accumulation of flows (Table A2).

The main inward investors are the USA, Sweden, the UK and West Germany. These same four countries were also the main destinations for Danish outward investment, with over 70% of outward investment going to OECD countries. Inward investment is most significant in the tertiary sector, but it also accounted for 9% of output in manufacturing. Chemicals, metals, electrical products and paper are the manufacturing sectors in which foreign firms play the most important role.

Denmark has a liberal policy towards inward direct investment; no general investment screening mechanisms exist and permission to invest is usually granted without difficulty. Except for investment in oil exploitation foreign investors may have full financial control over a business enterprise in Denmark. Outward investment is also freely permitted; and indeed, in developing countries actively encouraged.

MAIN SOURCES OF DATA:

A **Official**

1 Danmarks Nationalbank, *Monetary Review;* gives figures for flows and the *Yearbook* gives permits.

2 Danmarks Statistik, 1979, *A Survey of Foreign Owned Enterprises, 1976* (in Danish).

3 US Department of Commerce Investment Trade Administration, *Investment Climate in Foreign Countries,* Washington, 1985, vol I.

B **Private**

1 C Estrup, *Virksomhedsoverdragelser,* M & A International, Denmark, 1984.

2 P Schultz and H Vestergaard, *Danish Foreign Direct Investments — The General Pattern and Two Extreme Cases of Eager and Reluctant Investors,* presented at the Annual Conference of European International Business Association, Glasgow, Scotland, December 15-17, 1985.

Note:
Data do not allow us to complete Table A11 for Denmark.

Table A1

SUMMARY OF THE COUNTRY'S INTERNATIONAL INVESTMENT POSITION

		Inward Investment	Outward Investment
1	Number of foreign affiliates in host country, and of foreign affiliates of home country firms at the end of 1984	647[1]	823
2	Number of foreign firms with direct investments in host country, and home country firms with direct foreign affiliates	*N.A.*	*N.A.*
3	Total foreign direct capital stock at book value as a percentage of GNP at factor cost, 1983	1.54	1.55
4	Flow of foreign direct investment in the five year period 1979-83 (D Kr m)	4,204	5,095
5	Employment in foreign affiliates or abroad, 1984	86,685[2]	*N.A.*
6	Output of foreign affiliates or abroad, 1976 (D Kr m)	4,484[3]	*N.A.*

Source:

Danmarks Statistik 1979, *A Survey of Foreign Owned Enterprises, 1976* (in Danish); Danmarks Nationalbank, *Monetary Review, February 1985; Who Owns Whom,* Continental Europe, 1984, London: Dun & Bradstreet; C Estrup, unpublished data; Paul Schulta and Harold Vestergaard, *Danish Foreign Direct Investments – The General Pattern and Two Extreme Cases of Eager and Reluctant Investors, op cit.*

NOTES TO TABLE A1

1 Represents foreign owned firms with more than 20 employees.

2 Represents employment in foreign owned firms with more than 20 employees.

3 Value added.

Table A2

PRIVATE FOREIGN CAPITAL STOCK, 1983 - 84 (D Kr m)

	Inward Investment			Outward Investment		
	Portfolio	*Direct*	*Total*	*Portfolio*	*Direct*	*Total*
Book value of capital stock						
1983[1]	9,680[2]	14,952	*N.A.*	2,130[2]	4,589[3]	*N.A.*
1984	*N.A.*	15,048[4]	*N.A.*	*N.A.*	10,576[4]	*N.A.*

Source:
Danmarks Nationalbank, *Monetary Review, February 1985;* IMF, *Balance of Payments Statistics Yearbook*, various issues.

NOTES TO TABLE A2

1 Accumulated flows over period 1960-83.

2 Represents cumulative flows as from 1974 to 1983; the equivalent direct investment flows over the same period amounted to D Kr 7,671 m for inward investment, and D Kr 7,711 m for outward investment.

3 See Table A5 for an estimate of this figure based on the accumulation of permits.

4 Accumulated flows over period 1960-84.

Table A3

FLOW OF FOREIGN DIRECT INVESTMENT, 1971 - 84 (D Kr m)[1]

	Inward Investment			Outward Investment		
	Reinvested Profits	*Other*	*Total*[1]	*Reinvested Profits*	*Other*	*Total*[1]
1971	*Not Separately Available*		536	*Not Separately Available*		259
1972			970			468
1973			571			346
1974			736			369
1975			611			582
1976			632			399
1977			456			967
1978			490			179
1979			544			*N.A.*
1980			594			1,100
1981			714			1,000
1982			1,122			662
1983			587			909
1984			96			987

Source:

Danmarks Nationalbank, *Monetary Review, February 1985 and August 1982;* IMF, *Balance of Payments Yearbook*, various issues.

NOTES TO TABLE A3

1 Excluding reinvested profits.

Table A4

SECTORAL DISTRIBUTION OF FOREIGN DIRECT CAPITAL STOCK, 1983 (D Kr m)[1]

	Inward Investment			Outward Investment		
	Primary	*Secondary*	*Tertiary*	*Primary*	*Secondary*	*Tertiary*
1974-83	269.3	4,599.5	2,802.2	*Not Available*		

Source.

C Estrup, unpublished data.

NOTES TO TABLE A4

1 Estimates obtained by applying the percentage sectoral distribution of employment in foreign-owned firms, 1984, (with more than 20 employees), to the capital stock figure, 1983, from Table A2.

Table A5

GEOGRAPHICAL DISTRIBUTION OF FOREIGN DIRECT CAPITAL STOCK, 1983 (D Kr m)

	Inward Investment			Outward Investment		
	Developed Countries	*Developing Countries*	*Total*	*Developed Countries*	*Developing Countries*	*Total*
1974-83[1]	16,356[2]	753[3]	17,109	9,780[2]	4,081[3]	13,861

Source:

Danmarks Nationalbank, *Report and Accounts for the year 1983;* C Estrup, unpublished data.

NOTES TO TABLE A5

1 Accumulated permits for foreign direct investment over period 1974-83.

2 EEC (10), plus Finland, Norway, Switzerland, Sweden, Canada and the USA, for inward investment, and the EEC plus Norway, Switzerland, Sweden and the USA for outward investment.

3 Rest of the world.

Table A6

INDUSTRIAL DISTRIBUTION OF FOREIGN DIRECT CAPITAL STOCK, 1983 (D Kr m)[1]

	Inward Investment	Outward Investment
	1974-83	
Primary	269.3	
Mining & quarrying	47.7	
Oil	221.6	
Secondary	4,599.5	
Food & drink	569.4	
Chemicals & allied	367.0	
Metals	408.0	
Mechanical engineering	611.3	
Electrical equipment	1,625.5	*Not Available*
Textiles & clothing	87.4	
Paper & allied	384.5	
Rubber[2]	283.8	
Stone, clay & glass	49.2	
Other manufacturing	213.4	
Tertiary	2,802.2	
Distributive trade	1,884.8	
Other services	917.4	
TOTAL	7,671.0	

Source:

C Estrup, unpublished data.

NOTES TO TABLE A6

1 Estimates obtained by applying the percentage sectoral distribution of employment in foreign-owned firms, 1984, (with more than 20 employees), to the capital stock figure, 1983, from Table A2.

2 Represents plastics and polymers.

Table A7

LEADING SOURCE AND RECIPIENT COUNTRIES, 1983 (D Kr m)

	Inward Investment	Outward Investment
	1974-83[1]	*1974-83*[1]
DEVELOPED AREAS	16,356	9,780
Europe	12,390	7,784
EEC of which:	6,636	5,680
Belgium & Luxembourg	370	983
France	342	871
W. Germany	2,031	1,316
Italy[2]	411	121
Netherlands	1,281	445
UK[3]	2,201	1,944
Other Europe of which:	5,754	2,104
Finland	365[4]	*N.S.A.*
Norway	888	568
Sweden	3,547	993
Switzerland	974	543
North America of which:	3,966	1,966
Canada	199[4]	*N.S.A.*
USA	3,767	1,996
DEVELOPING AREAS[5]	753	4,081
TOTAL	17,109	13,861

Source:

Danmarks Nationalbank, Report and Accounts for the year 1983; C Estrup, unpublished data.

NOTES TO TABLE A7

1 Accumulated permits for foreign direct investment over period 1974-83.

2 Includes Greece.

3 Includes Ireland.

4 Estimated by applying percentage geographical distribution of employment in foreign-owned firms, 1984, (with more than 20 employees) to the total accumulated permits figure, 1974-83.

5 All countries except those listed above.

Table A8

INDICATORS OF THE SIGNIFICANCE OF INWARD FOREIGN DIRECT INVESTMENT OR THE ACTIVITIES OF FOREIGN-BASED COMPANIES TO THE NATIONAL ECONOMY, 1976 - 83

1	Direct capital stock of foreign affiliates in 1983 as a proportion of:	
	a GNP at factor cost	3.01
	b population (in D Kr per head)	2,926.03
2	Employment in foreign affiliates in 1984 as a percentage of all employment	
	a in all industry	3.5
	b in manufacturing	14.8
3	Output of foreign affiliates in 1976 as a percentage of all companies' output	
	a in primary (ie, extractive) industry	0.4
	b in secondary (ie, manufacturing) industry	8.8
	c in tertiary industry (ie, services etc)	13.4
4	Exports of foreign affiliates in 1976 as a percentage of all manufacturing exports	13.1
5	Percentage share of sales, value added and employment accounted for by foreign affiliates in selected sectors, 1976	

	Sales	*Value added*	*Employment*
Primary Goods Sector			
Oil	*N.A.*	*N.A.*	*N.A.*
Manufacturing Sector			
Food & drink	5.2	6.5	6.0
Chemicals & allied	36.2	24.9	20.2
Metals	22.1	19.9	17.8
Mechanical engineering	10.9	9.7	10.3
Electrical equipment	21.0	18.4	18.3
Textiles & clothing	7.9	7.3	5.7
Paper & allied	11.2	8.2	7.5
Stone, glass & clay	7.5	6.9	6.7
Other manufacturing	3.9	3.1	2.7

Source:

Danmarks Statistik 1979, A Survey of Foreign Owned Enterprises, 1976 (in Danish); C Estrup, unpublished data.

NOTES TO TABLE A8

[1] Represents employment in foreign owned firms with more than 20 employees as a percentage of all employment.

Table A9

INDICATORS OF THE SIGNIFICANCE OF OUTWARD FOREIGN DIRECT INVESTMENT OR THE ACTIVITIES OF HOME-BASED COMPANIES ABROAD FOR THE NATIONAL ECONOMY, 1983

1	Foreign capital stock of home-based firms at book value in 1983 as a proportion of:	
	a GNP at factor cost	1.55
	b population (in D Kr per head)	1,509.00

Source:
Danmarks Nationalbank, *Monetary Review,* Feb. 1985; IMF, *International Financial Statistics Yearbook, 1985.*

Table A10

DISTRIBUTION OF FOREIGN SUBSIDIARIES AND ASSOCIATES AND FOREIGN CAPITAL STOCK BY PERCENTAGE OWNERSHIP OF PARENT COMPANIES, 1976

	Inward Investment		Outward Investment	
	Number of Affiliates	*Value of Capital Stock*	*Number of Affiliates*	*Value of Capital Stock*
100% owned subsidiaries 50-99.9% owned subsidiaries and associates	1,177	*Not Available*	*Not Available*	
Less than 50% owned subsidiaries and associates	118			
TOTAL	1,295			

Source:
Danmarks Statistik, 1979, *A Survey of Foreign Owned Enterprises, 1976* (in Danish).

Table A12

LEADING FOREIGN AND DOMESTIC MULTINATIONAL COMPANIES, 1983

A Leading Foreign Multinational Companies in the country

	Name	*Home Country*	*Sector*	*No. of employees 1983*
1	British Leyland	UK	Motor vehicles	500
2	KFK	Norway	Food	530
3	Kodak	USA	Photography	550
4	Beauvais Felix	Sweden	Food	600
5	Rank-Xerox	USA	Office equipment	600
6	Neckelmann, K	W. Germany	Synthetic fibres	600
7	Fona Radio	UK	Electrical equipment	600
8	Burm. & Wain Ener	W. Germany	Electrical equipment	650
9	Brdr. Dahl	Sweden	Trade	650
10	Dumex	Norway	Pharmaceuticals	700
11	Metro	W. Germany	Distributive trade	700
12	Asea	Sweden	Electrical equipment	725
13	B P Oliekomp	UK	Oil	730
14	Siemens	W. Germany	Electrical equipment	750
15	Illum	UK	Distributive trade	750
16	Codan Forsikring	UK	Insurance	800
17	Dansk Shell	Netherlands/UK	Oil	825
18	Alpha Diesel	W. Germany	Transportation equipment	825
19	Da. Erhvervs Reng	UK	Services	850
20	NCR Danmark	USA	Office equipment	875
21	Nestle Nordisk	Switzerland	Food	900
22	Dansk Unilever	UK/Netherlands	Food	920
23	B & W Diesel	W. Germany	Transportation equipment	1000
24	Dansk Esso	USA	Oil	1000
25	BBC Brown Boven	Switzerland	Electrical equipment	1400

Table A12 (cont'd)

LEADING FOREIGN AND DOMESTIC MULTINATIONAL COMPANIES, end 1983

B	Leading Domestic Companies with Multinational Interests		
	Name[1]	*Sector*	*Employment abroad as a % of total employment*
1	Sophus Berendsen	Mechanical & electrical engineering, wholesale trade, insurance & services	87.5
2	Det Ostasiatiske Kompagni	Chemicals, mechanical engineering, timber & sea transport	*N.A.*
3	De Dansk Sukkerfabrikker (DDS)	Mechanical engineering, food & paper	30.0
4	J Lauritzen Holding	Sea transport	
5	ISS – International Service System	Office machinery, electrical & instrument engineering, services	80.0
6	F L Smidth	Mechanical engineering	25.0
7	The Grutenberghus Group	Paper & other manufacturing	*N.A.*
8	Nordisk Fjerfabrik	Textiles	*N.A.*
9	Novo Industri	Other manufacturing, wholesale trade	33.3
10	Sadolin og Holmblad	Chemicals	*N.A.*
11	Det Store Nordiske Telegraf-Selskab	Electrical engineering, telecommunications, and business services	*N.A.*
12	Danfoss	Mechanical engineering	54.5
13	Fosker and Nielsen	Electrical engineering	83.3
14	De Forenede Bryggerier	Drink & food	
15	Tjaereborg	Tourism, air and other transport	
16	Superfos	Chemicals, paper & agriculture	*Not*
17	Weston Taeppefabrik	Textiles	*Available*
18	Danisco	Chemicals, food and drink	
19	Kongskilde Koncernselskab	Mechanical engineering	
20	East Asiatic Co.	International trade	83.0
21	A P Moller	Shipping, oil, manufacturing	75.0
22	United Breweries	Drink	38.5
23	Lego	Plastic products	50.0
24	Grundfus	Mechanical engineering	40.0
25	Kampsax	Consulting engineers	66.7

NOTES TO TABLE A12

[1] Companies ranked by number of overseas subsidiaries.

DENMARK : DEFINITIONS

Official data on foreign direct investment in Denmark and direct investment abroad by Danish firms are provided by *Danmarks Nationalbank.* Such data refer only to flows of investment and does not include reinvested profits. Direct investment includes supplies of equity capital in various forms, such as acquisitions of large share interests in a company, intra-group loans with maturities of at least five years, and capital transfers towards current expenses. Shorter-term intra-group loans, on the other hand, are recorded as other business loans and credits and not as direct investments. Often Danish and foreign companies belonging to the same group will accumulate trade debts over a long period. If these debts are consolidated — thereby taking the form of intra-group loans or equity capital — they will then be reclassified as direct investments although the underlying capital supplies were effected earlier. One of the consequences of the alteration of the Foreign-Exchange Regulations as from 1 May 1983 is that inward intra-group loans are now recorded as ordinary financial loans and are hence no longer classified as foreign direct investment in Denmark.

Direct investment statistics are recorded at the time of payment or set-off. Permits for direct investments granted by the Ministry of Industry and the Bank are recorded as well. The statistics of permits cover also small investments in the form of equity capital, for which no permit proper is required. Discrepancies occur between payments and permits statistics primarily because settlements of direct investments may extend over several years, because capital transfers towards current expenses are included only in the payments statistics, and because, in some instances, planned investments are not implemented.

Source:

Danmarks Nationalbank, *Report and Accounts for the Year,* various issues.

FRANCE

France has had highly developed, albeit somewhat ambiguous, general policies towards inward direct investment, which have become more restrictive since the early 1960s. Particular efforts have been made to establish or maintain a distinct French position in major high-technology sectors.

A relatively pragmatic and discretionary system allows substantial scope for varying policies on foreign direct investment, the flow of which appears to have reached a peak in 1981 and has since fallen significantly.

Data on the geographical distribution of investment show that for the period 1975-83 outward investment has overtaken inward investment, which may be partly attributable to the investment policies of 1981-83. Outward investment to the developing countries has shifted away from French speaking Africa towards the newly industrialised countries, while amongst the developed countries, the USA has been the major growth area.

Regarding the sectoral distribution of inward investment, while the recent flow (between 1975 and 1983) has predominately gone into the tertiary sector, such a calculation leaves out of account the longer standing stock of investment in manufacturing.

MAIN SOURCES OF DATA:

A **Official**

1 Banque de France: publishes annual reports on the Balance of Payments position of France.

2 Ministere de l'Economie et des Finances: provides data on investment flows.

3 Ministere de l'Industrie: publishes information on imports and exports of foreign affiliates.

B **Private**

1 J Savary, *French Multinationals,* London: Frances Pinter, 1984.

2 C A Michalet & T Chevallier, 'France', in J H Dunning (Ed), *Multinational Enterprises, Economic Structure and International Competitiveness,* London: John Wiley, 1985.

Table A1

SUMMARY OF THE COUNTRY'S INTERNATIONAL INVESTMENT POSITION

		Inward Investment	Outward Investment
1	Number of foreign affilaites in host country, and of foreign affiliates of home country firms at Jan 1 1971	3,671	*N.A.*
2	Number of foreign firms with direct investments in host country, and home country firms with direct foreign affiliates at the end of 1981	980[1]	20
3	Total foreign direct capital stock at book value as a percentage of GNP at factor cost in 1982	2.79	3.64
4	Flow of foreign direct investment in the five year period 1979-83 (F Fr m)	61,674	81,128
5	Employment in foreign affiliates or abroad, 1981	4,473,000[2]	791,000
6	Output of foreign affiliates or abroad	*N.A.*	*N.A.*

Source:

J Savary, Les effets des enterprises multinationales sur l'emploi: le cas de la France: *Document de Travail,* No 24,. Bureau International du travail, Geneve, 1983; Stopford & Dunning, *Multinationals: Company Performance & Global Trends,* London, Macmillan, 1983; Les Participations etrangeres dans l'industries francaise en 1971, *Economic Statistique,* 1974.

NOTES TO TABLE A1

1 1971.

2 1980.

Table A2

PRIVATE FOREIGN CAPITAL STOCK, 1960-83 (F Fr bn)

	Inward Investment			Outward Investment		
	Portfolio	*Direct*	*Total*	*Portfolio*	*Direct*	*Total*
Book value of capital stock						
1960	*Not Available*	*N.A.*	*Not Available*	*Not Available*	20.10	*Not Available*
1967		14.76			29.52	
1971		*N.A.*			40.24	
1973		25.83			*N.A.*	
1975		42.60[1]			47.58	
1976		*N.A.*			56.88	
1977		*N.A.*			61.93	
1978		50.40			67.24	
1979		62.08[2]			74.34	
1980		76.00			84.52	
1981		89.22			109.65[3]	
1982		99.57			129.84	
1983		112.07			143.93	

Source:
Stopford & Dunning, *Multinationals: Company Performance & Global Trends,* London; Macmillan, 1983; *Les Cahiers Francais,* No 190, March-April 1979; J Savary, *French Multinationals,* London: Frances Pinter, 1984

NOTES TO TABLE A2

1 1974.

2 From 1979 onwards, calculations of direct inward investment based on cumulative net flows of long term capital.

3 From 1981 onwards, calculations of direct outward investment based on cumulative net flows.

Table A3

FLOW OF FOREIGN DIRECT INVESTMENT, 1970-83 (F Fr m)

	Inward Investment			Outward Investment		
	Reinvested Profits	*Other*	*Total*	*Reinvested Profits*	*Other*	*Total*
1970	955	2,500	3,455	117	1,955	2,072
1971	578	2,335	2,913	11	2,190	2,201
1972	515	2,946	3,461	38	2,952	2,990
1973	935	4,210	5,145	11	4,024	4,035
1974	497	7,075	7,572	35	3,713	3,748
1975	317	5,428	5,745	57	6,105	6,162
1976	348	3,745	4,093	*N.S.A.*	*N.S.A.*	8,428
1977	109	7,008	7,117	298	6,253	6,551
1978	51	11,074	11,125	*N.S.A.*	*N.S.A.*	8,131
1979	60	11,620	11,680	*N.S.A.*	*N.S.A.*	8,414
1980	187	13,733	13,920	77	13,230	13,307
1981	109	13,113	13,222	19	25,108	25,127
1982	261	10,082	10,343	*N.S.A.*	*N.S.A.*	20,195
1983	*N.S.A.*	*N.S.A.*	12,509	*N.S.A.*	*N.S.A.*	14,085

Source:

Banque de France & Ministere de l'Economie et des Finances, *Les Balance des Paiments de la France,* Annual Reports, various years; Ministere de l'Economie et des Finances, *Les Notes Bleues,* No 88, September 13-19, 1982.

Table A4

SECTORAL DISTRIBUTION OF FOREIGN DIRECT CAPITAL STOCK, 1975-83 (F Fr m)[1]

	Inward Investment			Outward Investment		
	Primary	*Secondary*	*Tertiary*	*Primary*	*Secondary*	*Tertiary*
1975-80	1,380	19,179	33,121	10,668	19,653	20,672
1975-83	1,438	33,215	55,101	30,185	38,491	41,724

Source:

Banque de France & Ministere de l'Economie et des Finances, *La Balance des Paiments de la France,* Annual Reports (Annexes), various years; Ministere de l'Economie et des Finances, *Les Notes Bleues,* No 88, September 13-19, 1982.

NOTES TO TABLE A4

1 Calculations based on cumulative net flows of long term capital.

Table A5

GEOGRAPHICAL DISTRIBUTION OF FOREIGN DIRECT CAPITAL STOCK, 1975-83 (F Fr m)[1]

	Inward Investment			Outward Investment		
	Developed Countries	*Developing Countries*	*Total*	*Developed Countries*	*Developing Countries*	*Total*
1975-80	47,482	6,198	53,680	37,816	13,297	51,113
1975-83	79,306	10,448	89,754	83,017	27,503	110,520

Source:

Banque de France & Ministere de l'Economie et des Finances, *Balance des Paiments de la France,* Annual Reports, various years; Ministere de l'Economie et des Finances, *Les Notes Bleues,* No 88, September 13-19, 1982.

NOTES TO TABLE A5

1 Calculations based on cumulative net flows of long term capital.

Table A6

INDUSTRIAL DISTRIBUTION OF FOREIGN DIRECT CAPITAL STOCK, 1975-83 (F Fr m)[1]

	Inward Investment		Outward Investment	
	1975-80	*1975-83*	*1975-80*	*1975-83*
Primary	1,380	1,438	10,668	30,185
Agriculture	201	283	430	622
Mining & quarrying	1	28	181	449
Oil[2]	1,178	1,127	10,057	29,114
Secondary	19,179	33,215	19,653	38,491
Food & drink	1,747	2,689	2,299	3,632
Chemicals & allied[3]	5,879	10,689	2,194	4,103
Metals, Mechanical engineering, Electrical equipment, Motor vehicles, Other transportation equipment	6,896	12,699	10,881	22,442
Textiles & clothing	949	1,448	379	866
Other manufacturing[4]	3,708	5,690	3,900	7,448
Tertiary	33,121	55,101[5]	20,672	41,724[5]
Transport & communications	528	686	409	1,957
Distributive trade[6]	8,770	16,702	6,826	10,817
Property	13,934	21,697	1,241	2,157
Banking & finance[7]	5,861	8,924	9,242	19,994
Other services	4,028	4,794	2,954	5,081
TOTAL	53,680	89,754	50,993	110,400

Source:
Banque de France & Ministere de l'Economie et des Finances, *La Balance des Paiments de la France*, Annual Reports, various issues; Ministere de l'Economie et des Finances, *Les Notes Bleues,* No 88, September 13-19, 1982.

NOTES TO TABLE A6

1 Calculations based on cumulative net flows of long term capital.
2 All sources of energy.
3 Including Rubber, Coal & Petroleum products.
4 Including Paper & allied, Stone, clay & glass.
5 Including items under indeterminate classification.
6 Represents commerce.
7 Including Insurance.

Table A7

LEADING SOURCE AND RECIPIENT COUNTRIES, 1975-83 (F Fr m)[1]

	Inward Investment		Outward Investment	
	1975-80	*1975-83*	*1975-80*	*1975-83*
DEVELOPED AREAS	47,482	79,306	37,816	83,017
Europe				
EEC of which:	30,936	49,056	15,247	29,443
Belgium & Luxembourg	5,022	7,752	3,641	6,662
Denmark	349	646	109	127
W. Germany	7,866	12,855	2,933	6,190
Ireland	58	105	315	548
Italy	1,901	3,288	3,138	5,923
Netherlands	8,746	13,163	375	3,118
UK	6,994	11,247	4,736	6,642
North America of which:	6,745	12,422	12,311	35,784
Canada	-30	348	1,896	-1,951
USA	6,775	12,074	10,415	37,735
Other developed countries[2]	9,801	17,828[3]	10,258	17,790[4]
DEVELOPING AREAS	6,198	10,448	13,297	27,503[5]
TOTAL	53,680	89,754	51,113	110,520

Source:
Banque de France & Ministere de l'Economie et des Finances, *La Balance des Paiments de la France,* Annual Reports, various years; Ministere de l'Economie et des Finances, *Les Notes Bleues,* No 88, September 13-19, 1982.

NOTES TO TABLE A7

1 Calculations based on cumulative net flows of long term capital.

2 Includes all developed countries except North America and the EEC.

3 Of this total, 5,045 million was accounted for by Switzerland, 1,279 million by Sweden and 1,230 million by Japan in the period 1981-83.

4 Of this total, 3,645 million was accounted for by Spain, and 2,965 million by Switzerland in the period 1981-83.

5 Of this total, 1,563 million was accounted for by Argentina and 1,365 million by Brazil in the period 1981-83.

Table A8

INDICATORS OF THE SIGNIFICANCE OF INWARD FOREIGN DIRECT INVESTMENT OR THE ACTIVITIES OF FOREIGN-BASED COMPANIES TO THE NATIONAL ECONOMY, 1977-82

1	Direct capital stock of foreign affiliates at book value in 1982 as a proportion of:	
	a GNP at factor cost	2.79
	b population (in F Fr per head)	1,836.41
2	Employment in foreign affiliates in 1982 as a percentage of all employment in manufacturing	20.2[1]
3	Output of foreign affiliates in 1982 as a percentage of all companies' output in secondary (ie, manufacturing) industry	25.3[2]
4	Exports of foreign affiliates in 1977 as a percentage of all manufacturing exports	25.9
5	Percentage share of sales accounted for by foreign affiliates in selected sectors, 1982	
		Sales
	Primary Goods Sector	
	Oil	51.4
	Manufacturing Sector	
	Chemicals & allied	40.0[3]
	Metals	15.0[3]
	Electrical equipment	34.0[3]
	Motor vehicles	14.9
	Other transportation equipment	6.0[3]
	Textiles & clothing	7.2[3]
	Paper & allied	24.1
	Rubber	24.8

Source:

Ministere de l'Industrie, *L'implantation etrangere dans l'industrie, 1 Jan 1983,* STISI, 1984; Ministere de l'Industrie, *Importations, Exportations et Fifiales Francaises de Firmes Multinationales,* STISI, 1982.

FRANCE NOTES TO TABLE A8

1 Includes only employment in French enterprises in which foreign participation is greater than 20% of capital (petroleum excluded).

2 Represents sales.

3 Represents re-restimated data in sectoral distribution by the Minsitere de l'Industrie.

Table A9

INDICATORS OF THE SIGNIFICANCE OF OUTWARD FOREIGN DIRECT INVESTMENT OR THE ACTIVITIES OF HOME-BASED COMPANIES ABROAD FOR THE NATIONAL ECONOMY, 1974-82

1	Foreign capital stock of home-based firms at book value in 1982 as a proportion of:	
	a GNP at factor cost	3.64
	b population (in F Fr per head)	2,394.69
2	Employment in foreign affiliates in 1977 as a percentage of domestic employment in all industry	25.20[1]
3	Sales of foreign affiliates of home-based firms as a percentage of that in selected domestic sectors, 1974	
		Sales[2]
	Primary Goods Sector	
	Mining & quarrying[3]	28.3
	Oil	21.2
	Manufacturing Sector	
	Chemicals & allied	12.1
	Metals	10.6
	Mechanical engineering	1.7
	Electrical equipment	4.1
	Motor vehicles	12.5
	Textiles & clothing	3.6
	Paper & allied } Rubber }	14.2[4]
	Services Sector	
	Construction	3.7
	Trade & distribution	0.3
	Other services	0.02

Source:

IMF, *International Financial Statistics, 1985;* J Savary, *French Multinationals,* London: Frances Pinter, 1982.

NOTES TO TABLE A9

1 Based on a sample of 67 French multinationals.

2 Based on a sample of firms; percentage represents the ratio of production abroad to total production in France & abroad.

3 Represents mining, construction, materials & class.

4 Including plastics.

Table A10

DISTRIBUTION OF FOREIGN SUBSIDIARIES AND ASSOCIATES AND FOREIGN CAPITAL STOCK BY PERCENTAGE OWNERSHIP OF PARENT COMPANIES, 1980 (F Fr m)

	Inward Investment		Outward Investment	
	Number of Affiliates	*Value of Capital Stock*[1]	*Number of Affiliates*	*Value of Capital Stock*
100% owned subsidiaries	*Not Available*	11,085	*Not Available*	
50-99.9% owned subsidiaries and associates				
Less than 50% owned subsidiaries and associates[2]		2,499		
TOTAL		13,584		

Source:

Les Echanges Internationaux, *Les Chiffres Cles,* SESSI, 1983.

NOTES TO TABLE A10

1 Flow of inward investment for 1980.

2 Represents 20-50% owned subsidiaries & associates.

Table A11

ROYALTY RECEIPTS AND PAYMENTS, 1975-82 (F Fr m)

	Payments			Receipts		
	To Affiliates	*To Non-affiliates*	*Total*	*From Affiliates*	*From Non-affiliates*	*Total*
1975	*Not Separately Available*		2,211.8	*Not Separately Available*		827.5
1976			2,803.2			965.7
1977			2,678.9			1,388.2
1978			3,062.3			1,559.4
1979			3,429.9			1,824.9
1980			4.345.2			2,095.6
1981			5,139.4			2,685.0
1982			5,949.9			2.467.0

Source:

IMF, *Balance of Payments Statistics Yearbook,* various issues.

Table A12

LEADING FOREIGN AND DOMESTIC MULTINATIONAL COMPANIES

A Leading Foreign Multinational Companies in the country, end 1980

Name		*Home Country*	*Sector*	*French Turnover (F Fr m)*
1	Shell	USA	Oil	41,956
2	Esso	USA	Oil	26,665
3	Francaise des Petroles BP	UK	Oil	17,581
4	IBM	USA	Data processing	13,698
5	Philips France	Netherlands	Electronic equipment	10,910
6	Mobil Oil	USA	Oil	8,003
7	Unilever	UK	Food products	6,997
8	Roussel-Uclaf (Hoechst)	W. Germany	Chemicals	5,292
9	Volkswagen France	W. Germany	Motor vehicles	4,524
10	Sopad (Nestle)	Switzerland	Food products	4,373
11	Ford	USA	Motor vehicles	4,214
12	Esso Chimie	USA	Petro-chemicals	3,896
13	Cargill	USA	Commodity trading agent and principal	3,710
14	Kodak Pathe (Eastman Kodak)	USA	Photographic equipment	3,547
15	Mercedes Benz (Daimler)	W. Germany	Motor vehicles	3,227
16	Shell Chimie	USA	Petro-chemicals	3,128
17	General Motors	USA	Motor vehicles	2,540
18	CEM (Brown Bovery)	Switzerland	Electrical equipment	2,530
19	Francaise BASF	W. Germany	Chemicals	2,500
20	Francaise Hoechst	W. Germany	Chemicals	2,431
21	Rank Xerox	USA	Scientific & photographic equipment	2,353
22	International Harvester France	USA	Industrial & agricultural equipment	2,159
23	DBA (Bifco)	USA	Motor vehicles	2,132
24	Colgate Palmolive	USA	Consumer products	1,992
25	Fiat	Italy	Motor vehicles	1,972

Source:
Article from 'Le Nouvel Economiste', December 14, 1981.

Table A12 (cont'd)

LEADING FOREIGN AND DOMESTIC MULTINATIONAL COMPANIES, 1974-82

B Leading Domestic Companies with Multinational Interests, 1974 and 1982

Name	Sector	Foreign Production (F Fr m), 1974	Employment abroad as a % of global employment, 1982
1 CFP	Oil	18,000	44.2
2 SGPM	Building materials	7,837	47.8
3 Michelin	Rubber	6,932	59.0
4 ERAP[1]	Oil	6,500	*N.A.*
5 PUK	Metals	4,857	29.1
6 Marine Wendel	Metals	3,905	*N.A.*
7 Compagnie Nord-Imetal	Metals	3,861	78.2[3]
8 Rhone-Poulenc	Chemicals	3,827	38.1
9 Renault	Motor vehicles	3,658	24.5
10 BSN-GD	Food	3,104	29.2
11 Citroën	Motor vehicles	3,000	*N.A.*
12 Lafarge	Building materials	2,615	49.6
13 Air Liquide	Chemicals	2,465	60.0
14 Vallourec	Metals	1,876	*N.A.*
15 Empain Schneider	Machinery	1,681	22.0
16 L'Oreal (Nestle group)	Drugs	1,418	49.0
17 Thomson	Electrical equipment	1,376	15.4
18 CGE	Electrical equipment	1,363	20.3
19 EMC	Chemicals	1,338	26.2
20 Automobiles Peugeot[2]	Motor vehicles	1,262	*N.A.*
21 DMC	Textiles	1,048	36.1
22 Roussel-Uclaf (Hoechst, West Germany)	Chemicals	1,000	39.3

Source:

J Savary, *The French Multinationals,* London: Frances Pinter.

NOTES TO TABLE A12

1 ERAP and SNPA were merged to form Elf Aquitaine, for which employment abroad as a percentage of global employment was 30.4%.

2 The group PSA Peugot-Citroën was formed in 1976 from the absorption of Citroën and the European subsidiaries of Chrysler, and had 26.5% foreign employment as a share of worldwide employment. See J Stopford *The World Directory of Multinational Enterprises,* London: Macmillan, 1982.

3 Imetal only.

FRANCE: DEFINITIONS

The definition of direct investment in terms of the balance of payments differs from the definition established by law. The former includes capital operations that have a participation of greater than 20% of the capital, increase of capital or the purchase of shares in a firm. It also includes loans made by the affiliates from the parent company that lasts more than a year as well as unguaranteed loans and subsidies. It also incorporates the purchase of property. The purchase of property may be made as a financial investment or it may include other elements such as guarantees and extension to other activities.

The statistics of the balance of payments include only financial flows between France and abroad (including overseas countries and the franc zone). They do not include self-financed investment or investments financed by local credits or reinvested profits. Neither do they include French stocks of capital abroad nor of foreign stocks of capital in France.

Until 1978, the balance of payments statistics allowed the breakdown between investments made by the private non-banking sector and the investments of the banking sector (investments abroad by French banks or investments in French banks by non-residents). The previous *Notes Bleues* only referred to the investments made by the private non-banking sector. Since 1979, the change of methodology adopted by the Bank of France does not allow the breakdown of investments by the banking sector according to sector or geographical area. The investment by the non-banking and banking private sectors have been contained, and in order to ensure some consistency, all the banking sector investments before 1979 have been aggregated.

Before 1978, French investments abroad did not include loans from residents to non-residents. These loans were included in another item in the balance of payments. After 1979, all the French investments abroad are included in only one item in the balance of payments. The same can be said for foreign investments in France. However, before 1978, the item long-term credits made the distinction between direct investment and others. Comparisons between inward and outward investments are not possible in the long term since they exclude investments in the oil and property sector. Inward direct investment in the energy sector is very insignificant although it represents an important, though decreasing, share of French investments abroad.

The gross figures (disinvestments not included) are more significant. Net figures may be disturbed by important disinvestments corresponding to the particular strategy of each firm or nationalisation measures made by each country.

All figures are in current francs.

Source:

Ministère de l'Economie et des Finances, *Les Notes Bleues.*

WEST GERMANY

Partly as a result of confiscations during two world wars, West Germany has only recently regained its position as one of the major outward direct investors. The stock of outward investment has now overtaken inward investment, which had risen after 1958 as US firms in particular attempted to gain greater access to an expanded EEC market. Outward investment in banking and services has been growing especially rapidly, though manufacturing investment still accounts for well over half of the total stock of both outward and inward investment. In recent years developing country investment in Germany appears to have been rising faster than that of developed countries, but within the latter the total capital of European firms has overtaken that of US corporations. Meanwhile, the outward investment of the Federal Republic in the USA has grown spectacularly during the 1970s, even though in that country it is still well behind the position of affiliates of firms based in the UK or the Netherlands.

MAIN SOURCES OF DATA:

A **Official**

1 Deutsche Bundesbank: since 1976 has provided an annual assessment of the book value of capital stock of foreign affiliates. Royalties paid by foreign affiliates are detailed over a longer time span.

2 Bundesministerium fur Wirtschaft: issues regular statements based on preliminary flow data made available by the Deutsche Bundesbank. The cumulative investment stocks deduced from this does not match the Bundesbank's own census.

3 Deutsche Bundesbank: a third set of investment flows enters into balance of payments figures published in statistical supplements.

B **Private**

1 P Juhl, 'The Federal Republic of Germany' in J H Dunning, *Multinational Enterprises, Economic Structure and International Competitiveness,* Chichester: John Wiley, 1985.

Table A1

SUMMARY OF THE COUNTRY'S INTERNATIONAL INVESTMENT POSITION

		Inward Investment	Outward Investment
1	Number of foreign affiliates in host country, and of foreign affiliates of home country firms at the end of 1983[1]	8,997	13,811
2	Number of foreign firms with direct investments in host country, and home country firms with direct foreign affiliates	*N.A.*	*N.A.*
3	Total foreign direct capital stock at book value as a percentage of GNP at factor cost in 1983	4.8	6.3
4	Flow of foreign direct investment in the five year period 1979-83 (DM m)	10,854	38,545
5	Employment in foreign affiliates or abroad, 1983[1]	1,485,000	1,619,000
6	Output of foreign affiliates or abroad 1983 (DM m)	565,700	436,700

Source:

Deutsche Bundesbank, *Monthly Report, March 1985;* and *Die Kapitalverflechtung der Unternehmen mit dem Ausland nach Ländern und Wirtschaftszweigen, Annex to the Statistical Supplements to Monthly Reports, Series 3, Balance of Payments Statistics, June 1985;* IMF, *International Financial Statistics, July 1985.*

NOTES TO TABLE A1

1 Figures refer to primary and secondary investments. See Definitions below.

Table A2

PRIVATE FOREIGN CAPITAL STOCK, 1960-83 (DM bn)

	Inward Investment			Outward Investment		
	Portfolio[1]	*Direct*[2]	*Total*	*Portfolio*[1]	*Direct*[2]	*Total*
Book value of capital stock						
1960	*Not Available*	7.00	*Not Available*	*Not Available*	3.20	*Not Available*
1965		19.56			7.85	
1970		35.11			17.33	
1975	93.85	60.51	154.36	112.73	37.64	150.36
1976	109.86	63.53	173.39	129.19	43.10	172.30
1977	130.23	62.31	192.54	139.12	46.54	185.66
1978	158.19	66.94	225.14	151.45	52.70	204.15
1979	185.38	70.27	255.65	163.78	61,16	224.93
1980	215.00	71.76	286.76	191.75	74.35	266.11
1981	244.33	74.74	319.07	218.76	88.43	307.19
1982	253.44	76.36	329.80	228.71	95.40	324.11
1983	257.64	80.59	338.24	240.66	106.05	346.70

Source:

Deutsche Bundesbank, *Monthly Report, April 1979, January 1981, August 1982, May 1983, July 1984, July 1985;* Deutsche Bundesbank, *Appendix to Statistical Supplements to Monthly Reports, Series 3, Balance of Payments Statistics, July 1982*

NOTES TO TABLE A2

1 External assets of German Banks plus external assets of domestic enterprises (excluding trade credits) and external liabilities of same.

2 Figures for 1976-81 presented in Deutsche Bundesbank *Monthly Reports,* figures for 1960 estimated by authors from US and UK data. Direct capital stock for 1961-75 was then obtained by dividing the change from 1960 to 1976 between years according to the proportional size of FDI flows (see Table A3) as given in the balance of payments data.

Table A3

PRIVATE FOREIGN DIRECT INVESTMENT, 1970-84 (DM m)

	Inward Investment			Outward Investment		
	Reinvested Profits	*Other*	*Total*	*Reinvested Profits*	*Other*	*Total*
1970	686	1,484	2,170	638	2,545	3,183
1971	891	3,014	3,905	756	2,900	3,656
1972	935	5,222	6,157	1,356	3,632	4,988
1973	880	4,444	5,324	1,128	3,289	4,417
1974	1,100	4,395	5,495	1,425	3,534	4,959
1975	1,142	548	1,690	1,031	3,909	4,940
1976	1,230	1,452	2,682	1,235	4,944	6,179
1977	−543	2,820	2,277	-532	5,654	5,122
1978	604	2,666	3,270	572	6,670	7,242
1979	1,847	1,302	3,149	1,772	6,463	8,235
1980	−1,112	1,869	757	-1,174	8,591	7,417
1981	−3,065	3,784	720	-3,008	11,784	8,776
1982	−1,152	3,161	2,009	-391	6,421	6,030
1983	−54	4,121	4,067	-157	8,244	8,087
1984	641	2,684	3,325	525	8,226	8,751

Source:

Deutsche Bundesbank, *Appendix to Statistical Supplements to Monthly Reports, Series 3, Balance of Payments Statistics,* July 1982, July 1984 and July 1985; IMF, *Balance of Payments Statistics, Yearbook, 1984.*
Yearbook, 1984.

Table A4

SECTORAL DISTRIBUTION OF FOREIGN DIRECT CAPITAL STOCK, 1966-83 (DM m)[1]

	Inward Investment				Outward Investment		
	Primary[2]	*Secondary*	*Tertiary*		*Primary*	*Secondary*	*Tertiary*
1966[3]	159	18,592	5,379		305	6,193	2,612
1976	236	41,997	21,298		1,727	26,054	15,321
1983	243	44,687	35,660		4,639	61,538	39,871

Source:

Deutsche Bundesbank, *Monthly Report, April 1984* and *March 1985,* and *Die Kapitalverflechtung der Unternehmen mit dem Ausland nach Landern und Wirtschaftszweigen,* Annex to the *Statistical Supplements to Monthly Reports, Series 3, Balance of Payments Statistics, June 1983* and *March 1985;* (for 1966) Deutsche Bundesbank, *Monthly Report, April 1979,* and Bundesministerium fur Wirtschaft, unpublished statements, *Runderlass Aussenwirtschaft.*

NOTES TO TABLE A4

1 The industrial distribution refers to the industry of the investing parent.

2 Mainly mining and oil.

3 Estimated by authors – see footnote 2 to Table A2.

Table A5

GEOGRAPHICAL DISTRIBUTION OF FOREIGN DIRECT CAPITAL STOCK 1965-83 (DM m)

	Inward Investment				Outward Investment		
	Developed Countries	*Developing Countries*	*Total*		*Developed Countries*	*Developing Countries*	*Total*
1965[1]	19,327	235	19,562		5,952	1,896	7,848
1970[1]	34,495	611	35,106		13,027	4,299	17,848
1976	61,727	1,270	63,531		34,506	8,597	43,105[2]
1983	77,418	2,139	80,590		88,770	17,278	106,048

Source:

As for West Germany Table A4.

NOTES TO TABLE A5

1 Authors' estimate. See footnote 2, Table A2.

2 Total slightly different to that given in Table A4 due to rounding in the source.

Table A6

INDUSTRIAL DISTRIBUTION OF FOREIGN CAPITAL STOCK, 1976-83 (DM m)[1]

	Inward Investment		Outward Investment	
	1976	*1983*	*1976*	*1983*
Primary	236	243	1,727	4,639
Agriculture	51	72	47	81
Mining & quarrying	185	48	596	1,796
Oil		123	1,084	2,762
Secondary	41,997	44,687	26,054	61,538
Food & drink	3,387	3,280	494	930
Chemicals & allied	5,992	7,460	8,134	17,518
Metals	5,477	3,453	2,153	4,570
Mechanical engineering[2]	4,157	8,162	3,257	8,841
Electrical equipment[2]	6,181	4,064	5,101	11,484
Motor vehicles	4,857	5,179	4,027	11,276
Other transportation equipment	256	137[3]	268	951
Textiles & clothing	546	425	353	817
Paper & allied	594	749	148	621
Rubber[4]	1,762	1,784	375	804
Stone, clay & glass	834	978	764	1,607
Coal & petroleum products	7,164	7,843	509	1,095
Other manufacturing	791	1,173	471	1,024
Tertiary	21,298	35,660	15,321	39,871
Construction	147	196	460	1,981
Transport & communications	518	826	939	1,343
Distributive trade	8,752	14,116	2,160	4,244
Property	6,588	11,393	6,010	11,785
Banking & finance	4,028	7,191	3,370	13,062
Other services	1,265	1,938	2,382[5]	7,456[5]
TOTAL	63,531	80,590	43,102	106,048

Source:
Deutsche Bundesbank, *Monthly Report,* April 1984 and March 1985, and *Die Kapitalverflechtung der Unternehmen mit dem Ausland nach Landern und Wirtschaftszweigen,* annex to the *Statistical Supplements, series 3, Balance of Payments Statistics, Monthly Report,* June 1983 & March 1985.

NOTES TO TABLE A6

1 The industrial distribution refers to the industry of the the investing parent.
2 Prior to 1980 data processing equipment is included in Electrical equipment, from 1980 this is included in Mechanical engineering.
3 Data for Shipbuilding is suppressed for inward investment in 1983, and is included in Other manufacturing.
4 From 1981 asbestos manufacture in stone, clay and glass. Prior to 1981 it is included in Rubber.
5 Outward direct investment by private individuals is included in Other services, being DM 1,998 million in 1976 and DM 5,208 million in 1983.

Table A7

LEADING SOURCE AND RECIPIENT COUNTRIES
1976-83 (DM m)

	Inward Investment		Outward Investment	
	1976	*1983*	*1976*	*1983*
DEVELOPED AREAS	61,727	77,418	34,506	88,770
Europe	33,744	39,413	25,570	49,513
EEC of which:	21,961	23,717	16,015	32,919
Belgium & Luxembourg	2,543	1,964	4,586	9,678
Denmark	388	596	365	675
France	4,331	5,339	4,468	8,388
Greece	23	37	277	600
Ireland	53	91	179	531
Italy	641	709	1,002	2,917
Netherlands	8,852	8,140	3,870	5,742
UK	5,130	6,841	1,268	4,388
Other Europe of which:[2]	11,783[1]	15,696[1]	9,555	16,594
Austria	722	1,060	1,900	3,261
Cyprus	*N.A.*[2]	*N.A.*[2]	9	43
Finland	75	191	78	106
Norway	115	150	78	361
Portugal	12	10	310	331
Spain	62	124	1,685	3,106
Sweden	1,389	1,747	366	474
Switzerland	9,114	11,521	4,917	8,498
Turkey	*N.A.*	*N.A.*	145	250
North America of which:	26,550	34,432	7,311	34,014
Canada	539	698	1,992	4,814
USA	26,011	33,734	5,319	29,200
Other developed countries of which:	1,433	3,573	1,625	5,243
Australia	*N.S.A.*	*N.S.A.*	285	1,388
Japan	1,415	3,475	473	1,583
New Zealand	*N.A.*	*N.A.*	10	46
South Africa	9	5	857	2,226
DEVELOPING AREAS	1,270	2,139	8,597	17,278
Africa of which:	8[3]	7[3]	1,673	3,885
Algeria	*Not Available*	*Not Available*	271	381
Cameroon			19	31
Egypt	3		134	912
Ethiopia	*Not Available*		4	*N.A.*
Ghana			17	4
Kenya			39	66

Table A7 (cont'd)

LEADING SOURCE AND RECIPIENT COUNTRIES
1976-83 (DM m)

	Inward Investment		Outward Investment	
	1976	*1983*	*1976*	*1983*
DEVELOPING AREAS (cont'd)				
Libya			109	274
Morocco			28	65
Nigeria			531	1,460
Senegal	*Not Available*	*Not Available*	4	9
Zaire			84	35
Zambia			10	16
Zimbabwe			*N.A.*	14
Asia & Pacific (except Japan or Middle East) of which:	96	181	793	2,563
Hong Kong	30	50	124	440
India	16	30	133	300
Indonesia	1	11	76	151
S. Korea	48	64	14	101
Malaysia		*N.A.*	68	200
Pakistan		8	40	43
Philippines			15	56
Singapore	*Not Available*	*Not Available*	234	983
Sri Lanka			*N.A.*	20
Taiwan		2	23	71
Thailand		14	43	94
Latin America of which:	688	1,143	5,436	9,876
Argentina	192	194	476	1,067
Bahamas	7	24	14	456
Brazil	56	104	3,620	5,789
Chile	*N.A.*	*N.A.*	53	99
Colombia	7	*N.A.*	57	147
Mexico	18	5	198	760
Netherlands Antilles	7	18	331	506
Panama	356	375	116	68
Paraguay	*N.A.*	*N.A.*	11	42
Peru	*N.A.*	*N.A.*	99	41
Uruguay	22	22	19	22
Venezuela	3	6	188	139
Middle East of which:	478[3]	808[3]	695	954
Iran	*N.A.*	743	454	379
Iraq	*N.A.*	*N.A.*	39	66

Table A7 (cont'd)

LEADING SOURCE AND RECIPIENT COUNTRIES 1976-83 (DM m.)

	Inward Investment		Outward Investment	
	1976	*1983*	*1976*	*1983*
DEVELOPING AREAS (cont'd)				
Israel	11	16	77	*N.S.A.*[4]
Kuwait	37	*N.A.*	*N.A.*	*N.A.*
Saudi Arabia	*N.A.*	7	48	330
United Arab Emirates	*N.A.*	*N.A.*	65	112
UNSPECIFIED	534	1,033	–	–
TOTAL	63,531	80,590	43,105[5]	106,048

Source:

As for West Germany Table A6.

NOTES TO TABLE A7

1 Includes Eastern Europe which accounted for DM 271 million and DM 835 million of inward German investments in 1976 and 1983 respectively.

2 For inward investment Cyprus is classified under Asia.

3 Certain OPEC countries not in the Middle East, such as Algeria, Ecuador, Gabon, Libya and Nigeria, are included in the Middle East total for inward investment. Africa's total is reduced accordingly.

4 Israel is classified under Asia in 1983 (outward only) while Lebanon is classified under Asia for outward and inward in both years.

5 Total slightly different from that in Table A6 due to rounding in the source.

Table A8

INDICATORS OF THE SIGNIFICANCE OF INWARD FOREIGN DIRECT INVESTMENT OR THE ACTIVITIES OF FOREIGN-BASED COMPANIES TO THE NATIONAL ECONOMY, 1982 - 1983

1	Direct capital stock of foreign affiliates at book value in 1983 as a proportion of:	
	a GNP at factor cost (as a %)	4.82
	b population (in DM per head)	1,307.6
2	Employment in foreign affiliates in 1982 as a percentage of all employment	
	a in all industry	8.33
	b in manufacturing	15.80
3	Output of foreign affiliates in 1982 as a percentage of all companies' output in manufacturing industry	26.15
4	Percentage share of sales and employment accounted for by foreign affiliates in selected sectors, 1982	

	Sales	*Employment*
Primary Goods Sector		
Agriculture		0.50
Mining and quarrying	30.53	10.05
Oil		25.00
Manufacturing Sector		
Food and drink	23.67	17.67
Chemicals and allied	29.24	21.76
Metals	23.49	30.36
Mechanical engineering	22.58	16.31
Electrical equipment	22.80	18.76
Motor vehicles	22.44	18.92
Other transportation equipment	10.01	9.73
Textiles and clothing	6.55	4.81
Paper and allied	11.28	7.57
Rubber	24.83	20.42
Stone, glass & clay	22.52	21.10
Coal and petroleum products	77.48	60.98
Timber and furniture	1.95	0.96
Other manufacturing	19.42	14.98
Services Sector		
Construction		1.78
Transport and communications		3.47
Trade and distribution		8.09
Banking and finance		6.27
Other services		2.57

Source:

Deutsche Bundesbank, *Monthly Report,* March 1985, supplement "Die Kapitalverflechtung der unternehmen mit dem Ausland nach Ländern und wirtschaftszweigen 1978 bis 1983"; Deutsche Bundesbank, *Monthly Report,* August 1985, supplement "saisonbereinigte wirtschaftszahlen"; statistisches bundesamt, *statistisches Jahrbuch, 1983*; IMF, *International Financial Statistics Yearbook, 1984.*

Table A9

INDICATORS OF THE SIGNIFICANCE OF OUTWARD FOREIGN DIRECT INVESTMENT OR THE ACTIVITIES OF HOME-BASED COMPANIES ABROAD FOR THE NATIONAL ECONOMY, 1982 - 1983

1	Foreign capital stock of home-based firms at book value in 1983 as a proportion of:		
	a GNP at factor cost		6.34
	b population (in DM per head)		1,719.7
2	Employment in foreign affiliates in 1982 as a percentage of domestic employment		
	a in all industry		10.21
	b in manufacturing		18.10
3	Output of foreign manufacturing affiliates in 1982 as a percentage of		
	a domestic manufacturing output		16.97
	b manufacturing exports from the home country		55.48
4	Sales and employment of foreign affiliates of home-based firms as a percentage of that in selected domestic sectors, 1982		
		Sales	*Employment*
	Primary Goods Sector		
	Agriculture		1.51
	Mining and quarrying	5.43	3.65
	Oil		25.00
	Manufacturing Sector		
	Food and drink	4.82	6.63
	Chemicals and allied	54.41	57.69
	Metals	10.18	12.54
	Mechanical engineering	13.56	12.91
	Electrical equipment	24.33	23.90
	Motor vehicles	25.40	28.88
	Other transportation equipment	0.00	0.00
	Textiles and clothing	8.73	12.59
	Paper and allied	8.09	5.59
	Rubber	9.49	4.50
	Stone, glass & clay	14.04	13.92
	Coal and petroleum products	2.00	4.88
	Timber and furniture	4.68	8.13
	Other manufacturing	24.97	22.22
	Services Sector		
	Construction		3.12
	Transport and communications		3.14
	Trade and distribution		9.95
	Banking and finance		4.18
	Other services		1.26

Source:

Deutsche Bundesbank, *Monthly Report,* March 1985, supplement "Die Kapitalverflechtung der unternehmen mit dem Ausland nach Ländern und wirtschaftszweigen 1978 bis 1983"; Deutsche Bundesbank, *Monthly Report,* August 1985, supplement "saisonbereinigte wirtschaftszahlen"; statistisches bundesamt, *statistisches Jahrbuch, 1983*; IMF, *International Financial Statistics Yearbook, 1984.*

Table A10

DISTRIBUTION OF FOREIGN SUBSIDIARIES AND ASSOCIATES AND FOREIGN CAPITAL STOCK BY PERCENTAGE OWNERSHIP OF PARENT COMPANIES, 1982

	Inward Investment		**Outward Investment**	
	Number of Affiliates	*Value of Capital Stock (DM m)*[1]	*Number of Affiliates*	*Value of Capital Stock (DM m)*[1]
50-100% owned subsidiaries and associates	*Not Available*	2,309.7	*Not Available*	5,553.1
Less than 50% owned subsidiaries and associates		806.6		468.7
TOTAL		3,116.3		6,021.8

Source:
Ministry of Economics, unpublished statement, *Aktuelle Beitrage zur Wirtschaft und Finanzpolitik*, 5th April 1983.

NOTES TO TABLE A10

1 Excluding advances and loans from parent companies.

Table A11

ROYALTY RECEIPTS AND PAYMENTS, 1967-83 (DM m)

	Payments			**Receipts**		
	To Affiliates	*To Non-affiliates*	*Total*	*From Affiliates*	*From Non-affiliates*	*Total*
1967-70[1]	654	286	940	10	383	393
1971-75[1]	1,120	367	1,487	33	601	634
1976	1,326	420	1,746	74	654	728
1977	1,433	462	1,895	54	724	778
1978	1,509	428	1,937	90	774	864
1979	1,516	436	1,952	81	820	901
1980	1,620	459	2,079	89	922	1,011
1981	1,607	536	2,143	102	993	1,095
1982	1,677	524	2,201	161	1,033	1,194
1983	2,045	436	2,481	300	1,013	1,313

Source:
Deutsche Bundesbank, *Monthly Report*, July 1984.

NOTES TO TABLE A11

1 Annual Average. The figures for 1967-74 have been supplemented by estimates.

Table A12

LEADING FOREIGN AND DOMESTIC MULTINATIONAL COMPANIES, end 1983

A	Leading Foreign Multinational Companies in the country, end 1983			
Name		*Home Country*	*Sector*	*German Turnover (US S bn)*
1	Esso	USA	Petroleum	6.40[1]
2	Adam Opel	USA	Motor vehicles and parts	5.87[2]
3	Ford-Werke	USA	Motor vehicles and parts	5.23[1]
4	IBM Deutschland	USA	Computers & Office equipment	4.12[1]
5	Mobil Oil	USA	Petroleum	3.69[1,3]
6	Deutsche Texaco	USA	Petroleum	2.99[1]
7	Standard Elektric, Lorenz	USA	Electronics, appliances	1.68[1]
8	ARBED Saarstahl	Luxembourg	Metal manufacturing – steel	0.77[3]
9	Eschweiler Bergwerks – Verein	Luxembourg	Mining – coal	0.77

Table A12 (cont'd)

LEADING FOREIGN AND DOMESTIC MULTINATIONAL COMPANIES

B Leading Domestic Companies with multinational interests, 1983

	Name	*Sector*	*Global Turnover (US $ bn)*	*Sales of overseas subsidiaries as a % of worldwide sales (1981)*
1	Siemens	Electronics, computers	15.72	15
2	Volkswagenwerk	Motor vehicles	15.69	33[4]
3	Daimler-Benz	Motor vehicles and parts	15.66	21
4	Bayer	Chemicals	14.62	51[5]
5	Hoechst	Chemicals	14.56	39[5]
6	BASF	Chemicals	13.25	57[4]
7	Thyssen	Metal mfg-steel, machinery	11.30	45[4]
8	Veba Oel	Petroleum, chemicals	7.57	*N.A.*
9	Ruhrkohle	Mining – coal	7.20	*N.A.*
10	Fried. Krupp	Metal mfg, industrial equipmt.	6.76	11[6]
11	Robert Bosch	Motor vehicle parts	5.62	26[5]
12	Mannesmann	Metal products, machinery	5.51	31
13	Gutehoffnungshutte	Industrial and transportation equipment	4.99	*N.A.*
14	Bayerische Motoren Werke	Motor vehicles and parts	4.68	*N.A.*
15	AEG – Telefunken	Electronics, appliances	4.51	17[5]
16	Degussa	Metal products, chemicals	4.42	15
17	Metallgesellschaft	Metal manufacturing – nonferrous	3.90	57[4]
18	Flick Group	Paper & wood products, chemicals	3.89	*N.A.*
19	Salzgitter	Metal manufacturing – steel	3.77	*N.A.*
20	Deutsche Babcock	Metal products, industrial equipmt.	2.82	*N.A.*
21	Bertelsmann	Publishing, printing	2.52	49[4]
22	VIAG	Metal manufacturing – aluminium	2.31	*N.A.*
23	Klockner-Werke	Metal manufacturing	2.09	*N.A.*
24	Henkel	Chemicals	1.74	62[4]
25	Schering	Pharmaceuticals, chemicals	1.68	70[4]

Source:

Fortune International, August 20 1984; J M Stopford and J H Dunning, *Multinationals Company Performance and Global Trends,* London: Macmillan, 1983; *Who Owns Whom, Continental Europe, 1981, Volumes 1 and 2,* London: Dun and Bradstreet Ltd.

NOTES TO TABLE A12

1 Revenue includes certain sales to foreign affiliates of the US parent company.
2 Fortune estimate.
3 Parent only.
4 Includes all exports, direct and intra-group.
5 Excludes all exports; any intra-group exports are therefore included with direct exports.
6 Data for Konzern.

WEST GERMANY TABLES : DEFINITIONS

Foreign affiliates: Foreign affiliates are made up of subsidiaries and branches, which foreign investors are required to report for statistical purposes where they have interest in affiliates whose combined operating assets total more than DM 500,000. Subsidiaries are companies in which economically connected foreign residents hold directly or indirectly 25% or more of the shares or voting rights. Branches are permanent business establishments set up by a parent company abroad, and do not include 'turnkey projects', ie, assembly plants, building sites etc, set up for a limited period to carry out a specific project.

Foreign direct capital stock: The stock of direct investment at the end of a given year is the level of foreign owned equity capital (share in nominal capital, reserves and reinvested profits) plus foreign loans and advances. This is the contribution of parents through equity or debt to the book value of the assets of affiliates.

Foreign direct investment: Direct investment flows are stated net of disinvestment. Here we refer to 'primary' direct investment, consisting of equity participations, reinvested earnings, and loans and advances including those in dependent holding companies abroad, but excluding the 'secondary' direct investment of those holding companies.

Royalties: Royalties comprise payments for the purchase or use and exploitation of patents, inventions, processes and other technological know-how, as well as copyrights and trademarks (shown separately). They exclude film rights.

Classification of activities: Inward investment and related data are classified by the industry of the affiliate. Outward data are classified by industry of the affiliate unless otherwise specified.

Source:

Deutsche Bundesbank, *Monthly Report, April 1979, July 1982, March 1985.*

GREECE

The official attitude to inward direct investment is welcoming, providing it helps to achieve certain economic objectives, eg job creation, promotion of exports, etc. Like other private investment, foreign investment is excluded from sectors under state control such as rail and air transport, telecommunications, broadcasting and armaments. The minerals sector is also coming under increasing Government supervision.

For most of the post-war period, there has been an influx of foreign direct investment into Greece, although over the last decade, the flow has fallen significantly. Nevertheless, foreign-owned subsidiaries remain an important part of Greek manufacturing in terms of assets, employment and capital.

Foreign investment has been concentrated in the more capital-intensive and modern branches of the economy, largely because Greek manufacturing lacks such essential high technology industries. Most investment in the manufacturing sector falls within five spheres; basic metals, chemicals, transport equipment, electrical goods and petroleum products. Sales originating from foreign controlled companies accounted for at least 50% of the market in those sectors in 1977. In the tertiary sector the majority of foreign investment is concentrated in transport and communications.

The main sources of investment are the USA and the EEC countries, particularly France.

There are no available data on Greek outward investment.

MAIN SOURCES OF DATA:

A Official

1 National Statistical Service of Greece; publishes data on employment in Greece.

2 Hellenic Industrial Development Bank; provides information about foreign direct investment in Greece, their sectoral and geographical distribution.

3 FGI, *Bulletin of Greek Industries*.

4 US Department of Commerce International Trade Administration, *Investment Climate in Foreign Countries*, Washington, 1985, vol I.

B Private

1 N Nanopoulos, 'A model of inward foreign direct investment, licensing and imports: its application across the Greek manufacturing industries', unpublished PhD thesis, University of Reading, 1982.

2 E Dokopoulou, 'The Pattern of MNC Activity in Greece', *Multinational Business* no 2, 1985.

Note:

Data do not allow us to complete Table A9 for Greece.

Table A1

SUMMARY OF THE COUNTRY'S INTERNATIONAL INVESTMENT POSITION

		Inward Investment	Outward Investment
1	Number of foreign affiliates in host country, and of foreign affiliates of home country firms at the end of 1981	798	*N.A.*
2	Number of foreign firms with direct investments in host country, and home country firms with direct foreign affiliates	*N.A.*	*N.A.*
3	Total foreign direct capital stock at book value as a percentage of GNP at factor cost in 1980	3.97	*N.A.*
4	Flow of foreign direct investment in the five year period 1976-80, (US $ m)	146.0	*N.A.*
5	Employment in foreign affiliates or abroad, 1977	75,744	*N.A.*
6	Output of foreign affiliates or abroad	*N.A.*	*N.A.*

Source:

Hellenic Industrial Development Bank, *Investment Guide in Greece,* Athens; IMF, *Balance of Payments Statistics Yearbook,* various issues; FGI, *Bulletin of Greek Industries,* various issues.

Table A2

PRIVATE FOREIGN CAPITAL STOCK, 1976 - 84 (US $ m)

	Inward Investment				Outward Investment		
	Portfolio	*Direct*	*Total*		*Portfolio*	*Direct*	*Total*
Book value of capital stock							
1976	*Not Available*	1,344.0	*Not Available*		*Not Available*		
1978		2,158.6					
1980		3,443.9					
1983		4,840.5					
1984		5,277.7					

Source:

Hellenic Industrial Development Bank, *Investment Guide in Greece,* Athens; IMF, *Balance of Payments Statistics Yearbook,* various issues.

Table A3

FLOW OF FOREIGN DIRECT INVESTMENT, 1970 - 84 (US S m)[1]

	Inward Investment				Outward Investment		
	Reinvested Profits	*Other*	*Total*		*Reinvested Profits*	*Other*	*Total*
1970	*Not Separately Available*		50.0		*Not Available*		
1971			42.1				
1972			55.4				
1973			62.0				
1974			67.4				
1975			24.3				
1976			304.8				
1977			386.4				
1978			428.2				
1979			612.4				
1980			672.9				
1981			520.0				
1982			437.2				
1983			439.4				
1984			485.8				

Source:

IMF, *Balance of Payments Statistics Yearbook,* various issues.

NOTES TO TABLE A3

1 Excluding reinvested profits.

Table A4

SECTORAL DISTRIBUTION OF FOREIGN DIRECT CAPITAL STOCK, 1953 - 78 (US $ m)

	Inward Investment				Outward Investment		
	Primary	*Secondary*	*Tertiary*		*Primary*	*Secondary*	*Tertiary*
1953 - 76[1]	30.2	741.5	277.9		*Not Available*		
1953 - 78[2]	*N.A.*	811.7	*N.A.*				

Source:

Hellenic Industrial Development Bank, *Investment Guide in Greece,* Athens.

NOTES TO TABLE A4

1 Calculations based on cumulative gross investment flows, 1953 - 76.

2 Calculations based on cumulative gross investment flows, 1953 - 78.

Table A5

GEOGRAPHICAL DISTRIBUTION OF FOREIGN DIRECT CAPITAL STOCK, 1953 - 78 (US $ m)

	Inward Investment[1]				Outward Investment		
	Developed Countries	*Other Countries*	*Total*		*Developed Countries*	*Developing Countries*	*Total*
1953 - 78	995.8	175.7	1,171.5		*Not Available*		

Source:

Hellenic Industrial Development Bank, *Investment Guide in Greece,* Athens.

NOTES TO TABLE A5

1 Calculations based on cumulative gross investment flows, 1953 - 78.

Table A6

INDUSTRIAL DISTRIBUTION OF FOREIGN DIRECT CAPITAL STOCK, 1953 - 78 (US $m)

	Inward Investment		Outward Investment
	1953-76[1]	*1953-78*[2]	
Primary	30.2		*Not Available*
Agriculture	1.6	*Not Separately Available*	
Mining & quarrying	28.6		
Secondary	741.5	811.7	
Food & drink	18.5	42.1	
Chemicals & allied	114.3	118.9	
Metals	239.1	247.3	
Mechanical engineering	3.9	4.6	
Electrical equipment	68.5	77.3	
Motor vehicles; Other transportation equipment	47.8	53.4	
Textiles & clothing	44.1	48.4	
Paper & allied	13.0	15.6	
Rubber	29.9	30.2	
Stone, clay & glass	34.7	36.7	
Coal & petroleum products	115.2	121.4	
Other manufacturing	12.3	15.8	
Tertiary	277.9		
Transport & communications	213.0	*Not Separately Available*	
Banking & finance	11.3		
Other services[3]	53.6		
TOTAL	1,049.6	1,171.5	

Source:

Hellenic Industrial Development Bank, *Investment Guide in Greece,* Athens

NOTES TO TABLE A6

1 Calculations based on cumulative gross investment flows, 1953 - 76.

2 Calculations based on cumulative gross investment flows, 1953 - 78.

3 Represents tourism.

Table A7

LEADING SOURCE AND RECIPIENT COUNTRIES, 1953 - 78 (US $m)

	Inward Investment[1]	Outward Investment
	1953-78	
DEVELOPED AREAS	995.8	*Not Available*
Europe	457.7	
EEC of which:	387.8	
France	257.3	
W. Germany	70.8	
Italy	29.2	
Netherlands	14.1	
UK	16.4	
Other Europe of which:	69.9	
Liechtenstein	9.1	
Switzerland	60.8	
North America of which:	538.1	
USA	538.1	
UNSPECIFIED	175.7	
TOTAL	1,171.5	

Source:
Hellenic Industrial Development Bank, *Investment Guide in Greece,* Athens.

NOTES TO TABLE A7

1 Calculations based on cumulative gross inflow of funds for FDI in Greece, 1953 - 78.

Table A8

INDICATORS OF THE SIGNIFICANCE OF INWARD FOREIGN DIRECT INVESTMENT OR THE ACTIVITIES OF FOREIGN-BASED COMPANIES TO THE NATIONAL ECONOMY, 1977 - 80

1	Direct capital stock of foreign affiliates at book value in 1980 as a proportion of:	
	a GNP at factor cost	3.97
	b population (in US S per head)	131.20
2	Employment in foreign affiliates in 1977 as a percentage of all employment in manufacturing	21.34
3	Output of foreign affiliates in 1977 as a percentage of all companies' output in secondary (ie, manufacturing) industry	25.50[1]
4	Exports of foreign affiliates in 1977 as a percentage of all manufacturing exports	18.50[2]

5 Percentage share of sales and employment accounted for by foreign affiliates in selected sectors, 1977

	Sales	*Employment*
Manufacturing Sector		
Food & drink	15.0	11.0
Chemicals & allied	56.0	34.5
Metals	36.4	88.6
Mechanical engineering	7.5	2.3
Electrical equipment	53.0	53.6
Motor vehicles } Other transportation equipment }	52.5	60.9
Textiles & clothing	10.2	9.8
Paper & allied	11.4	6.8
Rubber	24.6	19.0
Stone, glass & clay	12.4	23.7
Coal & petroleum products	71.1	82.7
Timber & furniture	3.3	5.8
Other manufacturing	4.1	34.2

Source:
National Statistical Service of Greece, *Statistical Yearbook,* Athens, various issues; International Labour Office, *Yearbook of Labour Statistics,* Geneva, 1981; FGI, Bulletin of Greek Industries, various issues; IMF, *Balance of Payments Statistics Yearbook,* various issues; IMF, *International Financial Statistics Yearbook, 1984.*

NOTES TO TABLE A8

1 Represents percentage of inward FDI sales as a fraction of total Greek industrial production; average of all sectors.

2 Represents percentage of FDI manufacturing exports as a fraction of total Greek manufacturing exports.

Table A10

DISTRIBUTION OF FOREIGN SUBSIDIARIES AND ASSOCIATES AND FOREIGN CAPITAL STOCK BY PERCENTAGE OWNERSHIP OF PARENT COMPANIES

	Inward Investment		Outward Investment	
	Number of Affiliates	*Value of Capital Stock*	*Number of Affiliates*	*Value of Capital Stock*
100% owned subsidiaries	93	*Not Available*	*Not Available*	
50–99.9% owned subsidiaries and associates	*N.A.*			
Less than 50% owned subsidiaries and associates	27			
TOTAL	120[1]			

Source:

E Dokopoulou, "The Pattern of MNC Activity in Greece", in *Multinational Business,* no 2, 1985.

NOTES TO TABLE A10

[1] Based on in depth interviews with the managers of 120 out of the 260 manufacturing firms listed with foreign shareholdings in Greece in 1979. This sample represents 65.5% of assets and 62.0% of employment of foreign firms in Greece at that time. that time.

Table A11

ROYALTY RECEIPTS AND PAYMENTS, 1976 - 82 (US $ m)

	Payments			Receipts		
	To Affiliates	*To Non-affiliates*	*Total*	*From Affiliates*	*From Non-affiliates*	*Total*
1976	*Not Separately Available*		13.85	*Not Available*		
1977			14.01			
1978			16.28			
1979			18.09			
1980			19.52			
1981			18.87			
1982			12.14			

Source:
IMF, *Balance of Payments Statistics Yearbook,* various issues.

Table A12

LEADING FOREIGN MULTINATIONAL COMPANIES, 1983

	Name	*Home Country*	*Sector*
1	AEG - Telefunken AG	W. Germany	Electrical engineering
2	L'Air Liquide SA	France	Industrial gases
3	Alfa - Laval AB	Sweden	Mechanical engineering
4	Beecham Group PLC	UK	Pharmaceuticals
5	Cadbury Schweppes PLC	UK	Food
6	The Colgate - Palmolive Company	USA	Consumer products
7	Compagnie Francaise des Petroles SA	France	Petroleum marketing
8	Daimler - Benz AG	W. Germany	Motor vehicles
9	The Dow Chemical Company	USA	Chemicals
10	ENI	Italy	Oil
11	General Motors Corp	USA	Motor vehicles
12	Goodyear Tyre and Rubber Company	USA	Rubber tyres
13	Metal Box PLC	UK	Metal containers
14	Nestle SA	Switzerland	Food products
15	Ing C Olivetti & C SpA	Italy	Office equipment
16	Petrofina SA	Belgium	Petroleum/petrochemicals
17	Procter and Gamble Company	USA	Consumer products
18	Roche/Sapae Group	Switzerland	Pharmaceuticals
19	Royal Dutch/Shell Group of Companies	Netherlands / UK	Petroleum
20	Siemens AG	Germany	Electrical and electronic engineering
21	Texaco Incorporated	USA	Petroleum
22	Thorn - EMI PLC	UK	Electrical consumer products
23	Unilver	UK / Netherlands	Consumer products
24	Union Carbide Corporation	USA	Chemicals
25	The Xerox Corporation	USA	Office equipment

Source:
John M Stopford, *The World Directory of Multinational Enterprises 1982-83,* Bath: The Pitman Press, 1982.

IRELAND

Government policy towards the attraction of direct foreign investment in industry has been a key element of Irish economic strategy for the past 25 years. The switch to an outward-looking policy, central to which was the encouragement of export orientated foreign investment in manufacturing industry, came in about 1958, and the foreign investment boom lasted to the mid 1970s. The Irish Development Authority administers an extensive programme of incentives for foreign investment.

Foreign firms have been the main source of growth in net employment, and have accounted for the bulk of the growth of Ireland's manufacturing exports during the past 20 years, now providing about three-quarters of those exports.

The USA and the UK are the main sources of investment in Ireland, with West Germany and other European countries playing a smaller role. The UK tends to be more important in the traditional sectors such as food and drink, textiles and footwear, while the USA dominates the newer, more technology based sectors.

No data are available on outward direct investment. The Central Bank operates a system of controls on capital outflows and applications to make direct investments are considered in the context of the likely benefit to the Irish economy in the form of increased foreign currency earnings and the profit generating capacity of the enterprise.

MAIN SOURCES OF DATA:

A **Official**

1. Central Statistics Office; publishes annually a balance of payments statement including FDI in Ireland.
2. National Economic & Social Council, provides data on the share of employment in Ireland accounted for by foreign affiliates.
3. Industrial Development Authority, *Annual Report,* contains data on employment and investment by manufacturing subsidiaries.

B **Private**

1. J Fitzpatrick, 'Foreign Investment in Ireland in the 1980s', *Multinational Business,* 1982.
2. M O Suilleabhain, 'The case of the Republic of Ireland', International Labour Office Working Papers on the Employment Effects of Multinational Enterprises, no 22, Geneva, 1982.

Note:
Data do not allow us to complete Tables A9, A10 or A11 for Ireland.

Table A1

SUMMARY OF THE COUNTRY'S INTERNATIONAL INVESTMENT POSITION

		Inward Investment	Outward Investment
1	Number of foreign affiliates in host country, and of foreign affiliates of home country firms at the end of 1983	854[2]	*N.A.*
2	Number of foreign firms with direct investments in host country, and home country firms with direct foreign affiliates	*N.A.*	*N.A.*
3	Total foreign direct capital stock[1] at book value as a percentage of GNP at factor cost in 1981	21.68	*N.A.*
4	Flow of foreign direct investment in in the five year period, 1978-82 (Ir £ m)	795.8	*N.A.*
5	Employment in foreign affiliates or abroad, 1981	83,128[2]	*N.A.*
6	Output of foreign affiliates or abroad	*N.A.*	*N.A.*

Source:

IMF, *Balance of Payments Statistics Yearbook,* various issues; IMF, *International Financial Statistics Yearbook, 1984;* International Labour Office, 'Employment effects of multinational enterprises: The case of the Republic of Ireland', working paper by M O Suilleabhain, Geneva, 1982; UK Department of Trade and Industry, 'Census of Overseas Assets, 1981', *Business Monitor,* Supplement, 1981; Deutschen Bundesbank, *Zahlungsbilanzstatistik,* no 6, June 1983; US Department of Commerce, *Survey of Current Business,* August, 1983; Central Statistics Office, *Irish Statistical Bulletin,* 1982.

NOTES TO TABLE A1

1 US, UK, and West German capital stock only.

2 For manufacturing only.

Table A2

PRIVATE FOREIGN CAPITAL STOCK, 1981 - 84 (Ir £ m)

	Inward Investment				Outward Investment		
	Portfolio	*Direct*	*Total*		*Portfolio*	*Direct*	*Total*
Book value of capital stock							
1981	*Not Available*	2,259.5[1]	*Not Available*		*Not Available*		
1984		2,503.4					

Source:

UK Department of Trade and Industry, 'Census of Overseas Assets, 1981', *Business Monitor,* Supplement, 1981; Deutschen Bundesbank, *Zahlungsbilanzstatistik,* no 6, June 1983; US Department of Commerce, *Survey of Current Business,* August, 1983.

NOTES TO TABLE A2

1 Represents stock of US, UK and West German investment only.

Table A3

FLOW OF FOREIGN DIRECT INVESTMENT, 1970 - 84 (Ir £ m)

	Inward Investment				Outward Investment		
	Reinvested Profits	*Other*	*Total*[1]		*Reinvested Profits*	*Other*	*Total*
1970	*Not Separately Available*		13.3		*Not Available*		
1971			10.3				
1972			12.6				
1973			21.9				
1974			22.1				
1975			71.6				
1976			96.1				
1977			78.1				
1978			195.7				
1979			164.5				
1980			139.4				
1981			126.2				
1982			170.0				
1983			134.2				
1984			109.7				

Source:

IMF, *Balance of Payments Statistics Yearbook,* various issues; Central Statistics Office, *Irish Statistical Bulletin,* 1982.

NOTES TO TABLE A3

1 Excluding reinvested profits.

Table A4

SECTORAL DISTRIBUTION OF FOREIGN DIRECT CAPITAL STOCK, 1981 (Ir £ m)[1]

	Inward Investment			Outward Investment		
	Primary	*Secondary*	*Tertiary*	*Primary*	*Secondary*	*Tertiary*
1981	77.9	1,690.5	491.1	*Not Available*		

Source:

UK Department of Trade and Industry, 'Census of Overseas Assets, 1981', *Business Monitor,* Supplement, 1981; Deutschen Bundesbank, *Zahlungsbilanzstatistik,* no 6, June, 1983; US Department of Commerce, *Survey of Current Business,* August 1983.

NOTES TO TABLE A4

1 Includes US, UK and West German investment only.

Table A5

GEOGRAPHICAL DISTRIBUTION OF FOREIGN DIRECT CAPITAL STOCK, 1981 (Ir £ m)[1]

	Inward Investment			Outward Investment		
	Developed Countries	*Developing Countries*	*Total*	*Developed Countries*	*Developing Countries*	*Total*
1981	2,259.5	*N.A.*	*N.A.*	*Not Available*		

Source:

As for Table A4.

NOTES TO TABLE A5

1 Includes US, UK and West German investment only.

Table A6

INDUSTRIAL DISTRIBUTION OF FOREIGN DIRECT CAPITAL STOCK, 1981 (Ir £ m)[1]

	Inward Investment 1981	Outward Investment
Primary	77.9	Not Available
Agriculture		
Mining & quarrying	0.5[2]	
Oil	44.0[2]	
Secondary	1,690.5	
Food & drink	426.2[3]	
Chemicals & allied	667.5	
Metals	33.7[3]	
Mechanical engineering	165.2	
Electrical equipment	29.6[4]	
Motor vehicles	} N.A.	
Other transportation equipment		
Textiles & clothing	27.2[5]	
Paper & allied	14.9[5]	
Rubber	N.A.	
Other manufacturing	282.5[3]	
Tertiary	491.1	
Construction	5.0[5]	
Transport & communications	6.0[5]	
Distributive trade	195.8	
Property	49.9[5]	
Banking & finance	198.5[6]	
Other services	35.9	
TOTAL	2,259.5	

Source:

UK Department of Trade and Industry, 'Census of Overseas Assets, 1981', *Business Monitor,* Supplement, 1981; Deutschen Bundesbank, 'Die Kapitalverflechtung der Unternehman mit dem Ausland nach Landern und Wirtschaftszweigen, 1976 bis 1981, *Zahlungsbilanzstatistik,* no 6, June 1983; US Department of Commerce, *Survey of Current Business,* August 1983.

NOTES TO TABLE A6

1 Includes US, UK and West German investment only.
2 US investment only.
3 Excluding German investment.
4 Excluding UK investment.
5 UK investment only.
6 Including US investment in property.

Table A7

LEADING SOURCE AND RECIPIENT COUNTRIES 1981 (Ir £ m)[1]

	Inward Investment		Outward Investment
	1981		
DEVELOPED AREAS[2]	2,259.5		*Not Available*
Europe[2]	843.9		
EEC of which:[2]	843.9		
W. Germany	109.3		
UK	734.6		
North America of which:	1,415.6		
USA	1,415.6		
TOTAL	2,259.5[1]		

Source:
As for Table A6.

NOTES TO TABLE A7

1 Includes US, UK, West German investment only.

2 Including only those countries shown below.

Table A8

INDICATORS OF THE SIGNIFICANCE OF INWARD FOREIGN DIRECT INVESTMENT OR THE ACTIVITIES OF FOREIGN-BASED COMPANIES TO THE NATIONAL ECONOMY, 1979-81

1	Direct capital stock of foreign affiliates[1] at book value in 1981 as a proportion of:	
	a GNP at factor cost	21.68
	b population (in Ir £ per head)	656.80
2	Employment in foreign affiliates[1] in 1981 as a percentage of all employment in manufacturing	34.60
3	Exports of foreign affiliates[2] in 1979 as a percentage of all manufacturing exports	70.00
4	Percentage share of employment accounted for by foreign affiliates in selected sectors, 1980.	

Manufacturing Sector	*Employment*
Food & drink	19.3
Chemicals & allied	80.0
Metals	} 49.1
Mechanical engineering	} 49.1
Electrical equipment	} 49.1
Motor vehicles[3]	*N.S.A.*
Other transportation equipment[3]	*N.S.A.*
Textiles & clothing	38.4
Paper & allied	13.6
Rubber[3]	*N.S.A.*
Stone, glass & clay	15.4
Coal & petroleum products[3]	*N.S.A.*
Timber & furniture	12.8
Other manufacturing	31.6

Source:

IMF, *International Financial Statistics Yearbook, 1984;* National Economic & Social Council, *Policies for Industrial Development: Conclusions & Recommendations,* no 66, Dublin, September 1982; International Labour Office, *Yearbook of Labour Statistics,* Geneva, 1981; UK Department of Trade and Industry, 'Census of Overseas Assets 1981', *Business Monitor,* Supplement, 1981; Deutschen Bundesbank, *Zahlungsbilanzstatistik*, no 6, June 1983; US Department of Commerce, *Survey of Current Business,* August 1983.

NOTES TO TABLE A8

1 US, UK and West German capital stock only.

2 For manufacturing only.

3 Motor vehicles, other transportation equipment, rubber, coal & petroleum products all included under other manufacturing.

Table A12

LEADING FOREIGN AND DOMESTIC MULTINATIONAL COMPANIES

A Leading Foreign Multinational Companies in the country, January 1982

	Name	*Home Country*	*Sector*
1	Nokia	Finland	Metals
2	Asahi Chemical International	Japan	Chemicals
3	Akzo	Netherlands	Chemicals
4	N V Philips Gloeilampenfabrieken	Netherlands	Electrical
5	Unilever	UK/Netherlands	Food
6	Ciba-Geigy AG	Switzerland	Chemicals
7	Beecham Group	UK	Pharmaceuticals
8	Cadbury Bros	UK	Food
9	Courtaulds	UK	Textiles
10	Glaxo Holdings	UK	Pharmaceuticals
11	Pilkington Bros	UK	Building materials
12	Reckitts & Colman	UK	Pharmaceuticals
13	Rowntree Mackintosh	UK	Food
14	Abbott Laboratories Inc	USA	Pharmaceuticals
15	Baker International Corp	USA	Machinery
16	Beatrice Foods Co	USA	Food
17	Borden Inc	USA	Food
18	Digital Equipment Corp	USA	Office equipment
19	Dresser Industries Inc	USA	Machinery
20	Emerson Electric Co	USA	Electrical
21	General Electric Co	USA	Electrical
22	Pfizer Co. Inc	USA	Pharmaceuticals
23	Revlon Inc	USA	Pharmaceuticals
24	Squibb Corp	USA	Pharmaceuticals
25	Westinghouse Electric Corp	USA	Electric

Source:
Department of Industry and Energy, 'Overseas Companies in Ireland', Dublin, January 1982.

Table A12 (cont'd)

LEADING FOREIGN AND DOMESTIC MULTINATIONAL COMPANIES

B Leading Domestic Companies with Multinational Interests, 1982			
Name	Sector	Global Turnover *(Ir £ m)*	Sales of overseas subsidiaries as % of worldwide sales (1982)
1 Jefferson Smurfit	Paper and paper products	501	84%
2 Cement – Roadstone	Building materials	418	*N.A.*
3 Waterford Glass	Glasswork	204	*N.A.*
4 Independent Group	Publications, newsprint, advertising agencies	59	*N.A.*
5 McInerney	Construction	56	*N.A.*
6 Rohan Group	Construction	25	*N.A.*

IRELAND : DEFINITIONS

Direct Investment: includes subscriptions by non-residents to share issues by Irish companies, other direct investment in Ireland by non-residents and direct investment by residents in other countries.

For balance of payments purposes, the Central Statistics Office conducts an annual non-statutory survey of Irish branches and subsidiaries of foreign parent companies. The results are not published but are used in the estimation of aggregates (eg, private direct investment) for entry in the Irish balance of payments statement. In principle, any company which has a non-domestic parent is included in the register of possible respondents; parent is intended to mean any corporation or group of affiliates which directly or indirectly controls enough of the voting stock to exert an important influence on the policies of the company.

Source:
Central Statistics Office, *Irish Statistical Bulletin,* June 1982.

ITALY

In terms of international comparisons, exports from Italy are more important than direct investment abroad: the country's share in world trade is four times its share in world direct investment. Nonetheless in recent years outward investment has grown rapidly, and since 1982 its stock of outward investment has been greater than the stock of invward investment. The activity of Italian firms abroad is mainly concentrated in the other EEC countries and in Latin America; the total share of developing countries is quite high in comparison with the geographical distribution of the outward investment of other industrialized countries.

Inward investment in Italy has mainly been concentrated in manufacturing, especially in the chemicals and engineering sectors. in the 1960s US companies accounted for a high share of direct investment in Italy, but over the last ten years the share of MNEs from other European countries has been rising much faster.

Official data regarding both inward and outward FDI is rather limited, and sometimes unreliable.

MAIN SOURCES OF DATA

A Official

1. Bank of Italy: provides annual data on investment flows (not including reinvested profits) and stocks.
2. Ufficio Italiano Cambi: provides annual data on the technological balance of payments.
3. Istituto Centrale di Statistica: published irregular data on foreign participations in Italian firms.

B Private

1. Ricerche & Progetti (Turin): has compiled a directory of a large number of foreign-owned Italian firms.
2. Istituto per la Ricerca Sociale (Milan): has established a data-base covering a large number of Italian firms with foreign production.
3. F Orida (Ed.), *L'Internazionalizzazione del Sistema Industriale Italiano*, Bologna: Il Mulino, 1986.
4. N Acocella (Ed.), *Le Multinazionali Italiane*, Bologna: Il Mulino, 1986.

Table A1

SUMMARY OF THE COUNTRY'S INTERNATIONAL INVESTMENT POSITION

		Inward Investment	Outward Investment
1	Number of foreign affiliates in host country, and of foreign affiliates of home country firms at the end of 1984[1]	850[2]	576
2	Number of foreign firms with direct investments in host country, and home country firms with direct foreign affiliates at the end of 1984[1]	560[2]	246
3	Total foreign direct capital stock at book value as a percentage of GNP at factor cost in 1983	2.28	2.65
4	Flow of foreign direct investment in the five year period 1979-83 (Lire bn)	4,774	7,311
5	Employment in foreign affiliates or abroad, 1980	793,282	142,599[3]
6	Output of foreign affiliates or abroad, 1980 (Lire bn)	74,563.8	7,343[3]

Source:

Ricerche e Progetti, *Rilevazione delle Partecipazioni Estere nelle Imprese Industriali Italiane;* Instituto per la Ricerca Sociale, unpublished data; Bank of Italy, *Annual Report, 1984;* Instituto Centrale di Statistica, unpublished data; N Acocella & R Schiatterella, 'Italian direct investment in developing countries', *Lo Spettatore Internazionale,* Vol. 17, No. 1, January - March 1982.

NOTES TO TABLE A1

1 Manufacturing only.

2 1981.

3 For a sample of 87 subsidiaries of 31 multinationals covering only their industrial production activity in the developing countries.

Table A2

PRIVATE FOREIGN CAPITAL STOCK, 1971-84 (Lire bn)

	Inward Investment			Outward Investment		
	Portfolio	*Direct*	*Total*	*Portfolio*	*Direct*	*Total*
Book value of capital stock						
1971	*Not Available*			*N.A.*	1,377	*N.A.*
1975	2,324	6,230	8,554	2,597	2,255	4,852
1976	2,012	4,990	7,002	3,062	2,941	6,003
1977	1,917	6,014	7,931	3,224	3,607	6,831
1978	2,323	6,667	8,990	4,231	3,956	8,187
1979	3,457	7,302	10,759	4,020	4,704	8,724
1980	5,580	8,274	13,854	5,117	6,486	11,603
1981	6,480	9,273	15,753	5,400	8,857	14,257
1982	6,439	10,106	16,545	6,028	11,118	17,146
1983	7,301	12,148	19,449	6,472	14,098	20,570
1984	9,288	18,031	27,319	8,905	20,498	29,403

Source:
Bank of Italy, *Annual Report, 1984*, and earlier issues.

Table A3

FLOW OF FOREIGN DIRECT INVESTMENT, 1972-85 (Lire bn)[1]

	Inward Investment				Outward Investment		
	Reinvested Profits	*Other*	*Total*		*Reinvested Profits*	*Other*	*Total*
1972	*Not Available*	1,052	1,052		*Not Available*	125	125
1973		361	361			152	152
1974		393	393			131	131
1975		412	412			227	227
1976		78	78			132	132
1977		1,002	1,002			486	486
1978		433	433			143	143
1979		301	301			456	456
1980		503	503			646	646
1981		1,303	1,303			1,596	1,596
1982		806	806			1,387	1,387
1983		1,807	1,807			3,230	3,230
1984		2,267	2,267			3,505	3,505
1985		1,916	1,916			3,586	3,586

Source:
Bank of Italy, *Annual Report, 1975, 1984, 1985.*

NOTES TO TABLE A3

1 Excluding reinvested profits.

Table A4

SECTORAL DISTRIBUTION OF FOREIGN DIRECT CAPITAL STOCK, 1974-83 (Lire bn)

	Inward Investment			Outward Investment		
	Primary	*Secondary*	*Tertiary*	*Primary*	*Secondary*	*Tertiary*
1974	618	3,108	1,723	645	629	1,011
1976	611	2,856	1,523	747	1,236	958
1978	787	4,188	1,692	1,034	1,831	1,088
1980	846	4,854	2,574	1,242	3,255	1,987
1982	946	5,264	3,896	2,471	5,061	3,586
1983	1,172	6,692	4,284	3,167	6,349	4,582
1984	1,253	10,699	6,079	4,617	9,224[1]	6,657[1]

Source:

Bank of Italy, *Annual Report, 1984, 1985.*

NOTES TO TABLE A4

1 A proportion of the investment recorded by the Bank of Italy under banking and finance has been reallocated to manufacturing (see Definitions).

Table A5

GEOGRAPHICAL DISTRIBUTION OF FOREIGN DIRECT CAPITAL STOCK, 1974-83 (Lire bn)

	Inward Investment			Outward Investment		
	Developed Countries	*Developing Countries*[1]	*Total*	*Developed Countries*	*Developing Countries*	*Total*
1974	*Not Separately Available*		5,449	*Not Separately Available*		2,285
1976			4,990			2,941
1978			6,667			3,956
1980			8,274			6,486
1982			10,106			11,118
1983			12,148	7,400	6,698	14,098
1984			18,031	*N.S.A.*	*N.S.A.*	20,498

Source:

Bank of Italy, *Annual Report, 1984, 1985.*

NOTES TO TABLE A5

1 Negligible for all years.

Table A6

INDUSTRIAL DISTRIBUTION OF FOREIGN DIRECT CAPITAL STOCK, 1974-84 (Lire bn)

	Inward Investment		Outward Investment	
	1974	*1984*	*1974*	*1984*[1]
Primary	718	1,253	645	4,617
Agriculture	46	41	2	4
Mining & quarrying } Oil }	572	1,212	643	4,613
Secondary	3,108	10,699	629	9,224
Food & drink	306	834	62	461
Chemicals & allied	595	2,938	189	1,218
Metals[2]	142	267	20	802
Mechanical engineering }	895	3,799	138	895
Electrical equipment }				1,070
Motor vehicles } Other transportation equipment }	97	1,757	15	2,306
Textiles & clothing	217	456	26	83
Paper & allied	*Not Separately Available*		*N.S.A.*	64
Rubber[3]			*Not Separately Available*	
Stone, clay & glass[2]				
Coal & petroleum products				
Other manufacturing	856	648	368[3]	2,325[3]
Tertiary	1,723	6,079	1,011	6,657
Construction	*N.S.A.*	*N.S.A.*	*N.S.A.*	*N.S.A.*
Transport & communications	123	451	26	93
Distributive trade	281	1,463	191	836
Property	*N.S.A.*	*N.S.A.*	*N.S.A.*	*N.S.A.*
Banking & finance	534	2,494	776	5,605
Other services	785	1,671	18	123
TOTAL	5,449	18,031	2,285	20,498

Source:
Bank of Italy, *Annual Report, 1984, 1985,* N Acocella (Ed.), *Le Multinazionali Italiane*, Bologna: Il Mulino, 1986.

NOTES TO TABLE A6

1 A proportion of the investment recorded by the Bank of Italy under banking and finance has been reallocated to manufacturing. The distribution of investment between manufacturing sectors has been adjusted using the distribution of the Acocella sample of 267 foreign affiliates of Italian multinationals.

2 Non-metallic mineral products are included under metals.

3 A significant proportion of outward investment stock is in the rubber products sector, and has been recorded under other manufacturing. In 1981 Lire 1,481 bn was invested in this sector by firms in the Acocella sample.

Table A7

LEADING SOURCE AND RECIPIENT COUNTRIES, 1974 - 84 (Lire bn)

	Inward Investment		Outward Investment	
	1974	*1984*	*1974*	*1983*
DEVELOPED AREAS				7,400
Europe				5,800
EEC	1,382	8,258	636	4,100
Other Europe of which:				1,700
Switzerland[1]				1,600
North America of which:				1,600
United States	909	3,374	112	1,600
DEVELOPING AREAS				6,600
Africa (except S. Africa)				1,600
Asia & Pacific				1,000
Latin America				4,000
UNALLOCATED		6,399		89
TOTAL	5,449	18,031	2,285	14,089

Source:
Bank of Italy, *Annual Report, 1984, 1985.*

NOTES TO TABLE A7

1 Lichtenstein included under Switzerland.

Table A8

INDICATORS OF THE SIGNIFICANCE OF INWARD FOREIGN DIRECT INVESTMENT OR THE ACTIVITIES OF FOREIGN-BASED COMPANIES TO THE NATIONAL ECONOMY, 1981 - 84

1	Direct capital stock of foreign affiliates at book value in 1984 as a proportion of:		
	a	GNP at factor cost	2.94
	b	population (in Lire per head)	327,801
2	Employment in foreign affiliates in 1981 as a percentage of all employment		
	a	in all industry	6.48
	b	in manufacturing	8.33
3	Output of foreign affiliates in 1982 as a percentage of all companies' output		
	a	in primary (ie, extractive) industry	19.5 (a–c combined)
	b	in secondary (ie, manufacturing) industry	
	c	in tertiary industry (ie, services etc)	
4	Exports of foreign affiliates in 1982 as a percentage of all manufacturing exports		14.6
5	Percentage share of assets accounted for by foreign affiliates in selected sectors, 1982		

	Assets[1]
Primary Goods Sector	
Mining and quarrying / Oil	2.8
Manufacturing Sector	9.0
Food & drink	10.0
Chemicals & allied	13.7
Metals	0.9
Mechanical engineering / Electrical equipment / Motor vehicles / Other transportation equipment	12.5
Textiles & clothing	4.2
Paper & allied	7.4
Rubber / Stone, glass & clay / Coal & petroleum products / Furniture / Other manufacturing	6.7
Services Sector	
Construction	4.5
Transport & communications	1.8
Distributive trade	33.2
Property / Banking & finance / Other services	2.2

Source:

Bank of Italy, *Annual Report, 1984*; Recerche e Progetti, *Rilevazione delle Partecipazioni Estere nelle Imprese Industriali Italiane*; ISTAT, *Situazione Patrimoniale e Conti Economici* delle Grandi Imprese nel 1982.

NOTES TO TABLE A8

1 Represents the share of 353 majority owned foreign affiliates in a total sample of 2,510 large Italian firms, as defined by ISTAT.

Table A9

INDICATORS OF THE SIGNIFICANCE OF OUTWARD FOREIGN DIRECT INVESTMENT OR THE ACTIVITIES OF HOME-BASED COMPANIES ABROAD FOR THE NATIONAL ECONOMY, 1981 - 84

1	Foreign capital stock of home-based firms at book value in 1984 as a proportion of:		
	a	GNP factor cost	3.34
	b	population (in Lire per head)	372,651
2	Employment in foreign affiliates in 1981 as a percentage of domestic employment		
	a	in all industry	1.63
	b	in manufacturing	2.11

Source:
Bank of Italy, *Annual Report, 1984*; Institute per la Ricerca Sociale, unpublished data.

Table A10

DISTRIBUTION OF FOREIGN SUBSIDIARIES AND ASSOCIATES AND FOREIGN CAPITAL STOCK BY PERCENTAGE OWNERSHIP OF PARENT COMPANIES, 1983

	Inward Investment		Outward Investment	
	Number of affiliates[1,2]	*Value of capital stock (Lire bn)*[3]	*Number of affiliates*[1]	*Value of capital stock (Lire bn)*
100% owned subsidiaries	204	2,104.6 (100% and 50-99.9% combined)	103	*Not Available*
50-99.9% owned subsidiaries and associates	166		71	
Less than 50% owned subsidiaries and associates	71	580.5	165	
TOTAL[4]	441	2,685.1	339	

Source:

Ricerche e Progetti, *Rilevazione delle Partecipazione Estere nelle Imprese Industriali Italiane;* Instituto per la Ricerca Sociale, unpublished data; Instituto Centrale di Statistica, unpublished data.

ITALY NOTES TO TABLE A10

1 Manufacturing only.

2 1981.

3 1980.

4 The discrepancy with other tables arises because of an unallocated proportion of affiliates and capital stock.

Table A11

ROYALTY RECEIPTS AND PAYMENTS, 1972 - 83 (Lire bn)

	Payments			Receipts		
	To Affiliates	*To Non-affiliates*[1]	*Total*	*From Affiliates*	*From Non-affiliates*[2]	*Total*
1972-75	*Not Separately Available*		192	*Not Separately Available*		39.7
1976			226.6			66.2
1977			379.6			132.9
1978			576.8			114.1
1979			445.3			145.1
1980	146.74	396.75	543.5	42.15	149.4	191.6
1981	*Not Separately Available*		647.8	*Not Separately Available*		225.4
1982			808.4			217.1
1983			911.5			224.7

Source:
A M Scarda & G Sirilli, "Technological transfer and the technological balance of payments", *Quaderni ISRDS, 1982*; Ufficio Italiano Cambi, *Bulletin.*

NOTES TO TABLE A11

1 Including payments made by Italian parent multinationals.

2 Including receipts of foreign owned affiliates.

3 Annual average.

Table A12

LEADING FOREIGN AND DOMESTIC MULTINATIONAL COMPANIES

A Leading Foreign Multinational Companies in the country

	Name	*Home Country*	*Sector*	*Italian sales 1983 (Lire bn)*
1	Esso Italiana	USA	Petroleum (sales)	5,359
2	IBM Italia	USA	Office Automation	3,021
3	Total	France	Petroleum (sales)	2,182
4	Fina Italiana	Belgium	Petroleum (sales)	1,799
5	Chevron Oil Italiana	USA	Petroleum (sales)	1,577
6	Renault Italia	France	Motor vehicles (sales)	1,215
7	Philips	Netherlands	Electronics	1,091
8	Tamoil Italia	Kuwait	Petroleum (sales)	1,053
9	Zanussi (Electrolux)	Sweden	Electrical appliances	1,021
10	Michelin Italiana	France	Rubber	896
11	Elf Italiana	France	Petroleum (sales)	834
12	Texaco	USA	Petroleum (sales)	777
13	Gulf Italiana	USA	Petroleum (sales)	690
14	Unil-It (Unilever)	UK-Netherlands	Chemicals, Food	645
15	Shell Italia	UK-Netherlands	Petroleum (sales)	600
16	Ire (Philips)	Netherlands	Household appliances	578
17	Riv-Skf	Sweden	Machinery	512
18	Honeywell Italia	USA	Office equipment	474
19	3M Italia	USA	Chemicals	471
20	Bayer Italia	W. Germany	Chemicals	461
21	Ciba-Geigy	Switzerland	Chemicals	448
22	Procter & Gamble Italia	USA	Chemicals	433
23	BMW Italia	W. Germany	Motor vehicles	420
24	Citroen Italia	France	Motor vehicles	384
25	Esso Chimica	USA	Chemicals	358

Source:
Instituto per la Ricerca Sociale, unpublished data.

Table A12 (contd)

B Leading Domestic Companies with Multinational Interests

Name		Sector	*Global Sales 1983 (Lire bn)*	*Sales of overseas subsidiaries as a % of worldwide sales (1983)*
1	AGIP[2]	Oil	51,123	26.1
2	FIAT	Motor vehicles, steel, telecommunications etc.	24,711	19.7
3	Montedison	Chemicals	10,660	*N.A.*
4	Enichem[2]	Chemicals	8,646	6.6
5	Pirelli	Tyres and cables	5,984	65.9
6	Olivetti	Office equipment	3,736	56.0
7	Alfa Romeo[3]	Motor vehicles	3,503	17.4
8	Ferruzzi	Food	2,139[4]	*N.A.*
9	Snia Bpd	Fibres, textiles, defence systems	1,920	6.6
10	Ferrero	Food	1,234[5]	33.4[6]
11	Italtel[3]	Telecommunications	1,098	*neg.*
12	Buitoni	Food	1,095	47.8
13	Star	Food	804	16.2
14	Benetton	Clothing	732	6.6
15	SMI	Metalworking	710	0.6
16	Parmalat	Food	701	15.4
17	Acraf	Pharmaceuticals	696	*N.A.*
18	Merloni	Household appliances	663	27.1
19	Unicem	Concrete	614	*N.A.*
20	Piaggio	Motorcycles	601[4]	*N.A.*
21	Martini e Rossi	Beverages	446[7]	52
22	Miroglio	Textiles & clothing	423	20.3
23	Necchi	Machinery	296	7.1
24	Bassani Ticino	Electrical equipment	279	7.9
25	Manuli	Cables	253	25.7

Source:
Istituto per la Ricerca Sociale, based on *R&S* Medicbanca.

NOTES TO TABLE A12

1 Some groups are excluded for lack of data (eg, Cinzano).
2 Part of the ENI group.
3 Part of the IRI group.
4 Sales of Italian companies.
5 Sales of Italian and German companies.
6 Only German subsidiary.
7 Sales of Italian and English companies.

DEFINITIONS

As for the other countries, Italy's stock of outward and inward foreign direct investment is approximately valued at historic cost. The only major qualification is that where a foreign company in which there is Italian participation is quoted on a foreign stock exchange, the company's assets are assessed according to the year end stock exchange valuation. One central difficulty with the Bank of Italy data on FDI stocks is the high proportion which is allocated to financial investments in holding companies, especially in Luxembourg. These investments are in fact channelled via the holding companies in Luxembourg (and Lichtenstein) to real sectors of activity in other countries. Research is currently underway to try and resolve this problem.

NETHERLANDS

The Netherlands has always been an important outward direct investor. In 1980, it accounted for 7.8% of the world stock of foreign direct investment and was ranked third after the USA and UK. In 1960, this percentage had been even greater (10.5%) but the growth of foreign direct investment from countries such as Japan and Germany has since led to a relative decline.

Dutch investments abroad are anticyclical – the boom years of 1972/73 and 1976/78 had smaller capital outflows than the recession years of 1974/75 and 1979/82. Inflows of capital show the same pattern. (Table A3.)

The recovery of economic activity in the Netherlands which began in 1983 persisted in a more pronounced way in 1984 (notably in manufacturing industry) and is expected to continue.

Data on the sectoral distribution of investment suggest that the major growth area for the activities of both Dutch MNEs and foreign MNEs in the Netherlands is the tertiary sector, with the main emphasis on distributive trade, banking and finance. However, considerable investments have also occurred in the primary sector (particularly the energy industries) and in the manufacturing sector (primarily in metals & electrical engineering).

Turning to the geographical distribution of investment, it appears that for the developing countries, inward investment has risen relative to outward investment. For the developed countries, inward and outward investments have increased by roughly equal proportions, much attributable to the USA.

Government policies with regards foreign investment are very liberal. Foreign firms are given equal treatment vis-a-vis domestic firms except those in broadcasting, military production and aviation which are considered to be sensitive areas. Government incentives and access to the capital market are extended to all firms regardless of nationality. Laws and regulations which affect investment are applied on a non-discriminatory basis to all firms. The extent to which the government actively pursues a policy of attraction is manifested by the presence of their foreign investment commissions abroad.

MAIN SOURCES OF DATA:

A Official

1. Bank of Netherlands: publishes quarterly and annual data on inward and outward investment.
2. Marius van Nieuwkerk and Robert P Sparling, *The Netherlands international direct investment position*, Monetary Monographs No. 4, De Nederlandsche Bank n.v.: Martinus Nijhoff Publishers, Dordrecht, 1985.

B Private

1. J T de Mare, 'Dutch Multinational Enterprises and the structure of the Dutch Economy', paper presented at EIBA Annual Conference', Rotterdam, Dec 1984.

Note:
Data do not allow us to complete Table A10 for the Netherlands.

Table A1

SUMMARY OF THE COUNTRY'S INTERNATIONAL INVESTMENT POSITION

		Inward Investment	Outward Investment
1	Number of foreign affiliates in host country, and of foreign affiliates of home country firms at the end of 1980[1]	54	327
2	Number of foreign firms with direct investments in host country, and home country firms with direct foreign affiliates at the end of 1980	579	99
3	Total foreign direct capital stock at book value as a percentage of GNP at factor cost in 1983	13.22	27.36
4	Flow of foreign direct investment in the five year period 1980-84 (N Fl m)	12,405	32,200
5	Employment in foreign affiliates or abroad 1980	195,100	1,071,200
6	Output of foreign affiliates or abroad	*N.A.*	*N.A.*

Source:

De Netherlandsche Bank, *Annual Reports,* various years

NOTES TO TABLE A1

1 Represents manufacturing companies only.

Table A2

PRIVATE FOREIGN CAPITAL STOCK, 1973 - 83 (N Fl m)

	Inward Investment			Outward Investment		
	Portfolio	*Direct*	*Total*	*Portfolio*	*Direct*	*Total*
Book value of capital stock						
1973	*Not Available*	20,659	*Not Available*	*Not Available*	44,173	*Not Available*
1975		26,382			53,561	
1976		28,426			51,517	
1977		30,179			57,805	
1978		31,565			60,572	
1979		36,147			71,974	
1980		40,817			89,685	
1981		45,432			99,508	
1982		47,176			104,291	
1983		51,865			119,886	
1984[1]		53,265			128,086	

Source:
Marius van Nieuwkerk and Robert P Sparling, *op cit;* De Nederlandsche Bank, *Annual Report,* 1984.

NOTES TO TABLE A2

1 The direct capital stock figures for 1984 has been estimated by adding the difference in direct capital stock between 1983 and 1984 as provided by the De Nederlandsche Bank Annual Report, to the revised 1983 stock figure presented in this table.

Table A3

FLOW OF FOREIGN DIRECT INVESTMENT, 1974 - 83 (N Fl m)[1]

	Inward Investment			Outward Investment		
	Reinvested Profits	*Other*	*Total*	*Reinvested Profits*	*Other*	*Total*
1974	*Not Separately Available*		3,028	*Not Separately Available*		5,449
1975			2,695			3,939
1976			2,044			–2,044
1977			1,753			6,288
1978			1,386			2,767
1979			4,582			11,402
1980			4,670			17,711
1981			4,615			9,823
1982			1,744			4,783
1983			4,689			15,595
1984[1]			1,400			8,200

Source:

Van Nieuwkerk and Sparling, *op cit.*

NOTES TO TABLE A3

1 The direct capital stock figures for 1984 have been estimated by adding the difference in direct capital stock between 1983 and 1984 as provided by the De Nederlandsche Bank Annual Report, to the revised 1983 stock figures presented in this table.

Table A4

SECTORAL DISTRIBUTION OF FOREIGN DIRECT CAPITAL STOCK, 1973 - 83 (N Fl m)

	Inward Investment			Outward Investment		
	Primary[1]	*Secondary*	*Tertiary*	*Primary*[1]	*Secondary*	*Tertiary*
1973	8,327	6,695	5,637	21,041	17,301	5,831
1975	11,058	8,091	7,233	25,055	20,659	7,847
1977	11,502	9,148	9,529	25,234	22,494	10,077
1979	11,384	11,467	13,296	32,961	25,807	13,206
1981	15,962	11,053	18,417	50,525	28,406	20,577
1983	17,263	12,395	22,207	64,593	28,117	27,176

Source:
Van Nieuwkerk and Sparling, *op cit.*

NOTES TO TABLE A4

1 Represents agriculture and fishing, mining and quarrying, oil and chemicals.

Table A5

GEOGRAPHICAL DISTRIBUTION OF FOREIGN DIRECT CAPITAL STOCK, 1973 - 83 (N Fl m)

	Inward Investment			Outward Investment		
	Developed Countries	*Developing Countries*	*Total*	*Developed Countries*	*Developing Countries*	*Total*
1973	19,458	1,201	20,659	35,719	8,454	44,173
1975	23,870	2,512	26,382	43,403	10,158	53,561
1977	26,891	3,288	30,179	46,534	11,271	57,805
1979	31,347	4,800	36,147	58,353	13,621	71,974
1981	37,861	7,571	45,432	80,820	18,688	99,508
1983	43,351	8,514	51,865	98,985	20,901	119,886

Source:
Van Nieuwkerk and Sparling, *op cit.*

Table A6

INDUSTRIAL DISTRIBUTION OF FOREIGN DIRECT CAPITAL STOCK, 1973 - 83 (N Fl m)

	Inward Investment		Outward Investment	
	1973	*1983*	*1973*	*1983*
Primary	8,327	17,263	21,041	64,593
Agriculture	11	779	127	737
Mining & quarrying / Oil	8,316[2]	16,484[2]	20,914[2]	63,856[2]
Secondary	6,695	12,395	17,301	28,117
Food & drink[3]	1,142	3,625	5,863	9,282
Chemicals & allied	*N.A.*	*N.A.*	*N.A.*	*N.A.*
Metals[4]	3,941	6,474	10,634	17,267
Mechanical engineering	*Not Available*		*Not Available*	
Electrical equipment				
Motor vehicles				
Other transportation equipment				
Textiles & clothing				
Paper & allied				
Rubber				
Stone, clay & glass				
Coal & petroleum products				
Other manufacturing	1,612	2,296	804	1,568
Tertiary	5,637	22,207	5,831	27,176
Construction	163	431	495	1,439
Transport & communications[5]	355	555	1,312	1,460
Distributive trade	2,776	9,810	2,365	9,078
Property	*N.A.*	*N.A.*	*N.A.*	*N.A.*
Banking & finance	1,167	4,801	941	7,366
Other services	1,176	6,610	718	7,833
TOTAL	20,659	51,865	44,173	119,886

Source:
Van Nieuwkerk and Sparling, *op cit.*

NOTES TO TABLE A6

1 Including fishing.
2 Including chemicals.
3 Including tobacco.
4 Including electrical engineering.
5 Including storage.

Table A7

LEADING SOURCE AND RECIPIENT COUNTRIES, 1973 - 83 (N Fl m)

	Inward Investment		Outward Investment	
	1973	*1983*	*1973*	*1983*
DEVELOPED AREAS	19,458	43,351	35,719	98,985
Europe	10,879	21,989	23,360	51,703
EEC of which	8,840	16,319	22,335	46,263
Belgium & Luxembourg	1,514	2,600	3,132	7,461
Denmark	11	157	345	1,303
France	934	2,386	2,815	4,773
W. Germany	2,614	2,875	8,324	8,365
Ireland	22	219	120	1,657
Italy	73	162	803	1,635
UK	3,672	7,920	6,796	21,069
Other Europe of which				
Switzerland	2,039	5,670	1,025	5,440
North America of which	7,689	18,020	6,200	33,398
USA	7,689	18,020	6,200	33,398
Other developed countries of which	890	3,342	6,159	13,884
Japan	159	1,291	*N.A.*	*N.A.*
DEVELOPING AREAS	1,201	8,514	8,454	20,901
Europe	10	56	1,237	1,627
Africa	396	135	201	1,680
Asia & Pacific	51	810	1,738	6,144
Latin America of which	744	7,513	5,278	11,450
Netherlands Antilles	604	6,287	2,575	6,996
TOTAL	20,659	51,865	44,173	119,886

Source:
Van Nieuwkerk and Sparling, *op cit.*

Table A8

INDICATORS OF THE SIGNIFICANCE OF INWARD FOREIGN DIRECT INVESTMENT OR THE ACTIVITIES OF FOREIGN-BASED COMPANIES TO THE NATIONAL ECONOMY, 1980 - 83

1	Direct capital stock of foreign affiliates at book value in 1983 as a proportion of:		
	a	GNP at factor cost	13.22
	b	population (in N Fl per head)	3,454.04
2	Employment in foreign affiliates in 1980 as a percentage of all employment		
	a	in all industry	7.50
	b	in manufacturing	19.20
3	Percentage share of employment accounted for by foreign affiliates in selected sectors		
			Employment
	Manufacturing Sector		
		Food & drink	19.7
		Chemicals & allied	36.9
		Metals	43.6
		Mechanical engineering	10.3
		Electrical equipment	23.6
		Motor vehicles } Other transportation equipment }	17.5
		Textiles & clothing	7.9
		Paper and allied	11.8
		Rubber	6.5
		Stone, glass & clay	26.4
		Other manufacturing	2.0
	Services Sector		
		Transport & communications	0.9
		Trade & distribution	2.8
		Banking and finance	2.8
		Other services	0.1

Source:
J T de Mare, calculations based on data provided by the Central Bureau of Statistics.

Table A9

INDICATORS OF THE SIGNIFICANCE OF OUTWARD FOREIGN DIRECT INVESTMENT OF THE ACTIVITIES OF HOME-BASED COMPANIES ABROAD FOR THE NATIONAL ECONOMY, 1980 - 83

1 Foreign capital stock of home-based firms at book value in 1983 as a proportion of:	
a GNP at factor cost	27.36
b population (in N Fl per head)	7,151.81
2 Employment in foreign affiliates in 1980 as a percentage of domestic employment in manufacturing	29.70

3 Sales, value added and employment of foreign affiliates of home-based firms as a percentage of that in selected domestic sectors, 1980

	Sales	*Value Added*	*Employment*
Manufacturing Sector			
Food & drink[1]	17.8	20.3	18.4
Chemicals & allied	25.9	21.1	24.2
Metals	25.2	29.2	25.6
Mechanical engineering	19.9	17.9	20.0
Electrical equipment / Motor vehicles / Other transportation equipment	60.6	58.2	57.4
Textiles & clothing	10.6	10.9	9.8
Paper & allied	15.6	16.3	13.9
Rubber	13.0	11.4	10.6
Stone, glass & clay	8.1	7.4	6.9
Services Sector			
Construction			11.7
Transport & communications	*Not Available*		11.1
Banking & finance[2]			11.0
Other services			7.5

NOTES TO TABLE A9

1 Including tobacco.

2 Including insurance.

Table A11

ROYALTY RECEIPTS AND PAYMENTS, 1975 - 84 (N Fl m)

	Payments			Receipts		
	To Affiliates	*To Non-affiliates*	*Total*	*From Affiliates*	*From Non-affiliates*	*Total*
1975	*Not Separately Available*		709.31	*Not Separately Available*		466.73
1976			940.17			552.56
1977			879.68			567.35
1978			964.33			631.15
1979			1,114.43			743.82
1980			1,278.27			830.62
1981			1,482.87			965.04
1982			1,532.91			910.90
1983			1,476.73			973.30
1984			1,789.16			963.64

Source:
IMF, *Balance of Payments Statistics Yearbook,* various issues.

Table A12

LEADING FOREIGN AND DOMESTIC MULTINATIONAL COMPANIES

A Leading Foreign Affiliates in the Country, 1983

	Name	*Home Country*	*Sector*	*Netherlands Turnover (N Fl bn)*
1	Esso Nederland	USA	Oil, chemicals	7.08
2	Chevron Nederland	USA	Oil	4.82
3	Dow Chemicals Nederland	USA	Chemicals	4.69
4	BP	UK	Oil	3.20
5	Hendrix Int	UK	Food	2.83
6	Douwe Egberts	USA	Food, tobacco	2.47
7	IBM Nederland	USA	Electrotech	2.01
8	ICI Holland	UK	Chemicals	1.74
9	Hoechst Holland	Germany	Chemicals	1.60
10	GM Nederland	USA	Motor vehicles	1.50
11	Mobil Nederland	USA	Oil	1.12
12	OTRA	France	Wholesale trade	1.07
13	T & D Verblifa	USA	Metals	1.05
14	KNP[1]	Canada	Paper	1.03
15	Nederland Stikstof Mij	Norway	Chemicals	0.80
16	Ford Nederland	USA	Motor vehicles	0.78
17	Mercedes Benz Nederland	Germany	Motor vehicles	0.75
18	Du Pont Nederland	USA	Chemicals	0.75
19	Scania Nederland	Sweden	Motor vehicles	0.71
20	Turmac Tobacco	UK	Tobacco	0.65
21	Mars Nederland	UK	Food	0.64
22	Total	USA	Oil	0.64
23	Van Nelle	USA	Food, tobacco	0.55
24	Pechiney	France	Metals	0.54
25	Peugeot-Talbot	France	Motor vehicles	0.52
26	Allied Breweries	UK	Beverages	0.52

Table A12

LEADING FOREIGN AND DOMESTIC MULTINATIONAL COMPANIES

B Leading Domestic Companies with Multinational Interests, 1983

	Name	*Sector*	*Global Turnover (N Fl bn)*	*Sales of overseas subsidiaries as % of worldwide sales (1983)*
1	Royal Dutch/Shell	Oil	229.56	60[2]
2	Unilever	Food	59.43	39[3]
3	Phillips	Electrotech	46.18	93[4]
4	DSM	Chemicals	19.77	14[5]
5	AKZO	Chemicals	15.09	67[5]
6	SHV Holdings	Wholesale trade, services	11.07	
7	Vendex International	Retail trade	10.50	
8	Ahold	Retail trade	9.69	
9	Hoogovens	Metals	6.05	*Not Available*
10	KLM	Transport	4.96	
11	NedLloyd Group	Transport	4.17	
12	Heineken	Beverages	3.65	
13	Wessanen	Food	3.49	62[3]
14	KBB	Retail trade	3.49	
15	Bührmann-Tetterode	Paper	2.78	
16	PolyGram	Records	2.77	
17	Internatio-Müller	Wholesale trade, services	2.57	
18	Hagemeyer	Wholesale trade	2.49	*Not Available*
19	Kon Van Leer	Metals	2.47	
20	Volker Stevin	Building	2.30	
21	Boskalis Westminster	Building	2.15	
22	Ballast-Nedam	Building	2.07	
23	VMF-Stork	Metals	1.86	
24	Hunter Douglas	Metals	1.74	
25	CCF	Food	1.71	

Source:
Met Financieele Dagblad, *Annual Survey,* various issues.

NOTES TO TABLE A12

1 KNP is 40% owned by McMillan Bloedel. However, this 40% means effective control because the company is not quoted on the Dutch stock market which means that the rest of the stocks are dispersed.

2 Outside EEC.

3 Sales outside EEC; including exports.

4 Includes all exports, direct & intra-group.

5 Excludes all exports; intra-group exports are therefore included with direct exports.

NETHERLANDS TABLES: DEFINITIONS

The delimitation of the concept of direct investment used in the Netherlands meets the criterion that direct investment is characterised by the acquisition of a more or less lasting interest in an enterprise, with the aim of having an effective voice in the management. In practice, the condition applies that this must be attended by a shareholding, irrespective of its percentage.

Purchases on the stock exchange are always classified as portfolio investment (security transactions). In the event that such purchases should lead in time to an actual direct investment relationship, intra-group transfers, etc. will often ensue, which will be recognised as such in the balance-of-payments registration. Hence, the direct investment relationship will become evident later. If residents sell or buy shareholdings direct, i.e. not on the stock exchange, the resident concerned is requested to state the nature of the transaction (portfolio investment or direct investment). Finally, information is obtained from annual reports and publications in the media.

As in France, transaction data about direct investment are primarily collected within the framework of the balance-of-payments registration; this registration is monolithic in nature in that each payment is recorded within a single uniform framework ('exchange control registration'). Moreover, since 1973 the Netherlands has also collected data by means of annual surveys of the positions of outward and inward direct investment.

The direct investment data included in the balance of payments relate to the direct investment flows between residents and non-residents. *Capital participations* are generally acquired by direct purchases of shares. However, capital participations can also be acquired without any payment, for instance by an exchange of shares or by the acquisitions of shares against the transfer of claims, goods, licenses or know-how. All these transactions are recorded in the statistics concerned. In addition to capital participations, the direct investment registration includes – in conformity with the IMF and OECD guidelines – all short and long-term intra-group *lending* and all intra-group *current accounts.*

The balance-of payments data are published in the Bank's Annual Reports and Quarterly Bulletins about two or three months after the period of registration.

The position figures, which are compiled by means of the annual surveys, may change as a result of the following factors: first, changes ensuing from changes in capital participation and/or in intra-group lending positions. These are the *capital flows*. They may be due to such transactions and purchases or sales of shares and the granting or repayment of intra-group credits and loans; second, changes ensuing from the retention of *profits* or the absorption of losses by subsidiaries; and third, changes ensuing from *exchange rate differences*, other revaluations and adjustments. As the Netherlands balance of payments includes only the capital flows under the first factor stated above, the changes in positions are more comprehensive than the changes in direct investment shown in the balance of payments; cases in point are retained profits, exchange rate differences and revaluations.

Source:
Van Nieuwkerk and Sparling, *op cit.*

UNITED KINGDOM

The United Kingdom, once the world's leading outward direct investor, fell to second place behind the USA in the postwar period, while inward investment into the UK became markedly more significant. Outward investment is primarily concentrated in petroleum and manufacturing activities but the relative importance of services has risen in recent years, especially when banking and finance is included. The primary product sector has held its place in total inward investment due to the attraction of North Sea oil. UK outward investment has traditionally been orientated towards Commonwealth countries, but in the 1960s it began to enter Europe more strongly. In the late 70s and early 80s the USA was the single most attractive destination; indeed between 1978 and 1981 it accounted for 50.7% of the increase in capital stock. US firms had offered the largest source of inward investment into the UK in the 1950s and 1960s, but by 1970s European investment was growing faster.

MAIN SOURCES OF DATA:

A **Official**

1 Department of Trade and Industry; provides annual data on investment flows and on royalties and exports of foreign affiliates.

2 Bank of England: publishes annual data on the external asset and liability position of the United Kingdom.

3 Department of Trade and Industry: also responsible for the annual Census of Production in which the sales, value added and employment of UK manufacturing affiliates of foreign firms are shown separately for alternate years.

4 Central Statistical Office: publishes information which draws on Department of Industry and Bank of England sources.

Further details of sources used in the compilation of this profile are presented at the end of each table.

B **Private**

1 J H Dunning and T Houston, *UK Industry Abroad,* London: Financial Times, 1976.

2 J H Dunning, *US Industry in Britain,* London: Financial Times, 1976.

3 J H Dunning (Ed) *Multinational Enterprises Economic Structure and International Competitiveness,* Chichester: John Wiley, 1985.

4 J M Stopford and L Turner, *Britain and the Multinationals,* Chichester: John Wiley, 1985.

5 J M Stopford and J H Dunning, *Multinationals: Company Performance and Global Trends,* London: Macmillan, 1983.

6 J H Dunning, *Japanese Participation in UK Industry,* London: Croom Helm, 1986.

Table A1

SUMMARY OF THE COUNTRY'S INTERNATIONAL INVESTMENT POSITION

		Inward Investment	Outward Investment
1	Number of foreign affiliates in host country, and of foreign affiliates of home country firms at the end of 1981[1]	3,070	9,092
2	Number of foreign firms with direct investments in host country, and home country firms with direct foreign affiliates at the end of 1981	2,935	1,509
3	Total foreign direct capital stock at book value as a percentage of GNP at factor cost in 1981	15.3	19.8
4	Flow of foreign direct investment in the five year period, 1979-83[2] (£ m)	9,499.9	16,442.2
5	Employment in foreign affiliates or abroad, 1981	858,100[3]	1,390,000[4]
6	Output of foreign affiliates or abroad, 1981 (£ m)	31,909.5[3]	60,728.7[4]

Source:

Department of Industry, *Census of Overseas Assets, 1978;* Bank of England, *Quarterly Bulletin, June 1982;* Central Statistical Office, *National Income and Expenditure, 1982;* Department of Industry, *Business Monitor M4, Overseas Transactions, 1980;* Department of Industry, *Business Monitor PA 1002, Census of Production Summary Tables, 1979;* J H Dunning and J M Stopford, *Multinationals: Company Performance and Global Trends, op cit.*

NOTES TO TABLE A1

1 Excluding oil, banking and insurance.

2 Includes oil, banking, insurance and property.

3 Manufacturing only, 1981.

4 For a sample of 67 of the largest UK based multinationals in 1981.

Table A2

PRIVATE FOREIGN CAPITAL STOCK, 1960 - 84 (£ m)

	Inward Investment				Outward Investment		
	Portfolio	*Direct*[1]	*Total*		*Portfolio*	*Direct*[1]	*Total*
Book value of capital stock							
1962	1,030	2,130	3,160		3,200	4,870	8,070
1966	1,150	3,130	4,280		3,650	6,285	9,935
1970	2,075	4,885	6,960		5,600	8,800	14,400
1975	3,000	12,103	15,103		6,900	18,286	25,186
1976	3,390	13,696	17,086		8,700	22,892	31,592
1977	4,700	15,716	20,416		8,600	23,770	32,370
1978	4,580	17,861	22,441		10,100	27,298	37,398
1979	4,530	21,908	26,438		12,000	31,063	43,063
1980	5,100	26,422	31,522		18,100	33,849	51,949
1981	5,800	30,040	35,840		24,400	46,238	70,638
1982	6,800	31,766	38,566		40,000	54,130	94,130
1983	9,600	36,330	45,930		59,900	61,039	120,939
1984	13,300	36,841	50,141		82,500	73,829	156,329

Source:
Bank of England, *Quarterly Bulletin,* June 1971, 1982, 1984 and September 1985; Central Statistical Office, *United Kingdom Balance of Payments* 1985.

NOTES TO TABLE A2

1 Including banking from 1976 onwards. From 1962 to 1970, outward direct investment stock includes insurance companies' investments in the USA only and inward investment excludes insurance.

Table A3

FLOW OF FOREIGN DIRECT INVESTMENT, 1970 - 84 (£ m)[1]

	Inward Investment			Outward Investment		
	Reinvested Profits	*Other*	*Total*	*Reinvested Profits*	*Other*	*Total*
1970	180.6	182.6	363.2	321.6	224.6	546.2
1971	184.2	266.1	450.3	329.2	346.3	675.5
1972	304.0	103.5	407.5	465.1	271.7	736.8
1973	344.2	370.2	734.4	839.8	781.0	1,620.8
1974	251.1	602.6	853.7	851.0	724.5	1,575.5
1975	247.1	368.3	615.4	879.4	291.9	1,171.3
1976	540.9	258.0	798.9	1,454.3	690.5	2,144.8
1977	837.5	488.5	1,326.0	1,291.6	593.2	1,884.8
1978	689.3	571.8	1,261.1	1,259.5	1,450.2	2,709.7
1979	1,226,3	514.6	1,740.9	1,622.0	1,412.6	3,034.6
1980	689.0	1,851.9	2,540.9	1,633.7	1,683.0	3,316.7
1981	637.8	360.2	998.0	2,031.7	3,102.5	5,134.2
1982	769.2	305.1	1,074.3	1,661.8	867.4	2,529.2
1983	1,096.5	1,099.0	2,195.5	2,180.9	1,354.4	3,535.3
1984	1,743.1	946.3	2,689.4	2,359.6	639.6	2,999.2

Source:

Department of Industry, *Business Monitor M4, Overseas Transactions, 1980, 1982 and 1983; British Business,* 18-24 May 1984; IMF, *Balance of Payments Statistics* 1985.

NOTES TO TABLE A3

1 Excluding oil.

Table A4

SECTORAL DISTRIBUTION OF FOREIGN DIRECT CAPITAL STOCK, 1962 - 81 (£ m)[1]

	Inward Investment			Outward Investment		
	Primary[2]	*Secondary*	*Tertiary*[3]	*Primary*	*Secondary*	*Tertiary*
1962	700.0	1,192.5	237.2		*Not Available*	
1965	800.0[4]	1,643.1	356.8	2,011.1[5]	2,103.4	1,470.5
1971	1,750.0	3,180.2	636.8	3,100.1	3.934.4	1,732.4
1974	3,050.0	4,763.1	1,804.1	4,024.7	6,110.8	3,200.3
1978	5,250.0	8,272.5	2,826.0[6]	5,380.4	11,920.6	5,886.6[7]
1981	9,550.0	12,188.3	4,773.8	11,563.8	16,166.9	9,914.7

Source:

Department of Industry, *Census of Overseas Assets, 1978 and 1981 and 1984;* Department of Trade and Industry, *Trade and Industry, 15 Nov. 1973;* Board of Trade, *Board of Trade Journal, 16 Jan 1968;* Central Statistical Office, *United Kingdom Balance of Payments, 1982;* Bank of England, *Quarterly Bulletin, September 1970.*

NOTES TO TABLE A4

1 Excluding banking and insurance.
2 Only oil companies.
3 Including agriculture and mining.
4 Average of figure for 1964 (£750 m) and 1966 (£850 m).
5 Oil component estimated as an average of figure for 1964 (£1,275 m) and 1966 £1,475 m).
6 £3,750.5 m including banking.
7 £7,196.6 m including banking, and £7,926.6 m including both banking and insurance companies' investments in the USA (only).

Table A5

GEOGRAPHICAL DISTRIBUTION OF FOREIGN DIRECT CAPITAL STOCK, 1960 - 81 (£ m)[1]

	Inward Investment			Outward Investment		
	Developed Countries	*Developing Countries*	*Total*	*Developed Countries*	*Developing Countries*	*Total*
1960	1,025.7	14.3	1,040.0	1,863.0	1,087.0	2,950.0
1965	1,964.2	35.7	1,999.9	2,825.4	1,384.6	4,210.0
1970	3,289.4	46.5	3,335.9	4,645.1	1,759.0	6,404.1
1974	6,255.0	312.2	6,567.2	8,276.4	2,159.4	10,435.8
1978	10,865.5	232.7	11,098.2	15,295.4	3,892.3	19,107.7
1981	16,131.0	831.0	16,962.0	22,319.4	6,225.4	28,545.1

Source:

As for United Kingdom Table A4.

NOTES TO TABLE A5

1 Excluding oil, banking and insurance. When including oil companies and banks, total outward forign direct capital stock was provisionally estimated at £24,924.4 m in 1978 of which £20,186.2 m was in developed countries, and £4,728.2 m in developing countries. The revised total is £24,724.9 m.

Table A6

INDUSTRIAL DISTRIBUTION OF FOREIGN DIRECT CAPITAL STOCK, 1971 - 81 (£ m)[1]

	Inward Investment		Outward Investment	
	1971	*1981*	*1971*	*1981*
Primary[2]	1,750.0	9,550.0	3,100.1	11,563.7
Agriculture[3]	*N.A.*	*N.A.*	441.5	762.2
Mining & quarrying[3]	*N.A.*	*N.A.*	558.6	1,701.5
Oil	1,750.0	9,550.0	2,100.0	9,100.0
Secondary	3,180.2	12,188.3	3,934.4	16,166.9
Food & drink	391.9	2,009.4	1,104.2	4,384.4
Chemicals & allied	460.4	2,401.7	683.9	4,532.8
Metals	258.6	654.6	142.7	320.8
Mechanical engineering	684.4	2,168.5	263.4	1,014.2
Motor vehicles	466.4	1,753.5	498.0	1,621.8
Textiles & clothing	30.9	119.9	298.6	691.8
Paper & allied	92.5	633.6	261.5	883.7
Rubber	194.6	351.2	134.1	553.5
Coal & petroleum products	*N.A.*	*N.A.*	*N.A.*	*N.A.*
Other manufacturing	215.2	772.4	454.6	1,605.9
Tertiary[4]	636.8	4,773.7	1,732.4	9,914.7
Construction	*N.A.*	179.2	88.6	681.1
Transport & communications	*N.A.*	121.4	309.3	1,039.2
Distributive trade	392.6	2,567.1	876.4	3,833.2
Property	*N.A.*	*N.A.*	140.0	2,017.7
Banking & finance[1]	*N.A.*	–	*N.A.*	–
Other services[1,3]	244.2	1,906.0	318.1	2,343.5
TOTAL	5,567.0	26,511.7	8,766.9	37,645.3

Source:

Department of Industry, *Census of Overseas Assets, 1978 and 1981;* Department of Trade and Industry, *Trade and Industry, 15 Nov 1973;* Central Statistical Office, *United Kingdom Balance of Payments 1982.*

NOTES TO TABLE A6

1 Excluding banking and insurance, figures for which in 1978 are to be found in the Notes to Table A4. Investment by financial institutions other than banking and insurance is included under *other services.*

2 For inward investment stock, only oil companies are included.

3 For inward investment stock, agriculture and mining are included under *other services.*

4 For inward investment stock, including agriculture and mining.

Table A7

LEADING SOURCE AND RECIPIENT COUNTRIES, 1971 - 81 (£ m)[1]

	Source Countries		Recipient Countries	
	1971	*1981*	*1971*	*1981*
DEVELOPED AREAS	3,766.8	16,131.0	4,911.9	22,319.4
Europe				
EEC of which:	498.4	2,585.5	1,198.4	5,493.8
Denmark	21.9	155.2	26.9	144.9
France	80.4	574.6	247.5	1,064.1
W. Germany	59.8	627.0	305.7	1,510.2
Ireland	3.6	76.3	179.6	734.6
Italy	74.0	71.6	93.0	384.3
Netherlands	218.3	737.5	189.3	1,097.6
Other Europe of which:	393.2	1,942.1	263.1	1,118.0
Portugal	*N.A.*	*N.A.*	35.4	95.1
Spain	*N.A.*	20.6	80.4	321.3
Sweden	75.8	470.7	38.4	157.3
Switzerland	280.4	1,224.7	53.4	287.4
Turkey	*N.A.*	*N.A.*	5.2	*N.A.*
North America of which:	2,718.7	10,451.4	1,465.7	9,883.9
Canada	270.7	892.0	671.0	1,904.7
USA	2,448.0	9,559.4	794.7	7,979.2
Other developed countries of which:	156.5	1,152.0	1,984.7	5,823.7
Australia	29.2	330.3	1,137.5	3,534.5
Japan	13.3	324.1	15.9	187.2
South Africa	108.4	472.8	651.7	1,786.7
DEVELOPING AREAS	50.2	831.0	1,755.0	6,225.7
Africa of which:			594.9	1,911.7
Ghana	*Not Available*	*Not Available*	73.0	54.5
Kenya			60.5	208.0
Nigeria			155.6	638.4
Zambia			36.5	134.7
Zimbabwe			78.7	479.4
Asia & other Pacific of which:	11.9	523.4	675.1	2,380.3
Hong Kong	*Not Available*	*Not Available*	47.4	835.3
India			289.8	318.7
Malaysia			195.9	560.1
Pakistan			48.3	59.4
Singapore			19.5	419.6

Table A7 (cont'd)

LEADING SOURCE AND RECIPIENT COUNTRIES, 1971 - 81 (£ m)[1]

	Source Countries		Recipient Countries	
	1971	*1981*	*1971*	*1981*
Latin America of which:	38.9	206.8	488.5	1,711.3
Argentina			58.4	95.2
Bahamas			43.8	61.6
Brazil			79.5	421.1
Mexico			52.1	277.9
Netherlands Antilles	*Not*	*Not*	*N.A.*	-50.2
Trinidad & Tobago	*Available*	*Available*	42.3	64.9
Middle East of which:			32.4	236.4
Iran			5.9	6.6
Israel			3.3	7.9
Saudi Arabia			*N.A.*	25.8
OTHER DEVELOPING COUNTRIES	-0.6	100.9	-35.9	-13.5
TOTAL	3,817.0	16,962.0	6,666.9	28,545.1

Source:

Department of Industry, *Census of Overseas Assets, 1981.*

NOTES TO TABLE A7

1 Excluding oil, banking and insurance.

Table A8

INDICATORS OF THE SIGNIFICANCE OF INWARD FOREIGN DIRECT INVESTMENT OR THE ACTIVITIES OF FOREIGN-BASED COMPANIES TO THE NATIONAL ECONOMY, 1978 - 81

1 Direct capital stock of foreign affiliates at book value in 1981 as a proportion of:	
a GNP at factor cost	12.6
b population (in £ per head)	475.7
2 Employment in foreign affiliates in 1981 as a percentage of all employment in manufacturing	14.8
3 Output of foreign affiliates in 1981 as a percentage of all companies' output in secondary (ie, manufacturing) industry	19.3
4 Exports of foreign affiliates in 1981 as a percentage of all manufacturing exports	38.0[1]
5 Profits of foreign affiliates in 1978 as a percentage of profits of all companies in the host country	
a in all sectors	10.0
b in manufacturing	15.7

6 Percentage share of assets, sales and employment accounted for by foreign affiliates in selected sectors

	Assets (1978)	*Sales* (1981)	*Employment* (1981)
Primary Goods Sector			
Agriculture, mining and quarrying	*N.A.*	*N.A.*	*N.A.*
Oil	37.9	*N.A.*	*N.A.*
Manufacturing Sector			
Food & drink	8.0	17.9	11.1
Chemicals & allied	15.2	33.5	30.8
Metals	16.4	14.0	9.20
Mechanical engineering	21.9	25.8	19.8
Electrical equipment	17.0	23.4	21.4
Motor vehicles	24.1	27.8	24.6
Other transportation equipment	*N.A.*	*N.A.*	*N.A.*
Textiles & clothing	2.4	8.2	3.7
Paper & allied	10.6	15.5	12.7
Rubber		24.8	19.7
Stone, glass & clay	*Not*	*N.A.*	*N.A.*
Coal & petroleum products	*Available*	*N.A.*	*N.A.*
Timber & furniture		2.0	1.4
Other manufacturing	9.0	17.9	13.2

Table A8 (cont'd)

INDICATORS OF THE SIGNIFICANCE OF INWARD FOREIGN DIRECT INVESTMENT OR THE ACTIVITIES OF FOREIGN-BASED COMPANIES TO THE NATIONAL ECONOMY, 1978 - 81

6 (cont'd)	*Assets*	*Sales*	*Employment*
Services Sector			
Construction	2.3		
Transport & communications	4.2		
Trade and distribution	10.3	*Not Available*	*Not Available*
Banking & finance	*N.A.*		
Other services	6.9		

Source:

Bank of England, *Quarterly Bulletin, June 1982;* Central Statistical Office, *National Income and Expenditure 1982;* Department of Industry, *Business Monitor PA 1002, Census of Production Summary Tables, 1979 and 1981;* Department of Industry, *Business Monitor M4, Overseas Transactions, 1980;* Department of Industry, *Business Monitor M3, Company Finance No 13 (November 1982);* Department of Industry, *Business Monitor M4, Census of Overseas Assets, 1978;* Central Statistical Office, *UK Balance of Payments 1982.*

Table A9

INDICATORS OF THE SIGNIFICANCE OF OUTWARD FOREIGN DIRECT INVESTMENT OR THE ACTIVITIES OF HOME-BASED COMPANIES ABROAD FOR THE NATIONAL ECONOMY, 1978 - 81

1	Foreign capital stock of home-based firms at book value in 1981 as a proportion of:	
	a GNP at factor cost	19.6
	b population (in £ per head)	738.3
2	Employment in foreign affiliates in 1981 as a percentage of domestic employment	
	a in all industry	6.6[1]
	b in manufacturing	22.9[2]
3	Output of foreign manufacturing affiliates in 1981 as a percentage of:	
	a domestic manufacturing output	121.7[3]
	b manufacturing exports from the home country	158.7[3]
4	Profits of foreign affiliates in 1978 as a percentage of all profits recorded by home-based companies[4]	
	a in all sectors	21.9
	b in manufacturing	17.3

5 Assets of foreign affiliates of home-based firms as a percentage of those in selected domestic sectors (Book value), 1978[5]

Primary Goods Sector		*Manufacturing Sector (cont'd)*	
Agriculture	34.4	Paper & allied	21.9
Mining and quarrying	29.5	Other manufacturing	15.4
Oil	30.3		
Manufacturing Sector			
Food and drink	23.4	*Services Sector*	
Chemicals & allied	34.4	Construction	10.5
Metals	23.7	Transport & communications communications	18.8
Mechanical engineering	8.7	Trade & distribution	22.8
Electrical equipment	10.2	Property	13.0
Motor vehicles	6.1	Other services	12.4
Other transportation equipment	32.7		
Textiles & clothing	16.1		

Source:

J M Stopford and J H Dunning, *Multinationals: Company Performance and Global Trends,* London: Macmillan, 1983; Central Statistical Office, *Monthly Digest of Statistics, no 446, February 1983; Business Monitor M3 Company Finance no 13, November 1982.*

NOTES TO TABLE A9

1 Foreign employment in a sample of 67 UK based multinationals. Including two Anglo-Dutch firms (Shell and Unilever) the figure is 9.5%.

2 Using the same estimate of foreign affiliate employment, given that the bulk of the 67 UK firms are in manufacturing activities.

3 Using the same survey of 67 firms (excluding Shell and Unilever) mentioned in preceding footnotes.

4 Including the profits of the UK affiliates of foreign companies as home-based. For definitions see footnote 2 of UK Table A8.

5 At book value

Table A10

DISTRIBUTION OF FOREIGN SUBSIDIARIES AND ASSOCIATES AND FOREIGN CAPITAL STOCK BY PERCENTAGE OWNERSHIP OF PARENT COMPANIES, 1981[1]

	Inward Investment		Outward Investment	
	Number of Affiliates	*Value of Capital Stock (£ m)*	*Number of Affiliates*	*Value of Capital Stock (£ m)*
100% owned subsidiaries	2,163	12,925.4	5,910	19,528.3
50-99.9% owned subsidiaries and associates	282	1,743.1	1,160	5,700.7
Less than 50% owned subsidiaries and associates	139	732.2	935	2,141.1
TOTAL	2,584	15,400.7	8,005	27,370.1

Source:

Department of Industry, *Census of Overseas Assets, 1981.*

NOTES TO TABLE A10

1 Excluding oil, banking and insurance, and excluding investments in branches.

Table A11

ROYALTY RECEIPTS AND PAYMENTS, 1966 - 82 (£ m)

	Payments			Receipts		
	To Affiliates	*To Non-affiliates*	*Total*	*From Affiliates*	*From Non-affiliates*	*Total*
1966 - 1970[1]	50.0	39.1	89.1	33.3	71.8	105.1
1971 - 1975[1]	102.7	68.8	171.6	62.9	144.0	206.9
1976	179.9	116.1	296.0	112.9	274.1	387.0
1977	214.1	114.1	328.2	127.0	296.3	423.3
1978	254.0	110.0	364.0	151.8	308.2	460.0
1979	288.3	66.7	355.1	170.2	296.9	467.1
1980	324.0	73.7	397.7	200.7	286.8	487.5
1981	361.7	86.4	448.2	235.5	338.4	575.9
1982	382.1	82.3	464.4	229.0	339.3	568.3
1983	435.1	110.7	545.8	307.3	393.3	700.6

Source:

Department of Industry, *Business Monitor M4, Overseas Transactions, 1976, 1980, 1982 and 1983.*

NOTES TO TABLE A11

1 Annual average.

Table A12

LEADING FOREIGN AND DOMESTIC MULTINATIONAL COMPANIES

A Leading Foreign Multinational Companies in the Country, 1983

	Name	*Home Country*	*Sector*	*UK Turnover (£000) 1983*
1	Esso UK	USA	Oil industry	7,565,200
2	Philbro-Salomon Inc	USA	Commodity brokers, etc.	4,036,181 (31.12.82)
3	Ford Motor Co	USA	Motor vehicle manufacturers	3,585,000
4	Gallaher Ltd	USA	Tobacco, optics, pumps & valve distribution	2,579,700
5	Texaco Ltd	USA	Oil industry	2,379,458 (31.12.82)
6	Amalgamated Metal Corp	W. Germany	Metal & ores	2,076,726
7	Mobil Holdings Ltd	USA	Petroleum products	1,758,466 (31.12.82)
8	Conoco	USA	Petroleum products	1,682,700 (31.12.82)
9	IBM UK Holdings	USA	Information handling equipment manufacturers	1,677,162
10	C.T. Bowring & Co	USA	Insurance brokers, etc	1,614,400 (31.12.82)
11	Rank Xerox	USA	Copiers & office systems	1,462,300 (28.10.83)
12	International Thomson Org	Canada	Oil, travel, printing & publishing	1,148,900
13	Vauxhall Motors Ltd	USA	Motor vehicle manufacturers	1,060,148 (31.12.82)
14	Philips Electronic & Assoc	Holland	Electrical & electronic products	965,776
15	Louis Dreyfus & Co	France	Merchants & shippers	943,168
16	Cargill UK	USA	Commodity trading agent & principal	933,632 (31.05.83)
17	NAFTA (GB)	USSR	Traders in petroleum products	930,856 (31.12.82)
18	Bunge & Co Ltd	Netherlands Antilles	Grain cotton & commodity merchants	930,606
19	Petrofina (UK)	Belgium	Petroleum products	837,782 (31.12.82)
20	Tampinex	USA	Oil traders	753,098 (31.12.82)
21	Elf Aquitaine UK Holings	France	Gas & condensate products oil & gas exploration	751,800
22	Food Manufacturers	UK	Food manufacturers	717,819 (1.1.83)
23	Gulf Oil (GB)	USA	Distribution of petroleum products	630,014 (31.12.82)
24	Nestle Holdings UK	Switzerland	Food manufacturers & distributors	596,862 (31.12.82)
25	Safeway Food Stores	USA	Food retailing	570,775 (1.10.83)

Source:

The Times 1000 1984-85, *The World's Top Companies,* London: Times 1984.

Table A12 (cont'd)

LEADING FOREIGN AND DOMESTIC MULTINATIONAL COMPANIES

B	Leading Domestic Companies with Multinational Interests, 1983			
	Name	*Sector*	*Global Turnover (£ th)*	*Sales of overseas subsidiaries as % of worldwide sales (1981)*
1	British Petroleum Co	Oil, chemicals, etc	37,960,000	63[1]
2	Shell Transport & Trading	Oil, chemicals, etc	24,411,000	60[2]
3	BAT Industries	Tobacco, retailing, paper, etc	11,652,000	78
4	Imperial Chemical Industries	Chemicals	8,256,000	44[3]
5	Unilever	Food & household products	5,355,000	39[4]
6	Rio Tinto-Zinc Corp	Mining, metals, etc	4,811,000	73[3]
7	General Electric Company	Electrical engineering	4,625,500 (31.3.83)	33[3]
8	Grand Metropolitan	Hotels, brewing, etc	4,468,800 (30.9.83)	27[3]
9	Imperial Group	Tobacco, food & drink, etc	4,381,500 (31.10.83)	17[3]
10	S W Berisford	Commodity trading	4,325,341 (30.9.83)	*N.A.*
11	British Leyland	Motor vehicles	3,421,000	17[3]
12	Rothmans International	Tobacco, consumer products, etc	3,411,732	81[3]
13	George Weston Holdings	Food manufacturers & distributors	3,376,195 (2.4.83)	36
14	Allied Lyons	Brewing, hotels, etc	2,850,500 (3.3.84)	24[3]
15	Dalgety	International merchants	2,842,000 (30.6.83)	49
16	Thorn-EMI	Electrical & electronic engineers, music, etc	2,715,900 (31.3.83)	28[3,5]
17	Lonrho	Mining, agric., textiles, construction, etc	2,356,500 (30.9.83)	*N.A.*
18	British Aerospace	Aircraft manufacturing	2,300,000	4[8]
19	Ultramar	Petroleum exploration	2,057,100	84[6]
20	Courtaulds	Fibres, textiles, etc	2,038,100 (31.3.84)	37[3]
21	Bass	Brewing	1,988,400 (30.9.83)	5[3]
22	Guest, Keen & Nettlefolds	Steel & engineering products	1,975,000	43[3]
23	BTR	Construction, energy, etc	1,969,500	49[6,7]
24	Sears Holdings	Footwear, stores, engineering	1,846,000	*N.A.*
25	Reed International	Paper products, publishing,	1,809,000	18[3]

Source:

The Times 1000, 1984-85, *The World's Top Companies,* London: Times, 1984; J M Stopford & J H Dunning, *Multinationals: Company Performance and Global Trends,* London: Macmillan, 1983.

NOTES TO TABLE A12(b)

1 Excluding UK-based international activities.
2 Outside EEC.
3 Excludes all exports; any intra-group exports are therefore included in direct exports.
4 1978 data.
5 Fiscal 1982 data.
6 Outside Europe.
7 Includes all exports, direct and intra-group.
8 Represents employment figures.

UNITED KINGDOM TABLES: DEFINITIONS

Foreign affiliates

Foreign affiliates are made up of subsidiaries, associates and branches. Subsidiaries are defined in section 154 of the Companies Act 1948, and in general are majority or wholly owned by the parent company. Associates are companies in which the investing firm participates in the management but does not exercise control. Branches are permanent establishments set up by the parent company in which there is no equity share capital apart from that of the parent.

Foreign direct capital stock

This is represented by the foreign owned portion of the book value of assets of foreign affiliates, as entered in UK company accounts. Book values are the historic cost of assets when purchased or last revalued, and in general, particularly in inflationary periods, are lower than market values or replacement costs.

The net book value of direct investment is defined in more detail as follows: For subsidiaries and branches; fixed assets (net of depreciation at historic cost), plus current assets, less current liabilities, excluding those due or from the investing company, less long-term loans, less deferred tax reserves and provisions, and less minority shareholders interests in subsidiaries. In the case of subsidiaries this equals the foreign-owned proportion of share capital and reserves, plus net loans and liabilities due to the investing company. For associates; usually the cost of share capital when purchased, less any amounts written off, plus the investing company's share of the post-acquisition retained profits and reserves, plus loans and net current balances due to the investing company.

Assets purchased by direct investment financed by UK companies through foreign currency borrowing from UK and overseas banks are included, but not the corresponding liability to the lender of foreign currency. Similarly, borrowings in the UK by foreign companies are not included in outward direct investment, but any inward direct investment it finances is included. However, local borrowing by foreign affiliates themselves is not included as direct investment since it does not increase the value of net assets attributable to the investing company.

Foreign direct investment

Direct investment is stated net of disinvestment and consists of the parent company's share of the unremitted profits, less losses of subsidiaries and associates; the cash acquisition, net of sales, of share and loan capital of subsidiaries and associates; and changes in indebtedness on inter-company accounts and on intra-company branch-head office accounts.

Net direct investment is a financial concept and is not the same as capital expenditure on fixed assets or as the growth in the net assets of affiliates themselves. Direct investment covers only the money invested by the parent company, and this can be less than the change in the value of the fixed assets of foreign affiliates if the latter is financed by local borrowing or by other shareholders or, greater, if part of the direct investment is used to finance working capital (eg, to repay past borrowing). Direct investment also includes acquisitions of foreign companies by means of an exchange of shares, such that a direct investment asset or liability is offset by an equivalent portfolio liability or asset.

Note that although both the UK and the USA adopt the definition of direct investment given in the IMF Balance of Payments Manual, there are differences between the operational definitions used by each country. Thus, estimates of UK direct investment (outward to and inward from the USA) tend to be higher than estimates of equivalent US inward and outward investment, particularly because UK company stocks and work-in-progress are valued on a first in — first out basis, whereas in US company accounts they are valued on a last in — first out basis.

Royalties

Royalties include licenses, patents, trade marks, design copyrights, manufacturing rights, use of technical 'know-how' and technical assistance, use of printed matter, sound recording royalties and performing rights; they exclude transactions relating to film and television rights.

Source:
Department of Industry, *Business Monitor M4, Census of Overseas Assets 1978* and *Overseas Transactions 1980.*

OTHER EUROPE

AUSTRIA

The 1981 biennial survey of the National Bank of Austria on foreign direct investment covered 1,754 Austrian companies with foreign participation and a nominal capital of at least A Sch 1 million. This coverage represents an estimated 80-90% of total foreign direct investment in Austria. 36% of these Austrian companies with foreign participation were responsible for 1,814 establishments engaged in manufacturing activities employing a total of 160,000 workers. 64% of these Austrian companies with foreign participation were responsible for 3,594 establishments engaged in non-manufacturing activities employing a total of 87,000 workers. The National Bank of Austria measures the degree of foreign penetration according to the share of employment accounted for by foreign affiliates. In 1981, the overall figure was 12%, representing 26% in manufacturing and 6% elsewhere. Public joint-stock (AG) and private limited (GmbH) companies comprised 83% of the companies surveyed with partnerships of one kind or another accounting for the remainde. Foreign majority holdings represented 85% of the companies surveyed and accounted for 77% of the total employees of direct foreign investors surveyed, or 7% of the total working force in Austria.

The total foreign nominal capital of the establishments surveyed amounted to A Sch 3.1 billion, of which 54% was invested in manufacturing and 46% elsewhere. 85% of the entire nominal foreign capital originated from within Europe, of which West Germany and other EEC countries had contributed 57%, Switzerland and Austria's EFTA partners 40% and other countries 3%.

A total number of 397 Austrian businesses had 724 holdings in companies outside Austria according to the 1982 biennial survey of the National Bank of Austria. This coverage represents an estimated 70-75% of total Austrial foreign direct investment. Of these, 370 holdings with capital investments of A Sch 5,346 million were engaged in manufacturing and 354 holdings with capital investments of A Sch 5,933 million were within non-manufacturing activities. Over 50% of these direct investments abroad were joint ventures and just under 50% consisted of partnerships, branches and other unincorporated branches. A vast majority of these direct investments abroad were greenfield investments rather than takeovers of existing firms. Such a survey revealed that Austrian foreign direct investment totalled A Sch 11.3 billion at the end of 1982.

Almost 25% of total Austrian nominal capital invested abroad had been chanelled to West Germany, 26% into other EEC countries, 16% into EFTA countries, notably Switzerland, 25% into America, predominantly the USA, and 6% into the rest of the world, mainly Asia.

MAIN SOURCES OF DATA:

Official

1 National Bank of Austria monthly publication, *Austria's Monetary Situation Survey,* abridged from *Mitteilungen des Direktoriums der Oesterreichischen Nationalbank*, provides data on the investment position of Austria.

Note:
Data do not allow us to complete Table A12 for Austria.

Table A1

SUMMARY OF THE COUNTRY'S INTERNATIONAL INVESTMENT POSITION

		Inward Investment	Outward Investment
1	Number of foreign affiliates in host country, and of foreign affiliates of home country firms at the end of 1981	5,408[1]	724[2]
2	Number of foreign firms with direct investments in host country, and home country firms with direct foreign affiliates at the end of 1981	1,754[1]	397[2]
3	Total foreign direct capital stock at book value as a percentage of GNP at factor cost in 1981	4.39	1.0
4	Flow of foreign direct investment in the five year period, 1979-83 (A Sch m)	18,201	11,625
5	Employment in foreign affiliates or abroad, 1981	247,000[1]	*N.A.*
6	Output of foreign affiliates or abroad abroad	*N.A.*	*N.A.*

Source:

National Bank of Austria, *Austria's Monetary Situation Survey,* abridged from *Mitteilungen des Direktoriums der Oesterreichischen Nationalbank,* various issues; IMF, *International Financial Statistics,* various issues; IMF, *Balance of Payments Yearbook,* various issues.

NOTES TO TABLE A1

1 Based on the biennial survey of the National Bank of Austria on foreign direct investment in Austria covering foreign-influenced Austrian establishments with a nominal capital of not less than A Sch 1 million, representing an estimated 80-90% of such investment as a whole. Agriculture, forestry and public services are excluded where there is little or no foreign investment interest.

2 Based on the 1982 biennial survey of the National Bank of Austria on Austrian direct investment abroad. This survey may be said to represent by value an estimated 70-75% of total Austrian foreign direct investment. Agriculture, forestry and public services are excluded where there is little or no foreign investment interest.

Table A2

PRIVATE FOREIGN CAPITAL STOCK, 1968-84 (A Sch m)

	Inward Investment			Outward Investment		
	Portfolio	*Direct*[1]	*Total*	*Portfolio*	*Direct*[2]	*Total*
Book value of capital stock						
1968	*Not Available*	17,566	*Not Available*	*Not Available*	*N.S.A.*	*Not Available*
1969		19,637			*N.S.A.*	
1970		20,331			*N.S.A.*	
1975		33,521			*N.S.A.*	
1976		33,436			*N.S.A.*	
1977		35,985			7,078	
1978		38,683			8,290	
1979		40,637			6,793	
1980		43,677			7,320	
1981		46,027			10,079	
1982		49,481			11,279	
1983		53,275			14,620	
1984		55,397			15,800	

Source:

National Bank of Austria, *Austria's Monetary Situation Survey,* abridged from *Mitteilungen des Direktoriums der Oesterreischischen Nationalbank,* various issues.

NOTES TO TABLE A2

1 Represents Austria's total foreign liabilities with respect to foreign direct investment. It consists of:

a equity capital (shareholder's funds) composed of nominal foreign capital, statutory and free reserves and profits and losses brought forward, and

b long-term loans.

2 Represents Austria's claims from its direct investment abroad. It consists of:

a nominal capital,

b other equity capital, and

c long-term loans.

Table A3

FLOW OF FOREIGN DIRECT INVESTMENT, 1970-83 (A Sch m)[1]

	Inward Investment			Outward Investment		
	Reinvested Profits	*Other*	*Total*	*Reinvested Profits*	*Other*	*Total*
1970	*Not Separately Available*		2,458.0	*Not Separately Available*		291.0
1971			2,013.0			904.0
1972			1,786.0			642.0
1973			2,071.0			700.0
1974			3,210.0			420.0
1975			1,742.0			519.0
1976			1,933.0			1,043.0
1977			1,582.3			1,427.9
1978			2,072.6			1,309.0
1979			2,504.3			1,139.9
1980			3,081.5			4,395.0
1981			5,296.0			3,342.8
1982			4,652.0			2,523.8
1983			5,204.0			3,302.9
1984			2,912.4			1,558.8

Source:
IMF, *Balance of Payments Statistics,* various issues.

NOTES TO TABLE A3

1 These data *exclude* reinvested profits which are not separately given.

Table A4

SECTORAL DISTRIBUTION OF FOREIGN DIRECT CAPITAL STOCK, 1974-82 (A Sch m)[1,2]

	Inward Investment				Outward Investment		
	Primary	*Secondary*	*Tertiary*		*Primary*	*Secondary*	*Tertiary*
1974	*Not Available*	15,066	14,221		*Not Available*	*Not Available*	*Not Available*
1975		16,374	17,147				
1977		21,109	14,876				
1979		23,745	16,892			3,110	3,683
1980		24,978	18,699			3,167	4,153
1981		25,559	20,468			4,575	5,504
1982		*N.A.*	*N.A.*			5,346	5,933

Source:

National Bank of Austria, *Austria's Monetary Situation Survey,* abridged from *Mitteilungen des Direktoriums der Oesterreichischen Nationalbank*, various issues.

NOTES TO TABLE A4

1 Agriculture, forestry and public services are excluded as in these cases there is little or no foreign investment.

2 Represents nominal capital.

Table A5

GEOGRAPHICAL DISTRIBUTION OF FOREIGN DIRECT CAPITAL STOCK, 1974-82 (A Sch m)[1]

	Inward Investment				Outward Investment		
	Developed Countries[2]	*Other Countries*	*Total*[3]		*Developed Countries*[2]	*Other Countries*	*Total*[3]
1974	15,604	5,130	20,734		*N.A.*	*N.A.*	*N.A.*
1975	17,503	5,410	22,913		*N.A.*	*N.A.*	*N.A.*
1977	19,534	5,864	25,398		*N.A.*	*N.A.*	*N.A.*
1979	21,496	6,472	27,968		2,695	1,970	4,665
1980	23,109	6,822	29,931		2,509	2,323	4,832
1981	31,517[4]	108[5]	31,625		3,345	3,025	6,370
1982	*N.A.*	*N.A.*	*N.A.*		6,802[6]	423[5]	7,225

Source:

National Bank of Austria, *Austria's Monetary Situation Survey,* abridged from *Mitteilungen des Direktoriums der Oesterreichischen Nationalbank,* various issues.

NOTES TO TABLE A5

1 Represents only nominal capital.

2 *Represents investment by West Germany, Switzerland, Liechtenstein and the USA.*

3 Total includes 'unspecified' figure.

4 Represents investment by European countries and America.

5 Represents investment by African and Asian countries.

6 Represents investment by European countries, America and Australasia.

Table A6

INDUSTRIAL DISTRIBUTION OF FOREIGN DIRECT CAPITAL STOCK, 1974-82 (A Sch m)[1]

	Inward Investment		Outward Investment	
	1974	*1981*	*1979*	*1982*
Primary				
Agriculture				
Mining & quarrying	*neg.*	*neg.*	*neg.*	*neg.*
Oil				
Secondary	15,066	25,559	3,110	5,346
Food & drink[2]	1,391	2,368	325	291[3]
Chemicals & allied[4]	3,936	7,567	615	1,060
Metals[5]	4,364	4,662	1,787	3,486
Mechanical engineering	*N.A.*	*N.A.*	*N.A.*	*N.A.*
Electrical equipment	1,770	5,981	68	101
Motor vehicles[5]	*N.A.*	*N.A.*	*N.A.*	*N.A.*
Other transportation equipment	*N.A.*	*N.A.*	*N.A.*	*N.A.*
Textiles & clothing	1,341	1,644	122	59[6]
Paper & allied	1,537	947	172	173
Rubber	*N.A.*	*N.A.*	*N.A.*	*N.A.*
Stone, clay & glass	727	1,398[7]	21[8]	
Coal & petroleum products	*N.A.*	*N.A.*	*N.A.*	*N.A.*
Other manufacturing	—	992	—	176
Tertiary	14,221	20,468	3,683	5,933
Construction	*N.A.*	*N.A.*	*N.A.*	*N.A.*
Transport & communications[9]	952	530	8	4
Distributive trade	8,741	8,458	251	377
Property	*N.A.*	*N.A.*	*N.A.*	*N.A.*
Banking & finance	1,653	6,324	1,952	3,667
Other services	2,875	5,156	1,472	1,885
TOTAL	29,287	46,027	6,793	11,279

Source:
National Bank of Austria, *Austria's Monetary Situation Survey,* abridged from *Mitteilungen des Direktoriums der Oesterreichischen Nationalbank,* various issues.

NOTES TO TABLE A6

1 Represents Austria's total foreign assets and liabilities with respect to foreign direct investment. Agriculture, forestry and public services are excluded as in these sectors there is little or no foreign investment.

2 Including leather and tobacco.

3 Represents food, drink and tobacco.

4 Including petroleum products.

5 Motor vehicles are included under metals.

6 Including leather.

7 Represents quarrying, pottery and construction.

8 Represents quarrying, pottery.

9 Including energy.

Table A7

LEADING SOURCE AND RECIPIENT COUNTRIES, 1974-82 (A Sch m)[1]

	Inward Investment		Outward Investment	
	1974	*1981*	*1979*	*1982*
DEVELOPED AREAS	*N.A.*	31,517	*N.A.*	6,802
Europe	12,896	26,871	2,324	5,014
EEC of which:	5,529	15,335	1,466	3,588
W. Germany	5,529	9,770	1,466	1,692
Other Europe of which:	7,367	11,536[2]	858	1,189
Switzerland[3]	7,367	10,155	858	1,112
North America of which:	*N.A.*	4,646	371	1,770
Canada	*N.A.*	204	*N.A.*	246
USA	2,708	4,442	371	1,524
Other developed countries of which:	neg	neg	*N.A.*	18
Australia	neg	neg	*N.A.*	18
DEVELOPING AREAS	*N.A.*	108	*N.A.*	423
Africa	*N.A.*	15	*N.A.*	45
Asia & Pacific	*N.A.*	93	*N.A.*	378
UNALLOCATED	5,130	–	1,970	–
TOTAL	20,734	31,625	4,665	7,225

Source:

National Bank of Austria, *Austria's Monetary Situation Survey,* abridged from *Mitteilungen des Direktoriums der Oesterreichischen Nationalbank,* various issues.

NOTES TO TABLE A7

1 Represents only nominal capital.

2 Represents EFTA A Sch 10,867 million, Eastern Europe A Sch 528 million and Other Europe A Sch 141 million.

3 Including Liechtenstein.

Table A8

INDICATORS OF THE SIGNIFICANCE OF INWARD FOREIGN DIRECT INVESTMENT OR THE ACTIVITIES OF FOREIGN-BASED COMPANIES TO THE NATIONAL ECONOMY, 1981

1	Direct capital stock of foreign affiliates at book value in 1981 as a proportion of:	
	a GNP at factor cost	4.39
	b population (in A Sch per head)	6,088.23
2	Employment in foreign affiliates in 1981 as a percentage of all employment[1]	
	a in all industry	12
	b in manufacturing	26

3 Percentage share of assets and employment accounted for by foreign affiliates in selected sectors, 1981

	Assets[2]	*Employment*
Manufacturing Sector		
Food and drink[3]	58.8	28.10
Chemicals and allied[4]	92.5	23.20
Metals[5]	75.2	16.40
Electrical equipment	79.3	58.90
Motor vehicles[5]	*N.A.*	*N.A.*
Other transportation equipment	*N.A.*	*N.A.*
Textiles and clothing	71.1	28.40
Paper and allied[6]	70.5	20.80
Stone, glass and clay[7]	66.8	34.40
Other manufacturing	37.0	25.00
Services Sector		
Transport and communications[8]	85.4	1.67
Trade and distribution	87.3	9.70
Banking and finance[9]	62.8	22.10
Other services	45.9	2.90

Source:

National Bank of Austria, *Austria's Monetary Situation Survey*, abridged from *Mitteilungen des Direktoriums der Oesterreichischen Nationalbank*, various issues; IMF, *International Financial Statistics.*

NOTES TO TABLE A8

1 Based on biennial survey of National Bank of Austria on foreign direct investment covering 1,754 foreign-influenced Austrian companies with a nominal capital of not less than A Sch 1 m, representing an estimated 80-90% of such investment as a whole.

2 Represents share of foreign nominal capital in total nominal capital.

3 Including tobacco and leather.

4 Including petroleum.

5 Motor vehicles are included under metals.

6 Including wood.

7 Represents pottery, quarrying and construction.

8 Represents transport and energy.

9 Including insurance.

Table A9

INDICATORS OF THE SIGNIFICANCE OF OUTWARD FOREIGN DIRECT INVESTMENT OR THE ACTIVITIES OF HOME-BASED COMPANIES ABROAD FOR THE NATIONAL ECONOMY, 1982

1	Foreign capital stock of home-based firms at book value in 1982 as a proportion of:	
	a GNP at factor cost	1.00
	b population (in A Sch per head)	1,489.96
2	Employment in foreign affiliates in 1982 as a percentage of domestic employment[1]	
	a in all industry	12.20
	b in manufacturing	34.10

3 Assets and employment of foreign affiliates of home-based firms as a percentage of that in selected domestic sectors, 1982

	Assets[2]	*Employment*
Manufacturing Sector		
Food and drink[3]	57.7	14.9
Chemicals and allied[4]	42.1	48.5
Metals[5]	34.5	45.1
Electrical equipment	42.0	35.7
Motor vehicles[5]	*N.A.*	*N.A.*
Other transportation equipment	*N.A.*	*N.A.*
Textiles and clothing[6]	23.9	14.3
Paper and allied[7]	33.8	21.7
Other manufacturing	*N.A.*	12.5
Services Sector		
Construction	19.3	30.0
Transport and communications[8]	25.0	1.2
Trade and distribution	64.3	2.2
Banking and finance[9]	9.7	25.0
Other services	18.1	4.3

Source:

National Bank of Austria, *Austria's Monetary Situation Survey,* abridged from *Mitteilungen des Direktoriums der Oesterreichischen Nationalbank,* various issues; I.M.F., *International Financial Statistics.*

NOTES TO TABLE A9

1 Based on biennial survey of National Bank of Austria on Austrian direct investment covering 724 Austrian companies with multinational interests, representing by value some 75% of the universe.

2 Represents share of Austrian nominal capital in total nominal capital.

3 Including tobacco.

4 Including petroleum.

5 Motor vehicles are included under metals.

6 Including leather.

7 Including wood.

8 Represents energy and transport.

9 Including insurance.

Table A10

DISTRIBUTION OF FOREIGN SUBSIDIARIES AND ASSOCIATES AND FOREIGN CAPITAL STOCK BY PERCENTAGE OWNERSHIP OF PARENT COMPANIES, 1981-82[1]

	Inward Investment		Outward Investment	
	Number of Affiliates	*Value of Capital Stock (S m)*	*Number of Affiliates*	*Value of Capital Stock (S m)*
100% owned subsidiaries 50-99.9% owned subsidiaries and associates	*N.S.A.*	28,875[2]	383[4]	*N.S.A.*
Less than 50% owned subsidiaries and associates	*N.S.A.*	2,755[3]	341[5]	*N.S.A.*
TOTAL	5,408	31,628	724	7,224

Source:

National Bank of Austria, *Austria's Monetary Situation Survey,* abridged from *Mitteilungen des Direktoriums der Oesterreichischen Nationalbank,* various issues.

NOTES TO TABLE A10

1 Based on biennial survey of National Bank of Austria and represents only nominal capital.

2 Includes foreign capital with 51% to 80% participation amounting to A Sch 3,179 million and those greater than 80% amounting to A Sch 25,696 million, in 1981.

3 Includes foreign capital up to 25% participation A Sch 727 million and those between 26 and 50% participation A Sch 2,028 million in 1981.

4 Represents Austrian capital whose participation is between 51 and 80% A Sch 50 million and those greater than 80% A Sch 333 million in 1982.

5 Represents Austrian capital with up to 25% Austrian participation A Sch 204 million and those between 26% and 50% Austrian participation, A Sch 137 million in 1982.

Table A11

ROYALTY RECEIPTS AND PAYMENTS, 1974-82 (A Sch m)

	Payments			Receipts		
	To Affiliates	*To Non-affiliates*	*Total*	*From Affiliates*	*From Non-affiliates*	*Total*
1974	*Not Separately Available*		774	*Not Separately Available*		*Not Available*
1975			922			
1977			1,211			
1979			1,332			
1980			1,461			
1981			1,775			72
1982						77

Source:

National Bank of Austria, *Austria's Monetary Situation Survey,* abridged from *Mitteilungen des Direktoriums der Oesterreichischen Nationalbank,* various issues.

AUSTRIAN TABLES: DEFINITIONS

By Austria's definition, foreign direct investment represents 'capital investment by non-residents undertaken with the aim of creating or maintaining permanent financial links with a domestic enterprise in order to influence its business operations'. Such investment may take one of these forms:

1 Holdings in existing or newly-established enterprises acquired either for cash or for other considerations (offsetting of claims, bringing in of fixed or intangible assets);

2 Long-term loans and other facilities extended to an enterprise by foreign investors, in addition to their share holdings, for the purpose of strengthening its capital resources;

3 Reinvestment -- retention in place of distribution – of profits, resulting, whether by an increase in issued capital or by appropriation to reserves and/or the balance carried forward, in an increase in shareholders' funds.

Data was gathered by the Austrian National Bank through biennial surveys, beginning in 1974. With Austria itself, directly foreign-owned businesses (the term foreign-owned embracing foreign ownership in part as well as whole) are classified both regionally (by head office location) and excludes sectors (like agriculture and forestry and public services) with little or no foreign investment interest. It is estimated that the companies covered in the survey represented 70-80% of the universe.

Source:

National Bank of Austria, *Austria's Monetary Situation Survey,* abridged from *Mitteilungen des Direktoriums des Oesterreichischen Nationalbank.*

FINLAND

Finnish direct investment abroad increased significantly during the period 1973–84. The growth was particularly notable after the mid-1970s, a trend which reflects the extent of the internationalisation of Finnish industry in the 1970s. Finnish investment abroad has focused on the country's major export markets in Western Europe and North America, while the majority of Finnish owned companies abroad are in Sweden. Similarly, most of the inflow of investment has come from Western Europe with Sweden being the most important investor country.

The flow of foreign direct investment in Finland fluctuated annually between 1971 and 1975 but has fallen substantially since the mid-1970s. The activities of foreign firms operating in Finland have been financed to an increasing extent from Finnish sources, thus contributing to the decline in the inflow of investment.

Inward investment has been concentrated in the manufacturing sector, especially chemicals and non-metalic minerals, and in the services sector, with the emphasis on distributive trade; while for outward investment, the major growth areas have been the chemical and the metal and engineering industries, and finance and property in the service sector.

No special conditions are imposed on foreign direct investment in Finland and foreign firms are treated on an equal basis with domestic firms. There is a Commission for Foreign Investments which acts as an advisory body for all foreign investments in Finland. This favours investment which creates employment, increases exports, substitutes imports, brings in advanced technology, and is made in the manufacturing sector. In some national resource based sectors foreign ownership is limited to minority equity stake. The Governments' attitude towards outward direct investment is also liberal.

MAIN SOURCES OF DATA:

A **Official**

1 Bank of Finland: publishes monthly and annual data on the external assets and liabilities position of Finland. Also provides data and unpublished papers on investment inflows and outflows.

2 Central Statistical Office of Finland: provides data on enterprises by industry and type of ownership.

3 US Department of Commerce International Trade Administration, *Investment Climate in Foreign Countries,* Washington, 1985 vol I.

B **Private**

1 Luostarinen, Reijo, 'International operations of foreign and multinational companies in Finland', FIBO 16, Helsinki, 1981.

Table A1

SUMMARY OF THE COUNTRY'S INTERNATIONAL INVESTMENT POSITION

		Inward Investment	Outward Investment
1	Number of foreign affiliates in host country, and of foreign affiliates of home country firms at the end of 1985	1,154	1,626
2	Number of foreign firms with direct investments in host country, and home country firms with direct foreign affiliates	*N.A.*	*N.A.*
3	Total foreign direct capital stock at book value as a percentage of GNP at factor cost in 1983	0.89	2.38
4	Flow of foreign direct investment in the five year period, 1980-84 (F M m)	524	6,154
5	Employment in foreign affiliates or abroad, 1980	42,018	*N.A.*
6	Output of foreign affiliates or abroad, 1980 (F M m)	26.1	16.5[1]

Source:

Bank of Finland, *Monthly Bulletin,* various issues; IMF, *International Financial Statistics Yearbook, 1984;* Central Statistical Office of Finland, *Register of Enterprises,* 1980.

NOTES TO TABLE A1

1 Figure refers to total turnover of the Finnish-owned manufacturing companies operating abroad in 1983.

Table A2

PRIVATE FOREIGN CAPITAL STOCK, 1978 - 84 (F M bn)

	Inward Investment			Outward Investment		
	Portfolio	*Direct*	*Total*	*Portfolio*	*Direct*	*Total*
Book value of capital stock						
1978	0.23[1]	1.89	2.12	0.96	1.85	2.81
1980	0.34[1]	2.08	2.42	1.05	2.81	3.86
1983	1.61	2.32	3.93	3.93	6.17	10.10
1984	3.10	2.65	5.75	1.92	8.69	10.61
1985	*N.A.*	3.03	*N.A.*	*N.A.*	10.73	*N.A.*

Source:
Bank of Finland, *Monthly Bulletin,* various issues.

NOTES TO TABLE A2

1 Coverage for portfolio investment is incomplete.

Table A3

FLOW OF FOREIGN DIRECT INVESTMENT, 1971 - 84 (F M m)[1]

	Inward Investment			Outward Investment		
	Reinvested Profits	*Other*	*Total*	*Reinvested Profits*	*Other*	*Total*
1971	*Not Separately Available*		103	*Not Separately Available*		187
1972			131			237
1973			60			88
1974			156			82
1975			251			96
1976			223			118
1977			188			293
1978			141			257
1979			106			487
1980			104			487
1981			75			612
1982			-67			1,125
1983			88			1,451
1984			324			2,479
1985			380			2,042

Source:
Bank of Finland, *Monthly Bulletin,* various issues.

NOTES TO TABLE A3

1 Excluding reinvested profits.

Table A4

SECTORAL DISTRIBUTION OF FOREIGN DIRECT CAPITAL STOCK, 1979 - 81 (F M m)

	Inward Investment[1]			Outward Investment[2]		
	Primary	*Secondary*	*Tertiary*	*Primary*	*Secondary*	*Tertiary*
1979-81	*Not Available*			20.7	720.6	843.1
1980	1.3	512.7	1,566.4	*Not Available*		

Source:

Bank of Finland, Foreign Financing Department, unpublished paper by Seija Kulkki; Central Statistical Office of Finland, *Register of Enterprises,* 1980

NOTES TO TABLE A4

1 Authors' estimates obtained by applying percentage distribution of production in industrial sector by foreign affiliates to total foreign direct capital stock.

2 Estimates based on cumulative investment flows for 1979-81 only.

Table A5

GEOGRAPHICAL DISTRIBUTION OF FOREIGN DIRECT CAPITAL STOCK, 1973 - 84 (F M m)[1]

	Inward Investment			Outward Investment		
	Developed Countries	*Developing Countries*	*Total*[2]	*Developed Countries*	*Developing Countries*	*Total*[2]
1973-79	1,032	96	1,125	1,288	90	1,421
1973-84	1,486	155	1,649	6,823	589	7,575

Source:

Bank of Finland, 'Finnish Direct Investment Abroad & Foreign Direct Investment in Finland', series of unpublished papers by Seija Kulkki.

NOTES TO TABLE A5

1 Estimates based on cumulative investment flows, 1973-84. Up to 1983 includes companies in which direct foreign/direct Finnish ownership accounts for more than 20% of the nominal value of the share capital, the co-operative capital or similar basic capital. From 1984, includes companies in which direct foreign/direct Finnish ownership accounts for at least 10%.

2 Total includes 'unspecified' figure.

Table A6

INDUSTRIAL DISTRIBUTION OF FOREIGN DIRECT CAPITAL STOCK, 1979 - 81 (F M m)

	Inward Investment 1980[1]	Outward Investment 1979-81[2]
Primary	1.3	20.7
Agriculture	*N.S.A.*	*N.S.A.*
Mining & quarrying	1.3	*N.S.A.*
Oil	*N.S.A.*	*N.S.A.*
Secondary	512.7	720.6
Food & drink	84.3	14.0
Chemicals & allied[3]	134.7	20.5
Metals	18.6	5.0
Mechanical engineering / Electrical equipment / Motor vehicles / Other transportation equipment	188.0[4]	365.6[4]
Textiles & clothing	55.0	0.8
Paper & allied	17.6	178.2
Rubber[3]	*N.S.A.*	*N.S.A.*
Stone, clay & glass	7.6	50.8
Coal & petroleum products[3]	*N.S.A.*	*N.S.A.*
Other manufacturing	6.9	85.7
Tertiary	1,566.4	843.1
Construction	15.1	*N.S.A.*
Distributive trade[5]	1,470.1	*N.S.A.*
Property / Banking & finance	53.2	469.0
Other services	28.0	374.1
TOTAL	2,080.4	1,584.4

Source:
Bank of Finland, Foreign Financing Department, unpublished paper by Seija Kulkki; Central Statistical Office of Finland, *Register of Enterprises,* 1980.

NOTES TO TABLE A6

1 Authors' estimates calculated by applying the percentage distribution of production across industrial sectors by foreign affiliates to total foreign direct capital stock.

2 Estimates based on cumulative investment flows for 1979-81 only.

3 Coal & petroleum products, rubber & plastic products are included under chemicals.

4 Represents fabricated metal products, machinery and equipment.

5 Including restaurants and hotels.

Table A7

LEADING SOURCE AND RECIPIENT COUNTRIES,[1] 1973 - 84 (F M m)

	Inward Investment 1973-79	Inward Investment 1973-84	Outward Investment 1973-79	Outward Investment 1973-84
DEVELOPED AREAS	1,032	1,486	1,288	6,823
Europe	869	1,110	953	4,483
EEC of which:	330	164	789	2,875
Belgium & Luxembourg	*N.S.A.*	*N.S.A.*	186[2]	586[2]
Denmark	49	57	42	203
France	*N.S.A.*	*N.S.A.*	121	265
W. Germany	63	74	250	782
Greece, Ireland, Italy	30	-60	15	107
Netherlands	58	90	*N.S.A.*	*N.S.A.*
UK	130	3	175	932
Other Europe	539	946	164	1,608
Norway			22	198
Sweden	358	736	142	1,410
Switzerland	181	210		
North America	151	348	244	1,698
Other developed countries	12	28	91	642
DEVELOPING AREAS	96	155	90	589
Latin America of which:			57	201
Brazil	*Not*	*Not*	57	201
Middle East of which:	*Separately*	*Separately*	7	30
Saudi Arabia	*Available*	*Available*	7	30
Other developing countries			26	358
UNSPECIFIED	-3	8	43	163
TOTAL	1,125	1,649	1,421	7,575

Source:
Bank of Finland, 'Finnish Direct Investment Abroad & Foreign Direct Investment in Finland, series of unpublished papers by Seija Kulkki.

NOTES TO TABLE A7

1 Estimates based on cumulative investment flows, 1973-84. Up to 1983, includes companies in which direct foreign/direct Finnish ownership accounts for more than 20% of the nominal value of the share capital, the co-operative capital or similar basic capital. From 1984, includes companies in which direct foreign/direct Finnish ownership accounts for at least 10%.

2 Including the Netherlands.

Table A8

INDICATORS OF THE SIGNIFICANCE OF INWARD FOREIGN DIRECT INVESTMENT OR THE ACTIVITIES OF FOREIGN-BASED COMPANIES TO THE NATIONAL ECONOMY, 1980 - 83

1	Direct capital stock of foreign affiliates at book value in 1983 as a proportion of:		
	a GNP at factor cost		0.89
	b population (in F M per head)		473.50
2	Employment in foreign affiliates in 1980 as a percentage of all employment		
	a in all industry		3.90
	b in manufacturing		3.70
3	Output of foreign affiliates in 1980 as a percentage of all companies' output		
	a in primary (ie, extractive) industry		0.55
	b in secondary (ie, manufacturing) industry		4.43
	c in tertiary industry (ie, services, etc)		9.57
4	Percentage share of sales and employment accounted for by foreign affiliates in selected sectors, 1980		
		Sales	*Employment*
	Primary Goods Sector		
	Mining & quarrying	2.66	1.75
	Manufacturing Sector		
	Food & drink	3.28	3.98
	Chemicals & allied[1]	5.49	7.41
	Metals	1.70	1.78
	Engineering & transportation equipment	6.30[2]	4.85[2]
	Textiles & clothing	6.08	8.20
	Paper & allied	0.54	0.59
	Stone, glass & clay	1.69	1.47
	Other manufacturing	3.23	0.39
	Services Sector		
	Construction	1.05	0.88
	Trade & distribution[3]	11.62	4.70
	Banking & finance	7.95	5.75
	Other services	2.17	7.20

Source:

Bank of Finland, *Monthly Bulletin,* various issues; IMF, *International Financial Statistics Yearbook,* 1984; Central Statistical Office of Finland, *Register of Enterprises,* Appendix 1 & 2, 1980.

NOTES TO TABLE A8

1 Coal and petroleum products and rubber and plastic products are included under chemicals.

2 Represents fabricated metal products, machinery and equipment.

3 Including restaurants and hotels.

Table A9

INDICATORS OF THE SIGNIFICANCE OF FORWARD FOREIGN DIRECT INVESTMENT OR THE ACTIVITIES OF HOME-BASED COMPANIES ABROAD FOR THE NATIONAL ECONOMY, 1981 - 83

1	Foreign capital stock of home-based firms at book value in 1983 as a proportion of:	
	a GNP at factor cost	2.38
	b population (in F M per head)	1,259.20
2	Output of foreign manufacturing affiliates in 1981 as a percentage of:	
	a domestic manufacturing output	5.80
	b manufacturing exports from the home country	13.80
3	Sales of foreign affiliates of home-based firms[1] as a percentage of that in selected domestic sectors, 1981	
		Sales
	Manufacturing Sector	
	Food & drink	0.4
	Chemicals & allied[2]	0.9
	Metals; Mechanical engineering; Electrical equipment; Motor vehicles; Other transporation equipment	8.2
	Textiles & clothing	1.2
	Paper & allied	12.9
	Rubber[2]	*N.S.A.*
	Stone, glass & clay	2.4
	Coal & petroleum products[2]	*N.S.A.*
	Other manufacturing	0.7

Source:
Bank of Finland, *Monthly Bulletin,* vol. 59, No. 4, April 1985; Central Statistical Office, *Register of Enterprises,* 1980.

NOTES TO TABLE A9

1 Total turnover of the Finnish-owned manufacturing companies operating abroad in 1981.

2 Coal and petroleum products, and rubber and plastic products are included under chemicals.

Table A10

DISTRIBUTION OF FOREIGN SUBSIDIARIES AND ASSOCIATES AND FOREIGN CAPITAL STOCK BY PERCENTAGE OWNERSHIP OF PARENT COMPANIES, 1980

	Inward Investment		Outward Investment	
	Number of Affiliates	*Value of Capital Stock*	*Number of Affiliates*	*Value of Capital Stock*
100% owned subsidiaries 50-99.9% owned subsidiaries and associates	545	*Not Available*	*Not Available*	
Less than 50% owned subsidiaries and associates[1]	83			
TOTAL	628			

Source:
Central Statistical Office of Finland, *Register of Enterprises*, 1980.

NOTES TO TABLE A10

1 Represents 20-50% owned subsidiaries and associates.

Table A11

ROYALTY RECEIPTS AND PAYMENTS, 1975 - 82 (F M m)

	Payments			Receipts		
	To Affiliates	*To Non-affiliates*	*Total*	*From Affiliates*	*From Non-affiliates*	*Total*
1974	*Not Separately Available*		163	*Not Separately Available*		14
1976			196			60
1977			201			82
1978			219			126[1]
1979			248			192[1]
1980			303			215[1]
1981			374			*N.A.*
1982			390			*N.A.*

Source:
OECD, 'The role of know-how trade in Finland's balance of payments', paper presented at the workshop on the Technological Balance of Payments, by Pirkko Miikkulainen.

NOTES TO TABLE A11

1 Author's estimate.

Table A12

LEADING FOREIGN AND DOMESTIC MULTINATIONAL COMPANIES

A Leading Foreign Multinational Companies in the country, 1985

	Name	*Home Country*	*Sector*
1	Astra - Yhtiöt	Sweden	Pharmaceuticals
2	BP-Petro OY	UK	Petroleum
3	Suomen BP OY	UK	Petroleum
4	A B Electrolux	Sweden	Electrical equipment
5	Alfra Zavre AB	Sweden	Engineering products
6	Asea AB	Sweden	Electrical equipment
7	Babcock International	UK	Engineering products
8	BAT	UK	Tobacco & paper products
9	Bristol Myers	USA	Pharmaceuticals
10	Brown Boveri	Switzerland	Electrical Engineering
11	Eastman Kodak	USA	Photographic equipment
12	Eli Lilly	USA	Pharmaceuticals
13	Exxon Corporation	USA	Petroleum
14	Firestone Tyre & Rubber	USA	Rubber tyres
15	Ford Motor	USA	Motor vehicles
16	Glaxo Holdings	UK	Pharmaceuticals
17	Honeywell	USA	Electronic appliances & control systems
18	IBM	USA	Computers
19	LM Ericsson	Sweden	Telecommunications
20	NU Philips Gloeilampenfabrieken	Netherlands	Electrical equipment
21	Pilkington	UK	Glass products
22	Procter & Gamble	USA	Detergents
23	Sandoz	Switzerland	Pharmaceuticals
24	Siemens	Germany	Electrical products
25	Unilever	UK/Netherlands	Consumer goods

Table A12 (cont'd)

LEADING FOREIGN AND DOMESTIC MULTINATIONAL COMPANIES

B Leading Domestic Companies with Multinational Interests, 1981			
	Name	*Sector*	*No. of overseas subsidiaries (1981)*
1	Kone OY	Mechanical engineering	35
2	Enso - Gutzeit OY	Trading & investments	28
3	A. Ahlström Osakeyhtiö	Trading & mechanical engineering	25
4	Kymi Kymmene Corp.	Paper	20
5	Nokia AB, OY	Paper, aluminium	18
6	Asko Upo OY	Metals, timber, electronics	14
7	Tampella OY	Paper, textiles	14
8	Ravma - Repola OY	Mechanical engineering	13
9	Yhtynect Paperitchtant OY	Paper	12
10	G.A. Serlachivs OY	Paper	9
11	Jaakko Pöyry International OY	Engineering	9
12	Outokumpu OY	Mechanical engineering	9
13	Orion - Yhtymä OY	Chemicals, mechanical engineering	9
14	Karl Fazer OY	Food	7
15	Suomen Trikou AB	Textiles	7
16	Vakuutus OY Pohjola	Banking & insurance	7
17	Valmet OY	Mechanical engineering	7
18	Wiik & Höglund AB	Processing of rubber and plastics	7
19	Wärtsilä AB	Mechanical engineering	7
20	Fiskars AB	Metals, mechanical engineering	6
21	Navire AB	Mechanical engineering	6
22	Converta - Finnish Paper & Board	Paper	5
23	Kansallis - Osake - Pankki	Banking	5

Source:

Dun & Bradstreet Ltd, *Who Owns Whom,* London: Business Marketing Division (Publications), 1984.

FINLAND: DEFINITIONS

Statistics on Finnish investment abroad and foreign investment in Finland were compiled according to the date of recording up to 1984 but from 1985, the transaction date is used in compilation.

Until 1983, direct investment statistics include companies in which direct Finnish/foreign ownership accounts for more than 20% of the nominal value of the share capital, the co-operative capital or similar basic capital. However, in 1984, in line with OECD's recommendation, direct investment statistics include companies in which direct Finnish/foreign ownership accounts for at least 10% of the nominal value of the share capital, the co-operative capital or similar basic capital.

The item "equity capital" includes bond issues up to 1981.

Source:
Suomen Pankki, Bank of Finland.

HUNGARY

Hungary and Yugoslavia are the two most open economies among the East European states. Since the introduction of a more flexible economic management in 1968, the Hungarians have been trying to create an economy which is more responsive to market signals while not abandoning central planning. As early as 1972, legislation was introduced that created a framework for admitting foreign direct investment. Yet so far the inflow of such investment has been modest. By mid 1984, some 31 inward joint ventures had been registered, with an estimated total foreign capitalisation of Ft 450 million, about US $ 9 million at the current exchange rate. There are also about 20 outward joint ventures, mostly in manufacturing, in which Hungarians are joint owners with foreign firms abroad.

The largest group of inward joint ventures is in manufacturing, ranging from heat pumps to pharmaceuticals and packaging. But the Hungarians have failed to capture any worthwhile invetments or big names. Though the German company, Siemens, has an office in Budapest, its main function is that of technical liaison and design rather than local production. There are 13 companies active in the service sector: these range from a casino to a colour photo processing outlet. There are two tourism firms, a travel agency and one building a holiday village, and two in the financial service sector. The Central European International Bank is the only consortium bank in the Comecon countries and the only one to have a majority foreign participation. The largest and only Hungarian shareholder is the central bank, the Hungarian National Bank (34 per cent) with two Japanese, an Italian, West German, French and Austrian bank (11 per cent each) being the foreign stake holders.

Most of the joint ventures have modest capitalisation (below Ft 20 million or US $ 0.4 million) with only four exceeding Ft 100 million (US $ 2 million). The total capital involved, including Hungarian money, is around Ft 1,500 million or US $ 30 million.

Table A1 shows that most investments involve other European countries with West Germany and Austria vying for first place. The total number of foreign investors is in excess of the total number of ventures, as some have several foreign partners.

Table 1

JOINT VENTURES IN HUNGARY 1984

Country of Investor	*Number of Firms*	*Industry*	*% of Licences*
West Germany	9	Metallurgy	12.3
Austria	8	Engineering	35.0
Switzerland	6	Chemicals	37.8
USA	4	Light Industry	8.2
Japan	3	Food processing	3.4
Italy	2	Other	3.3
France	2	Total	100.0
Sweden	2		
Belgium	1		
Netherlands	1		
Greece	1		
Saudi Arabia	1		
TOTAL	40		

Source:
Economist Intelligence Unit, *Multinational Business*, no. 1, 1985

The lukewarm interest of foreign direct investors in Hungary can be partly explained by the main conditions of the law: no foreigners can have more than 49 per cent of the equity (unless there is a government exemption, but only one, in banking, has been granted so far). There are no investment incentives or grants, and profit tax is at 40 per cent. Hungary cannot compete with developing countries in wage levels and there is a serious labour shortage.

There has been only one joint venture that has made use of the custom-free zones. Introduced in 1982, and aiming to process imported raw material for re-export, this unit, Hunflexbau Kft of Sopron, on the Austrian border, makes prefabricated housing elements with a Danish partner.

Joint ventures seem unlikely to prosper in Hungary, in spite of the guarantee of profit and capital repatriation in a hard currency initially agreed upon. However, a deal with the Hungarians may prove attractive to firms in the service industries with a readily transferable knowhow, or in manufacturing where there is no other access to the market.

In some instances, the initial foreign capital is contributed in the shape of equipment which may prove attractive to manufacturers of capital goods. As Hungary is unable to obtain a good volume of inflow of technology via joint ventures, it has to pay for it in the form of license and knowhow agreements. In 1983 total spending on licenses amounted to Ft 1,057 million (US $ 20.8 million), 60 per cent higher than two years earlier. 83 per cent of the licenses come from the West.

Outward Investments

Foreign investment by Hungarian firms, like all other Comecon firms, is undertaken exclusively by state enterprises. This 'Leninist' principle, adopted after the 1917 Revolution in Russia and consequently by Eastern European countries after WWII, has been modified over time only to the extent that a broader range of state enterprises has been granted the right to engage in international operations. Private individuals and enterprises have not been granted such authority. These private entities have to deal internationally through state enterprises.

Comecon firms are not only state owned, they are also subject to very stringent administrative control by central state agencies. Comecon companies, in general, and Hungarian companies in particular, enjoy far less autonomy than state-owned enterprises in developed countries.

Investing enterprises in Hungary represent state-owned enterprises from a broad spectrum of sectors. The number of investing state enterprises by category as at end-1981 is presented in Table 2.

Table 2

TYPES OF STATE ENTERPRISES IN HUNGARY ENGAGING IN FOREIGN DIRECT INVESTMENT ACTIVITY, END-1981

Category	*Number of State Enterprises*
Foreign trade enterprises and associations	14
Production enterprises and associations	5
Banks	4
Insurance companies	1
Transport and freight enterprises	1
Engineering and construction organizations	1
Tourist agencies	1
Others*	4
TOTAL	31

* Research and Design institutes, publishing houses, hotel and catering firms, etc.

Source:
Files of East-West Project, Institute of Soviet and East European Studies, Carleton University, Ottawa.

Almost half of Hungarian state enterprises engaged in foreign direct investment have been made by specialized foreign trade enterprises and associations and only 30% have been made by production enterprises and banks.

The geographical distribution of Hungarian investments in OECD countries and the distribution of these investments by activities as at end 1981 are presented in Tables 3 and 4. The data refer to the number of firms with Hungarian equity participation.

Table 3

GEOGRAPHICAL DISTRIBUTION OF HUNGARIAN INVESTMENTS IN OECD COUNTRIES AS OF END 1981

Host Country	
Austria	16
Belgium	1
Canada	1
Denmark	1
Finland	1
France	3
Federal Republic of Germany	15
Greece	1
Ireland	1
Italy	3
Japan	1
Liechtenstein	1
Luxembourg	1
Netherlands	3
Spain	3
Sweden	2
Switzerland	2
UK	5
USA	7
	68

Source:
The East-West Business Directory: A Listing of Companies in the West with Soviet and East European Capital Participation, London: Duncan Publishing for the East-West Project, Carleton University, 1983.

Table 4

DISTRIBUTION OF HUNGARIAN INVESTMENTS BY ACTIVITY AS AT END-1981

Principal Activity	
Importing and some related marketing functions	40
Marketing, including retailing	3
Marketing, retailing and servicing	0
Assembly and manufacturing	13
Extraction and processing of raw materials	1
Financial services	6
Transport services	2
Technical services	2
Consumer services	2
TOTAL	68

Source:
As for Table 3.

A number of foreign subsidiaries of Comecon enterprises have in turn established branches or affiliates in other foreign countries. Hungarian enterprises are no exception. Hungary has established a holding company in Luxembourg as a vehicle for profitable foreign ventures.

The value of capital invested in total Comecon investments abroad is estimated at US $ 550 million as at end-1981, which gives an average of US $ 1.4 million per company. The reason for the low capital investment average may be attributed to the fact that most Comecon companies, in general, and Hungarian companies in particular, are engaged in services, especially in the imprt and marketing of products and related activities. The capital invested in the more extensive manufacturing or service facilities is much greater than the average. In these sectors, firms have fixed assets in the range of US $ 10 to 15 million.

The distribution of ownership structure of Hungarian investments as of end 1981 reveal that 10.3% of total Hungarian investment abroad represented minority ownership, 48.3% represented a 50-50 ownership split, 17.2% represented a majority ownership and 24.1% represented 100% ownership.

Hungarian investments in the developing economies of the Third World have been less well documented, although the evidence suggests rapid growth over the 1970s. It has been noted that in contrast to investments in developed economies, a much larger share of companies with Comecon equity participation in developing countries are engaged in production. The value of capital invested in these countries is probably higher than that of Comecon companies in the OECD countries. The evidence also suggests that most investments in developing countries are in joint ventures in which Comecon state enterprises represent an equal, or minority holding, while wholly-owned Comecon companies are relatively rare.

Table 5 lists the more active Hungarian multinational companies and their areas of activity as at end 1981.

Table 5

HUNGARIAN STATE ENTERPRISES WITH DIRECT INVESTMENTS IN THE OECD ECONOMIES, AS AT END 1981

Enterprise	*Activity*	*Number of Investments*
1. Hungarotex	Textiles	8
2. Tungsram	Lighting	7
3. Monimpex	Wines, juices, foodstuffs	6
4. Medimpex	Pharmaceuticals	5
5. Hungarian Foreign Trade Bank	Financial operation	4
6. National Bank of Hungary	Financial operation	2

Source:
As for Table 2.

NORWAY

The major objective of Norwegian policy on inward direct investment has been to restore and maintain domestic control of the natural resource sector, and concession laws are far more stringent in the case of foreign ownership of natural resources than in other sectors. However, the current coalition Government has recently improved the climate for foreign investment in a variety of ways, including the liberalisation of foreign exchange control regulations offshore.

The flow of direct inward investment has fluctuated annually, reaching a peak in 1976 and again in 1981. Using foreign-owned share capital as a general proxy, we see that the main source areas for investment in Norway are Western Europe, North America, particularly Sweden, the UK and the USA – the latter has held the greatest part of the foreign owned share capital during 1971-81. Foreign ownership interests have been concentrated on enterprises in mining, hydrocarbon exploration, manufacturing and the wholesale and retail trade.

Since the end of the 1970s, Norwegian presence in economic activity abroad has increased considerably, again largely in Europe and the USA, with a significant investment in Asia. The major growth industries for Norwegian outward investment have been chemicals and engineering. In June 1974 the Government reduced controls on outward investment in a bid to assist the internationalisation of Norwegian industry and provide expanded market opportunities for businesses and banks.

MAIN SOURCES OF DATA:

A Official

1 Norges Bank, Economic Bulletin – publishes reports on Norwegian investments abroad.

2 Norwegian Central Bureau of Statistics – provides data on foreign investments in Norwegian joint stock companies.

3 US Department of Commerce International Trade Administration, *Investment Climate in Foreign Countries,* Washington PBT6 - 100104, August 1985.

Table A1

SUMMARY OF THE COUNTRY'S INTERNATIONAL INVESTMENT POSITION

		Inward Investment	Outward Investment
1	Number of foreign affiliates in host country, and of foreign affiliates of home country firms at the end of 1982	1,657[1]	2,145[2]
2	Number of foreign firms with direct investments in host country, and home country firms with direct foreign affiliates at the end of 1982	*N.A.*	307[3]
3	Total foreign direct capital stock at book value as a percentage of GNP at factor cost in 1983	6.83	3.11
4	Flow of foreign direct investment in the five year period, 1979-83 (Kr bn)	10.99	7.07
5	Employment in foreign affiliates or abroad, 1981	76,865[1]	44,872
6	Output of foreign affiliates or abroad, 1981 (Kr bn)	87.15[1]	40.522

Source:

IMF, *Balance of Payments Yearbook,* various issues; IMF, *International Financial Statistics Yearbook, 1984;* Central Bureau of Statistics, Norway, *Saertrykk Fra Statistisk Ukehefte,* SU no 19, 1983.

NOTES TO TABLE A1

1 Includes only enterprises where 10% or more of the share capital is foreign owned.

2 Includes only companies abroad registered as having Norwegian interests amounting to 10% or more of owner capital.

3 Manufacturing companies only.

Table A2

PRIVATE FOREIGN CAPITAL STOCK, 1975 - 83 (Kr bn)[1]

	Inward Investment				Outward Investment		
	Portfolio	*Direct*	*Total*		*Portfolio*	*Direct*	*Total*
Book value of capital stock							
1975	*Not Available*	8.61	*Not Available*		*Not Available*	4.07	*Not Available*
1978		15.85				6.65	
1981		20.72				8.46	
1982		24.63				9.51	
1983		26.54				12.09	

Source:
IMF, *Balance of Payments Yearbook,* various issues.

NOTES TO TABLE A2
1 Estimates based on cumulative investment flows, 1968-83.

Table A3

FLOW OF FOREIGN DIRECT INVESTMENT, 1970 - 83 (Kr m)[1]

	Inward Investment				Outward Investment		
	Reinvested Profits	*Other*	*Total*		*Reinvested Profits*	*Other*	*Total*
1970	*Not Separately Available*		457.2		*Not Separately Available*		228.6
1971			663.9				226.0
1972			794.0				*N.A.*
1973			1,202.9				288.7
1974			1,918.7				819.5
1975			1,129.6				888.5
1976			2,034.8				1,026.9
1977			4,077.2				665.0
1978			2,546.6				341.3
1979			2,028.3				222.5
1980			295.7				1,253.6
1981			3,911.8				1,049.0
1982			2,850.1				1,966.6
1983			1,903.2				2,581.7

Source:
IMF, *Balance of Payments Yearbook,* various issues.

NOTES TO TABLE A3
1 Excluding reinvested profits

Table A4

SECTORAL DISTRIBUTION OF FOREIGN DIRECT CAPITAL STOCK, 1971 - 81 (Kr m)

	Inward Investment[1]			Outward Investment[2]		
	Primary	*Secondary*	*Tertiary*	*Primary*	*Secondary*	*Tertiary*
1971	25.4	809.6	682.3	*Not Available*		
1981	323.4	1,593.0	2,236.0	*N.A.*	2,017	3,083

Source:
Central Bureau of Statistics, Norway, *Saertrykk Fra Statistisk Ukehefte,* various issues.

NOTES TO TABLE A4

1 Figures refer to foreign-owned share capital of Norwegian joint stock companies.

2 Figures refer to Norwegian share of equity capital. If we also include loans from Norwegian shareholders the total figure for 1981 is 8,711 Kr m, with 3,447 Kr m in manufacturing.

Table A5

GEOGRAPHICAL DISTRIBUTION OF FOREIGN DIRECT CAPITAL STOCK, 1971 - 81 (Kr m)

	Inward Investment[1]			Outward Investment[2]		
	Developed Countries	*Developing Countries*	*Total*	*Developed Countries*	*Developing Countries*	*Total*
1971	1,477.4	2.2	1,479.6	*Not Available*		
1981	3,929.2	99.9	4,029.1	7,404	1,307	8,711

Source:
Central Bureau of Statistics, Norway, *Saertrykk Fra Statistisk Ukehefte,* various issues.

NOTES TO TABLE A5

1 Figures refer to foreign-owned share capital of Norwegian joint-stock companies, and includes only data for enterprises where 10% or more of the share capital is foreign owned.

2 Including loans from Norwegian shareholders.

Table A6

INDUSTRIAL DISTRIBUTION OF FOREIGN DIRECT CAPITAL STOCK, 1971 - 81 (Kr m)

	Inward Investment[1]		Outward Investment[2]
	1971	*1981*	*1981*
Primary	25.4	323.4	*Not Available*
Agriculture	0.2	0.0	
Mining and quarrying	25.2	323.4	
Secondary	809.6	1,593.0	2,017
Food & drink	*Not Separately Available*	*Not Separately Available*	323
Chemicals & allied			798
Metals			534
Mechanical engineering			184
Electrical equipment			*N.S.A.*
Other manufacturing			178
Tertiary	682.3	2,236.0	3,083
Construction	19.3	97.6	933
Transport & communications	3.8	21.2	495[3]
Distributive trade	544.3	1,638.0	*N.S.A.*
Property } Banking & finance }	52.4	430.6	1,008
Other services	62.5	48.6	647
TOTAL	1,517.3	4,152.4	5,100

Source:
Central Bureau of Statistics, Norway, *Saertrykk Fra Statistisk Ukehefte,* various issues

NOTES TO TABLE A6

1 Figures refer to foreign-owned share capital of Norwegian joint stock companies.

2 Figures refer to Norwegian share of equity capital.

3 Represents shipping.

Table A7

LEADING SOURCE AND RECIPIENT COUNTRIES, 1971 - 81 (Kr m)

	Inward Investment[1]		Outward Investment
	1971	*1981*	*1981*
DEVELOPED AREAS	1,477.4	3,929.2	7,404
Europe	945.2	2,872.1	5,482
EEC of which:	550.9	1,554.4	2,684
Belgium & Luxembourg	87.5	109.7	*N.S.A.*
Denmark	63.9	259.2	450
France	112.0	349.5	*N.S.A.*
W. Germany	23.3	147.9	327
Netherlands	25.9	150.2	*N.S.A.*
UK	238.3	537.9	1,907
Other Europe of which:	394.3	1,317.7	2,798
Sweden	225.0	725.2	540
Switzerland	154.2	520.9	*N.S.A.*
North America of which:	532.2	1,057.1	1,310
Canada	144.0	38.3	93
USA	388.2	1,018.8	1,217
Other developed countries	–	–	612
DEVELOPING AREAS	2.2	99.9	1,307
Africa	0.5	30.3	187
Asia & Pacific	0.6	38.0	290
Latin America	1.1	31.6	830
TOTAL	1,479.6	4,029.1	8,711

Source:

Central Bureau of Statistics, Norway, *Saertrykk Fra Statistisk Ukehefte* various issues.

NOTES TO TABLE A7

1 Figures refer to foreign-owned share capital of Norwegian joint stock companies, and include only data for enterprises where 10% or more of the share capital is foreign owned.

2 Figures refer to Norwegian share of equity capital and investment loans from Norwegian mother companies.

Table A8

INDICATORS OF THE SIGNIFICANCE OF INWARD FOREIGN DIRECT INVESTMENT OR THE ACTIVITIES OF FOREIGN-BASED COMPANIES TO THE NATIONAL ECONOMY, 1981 - 83

1	Direct capital stock of foreign affiliates at book value in 1983 as a proportion of:	
	a GNP at factor cost	6.83
	b population (in Kr per head)[1]	5,992.70
2	Employment in foreign affiliates[2] in 1981 as a percentage of all employment	
	a in all industry	4.02
	b in manufacturing	19.76
3	Output of foreign affiliates[2] in 1981 as a percentage of all companies' output	
	a in primary (ie, extractive) industry	31.39
	b in secondary (ie, manufacturing) industry	12.56

4 Percentage share of sales and employment accounted for by foreign affiliates[2] in selected sectors, 1981

	Sales	*Employment*
Primary Goods Sector	31.39	19.80
Manufacturing Sector	12.56	8.83
Services Sector		
Construction	13.01	3.95
Transport & communications	*N.A.*	0.66
Trade & distribution	14.59	10.57

Source:

IMF, *Balance of Payments Statistics Yearbook,* various issues; IMF, *International Financial Statistics Yearbook, 1984;* Central Bureau of Statistics, *Saertrykk Fra Statistisk Ukehefte,* SU no 19, 1983; UN, *Statistical Yearbook, 1981.*

NOTES TO TABLE A8

1 1982.

2 Includes only enterprises where 10% or more of the share capital is foreign owned.

Table A9

INDICATORS OF THE SIGNIFICANCE OF OUTWARD FOREIGN DIRECT INVESTMENT OR THE ACTIVITIES OF HOME-BASED COMPANIES ABROAD FOR THE NATIONAL ECONOMY, 1981 - 83

1	Foreign capital stock of home-based firms at book value in 1983 as a proportion of:		
	a	GNP at factor cost	3.11
	b	population (in Kr per head)[1]	2,313.90
2	Employment in foreign affiliates in 1981 as a percentage of domestic employment		
	a	in all industry	5.91
	b	in manufacturing[2]	2.54
3	Output of foreign manufacturing affiliates in 1981 as a percentage of:		
	a	domestic manufacturing output	14.86
	b	manufacturing exports from the home country	51.50

Source:

IMF, *Balance of Payments Statistics Yearbook,* various issues; IMF, *International Financial Statistics Yearbook, 1984; Labour Market Statistics,* 1981; UN, *Statistical Yearbook, 1982;* various publications from Norges National Bank.

NOTES TO TABLE A9

1 1982.

2 Including tertiary industry.

Table A10

DISTRIBUTION OF FOREIGN SUBSIDIARIES AND ASSOCIATES AND FOREIGN CAPITAL STOCK BY PERCENTAGE OWNERSHIP OF PARENT COMPANIES, 1981

	Inward Investment		Outward Investment	
	Number of Affiliates	*Value of Capital Stock*[1] *(Kr m)*	*Number of Affiliates*	*Value of Capital Stock (Kr m)*
100% owned subsidiaries	1,400	3,422.1	1,036	*Not Available*
50-99.9% owned subsidiaries and associates			419	
Less than 50% owned subsidiaries and associates[2]	257	2,599.6	412	
TOTAL	1,657	6,021.7	1,867[3]	*N.A.*

Source:

Central Bureau of Statistics, Norway, *Saertrykk Fra Statistisk Ukehefte,* no 19, 1983.

NOTES TO TABLE A10

1 Refers to total share capital.

2 Includes 10-50% owned subsidiaries and associates.

3 Total does not match Table A1 due to ownership links between affiliates which are then counted as one.

Table A11

ROYALTY RECEIPTS AND PAYMENTS, 1975 - 82 (Kr m)

	Payments			Receipts		
	To Affiliates	*To Non-affiliates*	*Total*	*From Affiliates*	*From Non-affiliates*	*Total*
1975	*Not Separately Available*		253.9	*Not Separately Available*		158.7
1976			302.4			189.0
1977			310.8			254.8
1978			341.3			321.6
1979			386.0			314.1
1980			469.3			443.6
1981			534.7			439.9
1982			612.8			448.9

Source:

IMF, *Balance of Payments Statistics Yearbook, 1983.*

Table A12

LEADING FOREIGN AND DOMESTIC MULTINATIONAL COMPANIES, 1983 - 84

A Leading Foreign Multinational Companies in the Country, 1983

Name	*Home Country*	*Sector*
AEG-Telefunken AG	W. Germany	Electrical engineering
Alfa-Laval AB	Sweden	Mechanical engineering
The British Petroleum Company PLC	UK	Petroleum
Ciba-Geigy AG	Switzerland	Chemicals
Compagnie Francaise des Petroles SA	France	Petroleum products
Diamond Shamrock Corporation	USA	Energy & chemicals
E I Du Pont de Nomours & Company	USA	Chemicals & fibres
AB Electrolux	Sweden	Electrical equipment
ENI	Italy	Petroleum
Exxon Corporation	USA	Petroleum
Ford Motor Company	USA	Motor vehicles
General Motors Corporation	USA	Motor vehicles
ICL PLC	UK	Computers
International Business Machines Corporation	USA	Computers
Minnesota Mining and Manufacturing Co	USA	Diversified manufacturing
Philips Petroleum Company	USA	Petroleum
Régie Nationale des Usines Renault	France	Motor vehicles
Royal Dutch/Shell Group of Companies	Netherlands/UK	Petroleum
Saab-Scania AB	Sweden	Motor vehicles
Siemens AG	W. Germany	Electrical and electronic equipment
Sociéte Nationale Elf Aquitaire	France	Petroleum
Texaco Incorporated	USA	Petroleum
Thorn EMI PLC	UK	Electric consumer products
Xerox Corporation	USA	Copiers
NV Philips Gloeilampenfabricken	Netherlands	Electrotechnical equipment

Source:
John M Stopford, *The World Directory of Multinational Enterprises 1982-83,* Bath: The Pitman Press, 1982.

Table A12 (cont'd)

LEADING FOREIGN AND DOMESTIC MULTINATIONAL COMPANIES, 1984

B Leading Domestic Companies with Multinational Interests, 1984			
Name	*Sector*	*Global Turnover (US $m)*	*Sales of overseas subsidiaries as % of worldwide sales (1981)*
1 Norsk Hydro	Chemicals	4,077	84[1]
2 Statoil	Petroleum	3,603	*N.A.*
3 Elkhem	Metal manufacturing	652	*N.A.*

Source:

Fortune, August 20, 1984.

NORWAY NOTES TO TABLE A12

1 Includes all exports

NORWAY: DEFINITIONS

Data on inward investment in Norway are collected by the Central Bureau of Statistics, Oslo and are published as official data. Data on outward investment are collected by the Currency Control Department of the National Bank of Norway, but as they are collected for the sake of currency control they may not always be suitable for other purposes.

PORTUGAL

Traditionally, Portugal has not held any major position in the international investment league, and indeed after the early 1970s outward investment declined with the loss of colonial territories, while inward investment fell for a time after the April 1974 revolution. However, investment in Portugal has risen quite substantially recently. A good part of the increase is due to the trading and commercial sector, in which British firms have historically been quite active (selling Portuguese wine), but now it appears that other European and North American subsidiaries are growing much faster. Portugal's accession to the European Economic Community is likely to see further new inward investment, particularly in the modern labour intensive sectors.

In the last few years the Portuguese policy towards inward direct investment has been increasingly liberal (due to the accession to the EEC and to the internal developments of Portuguese economic policy), though since 1976 all new foreign investments have had to be in accord with a foreign investment code. This *inter alia* identifies priority sectors for foreign investors, and seeks to evaluate the likely consequences to the Portuguese economy of inward investment and technology transfer.

Outward investments are subject to authorisation by the Bank of Portugal. For most of the last decade they have been broadly discouraged unless they could be shown to contribute to broad developmental goals and for strengthening the Portuguese balance of payments. More than 40% of authorised investment in the period 1979–82 was in the banking sector. There are some manufacturing and trading investments in Latin America and North Africa.

MAIN SOURCES OF DATA:

A Official

1 Foreign Investment Institute: established in 1978, this provides survey information acquired from foreign affiliates in Portugal, on their capital stock, sales, exports, employment, and royalty payments abroad.

2 Bank of Portugal: publishes annual data on foreign direct investment flows.

B Private

1 V Simoes 'Portugal' in J H Dunning (Ed), *Multinational Enterprises, Economic Structure and International Competitiveness,* Chichester and New York: John Wiley, 1985.

2 E M Taveira, Foreign Direct Investment in Portugal. The Present Structure, Determinents and Future Evolution after the Accession to the EEC, PhD thesis, University of Reading, 1985.

3 V C Simoes 'Investimento Esbrangeiro en Portugal': Panorame Generico, *Economica,* vol IX, no 2, May 1985.

Note:
Data do not allow us to complete Table A9 for Portugal.

Table A1

SUMMARY OF THE COUNTRY'S INTERNATIONAL INVESTMENT POSITION

		Inward Investment		Outward Investment
1	Number of foreign affiliates in host country, and of foreign affiliates of home country firms at the end of 1981	1,058		*N.A.*
2	Number of foreign firms with direct investments in host country, and home country firms with direct foreign affiliates	*N.A.*		*N.A.*
3	Total foreign direct capital stock at book value as a percentage of GNP at factor cost in 1984	3.05		*N.A.*
4	Flow of foreign direct investment in the the five year period, 1979-83 (Esc m)	38,333		3,963
5	Employment in foreign affiliates or abroad, 1981	136,620		*N.A.*
6	Output of foreign affiliates or abroad, 1981[1] (Esc m)	382,600		*N.A.*

Source:
Instituto do Investimento Extrangeiro, *Annual Reports,* 1978, 1979, 1980, 1981, 1982 and 1983; Banco de Portugal, *Economic Indicators, 1974-79;* IMF, *International Financial Statistics, 1984;* Instituto do Investimiento Estrangeiro, *Investimento e Tecnologia, no 1, 1982;* OECD, *Geographical Distribution of Financial Flows to Developing Countries, 1980-83;* Banco de Portugal, *Boletim Trimestral Estatistica e Estudos Economicos, March 1982;* Instituto do Investimento, unpublished data on employment; Banco de Portugal, *Annual Reports,* various years.

Table A2

PRIVATE FOREIGN CAPITAL STOCK, 1974-84 (Esc m)

	Inward Investment			Outward Investment		
	Portfolio	*Direct*	*Total*	*Portfolio*	*Direct*[1]	*Total*
Book value of capital stock						
1975	*Not Available*	8,320	*Not Available*	*Not Available*	2,517	*Not Available*
1978		13,548			3,017	
1981		30,915			4,517	
1982		34,713			5,306	
1983		38,450			7,319	
1984		67,119			8,820	

Source:
Instituto do Investimento Estrangeiro, unpublished data.

NOTES TO TABLE A2

1 Represents cumulative investment flows from 1971

Table A3

FLOW OF FOREIGN DIRECT INVESTMENT 1971-84 (Esc m)

	Inward Investment			Outward Investment		
	Reinvested Profits	*Other*	*Total*[1]	*Reinvested Profits*	*Other*	*Total*[2]
1971	*Not Separately Available*	*Not Separately Available*	986	*Not Separately Available*		107
1972			1,330			356
1973			1,439			1,019
1974			2,007			877
1975	339	1,515	1,854			158
1976	753	809	1,562			136
1977	492	1,698	2,190			89
1978	220	2,695	2,915			275
1979	569	3,286	3,855			−379
1980	782	7,107	7,889			717
1981	799	9,946	10,745			1,162
1982	702	10,874	11,576			789
1983	947	14,682	15,629	118	1,894	2,013
1984	1,951	26,718	28,669	150	1,351	1,501

Source:
Banco de Portugal, *Boletim Trimestral (Estatistica e Estudos Economicos)*, June 1979, March 1982, March 1985 and *Relatorio do Conselho de Administracao, 1983.*

NOTES TOTABLE A3

1 Excluding reinvested earnings before 1975.

2 Excluding reinvested earnings from 1971 to 1982.

Table A4

SECTORAL DISTRIBUTION OF FOREIGN DIRECT CAPITAL STOCK, 1974-78 (Esc m)

	Inward Investment			Outward Investment		
	Primary	*Secondary*	*Tertiary*	*Primary*	*Secondary*	*Tertiary*
1974	300	4,352	3,055	*Not Available*		
1978	483	7,172	5,893			
1981	1,329	17,962	11,624			
1983	1,727	20,326	16,398			

Source:
Instituto do Investimento Estrangeiro, unpublished data.

Table A5

GEOGRAPHICAL DISTRIBUTION OF FOREIGN DIRECT CAPITAL STOCK, 1981-83 (Esc m)

	Inward Investment			Outward Investment		
	Developed Countries	*Developing Countries*	*Total*	*Developed Countries*	*Developing Countries*	*Total*
1981	29,493	1,422[1]	30,915	*Not Available*		
1983	36,526[2]	1,924	38,450			

Source:
Instituto do Investimento Estrangeiro, unpublished data.

NOTES TO TABLE A5

1 Estimation assuming a 4.6% share of developing countries in total FDI stock.

2 Includes EEC countries, EFTA countries, the USA, Canada, Spain and Japan.

Table A6

INDUSTRIAL DISTRIBUTION OF FOREIGN DIRECT CAPITAL STOCK, 1974-83 (Esc m)

	Inward Investment		Outward Investment
	1974	1983	
Primary	300	1,727	Not Available
Agriculture	58	700	
Mining & quarrying	242	1,027	
Secondary	4,352	20,326	
Food & drink	384	1,853	
Chemicals & allied[1]	1,050	4,994	
Metals	333	1,116	
Mechanical engineering, Electrical equipment, Motor vehicles, Other transportation equipment	1,346	7,346	
Textiles & clothing	353	1,341	
Paper & allied	638	2,655	
Rubber[1]			
Stone, clay & glass[2]	115	433	
Coal & petroleum products[1]			
Other manufacturing	133	588	
Tertiary	3,055	16,398	
Construction	54	312	
Transport & communication	100	481	
Distributive trade[3]	2,160	10,601	
Property, Banking & finance	709	4,493	
Other services	32	511	
TOTAL	7,706	38,450	

Source:

Instituto do Investimento Estrangeiro, unpublished data.

NOTES TO TABLE A6

1 Rubber and coal and petroleum products are included under chemicals and allied.

2 All non-metallic minerals.

3 Including hotels.

Table A7

LEADING SOURCE AND RECIPIENT COUNTRIES, 1981-83 (Esc m)

	Inward Investment		Outward Investment
	1981	*1983*	
DEVELOPED AREAS	29,493	36,526	
Europe	24,363	30,048	
EEC of which:	16,793	21,182	
Belgium & Luxembourg	2,214	2,401	
Denmark	534	582	
France	5,035	6,710	
W. Germany	2,989	3,660	
Greece	5	20	
Ireland	100	154	
Italy	112	171	
Netherlands	2,590	3,004	
UK	3,214	4,480	
Other Europe of which:	7,570	8,866	*Not Available*
Austria	6	8	
Finland	2	37	
Norway	93	148	
Spain	1,203	1,457	
Sweden	2,524	2,602	
Switzerland	3,739	4,609[1]	
North America of which:	*N.S.A.*	5,761	
Canada	*N.S.A.*	252	
USA	4,044	5,509	
Other developed countries of which:	*N.S.A.*	717	
Japan	495	717	
DEVELOPING AREAS	1,422[2]	1,924	
Hong Kong	*Not Separately Available*	85	
Netherland Antilles		174	
Panama		410	
TOTAL	30,915	38,450	

Source:
Instituto do Investimento Estrangeiro, unpublished data.

NOTES TO TABLE A7

[1] Including Liechtenstein

[2] See table A5, footnote [1]

Table A8

INDICATORS OF THE SIGNIFICANCE OF INWARD FOREIGN DIRECT INVESTMENT OR THE ACTIVITIES OF FOREIGN-BASED COMPANIES TO THE NATIONAL ECONOMY, 1978-84

1	Direct capital stock of foreign affiliates at book value in 1984 as a proportion of:		
	a	GNP at factor cost	3.05
	b	population (in Esc per head)	6,711.9
2	Employment in foreign affiliates in 1981 as a percentage of all employment:		
	a	in all industry	8.2
	b	in manufacturing	12.9
3	Output of foreign affiliates in 1978 as a percentage of all companies' output:[1]		
	a	in primary (ie, extractive) industry	8.3
	b	in secondary (ie, manufacturing) industry	19.6
	c	in tertiary industry (ie, services etc)	10.9
4	Exports of foreign affiliates in 1981 as a percentage of all manufacturing exports		25.0

5 Percentage share of sales and employment accounted for by foreign affiliates in selected sectors. 1978-81.

	Sales 1978	*Employment 1981*
Primary Goods Sector		
Agriculture	1.22	0.43
Mining and Quarrying	30.96	18.59
Oil	*N.A.*	*N.A.*
Manufacturing Sector		
Food and Drink	15.77	7.23
Chemicals and allied	31.01[2]	26.69[3]
Metals	22.56	17.64
Mechanical engineering	14.05	} 24.30 (Mechanical engineering to Other transportation equipment)
Electrical equipment	67.33	
Motor vehicles } Other transportation equipment	51.28	
Textiles and clothing	9.33	6.20
Paper and allied	25.38	12.57
Rubber	46.18	*N.A.*[3]
Stone, glass & clay[4]	10.60	7.47
Coal and petroleum products	26.04	*N.A.*[3]
Timber and furniture[5]	4.51	1.91
Other manufacturing	19.60	10.70

Table A8 (cont'd)

INDICATORS OF THE SIGNIFICANCE OF INWARD FOREIGN DIRECT INVESTMENT OR THE ACTIVITIES OF FOREIGN-BASED COMPANIES TO THE NATIONAL ECONOMY, 1978-81

5 (cont'd)	*Sales*	*Employment*
Services Sector		
Construction	9.80	2.22
Transport and communications	4.35	0.88
Trade and distribution	12.54	12.54[6]
Banking and finance	8.14	8.52
Other services	2.10	0.68

Source:
Instituto do Investimento Estrangeiro, *Investimento e Tecnologia, no 1, 1982; no 2, 1983;* unpublished data; OECD, Geographical Distribution of Financial Flows to Developing Countries, 1980-83; V Simoes in J H Dunning (Ed), *Multinational Enterprises, Economic Structure and International Competitiveness,* Chichester and New York: John Wiley, 1985.

NOTES TO TABLE A8

1 Sales of foreign affiliates as a percentage of all sales.

2 Calculated from the ratios for basic industrial chemicals, other chemicals and plastics. When all these categories and the sales of non-MNEs in other chemical products in which MNEs are not active are considered, the foreign affiliates share of assets falls to 9.7%, and their share of sales to 19.45%.

3 Rubber and coal and petroleum products are included under chemicals and allied.

4 All non-metallic minerals.

5 Wood and cork products.

6 Wholesale trade only (for trade and hotels, 6.77%).

Table A10

DISTRIBUTION OF FOREIGN SUBSIDIARIES AND ASSOCIATES AND FOREIGN CAPITAL STOCK BY PERCENTAGE OWNERSHIP OF PARENT COMPANIES, 1978

	Inward Investment			Outward Investment	
	Number of Affiliates[1]	*Value of Capital Stock*[2] *(Esc m)*		*Number of Affiliates*	*Value of Capital Stock (Esc m)*
100% owned subsidiaries	278[3]	7,032.0		*Not Available*	
50-99.9% owned subsidiaries and associates	127[4]	4,010.3			
Less than 50% owned subsidiaries and associates	146	5,580.6			
TOTAL	551	16,622.9			

Source:

Instituto do Investimento Estrangeiro, *Investimiento e Tecnologia, no 1, 1982.*

NOTES TO TABLE A10

1 Data on a sample of 551 foreign affiliates reported by the IIE.

2 Total capital stock of affiliates, not just the portion which is foreign-owned.

3 95 - 100% owned affiliates

4 50 - 94.9% owned affiliates

Table A11

ROYALTY RECEIPTS AND PAYMENTS, 1972-82 (Esc m)

	Payments				Receipts		
	To Affiliates	*To Non-affiliates*	*Total*		*From Affiliates*	*From Non-affiliates*	*Total*[1]
1972-74[2]	*Not Available*	*Not Available*	*Not Available*		*Not Separately Available*		36
1977							105
1978							83
1979	620	1,391	2,782				131
1980	2,164	2,039	4,204				186
1981	2,951	2,845	5,796				*N.A.*
1982	3,898	6,231	10,129				*N.A.*

Source:

Instituto do Investimento Estrangeiro, *Investimento e Tecnologia, no 1, 1982, Informacao Estatistica, 1980, 1981, 1982.*

NOTES TO TABLE A11

1 Total receipts of royalties and fees for patents and trademarks, not all contracts for the transfer of technology; the equivalent figures for payments are 389, 764, 779, 1,072 and 1,548 Esc m.

2 Annual average.

3 For a sample of firms, such that these do not add up to total payments made.

Table A12

LEADING FOREIGN MULTINATIONAL COMPANIES, 1983

Name	*Home Country*	*Sector*	*Portuguese sales (Esc m)*
1 Shell Portuguesa	UK/Netherlands	Oil	47.43
2 Mobil Oil Portuguesa	USA	Oil	31.47
3 Renault Portuguesa	France	Motor vehicles	28.00
4 CPP (BP)	UK	Oil	14.94
5 Grundig	W. Germany	Electrical equipment	13.25
6 Supas – CPS	Brazil	Distributive trade	12.40
7 Salvador Caetano	Japan	Motor vehicles	11.31
8 Philips Portuguesa	Netherlands	Electrical equipment	10.23
9 EPSI	France	Chemicals	9.23
10 Ford Lusitana	USA	Motor vehicles	8.73
11 Companhia IBM Portuguesa	USA	Electronic equipment	8.11
12 SAPEC	Belgium	Chemicals	7.99
13 Secil – CGCC	Denmark	Building materials	7.95
14 Promivi Portuguesa	USA	Food products	7.76
15 Celbi	Sweden	Chemicals	7.69
16 Siemens	W. Germany	Electrical equipment	7.52
17 General Motors de Portugal	USA	Motor vehicles	7.40
18 Isopor	USA	Chemicals	7.00
19 Nestlé	Switzerland	Food products	6.86
20 Efacec	Belgium	Electrical equipment	6.71
21 Esso Portuguesa	USA	Oil	6.04
22 Hoescht Portuguesa	W. Germany	Chemicals	5.70
23 Industrias Lever Portuguesa	UK /.Netherlands	Food products	5.62
24 Magnetic Peripherals	USA	Electrical equipment	5.21
25 Fiat Portuguesa	Italy	Motor vehicles	5.21
26 Standard Electrica	USA	Electrical & communications equipment	5.16

Source:

Expresso, 26th January 1985.

PORTUGAL: DEFINITIONS

The *Foreign Investment Institute of Portugal* compiles data on authorised foreign investment in Portugal by type of operation: acquisition, greenfield investment, investment for expansion, investment for stabilisation and other investment. Expansion investments are increases to the capital in which the foreign currency import attains at least 50% of the operation value. Investments for stabilisation are increases to the capital in which the foreign currency import is less than 50%. Other investments are those comprising, among others, the establishment of branches, the creation of joint accounts and direct foreign investment preliminary acts.

Banco de Portugal Relatorio provides data on the geographical and industrial flows of foreign direct investment in Portugal and direct investment abroad by Portuguese firms. Such data include reinvested profits.

According to Portuguese law, there is no minimum level of foreign holdings required for equity participation to be considered as foreign direct investment. Hence, Portuguese foreign direct investment statistics include both direct and portfolio investments.

Source:
Foreign Investment Institute of Portugal, *Annual Report*,various issues; Banco de Portugal, *Relatorio,* various issues.

SPAIN

Since the 1960s, over 200 multinational corporations have contributed significantly to Spain's industrial development. At first, foreign affiliates were attracted towards the heavy industrial sectors such as shipbuilding, steel, engineering and construction and to other sectors such as chemicals, pharmaceuticals and oil refining. Since the mid 1970s, however, the pattern of inward investment has considerably changed. For example, the banking and finance sector, which occupied only seventh place with a 1.2% share in the new foreign direct investment in 1974, increased its share to 18% in 1983. The metal products sector, which attracted only US $ 50 million of direct investment in 1974, received US $ 416 million in 1983.

The period 1980 to 1982 were peak years for the inflow of foreign direct investment. By 1982, total foreign investment had reached US $ 1,500 million from a level of US $ 200 million in 1974. This massive increase in the interest of foreign investors can be partly explained by the implementation of two domestic measures undertaken in 1981. The first was to designate certain sectors as 'critical' sectors which needed restructuring, and therefore were entitled to government assistance. The second measure was the encouragement given to foreign firms through the introduction of more flexible approval procedures. Other major factors that have influenced the attractiveness of Spain to foreign companies include its prospects of membership in the European Economic Community, its comparatively low tax rates and production costs and its generally welcoming policies towards foreign direct investment, even with the advent of a socialist government in 1983. Spain's economic difficulties, coupled with the worldwide recession, signified a noticable decline of foreign direct investments in 1983.

For many years, the USA has been the principal source of inward direct investment although in 1983 French companies led the field. The West Europeans have traditionally been the major investors. It is sometimes difficult to get a clear picture of the actual source of inward investment in Spain as some funds are channelled to Spain via third countries, eg, Switzerland and Luxembourg.

Since the early 1970s, Spanish outward investment has risen significantly and has been directed mainly towards Latin America and Europe. Such outward investments are concentrated mainly in manufacturing and in banking and finance. With the recent modifications (1985) of the foreign investment legislation, Spain now has very liberal legislation relating to FDI.

MAIN SOURCES OF DATA:

A **Official**

1 Ministerio de Economia y Comercio, Secretaria General Tecnica publications:

- i *Balanza de Pagos de Espana;*
- ii *Censo de Inversiones Extranjeras;*
- iii *Direccion General de Transacciones Exteriores;*
- iv *Inversiones Extranjeras en Espana, Informacion Comercial Espanola. (Boletin Semanal)*

B **Private**

1 J J Duran and P Sanchez, *La Internacionalizacion de la Empresa Espanola: Inversiones Espanolas en el Exterior,* Madrid: Ministerio de Economia y Comercio, Secretaria General Tecnica Libros, 1981.

2 P Nueno, N Martinez and J Sarle, *Las Inversiones Espanolas en el Extranjero,* Spain: LEVSA, 1981.

Table A1

SUMMARY OF THE COUNTRY'S INTERNATIONAL INVESTMENT POSITION

		Inward Investment	Outward Investment
1	Number of foreign affiliates in host country, and of foreign affiliates of home country firms at the end of 1977	6,232[1]	290
2	Number of foreign firms with direct investments in host country, and home country firms with direct foreign affiliates	*N.A.*	*N.A.*
3	Total foreign direct capital stock at book value as a percentage of GNP at factor cost in 1982[2]	2.91	0.75
4	Flow of foreign direct investment in the five year period, 1978-82 (Pta m)	358,375.4	107,037.1
5	Employment in foreign affiliates or abroad, 1977	1,244,724[3]	231,245
6	Output of foreign affiliates or abroad, 1977 (Pta m)	4.70[4]	9.78[5]

Source:

Ministerio de Economia y Comercio, *Balanza de Pagos de Espana; Censo de Inversiones Extranjeras, Direccion General de Transacciones Exteriores; Informacion Comercial Espanola, Inversiones Extranjeras en Espana;* J J Duran & P Sanchez, *op cit.*

NOTES TO TABLE A1

1 Represents corporations with net worth equal to or above 1 million pesetas.

2 Based on a calculation of cumulative flows between 1960 and 1982.

3 For majority-owned foreign affiliates, the employment is 298,317.

4 For majority-owned foreign affiliates, the output is 1.05 million pesetas.

5 Represents total sales of 84 major Spanish firms investing abroad.

Table A2

PRIVATE FOREIGN CAPITAL STOCK, 1960 - 84 (Pta bn)[1]

	Inward Investment			Outward Investment		
	Portfolio	*Direct*	*Total*	*Portfolio*	*Direct*	*Total*
Book value of capital stock						
1965	17.57	20.67	38.24	0.81	0.80	1.62
1970	27.17	80.25	107.41	1.87	6.12	7.99
1975	32.51	173.89	206.40	4.71	26.33	31.04
1976	26.74	188.57	215.30	5.60	29.95	35.55
1977	27.44	211.65	239.09	5.64	40.75	46.40
1978	30.76	258.11	288.88	5.97	50.93	56.90
1979	37.42	312.50	349.92	6.97	63.62	70.59
1980	38.64	378.90	417.54	7.97	82.06	90.02
1981	49.25	463.57	512.83	8.12	98.84	107.96
1982	50.41	570.02	620.43	17.97	147.79	165.96
1983	57.29	686.91	744.20	18.68	174.31	192.99
1984	87.59	834.58	922.17	22.75	204.49	227.24

Source:

Ministerio de Economia y Comercio, *Balanza de Pagos Espanola.*

NOTES TO TABLE A2

1 Represents cumulative flow of net investment as from 1960.

Table A3

FLOW OF FOREIGN DIRECT INVESTMENT, 1970 - 84 (Pta bn)[1]

	Inward Investment			Outward Investment		
	Reinvested Profits	*Other*	*Total*	*Reinvested Profits*	*Other*	*Total*
1970	*Not Separately Available*		15.51	*Not Separately Available*		3.03
1971			14.10			1.76
1972			17.76			3.66
1973			23.50			4.72
1974			20.66			4.95
1975			17.63			5.11
1976			14.67			3.63
1977			23.08			10.80
1978			46.47			10.18
1979			54.38			12.69
1980			66.40			18.44
1981			84.68			16.78
1982			106.45			48.95
1983			116.88			26.52
1984			147.66			39.18

Source:
Ministerio de Economia y Comercio, *Balanza de Pagos Espanola.*

NOTES TO TABLE A3

1 Excluding reinvested profits.

Table A4

SECTORAL DISTRIBUTION OF FOREIGN DIRECT CAPITAL STOCK, 1960 - 84 (Pta bn)[1]

	Inward Investment			Outward Investment		
	Primary	*Secondary*	*Tertiary*	*Primary*	*Secondary*	*Tertiary*
1960-75	2.65	108.89	31.23	3.27	9.32	12.32
1976	2.73	117.05	36.49	3.47	11.99	13.70
1977	3.05	140.59	40.67	4.48	19.62	18.55
1978	3.79	181.54	55.87	7.34	23.75	24.46
1979	6.71	237.26	78.02	9.06	29.90	30.82
1980	8.02	296.64	102.76	10.70	38.65	46.16
1981	9.83	347.31	128.89	13.65	45.89	66.04
1982	15.01	473.66	180.18	22.10	59.41	109.60
1983	19.42	570.61	237.01	23.61	66.62	135.32
1984	46.94	711.73	339.19	24.30	75.08	184.34

Source:

Ministerio de Economia y Comercio, *Direccion General de Transacciones Exteriores.*

NOTES TO TABLE A4

1 Represents cumulative flows of foreign direct investment authorized by the administration and constituting more than 50% of the value of capital, as from 1960, for inward investment and cumulative flows of direct investment abroad authorised by the administration, as from 1963.

Table A5

GEOGRAPHICAL DISTRIBUTION OF FOREIGN DIRECT CAPITAL STOCK, 1960 - 84 (Pta bn)[1]

	Inward Investment			Outward Investment		
	Developed Countries	*Developing Countries*	*Total*	*Developed Countries*	*Developing Countries*	*Total*
1960-75	139.19	3.58	142.78	14.69	11.83	26.53
1976	152.41	3.86	156.27	16.25	14.53	30.78
1977	180.19	4.12	184.31	19.76	24.51	44.27
1978	234.32	6.88	241.20	22.58	34.59	57.17
1979	309.47	12.53	322.00	33.98	47.41	81.39
1980	390.75	16.67	307.42	48.86	57.27	106.12
1981	463.35	22.68	486.02	53.28	82.92	136.20
1982	630.21	37.65	668.87	80.76	120.97	201.73
1983	771.82	55.22	827.05	97.45	138.72	236.17
1984	981.75	116.11	1,097.86	128.90	156.29	285.18

Source:

Ministerio de Economia y Comercio, *Direccion General de Transacciones Exteriores.*

NOTES TO TABLE A5

1 Represents cumulative flows of foreign direct investment authorized by the administration and constituting more than 50% of the value of capital, as from 1960, for inward investment and cumulative flows of direct investment abroad authorised by the administration, as from 1963.

Table A6

INDUSTRIAL DISTRIBUTION OF FOREIGN DIRECT CAPITAL STOCK, 1960 - 83 (Pta bn)[1]

	Inward Investment		Outward Investment	
	1960-75	*1960-83*[2]	*1963-75*	*1963-83*
Primary	2.65	19.42	3.27	23.61
Agriculture	0.86	13.47	0.67	13.36
Mining & quarrying	1.54	} 5.95	} 2.60	} 10.25
Oil	0.25[3]			
Secondary	108.89	570.61	9.32	66.62
Food & drink	9.30[4]	*N.S.A.*	*Not Separately Available*	*Not Separately Available*
Chemicals & allied	25.78	151.36[5]		
Metals	4.13	*Not Separately Available*		
Mechanical engineering	5.90			
Electrical equipment	7.37			
Motor vehicles	} 44.80			
Other transportation equipment				
Textiles & clothing	2.42[4]			
Paper & allied	1.98			
Rubber	*N.S.A.*			
Stone, clay & glass	2.09	*N.S.A.*[5]		
Coal & petroleum products	*N.S.A.*[3]	*N.S.A.*		
Other manufacturing	5.13	419.25		
Tertiary	31.23	237.01	12.32	135.32
Construction	2.58	10.93	0.77	10.08
Transport & communications[6]	1.20	9.39	0.88	3.65
Distributive trade	18.88	133.08	6.90	28.82
Property	*N.S.A.*	*N.S.A.*	*N.S.A.*	*N.S.A.*
Banking & finance	1.96	73.34	0.31	88.38
Other services	6.91	10.27	3.45	4.39
TOTAL	142.78	827.04	24.91	225.55

Source:
Ministerio de Economia y Comercio, *Direccion General de Transacciones Exteriores.*

NOTES TO TABLE A6

1 Represents cumulative flows of foreign direct investment authorized by the administration and constituting more than 50% of the value of capital, as from 1960, for inward investment and cumulative flows of direct investment abroad authorised by the administration, as from 1963.

2 Flows between 1976 and 1984 are arranged according to a slightly different sectoral classification than that for earlier years.

3 The extraction of petroleum, natural gas, combustible solids; petroleum refining; extraction and transformation of radioactive minerals; production, transport and distribution of electrical energy; gas & hot water & extraction, purification & distribution of water are included under oil. .

4 Represents food sector alone.

5 Stone, clay and glass, and leather products are included under chemicals & allied.

6 Including storage.

Table A7

LEADING SOURCE AND RECIPIENT COUNTRIES, 1960 - 84 (Pta bn)[1]

	Inward Investment		Outward Investment	
	1960-75	*1960-83*	*1963-75*	*1963-84*
DEVELOPED AREAS	139.19	771.82	14.70	128.90
Europe	78.31	552.06	11.64	70.27
EEC of which:	50.09	339.90	8.14	48.37
Belgium & Luxembourg	3.05	29.26	2.12	10.36
Denmark	0.36	1.30	*N.A.*	0.29
France	7.75	81.06	2.53	12.91
W. Germany	15.06	93.55	0.40	3.36
Greece	0.03	0.08[3]	*N.A*	0.01
Ireland	0.13	0.72	*N.A.*	1.17
Italy	3.00	15.03	0.21	3.26
Netherlands	6.25	54.03	0.16	3.98
UK	14.46	64.87	2.58	13.03
Other Europe of which:	28.22	212.16	3.50	21.90
Austria	0.31	0.76		
Czechoslovakia	*N.A.*	0.01		
Finland	0.47	2.40	*Not*	*Not*
Liechtenstein	0.93	13.79	*Available*	*Available*
Norway	0.01	0.25		
Poland	0.01	0.01		
Portugal	0.11	0.37	2.37	13.36
Spain[2]	0.40	69.94	*N.S.A.*	*N.S.A.*
Sweden	2.15	7.89	*N.S.A.*	*N.S.A.*
Switzerland	23.78	116.68	0.88	8.09
Turkey	0.01	0.01	*N.S.A.*	*N.S.A.*
USSR	0.01	0.05[4]	2.99	*N.S.A.*
North America of which:	60.49	215.24	1.90	46.46
Canada	2.50	9.58	1.09	2.58
USA	57.99	205.66	0.07	43.88
Other developed countries of which:	0.40	4.52	0.07	1.69
Australia	0.06	0.10[5]		1.25
Japan	0.33	4.41	*Not Available*	0.37
South Africa	*N.A.*	0.01		*N.A.*
DEVELOPING AREAS	3.58	55.22	11.83	156.29
Africa of which:	0.17	2.30	2.28	13.81
Algeria	0.15	0.20	0.50	1.04
Morocco	0.02	0.25	0.20	2.73
Nigeria	*N.A.*	*N.A.*	1.03	2.17
Tunisia	0.01	0.04	*N.A.*	0.09
Others	*N.A.*	*N.A.*	*N.A.*	6.03

Table A7 (cont'd)

LEADING SOURCE AND RECIPIENT COUNTRIES, 1960 - 84 (Pta bn)[1]

	Inward Investment		Outward Investment	
	1960-75	*1960-83*	*1963-75*	*1963-84*
DEVELOPING AREAS (cont'd)				
Asia & Pacific of which:	0.09	0.16	0.13	6.03
India	0.01	0.04	*N.A.*	*N.A.*
Philippines	0.09	0.12	*N.A.*	*N.A.*
Latin America of which:	1.52	23.83	7.82	148.20
Argentina	0.01	0.38	0.81	14.43
Brazil		0.01	1.83	10.90
Chile		0.01	0.79	22.10
Colombia		0.07	0.71	2.37
Costa Rica	*Not Available*	0.03	0.09	0.89
Dominican Republic			0.15	3.69
Ecuador			0.09	2.22
Guatemala			0.09	4.50
Mexico	0.58	3.11	1.17	16.61
Panama	0.54	6.98	0.54	18.42
Paraguay	*N.A.*	0.16	0.16	4.82
Peru	*N.A.*	*N N.A.*	0.05	2.78
Puerto Rico	0.05	0.05	0.73	16.70
Uruguay	0.03	0.11	0.13	7.27
Venezuela	0.24	7.72	0.52	12.05
Middle East of which:	0.30	7.06	1.58	2.12
Dubai	*N.A.*	0.01	1.53	1.55
Iran	*N.A.*	0.28	0.05	0.57
Kuwait	0.23	5.49	*N.A.*	*N.A.*
Syria	0.02	1.11	*N.A.*	*N.A.*
OTHER DEVELOPING COUNTRIES	1.51	21.87	0.02	0.01
TOTAL	142.78	827.05	26.53	285.18

Source:

Ministerio de Economia y Comercio, *Direccion General de Transacciones Exteriores.*

NOTES TO TABLE A7

1 Represents cumulative flows of foreign direct investment authorized by the administration and constituting more than 50% of the value of capital, as from 1960, for inward investment and cumulative flows of direct investment abroad authorised by the administration, as from 1963.

2 Represents new investments of foreign affiliates established in Spain in previous years.

3 1960-82.

4 1960-80.

5 1960-81.

Table A8

INDICATORS OF THE SIGNIFICANCE OF INWARD FOREIGN DIRECT INVESTMENT OR THE ACTIVITIES OF FOREIGN-BASED COMPANIES TO THE NATIONAL ECONOMY, 1977 - 82

1	Direct capital stock of foreign affiliates at book value in 1982 as a proportion of:	
	a GNP at factor cost	2.91[1]
	b population (in Pta per head)	15,028.31
2	Employment in foreign affiliates in 1977 as a percentage of all employment in all industry	46.60
3	Output of foreign affiliates in 1977 as a percentage of all companies' output[2] in secondary (ie manufacturing) industry	74.61
4	Exports of foreign affiliates in 1977 as a percentage of all manufacturing exports[3]	51.10

5 Percentage share of assets, sales and employment accounted for by foreign affiliates in selected sectors, 1977

	Assets[4]	*Sales*	*Employment*
Primary Good Sector			
Agriculture	2	14	17
Mining & quarrying	26	43	48
Oil	15	91	14
Manufacturing Sector			
Food & drink	12	60	52
Chemicals & allied	32	85	77
Metals	6	29	28
Mechanical engineering	23	52	45
Electrical equipment	55	85	82
Motor vehicles	59	99	99
Other transportation equipment	2	58	43
Textiles & clothing	10	23	17
Paper & allied	7	52	33
Rubber	31	68	63
Stone, glass & clay	5	49	39
Coal & petroleum products	2	31	12
Timber & furniture	1.5	16	11
Other manufacturing	10	23	22

Table A8 (cont'd)

INDICATORS OF THE SIGNIFICANCE OF INWARD FOREIGN DIRECT INVESTMENT OR THE ACTIVITIES OF FOREIGN-BASED COMPANIES TO THE NATIONAL ECONOMY, 1977 - 82

6 (cont'd)	*Assets*[4]	*Sales*	*Employment*
Services Sector			
Construction	3	36	26
Transport & communications	2	49	39
Trade & distribution	9	42	33
Banking & finance	3.5	90	93
Other services	*N.A.*	*N.A.*	*N.A.*

Source:

Ministerio de Economia y Comercio, *Censo de Inversiones Extranjeras.*

NOTES TO TABLE A8

1 Represents cumulative flows between 1960 and 1982.

2 Represents sales.

3 Represents share of foreign affiliates exports in total manufacturing exports of all firms with capital greater than 2 million pesetas.

4 Book value of capital stock.

Table A9

INDICATORS OF THE SIGNIFICANCE OF OUTWARD FOREIGN DIRECT INVESTMENT OR THE ACTIVITIES OF HOME-BASED COMPANIES ABROAD FOR THE NATIONAL ECONOMY, 1977 - 82

1	Foreign capital stock of home-based firms at book value in 1982 as a proportion of:	
	a GNP at factor cost	0.75
	b population (in pesetas per head)	3,896.38
2	Employment in foreign affiliates in 1977 as a percentage of domestic employment in all industry	46.6
3	Output of foreign manufacturing affiliates in 1977 as a percentage of manufacturing exports from the home country	74.61

Source:

Ministerio de Economia y Comercio, *op cit;* J J Duran and P Sanchez, *op cit.*

Table A10

DISTRIBUTION OF FOREIGN SUBSIDIARIES AND ASSOCIATES AND FOREIGN CAPITAL STOCK BY PERCENTAGE OWNERSHIP OF PARENT COMPANIES, 1977

	Inward Investment		Outward Investment[1]	
	Number of Affiliates	*Value of Capital Stock (Pta m)*	*Number of Affiliates*	*Value of Capital Stock (Pta m)*
100% owned subsidiaries	1,623	375,550	41	*Not Available*
50-99.9% owned subsidiaries and associates			77	
Less than 50% owned subsidiaries and associates	4,609[2]	2,103,060[2]	163	
TOTAL	6,232	2,478,610	290	

Source:
Ministerio de Economia y Comercio, *Censo de Inversiones Extranjeras en Espana; Direccion General de Transacciones Exteriores.*

NOTES TO TABLE A10

1 Represents authorised outward investment.

2 Represents 1,953 foreign affiliates that are more than 25% but less than 50% foreign owned with a value of capital stock of 243,350 million pesetas and 2,656 foreign affiliates that are less than 25% foreign owned with a value of capital stock of 1,859,710 million pesetas.

Table A11

ROYALTY RECEIPTS AND PAYMENTS, 1970 - 84 (Pta bn)

	Payments			Receipts		
	To Affiliates	*To Non-affiliates*	*Total*	*From Affiliates*	*From Non-affilaites*	*Total*
1970	*Not Separately Available*		9.36	*Not Separately Available*		1.12
1975			17.30			2.89
1976			31.24			4.06
1977			28.69			4.48
1978			30.46			5.56
1979			34.70			7.64
1980			44.39			10.87
1981			52.34			16.70
1982			78.98			15.71
1983			69.22			15.32
1984			61.34			17.56

Source:
Ministerio de Economia y Hacienda, *Balanza de Pagos de Espana.*

Table A12

LEADING FOREIGN AND DOMESTIC MULTINATIONAL COMPANIES

A Leading Foreign Multinational Companies in the Country, 1984

	Name	*Home Country*	*Sector*	*Turnover in Spain (Pta bn)*
1	Fasa Renault	France	Motor vehicles	206
2	Petronor	Mexico	Petroleum	192
3	Ford Espana	USA	Motor vehicles	137
4	General Motors Espana	USA	Motor vehicles	130
5	Simago	France	Retailing	103
6	Citreon Hispania	France	Motor vehicles	83
7	IBM	USA	Computers	79
8	Michelin	France	Rubber tires	75
9	Dow Chemical Iberica	Switzerland	Chemicals	72
10	Promotora Hipermercados	France	Retailing	64
11	Sociedad Nestle	Switzerland	Food products	62
12	Compania Industrial y Abastecimientos	USA	Commodities	60
13	Aumotoviles Talbot	France	Motor vehicles	55
14	Galerias Preciados	Venezuela	Retailing	55
15	Motor Iberica (Nissan)	Japan	Motor vehicles	51
16	Standard Electrica (ITT)	USA	Telephone & telegraph	48
17	Ford Credit	USA	Finance	47
18	Phillips Iberica	Netherlands	Electronics	46
19	Rio Tinto Minera	UK	Minerals	44
20	Hoechst Iberica	W. Germany	Pharmaceuticals	44
21	Petrolifera Espanola (Shell)	UK	Petroleum	44
22	Aluminio Espanol (Pechiney-Alcan)		Aluminium	40
23	Unilever Espana	UK	Food products	39
24	Firestone Hispania	USA	Rubber tires	38
25	Koipe (Lessieur group)	France	Food	36

Table A12 (cont'd)

LEADING FOREIGN AND DOMESTIC MULTINATIONAL COMPANIES

B Leading Domestic Companies with Multinational interests, 1984

	Name	*Sector*	*Global Turnover (Pta bn)*
1	Cia Espanola de Petroleos	Petroleum	449
2	Cia Telefonica Nacional de Espana	Telephone	313
3	El Corte Ingles	Retailing	215
4	Union Explosives Rio Tinto	Metals, chemical products	197
5	Sociedad Espanola de Automobiles de turismo (SEAT)	Tourism	147
6	Hispanoil	Petroleum	143
7	Dragados y Construcciones	Construction	138
8	Empresa Nacional de Autocamiones	Motor vehicles	72
9	Empresa Nacional des Gas	Gas	66
10	Astilleros Espanoles	Shipbuilding	64
11	Entrecanales y Tavora	Construction	62
12	Huarte y Cia	Construction	51
13	Construcciones Aeronauticas (CASA)	Aircraft	40
14	Cros	Chemical products	33
15	Ferrovial	Construction	31
16	Focoex	Trading	30
17	Alumina Espanola	Aluminium	28
18	Acerinox	Metal manufacturing	27
19	Viajes Melia	Tourism	27
20	Asland	Construction materials	26
21	Uralita	Construction materials	24
22	Sarrio	Paper & allied	22
23	Foret	Chemical products	21
24	Jose Maria Aristran	Metal manufacturing	19
25	Abengoa	Electronics	18

SPANISH TABLES : DEFINITIONS

There is no data source for foreign direct capital stock in Spain. The two main data sources for flows of foreign direct investment in Spain are the two publications from the Ministerio de Economia y Comercio, namely: *Balanza de Pagos de Espana* and *Direccion General de Transacciones Exteriores.* Foreign direct investment, as defined in these sources, represents authorised investment by foreign individuals, private foreign legal corporate bodies, Spaniards residing abroad and the International Finance Corporation. The foreign capital may be contributed in the following ways: foreign monetary contribution, capital goods, technical assistance, patents and manufacturing licenses and any other means subject to administrative authorization. Direct investment may be made either at the time a company is set up or through acquiring shares issued by a company, in whole or in part, or through acquiring capital holdings in the case of companies whose capital is not in the form of shares. For these purposes, the acquisition of subscription rights is equated with acquisition of shares. In general, there are no limitations to acquire the control of a Spanish company, although in a very few cases the authorization of the Government (Board of Ministeries) is needed.

Source:

Ministerio de Economia y Comercio.

SWEDEN

Sweden is a small, well developed and highly open economy. The major source country of Swedish inward investment is the USA, followed by the UK and West Germany. In recent years, the share of the USA has been falling and that of European countries increasing. While Sweden is a favourable location for the manufacturing industry, its own market size is small, despite a very high income per capita. This may help explain why a particularly high proportion of inward investment is in the distributive sector.

Sweden's outward direct foreign investment is strongly oriented towards Europe, and within Europe the EEC, of which West Germany is the single largest recipient. In recent years, however, Swedish investment has increasingly turned towards the USA. Swedish multinationals are notably internationally oriented. Hypotheses to explain this have centred around the small domestic market size of Sweden itself, prompting an earlier and more extensive degree of multinational operations on the part of its firms.

Swedish outward investment is also concentrated in particular industrial sectors, metals and engineering, machinery (including electronics) and a higher proportion in wood-derived products than typifies other western source countries.

MAIN SOURCES OF DATA:

A Official

1 Sveriges Riksbank (Swedish Central Bank) compiles data on the annual value of inward and outward direct investment permits, together with data on the actual values of transactions.

2 Statistiska Centralbyran (Swedish Central Bureau of Statistics) in the process of collecting data on all enterprises in Sweden produces an analysis of foreign owned firms. Also certain data are collected together from this source on the major Swedish firms investing abroad.

B Private

1 Industriens Utredningsinstitut (The Industrial Institute for Economic and Social Research) has organised surveys on Swedish direct investments abroad, which have subsequently been published in private sources.

2 C Soderstrom, *Swedish Enterprises Operating Abroad, the Seventies: A Decade of Change,* Sweden: National Central Bureau of Statistics, 1980.

3 B Swedenborg, *The Multinational Operations of Swedish Firms,* Stockholm: Industrial Institute for Economic and Social Research, 1979.

4 B Swedenborg, 'Sweden' in J H Dunning (Ed), *Multinational Enterprises, Economic Structure and International Competitiveness*, London: John Wiley, 1985.

Table A1

SUMMARY OF THE COUNTRY'S INTERNATIONAL INVESTMENT POSITION

		Inward Investment	Outward Investment
1	Number of foreign affiliates in host country, and of foreign affiliates of home country firms at the end of 1979	4,115	1,772
2	Number of foreign firms with direct investments in host country, and home country firms with direct foreign affiliates	*N.A.*	*N.A.*
3	Total foreign direct capital stock at book value as a percentage of GNP at factor cost in 1981	0.9[1]	4.2
4	Flow of foreign direct investment in the five year period, 1978-82 (S Kr m)	4,166	18,343
5	Employment of foreign affiliates or abroad, 1983	131,254[2]	301,205[3]
6	Output of foreign affiliates or abroad, 1979 (S Kr m)	84,944.8[4]	56,990[5]

Source:

Central Bureau of Statistics, *Statistika Neddelanden,* 1981; Industriens Utredningsinstitut, unpublished data; C Soderstrom, *Swedish Enterprises Operating Abroad, the Seventies: A Decade of Change,* Sweden: National Central Bureau of Statistics, 1980; IMF, *International Financial Statistics,* 1981; Bank of Sweden, *Annual Report,* various issues.

NOTES TO TABLE A1

1 Inward investment stock approximated by cumulated inward investment flows, 1976-81.

2 Represents employment in majority owned affiliates.

3 Represents employment in foreign manufacturing affiliates 227,820 and employment in foreign sales and service affiliates 73,385 in 1978. Employees of subsidiaries abroad of the twenty largest Swedish concerns operating abroad (The Big Twenty), who account for some 90% of Swedish industry's direct investment abroad, was 258,984 in 1979.

4 Represents gross operating income in 1979 of 756 over 20% foreign-owned enterprises.

5 Refers to the sales of foreign manufacturing affiliates of Swedish parents in 1978.

Table A2

PRIVATE FOREIGN CAPITAL STOCK, 1967 - 81 (S Kr m)

	Inward Investment			Outward Investment		
	Portfolio	*Direct*	*Total*	*Portfolio*	*Direct*[1]	*Total*
Book value of capital stock						
1967		2,599.5			8.780	
1970		4,502.6			12,328	
1975		6,256.6			20,482	
1976		6,601.6			23,260	
1977	*Not Available*	6,998.6	*Not Available*	*Not Available*	26,782	*Not Available*
1978		7,317.6			29,100	
1979		7,792.6			32,182	
1980		8,868.6			35,163	
1981		9,860.6			39,576	
1983		11,390.6			54,098	

Source:

B Swedenborg, *The Multinational Operations of Swedish Firms,* Stockholm: Industrial Institute for Economic and Social Research, 1979; C Soderstrom, *Swedish Enterprises Operating Abroad, The Seventies: A Decade of Change,* Stockholm: National Central Bureau of Statistics, 1980; Sveriges Riksbank, *Quarterly Review,* 1982/83.

NOTES TO TABLE A2

1 Data are estimates for total industry, obtained by the addition of cumulative annual direct investment outflows recorded by the Sveriges Riksbank, to a stock estimate for 1967. The data cover both majority-owned foreign affiliates and minority-owned foreign associates.

2 The figure represents cumulated annual direct investment flows into Sweden as from 1960.

Table A3

FLOW OF FOREIGN DIRECT INVESTMENT, 1970 - 83 (S Kr m)[1]

	Inward Investment			Outward Investment		
	Reinvested Profits	*Other*	*Total*	*Reinvested Profits*	*Other*	*Total*
1970			558			1,101
1971	*Not Separately Available*		438	*Not Separately Available*		924
1972			319			1,251
1973			338			1,367
1974			315			1,769
1975	236	108	344			1,822
1976	345	*N.A.*	*N.A.*			2,474
1977	374	23	397	91	3,488	3,579
1978	285	34	319	50	1,808	1,858
1979	218	257	475	49	2,562	2,611
1980	72	1,004	1,076			2,677
1981	67	925	992	*Not Separately Available*		4,591
1982	130	1,174	1,304			6,606
1983	*N.S.A.*	*N.S.A.*	226			7,916

Source:

IMF, *Balance of Payments Statistics Yearbook,* various years.

NOTES TO TABLE A3

1 The flows shown here do not quite match those recorded by the Sveriges Riksbank and used to calculate foreign capital stock in Table A2.

Table A4

SECTORAL DISTRIBUTION OF FOREIGN DIRECT CAPITAL STOCK, 1965 - 81 (S Kr m)

	Inward Investment			Outward Investment[1]		
	Primary	*Secondary*	*Tertiary*	*Primary*	*Secondary*	*Tertiary*
1965	*Not Available*			*N.A.*	3,317	*N.A.*
1970				*N.A.*	5,735	*N.A.*
1977				*N.A.*	10,429	*N.A.*
1981	*N.A.*	5,174[2]	*N.A.*	*Not Available*		

Source:

B Swedenborg, *The Multinational Operations of Swedish Firms,* Stockholm: The Industrial Institute for Economic and Social Research, 1979; C Soderstrom, *op cit.*

NOTES TO TABLE A4

1 Swedish direct investment is the book value of the Swedish parent's share in foreign affiliates equity plus affiliate long term debts to the Swedish parent. (Long term = in excess of one year.) The figures given in this table represent foreign affiliates of Swedish manufacturing firms which cover some 90% of all foreign affiliates and minority interests of Swedish firms.

2 Estimated by applying the percentage of manufacturing in cumulative investment flows for 1976-81 to the 1981 stock figure calculated in Table A2.

Table A5

GEOGRAPHICAL DISTRIBUTION OF FOREIGN DIRECT CAPITAL STOCK, 1965 - 81 (S Kr m)

	Inward Investment			Outward Investment		
	Developed Countries	*Developing Countries*	*Total*	*Developed Countries*	*Developing Countries*	*Total*
1965[1]	*Not Available*			2,960	355	3,317
1970[1]				4,964	772	5,735
1976-81[2]	4,758	20	4,881	16,836	3,023	19,922

Source:

B Swedenborg, *The Multinational Operations of Swedish Firms: An analysis of determinants and effects,* Stockholm: Almquist & Wiksell International 1979, based on IVI survey on Swedish manufacturing investment abroad; Sveriges Riksbank, *Quarterly Review,* 1982-83.

NOTES TO TABLE A5

1 Manufacturing only.

2 Data for 1981 are cumulated annual direct investment flows 1976-81.

Table A6

INDUSTRIAL DISTRIBUTION OF FOREIGN DIRECT CAPITAL STOCK, 1970 - 81 (S Kr m)

	Inward Investment[1]	Outward Investment	
	1981	*1970*	*1977*
Primary			
Agriculture	*Not*	*Not*	*N.A.*
Mining & quarrying	*Available*	*Available*	1
Oil			*N.A.*
Secondary	5,174[1]	5,735	10,429
Food & drink		54	80
Chemicals & allied[2]		605	400
Metals		485	1,717
Mechanical engineering		2,811	2,893
Electrical equipment		629	1,799
Motor vehicles	*Not*	202	1,512
Other transportation equipment	*Separately*		
Textiles & clothing	*Available*	17	60
Paper & allied		599	1,148
Rubber[2]		*N.S.A.*	*N.S.A.*
Stone, clay & glass		*N.S.A.*	262
Coal & petroleum products			
Other manufacturing		333	559
Tertiary			
Construction	*Not*		
Transport & communications	*Available*		
Distributive trade[3]	2,637 2,637	*Not*	
Property		*Available*	
Banking & finance	*Not*		
Other services	*Available*		
TOTAL	9,861	12,328	26,782

Source:

Central Bureau of Statistics, data supplied on operations of foreign companies in Sweden; B Swedenborg, *op cit;* C Soderstrom, *op cit.*

NOTES TO TABLE A6

1 The broad distribution for inward investment in manufacturing is obtained by applying the proportion of manufacturing in cumulative investment flow for 1976-81 to the 1981 stock figure calculated in Table A2.

2 Rubber and plastic products are included under chemicals.

3 Other services are included with distributive trade.

Table A7

LEADING SOURCE AND RECIPIENT COUNTRIES, 1970 - 81 (S Kr m)

	Inward Investment	Outward Investment	
	1976-81[1]	*1970*[2]	*1976-81*[1]
DEVELOPED AREAS	4,758	4,964	16,836
Europe	3,146	3,711	11,332
EEC of which:	2,349		7,888
Belgium & Luxembourg	169		847
Denmark	262		834
France	568		1,207
W. Germany	588		1,586
Ireland	*N.S.A.*		57
Italy	*N.S.A.*		249
Netherlands	43	*Not Separately Available*	719
UK	719		2,389
Other Europe[3] of which:	797		3,444
Austria	*N.S.A.*		87
Finland	245		614
Norway	293		1,839
Portugal	*N.S.A.*		45
Spain	*N.S.A.*		276
Switzerland	239		583
North America of which:	1,338	1,060	4,973
Canada	47	401	374
USA	1,291	659	4,599
Other developed countries[3] of which:	274	193	531
Australia		*N.S.A.*	245
Japan	32	*N.S.A.*	50
DEVELOPING AREAS	20	772	3,023
Africa of which:		26	43
Liberia		*N.S.A.*	43
Asia & Pacific of which:		107	218
Hong Kong			82
Philippines		*Not Separately Available*	21
Singapore	*Not Separately Available*		115
Latin America of which:		639	2,017
Argentina			368
Bahamas			29
Bermuda		*Not Separately Available*	55
Brazil			1,406
Mexico			159

Table A7 (cont'd)

LEADING SOURCE AND RECIPIENT COUNTRIES, 1970 - 81 (S Kr m)

	Inward Investment	Outward Investment	
	1976-81[1]	*1970*[2]	*1976-81*[1]
DEVELOPING AREAS (cont'd)			
Middle East of which:	*Not Separately Available*	*Not Separately Available*	115
Saudi Arabia			49
United Arab Emirates			66
OTHER DEVELOPING COUNTRIES			630
UNSPECIFIED	103		63
TOTAL	4,881	5,735	19,922

Source:

B Swedenborg, *op cit;* Sveriges Riksbank, *Quarterly Review,* 1982-83.

NOTES TO TABLE A7

1 Data for 1981 are the cumulated annual transaction values 1976-81 provided by the Sveriges Riksbank, and therefore represent the increase in direct foreign investment over the period 1976-81.

2 Stock of manufacturing investment only.

3 Countries not specified are included in other developed countries, apart from the Soviet Union which is included in Other Europe for inward investment 1981.

Table A8

INDICATORS OF THE SIGNIFICANCE OF INWARD FOREIGN DIRECT INVESTMENT OR THE ACTIVITIES OF FOREIGN-BASED COMPANIES TO THE NATIONAL ECONOMY, 1978 - 81

1	Direct capital stock of foreign affiliates at book value in 1981 as a proportion of:	
	a GNP at factor cost	0.9
	b population (in S Kr per head)	586.66
2	Employment in foreign affiliates in 1975-6 as a percentage of all employment	
	a in all industry	4.9
	b in manufacturing	5.7
3	Output of foreign affiliates in 1978 as a percentage of all companies' output[1]	
	a in primary (ie, extractive) industry	2.8
	b in secondary (ie, manufacturing) industry	14.4
4	Profits of foreign affiliates in 1979 as a percentage of profits of all companies in the host country in all sectors.	11.1[2]

5 Percentage share of sales, value added and employment accounted for by foreign affiliates in selected sectors, 1978

	Sales	*Value added*	*Employment*[3]
Primary Goods Sector			
Agriculture	*N.A.*	*N.A.*	0.3
Mining & quarrying	2.8	2.9	3.8
Oil	*N.A.*	*N.A.*	*N.A.*
Manufacturing Sector			
Food & drink	13.9	16.3	13.8
Chemicals & allied[4]	45.9	32.6	22.1
Metals[5]	19.1	12.2	11.4
Mechanical engineering, Electrical equipment, Motor vehicles, Other transportation equipment	9.6[6]	10.3[6]	9.1[6]
Textiles & clothing	8.0	9.3	7.2
Paper & allied	5.8	5.6	3.8
Rubber[4]	*N.A.*	*N.A.*	*N.A.*
Stone, glass & clay	22.1	22.1	14.8
Coal & petroleum products[4]	*N.A.*	*N.A.*	*N.A.*
Furniture	1.7	1.6	2.0
Other manufacturing	16.6	16.5	11.9

Table A8 (cont'd)

INDICATORS OF THE SIGNIFICANCE OF INWARD FOREIGN DIRECT INVESTMENT OR THE ACTIVITIES OF FOREIGN-BASED COMPANIES TO THE NATIONAL ECONOMY, 1978 - 81

6 (cont'd)	*Sales*	*Value added*	*Employment*[3]
Services Sector			
Construction	*Not Available*	*Not Available*	2.7
Transport & communications			9.1[7]
Distributive trade			10.0[8]
Property			5.3
Banking & finance			
Other services			2.4

Source:

Central Bureau of Statistics, *Utlandsagda Foretag* (Foreign Owned Enterprises), 1978 and 1979 and 1981; Central Bureau of Statistics, *Statistika Neddelanden,* 1981; Industriens Utredningsinstitut, unpublished data.

NOTES TO TABLE A8

1 Represents value of sales of over 20% foreign-owned enterprises.
2 Represents profits before tax of 756 over 20% foreign-owned enterprises.
3 Employment figures are for 1979.
4 Coal and petroleum products, and rubber and plastic products are included under chemicals.
5 Represents basic metal industries.
6 Including manufacture of fabricated metal products, machinery and equipment.
7 Including storage.
8 Including restaurants and hotels.

Table A9

INDICATORS OF THE SIGNIFICANCE OF OUTWARD FOREIGN DIRECT INVESTMENT OR THE ACTIVITIES OF HOME-BASED COMPANIES ABROAD FOR THE NATIONAL ECONOMY, 1974 - 78

1	Foreign capital stock of home-based firms at book value in 1977 as a proportion of:	
	a GNP at factor cost	2.20
	b population (in S Kr per head)	984.67
2	Employment in foreign affiliates in 1978 as a percentage of domestic employment in manufacturing	26.0
3	Output of foreign manufacturing affiliates in 1975 as a percentage of:	
	a domestic manufacturing output	15.41
	b manufacturing exports from the home country	44.24
4	Profits of foreign affiliates in 1977 as a percentage of all profits recorded by home-based companies in all sectors	112.1
5	Employment of foreign affiliates of home-based firms as a percentage of that in selected domestic sectors, 1978	
		Employment
	Primary Goods Sector	
	Mining and quarrying	44
	Manufacturing Sector	
	Food and drink	26
	Chemicals and allied	35[1]
	Metals	29[2]
	Mechanical engineering	40
	Electrical equipment	44
	Motor vehicles Other transportation equipment	} 37
	Textiles and clothing	30
	Paper and allied	23
	Rubber	*N.A.*
	Stone, clay and glass	33
	Furniture	24
	Other manufacturing	39

Source:
Industriens Utredningsinstitut, *Syssel sattnings — strukturen i industriella foretag en studie av utvedlingen i svensk industri 1966-80 expertrapport tran direktinvesteringskommiten,* Stockholm, 1983; IMF, International Financial Statistics Yearbook, 1984; B Swedenborg, *Svensk Industri i Utlandet*, Industriens Utredningsinstitut Stockholm, 1982.

NOTES TO TABLE A9

1 Rubber and plastic products are included under chemicals.

2 Represents basic metal industries.

Table A10

DISTRIBUTION OF FOREIGN SUBSIDIARIES AND ASSOCIATES AND FOREIGN CAPITAL STOCK BY PERCENTAGE OWNERSHIP OF PARENT COMPANIES, 1979

	Inward Investment		Outward Investment	
	Number of Affiliates	*Value of Capital Stock*	*Number of Affiliates*	*Value of Capital Stock*
100% owned subsidiaries 50-99.9% owned subsidiaries and associates	3,171[1]	*Not Available*	*Not Separately Available*	*Not Available*
Less than 50% owned subsidiaries and associates	944[2]			
TOTAL	4,115		1,772[3]	

Source:
Central Bureau of Statistics, *Statistika Neddelanden,* 1981; B Swedenborg, *The Multinational Operations of Swedish Firms: An analysis of determinants and effects,* Stockholm: Almquist & Wiksell International, 1979.

NOTES TO TABLE A10

1 Represents subsidiaries of foreign enterprises where one foreign company or company group directly or indirectly disposes (owns) **more** than 50 per cent of the votes (capital). This group is called enterprises with a foreign parent company.

2 Represents foreign enterprises who own minority interests, ie, 20% as a minimum and 50% as a maximum of the votes (capital) numbering 592 in 1979 and enterprises which are owned to 20% or more by foreign (natural) persons. A foreign natural person is considered here as a person permanently resident abroad. The number is 352 in 1979.

3 Represents foreign affiliates of Swedish manufacturing firms in 1974 which cover some 90% of all foreign affiliates and minority interests of Swedish firms. This figure can be broken down as follows:

Manufacturing affiliates	–	481
Sales affiliates	–	1,227
Other affiliates	–	64

Table A11

ROYALTY RECEIPTS AND PAYMENTS, 1972 - 82 (S Kr m)

	Payments			Receipts		
	To Affiliates	*To Non-affiliates*	*Total*	*From Affiliates*	*From Non-affiliates*	*Total*
1972	*Not Separately Available*		294.72	*Not Separately Available*		98.24
1975			478.93			171.41
1976			598.45			261.51
1977			591.26			334.87
1978			601.73			298.25
1979			797.60			387.72
1980			858.76			379.84
1981			1,009.03			519.44
1982			1,387.22			471.65

Source:
IMF, *Balance of Payments Statistics Yearbook,* various issues.

Table A12

LEADING FOREIGN AND DOMESTIC MULTINATIONAL COMPANIES

A Leading Foreign Multinational Companies in the Country, 1984

Name	*Home Country*	*Sector*
AMP Incorporated	USA	Electrical and electronic engineering
Abbott Laboratories	USA	Pharmaceuticals
Akai Electric Co Ltd	Japan	Electrical and electronic engineering
American Cyanamid Company	USA	Pharmaceuticals
BAT Industries PLC	UK	Pulp and paper
Babcock International	UK	Mechanical engineering
Barclays Bank PLC	UK	Banking & finance
Beecham Group PLC	UK	Pharmaceuticals
British Aerospace PLC	UK	Manufacture of aeroplanes
The British Petroleum Co PLC	UK	Chemicals
The Burmah Oil PLC	UK	Wholesale distribution of fuel
Burroughs Corp	USA	Manufacture of office machinery and data processing equipment
Cadbury Schweppes PLC	UK	Food and drink
Colgate-Palmolive Co	USA	Consumer products
Emhart Corp	USA	Chemicals
Exxon Corp	USA	Wholesale distribution of fuel
The General Electric Co PLC	UK	Electrical and electronic engineering
General Motors Corp	USA	Manufacture of motor vehicles and parts
The Goodyear Tire & Rubber Co	USA	Processing of rubber
Gulf Oil Corp	USA	Wholesale distribution of fuels
ICI	UK	Chemicals
IBM	USA	Manufacture of office machinery and data processing equipment
Johnson & Johnson	USA	Chemical, medical and pharmaceutical products
Thorn EMI PLC	UK	Electrical and electronic engineering
Xerox Corp	USA	Manufacture of office machinery

Table A12 (cont'd)

LEADING FOREIGN AND DOMESTIC MULTINATIONAL COMPANIES

B Leading Domestic Companies with Multinational Interests, end 1983				
	Name	*Sector*	*Global Turnover (US $ th)*	*Sales of overseas subsidiaries as % of worldwide sales (1983)*
1	Volvo	Motor vehicles & parts	12,693,008	60
2	Electrolux	Electronics, appliances	4,189,713	57
3	ASEA	Electronics, industrial equipment	3,939,863	35
4	L M Ericsson	Electronics, telecommunications	3,359,499[1]	40
5	Saab-Scania	Motor vehicles	2,707,397	19
6	SKF	Metal products	2,127,440	76
7	Statsforetag Group	Industrial & farming equipment	1,477,465	53[2, 4]
8	Sandvik Group	Metal manufacturing & steel	1,318,849	9
9	Svenska Cellulosa	Paper & wood products	1,273,101	39
10	Alfa-Laval	Industrial & farming equipment	1,219,534	60
11	Svenska Flakt	Machinery	1,179,000[2]	63
12	Boliden	Metals	1,140,000[2]	*N.A.*
13	Granges	Metals	1,129,000[2]	14[2, 3]
14	Swedish Match	Wood products, chemicals, building materials	1,101,582	56
15	Atlas Copco	Industrial equipment	1,054,753[1]	66[2]
16	Esselte	Office equipment, publishing, printing	1,030,811	60[2]
17	AGA	Chemicals	1,003,000	65
18	Skanska	Building	*N.A.*[5]	23
19	ESAB	Electrical machinery	*N.A.*[5]	68
20	Sonesson	Conglomerate	*N.A.*[5]	45
21	Euroc	Conglomerate	*N.A.*[5]	33
22	Incentive	Conglomerate	*N.A.*[5]	33
23	Astra	Pharmaceuticals	*N.A.*[5]	47

Source:
Fortune International, August 20 1984; *Veckans affarer,* 16/1984, Stockholm; J Stopford and J H Dunning, *Multinationals: Company Performance and Global Trends,* London: Macmillan, 1983; Dun and Bradstreet, *Who Owns Whom 1984,* London: Business Marketing Division (Publications), 1984.

NOTES TO TABLE A12(b)

1 Also includes certain subsidiaries owned 50% or less, either fully or on a prorated basis.
2 Figures are for 1981.
3 Excludes all exports: any intra-group exports are therefore included with direct exports.
4 Includes all exports, direct and intra-group.
5 Companies 18-23 are ranked in descending order of total exports from Sweden in 1983.

SWEDEN TABLES : DEFINITIONS

Data on Swedish multinationals' operations abroad are available from the surveys by the Swedish Industriens Utredningsinstitut (Industrial Institute for Economic and Social Research) and published in Swedenborg (1973 and 1979). The Institute conducted three surveys, for the years 1965 and 1970, for the year 1974 and for 1977 which covered foreign investing mining and manufacturing enterprises. The surveys included all Swedish incorporated parent enterprises with more than fifty employees in Sweden, with both majority and minority direct foreign investment ownership and a lower threshold of ten per cent. The estimable universe was established from those Swedish firms which had been granted direct foreign investment permits by the Sveriges Riksbank (Swedish Central Bank), under foreign exchange regulations. These surveys are then believed to cover 97-99% of this universe.

The detailed data by industry and country relate to majority-owned foreign affiliates, which accounted for 90% by value of all Swedish ownership of foreign nominal capital in 1970. The Swedish data are available for foreign output values in respect of the industry distribution. For the geographical distribution and broad sectoral distribution, the Swedish share of total assets is available. Data on the direct foreign investment position are not generally available, although Swedenborg (1979) presents some estimates for 1965 and 1970, calculated as the book value of the parent's share in foreign affiliates equity plus affiliates long-term debts to the Swedish parent (long-term being greater than one year). Estimates for 1977 can be derived from Soderstrom (1980).

All Swedish data on inward multinational involvement are drawn from the Official Register of Enterprises, kept by the Swedish Statistika Centralbyran (Central Bureau of Statistics). From this source, which covers all natural and legal persons with employees, is derived the Register of Foreign-Owned Enterprises. This covers foreign affiliated enterprises in Sweden, defined as operating joint-stock companies and other legal persons (associations) in which foreign residents hold 20% or more of the voting rights. Where the number of votes is unkown, the share of issued capital is applied. This source presents data on the sales of foreign affiliates in Sweden, and it is these that are used in the statistical analysis. While other operating statistics are available, the only financial figures are for total assets rather than the direct foreign investment position. Thus the values for the geographical and sectoral distribution of foreign multinational involvement in Sweden are for total assets.

According to Swedish classification, foreign-owned enterprises are distributed into three groups. The largest is composed of subsidiaries of foreign enterprises, ie, all enterprises where one foreign resident or group directly or indirectly owns more than 50% of the voting rights. This group is termed 'enterprises with a foreign parent company'. The second group consists of enterprises in which a foreign resident owns a minority interest of greater than 20% of the voting rights. The third group of enterprises are those owned 20% or more by foreign (natural) persons resident abroad. This group is minor and, while it is included in the total of all groups, is not presented separately.

SWITZERLAND

Switzerland's small market has led her to rely on exports and on outward direct investment as ways of securing efficient development in a number of high-technology sectors, and indeed, during the 1970s, Swiss industry as a whole extended its foreign-based activities considerably.

Swiss foreign direct investment consists almost entirely of the foreign operations of only about 90 multinational corporations. Much of the data shown in the following set of tables is drawn from the results of a survey of the largest Swiss industrial operations, conducted by the University of Basel, 15 of which account for at least 80% of foreign personnel and production of 1980. Nine of the multinationals surveyed employed more than two-thirds of their personnel outside of Switzerland.

The multinational activities of Swiss firms are concentrated to a high degree in the developed countries, particularly in Western Europe, although there is also a certain amount of activity in Latin America.

MAIN SOURCES OF DATA:

A **Official**

1 Union Bank of Switzerland, publishes concise statistics of the Swiss economy.

B **Private**

1 S Borner, B Stuckley, F Wehrle, & B Burgener, 'Global Structural Change and International Competition Among Industrial Firms: The Case of Switzerland', *Kyklos,* vol 38, 1985.

2 F Wehrle, 'Veränderung der Weltwirtschaftlichen Rahmenbedingungen und die Internationalisierung der Schweizer Industrie', Discussion paper No 2, University of Basel, July 1983.

3 S Borner, F Wehrle, "Die Sechste Schweiz – Uberleben auf dem Weltmarkt", Orell Fussli Verlag, Zurich, 1984.

4 Silvio Borner, *New Forms of Internationalization: An Assessment in the Light of Swiss Experience,* Switzerland: Institute of Applied Economics, 1983.

Note:
Data do not allow us to complete Tables A6, A7, A10 and A11 for Switzerland.

Table A1

SUMMARY OF THE COUNTRY'S INTERNATIONAL INVESTMENT POSITION

		Inward Investment	Outward Investment
1	Number of foreign affiliates in host country, and of foreign affiliates of home country firms	*N.A.*	*N.A.*
2	Number of foreign firms with direct investments in host country, and home country firms with direct foreign affiliates	*N.A.*	*N.A.*
3	Total foreign direct capital stock at book value as a percentage of GNP at factor cost in 1983	8.18	41.35
4	Flow of foreign direct investment in the five year period, 1980-84 (S Fr bn)	5.0	29.9
5	Employment in foreign affiliates or abroad, 1980[1]	*N.A.*	548,890
6	Output of foreign affiliates or abroad, 1980 (S Fr bn)[1]	*N.A.*	70.10

Source:

Union Bank of Switzerland, *Switzerland in Figures,* various issues; F Wehrle, 'Veränderung der Weltwirtschaftlichen Rachmenbedingungen und die Internationalisierung der Schweizer Industrie', Discussion paper No 2, University of Basel, July 1983; Borner & Wehrle, *op cit.*

NOTES TO TABLE A1

1 Refers to the 87 largest Swiss multinationals.

Table A2

PRIVATE FOREIGN CAPITAL STOCK, 1975 - 84 (S Fr bn)

	Inward Investment				Outward Investment		
	Portfolio	*Direct*	*Total*		*Portfolio*	*Direct*	*Total*
Book value for capital stock							
1975	*N.A.*	10.70	*N.A.*		*N.A.*	58.80	*N.A.*
1984	*N.A.*	18.50	*N.A.*		*N.A.*	99.14	*N.A.*

Source:
Union Bank of Switzerland, unpublished data.

NOTES TO TABLE A2

1 Figures have been re-estimated by the authors based on a multiplicative factor used by the Union Bank of Switzerland in revising its earlier data.

Table A3

FLOW OF FOREIGN DIRECT INVESTMENT, 1970 - 84 (S Fr bn)

	Inward Investment				Outward Investment		
	Reinvested Profits	*Other*	*Total*		*Reinvested Profits*	*Other*	*Total*
1970			0.9				5.8
1971			1.6				4.1
1972			0.3				4.1
1973			1.6				4.3
1974			1.0				8.4
1975			1.1				4.1
1976	*Not*		0.8		*Not*		4.7
1977	*Separately*		0.7		*Separately*		0.4
1978	*Available*		0.3		*Available*		−0.7
1979			1.0				5.8
1980			1.5				12.5
1981			1.6				1.7
1982			0.1				0.6
1983			0.8				4.3
1984			1.0				10.8

Source:
Union Bank of Switzerland, unpublished data.

Table A5

GEOGRAPHICAL DISTRIBUTION OF FOREIGN DIRECT CAPITAL STOCK, 1970 - 80 (S Fr bn)[1]

	Inward Investment				Outward Investment		
	Developed Countries	*Developing Countries*	*Total*		*Developed Countries*	*Developing Countries*	*Total*
1970-80	*Not Available*				13.9	2.4	16.3

Source:

S Borner, B Stuckley, F Wehrle, & B Burgener, 'Global Structural Change and International Competition Among Industrial Firms: The Case of Switzerland', *Kyklos*, vol 38, 1985.

NOTES TO TABLE A5

1 Data refers to the 15 largest Swiss multinational corporations only.

Table A8

INDICATORS OF THE SIGNIFICANCE OF INWARD FOREIGN DIRECT INVESTMENT OR THE ACTIVITIES OF FOREIGN-BASED COMPANIES TO THE NATIONAL ECONOMY, 1983

1	Direct capital stock of foreign affiliates at book value in 1983 as a proportion of:		
	a	GNP at factor cost	8.18
	b	population (in S Fr per head)	2,700.62

Source:
Union Bank of Switzerland, *Switzerland in Figures,* various issues.

Table A9

INDICATORS OF THE SIGNIFICANCE OF OUTWARD FOREIGN DIRECT INVESTMENT OR THE ACTIVITIES OF HOME-BASED COMPANIES ABROAD FOR THE NATIONAL ECONOMY, 1980 - 83

1	Foreign capital stock of home-based firms at book value in 1983 as a proportion of:		
	a	GNP at factor cost	41.35
	b	population (in S Fr per head)	13,635.80
2	Employment in foreign affiliates[1] in 1980 as a percentage of domestic employment		
	a	in all industry	18.22
	b	in manufacturing	79.35
3	Output of foreign manufacturing affiliates[1] in 1980 as a percentage of manufacturing exports from the home country		149.34

Source:
Union Bank of Switzerland, *Switzerland in Figures,* various issues; F Wehrle, 'Veränderung der Weltwirtschaftlichen Rahmenbedingungen und die Internationalisierung der Schweizer Industrie', Discussion paper No 2, University of Basel, July 1983.

NOTES TO TABLE A9

1 Figure refers to the largest 87 Swiss multinationals.

Table A12

LEADING FOREIGN AND DOMESTIC MULTINATIONAL COMPANIES, 1981-83

A Leading Foreign Multinational Companies in the Country, 1983		
Name	*Home Country*	*Sector*
BAT Industries PLC	UK	Tobacco
Beecham Group PLC	UK	Pharmaceuticals
The British Petroleum Company PLC	UK	Petroleum
The Burmah Oil Company	UK	Petroleum
Compagnie Francaise des Petroles SA	France	Petroleum marketing
Daimler - Benz AG	W. Germany	Motor vehicles
The Dow Chemical Company	USA	Chemicals
ENI	Italy	Petroleum
Exxon Corporation	USA	Petroleum
Fiat SpA	Italy	Motor vehicles
Ford Motor Company	USA	Motor vehicles
General Motors Corp	USA	Motor vehicles
Goodyear Tire and Rubber Company	USA	Rubber tyres
ICL PLC	UK	Computers
International Business Machines Corporation	USA	Computers
Minnesota Mining and Manufacturing Co	USA	Diversified manufacturing
Petrofina SA	Belgium	Petroleum/petrochemicals
Regie Nationale des Usines Renault	France	Motor vehicles
Royal Dutch / Shell Group of Companies	Netherlands/UK	Petroleum
Societe Nationale Elf Aquitaire	France	Petroelum
Standard Oil Company of California	USA	Petroleum
Texaco Incorporated	USA	Petroleum
Thorn EMI PLC	UK	Electrical consumer products
Unilever	UK/Netherlands	Consumer products
The Wellcome Foundation	UK	Pharmaceuticals

Source
John M Stopford, *The World Directory of Multinational Enterprises 1982-83,* Bath: The Pitman Press, 1982.

Table 12 (cont'd)

LEADING FOREIGN AND DOMESTIC MULTINATIONAL COMPANIES

B Leading Domestic Companies with Multinational Interests, 1981

Name	*Sector*	*Global Turnover ($ m)*	*Sales of overseas subsidiaries as % of worldwide sales (1981)*
1 Nestle	Food	14,120	97
2 Ciba-Geigy	Chemicals	6,924	57
3 Brown Boveri	Electrical	5,039	85[1]
4 Alusuisse	Metals	3,507	91[2]
5 Roche	Pharmaceuticals	3,450	97[2]
6 Sandoz	Pharmaceuticals	2,936	95[2]
7 Suizer	Machinery	2,057	80
8 Oerlikon-Burhrle	Machinery	2,031	*N.A.*
9 Holderbank	Building materials	1,496	86
10 Georg Fischer	Plastics, mechanical engineering	*N.A.*	*Not Available*
11 Schindler	Transportation equipment	860	
12 Asuag	Precision instruments	*Not Available*	
13 Landis & Gyr	Electrical equipment		
14 Von Roll	Mechanical engineering		
15 Hesta	Mechanical engineering		

Source:

S Borner, B Stuckley, F Wehrle, & B Burgener, 'Global Structural Change and International Competition among Industrial Firms: The Case of Switzerland', *Kyklos,* vol 38, 1985; J Stopford & J H Dunning, *Multinationals Company Performance and Global Trends,* Surrey: Macmillan, 1983.

NOTES TO TABLE A12

1 Outside EFTA – includes exports.

2 Includes all exports: direct and intragroup.

TURKEY

As part of her general post-world war II economic development strategy, Turkey decided to encourage direct foreign investment. For this purpose, a number of increasingly liberal foreign direct investment laws were enacted, most notably law 6224 (1954). This law contained no explicit restrictions on any kind of foreign direct investment, but was vague about where it might be permitted, stating only that it must 'aid the country's economic development'.

Nevertheless, the incentives for foreign investment in Turkey put forth in the early 1950s have created a favourable environment for foreign MNEs and indeed, since then, direct inward investment in Turkey has been on a rising trend. Since 1980 the Turkish government has been improving and simplifying foreign investment laws and regulations, and has been mounting active promotional campaigns. To coordinate foreign investment policy, a Foreign Investment Department was established in 1980. This department has the power to approve investments up to US $ 50 million, with foreign participation ratios up to 49%. For other investments, the FID has to refer applications to the Council of Ministers.

Most inward investment has been concentrated in the manufacturing sector, particularly in the chemical, machinery, electrical equipment and transportation vehicle industries.

The major sources of investment in Turkey continue to be West Germany, the USA, Switzerland and the Netherlands.

There are no data available on Turkish outward investment but, in recent years, Turkish construction companies have become extremely active in the Middle East. In 1983, for example, the number of Turkish construction companies working abroad was 283 compared with 22 in 1978. By the end of 1983 these companies held contracts worth more than $ 14 billion.

MAIN SOURCES OF DATA:

A **Official**

1 Turkish Ministry of Commerce: has conducted annual surveys of the DFI firms covered by law 6224, since 1973.

2 State Planning Organisation, Foreign Investment Department: provides data on inward investment in Turkey, by geographical and sectoral distribution.

3 UNCTC, *Transnational Corporation in World Development: A Reexamination,* New York: UN, 1978.

4 US Department of Commerce International Trade Administration, *Investment Climate in Foreign Countries,* Washington, 1985, vol I.

B **Private**

1 A Erdilek, *Direct Foreign Investment in Turkish Manufacturing,* Tubingen: Mohr, 1982.

2 Turkish Industrialists and Businessmen's Association, *The Turkish Economy 1984,* Istanbul, 1984.

Note:
Data do not allow us to complete Tables A9 or A10.

Table A1

SUMMARY OF THE COUNTRY'S INTERNATIONAL INVESTMENT POSITION

		Inward Investment	Outward Investment
1	Number of foreign affiliates in host country, and of foreign affiliates of home country firms at the end of 1984	267	*N.A.*
2	Number of foreign firms with direct investments in host country, and home country firms with direct foreign affiliates	*N.A.*	*N.A.*
3	Total foreign direct capital stock at book value as a percentage of GNP at factor cost in 1983	0.52	*N.A.*
4	Flow of foreign direct investment in the five year period, 1980-84 (T Lira bn)	75.53	*N.A.*
5	Employment in foreign affiliates or abroad, 1977	43,216[1]	*N.A.*
6	Output of foreign affiliates or abroad, 1977 (T Lira bn)	31.8[1,2]	*N.A.*

Source:

IMF, *Balance of Payments Yearbook*, various issues; IMF, *International Financial Statistics Yearbook, 1984;* A Erdilek, *Direct Foreign Investment in Turkish Manufacturing,* Tubingen: Mohr, 1982; State Planning Organisation, Foreign Investment Department, *Annual Report,* 1984.

NOTES TO TABLE A1

1 Estimate based on Ministry of Commerce Survey, 1977.

2 Sum of the total (domestic and foreign) sales of all DFI firms.

Table A2

PRIVATE FOREIGN CAPITAL STOCK, 1983 - 84 (T Lira bn)[1]

	Inward Investment			Outward Investment		
	Portfolio	*Direct*[1]	*Total*	*Portfolio*	*Direct*	*Total*
Book value of capital stock						
1975		8,558.8				
1978	*Not*	10,309.3	*Not*		*Not*	
1982	*Available*	33,572.5	*Available*		*Available*	
1984		85,167.9				

Source:

IMF, *Balance of Payments Yearbook,* various issues.

NOTES TO TABLE A2

1 Estimates based on cumulative investment flows as from 1960.

Table A3

FLOW OF FOREIGN DIRECT INVESTMENT, 1970 - 84 (T Lira m)

	Inward Investment			Outward Investment		
	Reinvested Profits	*Other*	*Total*[1]	*Reinvested Profits*	*Other*	*Total*
1970			667.0			
1971			673.2			
1972			614.4			
1973			1,113.4			
1974			1,222.8			
1975			2,208.8			
1976	*Not*		444.7			
1977	*Separately*		483.7		*Not*	
1978	*Available*		822.1		*Available*	
1979			2,331.1			
1980			1,384.6			
1981			10,591.7			
1982			8,955.8			
1983			10,346.4			
1984			41,249.0			

Source:

IMF, *Balance of Payments Yearbook,* various issues.

NOTES TO TABLE A3

1 Excluding reinvested profits.

Table A4

SECTORAL DISTRIBUTION OF FOREIGN DIRECT CAPITAL STOCK, 1979 - 84 (T Lira bn)

	Inward Investment[1]				Outward Investment		
	Primary	*Secondary*	*Tertiary*		*Primary*	*Secondary*	*Tertiary*
1973 - 79	0.16	13.84	2.28			*Not*	
1984	2.92	71.86	43.13			*Available*	

Source:

A Erdilek, *Direct Foreign Investment in Turkish Manufacturing,* Tubingen: Mohr, 1982; State Planning Organisation Foreign Investment Department as cited in US Department of Commerce unpublished data.

NOTES TO TABLE A4

1 Estimates based on cumulative approved investment flows, 1973-79, as monitored by the Foreign Investment Department of the State Planning Organisation.

Table A5

GEOGRAPHICAL DISTRIBUTION OF FOREIGN DIRECT CAPITAL STOCK, 1979 - 84 (T Lira bn)

	Inward Investment[1]				Outward Investment		
	Developed Countries	*Developing Countries*	*Total*		*Developed Countries*	*Developing Countries*	*Total*
1973 - 79	14.35	0.91	16.28[2]			*Not*	
1984	80.17	23.17	117.90[2]			*Available*	

Source:

A Erdilek, *Direct Foreign Investment in Turkish Manufacturing,* Tubingen: Mohr, 1982; State Planning Organisation Foreign Investment Department as cited in US Department of Commerce unpublished data.

NOTES TO TABLE A5

1 Estimates based on cumulative approved investment flows, 1973-79, as monitored by the State Planning Organisation.

2 Total includes 'unspecified' figure.

Table A6

INDUSTRIAL DISTRIBUTION OF FOREIGN DIRECT CAPITAL STOCK, 1973 - 79 (T Lira m)

	Inward Investment[1]	Outward Investment
	1973-79	
Primary	158.6	Not Available
Agriculture	7.1	
Mining & quarrying	151.5	
Oil	*neg.*	
Secondary	13,844.7	
Food & drink	1,002.6	
Chemicals & allied	2,401.1	
Metals	772.0	
Mechanical engineering	1,232.6	
Electrical equipment	2,086.5	
Motor vehicles Other transportation equipment	3,697.5	
Textiles & clothing	149.2	
Paper & allied	341.0	
Rubber	1,584.2	
Coal & petroleum products	571.7	
Other manufacturing	6.3	
Tertiary	2,277.6	
Construction	*N.S.A.*	
Transport & communications	22.6	
Distributive trade	4.6	
Property	*N.S.A.*	
Banking & finance	382.7	
Other services	1,867.7	
TOTAL	16,280.9	

Source:

A Erdilek, *Direct Foreign Investment in Turkish Manufacturing,* Tubingen: Mohr, 1982.

NOTES TO TABLE A6

1 Estimates based on cumulative approved investment flows, registered by the State Planning Organisation.

Table A7

LEADING SOURCE AND RECIPIENT COUNTRIES, 1973 - 79 (T Lira m)

	Inward Investment[1]	Outward Investment
	1973-79	
DEVELOPED AREAS	14,346.9	
Europe	10,901.2	
EEC of which:	8,690.1	
Belgium	405.1	
Denmark	561.6	
France	2,359.3	
W. Germany	2,374.8	
Italy	1,810.4	
Netherlands	768.7	
UK	410.2	
Other Europe of which:	2,211.1	
Austria	194.8	
Finland	34.7	*Not*
Sweden	28.5	*Available*
Switzerland	1,953.1	
North America of which:	2,931.7	
Canada	314.7	
USA	2,617.0	
Other developed countries of which:	514.0	
Japan	514.0	
DEVELOPING COUNTRIES	912.0	
Latin America of which:	108.0	
Bahamas	90.0	
Venezuela	18.0	
Middle East of which:	804.0	
Kuwait	804.0	
UNSPECIFIED	1,021.8	
TOTAL	16,280.7	

Source:

A Erdilek, *Direct Foreign Investment in Turkish Manufacturing,* Tubingen: Mohr, 1982.

NOTES TO TABLE A7

1 Estimates based on cumulative approved investment flows as monitored by the Foreign Investment Department of the State Planning Organisation.

Table A8

INDICATORS OF THE SIGNIFICANCE OF INWARD FOREIGN DIRECT INVESTMENT OR THE ACTIVITIES OF FOREIGN-BASED COMPANIES TO THE NATIONAL ECONOMY, 1974 - 83

1	Direct capital stock of foreign affiliates at book value in 1983 as a proportion of:		
	a	GNP at factor cost	0.52
	b	population (in T Lira per head)	1,267.40
2	Employment in foreign affiliates[1] in 1977 as a percentage of all employment		
	a	in all industry	1.97
	b	all manufacturing	5.71
3	Output of foreign affiliates[1] in 1977 as a percentage of all companies' output in secondary (ie, manufacturing industry)		7.78
4	Exports of foreign affiliates in 1977 as a percentage of all manufacturing exports		6.14
5	Percentage share of assets accounted for by foreign affiliates in selected sectors, 1974		
	Manufacturing Sector		44
		Food and Tobacco	58
		Non electrical machinery	43
		Electrical machinery	54
		Motor vehicles	38
		Metal goods	23
		Rubber	59
		Paper	56

Source:

IMF, *Balance of Payments Statistics Yearbook,* various issues; IMF, *International Financial Statistics Yearbook, 1984;* International Labour Office, *Yearbook of Labour Statistics, 1981;* A Erdilek, *Direct Foreign Investment in Turkish Manufacturing,* Tubingen: Mohr, 1982. T G Uras, *Research on Foreign Capital Investment in Turkey* as quoted in UNCTC, 1978, p 271.

NOTES TO TABLE A8

1 Estimates based on Ministry of Commerce survey, 1977.

Table A11

ROYALTY RECEIPTS AND PAYMENTS, 1977 - 81 (T Lira m)

	Payments			Receipts		
	To Affiliates	*To Non-affiliates*	*Total*	*From Affiliates*	*From Non-affiliates*	*Total*
1977	*Not Separately Available*		63.1	*Not Separately Available*		42.0
1978			*N.A.*			30.4
1979			40.2			40.2
1980			*N.A.*			99.0
1981			393.4			*N.A.*

Source:
IMF, *Balance of Payments Yearbook, 1983.*

Table A12

LEADING FOREIGN AND DOMESTIC MULTINATIONAL COMPANIES, 1979 - 83

A Leading Foreign Multinational Companies in the Country, 1979

Name		*Home Country*	*Sector*
1	Renault	France	Motor vehicles
2	BMC	UK	Motor vehicles
3	Fiat	Italy	Motor vehicles
4	M.A.N.	W. Germany	Motor vehicles
5	Henkel	W. Germany	Chemicals
6	Ciba-Geigy	Switzerland	Pharmaceuticals
7	Goodyear	USA	Rubber
8	General Electric	USA	Electronics, industrial equipment
9	Hoffman La Roche	Switzerland	Pharmaceuticals
10	Philips	Netherlands	Electronics
11	Pirelli	Italy	Rubber
12	Northern Electric	Canada	Electrical
13	Pfizer	USA	Pharmaceuticals
14	Mercedes Benz	W. Germany	Motor vehicles
15	Siemens	W. Germany	Electrical machinery and cables
16	Unilever	UK/Netherlands	Food products, soaps
17	Tuborg	Denmark	Food products

Source:
A Erdilek, *op cit.*

B Leading Domestic Companies with Multinational Interests, 1983

Name		*Sector*	*Global Turnover (US $ m)*
1	Turkiye Petrolleri	Petroleum	3.837
2	Koc Holding	Motor vehicles	2.298
3	Haci Omer Sabanci Holding	Textiles, rubber products	2.335
4	Beta	Construction	
5	ENKA	Construction	
6	Bimbol/Artek	Construction	
7	S Turkes/F Akkaya	Construction	
8	Soyak/M Bin Laden Co	Construction	
9	Tefken	Construction	*Not*
10	Goktas	Construction	*Available*
11	Saracoglu	Construction	
12	Oz-Su	Construction	
13	B Goren	Construction	
14	Dogus Insorat Ticaret	Construction	
15	Etrak Insaat	Construction	

Source:
Fortune, August 20, 1984.

DEFINITIONS

The Turkish legal definition of direct foreign investment includes any foreign equity capital participation in a firm, regardless of the distribution of either ownership or managerial control between the foreign and national partners.

A 'DFI firm' is one with any foreign equity participation.

Since 1973, the Turkish Ministry of Commerce (MOC) had conducted annual surveys of the FDI firms covered by Law 6224. The data on 50 variables obtained through these surveys were treated as confidential even on the sectoral level, and therefore were neither published nor disclosed. The apparent limitation of MOC surveys was due to the fact that not all the DFI firms reported by MOC to exist were in actual existence. Some existed only on paper, with founding decrees but without any manufacturing facilities or activities. Some were no longer DFI firms, ie their foreign partners had sold out their shares to local interests. All DFI firms are legally required to participate in the MOC surveys.

Source:

A Erdilek, 1982.

YUGOSLAVIA

Before 1967, foreign direct investment in Yugoslavia was not permitted, although there had been a number of agreements between Yugoslavia and foreign firms covering technical assistance, co-operation in production and the use of patents and other intellectual property. Legislation enacted in 1967 made possible foreign direct investment in Yugoslavia although the initial response was unenthusiastic. In an attempt to attract more interest by foreign companies, a liberalisation of the foreign investment regulations occurred during 1970-77, and since 1976 the flow of inward investment in Yugoslavia has shown an upward trend.

This investment largely takes the form of contractual joint stock ventures between foreign firms and domestic enterprises, in which the share of the foreign partner may not exceed 49%, and the resulting enterprise retains Yugoslav nationality.

The investment of foreign capital is permitted in areas other than banking and finance, domestic transport, trade and other services; until recently the bulk of investment has been in the manufacturing sector, especially in the chemicals, metal products and transportation equipment industries.

Western multinational enterprises have accounted for much of the foreign investment that has occurred; the major sources of inward investment into Yugoslavia have been Italy, West Germany, the UK and the USA.

MAIN SOURCES OF DATA:

A Official

1 Federal Committee for Energy & Industry.

2 OECD; publishes data on foreign investment in Yugoslavia, by geographical and sectoral distribution.

3 OECD, *Economic Review of Yugoslavia,* provides further investment data.

B Private

1 C Coughlin, 'An Economic Analysis of Yugoslav Joint Ventures', *Journal of World Trade Law*, Jan/Feb 1983.

2 C Chittle, 'Direct Foreign Investment in a Socialist Labour-managed Economy: The Yugoslav Experience', *Weltwirtschaftliches Archiv,* 1975.

3 M Svetlicic and M Rojec, 'New Forms of Equity Investment by Yugoslav Firms in Developing Countries', a study for the Research Centre for Co-operation with Developing Countries, Ljubljana, 1985.

4 M Verbic and M Miovic, 'New Forms of Investment; Yugoslav Involvement in Developing Countries' Investment Projects', a study for the Research Centre for Co-operation with Developing Countries, Ljubljana, 1985.

5 P Cory, 'Industrial Co-operation, Joint Ventures and the MNEs in Yugoslavia' in Rugman (Ed), *New Theories of MNEs,* London: Croom Helm, 1982

Note:
Data do not allow us to complete Table A9 and A11 for Yugoslavia.

Table A1

SUMMARY OF THE COUNTRY'S INTERNATIONAL INVESTMENT POSITION

		Inward Investment	Outward Investment
1	Number of foreign affiliates in host country, and of foreign affiliates of home country firms	*N.A.*	*N.A.*
2	Number of foreign firms with direct investments in host country, and home country firms with direct foreign affiliates at the end of 1980	199 [1]	316 [2]
3	Total foreign direct capital stock at book value as a percentage of GNP at factor cost in 1980	6.61 [3]	*N.A.*
4	Flow of foreign direct investment in the five year period, 1976-80 (Y Din m)	7,248	*N.A.*
5	Employment in foreign affiliates or abroad	*N.A.*	*N.A.*
6	Output of foreign affiliates or abroad	*N.A.*	*N.A.*

Source:
OECD, *Foreign Investment in Yugoslavia,* Paris, 1982; M Svetlicic and M Rojec, 'New Forms of Equity Investment by Yugoslav Firms in Developing Countries', a study for the Research Centre for Co-operation with Developing Countries, Ljubljana, 1985; IMF, *International Financial Statistics Yearbook, 1984.*

NOTES TO TABLE A1

1 Contracts involving foreign investment.

2 End 1982.

3 Represents total foreign direct capital stock as a percentage of Gross National Product.

Table A2

PRIVATE FOREIGN CAPITAL STOCK, 1980 (Y Din m)[1]

	Inward Investment			Outward Investment		
	Portfolio	*Direct*	*Total*	*Portfolio*	*Direct*	*Total*
Book value of capital stock 1980	*N.A.*	10,265	*N.A.*	*Not Available*		

Source:
OECD, *Foreign Investment in Yugoslavia,* Paris 1982.

NOTES TO TABLE A2

1 Represents cumulative investment flows from 1968 onwards.

Table A3

FLOW OF FOREIGN DIRECT INVESTMENT, 1968 - 80 (Y Din m)

	Inward Investment			Outward Investment		
	Reinvested Profits	*Other*	*Total*	*Reinvested Profits*	*Other*	*Total*
1968-71	*Not Separately Available*		1,104	*Not Available*		
1972-73			1,092			
1974-75			630			
1976			2,220			
1977			578			
1978-79			2,600			
1980			1,850			

Source:
OECD, *Foreign Investment in Yugoslavia,* Paris 1982.

Table A4

SECTORAL DISTRIBUTION OF FOREIGN DIRECT CAPITAL STOCK, 1968 - 80 (Y Din m)[1]

	Inward Investment			Outward Investment		
	Primary	*Secondary*	*Tertiary*	*Primary*	*Secondary*	*Tertiary*
1968-75	*N.A.*	2,196	*N.A.*	*Not Available*		
1968-80	*N.A.*	10,126	*N.A.*			

Source:
OECD, *Foreign Investment in Yugoslavia,* Paris, 1982.

NOTES TO TABLE A4
1 Represents cumulative investment flows from 1968 onwards.

Table A5

GEOGRAPHICAL DISTRIBUTION OF FOREIGN DIRECT CAPITAL STOCK, 1980 (Y Din m)[1]

	Inward Investment			Outward Investment		
	Developed Countries	*Developing Countries*	*Total*	*Developed Countries*	*Developing Countries*	*Total*
1968-80	10,214.2	51.0	10,265.0	*Not Available*		

Source:
OECD, *Foreign Investment in Yugoslavia,* Paris, 1982.

NOTES TO TABLE A5
1 Represents cumulative investment flows from 1968 onwards.

Table A6

INDUSTRIAL DISTRIBUTION OF FOREIGN DIRECT CAPITAL STOCK, 1980 (Y Din m)

	Inward Investment		Outward Investment
	1968-75	*1968-80*	
Primary	*N.A.*	*N.A.*	*Not Available*
Secondary	2,196	10,126	
Food & drink	112	553	
Chemicals & allied	516	2,503	
Metals	373	3,453	
Electrical equipment	72	234	
Motor vehicles / Other transportation equipment	547	1,753	
Paper & allied	201	442	
Rubber	260	597	
Other manufacturing	115	591	
Tertiary	*N.A.*	*N.A.*	
TOTAL	2,826[1]	10,265[1]	

Source:
OECD, *Foreign Investment in Yugoslavia,* Paris, 1982.

NOTES TO TABLE A6

1 Includes investment in the primary and tertiary sectors.

Table A7

LEADING SOURCE AND RECIPIENT COUNTRIES, 1980 (Y Din m)

	Inward Investment		Outward Investment
	1968-80		
DEVELOPED AREAS	10,214.2		Not Available
Europe	6,837.8		
EEC of which	4,459.0		
Belgium & Luxembourg	250.4		
Denmark	4.4		
France	290.0		
W. Germany	1,123.0		
Italy	937.6		
Netherlands	75.7		
UK	1,777.9		
Other Europe of which	2,378.8		
Austria	254.2		
Czechoslavakia	59.6		
Finland	19.2		
German Democratic Republic	138.3		
Leichtenstein	40.9		
San Marino	6.1		
Sweden	223.4		
Switzerland	1,637.1		
North America of which	3,376.4		
Canada	8.4		
USA	3,368.0		
DEVELOPING AREAS	51.0		
Asia & Pacific (except Japan or Middle East) of which	43.9		
India	43.9		
Latin America of which	7.1		
Panama	7.1		
TOTAL	10,265.2		

Source:
OECD, *Foreign Investment in Yugoslavia,* Paris 1982

Table A8

INDICATORS OF THE SIGNIFICANCE OF INWARD FOREIGN DIRECT INVESTMENT OR THE ACTIVITIES OF FOREIGN-BASED COMPANIES TO THE NATIONAL ECONOMY, 1980

1	Direct capital stock of foreign affiliates at book value in 1980 as a proportion of	
a	GNP at factor cost	6.61[1]
b	population (in Y Din per head)	460.3

Source:
OECD, *Foreign Investment in Yugoslavia,* Paris 1982; IMF, *International Financial Statistics Yearbook, 1984.*

NOTES TO TABLE A8

1 Represents direct capital stock of foreign affiliates as a percentage of Gross Material Product.

Table A10

DISTRIBUTION OF FOREIGN SUBSIDIARIES AND ASSOCIATES AND FOREIGN CAPITAL STOCK BY PERCENTAGE OWNERSHIP OF PARENT COMPANIES, 1980-82 (Y Din m)

	Inward Investment[1]		Outward Investment[2]	
	Number of Affiliates	*Value of Capital Stock*	*Number of Affiliates*	*Value of Capital Stock*
100% owned subsidiaries	–	–	211	
50–99.9% owned subsidiaries and associates	–	–	49	*Not Available*
Less than 50% owned subsidiaries and associates	199[3]	10.27	56	
TOTAL	199[3]	10.27	316	

Source:
OECD, *Foreign Investment in Yugoslavia,* Paris, 1982; M Svetlicic and M Rojec, 'New Forms of Equity Investment by Yugoslav Firms in Developing Countries', a study for the Research Centre for Co-operation with Developing Countries, Ljubljana, Yugoslavia, February 1985.

NOTES TO TABLE A10

1 1980

2 1982

3 Contracts involving foreign investment.

Table A12

LEADING FOREIGN MULTINATIONAL COMPANIES, 1980

Name	*Home Country*	*Sector*	*Yugoslav Partner*
Unilever	Netherlands	Food	P K Beograd
General Foods	USA	Food	Agrocoop
Rhone Poulenc	France	Plastics	OHIS
Dow Chemical	USA	Chemicals	OKI
ICI	UK	Chemicals	Soda-So
Bayer	W. Germany	Pharmaceuticals	Lek
Ciba-Geigy	Switzerland	Pharmaceuticals	Pliva
Hoechst	W. Germany	Chemicals	Pik Servo Mihalj, Jugohemija
Boots	UK	Pharmaceuticals	Galenika
Dunlop	UK	Rubber	Fadip, Jugohemija
Semperit	Austria	Rubber	Sava
Alusuisse	Switzerland	Metals	Bons Kidric
Gillette	USA	Metal products	Yugoslavia Commerce
SKF	Sweden	Industrial equipment	UNIS, IKL
Westinghouse	USA	Electrical engineering	Prva Petoletka
Atlas Copco	Switzerland	Industrial equipment	Fagram, Univerzal
Honeywell	USA	Office equipment/computers	Ei-Nis, Progres
Elektrolux	Switzerland	Electrical engineering	Universal
Fiat	Italy	Motor vehicles	Zeljezara Store
Volkswagenwerk	W. Germany	Motor vehicles	UNIS
Citroen	France	Motor vehicles	TOMOS, Iskra
Renault	France	Motor vehicles	IMV
Daimler-Benz	W. Germany	Motor vehicles	Fap-Famos
General Motors	USA	Motor vehicles	LZT Kikinda
Agfa-Gevaert	Belgium	Photographic equipment	Zorka

Source:
P Cory, 'Industrial Co-operation, Joint Ventures and the MNEs in Yugoslavia' in Rugman (Ed), *New Theories of MNEs*, London: Croom Helm, 1982.

NORTH AMERICA

CANADA

Canada is better known as a host country to, rather than as a source of, foreign investment. Foreign direct investment accounted for more than 50% of long-term capital inflows between the mid-fifties and mid-seventies but has since assumed a significantly lower share, and stood at 44% of these inflows at the end of 1981. At the end of 1981, companies whose equity was controlled abroad accounted for 50% of the capital in Canadian manufacturing, 44% in petroleum and natural gas, 46% in other mining and smelting and 26% of all industries outside of agriculture and finance. The United States continues to account for by far the largest portion of foreign ownership in Canada with a share of just under 80%.

Ever since the late 1950s there has been concern about the political and economic effects of such high degrees of foreign ownership in Canada. In particular, direct investment issues have brought about a series of issues of which three can be singled out. First, extra-territorial application of law and policy is not peculiar to the USA nor is it a one-sided issue. The underlying issue affects relations between other sovereign states and is far from being resolved. Secondly, the issue of the economic performance of foreign-owned firms in Canada led to the establishment of the Foreign Investment Review Agency (FIRA) in 1973. Thirdly, attempts by the Canadian federal government to regulate the petroleum and natural gas sector and to increase its share of the revenue generated have included a programme designed to substantially reduce foreign ownership in these sectors. In 1984, a Conservative government was returned to power since when a somewhat more liberal policy towards inward investment has been pursued; and early in 1985 FIRA was replaced by Investment Canada. In 1984 the Foreign Investment Review Act was passed, which required FIRA to review specified types of foreign investment to ensure significant benefit to Canada. This Act was repealed in April 1985 and subsequently replaced by the Investment Canada Act.

While Canada's share of inward flows of direct investment has declined sharply over time, its outward flow of direct investment has increased markedly. In 1967 the stock of accumulated Canadian direct investment abroad was roughly 20% of the foreign-owned stock in Canada; by the early 1980s this proportion had risen to one third. The stock of Canada's direct investment abroad is now about one half of its inward foreign asset stake.

The geographical distribution of Canadian foreign direct investment characterises that of a young investor country in that there is a high degree of concentration in a few regions. In recent years, however, there has been a steady trend towards a more diversified pattern. Worthy of particular note is the growing number of Canadian multinationals investing in developing countries and in Western Europe. One half of Canada's direct investment abroad in 1981 was in the manufacturing sector, 28% in the extractive sector (mining and petroleum), and 13% in financial services. Within manufacturing, beverages, non-ferrous metals, wood and paper and iron products have been the major sectors for Canadian investment abroad.

MAIN SOURCES OF DATA:

A Official

1 Statistics Canada

a Balance of Payments Division regular publication, *Canada's International Investment Position* provides data on inward and outward direct investment stocks.

b Business Finance Division (Corporations Section) regular publication, *Corporation and Labour Unions Returns Act* provides data on assets, sales and profits attributable to enterprises under foreign control.

c Financial Flows and Multinational Enterprises Division and Merchandising and Services Division regular publication, *Concentration and Foreign Control in Retail and Wholesale Trade in Canada.*

d Manufacturing and Primary Industries Division and Financial Flows and Multinational Enterprises Division regular publication, *Domestic and Foreign Control of Manufacturing, Mining and Logging Establishments in Canada.*

2 Canadian Balance of International Payments, capital accounts summary provides data on the annual flows of direct investment.

B Private

1 Maclean Hunter Ltd annually publishes *The Financial Post 500,* a report on Canada's largest businesses.

2 Talaat Abdel-Malek, 'Canada's Direct Investment in Western Europe', Technological Innovation Studies Program Research Report, Office of Industrial Innovation, Department of Regional Industrial Expansion, Government of Canada.

3 Steven Globerman, 'Direct Investment, Economic Structure, and Industrial Competitiveness: The Canadian Case', in J H Dunning *Multinational Enterprise: Economic Structure and Industrial Competitiveness,* Chichester: John Wiley & Sons, 1985.

4 A E Safarian, *Governments and Multinationals: Policies in the Developed Countries,* Washington, DC: British-North American Committee, 1983.

Table A1

SUMMARY OF THE COUNTRY'S INTERNATIONAL INVESTMENT POSITION

		Inward Investment	Outward Investment
1	Number of foreign affiliates in host country, and of foreign affiliates of home country firms at the end of 1978	10,023[1]	2,483[2]
2	Number of foreign firms with direct investments in host country, and home country firms with direct foreign affiliates at the end of 1981	5,786[3]	1,081
3	Total foreign direct capital stock at book value as a percentage of GNP at factor cost in 1984	19.75	9.84
4	Flow of foreign direct investment in the five year period, 1980-84 (C $m)	–1,920	50,022[5]
5	Employment in foreign affiliates or abroad, 1976	778,915[4]	*N.A.*
6	Output of foreign affiliates or abroad 1980 (C $m)	172,505	*N.A.*

Source:

Statistics Canada, *Canada's International Investment Position,* various issues; *Canadian Statistical Review,* various issues and Canadian Balance of International Payments, various issues in 'Direct Investment, Economic Structure and Industrial Competitiveness: The Canadian Case', paper presented at a conference by Steven Globerman; Statistics Canada, *Domestic and Foreign Control of Manufacturing, Mining and Logging Establishments in Canada,* 1976.

NOTES TO TABLE A1

1 Represents recorded number of Canadian concerns in which foreign capital is invested.

2 Represents the number of foreign concerns owned by Canadian enterprises.

3 Represents the number of foreign controlled corporations in Canada in 1980.

4 Represents the total number of employees of foreign enterprises and establishments in the logging industry, selected mining industries and manufacturing industries.

5 1978-82.

Table A2

PRIVATE FOREIGN CAPITAL STOCK, 1960 - 84
(C $m)

	Inward Investment			Outward Investment		
	Portfolio	*Direct*	*Total*	*Portfolio*	*Direct*	*Total*
Book value of capital stock						
1960	7,914	12,872	20,786	1,300	2,500	2,800
1965	10,076	17,356	27,432	1,897	3,523	5,420
1970	14,790	26,423	41,213	2,819	6,188	9,007
1975	28,077	37,389	65,466	4,250	10,526	14,776
1976	37,134	40,311	77,445	4,618	11,491	16,109
1977	42,345	43,683	86,028	5,312	13,509	18,821
1978	57,700	48,300	106,000	6,408	16,422	22,830
1979	63,600	54,300	117,900	8,100	20,027	28,127
1980	69,400	61,637	131,037	8,900	25,800	34,700
1981	82,400	66,525	148,925	9,300	32,537	41,837
1982	97,300	69,200	166,500	9,800	33,865	43,665
1983	104,200	74,570	178,770	11,300	35,833	47,133
1984	115,400	83,128	198,528	14,500	41,383	55,883

Source:

Statistics Canada, *Canada's International Investment Position*, various issues; Statistcs Canada Daily, 'Foreign Long-term investment in Canada', 28 October 1983; Statistics Canada Daily, 'Canadian Direct Investment Abroad', 27 April 1984; Statistics Canada, *Canada's System of National Accounts;* Talaat Abdel-Malek, 'Canada's Direct Investment in Western Europe', Technological Innovation Studies Program Research Report, Office of Industrial Innovation, Department of Regional Industrial Expansion, Government of Canada.

Table A3

FLOW OF FOREIGN DIRECT INVESTMENT, 1970-84
(C $m)

	Inward Investment			Outward Investment		
	Reinvested Profits	*Other*	*Total*[1]	*Reinvested Profits*	*Other*	*Total*
1970			905	1,915	315	2,230
1971			925	2,248	230	2,478
1972			620	2,183	400	2,583
1973			830	2,754	770	3,524
1974			845	3,247	810	4,057
1975	*Not*		725	3,734	915	4,649
1976	*Separately*		–300	3,933	590	4,523
1977	*Available*		475	4,928	740	5,668
1978			135	5,739	2,325	8,064
1979			750	7,309	2,550	9,859
1980			800	8,123	3,150	11,273
1981			–4,400	8,837	6,900	15,737
1982			–900	4,139	950	5,089
1983			200	*N.S.A.*	2,700	*N.A.*
1984			2,380	*N.S.A.*	4,025	*N.A.*

Source:
Statistics Canada, *Canada's International Investment Position,* various years.

NOTES TO TABLE A3

1 Excluding reinvested earnings.

Table A4

SECTORAL DISTRIBUTION OF FOREIGN DIRECT CAPITAL STOCK, 1970-84 (C $m)

	Inward Investment			Outward Investment		
	Primary	*Secondary*	*Tertiary*	*Primary*	*Secondary*	*Tertiary*
1970	9,805	10,767	5,851	870	3,207	2,111
1975	12,228	15,999	9,162	2,220	5,315	2,991
1977	14,541	18,397	11,745	3,003	6,570	3,936
1978	15,548	20,265	12,415	3,986	7,619	4,817
1979	18,192	22,124	13,944	5,191	9,876	4,960
1980	21,445	24,793	15,399	8,245	10,794	6,761
1981	22,876	25,839	17,780	9,161	15,244	8,296
1982	22,502	26,706	19,628			
1983	23,667	29,078	21,335		*Not Available*	
1984	25,893	32,301	23,582			

Source:

Statistics Canada, *Canada's International Investment Position,* various issues; Statistics Canada, *Canada's System of National Accounts;* Statistics Canada Daily, 'Foreign Long-term Investment in Canada', 28 October 1983; Statistics Canada Daily, 'Canadian Direct Investment Abroad', 27 April 1984.

Table A5

GEOGRAPHICAL DISTRIBUTION OF FOREIGN DIRECT CAPITAL STOCK, 1970-84 (C $m)

	Inward Investment			Outward Investment		
	Developed Countries	*Developing Countries*[1]	*Total*	*Developed Countries*	*Developing Countries*	*Total*
1970	25,995	428	26,423	4,620	1,568	6,188
1975	36,785	604	37,389	7,951	2,575	10,526
1977	42,976	707	43,683	10,446	3,063	13,509
1978	47,422	828	48,250	12,596	3,826	16,422
1979	53,273	987	54,260	16,696	3,331	20,027
1980	60,344	1,293	61,637	21,725	4,078	25,803
1981	65,296	1,229	66,525	27,969	4,568	32,537
1982	67,713	1,487	69,200	28,963	4,902	33,865
1983	72,849	1,721	74,570	30,277	5,556	35,833
1984	81,210	1,918	83,128	35,284	6,099	41,383

Source:

Statistics Canada, *Canada's International Investment Position,* various issues; Statistics Canada Daily, 'Foreign Long-term Investment in Canada', 28 October 1983; Statistics Canada Daily, 'Canadian Direct Investment Abroad, 27 April 1984; Statistics Canada, *Canada's System of National Accounts.*

NOTES TO TABLE A5

1 Including centrally planned economies.

Table A6

INDUSTRIAL DISTRIBUTION OF FOREIGN DIRECT CAPITAL STOCK, 1970 - 82 (C $m)

	Inward Investment		Outward Investment	
	1970	*1982*	*1971*	*1981*
Primary	9,805	22,502	940	9,161
Agriculture				
Mining & quarrying	3,231	3,969	393	3,143
Oil	6,574	18,533	547	6,018
Secondary	10,767	26,706	3,445	15,244
Food & drink[1]	1,400	4,198	974	2,434
Chemicals & allied[2]	1,611	5,256	121	2,296
Metals / Mechanical engineering / Electrical equipment / Motor vehicles	4,862	11,362	1,564	6,275
Textiles & clothing	221	612	*N.S.A.*	*N.S.A.*
Paper & allied	2,030	3,635	536	2,933
Stone, clay & glass	412	951	*N.S.A.*	*N.S.A.*
Coal & petroleum products[2]	*N.S.A.*	*N.S.A.*	*N.S.A.*	*N.S.A.*
Other manufacturing	231	692	250	1,306
Tertiary	5,851	19,628	2,153	8,296
Construction	*N.S.A.*	*N.S.A.*	*N.S.A.*	*N.S.A.*
Transport & communications	*N.S.A.*	*N.S.A.*	*N.S.A.*	*N.S.A.*
Distributive trade	1,699	5,216	273	1,371
Property	*N.S.A.*	*N.S.A.*	*N.S.A.*	*N.S.A.*
Banking & finance	2,910	10,969	406	4,164
Other services	800	3,443	191	2,761
TOTAL	26,423	68,836	6,538	32,701

Source:
As in Table 4.

NOTES TO TABLE A6

1 For inward investment represents vegetable and animal products. For outward investment represents drink only.

2 Rubber and coal & petroleum products are included under chemicals & allied.

Table A7

LEADING SOURCE AND RECIPIENT COUNTRIES, 1970 - 84
(C $ m)

	Inward Investment		Outward Investment	
	1970	*1984*	*1971*	*1984*
DEVELOPED AREAS	25,995	81,210	4,849	35,284
Europe	4,477	15,186	1,093	4,327
EEC of which:		13,349		3,446
Belgium & Luxembourg	255	357	35	64
Denmark	14	34	*N.S.A.*	80
France	405	1,250	87	305
W. Germany	240	2,359	87	257
Greece	*N.S.A.*	10	*N.S.A.*	*N.S.A.*
Ireland	6	22	47	414
Italy	68	135	46	128
Netherlands	446	1,837	34	348
UK	2,503	7,345	590	1,850
Other Europe of which:		1,837		881
Austria	3	22	*Not Separately Available*	*N.S.A.*
Norway	5	29		62
Spain	*N.S.A.*	*N.S.A.*		194
Sweden	126	375		*N.S.A.*
Switzerland	322	1,131	36	449
Others		280		176
North America of which:	21,403	64,210	3,399	29,629
USA	21,403	64,210	3,399	29,629
Other developed countries of which:	115	1,814	357	1,328
Australia	12	124	299	930
Japan	103	1,690	58	160
New Zealand	*N.S.A.*	*N.S.A.*	*N.S.A.*	103
South Africa	*N.S.A.*	*N.S.A.*	*N.S.A.*	135
DEVELOPING AREAS	428	1,918	1,689	6,099
Africa	180[1]	175[1]	187	148
Asia & Pacific (except Middle East or Japan of which:	98	427	114	2,188
Hong Kong	33	183	*Not Separately Available*	95
Indonesia	*N.S.A.*	*N.S.A.*		1,399
Others	65	244		694

Table A7 (cont'd)

LEADING SOURCE AND RECIPIENT COUNTRIES, 1970 - 84
(C $m)

	Inward Investment		Outward Investment	
	1970	*1984*	*1971*	*1984*
Latin America of which:	150	1,316	1,388	3,763
Argentina	*N.S.A.*	*N.S.A.*	*N.S.A.*	45
Bahamas	84	187	143	181
Bermuda	29	876	190	1,287
Brazil	*N.S.A.*	*N.S.A.*	*N.S.A.*	873
Jamaica	*N.S.A.*	*N.S.A.*	113	181
Mexico	5	2	50	271
Netherlands Antilles	7	99		*N.S.A.*
Panama	17	199	*Not*	*N.S.A.*
Trinidad & Tobago	*N.S.A.*	*N.S.A.*	*Separately*	11
Venezuela	3	3	*Available*	75
Others	5	30		839
TOTAL	26,423	83,128	6,538	41,383

Source:
As in Table A5.

NOTES TO TABLE A7

1 South Africa is included under Africa, and consequently appears within the developing area total.

Table A8

INDICATORS OF THE SIGNIFICANCE OF INWARD FOREIGN DIRECT INVESTMENT OR THE ACTIVITIES OF FOREIGN-BASED COMPANIES TO THE NATIONAL ECONOMY, 1976 - 84

1	Direct capital stock of foreign affiliates at book value in 1984 as a proportion of:		
	a	GNP at factor cost	19.75
	b	population (in C $ per head)	3,306.80
2	Employment in foreign affiliates in 1976 as a percentage of all employment		
	a	in all industry	41.18
	b	in manufacturing	44.69
3	Output of foreign affiliates in 1980 as a percentage of all companies' output[1]		
	a	in primary (ie, extractive) industry	49.70
	b	in secondary (ie, manufacturing) industry	50.63
	c	in tertiary industry (ie, services, etc)	18.34
4	Profits of foreign affiliates in 1980 as a percentage of profits of all companies in the host country[2]		
	a	in all sectors	38.40
	b	in manufacturing	53.46

5 Percentage share of assets, sales and employment accounted for by foreign affiliates in selected sectors 1976

	Assets	*Sales*[3]	*Value Added*	*Employment*
Primary Goods Sector				
Agriculture[4]	*N.S.A.*	7.6	30.4	30.2
Mining and Quarrying	57	} 60.0	51.4	49.6
Oil[5]	51		*N.A.*	*N.A.*
Manufacturing Sector				
Food and drink		36.4	39.8	34.1
Chemicals and allied	66	75.3	82.3	75.8
Metals[6]	11[7]	17.1	22.3	19.8
Mechanical engineering	*N.A.*	65.5	63.0	58.9
Electrical equipment	66	69.0	63.4	65.4
Motor vehicles	92	95.6	78.8	69.7
Other transportation equipment	45	46.8	*N.A.*	*N.A.*
Textiles and clothing[8]	27	37.6	50.7	43.6
Paper and allied	53	39.2	45.8	41.6
Rubber[9]	73	*N.A.*	69.1	62.5
Stone, glass & clay	*N.A.*	62.3	55.8	47.5
Coal and petroleum products	*N.A.*	90.4	93.8	92.8
Timber and furniture	*N.A.*	16.4	16.4	14.2
Other manufacturing	48	50.3	53.2	43.0

Table A8 (Cont'd)

INDICATORS OF THE SIGNIFICANCE OF INWARD FOREIGN DIRECT INVESTMENT OR THE ACTIVITIES OF FOREIGN-BASED COMPANIES TO THE NATIONAL ECONOMY, 1976 - 84

	Assets	*Sales* [3]	*Value Added*	*Employment*
Services Sector				
Construction		11.0		
Transport & communications	*Not*	8.3[10]	*Not*	*Not*
Trade & distribution	*Available*	28.7[11]	*Available*	*Available*
Banking & finance		9.8[12]		
Other services		23.8		

Source:
Statistics Canada, *Canada's International Investment Position,* various issues; Statistics Canada Daily, 'Foreign Long-term Investment in Canada', 28 Oct, 1983; IMF, *International Financial Statistics Yearbook, 1984;* Globerman, *op cit*; Statistics Canada, *Domestic and Foreign Control of Manufacturing, Mining and Logging Establishments in Canada,* 1976.

NOTES TO TABLE A8

1 Represents sales of foreign controlled companies to total sales of controlled companies (both foreign and Canadian) in Canada in 1980.

2 Represents profits of foreign controlled companies to total profits of controlled companies (both foreign and Canadian) in Canada in 1980.

3 Sales figures are for the year 1978.

4 The value added and employment figures refer to the share of foreign affiliates in the logging industry.

5 Represents petroleum and natural gas.

6 Represents primary metal industries.

7 Represents iron and steel mills. For aluminium, the foreign share in assets is 54%.

8 Represents textiles only. For clothing, the share of employment and value added accounted for by foreign affiliates are 12.8% and 14.2% respectively.

9 The figures for value added and employment include plastic products.

10 Includes other utilities.

11 Represents wholesale trade alone. For retail trade, the share of foreign sales to total industry sales is 15.9%.

12 Includes real estate.

Table A9

INDICATORS OF THE SIGNIFICANCE OF OUTWARD FOREIGN DIRECT INVESTMENT OR THE ACTIVITIES OF HOME-BASED COMPANIES ABROAD FOR THE NATIONAL ECONOMY, 1984

1	Foreign capital stock of home-based firms at book value in 1984 as a proportion of:	
	a GNP at factor cost	9.84
	b population (in C $ per head)	1,647.43

Source:

Statistics Canada, *Canada's International Investment Position;* Statistics Canada Daily, 'Canada's Direct Investment Abroad', 27 April 1984; International Monetary Fund, *International Financial Statistics,* 1985.

Table A10

DISTRIBUTION OF FOREIGN SUBSIDIARIES AND ASSOCIATES AND FOREIGN CAPITAL STOCK BY PERCENTAGE OWNERSHIP OF PARENT COMPANIES, 1978
(C $m)

	Inward Investment		Outward Investment	
	Number of Affiliates	*Value of Capital Stock*	*Number of Affiliates*	*Value of Capital Stock*
100% owned subsidiaries	9,298[1]	*Not Available*	1,787[3]	*Not Available*
50-99.9% owned subsidiaries and associates	725[2]		369[4]	
Less than 50% owned subsidiaries and associates	*N.A.*		327[5]	
TOTAL	10,023	48,228	2,483	

Source:

Statistics Canada, *Canada's International Investment Position,* 1978.

NOTES TO TABLE A10

1 Represents the total number of foreign subsidiaries.

2 Represents unincorporated branches.

3 Represents total number of subsidiaries owned by Canadian enterprises abroad.

4 Represents total number of affiliates owned by Canadian enterprises abroad.

5 Represents total number of unincorporated branches owned by Canadian enterprises abroad.

Table A11

ROYALTY RECEIPTS AND PAYMENTS, 1969 - 81
(C $m)

	Payments			Receipts		
	To Affiliates	*To Non-affiliates*	*Total*	*To Affiliates*	*To Non-affiliates*	*Total*
1969	*Not Separately Available*		168	*Not Separately Available*		4
1973			257			7
1977			460			31
1981			769			41

Source:

Statistics Canada, *Corporations and Labour Unions Returns Act,* various issues.

Table A12

LEADING FOREIGN AND DOMESTIC MULTINATIONAL COMPANIES, 1983

A Leading Foreign Multinational Companies in the Country

	Name	*Home Country*	*Sector*	*Canadian Turnover (C $ th)*
1	General Motors of Canada Ltd	USA	Motor vehicles and parts	13,805,450
2	Imperial Oil Ltd	USA	Petroleum	8,919,000
3	Ford Motor Co of Canada	USA	Motor vehicles and parts	8,580,600
4	Texaco Canada Ltd	USA	Petroleum	5,652,000
5	Shell Canada Ltd	UK	Petroleum	5,300,000
6	Gulf Canada Ltd	USA	Petroleum	5,078,000
7	Chrysler Canada Ltd	USA	Motor vehicles	4,325,500
8	Canada Safeway Ltd	USA	Retailing	3,437,683
9	Simpsons Sears Ltd	USA	Retailing	3,314,683
10	IBM Canada Ltd	USA	Computers	2,462,000
11	F W Woolworth Co	USA	Retailing	1,738,820
12	Mitsui & Co Canada	Japan	Retailing	1,663,932
13	Alberta & Southern Gas Co	USA	Natural gas	1,605,678
14	Amoco Canada Petroleum	USA	Petroleum and chemicals	1,501,040
15	Suncor Inc	USA	Petroleum, gas and chemicals	1,473,800
16	Anglo-Canadian Telephone Co	USA	Telecommunications	1,462,797
17	Canadian General Electric Co	USA	Electrical engineering	1,462,797
18	Mobil Oil Canada Ltd	USA	Petroleum	1,392,800
19	Mitsubishi Canada Ltd	Japan	Retailing	1,233,321
20	Dow Chemical Canada Ltd	USA	Chemicals	1,228,069
21	Ultramar Canada Inc	UK	Petroleum	1,175,838
22	Du Pont Canada Inc	USA	Chemicals	1,116,444
23	CIL Inc	UK	Chemicals	1,113,772
24	Cargill Grain Co	USA	Food Products	1,111,960
25	K-Mart Canada Ltd	USA	Retailing	1,001,979

Table A12 (cont'd)

LEADING FOREIGN AND DOMESTIC MULTINATIONAL COMPANIES, 1983

B Leading Domestic Companies with Multinational Interests

Name	*Sector*	*Sales (C $ th)*	*Sales of overseas subsidiaries as % of world wide sales (1981)*
Canadian Pacific Ltd	Metal refining, rail & other transportation services, retailing	12,759,297	27
(Northern Telecom) Bell Canada Ent	Telecommunications	8,874,700	
George Weston Ltd	Food products	7,799,500	
Alcan Aluminium Ltd	Mining & metals	6,418,339	78
Canadian National Railway	Railways, hotels, other transport services	4,625,100	
Hudson's Bay Co	Petroleum & gas, retailing, property	4,370,528	
Canada Development Corp	Petroleum & gas, mining & metals, chemicals	3,834,700	
Nova Corporation	Energy, chemicals, mechanical engineering	3,823,005	
Brascan Ltd	Beverages, paper, banking & insurance	3,555,000	
Hiram Walker Resources Ltd	Beverages, natural gas	3,402,826	47
Noranda Mines	Mining & metal refining	3,094,292	29
Canada Packers	Food products, chemicals & leather	3,001,447	15
International Thomson Org	Petroleum, printing & publishing, leisure services	2,808,989	
Dome Petroleum Ltd	Petroleum & mining	2,594,600	
Moore Corp	Paper products, printing & business services	2,235,047	90
Seagram Co	Beverages	2,222,934	93
MacMillan Bloedel Ltd	Wood products, pulp & paper	2,044,100	
Stelco Inc	Mining & metal refining	2,033,169	
John Labatt Ltd	Food products & beverages	1,928,712	
Massey-Ferguson Ltd	Agricultural & industrial mach.	1,894,344	92
Genstar Corp	Construction, mining, metals, chemicals, banking & property	1,826,700	50
Domtar Inc	Wood products, chemicals	1,820,000	
Atco Ltd	Petroleum, metals, timber & property	1,722,985	
Olympia & York Developments	Paper & wood products, mining banking and property	1,660,180 1,660,180	
Molson Cos	Beverages, forestry, chemicals & wholesale trade	1,461,008	25

Source:
The Financial Post Top 500, Summer 1984; Stopford & Dunning, *Multinationals: Company Performance and Global Trends.*

CANADIAN TABLES : DEFINITIONS

Foreign direct investment in Canada represents foreign investment in Canadian enterprises with some influence in or control of the management. It comprises the book value of long-term capital (debt and equity) owned by foreign direct investors in direct investment enterprises in Canada.

Canadian direct investment abroad is a measure of the stock of long-term capital at a point in time in equity and debt in foreign subsidiaries, affiliates and branches owned by Canadian companies.

In December 1982, a material change in the conceptual treatment of foreign direct investment was introduced by Statistics Canada. Direct investment estimates were changed to correspond more closely with the conceptual treatment of foreign direct investment flows as recorded in the balance of payments. Thus, foreign direct investment position estimates have been revised to include only the investment of foreign direct investors. Previously, the position estimates had included all the capital invested in direct investment enterprises in Canada from the country of the foreign direct investor. This meant that investment by foreign portfolio investors residing in the same country as the direct investor was previosuly included in the direct investment position estimates.

For example, if Company A (resident in country A) has a subsidiary, Company B (resident in country B), investments of other residents (not related to Company A) of country A in Company B would have been included as foreign direct investment under the previous treatment. Similarly, banks and insurance companies resident in country A, extending loans or debt to Company B would also have been included as foreign direct investment under the previous treatment.

The position estimates of foreign direct investment in Canada will be compiled on this basis in the future. Information has been collected on this conceptual basis only since 1975 and the data for the four years 1975 to 1978 have been presented on the revised conceptual basis. Total direct investment on the revised basis for 1975, 1976 and 1977 represent about 93% of the corresponding estimates on the previous conceptual basis.

It should be noted that the concept of direct investment as used in the position statistics continues to differ from the flow statistics in one important respect. Retained earnings accruing to direct investor is included in the position statistics whereas it is excluded from the flow statistics. However, short-term transactions with foreign direct investors are still excluded from the measurement of direct investment for both the flows and the position statistics.

Source:
Statistics Canada, *Canada's International Investment Position.*

UNITED STATES

The USA became the world's largest outward direct investor after 1945, though over the last twenty years its share has somewhat fallen back, while in the 1970s inward investment in the USA especially by European firms has taken off. In the 1960s US outward investment rose especially rapidly in European manufacturing, but more recently it has grown most notably in services, which have also proved a major area of expansion for inward investment. In recent years US firms have strengthened their activities abroad in developing countries almost as fast as in the industrialised ones, through for example, export platform or off shore investments in S.E.Asia. Investment from developing countries has also been expanding apace in the USA, accounting for 2.5% of total inward investment in 1970 and 7% in 1984 (excluding the Netherlands Antilles).

MAIN SOURCES OF DATA:

A **Official**

1 International Investment Division, Bureau of Economic Analysis (BEA), US Department of Commerce: publishes quarterly data on balance of payments income and capital flows, including fees and royalties, and summarises annually the direct investment posit position of the US. Also collects and publishes annually data on the operations of US parents and their foreign affiliates and of US affiliates of foreign direct investors, including information on assets, sales, employment and profitability. Comprehensive benchmark surveys are conducted periodically by the BEA, covering both balance of payments data and financial and operating data. Such information forms the basis of estimates derived from data collected in smaller sample surveys conducted in non-benchmark years.

2 US Department of Commerce, International Trade Administration: publishes lists of new foreign investments in the US.

B **Private**

1 *Forbes:* provides details of the largest 100 foreign affiliates in the USA.

2 *Fortune:* publishes a list of the largest 500 US and non-US companies in the world.

3 *Business Week:* gives figures on R & D expenditure by the largest US firms.

4 T Pugel, 'United States' in J H Dunnint (Ed), *Multinational Enterprises, Economic Structure and International Competitiveness,* Chichester & New York: John Wiley, 1985.

Table A1

SUMMARY OF THE COUNTRY'S INTERNATIONAL INVESTMENT POSITION

		Inward Investment	Outward Investment
1	Number of foreign affiliates in host country, and of foreign affiliates of home country firms at the end of 1980	12,510	35,789[1]
2	Number of foreign firms with direct investments in host country, and home country firms with direct foreign affiliates at the end of 1977	*N.A.*	3,540[2]
3	Total foreign direct capital stock at book value as a percentage of GNP at factor cost, 1984	4.36	6.37
4	Flow of foreign direct investment in the five year period, 1980-84 (US $ m)	89,571	34,319
5	Employment in foreign affiliates or abroad, 1982	2,435,143	7,196,691[1]
6	Output of foreign affiliates or a abroad, 1982 (US $ m)	515,722[3]	649,749[4]

Source:

Department of Commerce, *Survey of Current Business, August 1985, October 1984, August 1984, December 1984, November 1983, June 1982,* Department of Commerce, *US Direct Investment Abroad, 1977.*

NOTES TO TABLE A1

1. For 1977.
2. For those reporting in the 1977 survey, who had 24,666 foreign affiliates of the total 35,789.
3. Represents sales.
4. Sales of non-bank affiliates in 1977.

Table A2

PRIVATE FOREIGN CAPITAL STOCK, 1960 - 84 (US $ m)

	Inward Investment			Outward Investment		
	Portfolio	*Direct*	*Total*	*Portfolio*	*Direct*	*Total*
Book value of capital stock						
1960	11,508	6,910	18,418	12,632	31,865	44,497
1965	17,518	8,797	26,315	32,961	49,474	71,435
1970	67,491	13,270	80,761	43,275	75,480	118,755
1975	105,963	27,662	133,625	113,020	124,050	237,070
1976	128,284	30,770	159,054	145,609	136,809	282,418
1977	130,848	34,595	165,443	164,257	145,990	310,247
1978	156,202	42,471	198,673	212,270	162,727	374,997
1979	201,533	54,462	255,995	245,342	187,858	433,200
1980	241,716	83,046	324,762	301,191	215,375	516,566
1981	289,844	108,714	398,558	392,813	228,348	621,161
1982	378,110	124,677	502,787	508,833	221,843	730,676
1983	456,045	137,061	593,106	553,871	226,962	780,833
1984	527,856	159,571	687,427	561,713	233,412	795,125

Source:

Department of Commerce, *Survey of Current Business, October 1984, August 1984, August 1983, August 1982, August 1980, October 1972,* Department of Commerce, *Selected Data on U.S. Direct Investment Abroad, 1950-76,* Department of Commerce, *Selected Data on Foreign Direct Investment in the US, 1950-79.*

NOTES TO TABLE A2

[1] Represents the direct investment position of the USA which refers to the parents' equity in, and net outstanding loans to, their affiliates. (See Definitions.)

Table A3

FLOW OF FOREIGN DIRECT INVESTMENT, 1960 - 84 (US $ m)

	Inward Investment			Outward Investment		
	Reinvested Profits	*Other*	*Total*	*Reinvested Profits*	*Other*	*Total*
1970	434	-200	234	3,176	4,413	7,589
1971	542	-717	-175	3,176	4,441	7,617
1972	569	-189	380	4,532	3,214	7,746
1973	1,025	1,631	2,656	8,158	3,195	11,353
1974	1,065	3,695	4,760	7,777	1,275	9,052
1975	1,189	1,414	2,603	8,048	6,196	14,244
1976	1,659	2,687	4,346	7,696	4,253	11,949
1977	1,586	2,142	3,728	6,396	5,497	11,893
1978	2,583	5,313	7,897	11,343	4,713	16,056
1979	3,955	7,921	11,877	18,964	6,258	25,222
1980	5,177	11,741	16,918	17,017	2,205	19,222
1981	2,766	21,635	24,401	13,483	-3,859	9,624
1982	-2,379	16,171	13,792	6,706	-11,130	-4,424
1983	89	11,857	11,945	9,603	-4,209	5,394
1984	3,722	18,792	22,514	10,965	-6,462	4,503

Source:

Department of Commerce, *Survey of Current Business, August 1985, October 1984, August 1984, August 1983, August 1982, August 1980, October 1975, February 1973.*

Table A4

SECTORAL DISTRIBUTION OF FOREIGN DIRECT CAPITAL STOCK, 1959 - 84 (US $ m)[1]

	Inward Investment			Outward Investment		
	Primary	*Secondary*	*Tertiary*	*Primary*[4] 1	*Secondary*	*Tertiary*
1959	1,419[2,3]	2,885[2]	3,308[2]	13,281	9,692	6,762
1965	1,710[3]	3,609	3,609	19,229	19,339	10,906
1970	2,992[3]	6,140	4,138	25,159	31,049	19,272
1975	6,213[3]	11,386	10,063	32,520	55,886	35,644
1980	14,293	33,011	35,742	54,350	89,290	72,068
1981	18,346	40,533	49,835	59,511	92,388	75,351
1982	20,585	44,065	60,027	63,132	90,609	68,102
1983	21,285	47,665	68,111	67,135	90,171	69,656
1984	30,129	50,664	78,778	70,372	93,012	70,028

Source:

Department of Commerce, *Survey of Current Business, August 1985, October 1984, August 1984, August 1983, August 1982, October 1977, February 1973, November 1972;* Department of Commerce, *US Business Investments in Foreign Countries (Supplement to Survey of Current Business, 1960);* Department of Commerce, *Selected Data on on US Direct Investment Abroad, 1950-76.*

NOTES TO TABLE A4

1 Represents the direct investment position of the USA, which indicates the parents' equity in, and net outstanding loans to their affiliates. (See Definitions.)

2 For 1962.

3 Oil only.

4 Oil and mining only.

Table A5

GEOGRAPHICAL DISTRIBUTION OF FOREIGN DIRECT CAPITAL STOCK, 1959 - 84 (US $ m)[1]

	Inward Investment			Outward Investment		
	Developed Countries	*Developing Countries*	*Total*	*Developed Countries*	*Developing Countries*	*Total*
1959	7,423[2]	189[2]	7,612[2]	16,797	12,938	29,735
1965	8,582	215	8,797	32,312	17,612	49,474
1970	12,901	369	13,270	51,819	19,192	75,480
1975	24,563	3,099	27,662	90,695	26,288	124,050
1980	72,001	11,044	83,046[3]	158,350	53,277	215,375
1981	92,876	15,838	108,714	167,112	56,109	228,348
1982	105,414	19,263	124,677	164,312	52,618	221,843
1983	116,705	20,356	137,061	169,975	51,430	226,962
1984	137,751	21,820	159,571	174,057	53,932	233,412

Source:

As for Table A4.

NOTES TO TABLE A5

1 Represents the direct investment position of the USA, which indicates the parents' equity in, and net outstanding loans to their affiliates. (See Definitions.)

2 For 1962.

3 The previously reported estimate for the inward direct investment position for 1980 was S68,351m, of which S60,283m was from developed countries, and S8,068m from developing countries. This had been calculated on the basis of an extension of the 1974 benchmark survey using cumulative flows. It was revised as a result of the 1980 benchmark survey, largely taking account of previously unreported equity capital and intercompany debt transactions between 1974 and 1980.

Table A6

INDUSTRIAL DISTRIBUTION OF FOREIGN DIRECT CAPITAL STOCK, 1973 - 84 (US $ m)[1]

	Inward Investment		Outward Investment	
	1973	*1984*	*1973*	*1983*
Primary[2]	4,792	30,129	30,989	46,750
Agriculture[3]	*N.S.A.*	1,164		746
Mining & quarrying	*N.S.A.*	4,049	6,038	6,742
Oil[4]	4,792	24,916	24,951	39,262
Secondary[5]	8,231	50,664	44,370	110,647
Food & drink	1,279	8,141	3,781	9,078
Chemicals & allied	2,892	16,749	8,415	20,220
Metals	960	5,749	2,971	6,046
Mechanical engineering[6]	1,366 (Mechanical engineering and Electrical equipment)	3,513	11,811 (Mechanical engineering and Electrical equipment)	15,656
Electrical equipment		5,437		7,716
Motor vehicles		1,425	7,544 (Motor vehicles and Other transportation equipment)	10,613
Other transportation equipment		296		685
Textiles & clothing	*Not Separately Available*	420		1,550
Paper & allied		3,819	*Not Separately Available*	3,891
Rubber[7]		819		2,284
Stone, clay & glass		2,642		2,090
Coal & petroleum products		*N.S.A.*		20,523
Other manufacturing	1,733	1,679	9,848	10,295
Tertiary	7,533	78,778	25,955	68,720
Construction	*N.S.A.*	4,212		1,588
Transport & communications[8]	*N.S.A.*	1,649	2,837	2,746
Distributive trade	3,117	30,494	9,313	28,534
Property	600	16,899	*N.S.A.*	230
Banking & finance	*N.S.A.*	14,449	*N.S.A.*	418
Other services[3,9]	3,816	11,075	13,805	35,204
TOTAL	20,556	159,571	101,313	226,117

Source:

Department of Commerce, *Survey of Current Business, August 1985, October 1984 and August 1984;* Department of Commerce, *Selected Data on US Direct Investment Abroad, 1950-76;* Department of Commerce, *Bureau of Economic Analysis, International Investment Division, unpublished data.*

NOTES TO TABLE A6

1 Represents the direct investment position of the USA, which indicates the parents' equity in, and net outstanding loans to their affiliates. (See Definitions.)

2 For inward investment stock, only oil is included for 1973, while for outward investment stock, only oil and mining are included in 1973.

3 For inward investment stock, agriculture and mining are included under 'other services' for 1973; for outward investment stock in 1973 agriculture is included under 'other services'.

4 For inward investment stock 1973 and 1983, and outward investment stock 1970 also includes 'coal and petroleum products'.

5 Only includes 'coal and petroleum products' in 1983 for outward investment stock.

6 Represents machinery.

7 Including plastics.

8 Including public utilities.

9 Within other services, for inward investment stock finance and insurance accounts for S2,814m in 1973, while for outward investment stock it accounts for S9,726m. For inward investment stock, insurance accounts for S8,819m in 1984.

Table A7

LEADING SOURCE AND RECIPIENT COUNTRIES, 1970 - 84 (US $ m)[1]

	Inward Investment			Outward Investment	
	1970	*1984*		*1970*	*1983*
DEVELOPED COUNTRIES	12,901	137,751		51,819	169,975
Europe	9,554	106,567		25,255	102,461
EEC of which:		94,849			78,461
Belgium & Luxembourg	338	3,310		1,546	6,369
Denmark	*N.S.A.*	404		388	1,401
France	286	6,502		2,643	6,900
W. Germany	680	11,956		4,313	15,994
Greece	*N.S.A.*	60		*N.S.A.*	249
Ireland	*N.S.A.*	261		183	3,674
Italy	100	1,614		1,464	4,790
Netherlands	2,151	32,643		1,550	8,649
UK	4,127	38,099		8,016	30,851
Other Europe of which:		11,718			23,584
Austria		264		*N.S.A.*	551
Finland	*Not Separately Available*	80		*N.S.A.*	211
Lichtenstein		121			
Norway		304		306	3,460
Portugal		-2		*N.S.A.*	206
Spain		232		696	2,440
Sweden	208	2,222		656	968
Switzerland	1,545	8,349		2,631	15,065
Turkey	*N.S.A.*			*N.S.A.*	141
North America of which:	3,117	14,001		21,015	47,538
Canada	3,117	14,001		21,015	47,538
Other developed countries of which:	229[3]	17,183		5,549	19,583
Australia	*N.S.A.*	2,349		3,148	8,627
Japan	229	14,817		1,482	8,059
New Zealand	*N.S.A.*	52		140	578
South Africa	*N.S.A.*	-35		778	2,319
DEVELOPING AREAS	369[2]	21,821		19,192	51,430
Africa of which:		69		2,427	5,188
Algeria					66
Egypt					1,504
Ethiopia	*Not Separately Available*	*neg*		*Not Separately Available*	14
Ghana					181
Kenya					144
Liberia		73		896	*N.A.*

Table A7 (cont'd)

LEADING SOURCE AND RECIPIENT COUNTRIES, 1970 - 84 (US $ m)[1]

	Inward Investment		Outward Investment	
	1970	*1984*	*1970*	*1984*
DEVELOPING AREAS (cont'd)				
Libya			*N.S.A.*	193
Morocco		*neg*	*N.S.A.*	47
Nigeria			337	516
Senegal				29
Sudan		*N.S.A.*		263
Tunisia		*neg*	*Not Separately Available*	143
Zaire		*N.S.A.*		169
Zambia		*N.S.A.*		140
Zimbabwe		*N.S.A.*		44
Asia & Pacific of which:		929	2,260	13,297
Hong Kong		553	*N.S.A.*	3,310
India		12	295	463
Indonesia		*neg*	218	3,042
S. Korea		-112	*N.S.A.*	650
Malaysia		22	*N.S.A.*	1,118
Pakistan		19	*N.S.A.*	95
Philippines	*Not Separately Available*	121	640	1,102
Singapore		228	*N.S.A.*	1,965
Sri Lanka		*neg*	*N.S.A.*	7
Taiwan		70	*N.S.A.*	695
Thailand		17	*N.S.A.*	729
Latin America of which:		15,516	12,962	29,501
Argentina		243	1,022	3,054
Bahamas		182	408	4,061
Bermuda		1,091	242	11,455
Brazil		161	1,526	9,022
Chile		-5	758	627
Colombia		67	584	1,871
Ecuador		36	*N.S.A.*	
Guyana				12
Jamaica		900[1]	*N.S.A.*	553
Mexico		306	1,912	4,999
Netherlands Antilles		10,523	*N.S.A.*	-19,722
Panama		1,867	1,190	4,519
Paraguay		*neg*	*N.S.A.*	33

Table A7 (cont'd)

LEADING SOURCE AND RECIPIENT COUNTRIES, 1970 - 84 (US $ m)[1]

	Inward Investment		Outward Investment	
	1970	*1984*	*1970*	*1984*
DEVELOPING AREAS (cont'd)				
Peru	*Not Separately Available*	*neg*	744	2,992
Trinidad & Tobago		*N.S.A.*	*N.S.A.*	937
Uruguay		*N.S.A.*	*N.S.A.*	111
Venezuela		48	2,241	1,641
Others		96	–	–
Middle East of which:		5,159	1,545	2,992
Iran		17	*Not Separately Available*	43
Israel		497		443
Jordan		-8		38
Kuwait		4,211		-145
Lebanon		31		
Saudi Arabia		398		1,126
Syria		*N.S.A.*		4
United Arab Emirates		21		736
Other developing countries		148		5,557
TOTAL	13,270	159,571	75,480	226,962

Source:

Department of Commerce, *Survey of Current Business, August 1985 and February 1973;* Department of Commerce, *Selected Data on US Direct Investment Abroad, 1950-76;* Department of Commerce, *Bureau of Economic Analysis, International Investment Division, unpublished data.*

NOTES TO TABLE A7

1 Represents the direct investment position of the USA, which indicates the parents' equity in, and net outstanding loans to their affiliates. (See Definitions.)

2 Only Japan.

3 Including Australia, South Africa and New Zealand.

Table A8

INDICATORS OF THE SIGNIFICANCE OF INWARD FOREIGN DIRECT INVESTMENT OR THE ACTIVITIES OF FOREIGN-BASED COMPANIES TO THE NATIONAL ECONOMY, 1981 - 84

1	Direct capital stock of foreign affiliates at book value in 1984 as a proportion of:		
	a GNP at factor cost		4.36
	b population (in US $ per head)		584.48[1]
2	Employment in foreign affiliates in 1982 as a percentage of all employment		
	a in all industry		2.40
	b in manufacturing		6.60
3	Manufacturing output of foreign affiliates in 1982 as a percentage of all output in secondary (ie, manufacturing) industry		7.40
4	Exports of foreign affiliates in 1982 as a percentage of all manufacturing exports		6.70
5	Profits of foreign affiliates in 1981 as a percentage of profits of all companies in the host country[2]		
	a in all sectors		1.50
	b in manufacturing		1.00
6	Percentage share of sales and employment accounted for by foreign affiliates in selected sectors, 1982		
		Sales	*Employment*[3]
	Primary Goods Sector		
	Agriculture	*N.S.A.*	0.4
	Mining & quarrying	*N.S.A.*	3.4
	Manufacturing Sector		
	Food & drink	5.1	7.4
	Chemicals & allied	31.4	36.3
	Metals	6.1	4.4
	Mechanical engineering	6.9	5.8
	Electrical engineering	9.4	7.8
	Motor vehicles Other transportation equipment	4.6	3.9
	Textiles & clothing	4.7	1.9
	Paper & allied	7.9	7.7
	Rubber	4.2	3.7
	Stone, glass & clay	11.2	8.1
	Other manufacturing	*N.S.A.*	4.3
	Services Sector		
	Construction	3.1	1.3
	Transport & communications	2.3	1.1
	Trade & distribution	4.8	3.3
	Banking & finance	1.2	*N.S.A.*

Source:
Department of Commerce, *Survey of Current Business, August 1985, 1982, October 1984, December 1984.*

NOTES TO TABLE A8

1 1983.

2 Affiliates income (interest, dividends, earnings of unincorporated affiliates and reinvested earnings of incorporated affiliates) as a percentage of total profits (interest, dividends, personal rental income and proprietors' income).

3 Estimated using data on total employment in the USA as classified by establishment, and data regarding FDI as classified by enterprise.

Table A9

INDICATORS OF THE SIGNIFICANCE OF OUTWARD FOREIGN DIRECT INVESTMENT OR THE ACTIVITIES OF HOME-BASED COMPANIES ABROAD FOR THE NATIONAL ECONOMY, 1977 - 84

1	Foreign capital stock of home-based firms at book value in 1984 as a proportion of:		
	a GNP at factor cost		6.37
	b population (in US $ per head)		967.86
2	Employment in foreign affiliates in 1977 as a percentage of domestic employment		
	a in all industry		7.80
	b in manufacturing		27.00
3	Output of foreign manufacturing affiliates in 1977 as a percentage of:		
	a domestic manufacturing output		18.50[2]
	b manufacturing exports from the home country		247.20
4	Profits of foreign affiliates in 1981 as a percentage of all profits recorded by home-based companies[3]		
	a in all sectors		5.90
	b in manufacturing		8.10
5	Sales and employment of foreign affiliates of home-based firms as a percentage of that in selected domestic sectors, 1977		
		Sales	*Employment*
	Manufacturing Sector		
	Food & drink	13.5	28.3
	Chemicals & allied	38.0	69.6
	Metals	10.6	16.6
	Mechanical engineering	27.9	35.1
	Electrical equipment	26.0	35.1
	Motor vehicles	46.6	57.9[4]
	Textiles & clothing	9.8	7.1
	Paper & allied	15.5	23.7
	Other manufacturing	8.9	15.3
	Services Sector		
	Transport & communications	*Not*	3.6
	Trade & distribution	*Separately*	2.5
	Other services	*Available*	9.6[5]

Source:

Department of Commerce, *Survey of Current Business, August 1985, August 1984, August 1982, February 1982, April 1981, December 1979;* Department of Commerce, *US Direct Investment Abroad, 1977.*

NOTES TO TABLE A9

1 1983.

2 Sales of manufacturing affiliates as a percentage of sales of US-based manufacturing firms.

3 Affiliates income (interest, dividends, earnings of unincorporated affiliates, and reinvested earnings of incorporated affiliates) as a percentage of total profits (interest, dividends, personal rental income and proprietors' income).

4 All transportation equipment.

5 Finance (excluding banking) insurance and property.

Table A10

DISTRIBUTION OF FOREIGN SUBSIDIARIES AND ASSOCIATES AND FOREIGN CAPITAL STOCK BY PERCENTAGE OWNERSHIP OF PARENT COMPANIES, 1977[1]

	Inward Investment		Outward Investment	
	Number of Affiliates	*Value of Capital Stock (US $ m)*	*Number of Affiliates*	*Value of Capital Stock (US $ m)*
100% owned subsidiaries	*Not Available*		12 825[1]	132,526[3]
50-99.9% owned subsidiaries and associates				
Less than 50% owned subsidiaries and associates			11,841[2]	13,464[4]
TOTAL			24,666	145,990

Source:
Department of Commerce, *US Direct Investment Abroad, 1977.*

NOTES TO TABLE A10
1 Including 884 bank affiliates.
2 Consisting of 11,841 50% or less owned non-bank affiliates.
3 Including S4,370 m in bank affiliates.
4 Consisting of S13,465 m in 50% or less owned non-bank affiliates.

Table A11

ROYALTY RECEIPTS AND PAYMENTS, 1967 - 84 (US $ m)

	Payments			Receipts		
	To Affiliates	*To Non-affiliates*	*Total*	*From Affiliates*	*From Non-affiliates*	*Total*
1967-70[1]	88.5	111.0	199.5	1,321.5	472.3	1,793.8
1971-75[1]	185.8	162.0	347.8	2,412.2	698.6	3,110.8
1976	293.0	189.0	482.0	3,262.0	822.0	4,084.0
1977	243.0	191.0	434.0	3,554.0	920.0	4,474.0
1978	396.0	214.0	610.0	4,806.0	1,065.0	5,871.0
1979	471.0	235.0	706.0	5,042.0	1,150.0	6,192.0
1980	515.0	254.0	769.0	5,695.0	1,170.0	6,865.0
1981	429.0	264.0	693.0	5,867.0	1,386.0	7,253.0
1982	42.0	295.0	337.0	5,572.0	1,567.0	7,139.0
1983	170.0	282.0	452.0	6,275.0	1,579.0	7,854.0
1984	203.0	292.0	495.0	6,422.0	1,650.0	8,072.0

Source:
Department of Commerce, *Survey of Current Business, January 1980, March 1980, March 1981, March 1982, March 1983, March 1984, March 1985.*

NOTES TO TABLE A11
1 Annual average.

Table A12

LEADING FOREIGN AND DOMESTIC MULTINATIONAL COMPANIES, 1981

A Leading Foreign Multinational Companies in the country

Name	*Home Country*	*Sector*	*US Turnover (US $ m)*
1 Anglo American Corp of S. Africa	South Africa	Metals	27 805
2			
2 Royal Dutch Shell	Netherlands/UK	Oil & metals	26,329
3 Seagram	Canada	Drink	24,256
4 BP	UK	Oil	13,457
5 Fried Flick	W. Germany	Chemicals	6,521
6 Tengelmann	W. Germany	Retailing	6,227
7 BAT	UK	Paper/retailing & tobacco	5,794
8 Generale Occidentale	France	Retailing	5,426
9 Philips	Netherlands	Electrical	3,374
10 Bayer AG	W. Germany	Chemicals	3,030
11 Unilever NV	Netherlands	Food	2,706
12 Midland Bank	UK	Banking	2,654
13 Renault	France	Motor vehicles	2,589
14 Petrofina SA	Belgium	Oil	2,533
15 Nestle	Switzerland	Food	2,500
16 VW	W. Germany	Motor vehicles	2,500
17 Hong Kong & Shanghai Banking	Hong Kong	Banking	2,484
18 Cie Francaise des Petroles	France	Oil	2,354
19 Brascan	Canada	Paper	2,309
20 Schlumberger NV	Neths. Antilles	Electrical	2,300
21 Canadian Pacific	Canada	Railroad	2,150
22 ICI	UK	Chemicals	2,047
23 George Weston	Canada	Food	1,979
24 CIBA-GEIGY	Switzerland	Chemicals	1,887
25 Consolidated Gold Fields	UK	Mining	1,873

Table A12 (cont'd)

LEADING FOREIGN AND DOMESTIC MULTINATIONAL COMPANIES, 1984

B Leading Domestic Companies with Multinational Interests

	Name	*Sector*	*Global Turnover ($m)*	*Sales of overseas subsidiaries as a % of worldwide sales, 1981*
1	Exxon	Oil	90,854	74
2	General Motors	Motor vehicles & other transport	83,889	25
3	Mobil	Oil	56,047	65
4	Ford Motor	Motor vehicles	52,336	49
5	Texaco	Oil	47,334	67
6	IBM	Electrical & electronic equip.	45,937	48
7	Du Pont	Chemicals	35,915	17
8	ATT	Electrical equipment	33,188	*N.A.*
9	General Electric	Electrical equipment	27,947	23
10	Standard Oil (Indiana)	Oil	26,947	18
11	Chevron	Oil	26,798	*N.A.*
12	Atlantic Richfield	Oil	24,686	9
13	Shell Oil	Oil	20,701	*N.A.*
14	Chrysler	Motor vehicles	19,573	20
15	US Steel	Mining, metals, railways, wholesaling	18,274	*N.A.* *N.A.*
16	United Technologies	Aerospace	16,332	*N.A.*
17	Phillips Petroleum	Oil	15,537	21
18	Occidental Petroleum	Oil	15,373	32
19	Tenneco	Oil	14,779	19
20	SUN	Oil	14,466	26
21	ITT	Electrical equipment	14,001	47
22	Proctor & Gamble	Chemicals	12,946	32
23	R J Reynolds	Tobacco	11,902	21
24	Standard Oil (Ohio)	Oil	11,692	*N.A.*
25	DOW Chemicals	Chemicals	11,418	49

Source:

Forbes, July 1982; *Fortune,* April 1985; Stopford & Dunning, *Multinationals: Company Performance and Global Trends,* London: Macmillan, 1983.

UNITED STATES : DEFINITIONS

Foreign affiliates:

A foreign affiliate is defined as a business enterprise in which one foreign person owns, directly, or indirectly, 10% or more of the voting securities or the equivalent. After the 1977 survey, earlier data on the 1966 benchmark basis had to be revised to exclude those affiliates where no individual foreigner held at least 10%, but together foreigners of the same nationality (US citizens in the case of outward investment) between them held 50% or over. Affiliates report on a consolidated basis; the consolidation for a given affiliate includes all other affiliates in the same host country owned more than 50% by that affiliate. When a consolidated affiliate has operations in more than one industry, it is classified in theindustry that accounts for the largest proportion of its sales.

Foreign capital stock:

This is represented by the foreign owned portion of the book value of assets of foreign affiliates, consisting of foreign direct investors' equity in, and net outstanding loans to, their affiliates. Foreign capital stock is thus treated here as the direct investment position abroad or in the host country, or as parent companies' contribution to the total assets of foreign affiliates in the form of either equity or debt.

The position in incorporated foreign affiliates consists of the net book value of parent companies' holdings of capital stock and other contributions to affiliates, parents' equity in the retained earnings of affiliates, and parents' net inter-company accounts with their affiliates. The position in unincorporated affiliates is made up of parent companies' shares of the net worth of affiliates, plus affiliates' liabilities to investing companies, less affiliate claims on parents. For bank affiliates, the direct investment position is defined to include only their parents' permanent debt and equity investment in them.

The direct investment position at the end of a year is equal to the position at the beginning of the year plus equity and inter-company account flows, and reinvested earnings of incorporated affiliates (together FDI flows), and valuation adjustments. Valuation adjustments primarily reflect differences between transactions values recorded on the books of parent companies and foreign affiliates; parents' books are used to record FDI flows for outward investment, and affiliates' books to record foreign capital stock. Note that the valuation adjustment does not attempt to revolve assets at replacement cost; it is concerned with the net book value of affiliates' assets at historical cost.

Foreign direct investment

Direct investment flows are stated net of disinvestment and consist of equity and intercompany account flows to all foreign affiliates, and reinvested earnings of incorporated affiliates. Until 1980/82, unincorporated affiliates sometimes did not distinguish remittances of earnings from other cash remittances, such as the settlement of intercompany debt, so in their case reinvested earnings are included under equity and inter-company account flows. See the section on UK definitions for further qualification.

Royalties:

Royalties and fees measure payments for the use of rights or intangible property, and management fees. Royalties are payments for the use of copyrights, trademarks, franchises, designs, know how, formulas, techniques, manufacturing rights, and other intangible assets or proprietory rights; licensing fees refer to charges for the use of patents or industrial processes. Film and television tape rentals are excluded (here) as they do not relate to the transfer of technology.

Source:

Department of Commerce, *US Direct Investment Abroad, 1977,* Department of Commerce, *Survey of Current Business, August 1981, January 1980.*

OTHER DEVELOPED COUNTRIES

AUSTRALIA

Until the mid 1970s, Australia was mainly a host country to foreign direct investment, but as Australian firms have evolved their own competitive advantages, particularly in natural resource sectors, outward investment has begun to grow. At the same time, partly as a result of recent government policy, there has been a gradual indigenisation (or naturalisation) of foreign sudsidiaries in Australia; since 1983, domestic equity participation has been actively encouraged. In 1976, a Foreign Investment Review Board (FIRB) was set up, the task of which is to evaluate and monitor major inward investment proposals. In 1983, about one quarter of inward investment was directed to the primary sector, most of this being in mining. Services, notably distribution, finance and banking accounted for two fifths. Most direct investment originates from the USA, the UK and Japan, but inflows from the USA have been falling during the 1980s, while those from Japan and the UK have been rising. During the 1980s, the UK has been the leading source of portfolio investment, followed by Japan and the USA. In 1983, Australian companies owned direct investment assets abroad worth A S 3.4 billion, the leading recipient countries being the USA, New Zealand, Papua New Guinea and the ASEAN countries.

MAIN SOURCES OF DATA:

A Official

1 Australian Bureau of Statistics regular publications:

- a *Foreign Investment Australia*
- b *Foreign Ownership and Control of the Mining Industry*
- c *Foreign Ownership and Control of the Manufacturing Industry*
- d *Budget Paper on National Income and Expenditure*
- e *Research and Experimental Development Business Enterprises*

2 Bureau of Industry Economics: publishes occasional research reports on inward and outward direct investment.

B Private

1 Top 500 Corporations in Australia published in 'Australian Business', provides statistics on the largest companies in Australia.

Table A1

SUMMARY OF THE COUNTRY'S INTERNATIONAL INVESTMENT POSITION

		Inward Investment	Outward Investment
1	Number of foreign affiliates in host country, and of foreign affiliates of home country firms at 30 June 1983	3,221	1,614
2	Number of foreign firms with direct investments in host country, and home country firms with direct foreign affiliates at the end of 1983	*N.A.*	688
3	Total foreign direct capital stock at book value as a percentage of GNP at factor cost in 1983	10.68	1.98
4	Flow of foreign direct investment in the the five year period 1978-83 (A $ m)	8,377	2,486
5	Employment in foreign affiliates or abroad, 1982-83	266,155[1]	*N.A.*
6	Output of foreign affiliates or abroad abroad, 1982-83 (A $ m)	27,597[2]	*N.A.*

Source:

Australian Bureau of Statistics, *Foreign Investment Australia, 1982-83;* Australian Bureau of Statistics, *Foreign Ownership and Control in Manufacturing Industry, 1982-83;* Bureau of Industry Economics, *Australian Direct Investment Abroad: Effects on the Australian Economy,* Research Report 14; IMF, *International Financial Statistics,* 1984.

NOTES TO TABLE A1

1 Based on total employment in Australian manufacturing industry as at 30 June 1983 of 1,011,641, of which 26.7% is attributable to foreign ownership. This excludes single establishment enterprises employing fewer than four persons.

2 Based on total turnover in Australian manufacturing industry as at 30 June 1983 of A $ 82,320.6 million of which 33.5% is attributable to foreign ownership. This excludes single establishment enterprises employing fewer than four persons.

Table A2

PRIVATE FOREIGN CAPITAL STOCK, 1960 - 84
(A $ m)[1]

	Inward Investment			Outward Investment		
	Portfolio[2]	*Direct*	*Total*	*Portfolio*[2]	*Direct*	*Total*
Book value of capital stock						
1960	262	1,918	2,180	6	217	223
1965	506	3,439	3,945	28	288	316
1970	1,373	5,275	6,648	60	534	593
1975	2,891	7,037	9,928	104	882	986
1976	3,225	7,469	10,692	122	1,011	1,134
1977	3,988	8,121	12,109	154	1,204	1,359
1978	4,371	8,818	13,189	188	1,407	1,594
1979	5,095	9,985	15,080	176	1,522	1,698
1980	6,064	10,939	17,003	317	1,922	2,238
1981	8,709	13,428	22,137	221	2,142	2,363
1982	16,081	15,957	32,038	568	2,796	3,364
1983	24,979	18,082	43,060	866	3,359	4,225
1984	32,061	20,271	52,332	1,479	4,684	6,163

Source:
Australian Bureau of Statistics, *Foreign Investment Australia,* various issues.

NOTES TO TABLE A2

1 Equity investment is valued on a paid-up basis only while non-equity investment is based mainly on book value as at 30 June of the relevant year.

2 Represents portfolio investment and institutional loans.

Table A3

FLOW OF FOREIGN DIRECT INVESTMENT, 1970 - 84
(A $ m)

	Inward Investment			Outward Investment		
	Reinvested Profits	*Other*	*Total*	*Reinvested Profits*	*Other*	*Total*
1970-71	238	657	895	19	53	72
1971-72	224	646	870	30	91	121
1972-73	307	93	400	74	23	97
1973-74	430	186	616	100	145	244
1974-75	246	411	657	30	67	94
1975-76	612	-34	578	64	103	167
1976-77	655	408	1,063	99	156	255
1977-78	658	383	1,041	99	117	216
1978-79	824	513	1,338	160	65	225
1979-80	1,018	522	1,540	231	226	458
1980-81	829	1,560	2,389	199	246	445
1981-82	247	1,938	2,185	106	556	663
1982-83	-603	1,495	891	242	533	775
1983-84	591	1,450	2,042	296	1,224	1,519

Source:
Australian Bureau of Statistics, *Foreign Investment Australia,* 1982-83 and 1983-84.

Table A4

SECTORAL DISTRIBUTION OF FOREIGN DIRECT CAPITAL STOCK, 1975-83
(A $m)[1]

	Inward Investment			Outward Investment		
	Primary[2]	*Secondary*	*Tertiary*	*Primary*	*Secondary*	*Tertiary*
1975	1,566	2,418	3,054	*N.A.*	*N.A.*	*N.A.*
1978	1,710	3,003	4,106	257	488	661
1979	1,866	3,337	4,782	264	511	747
1980	2,162	3,467	5,309	376	644	901
1981	3,101	3,900	6,427	433	654	1,054
1982	3,748	4,778	7,432	593	909	1,293
1983	4,554	5,040	8,488	642	1,132	1,585

Source:
Australian Bureau of Statistics, *Foreign Investment Australia,* various issues.

NOTES TO TABLE A4

1 Figures are as at 30 June of the relevant year.

2 Excluding oil.

Table A5

GEOGRAPHICAL DISTRIBUTION OF FOREIGN DIRECT CAPITAL STOCK, 1978 - 83
(A $ m)[1]

	Inward Investment			Outward Investment		
	Developed Countries	*Developing Countries*	*Total*	*Developed Countries*	*Developing Countries*	*Total*
1978	8,216	602	8,818	769	638	1,407
1979	9,335	650	9,985	813	709	1,522
1980	10,183	756	10,939	1,005	917	1,922
1981	12,454	974	13,428	1,132	1,010	2,142
1982	14,313	1,644	15,957	1,582	1,214	2,796
1983	16,587	1,495	18,082	1,995	1,364	3,359

Source:
Australian Bureau of Statistics, *Foreign Investment Australia,* various issues.

NOTES TO TABLE A5

1 Figures are as at 30 June of the relevant year.

Table A6

INDUSTRIAL DISTRIBUTION OF FOREIGN DIRECT CAPITAL STOCK, 1978 & 1983 (A $ m)[1]

	Inward Investment		Outward Investment	
	1978	*1983*	*1978*	*1983*
Primary	1,710	4,553	257	642
Agriculture	130	292	23	57
Mining & quarrying Oil	1,580	4,261	234	585
Secondary	3,003	5,040	488	1,132
Food & drink	453	731	42	33
Chemicals & allied[2]	645	863	52	184
Metals	287	965	168	513
Mechanical engineering Electrical equipment	611	1,089	45	100
Motor vehicles Other transportation equipment	513	708	9	23
Textiles & clothing	122	162	8	14
Paper & allied	116	141	42	73
Rubber	*N.S.A.*	*N.S.A.*	*N.S.A.*	*N.S.A.*
Stone, clay & glass	90	168	97	165
Coal & petroleum products[2]	*N.S.A.*	*N.S.A.*	*N.S.A.*	*N.S.A.*
Other manufacturing	138	176	10	20
Tertiary	4,106	8,490	661	1,585
Construction	137	234	39	67
Transport & communications[3]	191	182	62	224
Distributive trade	2,023	4,326	220	352
Property Banking & finance	1,654	3,410	327	842
Other services[3]	101	338	13	91
TOTAL	8,818	18,082	1,407	3,359

Source:

Australian Bureau of Statistics, *Foreign Investment Australia, 1982-83.*

NOTES TO TABLE A6

1 Figures are as at 30 June of the relevant year.

2 Coal and petroleum products are included under chemicals and allied.

3 Communications are included in other services.

Table A7

LEADING SOURCE AND RECIPIENT COUNTRIES, 1978-83
(A $ m)[1]

	Inward Investment		Outward Investment	
	1978	*1983*	*1978*	*1983*
DEVELOPED AREAS	8,216	16,587	769	1,995
Europe	4,015	7,013	289	542
EEC of which:	3,635	6,410	281	537
Belgium & Luxembourg	102	117	9	14
Denmark	17	9	*N.A.*	*N.A.*
France	216	539	2	6
W. Germany	186	571	10	39
Greece	1	3	*N.A.*	*N.A.*
Ireland	6	55	1	11
Italy	47	108	5	2
Netherlands	170	507	49	113
UK	2,890	4,501	205	352
Other Europe of which:	380	603	8	5
Austria	5	4		
Finland	*N.A.*	1	*Not Available*	*Not Available*
Norway	3	4		
Spain	1	7	6	2
Sweden	118	181	*N.A.*	*N.A.*
Switzerland	226	367	*N.A.*	3
North America of which:	3,612	7,709	158	792
Canada	263	502	35	67
USA	3,349	7,207	123	725
Other developed countries of which:	589	1,865	322	661
Japan	504	1,654	5	140
New Zealand	72	163	304	508
South Africa	4	14	13	13
DEVELOPING AREAS	602	1,495	638	1,364
Africa	63	11	3	28
Asia & Pacific of which:	185	1,060	591	1,076
Fiji	*N.A.*	2	47	95
Hong Kong	110	330	55	128
India	*N.A.*	*N.A.*	*N.A.*	*N.A.*
Indonesia	1	2	53	73
S. Korea	*N.A.*	33	*N.A.*	*N.A.*

Table A7 (cont'd)

LEADING SOURCE AND RECIPIENT COUNTRIES, 1978-83
(A $ m)[1]

	Inward Investment		Outward Investment	
	1978	*1983*	*1978*	*1983*
Malaysia	6	72	31	62
Papua New Guinea	41	7	296	447
Philippines	-2	3	13	22
Singapore	18	519	51	195
Latin America of which:	359	409	36	254
Bahamas	62	50	*Not Available*	*Not Available*
Bermuda	60	149		
Brazil	3	7		
Netherlands Antilles	38	4	18	202
Panama	*N.A.*	32	*N.A.*	*N.A.*
Middle East	-5	15	2	1
Other developing countries	—	—	7	5
TOTAL	8,818	18,082	1,407	3,359

Source:
As for Table A5.

NOTES TO TABLE A7

1 Figures are as at 30 June of the relevant year.

Table A8

INDICATORS OF THE SIGNIFICANCE OF INWARD FOREIGN DIRECT INVESTMENT OF THE ACTIVITIES OF FOREIGN-BASED COMPANIES TO THE NATIONAL ECONOMY, 1982 - 83

1	Direct capital stock of foreign affiliates at book value in 1983 as a proportion of:	
	a GNP at factor cost	10.7
	b population (in A $ per head)	1,173.4
2	Employment in foreign affiliates in 1982-83 as a percentage of all employment in manufacturing	21.6
3	Profits of foreign affiliates in 1982-83 as a percentage of profits of all companies in the host country in all sectors	22.6[1]

4 Percentage share of sales, value added and employment accounted for by foreign affiliates in selected sectors, 1982-83

	Sales	*Value added*	*Employment*
Primary Goods Sector			
Mining	*N.A.*	33.6	24.8
Manufacturing Sector			
Food & drink	25.6	29.0	25.5
Chemicals & allied	65.7	66.8	59.6
Metals	30.7	28.7	22.5
Mechanical engineering	32.9	29.4	25.1
Electrical equipment	43.3	44.4	37.1
Motor vehicles; Other transportation equipment	61.9	51.8	43.0
Textiles & clothing	22.3	22.9	18.7
Paper & allied	15.6	15.2	12.2
Rubber	41.1	46.0	37.3
Stone, glass & clay	21.7	21.5	20.6
Coal & petroleum products	59.0	78.2	80.8
Timber & furniture	9.9	9.8	6.9
Other manufacturing	13.3	13.9	10.1

Sources:

Australian Bureau of Statistics, *Foreign Ownership and Control of the Mining Industry and Selected Mineral Processing Industries, 1982-83; Foreign Ownership and Control of the Manufacturing Industry, 1982-83;* Foreign Investment, *Australia, Preliminary, 1983-84; Budget Paper on National Income and Expenditure, 1983-84.*

NOTES TO TABLE A8

1 Based on net profits after tax of A $ 1,705 million attributable to foreign direct investors from all sectors expressed as a percentage of net profits after tax of all companies in Australia of A $ 7,577 million (after making appropriate allowances for stock valuation adjustment).

Table A9

INDICATORS OF THE SIGNIFICANCE OF OUTWARD FOREIGN DIRECT INVESTMENT OR THE ACTIVITIES OF HOME-BASED COMPANIES ABROAD FOR THE NATIONAL ECONOMY, 1983 - 84

1	Foreign capital stock of home-based firms at book value in 1983 as a proportion of:	
	a GNP at factor cost	1.98
	b population (in A $ per head)	217.98
2	Profits of foreign affiliates in 1983-84 as a percentage of all profits recorded by home-based companies	
	in all sectors	6.31[1]

Source:

Australian Bureau of Statistics, *Foreign Investment Australia: Preliminary 1983-84; Budget Paper on National Income and Expenditure, 1983-84.*

NOTES TO TABLE A9

1 Represents net profits after tax of Australian direct investors from abroad of A $ 477 million as a percentage of net profits of all companies in Australia.

Table A10

DISTRIBUTION OF FOREIGN SUBSIDIARIES AND ASSOCIATES AND FOREIGN CAPITAL STOCK BY PERCENTAGE OWNERSHIP OF PARENT COMPANIES, 1983 (A $ m)

	Inward Investment		Outward Investment	
	Number of Affiliates	*Value of Capital Stock*	*Number of Affiliates*	*Value of Capital Stock*
100% owned subsidiaries	2,579	15,461	*Not Available*	
50-99.9% owned subsidiaries and associates	358	1,904		
Less than 50% owned subsidiaries and associates[1]	284	717		
TOTAL	3,221	18,082	1,614	3,359

Source:
Australian Bureau of Statistics, *Foreign Investment Australia, 1982-83.*

NOTES TO TABLE A10

1 Represents 25-50% share of equity held by foreign direct investors.

Table A11

ROYALTY RECEIPTS AND PAYMENTS, 1976 - 82 (A $ m)[1]

	Payments			Receipts		
	To Affiliates	*From Non-affiliates*	*Total*	*From Affiliates*	*To Non-affiliates*	*Total*
1976-77	48.8	16.3	65.1	3.2	3.9	7.1
1978-79	79.0	27.6	106.6	5.9	5.7	11.6
1981-82	93.4	30.5	123.9	5.1	7.1	12.2

Source:
Australian Bureau of Statistics, *Research and Experimental Development, Business Enterprises,* 1981-82 and 1978-79 issues.

NOTES TO TABLE A11

1 Represents receipts and payments from technical know-how.

Table A12

LEADING FOREIGN AND DOMESTIC MULTINATIONAL COMPANIES

A Leading Foreign Multinational Companies in the Country, 1981

	Name	*Home Country*	*Sector*	*Australian Turnover (A $ th)*
1	Shell Australia	Netherlands/UK	Petroleum	2,484,850
2	CRA[1]	UK	Metals	1,828,100
3	BP Australia	UK	Petroleum	1,784,740
4	Mobil Oil Australia	USA	Petroleum	1,629,880
5	Mitsui Australia	Japan	Metals, machinery	1,300,000
6	ICI Australia	UK	Chemicals	1,265,480
7	Dalgety Australia	UK	Food Products	1,023,640
8	General Motors Holden	USA	Motor vehicles	991,187
9	Ford Motor Co	USA	Motor vehicles	878,800
10	Alcoa Australia	USA	Metals	868,900
11	C. Itoh Australia	Japan	Distributive trade	835,000
12	Marubeni Australia	Japan	Various	723,644
13	Esso Australia	USA	Petroleum	661,000
14	Australian Safeway	USA	Distributive trade	611,422
15	Metal Manufacturers Ltd	UK	Metals	461,577
16	Hamersley Ltd	UK	Metals	449,420
17	Unilever Australia	UK	Food products	445,000
18	Mitsubishi Australia	Japan	Engineering	428,000
19	Philip Morris Australia Ltd	USA	Tobacco	427,591
20	Philips Industries Holdings Ltd	Netherlands	Electrical engineering	416,000
21	AMOCO Holdings Pty Ltd	USA	Petroleum	414,000
22	George Weston Foods Ltd	UK	Food products	409,185
23	Sumitomo Australia Ltd	Japan	Metals, machinery	400,000
24	AM International	USA	Machinery	339,490
25	International Harvester Ltd Australia	USA	Machinery	292,539

Table A12 (cont'd)

LEADING FOREIGN AND DOMESTIC MULTINATIONAL COMPANIES

B Leading Domestic Companies with Multinational Interests, 1981

	Name	*Sector*	*Global Turnover (A $ th)*
1	BHP	Metals	4,577,740
2	CSR Ltd	Chemicals, food & mining	2,932,500
3	Elders IXL Ltd	Agriculture, chemicals, etc	2,457,270
4	Australia & New Zealand Banking Group	Banking	2,027,040
5	Amatil Ltd[1]	Tobacco	1,325,000
6	National Commercial Banking Group of Australia	Banking	1,233,070
7	Dunlop Olympic Ltd	Chemicals & commodities	1,114,080
8	News Corp Ltd	Paper, printing & publishing	1,064,300
9	Pioneer Concrete Services Ltd	Building	1,027,530
10	Thomas Nationwide Transport Ltd	Services	1,002,920
11	Burns, Philip & Co	Shipping	1,002,000
12	The National Mutual Life Association of Australasia	Services	910,901
13	Australian Paper Manufacturers Ltd	Paper	828,228
14	James Hardi Industries Ltd	Building	749,889
15	HC Sleight Ltd	Commodities, shipping, etc	727,287
16	MIM Holdings Ltd[1]	Mining & metals	721,429
17	Comalco Ltd[1]	Mining & metals	719,874
18	Wormald International Ltd	Engineering	718,113
19	Castlemaine Tooheys Ltd	Food & drink	674,106
20	Westralian Farmers Cooperative	Agriculture	630,403
21	David Jones Ltd	Distributive trade	586,592
22	Tubemakers of Australia Ltd	Mining & metals	570,314
23	Peko-Wallsend Ltd	Mining & metals	561,515
24	Australian National Industries Ltd	Finance, construction, distribution, etc	560,200
25	Repco Corp Ltd	Finance, automotive, mechanical engineering	554,849

Source:

Top 500 Corporations in 'Australian Businesses'.

NOTES TO TABLE A12

1 A naturalized company. A company is granted naturalized status by the Government if it is at least 51% Australian owned. Its articles of association provide that a majority of members of its board be Australian citizens and general understanding have been reached between the company, major shareholder interests and the government about the exercise of voting powers in respect of the company's business in Australia.

AUSTRALIAN TABLES: DEFINITIONS

In distinguishing between direct investment and portfolio investment, *direct investment* in Australia is defined as:

a investment in Australian branches of foreign enterprises by the foreign head office or other related foreign enterprises,

b investment (both equity and non-equity) in an enterprise in Australia:

i by a single foreign resident (individual enterprise) or group of related enterprises in the one foreign country which owns 25% or more of the ordinary shares or voting stock of that enterprise and by foreign enterprises related to that foreign resident or group of related enterprises;

or, if this condition does not apply,

ii by residents of one foreign country, who together own 50% or more of the ordinary shares or voting stock of that enterprise, and foreign enterprises related to these residents.

c investment in an enterprise in Australia, which is a subsidiary (in terms of the Companies Act) of another enterprise in Australia referred to in (a) or (b) above, by the direct foreign investor(s).

On the basis of the above definition, it is possible for an enterprise in Australia to have direct foreign shareholders in more than one foreign country, eg, in the case where two foreign enterprises in different countries each hold 25% or more of the equity of the enterprise in Australia.

Similarly, Australian direct investment abroad relates to investment in foreign branches by enterprises in Australia and to investment by enterprises, or a group of related enterprises, in Australia in foreign enterprises in which they own 25% or more of the ordinary shares or voting stock. However, it is not possible to identify foreign enterprises in which unrelated enterprises in Australia or individual Australian residents own 50% or more of the equity, as sufficient information is not available on shares held in foreign enterprises by Australian investors.

Portfolio investment and institutional loans in Australia is all foreign investment other than direct investment, eg, investment in public issues of shares, debentures, etc and loans by unrelated financial institutions. This component of foreign investment in Australia also includes investment in company securities by foreign investors who invest through a nominee in Australia or who use an Australian address for the purpose of investing in Australia, unless such investment constitutes direct investment as defined above. In addition, all investment in unit trusts, mutual funds and land trusts is regarded as portfolio investment even where a majority of units in these funds is held by related foreign investors. This treatment is adopted because of the generally limited voting rights attached to these types of units. The portfolio investment and institutional loans component of Australian investment abroad covers investment in securities issued by foreign enterprises (other than that classified as direct investment), including changes in Australian residents' holdings of securities registered on Australian branch registers of foreign enterprises; investments in real estate and amounts which enterprises hold abroad temporarily, such as proceeds from the sale of foreign assets, from exports or from foreign borrowings.

The purpose of classifying foreign investment into direct investment and portfolio investment and institutional loans is to attempt to distinguish between investment which is accompanied by some degree of control, or potential control, over the operations of the enterprise in which the funds are invested, and investment which is not accompanied by such control. It should be noted that, although direct investment enterprises in Australia are not necessarily foreign controlled as defined in Australian Bureau of Statistics foreign ownership and control statistics, a study has shown that this is so in virtually all cases. No corresponding study has yet been made of foreign enterprises receiving direct investment from Australian enterprises. As the latter could themselves be foreign controlled, their foreign direct investment subsidiaries could also be foreign controlled.

Accounting Year

In general, details obtained for enterprises included in the surveys of foreign investment relate to accounting data for the year ended 30 June. However, where respondents have difficulty in reporting precise figures on a 30 June basis, estimates based on their nearest accounting period are accepted.

Source:

Australian Bureau of Statistics, *Foreign Investment Australia.*

JAPAN

Like West Germany, due to expropriations, Japan had negligible outward and inward direct foreign investment at the end of the Second World War. Therefore Japan's direct foreign investment position is of very recent vintage.

Outward investment by Japanese firms in the 1950s and 1960s was mainly located in the geographically close countries of South-East Asia, and developing countries in general. Two factors were important; first, direct investment was concentrated in natural resource sectors; second, within manufacturing, foreign investment was concentrated in labour-intensive industries in which Japan was losing its comparative trade advantage, notably textiles and clothing. Early Japanese investment was therefore distinctively vertical in nature.

During the 1970s and to date the pattern has been moving towards that of the West, ie, market-orientated and horizontal in nature, where the hosts are themselves developed countries.

Direct investment in Japan has grown at a very much slower pace, because of the strong industrial policy of the Japanese government in the 1950s and 1960s, impeding foreign ownership as a means of generating powerful indigenous competitors in key industries. Although the policy of the Japanese government towards inward investment has since become more liberal, the resulting pattern of direct investment in Japan today is still highly distinctive. In major industries, there is a higher incidence of joint ownership by incoming firms. The USA accounts for the bulk of the stock of inward investment, much of which is in the chemicals and engineering sectors.

MAIN SOURCES OF DATA:

A **Official**

1 Ministry of Finance and the Ministry of International Trade and Industry: both provide data on the approved annual value of transactions in outward and inward investment.

B **Private**

1 *Fortune International,* August 20, 1984.

2 J H Dunning, *Japanese Multinationals in the UK,* London: Croom Helm, 1985.

3 F Marsh, *Japanese Overseas Investment,* London: Economist Intelligence Unit, 1983.

4 T Ozawa, 'Japan' in J H Dunning (Ed) *Multinational Enterprises, Economic Structure and International Competitiveness,* Chichester: John Wiley, 1985.

Table A1

SUMMARY OF THE COUNTRY'S INTERNATIONAL INVESTMENT POSITION

		Inward Investment	Outward Investment
1	Number of foreign affiliates in host country, and of foreign affiliates of home country firms at the end of March 1980	1,315	3,567[1]
2	Number of foreign firms with direct investments in host country, and home country firms with direct foreign affiliates	*N.A.*	*N.A.*
3	Total foreign direct capital stock at book value as a percentage of GNP at factor cost in 1983	0.34	5.18
4	Flow of foreign direct investment in the five year period, 1979-84 (US $ m)	1,296	20,937
5	Employment in foreign affiliates or abroad, 1981	412,000	*N.A.*
6	Output of foreign affiliates or abroad, 1980 (US $ m)	6,876[2]	9,326[2]

Source:

Ministry of Finance, *Zaisei Kinyu tokei Geppo,* various issues; Ministry of International Trade and Industry, *Wagakukuni Kigyo no Kaigai Jigyo Katsudo,* 1979; IMF, *International Financial Statistics Yearbook,* various years.

NOTES TO TABLE A1

1 Data for March 1978.

2 Manufacturing only.

Table A2

PRIVATE FOREIGN CAPITAL STOCK, 1960 - 84 (US $m)[1]

	Inward Investment			Outward Investment		
	Portfolio	*Direct*[2]	Total	Portfolio	Direct	Total
Book value of capital stock						
1960	*Not Available*	88	*Not Available*	*Not Available*	529	*Not Available*
1965		270			1,394	
1970		594			3,576	
1975		1,497			15,941	
1976		1,693			19,403	
1977		1,917			22,209	
1978		2,153			26,807	
1979		2,677			31,802	
1980		2,976			36,495	
1981		3,408			45,403	
1982		4,157			53,131	
1983		4,974			61,276	
1984		*N.A.*			71,431	

Source:
Ministry of International Trade and Industry, *Gaishikei Kigyo no Doko,* various years; Ministry of Finance, *Zaisei Kinyu tokei Geppo,* various issues.

NOTES TO TABLE A2

1 Data refer to cumulative investment flows from Fiscal Year ending March 1951 onwards. Each year refers to the situation in March of the succeeding year.

2 The totals for inward direct investment include investment in Japan by foreign affiliates of Japanese parent companies.

Table A3

FLOW OF FOREIGN DIRECT INVESTMENT 1970 - 84 (US $ m)[1]

	Inward Investment				Outward Investment		
	Reinvested Profits	*Other*	*Total*		*Reinvested Profits*	*Other*	*Total*
1970	*Not Separately Available*		94		*Not Separately Available*		355
1971			227				390
1972			168				723
1973			-40				1,918
1974			206				1,911
1975			218				1,656
1976			114				2,002
1977			32				1,705
1978			4				2,465
1979			245				2,956
1980			274				2,340
1981			189				4,850
1982			445				4,528
1983			403				3,532
1984			–10				5,685

Source:

IMF, *Balance of Payments Statistics Yearbook*, various years.

NOTES TO TABLE A3

1 Excluding reinvested profits.

Table A4

SECTORAL DISTRIBUTION OF FOREIGN DIRECT CAPITAL STOCK, 1960 - 84 (US $ m)

	Inward Investment				Outward Investment[1]		
	Primary	*Secondary*	*Tertiary*		*Primary*	*Secondary*	*Tertiary*
1960	24	65	2		236	192	101
1965	89	168	15		479	493	422
1970[2]	126	400	70		1,454	1,220	1,665
1975[2]	234	988	277		6,229	7,139	7,856
1980[2]	451	1,863	663		10,984	14,855	17,910
1983	589	3,159	1,226		11,790	19,542	29,944
1984	*N.A.*	*N.A.*	*N.A.*		12,325	22,048	37,059

Source:

Ministry of International Trade and Industry, *Gaishikei Kigyo no Doko,* various years; Ministry of Finance, *Zaisei Kinyu tokei Geppo,* various issues.

NOTES TO TABLE A4

1 Data for outward investment excludes that which cannot be allocated to an industrial sector in certain years, therefore the totals may be less than those in Table A2.

2 For outward investment the years are 1971, 1977 and 1981.

Table A5

GEOGRAPHICAL DISTRIBUTION OF FOREIGN DIRECT CAPITAL STOCK, 1976 - 84 (US $ m)

	Inward Investment				Outward Investment		
	Developed Countries	*Developing Countries*	*Total*		*Developed Countries*	*Developing Countries*	*Total*
1976	1,418	28	1,479[1]		8,613	10,791	19,405
1983	3,590	224	4,037[1]		28,622	32,654	61,276
1984	*N.A.*	*N.A.*	*N.A.*		34,062	37,369	71,431

Source:

Ministry of International Trade and Industry, *Gaishikei Kigyo no Doko,* various years; Ministry of Finance, *Zaisei Kinyu tokei Geppo,* various issues.

NOTES TO TABLE A5

1 Including an unallocated component, but excluding investment in Japan by foreign affiliates of Japanese firms.

Table A6

INDUSTRIAL DISTRIBUTION OF FOREIGN DIRECT CAPITAL STOCK 1976 - 84 (US $ m)

	Inward Investment		Outward Investment	
	1976	*1983*	*1977*	*1984*
Primary	242	589	6,229	12,325
Agriculture	*N.S.A.*	*N.S.A.*	558	1,167
Mining & quarrying	*N.S.A.*	*N.S.A.*	5,671	11,158
Oil	242	589	*N.S.A.*	*N.S.A.*
Secondary	1,130	3,159	7,139	22,048
Food & drink	74	136	362	1,002
Chemicals & allied	424[1]	1,390[1]	1,369	3,849
Metals	103	394	1,051	4,805
Mechanical engineering	407	928	513	1,619
Electrical equipment	(combined)	(combined)	843	3,234
Motor vehicles	*N.S.A.*	*N.S.A.*	538	2,746
Other transportation equipment	*N.S.A.*	*N.S.A.*	(combined)	(combined)
Textiles & clothing	12[1]	31[1]	1,285	2,055
Paper & allied	*N.S.A.*	*N.S.A.*	627	1,106
Rubber	*N.S.A.*	*N.S.A.*	*N.S.A.*	*N.S.A.*
Stone, clay & glass	29	108	*N.S.A.*	*N.S.A.*
Other manufacturing	81	172	545	1,633
Tertiary	322	1,226	7,856	37,059
Construction	5[2]	31[2]	*N.S.A.*	703
Transport & communications	10	14	*N.S.A.*	4,660
Distributive trade	193	655	2,955	11,128
Property	*N.S.A.*	*N.S.A.*	*N.S.A.*	1,326
Banking & finance	*N.S.A.*	*N.S.A.*	1,694	7,054
Other services	114[2]	526[2]	3,207[2]	12,188[2]
TOTAL	1,695[3]	4,974[3]	21,223	71,431

Source:

Ministry of International Trade and Industry, *Gaishikei Kigyo no Doko,* various years; Ministry of Finance, *Zaisei Kinyu tokei Geppo,* various issues.

NOTES TO TABLE A6

1 Leather and Rubber are included in Chemicals and Allied.

2 Includes other not separately available but excludes data which cannot be allocated to a sector, such as investment in branches, and therefore sums to a total less than that in Table A2.

3 Totals for inward investment include investment in Japan of foreign affiliates of Japanese parent companies.

Table A7

LEADING SOURCE AND RECIPIENT COUNTRIES, 1976 - 84 (US $ m)

	Inward Investment[1]		Outward Investment	
	1976	*1983*	*1976*	*1984*
DEVELOPED AREAS	1,418	3,590	8,613	34,062
Europe	360	1,039	2,855	9,072
EEC of which:	218	642[2]	2,370[2]	7,664[2]
Belgium & Luxembourg	3[1]	5[1]	121[3]	1,575
Denmark	2	11	*N.S.A.*[2]	*N.S.A.*[2]
France	23	110	184	751
W. Germany	56	208	207	1,170
Greece	*N.S.A.*[2]	*N.S.A.*[2]	*N.S.A.*[2]	*N.S.A.*[2]
Ireland	*N.S.A.*[2]	*N.S.A.*[2]	36	179
Italy	*N.S.A.*[2]	*N.S.A.*[2]	*N.S.A.*[2]	149
Netherlands	23	93	182	1,074
UK	111	215	1,640	2,766
Other Europe of which:	142	397[2]	485[2]	1,408[2]
Spain	*N.S.A.*	*N.S.A.*	*N.S.A.*	423
Sweden	24	68	*N.S.A.*	*N.S.A.*
Switzerland	104	299	119	602
North America of which:	1,058	2,551	4,666	21,469
Canada	40	110	585	1,575
USA	1,018	2,441	4,080	19,894
Other developed countries of which:	*N.S.A.*	*N.S.A.*	1,092	3,521
Australia	*N.S.A.*	*N.S.A.*	818	3,153
New Zealand	*N.S.A.*	*N.S.A.*	110	238
DEVELOPING AREAS	28	224	10,791	37,369
Africa of which:	*N.S.A.*	*N.S.A.*	773	3,198
Liberia	*N.S.A.*	*N.S.A.*	274	2,296
Nigeria	*N.S.A.*	*N.S.A.*	125	157
Zaire	*N.S.A.*	*N.S.A.*	219	282
Asia & Pacific of which:	16	197	5,463	18,224
Hong Kong	11	172	447	2,799
Indonesia	*N.S.A.*	*N.S.A.*	2,704	8,015
S. Korea	*N.S.A.*	*N.S.A.*	690	1,548
Malaysia	*N.S.A.*	*N.S.A.*	356	*N.S.A.*
Philippines	*N.S.A.*	*N.S.A.*	354	832
Singapore	*N.S.A.*	*N.S.A.*	304	1,930
Taiwan	5	25	226	647
Thailand	*N.S.A.*	*N.S.A.*	228	711

Table A7 (cont'd)

LEADING SOURCE AND RECIPIENT COUNTRIES, 1976 - 84 (US $ m)

	Inward Investment[1]		Outward Investment	
	1976	*1983*	*1976*	*1984*
DEVELOPING AREAS (cont'd)				
Latin America of which:			3,301	13,020
Brazil	*Not Available*	*Not Available*	1,804	4,274
Chile			90	179
Mexico			170	1,220
Panama	12	27	113	4,916
Peru			459	*N.S.A.*
Middle East of which:	*Not Available*	*Not Available*	1,254	2,927
Iran			293	1,003
Saudi Arabia			830	357
UNSPECIFIED	34	222	–	–
TOTAL	1,479	4,037	19,405	71,431

Source:
Ministry of International Trade and Industry, *Gaishikei Kigyo no Doko,* various years; Ministry of Finance, *Zaisei Kinyu tokei Geppo,* various issues.

NOTES TO TABLE A7

1 Cumulative investment flows from 1951, excluding investment in Japan by the foreign affiliates of Japanese companies.

2 Certain countries of the EEC are included in Other Europe.

3 Belgium only.

Table A8

INDICATORS OF THE SIGNIFICANCE OF INWARD FOREIGN DIRECT INVESTMENT OR THE ACTIVITIES OF FOREIGN-BASED COMPANIES TO THE NATIONAL ECONOMY, 1980 - 83

1	Direct capital stock of foreign affiliates at book value in 1983 as a proportion of:		
	a	GNP at factor cost	0.34
	b	population (in US $ per head)	33.85
2	Employment in foreign affiliates in 1980 as a percentage of all employment		
	a	in all industry	0.80
	b	in manufacturing	1.60
3	Output of foreign affiliates in 1980 as a percentage of all companies' output[1]		
	a	in primary (ie, extractive) industry	38.10
	b	in secondary (ie, manufacturing) industry	4.70
	c	in tertiary industry (ie, services, etc)[2]	1.30
4	Profits of foreign affiliates in 1980 as a percentage of profits of all companies in the host country[3]		
	a	in all sectors	3.30
	b	in manufacturing	5.00

5 Percentage share of assets, sales and employment accounted for by foreign affiliates in selected sectors, 1980

	Assets	*Sales*	*Employment*
Primary Goods Sector			
Oil	33.6	38.1	22.0
Manufacturing Sector	4.5	4.7	1.6
Food & drink	*Not Available*	0.7	*Not Available*
Chemicals & allied		7.1	
Metals[4]		5.3	
Mechanical engineering		4.2	
Electrical equipment		2.4	
Motor vehicles		3.7	
Other transportation equipment			
Rubber		10.8	

Source:

Ministry of International Trade and Industry, *Gaishikei Kigyo no Doko,* March 1981, March 1983; Ministry of International Trade and Industry, *Survey of Foreign Affiliates in FY 1983 (Summary),* October 8, 1984.

NOTES TO TABLE A8

1 Refers to total sales in Japan. Data obtained from respondents to a MITI survey.

2 Figure for 1982.

3 After tax profits.

4 Non-ferrous metals only.

Table A9

INDICATORS OF THE SIGNIFICANCE OF OUTWARD FOREIGN DIRECT INVESTMENT OR THE ACTIVITIES OF HOME-BASED COMPANIES ABROAD FOR THE NATIONAL ECONOMY, 1979 - 83

1	Foreign capital stock of home-based firms at book value in 1983 as a proportion of:		
	a GNP at factor cost		5.18
	b population (in US $ per head)		513.82
2	Output of foreign manufacturing affiliates in 1982 as a percentage of:		
	a domestic manufacturing output		2.17
	b manufacturing exports from the home country		17.77
3	Assets and sales of foreign affiliates of home-based firms as a percentage of that in selected domestic sectors, end March 1979[1]		
		Assets	*Sales*
	Primary Goods Sector		
	Agriculture	20.0	46.7
	Mining & quarrying	49.1	61.2
	Manufacturing Sector	*N.A.*	5.9
	Food & drink	5.1	21.7
	Chemicals & allied	*N.A.*	4.6
	Metals[2]	30.6	4.8
	Mechanical engineering	5.1	1.7
	Electrical equipment	17.2	4.8
	Motor vehicles } Other transportation equipment }	20.1	3.1
	Textiles & clothing	47.8	5.3
	Paper & allied	18.4	41.9
	Services Sector	12.1	32.4

Source:

Ministry of International Trade and Industry, *Wagakuni Kigyo no Kaigai Jigyo Katsudo,* (Overseas Business Activities of Japanese Enterprises), 9th Report, 1980; IMF, *International Financial Statistics Yearbook,* 1984. *Statistics Yearbook,* 1984.

NOTES TO TABLE A9

1 Data to refer to respondents to a MITI survey, and account for approximately 85% of the total Japanese direct investment stock abroad. The percentages in section (5) are expressed with respect to those respondent firms' domestic capital/sales.

2 Non ferrous metals only.

Table A10

DISTRIBUTION OF FOREIGN SUBSIDIARIES AND ASSOCIATES AND FOREIGN CAPITAL STOCK BY PERCENTAGE OWNERSHIP OF PARENT COMPANIES, 1980

	Inward Investment		Outward Investment[1]	
	Number of Affiliates	*Value of Capital Stock*	*Number of Affiliates*	*Value of Capital Stock*
100% owned subsidiaries	490	*Not Available*	1,458	*Not Available*
50-99.9% owned subsidiaries and associates	565		1,004	
Less than 50% owned subsidiaries and associates	260		1,105	
TOTAL	1,315		3,567	

Source:

Ministry of Finance, *Zaisei Kinyu tokei Geppo,* various issues; Ministry of International Trade and Industry, *Wagakuni Kigyo no Kaigai Jigyo Katsudo,* 1979.

NOTES TO TABLE A10

1 For 1978.

Table A11

ROYALTY RECEIPTS AND PAYMENTS, 1974 - 84 (US $ m)

	Payments			Receipts		
	To Affiliates	*To Non-affiliates*	*Total*	*From Affiliates*	*From Non-affiliates*	*Total*
1974	*Not Separately Available*		747	*Not Separately Available*		110
1975			667			140
1976			802			174
1977			1,045			217
1978			1,212			287
1979			1,291			329
1980			1,301			344
1981			1,688			477
1982	345	1,409	1,754			563
1983	*N.A.*	*N.A.*	1,937			555
1984	*N.A.*	*N.A.*	2,176			657

Source:

IMF, *Balance of Payments Statistics Yearbook,* various years; Ministry of International Trade and industry, *Survey on Foreign Affiliates in FY 1983 (Summary),* October 8, 1984.

Table A12

LEADING FOREIGN AND DOMESTIC MULTINATIONAL COMPANIES

A Leading Foreign Affiliates in the country in terms of sales, end 1983

	Name	*Home Country*	*Sector*	*Turnover in Japan (US $m)*
1	Mitsubishi Oil	Japan/USA[1]	Petroleum	4,916,879
2	Nippondenso	Japan[1]/Germany[1]	Motor vehicle parts	2,961,173
3	IBM Japan	USA	Office equipment	2,578,368[2,3]
4	Nippon Light Metal	Japan[1]/Canada[1]	Metal products	1,470,257
5	Yokohama Rubber	Japan/USA[1]	Rubber products	1,089,083
6	Sumitomo Rubber	Japan/UK[1]	Rubber and plastic products	945,205
7	Prima Meat Packers	Japan[1]/USA[1]	Food products	819,436
8	Esso Standard Sekiyu KK	USA	Petroleum	*N.A.*
9	Texaco Japan Ltd	USA[1]	Petroleum	*N.A.*
10	A G International Chemical Co	USA[1]	Chemicals	*N.A.*
11	Ford Motor Co Japan	USA	Motor vehicles	*N.A.*
12	General Electric Japan	USA	Electrical	*N.A.*
13	Nippon Lever KK	UK/Netherlands	Food Products	*N.A.*
14	Du Pont Japan KK	USA	Chemicals	*N.A.*
15	Wiggins Teape (Japan) Ltd	UK	Paper	*N.A.*
16	Phillips Petroleum International	USA	Petroleum	*N.A.*
17	Siemens KK	Germany	Electrical	*N.A.*
18	Hoechst Japan Ltd	Germany	Chemicals	*N.A.*
19	Nestlé Japan Ltd	Switzerland	Food Products	*N.A.*
20	Dow Chemical (Japan) Ltd	USA	Chemicals	*N.A.*
21	Proctor & Gamble Sunhome Co Ltd	USA	Drugs	*N.A.*
22	W R Grace KK	USA	Chemicals	*N.A.*
23	Ciba-Geigy Japan Ltd	Switzerland	Chemicals	*N.A.*
24	Kanebo Cadbury Ltd	UK[1]	Food Products	*N.A.*

Source:

Fortune, August 20, 1984; *Who Owns Whom, Australia and Far East,* Dun and Bradstreet, 1984.

Table A12

LEADING FOREIGN AND DOMESTIC MULTINATIONAL COMPANIES

B Leading Domestic Multinational Companies in terms of sales, end 1981				
	Name	*Sector*	*Global Turnover (US $m)*	*Sales of overseas subsidiaries as % of worldwide sales*
1	Nissan	Motor vehicles	17,148	*N.A.*
2	Toyota	Motor vehicles	16,377[4]	*N.A.*
3	Matsushita	Electrical	15,700	11[5]
4	Hitachi	Electrical	15,480	*N.A.*
5	Nippon Steel	Metals	14,344[4]	*N.A.*
6	Mitsubishi Heavy Ind.	Motor vehicles	12,406	*N.A.*
7	Toshiba	Electrical	9,676	*N.A.*
8	Honda	Motor vehicles	7,607	*N.A.*
9	Nippon Kokan	Metals	6,783	*N.A.*
10	Mitsubishi Electric	Electrical	6,335	*N.A.*
11	Sumitomo Metal	Metals	6,025	*N.A.*
12	Kawasaki Steel	Metals	5,546[4]	*N.A.*
13	Toyo Kogyo	Motor vehicles	5,313[4]	*N.A.*
14	Kobe Steel	Metals	5,254[4]	*N.A.*
15	Nippon Electric	Electrical	4,841	30[6]
16	Sony	Electrical	4,801	71[6]
17	Sanyo	Electrical	4,437	61[6]
18	Taiyo Fishery	Food	4,429	8
19	Asahi Chemical	Chemicals	3,687	*N.A.*
20	Mitsubishi Chemical	Chemicals	3,550[4]	*N.A.*
21	Isuzu Motors	Motor vehicles	3,323[4]	*N.A.*
22	Fijitsu	Office equipment	3,201	*N.A.*
23	Komatsu	Machinery	3,191	*N.A.*
24	Ishikawajima-Harima	Machinery	3,139[4]	*N.A.*
25	Bridgestone	Rubber	3,090	*N.A.*

Source:

J M Stopford and J H Dunning, *Multinationals Company Performance and Global Trends,* London: Macmillan, 1983.

JAPAN NOTES TO TABLE A12

1 The company named is an associate, ie, owned 50% or less (but more than 10%) by firms from the countries cited.
2 Parent only.
3 Revenues include certain sales to foreign affiliates of the US parent company.
4 Parent company figures only.
5 1980 data.
6 Includes all exports, direct and intra-group.

JAPAN : DEFINITIONS

Foreign affiliates

The data for outward and inward direct foreign investment covers all foreign projects in which participation in management is intended, and thus includes both subsidiaries and associates. For certain operating data, taken from special surveys, ownership of 25% or more of equity capital is the minimum for a direct foreign investment to be deemed.

Foreign direct capital stock

Data on direct foreign investment stock derive from the cumulated approved value of specific projects submitted to the Japanese Ministry of Finance, under the Foreign Exchange Control Act (1949). The statistics yield information on both industry and partner country. The cumulation of values began in 1951, although in the earlier years very few projects were recorded. The cumulation of approved values in this way necessarily means that there is no opportunity to revalue earlier investments, or even to account for divestments or other sources of error.

Foreign direct investment

Because of the nature of the estimate of foreign direct capital stock the value of a direct foreign investment, given intended participation in management, is the value of equity capital outstanding plus any loan capital owed to the investing parent. The Japanese fiscal year begins on April 1st and runs until end March the following year. In accordance with this, as an example, fiscal year 1983 refers to the period April 1st 1983 to end March 1984. This corresponds closest to the calendar year 1983, and is reported as such in these tables.

NEW ZEALAND

A spate of regulations, restrictions and guidelines in the early 1970s were designed to allow inward direct investment only in those activities deemed to be 'in the national interest'. Since 1975, such regulations have been modified and liberalised to some extent. Indeed, in July 1979 a revised set of criteria was announced, the aim of which was to emphasise that foreign investment is welcome if it can contribute to the economic development of New Zealand.

The flow of outward investment increased annually to 1981, but since then has fallen slightly although it remains much higher than it was ten years previously.

The sources of inward investment have been very concentrated with the UK, the USA and Australia accounting for almost all the inflow.

The direction of investment has also been fairly concentrated with investment occurring mainly in the manufacturing and services sector, although the proportion of investment flowing to these sectors vary greatly from year to year. Nevertheless, the manufacturing sector is no longer the major destination for capital inflows that it was in the 1960s; in the period 1970-80, 54% of new investment was directed to the tertiary sector.

Within the manufacturing sector, there have been major shifts in the distribution of foreign direct investment over the period 1963-80; two of the major recipients of overseas investment flows — metal-working and engineering and transport equipment industries — have decreased in both absolute and relative importance, with the chemicals and mineral products industries receiving an increasing proportion of total foreign direct investment.

Within the service sector, the dominant recipients of overseas investment have been wholesale and retail trade, the banking and insurance and ownership of property industry groups.

MAIN SOURCES OF DATA:

A **Official**

1. Overseas Investment Commission: provide information on foreign takeovers and commencement of business in New Zealand.
2. Department of Statistics: publishes annually a comparative analysis of overseas companies and all companies, and provides balance of payments data indicating investment flows.
3. Reserve Bank of New Zealand: publishes Corporate Financial Statistics; an aggregate analysis of the annual accounts of New Zealand public companies.
4. Bureau of Industry Economics, *Australian direct investment in New Zealand*, Information Bulletin 3, Australian Government Publishing Service, Canberra, 1983.

Note:
Data do not allow us to complete Table A11 or A12 for New Zealand.

Table A1

SUMMARY OF THE COUNTRY'S INTERNATIONAL INVESTMENT POSITION

		Inward Investment	Outward Investment
1	Number of foreign affiliates in host country, and of foreign affiliates of home country firms at the end of 1984	345	*N.A.*
2	Number of foreign firms with direct investments in host country, and home country firms with direct foreign affiliates	*N.A.*	*N.A.*
3	Total foreign direct capital stock at book value as a percentage of GNP at factor cost in 1982	10.04	1.68
4	Flow of foreign direct investment in the five year period, 1979-83 (NZ $ m)	1,587.10	563.00
5	Employment in foreign affiliates or abroad	*N.A.*	*N.A.*
6	Output of foreign affiliates or abroad	*N.A.*	*N.A.*

Source:

Reserve Bank of New Zealand, *Foreign Investment in New Zealand,* supplement to Reserve Bank of New Zealand Bulletin, November 1981; IMF, *International Financial Statistics Yearbook,* 1984.

Table A2

PRIVATE FOREIGN CAPITAL STOCK, 1951 - 83 (NZ $ m)

	Inward Investment[1]			Outward Investment[2]		
	Portfolio	*Direct*	*Total*	*Portfolio*	*Direct*	*Total*
Book value of capital stock						
1951-59		554.2				
1970		630.4				
1975		1,296.7				
1976		1,411.4				
1977	*Not Available*	1,690.3	*Not Available*		*Not Available*	
1978		1,849.5				
1979		2,113.4				
1980		2,456.1				
1981		2,854.2				
1982		3,150.9		*N.A.*	529.5	*N.A.*
1983		3,437.2		*N.A.*	645.5	*N.A.*

Source:

Reserve Bank of New Zealand, *Foreign Investment in New Zealand,* supplement to Reserve Bank of New Zealnd Bulletin, November 1981; IMF, *Balance of Payments Statistics Yearbook,* 1984.

NOTES TO TABLE A2

1 Calculations based on cumulative investment flows, 1951-83.

2 Estimate based on cumulative flows 1970-83.

Table A3

FLOW OF FOREIGN DIRECT INVESTMENT, 1970 - 83 (NZ $ m)

	Inward Investment			Outward Investment		
	Reinvested Profits	*Other*	*Total*	*Reinvested Profits*	*Other*	*Total*
1970	42.3	33.9	76.2			0.9
1971	2.3	127.7	130.0			*N.A.*
1972	35.6	61.9	97.5			7.3
1973	64.3	42.1	106.4			*N.A.*
1974	91.4	61.3	152.7	*Not*		0.9
1975	59.1	120.6	179.7	*Separately*		3.4
1976	69.1	45.6	114.7	*Available*		*N.A.*
1977	170.5	108.4	278.9			33.4
1978	122.7	36.5	159.2			36.6
1979	172.9	91.0	263.9			94.8
1980	83.9	258.8	342.7			118.0
1981	100.2	297.9	398.1			119.0
1982	116.0	180.7	296.7			116.0
1983	115.2	171.1	286.3			115.2

Source:

Reserve Bank of New Zealand, *Foreign Investment in New Zealand,* supplement to Reserve Bank of New Zealand Bulletin, November 1981; IMF, *Balance of Payments Statistics Yearbook,* 1984.

Table A4

SECTORAL DISTRIBUTION OF FOREIGN DIRECT CAPITAL STOCK, 1963 - 80 (NZ $ m)[1]

	Inward Investment			Outward Investment		
	Primary	*Secondary*	*Tertiary*	*Primary*	*Secondary*	*Tertiary*
1963-70	8.6	199.7	163.6	*Not Available*		
1963-80	34.0	1,023.1	1,140.7			

Source:

Reserve Bank of New Zealand, *Foreign Investment in New Zealand,* supplement to Reserve Bank of New Zealand Bulletin, November 1981.

NOTES TO TABLE A4

1 Calculations based on cumulative investment flows, 1963-80. Total does not match Table A2 due to the non allocation of investment flows for 1951-62.

Table A5

GEOGRAPHICAL DISTRIBUTION OF FOREIGN DIRECT CAPITAL STOCK, 1951 - 80 (NZ $ m)[1]

	Inward Investment			Outward Investment		
	Developed Countries	*Other Countries*	*Total*[2]	*Developed Countries*	*Developing Countries*	*Total*
1951-70	586.4	44.0	630.4	*Not Available*		
1951-80	2,280.6	175.5	2,456.1			

Source:

Reserve Bank of New Zealand, *Foreign Investment in New Zealand,* supplement to Reserve Bank of New Zealand Bulletin, November 1981.

NOTES TO TABLE A5

1 Calculations based on cumulative investment flows, 1951-80.

2 Totals include 'unspecified' figures.

Table A6

INDUSTRIAL DISTRIBUTION OF FOREIGN DIRECT CAPITAL STOCK, 1963 - 80 (NZ $ m)[1]

	Inward Investment		Outward Investment
	1963-70	*1963-80*	
Primary	8.6	34.0	*Not Available*
Agriculture[2]	0.0	6.8	
Mining & quarrying	8.6	27.2	
Oil			
Secondary	199.7	1,023.1	
Food & drink	52.9	154.6	
Chemicals & allied	32.7	289.6	
Metals	28.5	162.4	
Mechanical engineering Electrical equipment Motor vehicles Other transportation equipment	43.2	197.6	
Textiles & clothing	7.8	26.2	
Paper & allied	13.2	65.3	
Rubber[3]	4.7	22.2	
Other manufacturing	16.7	105.2	
Tertiary	163.6	1,140.7	
Construction	2.4	23.3	
Transport & communications	9.7	-22.0	
Distributive trades	106.5	603.8	
Property Banking & finance	41.0	508.6	
Other services	4.0	27.0	
TOTAL	371.9	2,197.8	

Source:

Reserve Bank of New Zealand, *Foreign Investment in New Zealand,* supplement to Reserve Bank of New Zealand Bulletin, November 1981.

NOTES TO TABLE A6

1 Calculations based on cumulative investment flows, 1963-80. Total does not match Table A2 due to the non allocation of investment flows for 1951-62.

2 Represents farming, hunting, fishing, forestry and logging.

3 Represents leather and rubber products.

Table A7

LEADING SOURCE AND RECIPIENT COUNTRIES, 1970 - 80 (NZ $ m)[1]

	Inward Investment		Outward Investment
	1951-70	*1951-80*	
DEVELOPED AREAS[2]	586.4	2,280.6	*Not Available*
Europe[2]	317.3	1,069.0	
UK	317.3	1,069.0	
North America	95.0	511.4	
Other developed countries of which:[2]	174.1	700.2	
Australia[3]	174.1	700.2	
OTHER AREAS	44.0	175.5	
TOTAL	630.4	2,456.1	

Source:

Reserve Bank of New Zealand, *Foreign Investment in New Zealand,* supplement to Reserve Bank of New Zealand Bulletin, November 1981.

NOTES TO TABLE A7

1 Calculations based on cumulative flows, 1951-80.

2 Including only those countries shown below.

3 Other sterling countries are included with Australia up to 1969 but the investment involved is small.

Table A8

INDICATORS OF THE SIGNIFICANCE OF INWARD FOREIGN DIRECT INVESTMENT OR THE ACTIVITIES OF FOREIGN-BASED COMPANIES TO THE NATIONAL ECONOMY, 1980 - 82

1	Direct capital stock of foreign affiliates at book value in 1982 as a proportion of:	
	a GNP at factor cost	10.04
	b population (in NZ $ per head)	997.12
2	Profits[1] of foreign affiliates in 1980 as a percentage of profits of all companies in the host country	
	a in all sectors	28.88
	b in manufacturing	29.56
3	Percentage share of assets accounted for by foreign affiliates in selected sectors, 1980	
		Assets
	Primary Goods Sector	
	Agriculture[2]	2.08
	Manufacturing Sector	
	Food & drink	17.05
	Chemicals & allied	86.40
	Metals } Mechanical engineering }	56.54
	Electrical equipment	55.50
	Textiles & clothing	51.13
	Paper & allied	16.97
	Stone, glass & clay	19.54
	Other manufacturing	50.98
	Services Sector	
	Construction	34.42
	Transport & communications	20.37
	Trade & distribution	24.26
	Banking & finance	59.81
	Other services[2]	20.27

Source:

Reserve Bank of New Zealand, *Foreign Investment in New Zealand,* supplement to Reserve Bank of New Zealand Bulletin, November 1981; IMF, *International Financial Statistics Yearbook,* 1984.

NOTES TO TABLE A8

1 Net profits after deducting current year tax and minority interest.

2 Represents forestry and wood.

3 Including property.

Table A9

INDICATORS OF THE SIGNIFICANCE OF OUTWARD FOREIGN DIRECT INVESTMENT OR THE ACTIVITIES OF HOME-BASED COMPANIES ABROAD FOR THE NATIONAL ECONOMY, 1982

1	Foreign capital stock of home-based firms at book value in 1982 as a proportion of:	
	a GNP at factor cost	1.68
	b population (in NZ $ per head)	167.60

Source:

IMF, *International Financial Statistics Yearbook,* 1984.

Table A10

DISTRIBUTION OF FOREIGN SUBSIDIARIES AND ASSOCIATES AND FOREIGN CAPITAL STOCK BY PERCENTAGE OWNERSHIP OF PARENT COMPANIES, 1980

	Inward Investment		Outward Investment	
	Number of Affiliates[1]	*Value of Capital Stock*	*Number of Affiliates*	*Value of Capital Stock*
100% owned subsidiaries 50-99.9% owned subsidiaries and associates	329	*Not Available*	*Not Available*	
Less than 50% owned subsidiaries and associates	42			
TOTAL	371			

Source:

Reserve Bank of New Zealand, *Foreign Investment in New Zealand,* supplement to Reserve Bank of New Zealand Bulletin, November 1981.

NOTES TO TABLE A10

1 Represents takeovers and greenfield ventures only.

NEW ZEALAND : DEFINITIONS

Direct private foreign investment in New Zealand can be generally defined as investment by non-residents in New Zealand business, where the non-resident ownership of the business is sufficient to give the overseas investor an effective element of control over the management and activities of the business. If this element of control is present, then direct investment includes all capital transactions between the overseas investor and the New Zealand business, whether involving equity capital, long- or short-term borrowing, or changes in branch assets and liabilities. If this control is not present, then equity investment and borrowing from overseas are treated as portfolio investments and are not regarded as direct investments.

The general practice in New Zealand is to treat companies with 25% or more of their voting share capital controlled by foreign investors as 'overseas companies'.

Source:
Reserve Bank of New Zealand, 1981.

SOUTH AFRICA

Limited data on the investment position of South Africa is provided by the South African Reserve Bank. The inflow of foreign direct investment in South Africa has fluctuated annually, and since the mid-1970s, has been overtaken by South Africa's outward investment; this partly reflects the uncertain domestic political situation, and the indigenisation programme of the South African Government. In 1978 and 1979, in particular, several foreign affiliates were taken over or merged with South African companies.

The main source of investment in South Africa is the EEC, mainly attributed to the UK and West Germany. The USA is also a significant source of investment. South Africa's outward investment shows a similar geographical pattern, with the bulk of her investment going to the EEC and North and South America.

Reserve Bank statistics do not disaggregate South Africa's investment position by industrial sector. However, Table A6 indicates the sectoral pattern of UK, US and West German investment in South Africa, which, according to the data, accounts for about 45% of total foreign direct investment in the country. This is probably an underestimation of the situation, due to the undervaluation of US and UK stocks; other sources suggest that these two countries combined may account for over 50% of total FDI in South Africa. Some 85% of the country's oil industry is controlled by five major oil MNEs. Foreign mining companies continue to play an important role, but the bulk of non oil investment is concentrated on the manufacturing sector, particularly chemicals, metals, motor vehicles and electrical equipment, and to a lesser extent, in the services sector, notably the distributive trade. In policy, the South African Government is trying to steer a middle course between encouraging local industry and not discouraging inward direct investment. In particular, attention is being given to promoting the local interest of output produced by foreign affiliates.

MAIN SOURCES OF DATA:

A Official

1 South African Reserve Bank: compiles data on the investment position of the country.

2 US Department of Commerce, International Trade Administration, *Investment Climate in Foreign Countries,* Washington, 1985.

3 UN, Economic and Social Council, "Activities of Transnational Corporations in Southern Africa: Impact on Financial and Social Structures", Report of the Secretariat, New York, 1978.

4 UNCTC, *Activities of Transnational Corporations in the Industrial, Mining and Military Sectors of Southern Africa,* New York: UN, 1980.

5 UNCTC, *Activities of Transnational Corporations in South Africa and Namibia and the Responsibilities of Home Countries with respect to their Operations in this Area,* New York: UN, 1986.

Note:
Data do not allow us to complete Table A10 for South Africa.

Table A1

SUMMARY OF THE COUNTRY'S INTERNATIONAL INVESTMENT POSITION

		Inward Investment	Outward Investment
1	Number of foreign affiliates in host country, and of foreign affiliates of home country firms in 1978.	1,884	*N.A.*
2	Number of foreign firms with direct investments in host country, and home country firms with direct foreign affiliates in 1984	1,068[1]	*N.A.*
3	Total foreign direct capital stock at book value as a percentage of GNP at factor cost in 1982	22.84	8.99
4	Flow of foreign direct investment in the five year period, 1980-84 (Rand m)	539.6	1,335.5
5	Employment in foreign affiliates or abroad	*N.A.*	*N.A.*
6	Output of foreign affiliates or abroad	*N.A.*	*N.A.*

Source:
South African Reserve Bank, data as cited in US Department of Commerce, *Investment Climate in Foreign Countries,* Washington, 1983; IMF, *Balance of Payments Statistics Yearbook, 1984;* IMF, *International Financial & Statistics Yearbook, 1984;* UNCTC, 1986, *op cit.*

NOTES TO TABLE A1

1 Of these foreign firms 406 were of US origin, 364 of UK origin and 142 of West German origin.

Table A2

PRIVATE FOREIGN CAPITAL STOCK, 1970 - 84 (Rand bn)

	Inward Investment			Outward Investment		
	Portfolio	*Direct*	*Total*	*Portfolio*	*Direct*	*Total*
Book value of capital stock						
1970	1.88	3.94	5.82		*Not Available*	
1975	9.03	7.43	16.46			
1979	12.75	10.40	23.15	7.04	3.63	10.67
1980	13.07	12.22	25.29	8.98	4.23	13.21
1981	17.34	14.71	32.05	7.90	5.40	13.30
1982	22.26	17.14	39.40	8.50	6.75	15.25
1983	*N.A.*	17.22	*N.A.*	*N.A.*	6.94	*N.A.*
1984	*N.A.*	17.25	*N.A.*	*N.A.*	6.93	*N.A.*

Source:

South African Reserve Bank, data as cited in US Department of Commerce, *Investment Climate in Foreign Countries,* Washington, 1983; UN Economic and Social Council, 'Activities of Transnational Corporations in Southern Africa: Impact on Financial and Social Structures', Report of the Secretariat, New York, 1978.

Table A3

FLOW OF FOREIGN DIRECT INVESTMENT, 1970 - 84 (Rand m)[1]

	Inward Investment			Outward Investment		
	Reinvested Profits	*Other*	*Total*	*Reinvested Profits*	*Other*	*Total*
1970			239.3			12.1
1971			185.8			20.8
1972			90.1			15.0
1973			19.0			34.7
1974			470.5			77.6
1975			135.1			88.9
1976	*Not*		16.1	*Not*		28.1
1977	*Separately*		−109.9	*Separately*		61.3
1978	*Available*		−114.4	*Available*		234.5
1979			−409.6			8.7
1980			−7.6			552.3
1981			69.0			609.0
1982			370.4			−10.7
1983			80.6			186.8
1984			27.2			−1.9

Source:

IMF, *Balance of Payments Statistics Yearbook,* various issues.

NOTES TO TABLE A3

1 Excluding reinvested profits.

Table A4

SECTORAL DISTRIBUTION OF FOREIGN DIRECT CAPITAL STOCK, 1981 (Rand m)

	Inward Investment				Outward Investment		
	Primary	*Secondary*	*Tertiary*		*Primary*	*Secondary*	*Tertiary*
1981	389.5[1]	4,234.7[2]	1,126.8[2]		*Not Available*		

Source:

UK Department of Trade and Industry, *Business Monitor,* Supplement, 1981; US Department of Commerce, *Survey of Current Business,* August 1983; Deutschen Bundesbank, *Monthly Report,* Supplement, 1983.

NOTES TO TABLE A4

1 UK & US investment only.

2 UK, US and West German investment only. Total therefore does not match Table A2.

Table A5

GEOGRAPHICAL DISTRIBUTION OF FOREIGN DIRECT CAPITAL STOCK, 1979 - 82 (Rand m)

	Inward Investment				Outward Investment		
	Developed Countries	*Developing Countries*	*Total*		*Developed Countries*	*Developing Countries*	*Total*
1979	*Not Available*				1,597.2[3]	*N.S.A.*	3,630.0[2]
1981	6,553.3[1]	*N.S.A.*	14,710.0[2]		*Not Available*		
1982	*Not Available*				4,252.5[3]	*N.S.A.*	6,750.0[2]

Source:

UK Department of Trade and Industry, *Business Monitor,* Supplement, 1981; US Department of Commerce, *Survey of Current Business,* August 1983; Deutschen Bundesbank, *Monthly Report,* Supplement, 1983; South African Reserve Bank, data as cited in US Department of Commerce, *Investment Climate in Foreign Countries,* Washington, 1983.

NOTES TO TABLE A5

1 US, UK and West German investment only.

2 Total includes 'unspecified' figure.

3 Includes South African investment in Latin America.

Table A6

INDUSTRIAL DISTRIBUTION OF FOREIGN DIRECT CAPITAL STOCK, 1981 (Rand m)

	Inward Investment	Outward Investment
	1981	
Primary	389.5[1]	Not Available
Agriculture		
Mining & quarrying	389.5[1]	
Oil		
Secondary	4,234.7[2]	
Food & drink	449.5[1]	
Chemicals & allied	1,041.3[2]	
Metals	173.3[1]	
Mechanical engineering	632.5[2]	
Electrical equipment	550.2[2]	
Motor vehicles	368.9[3]	
Other transportation equipment	*N.A.*	
Textiles & clothing	124.5[4]	
Paper & allied	65.3[4]	
Rubber	76.5[4]	
Stone, clay & glass	*N.A.*	
Coal & petroleum products	*N.A.*	
Other manufacturing	344.6[4]	
Tertiary	1,126.8[2]	
Construction	103.9[4]	
Transport & communications	67.0[4]	
Distributive trade	665.1[2]	
Property	*N.A.*	
Banking & finance	118.2[1]	
Other services	172.6[2]	
TOTAL	6,553.3[5]	

Source:

UK Department of Trade and Industry, 'Census of Overseas Assets 1981', *Business Monitor,* Supplement, 1981; US Department of Commerce, *Survey of Current Business,* August, 1983; Deutschen Bundesbank, 'Die Kapitalverflechtung der Unternehmen mit dem Ausland nach Ländern und Wirtschaftszweigen 1976 bis 1981', *Monthly Report,* Supplement, June 1983.

NOTES TO TABLE A6

1 UK & US investment only.

2 UK, US and West German investment only.

3 UK & West German investment only.

4 UK investment only.

5 Total includes UK, US and West German investment only and thus does not match Table A2.

Table A7

LEADING SOURCE AND RECIPIENT COUNTRIES, 1979 - 82 (Rand m)

	Inward Investment	Outward Investment	
	1981	*1979*	*1982*
DEVELOPED AREAS[1]	6,553.3	1,597.2	4,252.5
EEC of which[1]:	4,048.0	1,270.5	2,767.5
W. Germany	787.0	*N.S.A.*	*N.S.A.*
UK	3,261.0	*N.S.A.*	*N.S.A.*
North America of which[1]:	2,505.3	326.7[2]	1,485.0[2]
Canada			
USA	2,505.3	*N.S.A.*	*N.S.A.*
UNSPECIFIED COUNTRIES	8,156.7	2,032.8	2,497.5
TOTAL	14,710.0	3,630.0	6,750.0

Source:

UK Department of Trade and Industry, 'Census of Overseas Assets 1981', *Business Monitor,* Supplement 1981; US Department of Commerce, *Survey of Current Business,* August 1983; Deutschen Bundesbank, 'Die Kapitalverflechtung der Unternehmen mit dem Ausland nach Ländern und Wirtschaftszweigen 1976 bis 1981', *Monthly Report,* Supplement, June 1983; South African Reserve Bank, data as cited in US Department of Commerce, *Investment Climate in Foreign Countries,* Washington, 1983.

NOTES TO TABLE A7

1 Including only those countries shown below.

2 Represents South African investment to North and South America combined.

Table A8

INDICATORS OF THE SIGNIFICANCE OF INWARD FOREIGN DIRECT INVESTMENT OR THE ACTIVITIES OF FOREIGN-BASED COMPANIES TO THE NATIONAL ECONOMY, 1982

1	Direct capital stock of foreign affiliates at book value in 1982 as a proportion of:		
	a	GNP at factor cost	22.84
	b	population (in Rand per head)	570.57
2	Assets in foreign affiliates in 1972 as a percentage of assets in all industry		42.0
3	Percentage share of sales accounted for by foreign affiliates in selected sectors in 1978		
	Primary Goods Sector		
		Oil	85
	Manufacturing Sector		
		Computers	98
		Pharmaceuticals	66
		Motor vehicles	65

Source:

South African Reserve Bank, data as cited in US Department of Commerce, *Investment Climate in Foreign Countries,* Washington, 1983; IMF, *International Financial Statistics Yearbook, 1984.*

Table A9

INDICATORS OF THE SIGNIFICANCE OF OUTWARD FOREIGN DIRECT INVESTMENT OR THE ACTIVITIES OF HOME-BASED COMPANIES ABROAD FOR THE NATIONAL ECONOMY, 1982

1	Foreign capital stock of home-based firms at book value in 1982 as a proportion of:		
	a	GNP at factor cost	8.99
	b	population (in £ per head)	224.70

Source:

South African Reserve Bank, data as cited in US Department of Commerce, *Investment Climate in Foreign Countries,* Washington, 1983; IMF, *International Financial Statistics Yearbook, 1984.*

Table A11

ROYALTY RECEIPTS AND PAYMENTS, 1975 - 84 (Rand m)

	Payments				Receipts		
	To Affiliates	*To Non-affiliates*	*Total*		*From Affiliates*	*From Non-affiliates*	*Total*
1975			52.4				4.4
1976			95.4				9.0
1977			122.5				10.6
1978	*Not*		154.1		*Not*		9.1
1979	*Separately*		135.1		*Separately*		8.7
1980	*Available*		147.4		*Available*		12.4
1981			204.9				16.7
1982			209.0				20.2
1983			245.6				21.7
1984			311.3				27.2

Source:

IMF, *Balance of Payments Statistics Yearbook,* various issues.

Table A12

LEADING FOREIGN MULTINATIONAL COMPANIES, 1980

Name	*Home Country*	*Sector*	*Total African Employees*
1. Consolidated Goldfield Ltd	UK	Extraction and preparation of ores	51,700
2. Wittington Investments UK Ltd	UK	Food	15,500
3. British Steel Corp	UK	Metal manufacturing	15,180
4. Newmont Mining Corp	USA	Extraction and preparation of ores	10,882
5. Imperial Chemical Industries PLC	UK	Chemicals	9,600
6. Lonhro Ltd	UK	Extraction and manufacture of solid fuels, ores, metals	7,176
7. Metal Box PLC	UK	Manufacture of finished metal goods	4,754
8. Charter Consolidated PLC	UK	Manufacture of metals and finished metal goods	4,724
9. Unilever, NV	Netherlands/ UK	Chemicals, food, paper, rubber and plastics	3,601
10. The British Electric Traction Co. PLC	UK	Inland transport, sea transport	3,288
11. General Electric Company Ltd	UK	Electrical and electronic engineering	3,200
12. The Coca-Cola Co	USA	Beverage	3,000
13. Dunlop Holdings PLC	UK	Processing of rubber and plastics	2,880
14. AMAX Inc	USA	Coal extraction and manufacture of solid fuels, extraction and preparation of ores.	2,825
15. Barclays Bank International Ltd	UK	Banking	2,417
16. BAT Industries Ltd	UK	Tobacco, food, engineering, paper and insurance	1,811
17. Standard Chartered Bank PLC	UK	Banking	1,797
18. Carnation Corp	USA	Food	1,587
19. United Technologies Corp	USA	Mechanical engineering	1,500
20. Union Carbide Corp	USA	Chemicals	1,487
21. Babcock International PLC	UK	Mechanical engineering	1,418
22. Ford Motor Co	USA	Motor vehicles and parts	1,327
23. Firestone Tyre and Rubber Co	USA	Processing of rubber	1,286
24. Del Monte Corp	USA	Food	1,200
25. Mobil Oil Corp	USA	Petroleum	918

Source:
UN, *The Activities of Transnational Corporations in the Industrial, Mining and Military Sectors of Southern Africa,* UN: New York, 1986.

DEVELOPING AREAS

AFRICA

(except South Africa)

BOTSWANA

The inflow of foreign direct investment to Botswana has fluctuated annually since the mid 1970s; reinvested earnings have been negative throughout this period, as indicated by Table A3.

The bulk of foreign investment is concentrated in the primary sector, notably mining. It originates largely from South Africa, although the USA does have significant interests in this sector.

Foreign investment in the manufacturing sector is again dominated by South Africa, with the UK and France having smaller investments.

The Government of Botswana pursues a free market policy and encourages inward investment in several ways. The Industrial Development Policy, adopted by Parliament in October 1984, articulates the Government's policy towards, and expectations of, foreign direct investment. Basically foreign investors are expected to identify with Botswana's development aspirations and participate fully in the country's economic life. Specifically foreign investors should assist in the training of local personnel and offer shares and other economic benefits for citizen participation. Botswana has few regulations governing inward investment and no formal screening procedures exist; neither does the Government impose any performance requirements on foreign affiliates.

MAIN SOURCES OF DATA:

A Official

1. Central Bank of Botswana: provides data on FDI flows for balance of payments purposes.
2. US Department of Commerce International Trade Administration, *Investment Climate in Foreign Countries*, Washington, 1983 and 1985, vol II.
3. UNESC, List of Major Transnational Corporations and Foreign Companies in Selected African Countries, ECA/UNCTC, October 1983.
4. UNCTC, *Transnational Corporations and World Development: Third Survey,* New York: UN, 1983.

Note:
Data do not allow us to complete Tables A9, A10 or A11 for Botswana.

Table A1

SUMMARY OF THE COUNTRY'S INTERNATIONAL INVESTMENT POSITION

	Inward Investment	Outward Investment
1 Number of foreign affiliates in host country, and of foreign affiliates of home country firms at the end of 1980	38[1]	*N.A.*
2 Number of foreign firms with direct investments in host country, and home country firms with direct foreign affiliates	*N.A.*	*N.A.*
3 Total foreign direct capital stock at book value as a percentage of GNP at factor cost in 1979	71.83	*N.A.*
4 Flow of foreign direct investment in the five year period, 1980-84 (Pula m)	269.8	0.3
5 Employment in foreign affiliates or abroad	*N.A.*	*N.A.*
6 Output of foreign affiliates or abroad	*N.A.*	*N.A.*

Source:

IMF, *Balance of Payments Statistics Yearbook, 1984;* IMF, *International Financial Statistics Yearbook, 1984;* US Department of Commerce, *Investment Climate in Foreign Countries*, Washington, 1983.

NOTES TO TABLE A1

[1] Represents affiliates of foreign MNEs from selected home countries as identified by UNCTC, 1983.

Table A2

PRIVATE FOREIGN CAPITAL STOCK, 1971 - 84 (Pula m)

	Inward Investment			Outward Investment		
	Portfolio	*Direct*[1]	*Total*	*Portfolio*	*Direct*	*Total*
Book value of capital stock						
1971		13.1				
1975		51.8				
1978	*Not Available*	68.8	*Not Available*		*Not Available*	
1981		334.0				
1984		442.8				

Source:
UNCTC, *op cit.*

NOTES TO TABLE A2

1 Foreign direct capital stock figures for 1981 and 1984 have been estimated by adding cumulative investment flows to the UNCTC stock figure of 1978.

Table A3

FLOW OF FOREIGN DIRECT INVESTMENT, 1975 - 84 (Pula m)

	Inward Investment			Outward Investment		
	Reinvested Profits	*Other*	*Total*	*Reinvested Profits*	*Other*	*Total*
1975	−37.3	8.8	28.5			*N.A.*
1976	−25.1	35.1	10.0			*N.A.*
1977	−33.1	43.4	10.3			0.2
1978	−23.9	57.7	33.8			*N.A.*
1979	−21.0	125.2	104.2	*Not Separately Available*		*N.A.*
1980	−12.1	99.1	97.0			1.8
1981	−67.7	141.7	74.0			−0.1
1982	−96.3	118.0	21.7			*N.A.*
1983	−76.3	102.4	26.1			−1.4
1984	−61.0	122.0	61.0			*N.A.*

Source:
IMF, *Balance of Payments Statistics Yearbook,* various issues.

Table A4

SECTORAL DISTRIBUTION OF FOREIGN DIRECT CAPITAL STOCK, 1981 (Pula m)

	Inward Investment			Outward Investment		
	Primary	*Secondary*	*Tertiary*	*Primary*	*Secondary*	*Tertiary*
1981	528.1	42.4[1]	*N.S.A.*	*Not Available*		

Source:

US Department of Commerce, *Investment Climate in Foreign Countries*, Washington, 1983.

NOTES TO TABLE A4

1 Represents secondary and tertiary sectors combined.

Table A5

GEOGRAPHICAL DISTRIBUTION OF FOREIGN DIRECT CAPITAL STOCK, 1981 (Pula m)

	Inward Investment			Outward Investment		
	Developed Countries	*Other Countries*	*Total*	*Developed Countries*	*Developing Countries*	*Total*
1981	530.6[1]	39.9	570.5[2]	*Not Available*		

Source:

US Department of Commerce, *Investment Climate in Foreign Countries*, Washington, 1983.

NOTES TO TABLE A5

1 Including South Africa, the USA and the UK only.

2 Total includes 'unspecified' figure, of which some part originates from South Africa.

Table A6

INDUSTRIAL DISTRIBUTION OF FOREIGN DIRECT CAPITAL STOCK, 1981 (Pula m)

	Inward Investment		Outward Investment
Primary	528.1		*Not Available*
Agriculture	*neg.*		
Mining & quarrying	528.1		
Oil	*neg.*		
Secondary & Tertiary	42.4		
TOTAL	570.5[1]		

Source:
US Department of Commerce, *Investment Climate in Foreign Countries,* Washington, 1983.

Table A7

LEADING SOURCE AND RECIPIENT COUNTRIES, 1981 (Pula m)

	Inward Investment		Outward Investment
	1981		
DEVELOPED AREAS[1]	530.6		*Not Available*
UK	2.5		
USA	97.6		
South Africa	430.5[2]		
UNSPECIFIED	39.9[2]		
TOTAL	570.5		

Source:
US Department of Commerce, *Investment Climate in Foreign Countries*, Washington, 1983; UK Department of Industry "Census of Overseas Assets, 1981", *Business Monitor*, Supplement, 1981; US Department of Commerce, *Survey of Current Business*, November, 1984.

NOTES ON TABLE A7

1 Including only those countries shown below.

2 A significant proportion of the "unspecified" figure originates from South Africa.

Table A8

INDICATORS OF THE SIGNIFICANCE OF INWARD FOREIGN DIRECT INVESTMENT OR THE ACTIVITIES OF FOREIGN-BASED COMPANIES TO THE NATIONAL ECONOMY, 1979

1	Direct capital stock of foreign affiliates at book value in 1979 as a proportion of:		
	a	GNP at factor cost	71.83
	b	population (in Pula per head)	518.73
2	Foreign investment as a percentage of domestic investment		0.5

Source:

US Department of Commerce, *Investment Climate in Foreign Countries,* Washington, 1983; IMF, *International Financial Statistics Yearbook, 1984.*

Table A12

LEADING FOREIGN MULTINATIONAL COMPANIES, 1983

Name	*Home Country*	*Sector*
Kier International	UK	Construction
Sir Alfred McAlpine	UK	Construction
Stirling International	UK	Construction
Macmillan	UK	Paper
Wardell Armstrong	UK	Mining
BRGM	France	Mining
CDF	France	Mining
Holiday Inn	USA	Hostels
Amax Inc	USA	Metals
De Beers Consolidated Mines Ltd	South Africa	Diamond trading

Source:
UNESC, List of Major Transnational Corporations and Foreign Companies in Selected African Countries, ECA/UNCTC, October 1983.

CAMEROON

There is little information on the international investment position of Cameroon. The inflow of foreign direct investment has been on a rising trend since the early 1970s, with reinvested earnings playing an important role.

The Government of Cameroon has a well defined set of foreign investment regulations and pursues a liberal policy towards the repatriation of profits. The economic and political stability of Cameroon provides the country with one of the most favourable atmospheres for private investment in Africa. In addition the Government offers foreign investors favourable investment incentives.

Foreign ownership of capital within the manufacturing sector is substantial, particularly in food, metals, textiles and wood processing. France is the main investor country in Cameroon; the USA and the UK have only small investment stakes in the country.

MAIN SOURCES OF DATA:

A Official

1 Central Bank of the United Republic of the Cameroons: provides data on FDI flows for balance of payments purposes;

2 US Department of Commerce International Trade Administration, *Investment Climate in Foreign Countries,* Washington, 1985, vol II.

3 UNESC, List of Major Transnational Corporations and Foreign Companies in Selected African Countries, ECA/UNCTC, October 1983.

4 L'Industrie Africaine en 1979, data as cited in the Report of the UN Economic Commission for Africa Mission on the Evaluation of UDEAC and the Feasibility of Enlarging Economic Co-operation in Central Africa, presented at the Annual Conference of the UDEAC Council of Heads of State, December 1981.

Note:

Data do not allow us to complete Tables A9, A10 or A11 for Cameroon.

Table A1

SUMMARY OF THE COUNTRY'S INTERNATIONAL INVESTMENT POSITION

		Inward Investment	Outward Investment
1	Number of foreign affiliates in host country, and of foreign affiliates of home country firms at the end of 1980	101[1]	*N.A.*
2	Number of foreign firms with direct investments in host country, and home country firms with direct foreign affiliates	*N.A.*	*N.A.*
3	Total foreign direct capital stock at book value as a percentage of GNP at factor cost in 1982	12.15	*N.A.*
4	Flow of foreign direct investment in the five year period 1979-83 (US $ m)	647.65	*N.A.*
5	Employment inforeign affiliates or abroad	*N.A.*	*N.A.*
6	Output of foreign affiliates or abroad	*N.A.*	*N.A.*

Source:

UNCTC, *Transnational Corporations in World Development: Third Survey*, New York: UN, 1983; IMF, *Balance of Payments Statistics Yearbook, 1984*; OECD, *Geographical Distribution of Financial Flows to Developing Countries*, Paris, 1984.

NOTES TO TABLE A1

1 Representing number of foreign affiliates of MNEs from selected home countries, as identified by UNCTC, 1983.

Table A2

PRIVATE FOREIGN CAPITAL STOCK, 1975 - 83 (US $m)

	Inward Investment			Outward Investment		
	Portfolio	*Direct*[1]	*Total*	*Portfolio*	*Direct*	*Total*
Book value of capital stock						
1975	*Not Available*	300.0	*Not Available*	*Not Available*		
1978		370.0				
1981		696.9				
1983		1,017.6				

Source:

UNCTC, *Transnational Corporations in World Development; Third Survey,* New York: UN, 1983;
IMF, *Balance of Payments Statistics Yearbook,* 1984.

NOTES TO TABLE A2

1 Foreign direct capital stock for 1981 and 1983 has been estimated by adding cumulative investment flows to the UNCTC stock figure for 1978.

Table A3

FLOW OF FOREIGN DIRECT INVESTMENT, 1970 - 83 (US $m)

	Inward Investment			Outward Investment		
	Reinvested Profts	*Other*	*Total*	*Reinvested Profits*	*Other*	*Total*
1970	*Not Separately Available*	*Not Separately Available*	16.0	*Not Separately Available*		*Not Available*
1971			2.0			
1972			3.3			
1973	7.2	–3.6	3.6			3.6
1974	16.8	4.8	21.6			–8.4
1975	17.0	9.7	26.7			2.4
1976	17.2	–0.8	16.4			8.2
1977	*N.S.A.*	*N.S.A.*	8.8			4.4
1978	32.8	7.8	40.6			6.9
1979	22.4	39.8	62.1			–2.1
1980	54.8	75.1	129.8			–8.3
1981	35.6	99.4	135.0			–0.5
1982	50.6	58.2	108.7			4.4
1983	27.9	184.0	212.0			5.2

Source:

IMF, *Balance of Payments Statistics Yearbook*, various issues.

NOTES TO TABLE A3

1 Excludes reinvested profits.

Table A4

SECTORAL DISTRIBUTION OF FOREIGN DIRECT CAPITAL STOCK, 1981 (US $ m)[1]

	Inward Investment				Outward Investment		
	Primary	*Secondary*	*Tertiary*		*Primary*	*Secondary*	*Tertiary*
1981	74	622.4	1.4		*Not Available*		

Source:

L'Industrie Africaine en 1979, data as cited in the Report of the UN Commission for Africa Mission on the Evaluation of UDEAC and the Feasibility of Enlarging Economic Co-operation in Central Africa, presented at the Annual Conference of the UDEAC Council of Heads of State, December, 1981.

NOTES TO TABLE A4

1 Estimated by applying the percentage sectoral distribution of foreign ownership of social capital, 1979, to the FDI stock figure of 1981.

Table A5

GEOGRAPHICAL DISTRIBUTION OF FOREIGN DIRECT CAPITAL STOCK, 1981 (US $ m)

	Inward Investment				Outward Investment		
	Developed Countries	*Other Countries*	*Total*		*Developed Countries*	*Developing Countries*	*Total*
1981	152.2[1]	545.6	697.8[2]		*Not Available*		

Source:

US Department of Commerce, *Survey of Current Business*, November 1984; UK Department of Industry, *Business Monitor*, Supplement 1981; UNCTC, *Transnational Corporations in World Development: Third Survey*, New York: UN, 1983; IMF, *Balance of Payments Statistics Yearbook*, 1984

NOTES TO TABLE A5

1 US and UK investments only.

2 Estimated by applying cumulative investment flows, 1979-81 to the UNCTC stock figure of 1978.

Table A6

INDUSTRIAL DISTRIBUTION OF FOREIGN DIRECT CAPITAL STOCK, 1981 (US $ m)[1]

	Inward Investment	Outward Investment
	1981	
Primary	74.0	*Not Available*
Agriculture	74.0	
Mining & quarrying	*neg.*	
Oil	*neg.*	
Secondary	622.4	
Food & drink [2]	172.4	
Chemicals & allied	62.8	
Metals	169.6	
Textiles & clothing	82.3	
Paper & allied	*N.S.A.*	
Rubber	*N.S.A.*	
Stone, clay & glass	36.3	
Coal & petroleum products	*N.S.A.*	
Other manufacturing [3]	99.0	
Tertiary	1.4	
Other services [4]	1.4	
TOTAL	697.8[5]	

Source:
L'Industrie Africaine en 1979, data as cited in the Report of the UN Economic Commission for Africa Mission on the Evaluation of UDEAC and the Feasibility of Enlarging Economic Co-operation in Central Africa, presented at the Annual Conference of the UDEAC Council of Heads of State, December, 1981; UNCTC, *Transnational Corporations in World Development: Third Survey*, New York: UN, 1983; IMF, *Balance of Payments Statistics Yearbook, 1984.*

NOTES TO TABLE A6

1 Estimated by applying the percentage sectoral distribution of foreign ownership of social capital in 1979, to the FDI stock figure of 1981.
2 Including tobacco.
3 Represents wood processing.
4 Represents electricity & water.
5 Estimated by adding cumulative investment flows 1979-81 to the UNCTC stock figure of 1978.

Table A7

LEADING SOURCE AND RECIPIENT COUNTRIES, 1981 (US $ m)

	Inward Investment	Outward Investment
DEVELOPED AREAS[1]	152.2	*Not Available*
UK	37.2	
USA	115.0	
UNSPECIFIED	545.6	
TOTAL	697.8[2]	

Sources:

US Department of Commerce, *Survey of Current Business*, November 1984; UK Department of Industry, *Census of Overseas Assets 1981, Business Monitor,* Supplement, 1981; UNCTC, *Transnational Corporations in World Development, Third Survey,* New York: UN, 1983; IMF, *Balance of Payments Statistics Yearbook,* 1984.

NOTES TO TABLE A7

1 Including only those countries shown below.

2 Estimated by adding cumulative investment flows, 1979-81 to the UNCTC stock figure of 1978.

Table A8

INDICATORS OF THE SIGNIFICANCE OF INWARD FOREIGN DIRECT INVESTMENT OR THE ACTIVITIES OF FOREIGN-BASED COMPANIES TO THE NATIONAL ECONOMY, 1979 - 82

1	Direct capital stock of foreign affiliates at book value in 1982 as a proportion of:	
	a GNP at factor cost	12.15
	b population (in US $ per head)	90.68
2	Foreign investment as a percentage of domestic investment 1978-80	1.9
3	Percentage share of assets, accounted for by foreign affiliates in selected sectors, 1979[1]	
		Assets
	Primary Goods Sector	
	Agriculture	19
	Manufacturing Sector	
	Food & drink	81[2]
	Chemicals & allied	57
	Metals	76
	Textiles & clothing	73[3]
	Paper & allied	0
	Stone, glass & clay	48
	Timber & furniture	80
	Services Sector	
	Other services	1[4]

Source:

UNCTC, *Transnational Corporations in World Development: Third Survey,* New York: UN, 1983; IMF, *Balance of Payments Statistics Yearbook, 1984;* OECD, *Geographical Distribution of Financial Flows to Developing Countries,* Paris, 1984. L'Industrie Africaine en 1979, data as cited in the Report of the ECA Mission on the Evaluation of UDEAC and the Feasibility of Enlarging Economic Co-operation in Central Africa, presented at the Annual Conference of the UDEAC Council of Heads of State, December, 1981.

NOTES TO TABLE A8

1 Represents foreign share of the ownership of capital in 1979.

2 Food only. For beverages, the foreign share is 69%; for tobacco, 75%.

3 Textiles only. For leather and footwear, the foreign share is 23%.

4 Represents electricity and water.

Table A12

LEADING FOREIGN MULTINATIONAL COMPANIES, 1983

Name	*Home Country*	*Sector*
Bourdin & Chausse Travaux	France	Construction
Compagnie Francaise Fibres Textiles	France	Agriculture
CFP-Total	France	Oil
Dumez	France	Mining
ELF Aquitaire	France	Oil
IFP	France	Gas
Hachetta	France	Distribution
Societe anonyme des travaux d'autre-mer	France	Construction
Optorg	France	Distribution
Ruhrgas	W. Germany	Gas
Peter Frankel & Partners	UK	Construction
Macmillan	UK	Paper
Walsh & Brais	Canada	Construction

Source:

UNESC, List of Major Transnational Corporations and Foreign Companies in Selected African Countries, ECA/UNCTC, October 1983.

CENTRAL AFRICAN REPUBLIC

The inflow of foreign direct investment to the Central African Republic has varied widely since the mid-1970s, reaching a peak in 1979.

There is little detailed information about the geographical and sectoral distribution of the stock of private foreign capital. Investor countries include Portugal, Belgium, Yugoslavia, Canada, Romania and Greece, although the bulk of foreign direct investment originates from France.

Commerce accounts for 25% of the total foreign capital stock in 1981, while a further 20% is directed to forestry. The diamond sector is also a significant recipient of investment particularly from Belgium and Israel. Other recipient industries include banking, beverages and tourism. In 1985 new investment in hotels amounted to US $ 5 million.

The Government of the Central African Republic unreservedly welcomes inward investment and has an extremely liberal investment code. The Government has identified certain sectors eligible for preference benefits by both domestic and foreign owned enterprises. There are no legal requirements concerning the extent of local participation in CAR enterprises.

MAIN SOURCES OF DATA:

A Official

1. Central Bank of the CAR: issues data on FDI flows for balance of payments purposes.
2. US Department of Commerce International Trade Administration, *Investment Climate in Foreign Countries,* Washington, 1983 and 1985 Vol II.
3. UNCTC, *Transnational Corporations in World Development: Third Survey,* New York: UN, 1983.
4. Report of the UN Economic Commission for Africa Mission on the Evaluation of UDEAC and the Feasibility of Enlarging Economic Co-operation in Central Africa, presented at the Annual Conference of the UDEAC Council Heads of State, December, 1981.

Note:
Data do not allow us to complete Tables A9, A10 or A11 for the Central African Republic.

Table A1

SUMMARY OF THE COUNTRY'S INTERNATIONAL INVESTMENT POSITION

		Inward Investment	Outward Investment
1	Number of foreign affiliates in host country, and of foreign affiliates of home country firms at the end of 1980[1]	20	*N.A.*
2	Number of foreign firms with direct investments in host country, and home country firms with direct foreign affiliates	*N.A.*	*N.A.*
3	Total foreign direct capital stock at book value as a percentage of GNP at factor cost in 1981	19.20	*N.A.*
4	Flow of foreign direct investment in the five year period 1979-83 (US $ m)	45.3	*N.A.*
5	Employment in foreign affiliates or abroad	*N.A.*	*N.A.*
6	Output of foreign affiliates or abroad	*N.A.*	*N.A.*

Source:

IMF, *Balance of Payments Statistics Yearbook, 1984;* OECD, *Geographical Distribution of Financial Flows to Developing Countries,* Paris, 1984.

NOTES TO TABLE A1

1 Represents number of affiliates of MNEs from selected home countries as identified by UNCTC, 1983.

Table A2

PRIVATE FOREIGN CAPITAL STOCK, 1981 (US $ m)

	Inward Investment			Outward Investment		
	Portfolio	*Direct*	*Total*	*Portfolio*	*Direct*	*Total*
Book value of capital stock						
1975	*Not Available*	60[1]	*Not Available*	*Not Available*		
1978		70				
1981		130				
1983		141[2]				

Source:
US Department of Commerce, *Investment Climate in Foreign Countries,* Washington, 1983.

NOTES TO TABLE A2
[1] From OECD countries only.
[2] 1981 stock plus new investment 1982-83.

Table A3

FLOW OF FOREIGN DIRECT INVESTMENT, 1970 - 83 (US $ m)

	Inward Investment			Outward Investment		
	Reinvested Profits	*Other*	*Total*[1]	*Reinvested Profits*	*Other*	*Total*
1970	*Not Separately Available*		1.0	*Not Separately Available*		*Not Available*
1971			1.0			
1972			1.1			
1974			6.0			
1975			6.1			1.2
1976			3.5			0.1
1977			2.3			0.1
1978			6.3			1.3
1979			23.3			*Not Available*
1980			5.2			
1981			5.9			
1982			8.8			
1983			2.1			

Source:
IMF, *Balance of Payments Statistics Yearbook,* various issues.

NOTES TO TABLE A3
[1] Excluding reinvested profits.

Table A4

SECTORAL DISTRIBUTION OF FOREIGN DIRECT CAPITAL STOCK, 1981 (US $m)

	Inward Investment			Outward Investment		
	Primary	*Secondary*	*Tertiary*	*Primary*	*Secondary*	*Tertiary*
1981	44	53[1]	33[2]	*Not Available*		

Source:

US Department of Commerce, *Investment Climate in Foreign Countries,* Washington, 1983.

NOTES TO TABLE A4

1 Includes tertiary sector other than commerce.

2 Includes commerce only.

Table A5

GEOGRAPHICAL DISTRIBUTION OF FOREIGN DIRECT CAPITAL STOCK, 1981 (US $m)

	Inward Investment			Outward Investment		
	Developed Countries	*Other Countries*	*Total*	*Developed Countries*	*Developing Countries*	*Total*
1981	102[1]	28	130	*Not Available*		

Source:

US Department of Commerce, *Investment Climate in Foreign Countries,* Washington, 1983; US Department of Commerce, *Survey of Current Business,* November, 1984.

NOTES TO TABLE A5

1 Includes France, Portugal, Belgium and the USA only.

Table A6

INDUSTRIAL DISTRIBUTION OF FOREIGN DIRECT CAPITAL STOCK, 1981 (US $m)

	Inward Investment		Outward Investment
	1981		
Primary	44		
Agriculture[1]	26		
Mining & Quarrying	18		
Secondary	*Not Available*		*Not Available*
Tertiary			
Construction			
Transport & communications			
Distributive trades	33		
Property	*Not Available*		
Banking & finance			
Other services			
TOTAL	130		

Source:
US Department of Commerce, *Investment Climate in Foreign Countries,* Washington, 1983.

NOTES TO TABLE A6

1 Represents forestry.

Table A7

LEADING SOURCE AND RECIPIENT COUNTRIES, 1981 (US $m)

	Inward Investment		Outward Investment
	1981		
DEVELOPED AREAS[1]	102		*Not Available*
Belgium	7		
France	80		
Portugal	14		
USA	1		
UNSPECIFIED	28		
TOTAL	130		

Source:
US Department of Commerce, *Investment Climate in Foreign Countries,* Washington, 1983; US Department of Commerce, *Survey of Current Business,* November 1984.

NOTES TO TABLE A7

1 Including only those countries shown below.

Table A8

INDICATORS OF THE SIGNIFICANCE OF INWARD FOREIGN DIRECT INVESTMENT OR THE ACTIVITIES OF FOREIGN-BASED COMPANIES TO THE NATIONAL ECONOMY, 1979 - 81

1	Direct capital stock of foreign affiliates at book value in 1981 as a proportion of:	
	a GNP at factor cost	19.20
	b population (in US $ per head)	55.79
2	Foreign Investment in affiliates as a percentage of domestic investment, 1978 - 80	2.1
3	Percentage share of assets accounted for by foreign affiliates in selected sectors, 1979[1]	*Assets*[1]
	Primary Goods Sector	
	Agriculture	37
	Manufacturing Sector	
	Food & drink	0
	Tobacco	95
	Chemicals and allied	100
	Metals / Mechanical engineering	95
	Textiles	5
	Leather and clothing	100
	Wood processing	88

Source:
IMF, *International Financial Statistics Yearbook, 1984;* L'Industrie Africaine en 1979, data as cited in the Report of the ECA Mission on the Evaluation of UDEAC and the Feasibility of Enlarging Economic Co-operation in Central Africa, December 1981; US Department of Commerce, *Investment Climate in Foreign Countries,* Washington, 1983; OECD, *Geographical Distribution of Financial Flows to Developing Countries,* Paris, 1984.

NOTES TO TABLE A8

1 Represents foreign share of ownership of capital in the Central African Republic.

Table A12

LEADING FOREIGN MULTINATIONAL COMPANIES, 1985

	Name	*Home Country*	*Sector*
1	Conoco	USA	Oil
2	Diamond Distributors International	USA	Mining
3	L'Air Liquide SA	France	Industrial gases
4	Brosette SA Holding	France	Fuels, ores, metals and industrial material, plastics and rubber
5	Credit Lyonnais SA	France	Banking and finance
6	Enterprise Miniere Et Chimique	France	Mineral extraction, chemicals, food, sea transport
7	Faugere Et Jutheau	France	Insurance
8	Financement Industriel, Commercial Et Agricole, SA	France	Mechanical engineering, drink, tobacco
9	Francaise de L'Afrique Occidentale SA	France	Banking and finance
10	Gerance Et D'Armement (Holding) SA	France	Sea transport
11	La Motoconfort	France	Manufacture of transport equipment, shipbuilding, aerospace, railway
12	Nationale D'Exploitation Industrielle des Tabacs et des Alumettes	France	Tobacco
13	Optorg SA Cie	France	Electrical and electronic equipment
14	Regie Nationale Des Usines Renault	France	Motor vehicles & parts
15	Imetal SA	France	Metal manufacturing
16	Nouvelle D'Exploitation des Ets, Dofan SA	France	Manufacture of leather & leather products
17	Rougier SA	France	Chemicals
18	SCAC SA	France	Coal extraction, mineral oil processing, timber, other transport services

Source:
UNESC, List of Major Transnational Corporations and Foreign Companies in selected African countries, ECA/UNCTC, October 1983; Dun and Bradstreet, *Who Owns Whom 1985,* London: Business Marketing Division (Publications), 1985.

CONGO

The inflow of foreign direct investment in Congo rose in 1975, falling sharply in 1976. Nevertheless, since then it has been on a steadily rising trend.

Foreign ownership of capital is substantial in both the primary and secondary sectors. Within manufacturing, foreign interests are particularly strong in beverages, tobacco, engineering, chemicals and pulp and paper. The USA, France and Belgium are the main investing countries in Congo.

The attitude of the Congolese Government towards inward direct investment is most favourable. An investment code, promulgated in 1982, sets out the rights and obligations of foreign investors and offers five categories of incentives to encourage investment consistent with national and regional development priorities. In particular, the Government encourages foreign investors to engage in joint ventures with Congolese nationals or with the State itself.

Capital outflows are permitted and outward direct investment in other UDEAC countries.

MAIN SOURCES OF DATA:

A **Official**

1 Central Bank of the Congo: provides data on FDI flows for balance of payments purposes.

2 UNESC, List of Major Transnational Corporations and Foreign Companies in selected African Countries, ECA/UNCTC, October 1983.

3 Report on the UN Economic Commission for Africa Mission on the Evaluation of UDEAC and the Feasibility of Enlarging Economic Co-operation in Central Africa, presented at the Annual Conference of the UDEAC Council of Heads of State, December, 1981.

4 US Department of Commerce International Trade Administration, *Investment Climate in Foreign Countries,* Washington 1985, vol II.

5 UNCTC, *Transnational Corporations in World Development Third Survey,* New York: UN, 1983.

Note:
Data do not allow us to complete Tables A9, A10 or A11 for the Congo.

Table A1

SUMMARY OF THE COUNTRY'S INTERNATIONAL INVESTMENT POSITION

		Inward Investment	Outward Investment
1	Number of foreign affiliates in host country, and of foreign affiliates of home country firms at the end of 1980	43[1]	*N.A.*
2	Number of foreign firms with direct investments in host country, and home country firms with direct foreign affiliates	*N.A.*	*N.A.*
3	Total foreign direct capital stock at book value as a percentage of GNP at factor cost in 1982	18.91	*N.A.*
4	Flow of foreign direct investment in the five year period 1979-83 (C Fr bn)	53.4	*N.A.*
5	Employment in foreign affiliates or affiliates abroad	*N.A.*	*N.A.*
6	Output of foreign affiliates or abroad	*N.A.*	*N.A.*

Source:

IMF, *Balance of Payments Statistics Yearbook*, various issues; IMF, *International Financial Statistics Yearbook, 1984.*

NOTES TO TABLE A1

1 Represents number of affiliates of foreign MNEs from selected countries identified in UNCTC, 1983.

Table A2

PRIVATE FOREIGN CAPITAL STOCK, 1983 (C Fr bn)[1]

	Inward Investment			Outward Investment		
	Portfolio	*Direct*	*Total*	*Portfolio*	*Direct*	*Total*
Book value of capital stock						
1975	*Not Available*	77.5	*Not Available*	*Not Available*		
1978		79.2				
1981		99.6				
1983		132.6				

Source:

IMF, *Balance of Payments Statistics Yearbook*, various issues; UNCTC, 1983, *op cit.*

NOTES TO TABLE A2

[1] Represents cumulative investment flows as from 1971.

Table A3

FLOW OF FOREIGN DIRECT INVESTMENT, 1971 - 83 (C Fr bn)

	Inward Investment			Outward Investment		
	Reinvested Profits	*Other*	*Total*	*Reinvested Profits*	*Other*	*Total*
1971	*Not Separately Available*		13.3	*Not Available*		
1972			16.7			
1973			15.4			
1974			11.3			
1975			20.8			
1976			0.3			
1977			0.5			
1978			0.9			
1979			3.5			
1980	1.3	7.2	8.5			
1981	0.5	7.9	8.4			
1982	0.4	11.2	11.6			
1983	6.5	14.9	21.4			

Source:
IMF, *Balance of Payments Statistics Yearbook,* various issues.

Table A4

SECTORAL DISTRIBUTION OF FOREIGN DIRECT CAPITAL STOCK, 1983 (C Fr bn)[1]

	Inward Investment			Outward Investment		
	Primary	*Secondary*	*Tertiary*	*Primary*	*Secondary*	*Tertiary*
1983	56.5	75.9	*N.A.*	*Not Available*		

Source:

L'Industrie Africaine en 1979, data as cited in the Report of the UN Commission for Africa Mission on the Evaluation of the UDEAC and the Feasibility of Enlarging Economic Co-operation in Central Africa, *op cit;* IMF, *Balance of Payments Statistics Yearbook,* various issues.

NOTES TO TABLE A4

1 Estimated by applying the percentage sectoral distribution of foreign ownership of social capital, 1979, to the FDI stock figure of 1983 (Table A2)

Table A5

GEOGRAPHICAL DISTRIBUTION OF FOREIGN DIRECT CAPITAL STOCK, 1983 (C Fr bn)

	Inward Investment			Outward Invesment		
	Developed Countries	*Other Countries*	*Total*	*Developed Countries*	*Developing Countries*	*Total*
1983	10.9[1]	121.5	132.4[2]	*Not Available*		

Source:

US Department of Commerce, *Survey of Current Business,* November 1984; IMF, *Balance of Payments Statistics Yearbook*, various issues.

NOTES TO TABLE A5

1 USA only.

2 Cumulative investment flow, 1971-83.

Table A6

INDUSTRIAL DISTRIBUTION OF FOREIGN DIRECT CAPITAL STOCK, 1983 (C Fr bn)[1]

	Inward Investment	Outward Investment
	1983	
Primary	56.5	
Agriculture	*neg.*	
Mining & quarrying	56.5	
Oil	*neg.*	
Secondary	75.9	
Food & drink[2]	31.9	
Chemicals & allied	12.2	
Mechanical engineering	3.6	
Textiles & clothing	11.5	
Other manufacturing[3]	16.7	
Tertiary		
Construction		
Transport & communications		
Distributive trade	*Not Available*	*Not Available*
Property		
Banking & finance		
Other services		
TOTAL	132.4	

Source:
L'Industrie Africaine en 1979, data as cited in the Report of the UN Commission for Africa Mission on the Evaluation of UDEAC and the Feasbility of Enlarging Economic Co-operation on Central Africa, presented at the Annual Conference of the UDEAC Council of Heads of State, December 1981; IMF, *Balance of Payments Statistics Yearbook,* various issues.

NOTES TO TABLE A6

1 Estimated by applying the percentage sectoral distribution of foreign ownership of social capital, 1979, to the FDI stock figure of 1983 (Table A2).

2 Represents beverages and tobacco.

3 Represents wood processing.

Table A7

LEADING SOURCE AND RECIPIENT COUNTRIES, 1983 (C Fr bn)

	Inward Investment	Outward Investment
	1983	
DEVELOPED AREAS		
USA	10.9	*Not Available*
UNSPECIFIED	121.5	
TOTAL	132.4[1]	

Source:
US Department of Commerce, *Survey of Current Business,* November 1984; IMF, *Balance of Payments Statistics Yearbook,* various issues.

NOTES TO TABLE A7

1 Cumulative investment flow, 1971-83.

Table A8

INDICATORS OF THE SIGNIFICANCE OF INWARD FOREIGN DIRECT INVESTMENT OR THE ACTIVITIES OF FOREIGN-BASED COMPANIES TO THE NATIONAL ECONOMY, 1979 - 82

1	Direct capital stock of foreign affiliates at book value in 1982 as a proportion of:	
	a GNP at factor cost	18.91
	b population (in C Fr per head)	68,641.98
2	Percentage share of assets accounted for by foreign affiliates in selected sectors, 1979[1]	
		Assets
	Primary Goods Sector	
	Mining & quarrying	83
	Manufacturing Sector	
	Food & drink	98.5[2]
	Chemicals & allied	89
	Mechanical engineering	100
	Textiles & clothing	70[3]
	Timber & furniture	70

Source:
L'Industrie Africaine en 1979, data as cited in the Report of the UN Economic Commission for Africa Mission on the Feasibility of Enlarging Economic Co-operation in Central Africa, presented at the Annual Conference of the UDEAC Council of Heads of State, December 1981; IMF, *Balance of Payments Statistics Yearbook*, various issues; IMF, *International Financial Statistics Yearbook, 1984.*

NOTES TO TABLE A8

1 Represents foreign share of the ownership of social capital in Congo, 1979

2 Beverages only. For tobacco, the foreign share is 100%.

3 Textiles only. For footwear, the foreign share is 100%.

Table A12

LEADING FOREIGN MULTINATIONAL COMPANIES, 1983

Name	*Home Country*	*Sector*
Banque Internationale pour l'Afrique Occidentale	France	Banking
Novotel	France	Hotels
L'Air Liquide SA	France	Industrial gases
Amrep SA	France	Mineral extraction, mineral oil processing
BSN - Gervais Danone SA	France	Food
Banque Nationale de Paris	France	Banking and finance
Bouygues SA	France	Construction
Brosette SA Holding	France	Fuels, ores, metals and industrial material, plastics and rubber
Chimique, Routiere Et D'Entreprise Generale	France	Civil engineering
C G Doris SA	France	Mechanical engineering
Commerciale De Metaux et Minerais (Rene Aumas)	France	Minerals, ores and metals
Credit Lyonnais SA	France	Banking and finance
Entreprise de Travaux Publics de L'Ouest SA	France	Civil engineering
Gevance Et D'Armement (Holding)	France	Sea transport
Omnium International De Parfumerie et Cosmetiques 'Interparco' SA	France	Cosmetics
Schaeffer Et Cie, Ets	France	Textiles
SCOA SA	France	Banking and finance
Generale SA	France	Public administration
Hachette	France	Paper, printing and publishing
Societe Nationale Elf Aquitaine	France	Extraction of mineral oil and natural gas and mineral oil processing
Optorg SA	France	Electrical and electronic equipment
Inchape PLC	UK	Business services
Iena Industries	UK	Timber
ENI	Italy	Oil

Source:
John M Stopford, *The World Directory of Multinational Enterprises 1982-83,* Bath: The Pitman Press, 1982.

EGYPT

Since President Anwar al-Sadat invited an open door policy towards inward direct investment in 1974, the investment climate in Egypt has become progressively more favourable. Nevertheless, the inflow of foreign direct investment has fluctuated since the mid-1970s, reaching a peak in 1979. By January 1984, approval had been given to 531 foreign investment projects.

The main investor countries in Egypt are other Arab countries, the USA, the UK and West Germany, and the bulk of their investment is concentrated in the petroleum and allied sectors. Within the tertiary sector, the main emphasis lies on banking, finance and real estate. There is little foreign investment in the manufacturing sector.

Egypt does not promote foreign investments by its own companies. Nevertheless as Table A3 shows there has been a consistent outflow of foreign investment since 1977.

MAIN SOURCES OF DATA:

A Official

1 *Central Bank of Egypt:* issues data on investment flows for balance of payment purposes.

2 US Department of Commerce International Trade Administration, *Investment Climate in Foreign Countries*, Washington, 1985 Vol. II.

3 UNESC, List of Transnational Corporations and Foreign Companies in Selected African Countries, ECA/UNCTC, October 1983.

Note:
Data do not allow us to complete Tables A9, A10, or A11 for Egypt.

Table A1

SUMMARY OF THE COUNTRY'S INTERNATIONAL INVESTMENT POSITION

		Inward Investment	Outward Investment
1	Number of foreign affiliates in host country, and of foreign affiliates of home country firms	*N.A.*	*N.A.*
2	Number of foreign firms with direct investments in host country, and home country firms with direct foreign affiliates	*N.A.*	*N.A.*
3	Total foreign direct capital stock at book value as a percentage of GNP at factor cost in 1982	11.34	*N.A.*
4	Flow of foreign direct investment in the five year period, 1979-83 (E £ m)	2,826.4	32.0
5	Employment in foreign affiliates or abroad	*N.A.*	*N.A.*
6	Output of foreign affiliates or abroad	*N.A.*	*N.A.*

Source:
IMF, *Balance of Payments Statistics Yearbook,* 1984; IMF, *International Financial Statistics Yearbook,* 1984.

Table A2

PRIVATE FOREIGN CAPITAL STOCK, 1982 (E £ m)

	Inward Investment				Outward Investment		
	Portfolio	*Direct*	*Total*		*Portfolio*	*Direct*	*Total*
Book value of capital stock							
1975		27.39					
1981	*Not*	1,977.99	*Not*			*Not*	
1982	*Available*	2,438.59	*Available*			*Available*	
1983		3,043.19					

Source:
IMF, *Balance of Payments Statistics Yearbook,* various issues; UNCTC, *Transnational Corporations in World Development: Third Survey,* New York: UN, 1983.

NOTES TO TABLE A2

1 The figure for 1975 represents UNCTC stock estimate. The figures for other years have been estimated by adding cumulative investment flow figures to the stock figure of 1975.

Table A3

FLOW OF FOREIGN INVESTMENT, 1975 - 83 (E £ m)

	Inward Investment				Outward Investment		
	Reinvested Profits	*Other*	*Total*		*Reinvested Profits*	*Other*	*Total*
1975			*N.A.*				−4.8
1976			23.9				−25.3
1977			41.1				2.7
1978	*Not*		124.4		*Not*		7.8
1979	*Separately*		851.0		*Separately*		3.6
1980	*Available*		383.6		*Available*		4.6
1981			526.6				4.1
1982			460.6				6.2
1983			604.6				13.5

Source:
IMF, *Balance of Payments Statistics Yearbook,* various issues.

Table A4

SECTORAL DISTRIBUTION OF FOREIGN DIRECT CAPITAL STOCK, 1981 (E £ m)

	Inward Investment				Outward Investment		
	Primary	*Secondary*	*Tertiary*		*Primary*	*Secondary*	*Tertiary*
1981	779.1[1]	27.5[2]	92.8[3]		*Not Available*		

Source:

UK Department of Industry, "Census of Overseas Assets 1981," *Business Monitor*, Supplement, 1981;
US Department of Commerce, *Survey of Current Business*, Washington, August 1983;
Deutschen Bundesbank, *Monthly Report*, Supplement, June 1983.

NOTES TO TABLE A4

1 US & West German investment only.

2 US, UK & West German investment only.

Table A5

GEOGRAPHICAL DISTRIBUTION OF FOREIGN DIRECT CAPITAL STOCK, 1981 (E £ m)

	Inward Investment				Outward Investment		
	Developed Countries	*Other Countries*	*Total*		*Developed Countries*	*Developing Countries*	*Total*
1981	917.6[1]	1,033.0	1,950.6[2]		*Not Available*		

Source:

UK Department of Industry, *Business Monitor,* M4 Supplement, 1981; US Department of Commerce, *Survey of Current Business,* August 1983; Deutschen Bundesbank, *Monthly Report,* Supplement, June 1983.

NOTES TO TABLE A5

1 US, UK & West German investment only.

2 Cumulative investment flow 1976-81.

Table A6

INDUSTRIAL DISTRIBUTION OF FOREIGN DIRECT CAPITAL STOCK, 1981 (E £ m)[1]

	Inward Investment	Outward Investment
	1981	
Primary	779.1[2]	Not Available
Oil	653.1[3]	
Secondary	27.5[4]	
Food & drink	0.6	
Chemicals & allied	14.8	
Metals	2.1	
Paper & allied	7.1	
Stone, clay & glass	2.1	
Other manufacturing	0.7	
Tertiary	92.8	
Construction	2.5[5]	
Distributive trade	7.7[3]	
Property) Banking & finance)	56.0[3]	
Other services	26.6	
TOTAL	917.6	

Source:
UK Department of Industry, "Census of Overseas Assets 1981", *Business Monitor,* Supplement 1981; US Department of Commerce, *Survey of Current Business,* August 1983; Deutschen Bundesbank, *Monthly Report,* Supplement, June 1983.

NOTES TO TABLE A6

1 Includes US, UK and West German investment only.

2 USA & West Germany only.

3 USA only.

4 Estimates within the manufacturing sector obtained by applying percentage sectoral distribution of total foreign participation in Free Zone projects in production, to the total stock of US, UK & West German investment in that sector.

5 UK only.

Table A7

LEADING SOURCE AND RECIPIENT COUNTRIES, 1981 (E £ m)

	Inward Investment		Outward Investment
	1981		
DEVELOPED AREAS[1]	917.6		
W. Germany	136.9		
UK	24.0		*Not Available*
USA	756.7		
UNSPECIFIED	1,033.0		
TOTAL	1,950.6[2]		

Source:
UK Department of Industry, "Census of Overseas Assets 1981", *Business Monitor*, Supplement, 1981; US Department of Commerce, *Survey of Current Business,* Washington, August 1983; Deutschen Bundesbank, "Die Kapitalverflechtung der Unternehmen mit dem Ausland nach Ländern und Wirtschaftsweigen 1976 bis 1981", *Monthly Report,* Supplement, June 1983.

NOTES TO TABLE A7

1 Including only those countries shown below.

2 Cumulative investment flow, 1976-81.

Table A8

INDICATORS OF THE SIGNIFICANCE OF INWARD FOREIGN DIRECT INVESTMENT OR THE ACTIVITIES OF FOREIGN-BASED COMPANIES TO THE NATIONAL ECONOMY, 1978 - 82

1	Direct capital stock of foreign affiliates at book value in 1982 as a proportion of	
	a GNP at factor cost	11.34
	b population (in E £ per head)	53.98
2	Foreign investment as a percentage of domestic investment 1978-80	0.4

Source:
IMF, *Balance of Payments Statistics Yearbook,* various issues; IMF, *International Financial Statistics Yearbook, 1984.*

Table A12

LEADING FOREIGN MULTINATIONAL COMPANIES, 1983

Name	*Home Country*	*Sector*
Maruberu Corp	Japan	Petrochemicals
Mitsui Oil Exploration Co	Japan	Oil
Nippon Kotran	Japan	Metals
Teikoku Oil Co	Japan	Oil
Toyo Engineering Co	Japan	Petrochemicals
Toyo Menka Kaisha	Japan	Metals
AMF	Japan	Rubber
Black & Ceatch	Japan	Public utilities
FMC Corp	USA	Transportation
Harbert Const Co	USA	Public utilities
Intercontinental Hotels	USA	Hotels
J A Jones	USA	Construction
Pau N Houkrd Co	USA	Public utilities
Peerless Instruments	USA	Electrical
Sadelini New York	USA	Public utilities
Babcock Contractors	UK	Oil
Bernard Sunley & Sons	UK	Construction
Arab Sunley & Sons	UK	Construction
Otto Buchwitz	E. Germany	Construction
Thyssen Rheinstahl Technik	W. Germany	Manufacturing
Oberoi Hotels	India	Hotels
Belgian Contractors	Belgium	Construction
Kuwait Real Estate Investment	Kuwait	Construction
Norrlandsvagnar	Sweden	Construction
Saevar Soickerfabrik	Sweden	Construction
Eastman Kodak	USA	Photographic films
Marathon Petroleum	USA	Oil

Source:

United Nations Economic & Social Council, List of Major Transnational Corporations and Foreign Companies in Selected African Countries, ECA/UNCTC, October 1983.

GABON

There are few detailed statistics available on foreign direct investment in Gabon despite a significant foreign presence there.

France is the most important investor country in Gabon, and accounts for over three quarters of the inward capital stake investment. The USA, Netherlands, UK and West Germany are playing a more important role, and in the 80s have made several substantial new investments in the oil and mining sectors.

Foreign ownership of capital is greatest in the primary sector, particularly oil and mining. Within the manufacturing sector, the main emphasis lies on chemicals, construction materials and wood processing. US banking exposure in Gabon is estimated to be about US $ 200 million.

Gabon offers a long history of potential stability and conservative financial management; and adopts a favourable stance to inward investment. However, all foreign firms incorporated in Gabon must give 10% of their equity ownership to the Government; and in general foreign companies are encouraged to form joint ventures with Gabonese firms. The screening procedure used to evaluate foreign investment is variable, but generally significant proposals have to be approved by the appropriate Government ministry.

MAIN SOURCES OF DATA:

A Official

1. Central Bank of Gabon: provides data on FDI flows for balance of payments purposes.
2. US Department of Commerce International Trade Administration, *Investment Climate in Foreign Countries,* Washington, 1983 and 1985 vol II.
3. UNESC, List of Major Transnational Corporations in Selected African Countries, ECA/UNCTC, October 1983.
4. UNCTC, *Transnational Corporations in World Development: Third Survey*, New York: UN, 1983.

B Private

1. L'Industrie Africaine en 1979, data as cited in the Report of the UN Economic Commission for Africa mission on the Evaluation of the UDEAC and the Feasibility of Enlarging Economic Co-operation in Central Africa, presented at the Annual Conference of the UDEAC Council of Heads of State, December 1981.

Note:
Data do not allow us to complete Tables A9, A10 or A11 for Gabon.

Table A1

SUMMARY OF THE COUNTRY'S INTERNATIONAL INVESTMENT POSITION

	Inward Investment	Outward Investment
1 Number of foreign affiliates in host country, and of foreign affiliates of home country firms at the end of 1980	96[1]	*N.A.*
2 Number of foreign firms with direct investments in host country, and home country firms with direct foreign affiliates	*N.A.*	*N.A.*
3 Total foreign direct capital stock at book value as a percentage of GNP at factor cost in 1981	30.15	*N.A.*
4 Flow of foreign direct investment in the five year period 1979-83 (US $ m)	384.7	32.4
5 Employment in foreign affiliates or abroad	*N.A.*	*N.A.*
6 Output of foreign affiliates or abroad	*N.A.*	*N.A.*

Source:

IMF, *Balance of Payments Statistics Yearbook,* various issues; OECD, *Geographical Distribution of Financial Flows to Developing Countries,* Paris, 1984; UNCTC, *Transnational Corporations in World Development: Third Survey*, New York: UN, 1983.

NOTES TO TABLE A1

1 Represents number of affiliates of foreign MNEs from selected foreign countries as identified by UNCTC, 1983.

Table A2

PRIVATE FOREIGN CAPITAL STOCK, 1975 - 83 (US $ m)

	Inward Investment			Outward Investment		
	Portfolio	*Direct*[1]	*Total*	*Portfolio*	*Direct*	*Total*
Book value of capital stock						
1975		620.0				
1978	*Not*	780.0	*Not*		*Not*	
1981	*Available*	921.1	*Available*		*Available*	
1983		1164.7				

Source:

IMF, *Balance of Payments Statistics Yearbook, 1984;* UNCTC, *Transnational Corporations in World Development: Third Survey,* New York: UN, 1983.

NOTES TO TABLE A2

1 Foreign direct capital stock for 1981 and 1983 have been estimated by adding cumulative investment flows to the UNCTC stock figure for 1978.

Table A3

FLOW OF FOREIGN DIRECT INVESTMENT, 1970 - 83 (US $ m)

	Inward Investment			Outward Investment		
	Reinvested Profits	*Other*	*Total*	*Reinvested Profits*	*Other*	*Total*
1970			–1.0			
1971			16.0			*Not*
1972			17.4			*Available*
1973		*Not*	15.5			
1974		*Separately*	79.4			–3.6
1975		*Available*	167.6			7.3
1976			38.7		*Not*	37.6
1977			35.0		*Separately*	20.3
1978			56.6		*Available*	*N.A.*
1979	46.0	9.0	55.0			6.7
1980	54.8	–23.3	31.5			7.9
1981	56.2	–1.6	54.6			7.1
1982	69.0	62.8	131.8			4.9
1983	92.5	19.3	111.8			5.8

Source:

IMF, *Balance of Payments Statistics Yearbook*, various issues.

Table A4

SECTORAL DISTRIBUTION OF FOREIGN DIRECT CAPITAL STOCK, 1981 (US $ m)[1]

	Inward Investment			Outward Investment		
	Primary	*Secondary*	*Tertiary*	*Primary*	*Secondary*	*Tertiary*
1981	645	262	15	*Not Available*		

Source:

L'Industrie Africaine en 1979, data as cited in the Report of the UN Economic Commission for Africa, *op cit.*

NOTES TO TABLE A4

1 Estimated by applying the percentage sectoral distribution of foreign ownership of social capital, 1979, to the FDI stock figure of 1981 (Table A2).

Table A5

GEOGRAPHICAL DISTRIBUTION OF FOREIGN DIRECT CAPITAL STOCK, 1981 (US $ m)[1]

	Inward Investment			Outward Investment		
	Developed Countries	*Developing Countries*	*Total*	*Developed Countries*	*Developing Countries*	*Total*
1981	902	19	921[2]	*Not Available*		

Source:

US Department of Commerce, *Investment Climate in Foreign Countries*, Washington, 1983.

NOTES TO TABLE A5

1 Estimates obtained by applying the source country distribution of FDI stock as found by an OECD study for 1976, to the stock figure of 1981 (Table A2).

2 Total includes unspecified figure.

Table A6

INDUSTRIAL DISTRIBUTION OF FOREIGN DIRECT CAPITAL STOCK, 1981 (US $ m)[1]

	Inward Investment	Outward Investment
	1981	
Primary	644.7	*Not Available*
Agriculture	25.8	
Mining & quarrying	257.9	
Oil[2]	361.0	
Secondary	261.5	
Food & drink[3]	21.2	
Chemicals & allied	63.5	
Metals	} 20.3	
Mechanical engineering		
Electrical equipment	*Not Available*	
Motor vehicles		
Other transportation equipment		
Textiles & clothing	4.6	
Paper & allied	*N.S.A.*	
Rubber	*N.S.A.*	
Stone, clay & glass	81.0	
Coal & petroleum products	*N.S.A.*	
Other manufacturing[4]	70.9	
Tertiary	14.8	
Construction	*Not Available*	
Transport & communications		
Distributive trade		
Property		
Banking & finance		
Other services[5]	14.8	
TOTAL	921.0	

Source:
L'Industrie Africaine en 1979, data as cited in the Report of the UN Economic Commission for Africa mission on the Evaluation of UDEAC and the Feasibility of Enlarging Economic Co-operation in Central Africa, presented at the Annual Conference of the UDEAC Council of Heads of State, December, 1981.

NOTES TO TABLE A6

1 Estimated by applying the percentage sectoral distribution of foreign ownership of social capital, 1979, to the FDI stock figure of 1981 (Table A2).

2 Petrol and gas.

3 Including tobacco.

4 Represents wood processing.

5 Represents electricity and water.

Table A7

LEADING SOURCE AND RECIPIENT COUNTRIES, 1981 (US $ m)[1]

	Inward Investment	Outward Investment
	1981	
DEVELOPED AREAS	902	*Not Available*
Europe	824	
EEC of which	824	
France	709	
W. Germany	11	
Netherlands	63	
UK	41	
North America of which	78	
USA	78[2]	
UNSPECIFIED	19	
TOTAL	921	

Source:

US Department of Commerce, *Investment Climate in Foreign Countries*, Washington, 1983; US Department of Commerce, *Survey of Current Business*, November, 1984.

NOTES TO TABLE A7

1 Estimates obtained by applying the source country distribution of FDI stock as found by an OECD study for 1976, to the stock figure at 1981 (Table A2).

2 US Department of Commerce estimate for 1981 is US $ 144 million.

Table A8

INDICATORS OF THE SIGNIFICANCE OF INWARD FOREIGN DIRECT INVESTMENT OR THE ACTIVITIES OF FOREIGN-BASED COMPANIES TO THE NATIONAL ECONOMY, 1978 - 81

1	Direct capital stock of foreign affiliates at book value in 1981 as a proportion of:	
	a GNP at factor cost	30.15
	b population (in US $ per head)	844.95
2	Foreign investment as a percentage of domestic investment 1978-80	1.8
3	Percentage share of assets accounted for by foreign affiliates in selected sectors, 1979	
		Assets[1]
	Primary Goods Sector	
	Agriculture	49
	Mining and quarrying	85
	Oil	75[2]
	Manufacturing Sector	
	Food & drink	26[3]
	Chemicals & allied	71
	Metals	} 89
	Mechanical engineering	
	Textiles & clothing	71
	Paper & allied	*N.A.*
	Stone, glass & clay	49
	Timber & furniture	83
	Services Sector	36[4]

Source:

UNCTC, *Transnational Corporations in World Development: Third Survey,* New York: UN, 1983; IMF, *Balance of Payments Statistics Yearbook, 1984;* IMF, *International Financial Statistics Yearbook, 1984;* OECD, *Geographical Distribution of Financial Flows to Developing Countries,* Paris, 1984; L'Industrie Africaine en 1979, data as cited in the Report of the UN Economic Commission for Africa Mission on the Evaluation of UDEAC and the Feasibility of Enlarging Economic Co-operation in Central Africa, presented at the Annual Conference of the UDEAC Council of Heads of State, December, 1981.

NOTES TO TABLE A8

1 Represents foreign share of the ownership at capital in 1979.

2 Petrol and gas.

3 Food only. For beverages, foreign share is 92.5%; for tobacco, 90%.

4 Represents electricity and water.

Table A12

LEADING FOREIGN MULTINATIONAL COMPANIES, 1983

Name		*Home Country*	*Sector*
1	Aeroservice Corp	USA	Aerospace
2	Amoco	USA	Oil
3	Gulf Oil	USA	Oil
4	Houston Oil	USA	Oil
5	Ocean	USA	Oil
6	Odeco	USA	Oil
7	Standard Oil of Indiana	USA	Oil
8	Barclays Bank	UK	Banking
9	George Wimpey Int	UK	Construction
10	Stirling International	UK	Civil works
11	Taylor Woodrow Int	UK	Construction
12	Bureau Central d'Etudes pour les Equipments d'autre mer	France	Consultancy work
13	Elf Quitaine	France	Oil
14	Sofrerail	France	Consultancy work
15	Techfor	France	Oil
16	Banco de Brasil	Brazil	Finance
17	Arcom	Romania	Construction
18	Geri Consult	W. Germany	Construction
19	C Itoh & Co	Japan	Oil
20	Abbdi Fecsult	Canada	Consultancy work
21	City Bank	USA	Banking
22	US Steel	USA	Steel products
23	L'Air Liquide	France	Industrial gases
24	La Farge	France	Cement products
25	Unilever	UK/Netherlands	Food products

Source:
UNESC, List of Major Transnational Corporations and Foreign Companies in Selected African Countries, ECA/UNCTC, October, 1983.

GHANA

There has been no consistent policy in the past decade towards foreign direct investment in Ghana, although the general attitude has been negative. Since Independence (March 1957), the rise of economic nationalism in Ghana has been apparent. In 1975, under the Investment Policy Decree, foreign companies operating in Ghana were obliged to sell between 40% and 60% of their assets to Ghanians, with few exceptions. Since then, there has been virtually no new FDI into Ghana; the importance of reinvested earnings is indicated in table A3.

In 1983 a 'reconstruction programme' was announced, with the government stating that foreign investment will be encouraged in certain mining and manufacturing activities. However, despite the incentives offered, little further new investment has occurred, a reflection of Ghana's general economic and political uncertainty.

The main investor countries are European, mainly the UK, and the USA. Foreign investment is concentrated on wholesale and retail trading, oil distribution and banking and insurance. Within the manufacturing sector, the main growth areas have been food and drink, textiles and garments.

MAIN SOURCES OF DATA:

A **Official**

1 Bank of Ghana; provides information on royalty payments, and other industrial statistics.

2 Investment Policy Implementation Committee; gives data on foreign companies operating in Ghana.

3 UN, Economic and Social Council; provides a list of major foreign companies operating in Ghana.

B **Private**

1 A N Hakam, 'Impediments to the Growth of Indigenous Industrial Entrepreneurship in Ghana, 1946-63', *Economic Bulletin for Ghana 2,* 1973.

2 A Adei, 'The growth of foreign investment and economic nationalism in post Independence Ghana, 1957-1975', working paper no 34, University of Sydney, 1980.

3 J Currie, 'Comparison of export oriented investment: Senegal, Ghana and Mauritius', paper prepared for the Commonwealth Secretariat, May 1985.

4 G Botchie, 'Employment and MNEs in export processing zones: The cases of Liberia and Ghana', International Labour Office Working Papers on the Employment Effects of MNEs, Geneva, 1984.

Note:
Data do not allow us to complete Tables A4, A6, A9 or A10 for Ghana.

Table A1

SUMMARY OF THE COUNTRY'S INTERNATIONAL INVESTMENT POSITION

		Inward Investment	Outward Investment
1	Number of foreign affiliates in host country, and of foreign affiliates of home country firms at the end of 1975	280	*N.A.*
2	Number of foreign firms with direct investments in host country, and home country firms with direct foreign affiliates	*N.A.*	*N.A.*
3	Total foreign direct capital stock at book value as a percentage of GNP at factor cost in 1981	1.11	*N.A.*
4	Flow of foreign direct investment in the five year period, 1979-83 (Cedi m)	104.6	*N.A.*
5	Employment in foreign affiliates or abroad	*N.A.*	*N.A.*
6	Output of foreign affiliates or abroad, 1969 (Cedi m)	464.6[1]	*N.A.*

Source:

UNCTC, *Transnational Corporations in World Development, Third Survey,* New York: UN, 1983; IMF, *Internationa Financial Statistics Yearbook, 1984;* IMF, *Balance of Payments Statistics Yearbook,* various issues; S Adei, *op cit;* A Hakim, *op cit.*

NOTES TO TABLE A1

1 Estimate obtained by adding 75% of total gross output of joint-ventures to total gross output of non-Ghanian firms, for manufacturing, mining and services sectors only.

Table A2

PRIVATE FOREIGN CAPITAL STOCK, 1975 - 84 (Cedi m)

	Inward Investment				Outward Investment		
	Portfolio	*Direct*	*Total*		*Portfolio*	*Direct*	*Total*
Book value of capital stock							
1975	*Not Available*	345.0	*Not Available*		*Not Available*		
1978		770.1					
1981		793.7					
1984		812.7					

Source:
UNCTC, *Transnational Corporations in World Development, Third Survey,* New York: UN, 1983; IMF, *Balance of Payments Statistics Yearbook,* various issues.

NOTES TO TABLE A2

1 Estimates for 1981 and 1984 obtained by adding cumulative investment flow figures 1979-81 or 1979-84, to the stock figures of 1978.

Table A3

FLOW OF FOREIGN DIRECT INVESTMENT, 1970 - 84 (Cedi m)

	Inward Investment				Outward Investment		
	Reinvested Profits	*Other*	*Total*		*Reinvested Profits*	*Other*	*Total*
1970	8.2	61.2	69.4		*Not Available*		
1971	12.4	19.6	32.0				
1972	12.9	2.9	15.8				
1973	15.3	1.4	16.7				
1974	8.3	4.2	12.5				
1975	19.5	61.5	81.0				
1976	11.9	2.7	14.6				
1977	2.1	14.4	16.5				
1978	3.4	4.4	7.7				
1979	*N.S.A.*	−2.2	−2.2				
1980	9.4	2.6	12.0				
1981	9.8	4.0	13.8				
1982	9.6	5.2	14.8				
1983	1.5	0.7	2.2				
1984	2.0	*N.S.A.*	2.0				

Source:
IMF, *Balance of Payments Statistics Yearbook,* various issues.

Table A5

GEOGRAPHICAL DISTRIBUTION OF FOREIGN DIRECT CAPITAL STOCK, 1981 (Cedi m)

	Inward Investment				Outward Investment		
	Developed Countries	*Other Countries*	*Total*		*Developed Countries*	*Developing Countries*	*Total*
1981	775.5[1]	75.8	851.3[2]		*Not Available*		

Source:
UK Department of Trade and Industry, 'Census of Overseas Assets 1981', *Business Monitor,* Supplement 1981; US Department of Commerce, *Survey of Current Business,* November 1984.

NOTES TO TABLE A5

1 Includes US & UK investment only.

2 Estimate obtained by adding cumulative investment flow figures 1979-81 to the stock figure of 1978.

Table A7

LEADING SOURCE AND RECIPIENT COUNTRIES, 1981 (Cedi m)

	Inward Investment		Outward Investment
	1981		
DEVELOPED AREAS	775.5[1]		*Not Available*
Europe			
UK	286.0		
North America of which:			
USA	489.5		
TOTAL	851.3[3]		

Source:
UK Department of Trade and Industry, 'Census of Overseas Assets 1981', *Business Monitor,* Supplement 1981; US Department of Commerce, *Survey of Current Business,* November 1984.

NOTES TO TABLE A7

1 Includes UK & US investment only.

2 Stock estimate obtained by adding cumulative investment flows, 1979-81, to the stock figure of 1978.

Table A8

INDICATORS OF THE SIGNIFICANCE OF INWARD FOREIGN DIRECT INVESTMENT OR THE ACTIVITIES OF FOREIGN-BASED COMPANIES TO THE NATIONAL ECONOMY, 1969 - 81

1	Direct capital stock of foreign affiliates at book value in 1981 as a proportion of:		
	a	GNP at factor cost	1.11
	b	population (in Cedi per head)	72.1
2	Output of foreign affiliates in 1969 as a percentage of all companies' output		
	a	in primary (ie extractive) industry	85
	b	in secondary (ie manufacturing) industry	67
	c	in tertiary industry (ie services etc)	65

Source:

UNCTC, *Transnational Corporations in World Development, Third Survey,* New York: UN, 1983; IMF, *Balance of Payments Statistics Yearbook,* various issues; IMF, *International Financial Statistics Yearbook, 1984;* S Adei, 'The growth of Foreign Investment and Economic Nationalism in Post Independence Ghana; 1957-1975', working paper no 34, University of Sydney, 1980.

Table A11

ROYALTY RECEIPTS AND PAYMENTS, 1970 - 75 (Cedis m)

	Payments			Receipts		
	To Affiliates	*To Non-affiliates*	*Total*	*From Affiliates*	*From Non-affiliates*	*Total*
1970	*Not Separately Available*		51.3	*Not Available*		
1975			1,012.0			

Source:

Bank of Ghana.

Table A12

LEADING FOREIGN MULTINATIONAL COMPANIES, 1983

	Name	*Home Country*	*Sector*
1	Trumpy & Fjell	Norway	Hotels
2	Bankers Trust Int	UK	Banking
3	British Aluminium Company	UK	Mining
4	Macmillan	UK	Publishing
5	Agri Petco-International	USA	Oil
6	Brown & Root	USA	Mining
7	Philips Petroleum	USA	Oil
8	Texas Pacific Oil Co	USA	Oil
9	Compagnie Francais des petroles	France	Mining
10	Interagra	France	Mining
11	Alusuisse	Switzerland	Mining
12	Impregilo Recchi	Italy	Construction
13	Mazzoni	Italy	Construction
14	Granges Int Mining	Sweden	Mining
15	Allgemeine Ball-Union	W. Germany	Construction

Source:

UN, Economic & Social Council, "List of Major Transnational Corporations and Foreign Companies in Selected African Countries", paper for the Economic Commission for Africa, October, 1983.

IVORY COAST

The inflows of foreign direct investment to the Ivory Coast vary from year to year, but not in large swings. Reinvested earnings play an important role in the determination of total foreign direct investment.

The main investor country is France; the UK, the USA, Lebanon, Belgium and Luxembourg follow at considerable distance. In addition, a substantial number of other countries have smaller investments in Ivory Coast.

There are few detailed statistics on the sectoral distribution of foreign investment in the Ivory Coast. Much of the French investment is directed towards the manufacturing sector, while US investment is primarily concentrated in the oil industry.

The Ivory Coast encourages foreign direct investment and gives special incentives to foreign owned firms entering the Ivory Coast market.

MAIN SOURCES OF DATA:

A Official

1. Ministry of Economy and Finance: provides data on the geographical and sectoral distribution of foreign investment in the Ivory Coast.

2. US Department of Commerce International Trade Administration, *Investment Climate in Foreign Countries,* Washington 1985.

3. UNESC, List of Transnational Corporations and Foreign Companies in Selected African Countries, ECA/UNCTC, October 1983.

4. UNCTC, *Transnational Corporations in World Development: Third Survey*, New York: UN, 1983.

Note:
Data do not allow us to complete Table A9 or A10 for the Ivory Coast.

Table A1

SUMMARY OF THE COUNTRY'S INTERNATIONAL INVESTMENT POSITION

		Inward Investment	Outward Investment
1	Number of foreign affiliates in host country, and of foreign affiliates of home country firms at the end of 1980	173	*N.A.*
2	Number of foreign firms with direct investments in host country, and home country firms with direct foreign affiliates	*N.A.*	*N.A.*
3	Total foreign direct capital stock at book value as a percentage of GNP at at factor cost in 1981	16.81	*N.A.*
4	Flow of foreign direct investment in the five year period, 1977-81 (IC Fr bn)	73.13	*N.A.*
5	Employment in foreign affiliates or abroad	*N.A.*	*N.A.*
6	Output of foreign affiliates or abroad	*N.A.*	*N.A.*

Source:

US Department of Commerce, *Investment Climate in Foreign Countries,* Washington, 1983; IMF, *Balance of Payments Statistics Yearbook, 1984;* OECD, *Geographical Distribution of Financial Flows to Developing Countries,* Paris, 1984.

NOTES TO TABLE A1

1 Represents number of affiliates of MNEs from selected home countries, as identified by UNCTC, 1983.

Table A2

PRIVATE FOREIGN CAPITAL STOCK, 1971 - 81 (IC Fr bn)

	Inward Investment			Outward Investment		
	Portfolio	*Direct*	*Total*	*Portfolio*	*Direct*	*Total*
Book value of capital stock						
1971	*Not Available*	85.1	*Not Available*	*Not Available*		
1975		110.3				
1978		144.3				
1979		202.2				
1980		274.9				
1981		302.7				

Source:
Ministry of Economy and Finance, data as cited in US Department of Commerce, *Investment Climate in Foreign Countries,* Washington 1983; UNCTC, 1983, *op cit* for years up to 1978; Cumulative flow figures have been added on to this to get an estimate of capital stock for other years.

Table A3

FLOW OF FOREIGN DIRECT INVESTMENT, 1970 - 81 (IC Fr bn)

	Inward Investment			Outward Investment		
	Reinvested Profits	*Other*	*Total*	*Reinvested Profits*	*Other*	*Total*
1970	2.78	5.83	8.61	*Not Available*		0.28
1971	5.28	-0.83	4.45			0.28
1972	4.38	0.28	4.66			0.82
1973	7.70	3.72	11.42			*Not Available*
1974	4.34	3.47	7.81			
1975	10.93	6.50	17.43			
1976	8.83	1.93	10.76			
1977	27.2	–14.7	12.6			
1978	47.4	19.1	66.5			
1979	35.7	22.2	57.9			
1980	50.5	22.1	72.7			
1981	16.2	11.6	27.8			

Source:

IMF, *Balance of Payments Statistics Yearbook,* various issues.

Table A4

SECTORAL DISTRIBUTION OF FOREIGN DIRECT CAPITAL STOCK, 1980 (IC Fr bn)

	Inward Investment				Outward Investment		
	Primary	Secondary	Tertiary		Primary	Secondary	Tertiary
1980	16[1]	40[2]	29[2]		Not Available		

Source:

Ministry of Economy and Finance, data as cited in US Department of Commerce, *Investment Climate in Foreign Countries,* Washington, 1983.

NOTES TO TABLE A4

1 US investment only.

2 French investment only.

Table A5

GEOGRAPHICAL DISTRIBUTION OF FOREIGN DIRECT CAPITAL STOCK, 1980 (IC Fr bn)

	Inward Investment				Outward Investment		
	Developed Countries	Developing Countries	Total		Developed Countries	Developing Countries	Total
1980	153	19	177[1]		Not Available		

Source:

US Ministry of Economy & Finance, data as cited in US Department of Commerce, *Investment Climate in Foreign Countries,* Washington, 1983.

NOTES TO TABLE A5

1 Total includes 'unspecified' figure.

Table A6

INDUSTRIAL DISTRIBUTION OF FOREIGN DIRECT CAPITAL STOCK, 1980 (IC Fr bn)

	Inward Investment	Outward Investment
	1980	
Primary	16[1]	
Oil	16	
Secondary	40[2]	
Tertiary	29[2]	
Commercial Activities	29	
TOTAL	85	

Source:
Ministry of Economy and Finance, data as cited in US Department of Commerce, *Investment Climate in Foreign Countries,* Washington 1983.

NOTES TO TABLE A6

1 US investment only.

2 French investment only.

Table A7

LEADING SOURCE OF RECIPIENT COUNTRIES, 1980 (IC Fr bn)

	Inward Investment	Outward Investment
	1980	
DEVELOPED AREAS	153	
Europe	131	
EEC of which:	119	
Belgium & Luxembourg	5	
France	102	
W. Germany	2	
Italy	2	*Not Available*
UK	8	
Other Europe of which:	12	
Switzerland	8	
North America of which:	22	
USA	22[1]	
DEVELOPING AREAS	19	
Africa (except S. Africa)	12	
Middle East of which:	7	
Israel	1	
Syria/Lebanon	6	
UNSPECIFIED	5	
TOTAL	177	

Source:
Ministry of Economy and Finance, data as cited in US Department of Commerce, *Investment Climate in Foreign Countries,* Washington, 1983.

NOTES TO TABLE A7

1 The US Department of Commerce estimate for 1980 is IC Fr 28.5 billion.

Table A8

INDICATORS OF THE SIGNIFICANCE OF INWARD FOREIGN DIRECT INVESTMENT OR THE ACTIVITIES OF FOREIGN-BASED COMPANIES TO THE NATIONAL ECONOMY, 1981

1	Direct capital stock of foreign affiliates at book value in 1981 as a proportion of:	
	a GNP at factor cost	16.81
	b population (in IC Fr per head)	36,690.91
2	Foreign investment in affiliates as a percentage of domestic investment 1978-80	0.3

Source:

US Department of Commerce, *Investment Climate in Foreign Countries,* Washington, 1983; OECD, *Geographical Distribution of Financial Flows to Developing Countries,* Paris, 1984.

Table A11

ROYALTY RECEIPTS AND PAYMENTS, 1975 - 80 (IC Fr bn)

	Payments			Receipts		
	To Affiliates	*To Non-affiliates*	*Total*	*From Affiliates*	*From Non-affiliates*	*Total*
1975	*Not Separately Available*		0.26	*Not Separately Available*		0.03
1976			0.30			0.03
1977			1.0			0.03
1978			1.4			0.03
1979			9.8			0.03
1980			7.6			0.03
1981			8.1			0.03

Source:

IMF, *Balance of Payments Statistics Yearbook,* 1983.

Table A12

LEADING FOREIGN MULTINATIONAL COMPANIES, 1985

	Name	*Home Country*	*Sector*
1	Banque Nationale de Paris	France	Banking
2	BRGM	France	Mining
3	Dumez	France	Mining
4	Credit du Nord	France	Banking
5	Credit Industrial & Commercial	France	Banking
6	Ponticelli	France	Construction (oil)
7	Bankers Trust Co	USA	Banking
8	Chase Manhattan	USA	Banking
9	Citibank	USA	Banking
10	Chemical Bank	USA	Banking
11	Fluor	USA	Oil
12	Exxon	USA	Oil
13	McDermott	USA	Construction (oil)
14	Mobil	USA	Oil
15	Colgate – Palmolive	USA	Pharmaceuticals
16	Philips Petroleum	USA	Oil
17	Tenneco	USA	Oil
18	Texaco	USA	Oil
19	Union Texas Petroleum	USA	Oil
20	DAF	Netherlands	Motor vehicles
21	Abay	Belgium	Construction
22	Solei Boneh	Isreal	Construction

Source:
UNESC' List of Transnational Corporations and Foreign Companies in Selected African countries, ECA/UNCTC, October 1983.

KENYA

Since Independence in 1963, the government has stressed the importance of foreign direct investment in Kenya, and has attempted to establish and maintain a favourable climate for it. Like several other developing African countries, Kenya pursues an 'Open Door' policy toward FDI, offering the usual package of fiscal incentives.

The inflow of FDI has been on a rising trend since the mid-1970s; table A3 indicates the importance of reinvested earnings.

By far the greatest source of foreign capital is the UK, with the USA following at considerable distance.

Although private foreign investment was significant in all sectors of the economy immediately following Independence, in recent years it has fallen substantially in the primary and tertiary sectors (with the notable exception of tourism). FDI is now largely concentrated in large-scale manufacturing, particularly food processing, chemicals and rubber, textiles and paper.

Kenyan direct investment abroad is mainly in neighbouring territories, with a limited amount in Europe and North America.

MAIN SOURCES OF DATA:

A Official

1 Kenya Central Bureau of Statistics; provides data on the sectoral distribution of FDI in Kenya, and information about employment.

B Private

1 R Kaplinsky, 'Employment effects of multinational enterprises: A case study of Kenya', *ILO Papers on the Employment Effects of MNEs,* no 8, Geneva, 1979.

2 N Rweyemamu, 'Foreign Investment Policy: Kenya's Experience', paper prepared for the Commonwealth Secretariat, August 1984.

3 N Swainson, *The Development of Corporate Capitalism in Kenya, 1918-1977,* London, Heinemann, 1980.

Note:
Data do not allow us to complete Tables A10 or A11 for Kenya. However in 1978, some 31.1% of investment by UK companies was in fully owned subsidiaries compared with 66.9% in 1974.

Table A1

SUMMARY OF THE COUNTRY'S INTERNATIONAL INVESTMENT POSITION

		Inward Investment	Outward Investment
1	Number of foreign affiliates in host country, and of foreign affiliates of home country firms at the end of 1980	481	*N.A.*
2	Number of foreign firms with direct investments in host country, and home country firms with direct foreign affiliates	*N.A.*	*N.A.*
3	Total foreign direct capital stock at book value as a percentage of GNP at factor cost in 1984	9.52	0.28
4	Flow of foreign direct investment in the five year period, 1980-84 (K Sh m)	3,407.8	196.3
5	Employment in foreign affiliates or abroad, 1976	49,820	*N.A.*
6	Output of foreign affiliates or abroad	*N.A.*	*N.A.*

Source:

UNCTC, *Transnational Corporations in World Development, Third Survey,* New York: UN, 1983; IMF, *Balance of Payments Statistics Yearbook,* various issues; IMF, *International Financial Statistics Yearbook, 1984;* Central Bureay of Statistics, *Statistical Abstract, 1976,* Nairobi, 1977; N Swainson, *The Development of Corporate Capitalism in Kenya, 1918-1977,* Heinemann, 1980.

NOTES TO TABLE A1

[1] Represents affiliates of MNEs from selected home countries as identified by UNCTC, 1983.

Table A2

PRIVATE FOREIGN CAPITAL STOCK, 1971 - 83 (K Sh m)

	Inward Investment			Outward Investment		
	Portfolio	*Direct*	*Total*	*Portfolio*	*Direct*	*Total*
Book value of capital stock						
1971	*Not Available*	1,428.6	*Not Available*	*Not Available*		
1978		3,850.0				
1981		5,629.6[1]				
1983		7,065.7[2]		*Not Available*	191.6[3]	*Not Available*
1984		7,885.7[2]			233.0[3]	

Source:
UNCTC, *Transnational Corporations in World Development, Third Survey,* New York: UN, 1983; IMF, *Balance of Payments Statistics Yearbook,* various issues.

NOTES TO TABLE A2

1 Estimate obtained by adding cumulative investment flow 1979-81 to the stock figure of 1978.

2 Estimate obtained by adding cumulative investment flows to the stock figure of 1978.

3 Cumulative investment flow 1975-83 and 1975-84.

Table A3

FLOW OF FOREIGN DIRECT INVESTMENT, 1970 - 83 (K Sh m)

	Inward Investment			Outward Investment		
	Reinvested Profits	*Other*	*Total*	*Reinvested Profits*	*Other*	*Total*
1970	100.0	0.0	100.0	*Not Available*		
1971	86.0	0.0	86.0			
1975	222.9	133.7	356.6	8.9	17.8	26.7
1976	231.8	144.9	376.7	9.7	19.3	29.0
1977	338.1	125.6	463.7	19.3	0.0	19.3
1978	318.8	–58.0	260.8	29.0	–9.7	19.3
1979	512.0	115.9	627.9	48.3	0.0	48.3
1980	386.4	202.9	589.3	9.7	0.0	9.7
1981	456.3	106.1	562.4	21.2	0.0	21.2
1982	554.1	156.6	710.7	68.7	–106.1	–37.4
1983	355.6	369.8	725.4	55.5	0.0	55.5
1984	534.8	285.1	820.0	41.4	0.0	41.4

Source:
IMF, *Balance of Payments Statistics Yearbook,* various issues.

Table A4

SECTORAL DISTRIBUTION OF FOREIGN DIRECT CAPITAL STOCK, 1976 (K Sh m)

	Inward Investment			Outward Investment		
	Primary	*Secondary*	*Tertiary*	*Primary*	*Secondary*	*Tertiary*
1976[1]	*N.A.*	3,976.3	178.7	*Not Available*		
1981[1]	583.8	2,061.7	1,437.1			

Source:

Kenyan Central Bureau of Statistics, cited in R Kaplinsky, 'Employment Effects of MNEs: a case study of Kenya'. *ILO Papers on the Employment Effects of MNEs,* no 8, Geneva, 1979; US Department of Industry, *Census of Overseas Assets.*

NOTES TO TABLE A4

1 Estimates obtained by applying the percentage sectoral distribution of the stock of FDI in Kenya to the stock figure of 1976 (Table A2).

2 Represents UK investment only. Total US investment in Kenya in 1981 is 1234.3 million Kenyan shillings.

Table A5

GEOGRAPHICAL DISTRIBUTION OF FOREIGN DIRECT CAPITAL STOCK, 1981 (K Sh m)

	Inward Investment			Outward Investment		
	Developed Countries	*Other Countries*	*Total*	*Developed Countries*	*Developing Countries*	*Total*
1981	5,316.9[1]	312.7	5,629.6[2]	*Not Available*		

Source:

US Department of Commerce, *Survey of Current Business,* November 1984; HMSO, 'Census of Overseas Assets 1981', *Business Monitor,* supplement 1981.

NOTES TO TABLE A5

1 Includes UK and US investment only.

2 Estimate obtained by adding cumulative investment flow, 1979-81, to the stock figure of 1978.

Table A6

INDUSTRIAL DISTRIBUTION OF FOREIGN DIRECT CAPITAL STOCK, 1976 (K Sh m)

	Inward Investment		Outward Investment
	1976[1]	*1981*[5]	
Primary	*N.A.*	583.8	*Not Available*
Secondary	3,976.3	2,061.7	
Food & drink	1,171.7	1,090.1	
Chemicals & allied[2]	1,205.0	563.4	
Metals[3]	394.7		
Electrical equipment		73.5	
Other transportation equipment			
Textiles & clothing	743.7		
Paper & allied	290.9	138.8	
Stone, clay & glass	91.4		
Coal & petroleum products			
Other manufacturing	78.9	142.9	
Tertiary	178.7	1,437.1	
Construction		110.2	
Distributive trade		1,118.6	
TOTAL	4,155.0[4]	4,082.6	

Source:

Kenyan Central Bureau of Statistics, cited in R Kaplinsky, 'Employment effects of MNEs: a case study of Kenya', *ILO Papers on the Employment Effects of MNEs,* no 8, Geneva, 1979; UNCTC, *Transnational Corporations in World Development, Third Survey,* New York: UN, 1983; UK Department of Industry, *Census of Overseas Assets.*

NOTES TO TABLE A6

1 Estimates obtained by applying the percentage sectoral distribution of the stock of FDI in Kenya to the stock figure of 1976 (Table A2).

2 Rubber is included under 'chemicals and allied'.

3 Fabricated metal products only.

4 Excluding capital invested in the primary sector.

5 Represents UK investment only. Total US investment in Kenya in 1981 is 1,234.3 million Kenyan shillings.

Table A7 LEADING SOURCE AND RECIPIENT COUNTRIES, 1981 (K Sh m)

	Inward Investment	Outward Investment
	1981	
DEVELOPED AREAS	5,316.9[1]	*Not Available*
Europe		
UK	4,082.6	
North America of which:		
USA	1,234.3	
TOTAL	5,629.6[2]	

Source:

US Department of Commerce, *Survey of Current Business,* November 1984; HMSO, 'Census of Overseas Assets 1981', *Business Monitor,* Supplement 1981.

NOTES TO TABLE A7

1 Includes US and UK investment only.

2 Estimate obtained by adding cumulative investment flow 1979-81 to the stock figure of 1978.

Table A8

INDICATORS OF THE SIGNIFICANCE OF INWARD FOREIGN DIRECT INVESTMENT OR THE ACTIVITIES OF FOREIGN-BASED COMPANIES TO THE NATIONAL ECONOMY, 1976 - 84

1	Direct capital stock of foreign affiliates at book value in 1984 as a proportion of:		
	a GNP at factor cost		9.52
	b population (in K Sh per head)		419.45
2	Employment in foreign affiliates[1] in 1976 as a percentage of all employment		
	a in all industry		5.80
	b in manufacturing		55.10
3	Foreign direct investment as a percentage of domestic investment, 1978-80		3.10
4	Percentage share of assets and employment accounted for by foreign affiliates in selected sectors, 1976		
		Assets	*Employment*[1]
	Manufacturing Sector		
	Food & drink	28.9	52.3
	Chemical & allied[2]	71.2	79.6
	Metals	46.3	59.2
	Textiles & clothing	56.5[3]	63.9
	Paper & allied	40.5	33.3
	Stone, glass & clay	44.4	65.1
	Timber & furniture	15.0	8.5
	Other manufacturing	32.4	20.0
	Tertiary Sector		
	Tourism	22.2	*N.A.*

Source:
UNCTC, *Transnational Corporations in World Development: Third Survey,* New York: UN, 1983; IMF, *Balance of Payments Statistics Yearbook,* various issues; IMF, *International Financial Statistics Yearbook,* 1984; Central Bureau of Statistics, *Statistical Abstract, 1976,* Nairobi, 1977; R Kaplinsky, *op cit;* ILO, *Yearbook of Labour Statistics,* Geneva, 1981.

NOTES TO TABLE A8

1 Includes only employment in large scale manufacturing for which foreign ownership is 10% or more.

2 Rubber is included under 'chemicals and allied'.

3 Textiles and leather.

Table A9 INDICATORS OF THE SIGNIFICANCE OF OUTWARD FOREIGN DIRECT INVESTMENT OR THE ACTIVITIES OF HOME-BASED COMPANIES ABROAD FOR THE NATIONAL ECONOMY, 1984

1	Foreign capital stock of home-based firms at book value in 1984 as a proportion of:	
	a GNP at factor cost	0.28
	b population (in K Sh per head)	12.39

Source:
IMF, *Balance of Payments Statistics Yearbook,* various issues; IMF, *International Financial Statistics Yearbook, 1984.*

Table A12

LEADING FOREIGN MULTINATIONAL COMPANIES, 1983

	Name	*Home Country*	*Sector*
1	B. Kang International Consultancy	Korea	Construction
2	Brown Boveri & Co	Switzerland	Electrical
3	Horizon Insurance Consultants	UK	Insurance
4	Brooke Bond Liebig	UK	Food
5	Macmillan	UK	Paper
6	Metal Box	UK	Metals
7	Mabib Bank	USA	Banking
8	Total Oil Products Ltd	USA	Oil
9	Singer Co	USA	Electrical
10	Pepsico Inc	USA	Drink
11	Pan American	USA	Air transport
12	Intercontinental Hotels Group	USA	Hotels
13	Esso	USA	Oil
14	ITT	USA	Electrical
15	IBM	USA	Office equipment
16	Coca Cola	USA	Drink
17	BASF	W. Germany	Chemicals
18	Alitalia	Italy	Air transport
19	Agip	Italy	Oil
20	Phillips	Netherlands	Electrical
21	Royal Dutch/Shell	Netherlands/UK	Oil
22	Hoechst	W. Germany	Pharmaceuticals

Source:

UNESC, List of Major Transnational Corporations and Foreign Companies in selected African Countries, paper for the Economic Commission for Africa, October, 1983.

LIBERIA

Since the declaration of the 'Open Door Policy' in 1944, government policies have generally been favourable towards foreign investment. The US dollar, on a par with the Liberian dollar, remains legal tender in Liberia, and is a particular attraction for foreign investors.

A large inflow of FDI into Liberia occurred in the 1950s and 1960s. However, recent developments in the country have marred the investment climate to some extent, and the flow of foreign capital has since declined significantly.

FDI into Liberia has been largely directed to plantation agriculture, namely forestry and rubber. Yet, despite the substantial production of rubber, Liberia has no significant rubber-based manufacturing industry. Foreign investment in the service sector is also important, with most of the financial institutions and insurance companies being foreign-owned. In addition, for tax and other reasons there is a great deal of investment in shipping and sea transport services.

The relatively little foreign activity in the manufacturing sector prompted the adoption of various corrective measures in an attempt to attract foreign investment to this sector. Among these measures were an 'Investment Code' of 1966 (amended in 1973), and the establishment of the National Investment Commission and the Liberian Industrial Free Zone Authority, in 1979. All offer generous incentives, but have attracted little new foreign investment to date.

The USA is the major investor in Liberia, significant in all key sectors of the economy. Other investor countries include West Germany, Italy, Sweden and the Lebanon.

MAIN SOURCES OF DATA:

A Official

1. *Liberian Ministry of Finance;* provides data on the geographical distribution of the stock of FDI.
2. *National Investment Commission;* provides unpublished data on stock of FDI, and sectoral distribution.
3. UNCTC, *Transnational Corporations in World Development: Third Survey*, New York: UN, 1983.

B Private

1. *International Labour Office*, 'Multinationals and employment in a West African sub-region: Liberia and Sierra Leone', Working paper no. 29 by O Iyanda, Geneva, 1984.
2. Seminar on Foreign Investment Policies and Prospects in Africa, 'Foreign Investment Policy: Liberia's Experience', paper prepared by *Commonwealth Secretariat,* London, June 1985.
3. *International Labour Office*, 'Employment and multinational enterprises in export processing zones: The cases of Liberia and Ghana', Working paper no 30 by G Botchie, Geneva, 1984.

Note:
Data do not allow us to complete Tables A9, A10 or A11 for Liberia.

Table A1

SUMMARY OF THE COUNTRY'S INTERNATIONAL INVESTMENT POSITION

		Inward Investment	Outward Investment
1	Number of foreign affiliates in host country, and of foreign affiliates of home country firms at the end of 1980	423[1]	*N.A.*
2	Number of foreign firms with direct investments in host country, and home country firms with direct foreign affiliates at	*N.A.*	*N.A.*
3	Total foreign direct capital stock at book value as a percentage of GNP at factor cost in 1981	158.5	*N.A.*
4	Flow of foreign direct investment in the five year period, 1980-84 (L $ m)	122.9	*N.A.*
5	Employment in foreign affiliates or abroad, 1981	124,420	*N.A.*
6	Output of foreign affiliates or abroad	*N.A.*	*N.A.*

Source:

Liberian National Investment Commission, unpublished data; IMF, *International Financial Statistics Yearbook, 1984*; International Labour Office, 'Multinationals and employment in a West African sub-region: Liberia and Sierra Leone', Working paper no 29 by O Iyanda, Genera, 1984; OECD, *Geographical Distribution of financial flows to developing countries,* Paris, 1984.

NOTES TO TABLE A1

1 Represents foreign affiliates of MNEs from selected home countries, as identified by UNCTC, 1983.

Table A2

PRIVATE FOREIGN CAPITAL STOCK, 1978-84 (L $ m)[1]

	Inward Investment			Outward Investment		
	Portfolio	*Direct*	*Total*	*Portfolio*	*Direct*	*Total*
Book value of capital stock						
1978	*Not Available*	804.7	*Not Available*	*Not Available*		
1981		839.5				
1984		927.6				

Source:
Liberian National Investment Commission, unpublished data; OECD, *Geographical Distribution of Financial Flows to Developing Countries,* Paris 1984.

NOTES TO TABLE A2

1 Estimates for 1981 and 1984 obtained by adding cumulative investment flow figures to the stock figure of 1978.

Table A3

FLOW OF FOREIGN DIRECT INVESTMENT, 1970-84 (L $ m)

	Inward Investment			Outward Investment		
	Reinvested Profits	*Other*	*Total*	*Reinvested Profits*	*Other*	*Total*
1975	*Not Separately Available*		80.7	*Not Available*		
1976			39.1			
1977			44.7			
1982			34.8			
1983			49.1			
1984			39.0			

Source:
UN Centre on Transnational Corporations, *Transnational Corporations in World Development, Third Survey,* New York: UN, 1983; OECD, *Geographical Distribution of Financial Flows to Developing Countries,* Paris 1984. IMF, *Balance of Payments Statistics,* various issues.

Table A4

SECTORAL DISTRIBUTION OF FOREIGN DIRECT CAPITAL STOCK, 1979 (L $ m)

	Inward Investment			Outward Investment		
	Primary	*Secondary*	*Tertiary*	*Primary*	*Secondary*	*Tertiary*
1979	622.9	*N.A.*	236.8[1]	*Not Available*		

Source:
Liberian National Investment Commission, unpublished data.

NOTES TO TABLE A4

1 Represents manufacturing and services.

Table A5

GEOGRAPHICAL DISTRIBUTION OF FOREIGN DIRECT CAPITAL STOCK, 1979 (L $ m)

	Inward Investment			Outward Investment		
	Developed Countries	*Developing Countries*	*Total*	*Developed Countries*	*Developing Countries*	*Total*
1979	825.8	34.8	859.6	*Not Available*		

Source:
Liberian Ministry of Finance, unpublished data.

Table A6

INDUSTRIAL DISTRIBUTION OF FOREIGN DIRECT CAPITAL STOCK, 1979 (L $ m)

	Inward Investment	Outward Investment
	1979	
Primary	622.9	*Not Available*
Agriculture[1]	256.1	
Mining & quarrying	366.8	
Oil	*N.S.A.*	
Secondary & Tertiary	236.8[2]	
TOTAL	859.6	

Source:
Liberian National Investment Commission, unpublished data.

NOTES TO TABLE A6

1 Represents forestry, $ 136.6 m and rubber plantations, $ 119.5 m.

2 Represents manufacturing & services.

Table A7

LEADING SOURCE AND RECIPIENT COUNTRIES, 1979 (L S m)

	Inward Investment *1979*	Outward Investment
DEVELOPED AREAS	825.8	*Not Available*
Europe	472.9	
EEC of which	362.9	
Denmark	0.3	
France	40.0	
W. Germany	218.9	
Italy	64.5	
Netherlands	39.2	
Other Europe of which	110.0	
Sweden	110.0	
North America of which	352.9	
Canada	12.9	
USA	340.0	
DEVELOPING AREAS	34.8	
Middle East of which	34.8	
Lebanon	34.8	
TOTAL	859.6	

Source:
Liberian Ministry of Finance, unpublished data.

Table 8

INDICATORS OF THE SIGNIFICANCE OF INWARD FOREIGN DIRECT INVESTMENT OR THE ACTIVITIES OF FOREIGN-BASED COMPANIES TO THE NATIONAL ECONOMY

1	Direct capital stock of foreign affiliates at book value in 1981 as a proportion of		
	a	GNP at factor cost	158.5
	b	population (in L $ per head)	631.9
2	Employment in foreign affiliates in 1981 as a percentage of all employment		
	a	of all employment	19.2
	b	of paid employment	64.5
3	Foreign investment as a percentage of domestic investment 1978-80		23.7

Source:
Liberian National Investment Commission, unpublished data; OECD, *Geographical Distribution of Financial Flows to Developing Countries*, Paris 1984; IMF, *International Financial Statistics Yearbook 1984;* International Labour Office, 'Multinationals and employment in a West African sub-region: Liberia and Sierra Leone', Working paper no 29 by O Iyanda, Geneva, 1984.

Table A12

LEADING FOREIGN MULTINATIONAL COMPANIES, 1985

	Name	*Home Country*	*Sector*
1	Keihin Raefer	Japan	Sea transport
2	Konoike Construction Co	Japan	Construction
3	Fried Krupp Gmbh	W. Germany	Bulk carriers
4	Hans Mehr	W. Germany	Mechanical engineering, textile, food, drink, tobacco, chemical & pharmaceutical
5	Nordmann, Rassmann Gmbh & Co	W. Germany	Wholesale distribution
6	Alfa-Laval AB	Sweden	Mechanical engineering
7	Electrolux AB	Sweden	Mining exploration
8	Nordstrom & Thulin AB	Sweden	Sea transport
9	Amax Inc.	USA	Mining & metals manufacture
10	Aluminium Co of America	USA	Mining & metals manufacture
11	Chemical New York Corp	USA	Banking & finance
12	Exxon Corp	USA	Petroleum
13	Gatx Corp	USA	Shipping
14	Getty Oil Co	USA	Petroleum
15	International Telephone & Telegraph	USA	Telecommunications
16	Koppers Co Inc	USA	Chemicals
17	Marathon Oil Co	USA	Petroleum
18	Marcona Corp	USA	Shipping
19	Mobil Corp	USA	Petroleum, shipping
20	Occidental Petroleum	USA	Petroleum
21	Ogden Corp	USA	Shipping
22	Philips Petroleum Co	USA	Petroleum
23	Sea Containers Inc	USA	Sea transport
24	Standard Oil Co	USA	Petroleum
25	Steuber Co Inc	USA	Shipping

Source:
UN Economic & Social Council, List of Major Transnational Corporations & Foreign Companies in Selected African Countries, Paper for the Economic Commission for Africa, October 1983; Dun and Bradstreet, *Who Owns Whom 1984.*

LIBYA

Since the early 1970s, there has been substantial disinvestment in Libya by foreign investors, while the outflow of Libyan investment abroad has been on a rising trend through the 1970s.

The USA and West Germany are the main sources of investment in Libya. As Table A6 indicates, the bulk of US investment is concentrated in the oil sector.

MAIN SOURCES OF DATA:

A Official

1 *The Bank of Libya:* provides data on FDI flows for balance of payments purposes.

2 UNESC, Economic Commission for Africa, 'List of Major Transnational Corporations and Foreign Companies in Selected African Countries', October 1983.

3 UNCTC, *Transnational Corporations in World Development: Third Survey, New York:* UN, 1983.

4 US Department of Commerce, *Survey of Current Business,* Washington, August 1983.

Note:
Data do not allow us to complete Tables A5, A10 or A11 for Libya.

Table A1

SUMMARY OF THE COUNTRY'S INTERNATIONAL INVESTMENT POSITION

		Inward Investment	Outward Investment
1	Number of foreign affiliates in host country, and of foreign affiliates of home country firms at the end of 1980	30[1]	*N.A.*
2	Number of foreign firms with direct investments in host country, and home country firms with direct foreign affiliates	*N.A.*	*N.A.*
3	Total foreign direct capital stock at book value as a percentage of GNP at factor cost in 1978	3.77	0.66[2]
4	Flow of foreign direct investment in the five year perid 1979-83 (L Din m)	–929.6	41.1[3]
5	Employment in foreign affiliates or abroad	*N.A.*	*N.A.*
6	Output of foreign affiliates or abroad	*N.A.*	*N.A.*

Source:
UNCTC, *Transnational Corporations in World Development: Third Survey,* New York, 1983; IMF, *Balance of Payments Statistics Yearbook,* various issues; IMF, *International Financial Statistics Yearbook, 1984.*

NOTES TO TABLE A1

1 Represents affiliates of foreign MNEs from selected home countries as identified by UNCTC, 1983.

2 Represents total foreign direct capital stock, 1982, as a percentage of GNP, 1978.

3 Flow of FDI, 1978-82.

Table A2

PRIVATE FOREIGN CAPITAL STOCK, 1975-82 (L Din m)

	Inward Investment			Outward Investment		
	Portfolio	*Direct*	*Total*	*Portfolio*	*Direct*	*Total*
Book value of capital stock						
1975	*Not Available*	186.5	*Not Available*	*Not Available*		
1978		195.4				
1981		255.4				
1982		179.4			60.1[2]	

Source:
UNCTC, Transnational Corporations in World Development: Third Survey, New York: UN, 1983; IMF, *Balance of Payments Statistics Yearbook,* various issues.

NOTES TO TABLE A2

1 Represents US and German investments only. In 1978, investments by these countries amounted to 84.34% of total foreign direct stock in Libya.

2 Cumulative investment flow, 1974-82.

Table A3

FLOW OF FOREIGN DIRECT INVESTMENT, 1970-83 (L Din m)

	Inward Investment			Outward Investment		
	Reinvested Profits	*Other*	*Total*	*Reinvested Profits*	*Other*	*Total*
1970	*Not Separately Available*		49.6	*Not Available*		
1971			50.0			
1972			−0.7			
1973			−43.9			
1974			−72.1	*Not Separately Available*		0.4
1975			186.5			0.3
1976			−155.5			0.3
1977	33.9	−167.6	−133.8			18.0
1978	34.5	−239.5	−205.0			8.2
1979	27.5	−201.5	−174.0			6.1
1980	42.0	−364.5	−322.5			13.9
1981	42.2	−262.5	−220.3			7.3
1982	37.2	−153.2	−116.0			5.6
1983	40.5	−137.3	−96.8			*N.A.*

Source:
IMF, *Balance of Payments Statistics Yearbook,* various issues.

Table A4

SECTORAL DISTRIBUTION OF FOREIGN DIRECT CAPITAL STOCK, 1981 (L Din m)[1]

	Inward Investment				Outward Investment		
	Primary	*Secondary*	*Tertiary*		*Primary*	*Secondary*	*Tertiary*
1981	136.5	4.1	3.6		*Not Available*		

Source:
US Department of Commerce, 'Survey of Current Business', Washington, August 1983.

NOTES TO TABLE A4

1 Figures refer to US investment in Libya only.

Table A6

INDUSTRIAL DISTRIBUTION OF FOREIGN DIRECT CAPITAL STOCK, 1981 (L Din m)[1]

	Inward Investment		Outward Investment
	1981		
Primary	136.5		*Not Available*
Agriculture	*N.S.A.*		
Mining & quarrying	*N.S.A.*		
Oil	136.5		
Secondary	4.1		
Tertiary	3.6		
TOTAL	144.2		

Source:
US Department of Commerce, *Survey of Current Business,* Washington, August 1983.

NOTES TO TABLE A6

1 Figures refer to US investment in Libya only.

Table A7

LEADING SOURCE AND RECIPIENT COUNTRIES, 1981 (L Din m)

	Inward Investment	Outward Investment
	1981	
DEVELOPED AREAS[1]	170.2	*Not Available*
W. Germany	26.0	
USA	144.2	
TOTAL	170.2[2]	

Source:
US Department of Commerce, *Survey of Current Business,* Washington, August 1983; Deutschen Bundesbank, "Die Kapitalverflechtung der Unternehmen mit dem Ausland nach Ländern und Wirtschaftszweigen 1976 bis 1981", *Monthly Report,* Supplement, June 1983.

NOTES TO TABLE A7

1 Including only those countries shown below.

2 Including USA and West German investment only.

Table A8

INDICATORS OF THE SIGNIFICANCE OF INWARD FOREIGN DIRECT INVESTMENT OR THE ACTIVITIES OF FOREIGN-BASED COMPANIES TO THE NATIONAL ECONOMY, 1981

1	Direct capital stock of foreign affiliates at book value in 1978 as a proportion of		
	a	GNP at factor cost	3.77
	b	population (in D per head)	71.31

Source:
UNCTC, *Transnational Corporations in World Development: Third Survey,* New York: UN, 1983; IMF, *International Financial Statistics Yearbook, 1984.*

Table A9

INDICATORS OF THE SIGNIFICANCE OF OUTWARD FOREIGN DIRECT INVESTMENT OR THE ACTIVITIES OF HOME-BASED COMPANIES ABROAD FOR THE NATIONAL ECONOMY, 1982

1	Foreign capital stock of home-based firms at book value in 1982 as a proportion of		
	a	GNP at factor cost	0.66[1]
	b	population (in L D per head)	10.56

Source:

IMF, *Balance of Payments Statistics Yearbook,* various issues; IMF, *International Financial Statistics Yearbook, 1984.*

NOTES TO TABLE A9

1 Represents foreign capital stock, 1982, as a percentage of GNP, 1978.

Table A12

LEADING FOREIGN MULTINATIONAL COMPANIES, 1983

Name	*Home Country*	*Sector*
Bellei Industrie Meccanicha	Italy	Chemicals
ENI	Italy	Oil
Recchi	Italy	Construction
Deminex	W. Germany	Oil
Vebá Oil	W. Germany	Oil
Daewoo Corp	S. Korea	Construction
Hyundaiconst & Engineering Corp	S. Korea	Construction
Samsung Construction Co	S. Korea	Construction
Mother Well Bridge Engineering	UK	Mechanical engineering
Neste	Finland	Oil
ABV	Sweden	Construction
Stone & Webister Eng Corp	USA	Chemicals
Hojgaard & Shultz	Denmark	Construction

Source:

UNESC, Economic Commission for Africa, 'List of Major Transnational Corporations and Foreign Companies in Selected African Countries', October, 1983.

MALAWI

There is little reliable information about foreign direct investment in Malawi. The inflow of foreign investment has fluctuated annually since the 1970s.

The main source of gross foreign investment is the UK; South Africa, the USA and Zimbabwe have small investments in Malawi.

Gross foreign investment is concentrated in agriculture and food, drink and tobacco. There is relatively little foreign interest in the tertiary sector.

MAIN SOURCES OF DATA:

A **Official**

1 Central Bank of Malawi: provides data on FDI flows for balance of payments purposes.

B **Private**

1 US Department of Commerce International Trade Administration, *Investment Climate in Foreign Countries,* Washington, 1983.

Note:
Data do not allow us to complete Tables A9, A10 or A11 for Malawi.

Table A1

SUMMARY OF THE COUNTRY'S INTERNATIONAL INVESTMENT POSITION

		Inward Investment	Outward Investment
1	Number of foreign affiliates in host country, and of foreign affiliates of home country firms	*N.A.*	*N.A.*
2	Number of foreign firms with direct investments in host country, and home country firms with direct foreign affiliates	*N.A.*	*N.A.*
3	Total foreign direct capital stock at book value as a percentage of GNP at factor cost in 1981	29.78[1]	*N.A.*
4	Flow of foreign direct investment in the five year period, 1977-81 (US $ m)	36.4	*N.A.*
5	Employment in foreign affiliates or abroad	*N.A.*	*N.A.*
6	Output of foreign affiliates or abroad	*N.A.*	*N.A.*

Source:
IMF, *Balance of Payments Statistics Yearbook*, various issues; IMF, *International Financial Statistics Yearbook*, 1984; US Department of Commerce, *Investment Climate in Foreign Countries,* Washington, 1983.

NOTES TO TABLE A1

1 Represents stock of gross foreign investments as a percentage of GNP.

Table A2

PRIVATE FOREIGN CAPITAL STOCK, 1981 (US $ m)[1]

	Inward Investment			Outward Investment		
	Portfolio	*Direct*	*Total*	*Portfolio*	*Direct*	*Total*
Book value of capital stock 1981	*N.A.*	366[1]	*N.A.*	*Not Available*		

Source:
US Department of Commerce, *Investment Climate in Foreign Countries*, Washington, 1983.

NOTES TO TABLE A2

1 Represents stock of gross foreign investment.

Table A3

FLOW OF FOREIGN DIRECT INVESTMENT, 1970 - 81 (US $ m)

	Inward Investment			Outward Investment		
	Reinvested Profits	*Other*	*Total*	*Reinvested Profits*	*Other*	*Total*
1970	2.0	7.0	9.0	*Not Available*		
1971	2.0	8.0	10.0			
1972	5.4	4.4	9.8			
1973	4.8	3.5	8.3			
1974	4.8	18.1	22.9			
1975	4.9	12.1	17.0			
1976	5.8	3.4	9.2			
1977	*Not Separately Available*		5.8			
1978			10.0			
1979			12.9			
1980			6.5			
1981			1.2			

Source:
IMF, *Balance of Payments Statistics Yearbook,* various issues.

Table A4

SECTORAL DISTRIBUTION OF FOREIGN DIRECT CAPITAL STOCK, 1981 (US $ m)[1]

	Inward Investment				Outward Investment		
	Primary	*Secondary*	*Tertiary*		*Primary*	*Secondary*	*Tertiary*
1981	200	120	45		*Not Available*		

Source:
US Department of Commerce, *Investment Climate in Foreign Countries,* Washington, 1983.

NOTES TO TABLE A4
1 Gross Foreign Investment.

Table A5

GEOGRAPHICAL DISTRIBUTION OF FOREIGN DIRECT CAPITAL STOCK, 1981 (US $ m)[1]

	Inward Investment				Outward Investment		
	Developed Countries	*Developing Countries*	*Total*		*Developed Countries*	*Developing Countries*	*Total*
1981	343	23	366		*Not Available*		

Source:
US Department of Commerce, *Investment Climate in Foreign Countries,* Washington, 1983.

NOTES TO TABLE A5
1 Gross Foreign Investment.

Table A6

INDUSTRIAL DISTRIBUTION OF FOREIGN DIRECT CAPITAL STOCK, 1981 (US $ m)[1]

	Inward Investment	Outward Investment
Primary	200	*Not Available*
Agriculture [2]	200	
Secondary	120	
Food & drink [3]	60	
Chemicals & allied	*Not Separately Available*	
Metals		
Mechanical engineering		
Electrical equipment		
Motor vehicles	30	
Other transportation equipment	*Not Separately Available*	
Textiles & clothing		
Paper & allied		
Rubber		
Stone, clay & glass		
Coal & petroleum products		
Other manufacturing	30	
Tertiary	45	
Construction	20	
Distributive trade	10	
Banking & finance	15	
TOTAL	365	

Source:
US Department of Commerce, *Investment Climate in Foreign Countries*, Washington, 1983.

NOTES TO TABLE A6

1 Represents Gross Foreign Investment.

2 Sugar & Tea.

3 Including tobacco ($30m)

Table A7

LEADING SOURCE AND RECEIPIENT COUNTRIES 1981 (US $ m)[1]

	Inward Investment	Outward Investment
DEVELOPED AREAS	343	Not Available
Europe	275	
EEC of which	275	
Denmark	15	
W. Germany	10	
UK	250	
North America of which	33	
Canada	3	
USA	30	
Other developed countries of which	35	
South Africa	35	
DEVELOPING AREAS	23	
Africa (except S. Africa) of which	20	
Zimbabwe	20	
Middle East of which	3	
Israel	3	
TOTAL	366	

Source:
US Department of Commerce, *Investment Climate in Foreign Countries*, Washington, 1983.

NOTES TO TABLE A7

1 Gross Foreign Investment.

Table A8

INDICATORS OF THE SIGNIFICANCE OF INWARD FOREIGN DIRECT INVESTMENT OR THE ACTIVITIES OF FOREIGN-BASED COMPANIED TO THE NATIONAL ECONOMY 1981

1	Direct capital stock[1] of foreign affiliates at book value in 1981 as a proportion of:		
	a	GNP at factor cost	29.78
	b	population (in US $ per head)	59.90

Source:
US Department of Commerce, *Investment Climate in Foreign Countries,* Washington, 1983;
IMF, *International Financial Statistics Yearbook, 1984.*

NOTES TO TABLE A8
1 Represents stock of Gross Foreign Investment.

Table A12

LEADING FOREIGN MULTINATIONAL COMPANIES, 1983

Name	*Home Country*	*Sector*
Kier International	UK	Construction
Walford Maritime Holdings	UK	Shipping
BAT Industries PLC	UK	Tobacco
British Leyland PLC	UK	Motor vehicles and parts
SBOC Group PLC	UK	Industrial gases
Brooke Bond Group PLC	UK	Tea
ICL PLC	UK	Computers
Massey-Ferguson	Canada	Farm and industrial machinery
Squibb Corp	USA	Pharmaceuticals
Unilever	UK/Netherlands	Consumer products

Source:
UNESC, List of Major Transnational Corporations & Foreign Companies in Selected African Countries, ECA/UNCTC, October 1983; John M Stopford, *The World Directory of Multinational Enterprises 1982-83,* Bath: The Pitman Press, 1982.

MAURITIUS

There is little reliable information about foreign direct investment in Mauritius. Any indication of the importance of FDI in Mauritius can only be obtained from statistics on outward direct investment from several major home countries of which the most important are the UK and the USA. In 1981, the stock of FDI in Mauritius owing to US and UK investments amounted to US $ 62.7 million.

MAIN SOURCES OF DATA:

A Official

1 US Department of Commerce unpublished data on US direct investment in Mauritius.

2 UK Department of Industry, *Census of Overseas Assets* provides statistics on UK direct investment in Mauritius.

3 UNCTC, *Transnational Corporations in World Development: A Reexamination,* New York: UN, 1978.

4 UNCTC, *Transnational Corporations in World Development: Third Survey*, New York: UN, 1983.

B Private

1 John Cantwell, "Recent Trends in Foreign Direct Investment in Africa", paper submitted to the Commonwealth Secretariat, 1985.

2 John M Stopford, *The World Directory of Multinational Enterprises 1982-83*, Bath: The Pitman Press, 1982.

Note:
Data do not allow us to complete Tables A4, A5, A6, A9, A10 or A11 for Mauritius.

Table A1

SUMMARY OF THE COUNTRY'S INTERNATIONAL INVESTMENT POSITION

		Inward Investment	Outward Investment
1	Number of foreign affiliates in host country, and of foreign affiliates of home country firms	*N.A.*	*N.A.*
2	Number of foreign firms with direct investments in host country, and home country firms with direct foreign affiliates	*N.A.*	*N.A.*
3	Total foreign direct capital stock at book value as a percentage of GNP at factor cost in 1984	12.25	*N.A.*
4	Flow of foreign direct investment in the five year period, 1980-84 (US $ m)	10.17	*N.A.*
5	Employment in foreign affiliates or abroad	*N.A.*	*N.A.*
6	Output of foreign affiliates or abroad	*N.A.*	*N.A.*

Source:
IMF, *Balance of Payments Statistics,* various issues; IMF, *International Financial Statistics*, various issues.

Table A2

PRIVATE FOREIGN CAPITAL STOCK, 1981 (US $ m)

	Inward Investment			Outward Investment		
	Portfolio	*Direct*	*Total*	*Portfolio*	*Direct*	*Total*
Book value of capital stock						
1975	*Not Available*	22.0	*Not Available*	*Not Available*		
1977		23.0				
1978		24.0				
1981		62.7[1]				
1982		64.5[2]				
1983		66.1[2]				
1984		71.0[2]				

Source:
US Department of Commerce, unpublished data; UK Department of Industry, *Census of Overseas Assets, 1981.*

NOTES TO TABLE A2

1 Represents US FDI stock in Mauritius of US $ 7.0 million and UK FDI stock in Mauritius of US $ 55.7 million.

2 The stock of FDI in 1982, 1983 and 1984 have been estimated by adding cumulative flow figures to the stock of FDI in 1981.

Table A3

FLOW OF FOREIGN DIRECT INVESTMENT, 1977 - 84 (US $ m)

	Inward Investment				Outward Investment		
	Reinvested Profits	*Other*	*Total*		*Reinvested Profits*	*Other*	*Total*
1977	*Not Separately Available*		2.22		*Not Separately Available*		0.70
1978			4.38				0.13
1979			1.81				2.45
1980			1.17				*Not Available*
1981			0.71				
1982			1.77				
1983			1.60				
1984			4.92				

Source:
IMF, *Balance of Payments Statistics,* various issues.

Table A7

LEADING SOURCE AND RECIPIENT COUNTRIES, 1971 - 81 (US $ m)[1]

	Inward Investment			Outward Investment
	1971	*1981*		
UK	5.6	55.7		*Not Available*
USA	7.0[2]	7.0		
TOTAL	12.6	62.7		

Source:
US Department of Commerce, unpublished data; UK Department of Industry, *Census of Overseas Assets, 1981.*

NOTES TO TABLE A7

1 Refers to UK and US investments only.

2 Refers to year 1977.

Table A8

INDICATORS OF THE SIGNIFICANCE OF INWARD FOREIGN DIRECT INVESTMENT OR THE ACTIVITIES OF FOREIGN-BASED COMPANIES TO THE NATIONAL ECONOMY,

1	Direct capital stock of foreign affiliates at book value in 1984 as a proportion of	
	a GNP at factor cost	12.25
	b population (in US $ per head)	73.96
2	Foreign direct investment as percentage of domestic investment in 1979	2.1

Source:
UNCTC, 1983, *op cit*; IMF, *International Financial Statistics*, 1985.

Table A12

LEADING FOREIGN MULTINATIONAL COMPANIES, 1983

Name	*Home Country*	*Sector*
L'Air Liquide SA	France	Industrial gases
BAT Industries PLC	UK	Tobacco products

Source:
John M Stopford, *The World Directory of Multinational Enterprises 1982-83*; Bath: The Pitman Press, 1982.

MOROCCO

Economic policy of post-Independence Morocco has been reflected in a series of broad development plans. With regard to attitudes towards foreign direct investment, the government has adopted a liberal policy whereby successive Investment Acts (the latest of which is 1983) offer generous incentives, aiming to attract foreign investment into the country.

The inflow of FDI into Morocco was very low immediately following Independence in 1956 but has generally been rising over the past decade.

The main investor country is France; other sources of investment include West Germany, Switzerland, the USA and some Arab-oil countries, notably Saudi Arabia and Kuwait.

The main recipient areas for foreign investment have been the services and manufacturing sectors, with relatively little foreign activity in the extractive industries.

MAIN SOURCES OF DATA:

A Official

1. Banque Marocaine du Commerce Exterieur: publishes monthly reviews on the investment and foreign trade position of Morocco.
2. Bank of Morocco: provides annual reports and statistics on foreign investment into Morocco.
3. Banque Nationale pour le Developpement Economique: gives data on inward investment and its sectoral distribution.
4. Office des Changes du Maroc: issues various publications about foreign investment by geographical distribution.
5. UNESC: provides a list of major foreign companies operating in Morocco.

Note:

Data do not allow us to complete Tables A9 or A10 for Morocco.

Table A1

SUMMARY OF THE COUNTRY'S INTERNATIONAL INVESTMENT POSITION

		Inward Investment	Outward Investment
1	Number of foreign affiliates in host country, and of foreign affiliates of home country firms	*N.A.*	*N.A.*
2	Number of foreign firms with direct investments in host counrty, and home country firms with direct foreign affiliates	*N.A.*	*N.A.*
3	Total foreign direct capital stock at book value as a percentage of GNP at factor cost in 1982	5.00	*N.A.*
4	Flow of foreign direct investment in the five year period 1979-83 (M Dir m)	2,976.3	*N.A.*
5	Employment in foreign affiliates or abroad	*N.A.*	*N.A.*
6	Output of foreign affiliates or abroad	*N.A.*	*N.A.*

Source:

Banque Marocaine du Commerce Exterieur, *Monthly Information Review*, various issues; Bank of Morocco, *Annual Report*, various issues; Banque Nationale pour le Developpement Economique, *Annual Report*, various issues; IMF, *International Financial Statistics Yearbook 1984.*

Table A2

PRIVATE FOREIGN CAPITAL STOCK, 1975 - 82 (M Dir m)

	Inward Investment[1]			Outward Investment		
	Portfolio	*Direct*	*Total*	*Portfolio*	*Direct*	*Total*
Book value of capital stock						
1975	*Not Available*	845.9	*Not Available*	*Not Available*		
1982		4,485.7				
1983		5,073.4				

Source:

Banque Marocaine du Commerce Exterieur, *Monthly Information Review*, various issues; Bank of Morocco, *Annual Report*, various issues; Banque Nationale pour le Developpement Economique, *Annual Report*, various issues.

NOTES TO TABLE A2

1 Estimate obtained from cumulative investment flows as from 1968.

Table A3

FLOW OF FOREIGN DIRECT INVESTMENT, 1970 - 83 (M Dir m)

	Inward Investment			Outward Investment		
	Reinvested Profits[1]	*Other*	*Total*	*Reinvested Profits*	*Other*	*Total*
1970	52.4	78.6	131.0			
1971	23.5	111.6	135.1			
1972	37.3	111.5	148.8			
1973	*Not Separately Available*		86.0			
1974			86.5		*Not Available*	
1975			136.6			
1976	71.5	223.5	295.0			
1977	62.6	375.5	438.1			
1978	122.9	395.5	518.4			
1979	75.2	301.1	376.3			
1980	24.5	538.0	562.5			
1981	48.9	562.8	611.7			
1982	23.3	814.8	838.1			
1983	41.0	546.7	587.7			

Source:

Banque Marocaine du Commerce Exterieur, *Monthly Information Review*, various issues; Bank of Morocco, *Annual Report*, various issues; Banque Nationale pour le Developpement Economique, *Annual Report*, various issues.

NOTES TO TABLE A3

1 Estimates obtained by applying the annual percentage of reinvested profits to total investment flows as given in the IMF data, to the total investment flows of this series.

Table A4

SECTORAL DISTRIBUTION OF FOREIGN DIRECT CAPITAL STOCK, 1968 - 82 (M Dir m)

	Inward Investment[1]				Outward Investment		
	Primary	*Secondary*	*Tertiary*		*Primary*	*Secondary*	*Tertiary*
1975	112.1	329.8	404.0		*Not Available*		
1982	503.6	1,534.1	2,448.0				

Source:

Banque Marocaine du Commerce Exterieur, *Monthly Information Review,* various issues; Bank of Morocco, *Annual Report*, various issues; Bank of Morocco, *Etudes et Statistiques*, 1980; Banque Nationale pour le Developpement Economique, *Annual Report*, various issues.

NOTES TO TABLE A4

1 Represents cumulative investment flows as from 1968.

Table A5

GEOGRAPHICAL DISTRIBUTION OF FOREIGN DIRECT CAPITAL STOCK, 1969 - 76 (M Dir m)[1]

	Inward Investment				Outward Investment		
	Developed Countries	*Other Countries*	*Total*		*Developed Countries*	*Developing Countries*	*Total*
1969-76	803.9[2]	283.9	1,087.8		*Not Available*		

Source:

Banque Nationale pour le Developpement Economique, *Annual Report,* various issues; Banque Marocaine du Commerce Exterieur, *Monthly Information Review*, various issues; Office des Changes du Maroc, publications from 1960-83.

NOTES TO TABLE A5

1 Author's estimates from cumulative investment flow data, 1969-76.

2 Including only those countries as specified in Table A7.

Table A6

INDUSTRIAL DISTRIBUTION OF FOREIGN DIRECT CAPITAL STOCK, 1968 - 82 (M Dir m)

	Inward Investment[1]		Outward Investment
	1968-75[1]	*1968-82*[2]	
Primary	112.1	503.6	*Not Available*
Agriculture	32.6	223.0	
Mining & quarrying	20.7	178.4	
Oil	58.8	102.2	
Secondary	329.8	1,534.1	
Food & drink[3]	*N.S.A.*	*N.S.A.*	
Chemicals & allied	22.3	60.5	
Metals	*Not Separately Available*		
Mechanical engineering			
Electrical equipment			
Motor vehicles			
Other transportation equipment			
Textiles & clothing	16.9	79.9	
Paper & allied[3]	*Not Separately Available*		
Rubber[3]			
Stone, clay & glass			
Coal & petroleum products			
Other manufacturing[3]	290.6	1,393.7	
Tertiary	404.0	2,448.0	
Transport & communications	16.4	115.7	
Distributive trade	96.5	229.5	
Property	37.2	785.2	
Banking & finance	57.4	238.4	
Other services	196.5	1,079.2	
TOTAL	845.9	4,485.7	

Source:

Banque Marocaine du Commerce Exterieur, *Monthly Information Review*, various issues; Bank of Morocco, *Annual Report*, various issues; Bank of Morocco, *Etudes et Statistiques*, 1980; Banque Nationale pour le Developpement Economique, *Annual Report*, various issues.

NOTES TO TABLE A6

1 Cumulative investment flows, 1968-75.

2 Cumulative investment flows, 1968-82.

3 Food, plastics, paper, furniture are all included under 'other manufacturing'.

Table A7

LEADING SOURCE AND RECIPIENT COUNTRIES, 1969 - 76 (M Dir m)[1]

	Inward Investment	Outward Investment
	1969-76	
DEVELOPED AREAS[2]	803.9	*Not Available*
Europe[2]	667.9	
EEC of which[2]	578.7	
Belgium	29.4	
France	370.9	
W. Germany	105.5	
Italy	52.2	
UK	20.7	
Other Europe of which[2]	89.2	
Switzerland	89.2	
North America of which[2]	136.0	
USA	136.0	
TOTAL	1,087.8	

Source:
As for Table A5

NOTES TO TABLE A7

1 Author's estimates obtained from cumulative investment flows 1969-76.

2 Including only those countries shown below

Table A8

INDICATORS OF THE SIGNIFICANCE OF INWARD FOREIGN DIRECT INVESTMENT OR THE ACTIVITIES OF FOREIGN-BASED COMPANIES TO THE NATIONAL ECONOMY, 1981

1	Direct capital stock of foreign affiliates at book value in 1981 as a proportion of		
	a	GNP at factor cost	5.00
	b	population (in M Dir head)	209.7

Source:
Banque Marocaine du Commerce Exterieur, *Monthly Information Review,* various issues; Bank of Morocco, *Annual Report*, various issues; Banque Nationale pour le Developpement Economique, *Annual Report*, various issues; IMF, *International Financial Statistics Yearbook, 1984.*

Table A11

ROYALTY RECEIPTS AND PAYMENTS, 1975 - 84 (M Dir m)

	Payments				Receipts		
	To Affiliates	*To Non-affiliates*	*Total*		*From Affiliates*	*From Non-affiliates*	*Total*
1975	*Not Separately Available*		93.5		*Not Separately Available*		4.9
1976			127.6				*N.A.*
1977			157.7				5.3
1978			125.2				*N.A.*
1979			115.9				5.0
1980			143.5				5.1
1981			128.1				12.2
1982			86.4				6.6
1983			83.6				15.2
1984			117.4				9.0

Source:
IMF, *Balance of Payments Statistics Yearbook,* various issues.

Table A12

LEADING FOREIGN MULTINATIONAL COMPANIES, 1983

Name	*Home Country*	*Sector*
Matt Hay & Anderson	UK	Construction
Atlantic Richfield Co (ARCO)	USA	Oil
Holiday Inn	USA	Hotels
Standard Oil of Indiana	USA	Oil
Campenon Bernard	France	Construction
Heurtey Industries	France	Chemicals
Dumez	France	Mining
Marubeni	Japan	Food
Krupp Industrie & Statuban	W. Germany	Construction
Instituto National de Industria	Spain	Mining
Intesca	Spain	Construction
Lonrho	UK	Oil

Source:
UNESC, "List of Major Transnational Corporations and Foreign Companies in selected African Countries", paper for the Economic Commission for Africa, October 1983.

NIGERIA

Various Nigerian governments have attempted to provide foreign investors with a favourable investment climate as well as generous tax incentives. However, despite Nigeria's liberal investment policies in the past, the growth of foreign private investment has not kept pace with its economic development.

Over the last decade, government regulation of the patterns of foreign private investment have restricted the sphere of foreign investment: one direct consequence of the 'Nigerian Enterprises Promotion Decrees' of 1972, 1977 and 1981 is that any new foreign investment has to be joint venture in nature.

The most important investing country in Nigeria is the UK, with West Germany, the USA and Japan following at considerable distance.

The three main recipient areas of foreign direct investment are mining and oil, trading and business services, and manufacturing and processing; while the two sectors attracting least foreign investment are agriculture, and transport and communications.

The bulk of US foreign direct investment in Nigeria has been directed to the oil industry, although the share of FDI in oil has fallen since the early 1970s. The manufacturing sector, on the other hand, has received a steadily increasing share of FDI from 1962 onwards.

MAIN SOURCES OF DATA:

A **Official**

1. Central Bank of Nigeria: provides data on stocks of FDI by geographical and sectoral distribution.
2. UNCTC, *Transnational Corporations in World Development: Third survey,* New York: UN, 1983.
3. J S Osakwe, 'Foreign Private Investment Policies in Nigeria', *Economic and Financial Review,* Central Bank of Nigeria, 19 December 1981.

B **Private**

1. J Cantwell, 'Recent Trends in Foreign Direct Investment in Africa', paper prepared for the Commonwealth Secretariat, 1985.
2. Africa 400, in *South, The Third World Magazine,* March 1986.

Note:
Data do not allow us to complete Tables A9, A10 or A11 for Nigeria.

Table A1

SUMMARY OF THE COUNTRY'S INTERNATIONAL INVESTMENT POSITION

		Inward Investment	Outward Investment
1	Number of foreign affiliates in host country, and of foreign affiliates of home country firms at the end of 1978	1,242	*N.A.*
2	Number of foreign firms with direct investments in host country, and home country firms with direct foreign affiliates	*N.A.*	*N.A.*
3	Total foreign direct capital stock at book value as a percentage of GNP at factor cost in 1982	6.41	*N.A.*
4	Flow of foreign direct investment in the five year period, 1979-83 (₦ m)	663	*N.A.*
5	Employment in foreign affiliates or abroad, 1977	166,000	*N.A.*
6	Output of foreign affiliates or abroad	*N.A.*	*N.A.*

Source:

Central Bank of Nigeria, *Economic and Financial Review,* December 1981; IMF, *Balance of Payments Statistics Yearbook,* various issues; IMF, *International Financial Statistics Yearbook, 1984.*

Table A2

PRIVATE FOREIGN CAPITAL STOCK, 1971 - 83 (₦ m)

	Inward Investment			Outward Investment		
	Portfolio	*Direct*	*Total*	*Portfolio*	*Direct*	*Total*
Book value of capital stock						
1971	*Not Available*	2584.0	*Not Available*	*Not Available*		
1975		4627.5				
1978		1745.2				
1981		1863.1				
1983		2633.0				

Source:
Central Bank of Nigeria, *Economic and Financial Review,* December 1981; IMF, *Balance of Payments Statistics Yearbook,* various issues.

Table A3

FLOW OF FOREIGN DIRECT INVESTMENT, 1970 - 83 (₦ m)

	Inward Investment			Outward Investment		
	Reinvested Profits	*Other*	*Total*	*Reinvested Profits*	*Other*	*Total*
1970	37.9	108.5	146.4	*Not Available*		
1971	57.9	145.8	203.7			
1972	40.7	160.0	200.7			
1973	20.4	225.1	245.5			
1974	57.5	104.3	161.8			
1975	80.7	176.4	257.1			
1976	82.5	159.8	242.3			
1977	48.2	234.8	283.0			
1978	*Not Separately Available*		135.2			
1979			186.9	*N.S.A.*	*N.S.A.*	3.1
1980			-404.1	*Not Available*		
1981			335.1			
1982			289.1			
1983			256.0			
1984			224.8			

Source:
IMF, *Balance of Payments Statistics Yearbook,* various issues.

Table A4

SECTORAL DISTRIBUTION OF FOREIGN DIRECT CAPITAL STOCK, 1962 - 78 (₦ m)[1]

	Inward Investment			Outward Investment		
	Primary	*Secondary*	*Tertiary*	*Primary*	*Secondary*	*Tertiary*
1962	142.3	78.0	93.1	*Not Available*		
1973	1,265.1	765.5	349.3			
1978	621.4	1,163.4	772.2			

Source:

Central Bank of Nigeria, *Economic and Financial Review,* December 1981.

NOTES TO TABLE A4

1 Represents book value of fixed assets.

Table A5

GEOGRAPHICAL DISTRIBUTION OF FOREIGN DIRECT CAPITAL STOCK, 1981 (₦ m)

	Inward Investment			Outward Investment		
	Developed Countries	*Other Countries*	*Total*	*Developed Countries*	*Other Countries*	*Total*
1973	1,222.9[1]	92.0	1,314.9	*Not Available*		
1981	1,321.0[2]	1,353.9	2,674.9[3]			

Source.

UK Department of Trade and Industry, "Census of Overseas Assets 1981", *Business Monitor,* Supplement, 1981; US Department of Commerce, *Survey of Current Business,* August 1983; Japanese Ministry of Finance, data as cited in F. Marsh, *Japanese Overseas Investment,* EIU, 1983; Deutsche Bundesbank, *Monthly Report,* Supplement, June 1983.

NOTES TO TABLE A5

1 Represents US, UK and other Europe only.

2 Includes UK, US, West German and Japanese investment only.

3 Estimated by adding cumulative investment flows to the book value of fixed assets at the end of 1978.

Table A6

INDUSTRIAL DISTRIBUTION OF FOREIGN DIRECT CAPITAL STOCK, 1962 - 78 (₦ m)[1]

	Inward Investment		Outward Investment
	1962	*1978*	
Primary	142.3	621.4	*Not Available*
Agriculture	12.2	25.6	
Mining & quarrying Oil	130.1	595.8	
Secondary	78.0	1,163.4	
Tertiary	93.1	772.2	
Construction	9.8	107.4	
Transport & communications	3.1	30.7	
Distributive trade	79.6	498.6	
Other services	0.6	135.5	
TOTAL	313.4	2,557.0	

Source:
Central Bank of Nigeria, *Economic and Financial Review,* December 1981.

NOTES TO TABLE A6

1 Represents book value of fixed assets.

Table A7

LEADING SOURCE AND RECIPIENT COUNTRIES, 1981 (₦ m)

	Inward Investment		Outward Investment
	1973	*1981*	
DEVELOPED AREAS	838.9	1,321.0[1]	*Not Available*
Europe	*Not Available*	1,083.4	
EEC of which:		1,083.4	
W. Germany		307.6	
UK	581.2	775.8	
Other Europe	257.7	*N.A.*	
North America of which:	*N.A.*	139.5	
USA	384.0	139.5	
Other developed countries of which:	*N.S.A.*	98.1	
Japan	*N.S.A.*	98.1	
UNSPECIFIED	92.0	1,353.9	
TOTAL	2,674.9[2]	1,314.9	

Source:
For 1973 data, Central Bank of Nigeria *Economic and Financial Review,* various issues.
For 1981 data, UK Department of Trade and Industry, "Census of Overseas Assets 1981", *Business Monitor,* Supplement, 1981; US Department of Commerce, *Survey of Current Business,* August 1983; Deutsche Bundesbank, "Die Kapitalverflechtung der Unternehmen mit dem Ausland nach Landern und Wirtschaftszweigen 1976 bis 1981", *Monthly Report,* Supplement, June 1983; Japanese Ministry of Finance, data as cited in F Marsh, *Japanese Overseas Investment,* EIU, 1983.

NOTES TO TABLE A7

1 Includes UK, US, West German and Japanese investment only.

2 Estimated by adding cumulative investment flows to the book value of fixed assets in 1978.

Table A8

INDICATORS OF THE SIGNIFICANCE OF INWARD FOREIGN DIRECT INVESTMENT OR THE ACTIVITIES OF FOREIGN-BASED COMPANIES TO THE NATIONAL ECONOMY, 1968 - 82

1	Direct capital stock of foreign affiliates at book value in 1982 as a proportion of		
	a	GNP at factor cost	6.41
	b	population (in ₦ per head)	34.41
2	Investment by foreign affiliates as a percentage of		
	a	capital expenditure 1970-78	10.8
	b	domestic investment 1978-80	0.5[1]
3	Assets in manufacturing industry held by foreign enterprises as a percentage of all manufacturing assets in 1968.		70.0

Source:
IMF, *International Financial Statistics Yearbook, 1984;* Central Bank of Nigeria, *Economic and Financial Review,* December 1981; Federal Office of Statistics, *Industrial Survey of Nigeria, 1968,* Lagos, 1971; UNCTC, *Transnational Corporations in World Development: Third Survey,* New York: UN, 1983.

NOTES TO TABLE A8

1 Investment of affiliates from OELD countries.

Table A12

LEADING FOREIGN MULTINATIONAL COMPANIES, 1984

Name	Home Country	Sector	Turnover (US $m)
1 Unilever	UK/Netherlands	Manufacturing, merchants	994.0
2 Peugeot	France	Motor vehicles	890.0
3 Gulf Oil	USA	Petroleum	766.0
4 Scoa	France	Motor vehicles	519.2
5 Agip	Italy	Petroleum	395.0
6 Nigerian Breweries (sub name)	UK	Brewing	392.5
7 Total Nigeria	USA	Petroleum	390.0
8 Mobil Oil	USA	Petroleum marketing	356.8
9 UTC (subsidiary name)	UK	Metals, textiles	336.0
10 Flour Mills of Nigeria	USA	Flour milling	284.1
11 Nigerian Bottling Co (sub name)	Greece	Beverages	252.0
12 Guinness	UK	Brewery	240.4
13 Texaco	USA	Petroleum	227.0
14 Unipetrol Nigeria (sub name)	USA	Petroleum	214.0
15 United Nigerian Textiles (sub name)	India	Textiles	187.9
16 West African Portland Cement (sub name)	UK	Building materials	166.0
17 Cadbury Schweppes	UK	Confectionery	148.6
18 B A T	UK	Tobacco	146.0
19 A G Leventis & Co (sub name)	Greece	Manufacturing, retail	124.5
20 Chemical & Allied Products	UK	Chemicals	92.8
21 Seven-Up Bottling	Lebanon	Beverages	82.8
22 Management Enterprises	USA	Trading, building	78.1
23 Tate & Lyle Nigeria	UK	Sugar, plastics	74.1
24 G Cappa	Italy	Civil engineering	49.1
25 Westminster Dredging	UK	Reclamation, infrastructure	47.3

Source:

Africa 400, in *South, The Third World Magazine,* March 1986.

SENEGAL

Senegal has provided a favourable climate for foreign investment, with its Industrial Free Trade Zone in Dakar, and the 1981 Investment Code which offers generous taxation and other incentives. Nevertheless, apart from reinvested earnings by existing firms, there has been little new foreign direct investment in Senegal throughout the 1970s and early 1980s.

The bulk of foreign investment originates from France, much of which is concentrated in tourism. US investment is largely directed towards petroleum, phosphate mining and manufacturing activities in the Free Trade Zone. Other investor countries include West Germany, Norway, Japan, Denmark and South Korea. There is some outward investment from Senegal mainly in other West African countries.

MAIN SOURCES OF DATA:

A Official

1 Central Bank of Senegal: provides data on FDI flows for balance of payments purposes.

2 UNCTC, *Transnational Corporations in World Development*, Third Survey, New York: UN, 1983.

3 UNESC, List of Major Transnational Corporations and Foreign Companies in Selected African Countries, ECA/UNCTC, October 1983.

4 US Department of Commerce International Trade Administration, *Investment Climate in Foreign Countries*, Washington, 1983 and 1985, vol II.

B Private

1 J Currie, "Comparison of Export Oriented Investment: Senegal, Ghana & Mauritius", paper presented at the Commonwealth Secretariat Seminar on Foreign Investment Policies & Prospects in Africa, July 1985.

Note:
Data do not allow us to complete Tables A4, A6, A9 or A10 for Senegal.

Table A1

SUMMARY OF THE COUNTRY'S INTERNATIONAL INVESTMENT POSITION

		Inward Investment	Outward Investment
1	Number of foreign affiliates in host country, and of foreign affiliates of home country firms in 1980	106[1]	*N.A.*
2	Number of foreign firms with direct investments in host country, and home country firms with direct foreign affiliates	*N.A.*	*N.A.*
3	Total foreign direct capital stock at book value as a percentage of GNP at factor cost in 1982	14.73	*N.A.*
4	Flow of foreign direct investment in the five year period, 1978-82 (US $m)	10.50	*N.A.*
5	Employment in foreign affiliates or abroad	*N.A.*	*N.A.*
6	Output of foreign affiliates or abroad	*N.A.*	*N.A.*

Source:

IMF, *Balance of Payments Statistics Yearbook, 1984;* UNCTC, *Transnational Corporations in World Development: Third Survey,* New York: UN, 1983; OECD, *Geographical Distribution of Financial Flows to Developing Countries*, Paris, 1984.

NOTES TO TABLE A1

[1] Represents number of affiliates of foreign MNEs of selected home countries, as identified by UNCTC, 1983.

Table A2

PRIVATE FOREIGN CAPITAL STOCK, 1975 - 82 (US $m)

	Inward Investment			Outward Investment		
	Portfolio	Direct	Total	Portfolio	Direct	Total
Book value of capital stock						
1975	*Not Available*	300.0	*Not Available*	*Not Available*		
1978		340.0				
1982		355.5[1]				

Source:
UNCTC, *Transnational Corporations in World Development: Third Survey*, New York: UN, 1983; OECD, *Geographical Distribution of Financial Flows in Developing Countries*, Paris, 1984.

NOTES TO TABLE A2
1 Estimated by adding cumulative investment flow, 1979-82, to the UNCTC stock figure for 1978.

Table A3

FLOW OF FOREIGN DIRECT INVESTMENT, 1970 - 82 (US $m)

	Inward Investment			Outward Investment		
	Reinvested Profits	*Other*	*Total*	*Reinvested Profits*	*Other*	*Total*
1970	5.0	0.0	5.0	*Not Separately Available*		*N.A.*
1971	6.0	4.0	10.0			*N.A.*
1972	10.9	4.3	15.2			2.2
1973	20.3	−15.5	4.8			*N.A.*
1974	12.0	−1.2	10.8			3.6
1975	18.2	4.9	23.1			7.3
1976	19.6	16.2	35.8			*N.A.*
1977	14.0	14.0	28.0			2.3
1978	25.0	−30.0	5.0			*Not Available*
1979	*Not Separately Available*		3.9			
1980			1.9			
1981			5.2			
1982			4.5			

Source:
IMF, *Balance of Payments Statistics Yearbook*, various issues; OECD, *Geographical Distribution of Financial Flows to Developing Countries*, Paris, 1984.

Table A5

GEOGRAPHICAL DISTRIBUTION OF FOREIGN DIRECT CAPITAL STOCK, 1980 (US $m)

	Inward Investment				Outward Investment		
	Developed Countries	*Other Countries*	*Total*		*Developed Countries*	*Developing Countries*	*Total*
1980	85[1]	260.8	345.8[2]		*Not Available*		

Source:

US Department of Commerce, *Investment Climate in Foreign Countries*, Washington, 1983; US Department of Commerce, *Survey of Current Business*, November 1984.

NOTES TO TABLE A5

1 Including France, the USA and W. Germany only.

2 Estimated by adding cumulative investment flow 1979-80 to the UNCTC stock figure of 1978.

Table A7

LEADING SOURCE AND RECIPIENT COUNTRIES 1980 (US $m)

	Inward Investment		Outward Investment
	1980		
DEVELOPED AREAS[1]	85		*Not Available*
France	62		
W. Germany	5		
USA	18		
UNSPECIFIED	260.8		
TOTAL	345.8[2]		

Source:

US Department of Commerce, *Investment Climate in Foreign Countries*, Washington, 1983; US Department of Commerce, *Survey of Current Business*, November 1984; UNCTC, *Transnational Corporations in World Development: Third Survey*, New York: UN, 1983; OECD, *Geographical Distribution of Financial Flows to Developing Countries*, Paris, 1984.

NOTES TO TABLE A7

1 Including only those countries shown below.

2 Estimated by adding cumulative investment flows, 1979-80, to the UNCTC stock figure of 1978.

Table A8

INDICATORS OF THE SIGNIFICANCE OF INWARD FOREIGN DIRECT INVESTMENT OR THE ACTIVITIES OF FOREIGN-BASED COMPANIES TO THE NATIONAL ECONOMY, 1982

1	Direct capital stock of foreign affiliates at book value in 1982 as a proportion of:	
	a GNP at factor cost	14.73
	b population (in US $ per head)	59.25
2	Foreign investment as a percentage of domestic investment, 1978-80	0.1

Source:
UNCTC, *Transnational Corporations in World Development: Third Survey,* New York: UN, 1983; OECD, *Geographical Distribution of Financial Flows to Developing Countries,* Paris, 1984.

Table A11

ROYALTY RECEIPTS AND PAYMENTS, 1974 - 78 (US $ m)

	Payments				Receipts		
	To Affiliates	*To Non-affiliates*	*Total*		*From Affiliates*	*From Non-affiliates*	*Total*
1974	*Not Separately Available*		0.12		*Not Available*		
1975			0.12				
1976			0.12				
1977			0.12				
1978			0.25				
1979			0.26		*Not Separately Available*		0.12
1980			0.26				0.12

Source:
IMF, *Balance of Payments Statistics Yearbook, 1983.*

Table A12

LEADING FOREIGN MULTINATIONAL COMPANIES, 1983

Name	*Home Country*	*Sector*
James Park	S. Korea	Manufacturing
Main L Park	S. Korea	Manufacturing
STC	S. Korea	Miscellaneous Manufacturing
International Housing Corp.	USA	Construction
Faromar	Denmark	Fishery
Lauritzen	Denmark	Fishery
Beliard & Murdoch	Belgium	Transportation equipment (ship repair)
Chanic	Belgium	Miscellaneous Manufacturing
Hachetta	France	Distribution
Novotel	France	Hotels
Optorg	France	Transportation equipment (distributing)
Petro-Canada	Canada	Oil
Fincantieri	Italy	Transportation equipment (ship repair)
Weser	W. Germany	Transportation equipment (ship repair)
Compagnie Francaise des Petroles	France	Oil
Lafarge	France	Cement
Mobil	USA	Oil
Nestle	Switzerland	Food products
Schneider	France	Mechanical engineering

Source:
UNESC, List of Major Transnational Corporations & Foreign Companies in Selected African Countries, ECA/UNCTC, October 1983.

SEYCHELLES

There are limited official statistics regarding the investment position of the Seychelles. The inflow of foreign direct investment has been on a steadily rising trend during the mid-1970s and early 1980s, with the level of reinvested earnings remaining largely unchanged. The flow of the Seychelles' outward investment follows a similar pattern. Part of the investment represents flight money from an uncertain domestic potential situation.

There are no data available on the sectoral or geographical distribution of either inward or outward investment. However, the main source of investment in the Seychelles is the UK, accounting for over 45% of total FDI in 1981. The bulk of the UK's investment is concentrated in the services industry, notably property. Within the manufacturing sector, the emphasis lies on food and drink.

The Government officially welcomes foreign investment providing it makes a genuine contribution to the Seychelles' economy. Screening mechanisms tend to be less formal than in most developed countries. There are no foreign exchange controls; profits and other monies may be freely converted and repatriated.

MAIN SOURCES OF DATA:

A Official

1 UNESC, Economic Commission for Africa, 'List of Major Transnational Corporations and Foreign Companies in Selected African Countries', October 1983.

2 US Department of Commerce International Trade Administration, *Investment Climate in Foreign Countries,* Washington, 1985 vol II.

Note:
Data do not allow us to complete Table A4, A6 or A10 for the Seychelles.

Table A1

SUMMARY OF THE COUNTRY'S INTERNATIONAL INVESTMENT POSITION

		Inward Investment	Outward Investment
1	Number of foreign affiliates in host country, and of foreign affiliates of home country firms	*N.A.*	*N.A.*
2	Number of foreign firms with direct investments in host country, home country firms with direct foreign affiliates	*N.A.*	*N.A.*
3	Total foreign direct capital stock at book value as a percentage of GNP at factor cost in 1982[1]	33.50	17.52
4	Flow of foreign direct investment in the five year period, 1980-84 (US $ m)	36.8	20.1
5	Employment in foreign affiliates or abroad	*N.A.*	*N.A.*
6	Output of foreign affiliates or abroad	*N.A.*	*N.A.*

Source:
IMF, *Balance of Payments Statistics Yearbook*, various issues; IMF, *International Financial Statistics Yearbook, 1984.*

NOTES TO TABLE A1

1 Cumulative investment flow, 1976-82.

Table A2

PRIVATE FOREIGN CAPITAL STOCK, 1976 - 84 (US $m)

	Inward Investment			Outward Investment		
	Portfolio	*Direct*	*Total*	*Portfolio*	*Direct*	*Total*
Book value of capital stock						
1976	*Not Available*	10.0[1]	*Not Available*	*Not Available*	*N.A.*	*Not Available*
1981		43.4[2]			21.2[3]	
1983		58.6[2]			29.4[3]	
1984		64.1[2]			33.3[3]	

Source

IMF, *Balance of Payments Statistics Yearbook*, various issues.

NOTES TO TABLE A2

1 Estimated stock of FDI in the Seychelles by OECD countries.

2 Estimated from capital stock in 1976 plus investment flows since that date

3 Estimated from cumulative investment flows 1976 onwards

Table A3

FLOW OF FOREIGN DIRECT INVESTMENT, 1976 - 84 (US $m)

	Inward Investment			Outward Investment		
	Reinvested Profits	*Other*	*Total*	*Reinvested Profits*	*Other*	*Total*
1976	*N.S.A.*	*N.S.A.*	5.8	*N.S.A.*	*N.S.A.*	2.3
1977	1.2	4.6	5.8	0.4	1.9	2.3
1978	1.3	3.7	5.0	0.5	2.0	2.5
1979	1.3	5.2	6.5	1.3	1.9	3.1
1980	1.3	6.5	7.8	1.4	2.3	3.9
1981	1.2	7.1	8.3	1.8	5.4	7.1
1982	1.1	7.7	8.8	1.4	3.5	5.0
1983	1.1	5.3	6.4	1.6	1.6	3.2
1984	1.0	4.5	5.5	1.6	2.3	3.9

Source:

IMF, *Balance of Payments Statistics Yearbook*, various issues.

Table A5

GEOGRAPHICAL DISTRIBUTION OF FOREIGN DIRECT CAPITAL STOCK, 1981 (US $m)

	Inward Investment			Outward Investment		
	Developed Countries	*Other Countries*	*Total*	*Developed Countries*	*Other Countries*	*Total*
1981	19.7[1]	19.5	39.2[2]	*Not Available*		

Source:

UK Department of Trade and Industry, *Business Monitor,* Supplement, 1981; US Department of Commerce, *Survey of Current Business,* November 1984; IMF, *Balance of Payments Statistics Yearbook,* various issues.

NOTES TO TABLE A5

1 Including US & UK investment only.

2 Total includes unspecified figure. (Estimated from cumulative investment flows, 1976-81).

Table A7

LEADING SOURCE AND RECIPIENT COUNTRIES, 1981 (US $m)

	Inward Investment	Outward Investment
	1981	*1981*
DEVELOPED AREAS[1]	19.7	*Not Available*
Europe		
UK	17.7	
North America		
USA	2.0	
UNSPECIFIED	19.5	
TOTAL	39.2[2]	

Source:

US Department of Commerce, *Survey of Current Business,* November 1984; UK Department of Trade and Industry, 'Census of Overseas Assets, 1981', *Business Monitor,* Supplement, 1981; IMF, *Balance of Payments Statistics Yearbook,* various issues.

NOTES TO TABLE A7

1 Including only those countries shown below.

2 Cumulative investment flow, 1976-81.

Table A8

INDICATORS OF THE SIGNIFICANCE OF INWARD FOREIGN DIRECT INVESTMENT OR THE ACTIVITIES OF FOREIGN-BASED COMPANIES TO THE NATIONAL ECONOMY, 1982

1	Direct capital stock[1] of foreign affiliates at book value in 1982 as a proportion of of:	
	a GNP at factor cost	33.50
	b population (in US $ per head)	750.00

Source
IMF, *Balance of Payments Statistics Yearbook,* various issues; IMF, *International Financial Statistics Yearbook, 1984.*

NOTES TO TABLE A8
1 Cumulative investment flow, 1976-82.

Table A9

INDICATORS OF THE SIGNIFICANCE OF OUTWARD FOREIGN DIRECT INVESTMENT OR THE ACTIVITIES OF HOME-BASED COMPANIES ABROAD FOR THE NATIONAL ECONOMY, 1982

1	Foreign capital stock[1] of home-based firms at book value in 1982 as a proportion of:	
	a GNP at factor cost	17.52
	b population (in US $ per head)	392.19

Source
IMF, *Balance of Payments Statistics Yearbook,* various issues; IMF, *International Financial Statistics Yearbook, 1984.*

NOTES TO TABLE A9
1 Cumulative investment flow, 1976-82.

Table A11

ROYALTY RECEIPTS AND PAYMENTS, 1976-84 (US $ m)

	Payments			Receipts		
	To Affiliates	*To Non-affiliates*	*Total*	*From Affiliates*	*From Non-affiliates*	*Total*
1976			1.04			
1977			1.05			
1978			1.13			*Not*
1979	*Not*		1.29	*Not*		*Available*
1980	*Separately*		1.30	*Separately*		
1981	*Available*		1.30	*Available*		
1982			1.10			.55
1983			1.20			.21
1984			1.10			.10

Source
IMF, *Balance of Payments Statistics Yearbook,* various issues

Table A12

LEADING FOREIGN MULTINATIONAL COMPANIES, 1983

Name		*Home Country*	*Sector*
1	Hunting Geology & Geophysical	UK	Oil
2	Amoco International	USA	Oil

Source:

UNESC, Economic Commission for Africa, 'List of Major Transnational Corporations and Foreign Companies in Selected African Countries', October 1983.

SIERRA LEONE

Sierra Leone's economic performance has been heavily dependent on developments in the mining sector, and the flow of foreign direct investment has fluctuated over the years, according to the fortunes of this sector.

In the early 1980s, the significance of FDI was recognised, and the government of Sierra Leone adopted a liberal policy, offering various fiscal and tariff incentives to foreign investors as set out in the industrial Development Act of 1983. There is little attempt to restrict the pattern of foreign investment, although joint-venture arrangements are favoured. However, the flow of foreign direct investment fell after 1978, and the economic difficulties thereafter have not encouraged new foreign investment in the country, despite the generous incentives offered. Reinvested profits have been important in relation to new equity investments.

Foreign direct investment in Sierra Leone, arise mainly from the UK, the USA and other developed countries. They are concentrated in the mining sector, certain manufacturing industries and the services sector, particularly banking and insurance. Within the manufacturing sector, investment in the food, drink and tobacco group is high, followed by the textile industry.

MAIN SOURCES OF DATA:

A **Official**

1 Central Statistical Office, *Annual Statistical Digest, 1980*, Freetown, Sierra Leone, July 1982.

2 Ministry of Labour: provides census data on employment in Sierra Leone.

3 UN Economic and Social Council; provides a list of major companies operating in Sierra Leone.

4 UNCTC, *Transnational Corporations in World Development: Third Survey,* New York: UN, 1983.

B **Private**

1 'Foreign Investment Policy: Sierra Leone's Experience'', paper prepared for the Commonwealth Secretariat, June 1985.

2 O Iyanda, 'Multinationals and Employment in a West African Sub-region: Liberia & Sierra Leone', *International Labour Office Working Papers on the Employment Effects of MNEs,* Geneva, 1984.

Note:
Data do not allow us to complete Tables A9, A10 or A11 for Sierra Leone.

Table A1

SUMMARY OF THE COUNTRY'S INTERNATIONAL INVESTMENT POSITION

		Inward Investment	Outward Investment
1	Number of foreign affiliates in host country, and of foreign affiliates of home country firms at the end of 1980	48	*N.A.*
2	Number of foreign firms with direct investments in host country, and home country firms with direct foreign affiliates	*N.A.*	*N.A.*
3	Total foreign direct capital stock at book value as a percentage of GNP at factor cost in 1982	6.30	*N.A.*
4	Flow of foreign direct investment in the five year period 1979-83 (Le m)	15.11	*N.A.*
5	Employment in foreign affiliates or abroad	39,000[1]	*N.A.*
6	Output of foreign affiliates or abroad	*N.A.*	*N.A.*

Source:

UN Centre on Transnational Corporations, *Transnational Corporations in World Development, Third Survey*, 1983; IMF, *Balance of Payments Statistics Yearbook,* various issues; IMF, *International Financial Statistics Yearbook, 1984;* International Labour Office. 'Multinationals and Employment in a West African Sub-region: Liberia & Sierra Leone', working paper 29 by O Iyanda, Geneva, 1984.

NOTES TO TABLE A1

1 Estimated MNE employment.

Table A2

PRIVATE FOREIGN CAPITAL STOCK, 1974 - 83 (Le m)

	Inward Investment			Outward Investment		
	Portfolio	*Direct*[1]	*Total*	*Portfolio*	*Direct*	*Total*
Book value of capital stock						
1974	*Not Available*	90.0	*Not Available*	*Not Available*		
1978		86.1				
1981		92.2				
1983		101.2				

Source:
UNCTC, *Transnational Corporations in World Development, Third Survey*, New York: UN, 1983; IMF, *Balance of Payments Statistics Yearbook*, various issues.

NOTES TO TABLE A2

1 Foreign direct capital stock for 1981 and 1983 have been estimated by adding cumulative investment flows to the stock figure of 1978.

Table A3

FLOW OF FOREIGN DIRECT INVESTMENT, 1970 - 83 (Le m)

	Inward Investment			Outward Investment		
	Reinvested Profits	*Other*	*Total*	*Reinvested Profits*	*Other*	*Total*
1970	*N.S.A.*	*N.S.A.*	6.67	*Not Available*		
1971	1.66	2.50	4.16			
1972	0.87	2.60	3.47			
1973	0.97	1.95	2.92			
1974	1.03	8.22	9.25			
1975	2.19	6.55	8.74			
1976	1.80	7.71	9.51			
1977	0.67	5.09	5.76			
1978	10.36	15.08	25.43			
1979	13.66	3.28	16.93			
1980	0.14	−19.67	−19.54			
1981	*N.S.A.*	*N.S.A.*	8.75			
1982	25.57	−19.83	5.74			
1983	10.48	−7.26	3.22			

Source:
IMF, *Balance of Payment Statistics Yearbook,* various issues.

Table A4

SECTORAL DISTRIBUTION OF EMPLOYMENT IN FOREIGN AFFILIATES (th)

	Primary[1]	*Secondary*	*Tertiary*
1974	9.66	6.24	20.14
1979	6.90	6.50	24.51
1981	6.90	6.89	26.16

Source:
Iyanda, 1984, *op cit.*

NOTES TO TABLE A4

1 Mining and quarrying only.

Table A5

GEOGRAPHICAL DISTRIBUTION OF FOREIGN DIRECT CAPITAL STOCK, 1981 (Le m)

	Inward Investment				Outward Investment		
	Developed Countries	*Other Countries*	*Total*		*Developed Countries*	*Developing Countries*	*Total*
1981	42.0[1]	49.6	91.6[2]		*Not Available*		

Source:
HMSO, 'Census of Overseas Assets 1981', *Business Monitor,* Supplement 1981; US Department of Commerce, *Survey of Current Business*, November 1984.

NOTES TO TABLE A5

1 Includes UK and US investment only.

2 Estimated by adding cumulative investment flows 1979-81 to the stock figure of 1978.

Table A6

INDUSTRIAL DISTRIBUTION OF FOREIGN DIRECT CAPITAL STOCK, 1981 (Le m)

	Inward Investment		Outward Investment
	1981		
Primary			
Agriculture			
Mining & quarrying	*N.S.A.*		
Oil			
Secondary	18.4[1]		*Not Available*
Food & drink	17.7[1]		
Tertiary	10.8[1]		
Distributive trade	9.2[1]		
TOTAL	91.6[2]		

Source:
HMSO, 'Census of Overseas Assets, 1981', *Business Monitor*, Supplement 1981.

NOTES TO TABLE A6
1 UK investment only.
2 Estimated by applying cumulative investment flow figures 1979-81 to the stock figure of 1978.

Table A7

LEADING SOURCE AND RECIPIENT COUNTRIES, 1981 (Le m)

	Inward Investment		Outward Investment
	1981		
DEVELOPED AREAS	42.0[1]		
EEC of which			
UK	29.1		*Not Available*
North America of which			
USA	12.9		
TOTAL	91.6[2]		

Source:
HMSO, 'Census of Overseas Assets 1981', *Business Monitor*, Supplement 1981.
US Department of Commerce, *Survey of Current Business,* November 1984.

NOTES TO TABLE A7
1 Includes UK and US investment only.
2 Estimated by adding cumulative investment flows, 1979-81, to the stock figure of 1978.

Table A8

INDICATORS OF THE SIGNIFICANCE OF INWARD FOREIGN DIRECT INVESTMENT OR THE ACTIVITIES OF FOREIGN-BASED COMPANIES TO THE NATIONAL ECONOMY, 1978 - 82

1	Direct capital stock of foreign affiliates at book value in 1982 as a proportion of		
	a	GNP at factor cost	6.30
	b	population (in Le per head)	28.4
2	Employment in foreign affiliates in 1981 as a percentage of all employment[1]		
	a	in all industry	17.0
	b	in manufacturing	13.0
3	Foreign investment as a percentage of domestic investment, 1978-80		1.9
4	Percentage share of employment accounted for by foreign affiliates in selected sectors, 1981		
			Employment
	Primary Goods Sector		
		Mining & quarrying	46
	Manufacturing Sector		13
	Services Sector		
		Construction	43
		Transport & communications	34
		Trade & distribution	6

Source:

International Labour Office, 'Multinationals and Employment in a West African Sub-region: Liberia & Sierra Leone', Working paper no 29 by O Iyanda, Geneva, 1984; IMF, *International Financial Statistics Yearbook*, 1984; IMF, *Balance of Payments Statistics Yearbook*, various issues.

NOTES TO TABLE A8

1 Excluding employment in agriculture, where MNE investment is relatively insignificant; MNE employment as a fraction of the total working population (including agriculture) in 1981 is 3.4%.

Table A12

LEADING FOREIGN MULTINATIONAL COMPANIES

Name	*Home Country*	*Sector*
Caldeonian Hotel Holding	UK	Hotels
Aracca Petroleum Corp	USA	Oil
Bethlehem Steel	USA	Mining
Nord Resources	USA	Oil
Transierra Exploration Corp	USA	Mining
Austro Mineral	Austria	Mining
Alu Suisse	Switzerland	Mining
BAT Industries PLC	UK	Tobacco

Source:
UN, Economic and Social Council, List of Major Transnational Corporations and Foreign Companies in Selected African Countries, paper for the Economic Commission for Africa, October 1983.

TANZANIA

There are no official published sources of statistics on foreign direct investment in Tanzania. The only relevant statistics that have been recently compiled pertain to the investment activity of the private sector as a whole, both foreign and domestic, with no disaggregation between them.

The UK is by far the largest source of foreign direct investment in Tanzania, with some twenty private enterprises operating in Tanzania in recent years. Other important, although substantially less significant investor countries are Sweden, Japan, West Germany and Holland. US investment is concentrated largely in tyre production and oil distribution.

MAIN SOURCES OF DATA:

A Official

1. OECD, *Geographic Distribution of Financial Flows to Developing Countries*, Paris: OECD, 1984 gives statistical information on flows of foreign direct investment in several countries.
2. US Department of Commerce provides data on the stock of US investment in Tanzania as well as its sectoral distribution.
3. UK Department of Industry, *Census of Overseas Assets* provides data on the stock of UK investment in Tanzania as well as its sectoral distribution.
4. UNCTC, *Transnational Corporations in World Development: Third Survey*, New York: UN, 1983.

B Private

1. John Cantwell, "Recent Trends in Foreign Direct Investment in Africa", paper submitted to the Commonwealth Secretariat, 1985.
2. John M Stopford, *The World Directory of Multinational Enterprises 1982–83,* Bath: The Pitman Press, 1982.

Note:
Data do not allow us to complete Tables A6, A9, A10 and A11 for Tanzania.

Table A1

SUMMARY OF THE COUNTRY'S INTERNATIONAL INVESTMENT POSITION

		Inward Investment	Outward Investment
1	Number of foreign affiliates in host country, and of foreign affiliates of home country firms	*N.A.*	*N.A.*
2	Number of foreign firms with direct investments in host country, and home country firms with direct foreign affiliates	*N.A.*	*N.A.*
3	Total foreign direct capital stock at book value as a percentage of GNP at factor cost in 1978	3.96	*N.A.*
4	Flow of foreign direct investment in the five year period, 1979-82 (US $ m)	45.8	*N.A.*
5	Employment in foreign affiliates or abroad	*N.A.*	*N.A.*
6	Output of foreign affiliates or abroad	*N.A.*	*N.A.*

Source:
OECD, *Geographic Distribution of Financial Flows to Developing Countries*, Paris: OECD, 1984.

Table A2

PRIVATE FOREIGN CAPITAL STOCK, 1981 (US $ m)

	Inward Investment			Outward Investment		
	Portfolio	*Direct*	*Total*	*Portfolio*	*Direct*	*Total*
Book value of capital stock						
1971	*Not Available*	65.0	*Not Available*	*Not Available*		
1975		140.0				
1978		170.0				
1981		201.5[1]				

Source:
US Department of Commerce, unpublished data; UK Department of Industry, *Census of Overseas Assets,* 1981; UNCTC, 1983, *op cit.*

NOTES TO TABLE A2

1 Represents US FDI stock in Tanzania of US $ 29.0 million and UK FDI stock in Tanzania of US $ 60.9 million.

Table A3

FLOW OF FOREIGN DIRECT INVESTMENT, 1979-82 (US $ m)

	Inward Investment			Outward Investment		
	Reinvested Profits	*Other*	*Total*	*Reinvested Profits*	*Other*	*Total*
1979	*Not Separately Available*		8.0	*Not Available*		
1980			4.6			
1981			18.9			
1982			14.3			

Source:
OECD, *Geographic Distribution of Financial Flows to Developing Countries,* Paris: OECD, 1984.

Table A4

SECTORAL DISTRIBUTION OF FOREIGN DIRECT CAPITAL STOCK, 1981 (US $ m)

	Inward Investment				Outward Investment		
	Primary	*Secondary*	*Tertiary*		*Primary*	*Secondary*	*Tertiary*
1981[1]	*N.A.*	44.27	*N.A.*		*Not Available*		

Source:
UK Department of Industry, *Census of Overseas Assets,* 1981.

NOTES TO TABLE A4

1 Represents UK investment only, of a total stock of UK investment of US $ 60.9 m.

Table A5

INDUSTRIAL DISTRIBUTION OF FOREIGN DIRECT CAPITAL STOCK, 1981 (US $ m)

	Inward Investment[1]	Outward Investment
	1981	
Primary	*N.S.A.*	*Not Available*
Agriculture	*N.A.*	
Mining & quarrying	0.0	
Oil	*N.A.*	
Secondary	44.27	
Food & drink	*N.S.A.*	
Chemicals & allied	6.09	
Metals	0.0	
Mechanical engineering	0.0	
Electrical equipment	*N.S.A.*	
Textiles & clothing	0.0	
Paper & allied	*N.S.A.*	
Rubber	0.0	
Other manufacturing	*N.S.A.*	
Tertiary	*N.S.A.*	
Construction	*N.A.*	
Transport & communications	*N.A.*	
Distributive trade	6.52	
TOTAL	60.9	

Source:
UK Department of Industry, *Census of Overseas Assets,* 1981.

NOTES TO TABLE A5

1 Represents UK investment only.

Table A7

LEADING SOURCE AND RECIPIENT COUNTRIES, 1971-81 (US $ m)[1]

	Inward Investment			Outward Investment
	1971	*1981*		
UK	17.1	60.9		*Not Available*
USA	*N.S.A.*	29.0		
Other unspecified countries	47.9	–		
TOTAL	65.0	90.0		

Source:
US Department of Commerce, unpublished data; UK Department of Industry, *Census of Overseas Assets,* various issues.

NOTES TO TABLE A7

1 Represents UK and US investments only.

Table A8

INDICATORS OF THE SIGNIFICANCE OF INWARD FOREIGN DIRECT INVESTMENT OR THE ACTIVITIES OF FOREIGN-BASED COMPANIES TO THE NATIONAL ECONOMY, 1978-80

1	Direct capital stock of foreign affiliates at book value in 1978 as a proportion of	
	a GNP at factor cost	3.96
	b population (in US $ per head)	9.75
2	Foreign direct investment as a percentage of domestic investment, 1978-80	0.6

Source:
UN, *International Financial Statistics 1985,* New York: UN, 1985; UNCTC, 1983, *op cit.*

Table A12

LEADING FOREIGN MULTINATIONAL COMPANIES, 1983

Name	*Home Country*	*Sector*
Brooke Bond Group PLC	UK	Food products
Compagnie Francaise des Petroles SA	France	Marketing of oil products
ENI	Italy	Petroleum refining
ICL PLC	UK	Manufacture of computers
Matsushita Electric Industrial Company Ltd	Japan	Electrical and electronic products
Metal Box PLC	UK	Manufacture of metal containers
Pfizer Incorporated	USA	Pharmaceuticals
NV Philips Gloecilampenfabriecken	Netherlands	Electrotechnical equipment
Unilever PLC/NV	Netherlands/ UK	Consumer products
The Wellcome Foundation Limited	UK	Pharmaceuticals

Source:
John M Stopford, *The World Directory of Multinational Enterprises 1982-83,* Bath: The Pitman Press, 1982.

TOGO

There is little information about the investment position of Togo. The inflow of foreign direct investment fluctuated throughout the 1970s; the level of reinvested profits has been on a rising trend. The negligible flow of outward investment has changed little since the early to mid-1970s.

There are no detailed statistics available on the sectoral or geographical distribution of either inward or outward investment. Investor countries into Togo include West Germany, France, the UK and the USA.

The Government of Togo welcomes inward investment as a means of promoting the country's economic development. There is a Tongolese investment code which identifies sectors in which investment is especially needed. There are few performance requirements and the Tongolese Government does not require foreign investors to enter into joint ventures with either private or government partners.

MAIN SOURCES OF DATA:

A Official

1. Chamber of Commerce, Togo: provides broad data about the inflow and outflow of investment.
2. US Department of Commerce, International Trade Administration, *Investment Climate in Foreign Countries,* Washington, 1983 and 1985, vol. II.
3. UNCTC, *Transnational Corporations in World Development: Third Survey,* New York: UN, 1983.

Note:
Data do not allow us to complete Tables A4, A6, A10 or A11 for Togo.

Table A1

SUMMARY OF THE COUNTRY'S INTERNATIONAL INVESTMENT POSITION

		Inward Investment	Outward Investment
1	Number of foreign affiliates in host country, and of foreign affiliates of home country firms at the end of 1980	34[1]	*N.A.*
2	Number of foreign firms with direct investments in host country, and home country firms with direct foreign affiliates	*N.A.*	*N.A.*
3	Total foreign direct capital stock at book value as a percentage of GNP at factor cost in 1979	15.15	0.44[1]
4	Flow of foreign direct investment in the five year period, 1977-81 (US $m)	212.7	2.1[2]
5	Employment in foreign affiliates or abroad	*N.A.*	*N.A.*
6	Output of foreign affiliates or abroad	*N.A.*	*N.A.*

Source:

UNCTC, *Transnational Corporations in World Development: Third Survey,* New York: UN, 1983; UNCTC, *Salient Features and Trends in Foreign Direct Investment,* New York, 1983; IMF, *Balance of Payments Statistics Yearbook,* various issues; IMF, *International Financial Statistics Yearbook, 1984.*

NOTES TO TABLE A1

1 Represents affiliates of foreign MNEs from selected home countries as identified by UNCTC, 1983.

2 1975.

3 1971-1975.

Table A2

PRIVATE FOREIGN CAPITAL STOCK, 1975 - 81 (US $m)

	Inward Investment			Outward Investment		
	Portfolio	*Direct*	*Total*	*Portfolio*	*Direct*	*Total*
Book value of capital stock						
1975	*Not Available*	90.0	*Not Available*	*Not Available*	2.6[1]	*Not Available*
1978		100.0			*N.A.*	
1981		203.8			*N.A.*	

Source:

UNCTC, *Transnational Corporations in World Development: Third Survey,* New York: UN, 1983, UNCTC, *Salient Features and Trends in Foreign Direct Investment,* New York, 1983; IMF, *Balance of Payments Statistics Yearbook,* various issues.

NOTES TO TABLE A2

1 Cumulative investment flow, 1967-75.

Table A3

FLOW OF FOREIGN DIRECT INVESTMENT, 1970 - 81 (US $m)

	Inward Investment			Outward Investment		
	Reinvested Profits	*Other*	*Total*	*Reinvested Profits*	*Other*	*Total*
1970	*N.S.A.*	*N.S.A.*	1.0	*Not Separately Available*		0.2
1971	1.0	4.0	5.0			1.0
1972	1.1	0.0	1.1			−1.1
1973	1.2	2.4	3.6			1.2
1974	1.2	−40.9	−39.7			0.5
1975	*N.S.A.*	*N.S.A.*	*N.A.*			0.5
1976	3.5	2.3	5.8	*Not Available*		
1977	2.9	9.1	12.0			
1978	3.3	93.6	96.9			
1979	4.1	49.8	53.9			
1980	−14.3	55.7	41.4			
1981	−19.4	27.9	8.5			

Source:

IMF, *Balance of Payments Statistics Yearbook,* various issues; UNCTC, *Salient Features and Trends in Foreign Direct Investment,* New York, 1983.

Table A5

GEOGRAPHICAL DISTRIBUTION OF FOREIGN DIRECT CAPITAL STOCK, 1980 (US $m)

	Inward Investment			Outward Investment		
	Developed Countries	*Other Countries*	*Total*	*Developed Countries*	*Developing Countries*	*Total*
1980	30.0[1]	166.0	196.0[2]	*Not Available*		

Source:
The French Embassy; Deutschen Bundesbank; data as cited in US Department of Commerce, *Investment Climate in Foreign Countries,* Washington, 1983; US Department of Commerce, *Survey of Current Business,* November, 1984.

NOTES TO TABLE A5

1 Including France, West Germany and the USA only.

2 Total includes unspecified figure. (Estimated by adding cumulative investment flows, 1979-80, to the UNCTC stock figure of 1978.

Table A7

LEADING SOURCE AND RECIPIENT COUNTRIES, 1980 (US $m)

	Inward Investment	Outward Investment
	1980	
DEVELOPED AREAS[1]	30.0	*Not Available*
Europe		
EEC of which:[1]	24.0	
France	2.0	
W. Germany	22.0	
North America		
USA	6.0[2]	
UNSPECIFIED	166.0	
TOTAL	196.0[3]	

Source:
The French Embassy; Deutschen Bundesbank, data as cited in US Department of Commerce, *Investment Climate in Foreign Countries,* Washington, 1983; US Department of Commerce, *Survey of Current Business,* November, 1984.

NOTES TO TABLE A7

1 Including only those countries shown below.

2 1979 estimate.

3 Estimated by adding cumulative investment flow, 1979-80 to the UNCTC stock figure of 1978.

Table A8

INDICATORS OF THE SIGNIFICANCE OF INWARD FOREIGN DIRECT INVESTMENT OR THE ACTIVITIES OF FOREIGN-BASED COMPANIES TO THE NATIONAL ECONOMY, 1979

1	Direct capital stock of foreign affiliates at book value in 1979 as a proportion of:		
	a	GNP at factor cost	15.15
	b	population (in US $ per head)	61.94

Source:

UNCTC, *Transnational Corporations in World Development: Third Survey,* New York: UN, 1983; IMF, *Balance of Payments Statistics Yearbook, 1984;* IMF, *International Financial Statistics Yearbook, 1984.*

Table A9

INDICATORS OF THE SIGNIFICANCE OF OUTWARD FOREIGN DIRECT INVESTMENT OR THE ACTIVITIES OF HOME-BASED COMPANIES ABROAD FOR THE NATIONAL ECONOMY, 1975

1	Foreign capital stock of home-based firms at book value in 1975 as a proportion of:		
	a	GNP at factor cost	0.44
	b	population (in US $ per head)	1.17

Source:

UNCTC, *Salient Features and Trends in Foreign Direct Investment,* New York, 1983; IMF, *Balance of Payments Statistics Yearbook,* various issues; IMF, *International Financial Statistics Yearbook, 1984.*

Table A12

LEADING FOREIGN AFFILIATES, 1983

	Name	*Home Country*	*Sector*
1	Campenon Bernard	France	Construction
2	Dyckerhoff & Widmann	W. Germany	Construction
3	OT Africa Line	UK	Shipping
4	Ste Nat Du Commerce	France	Commerce
5	SGGG Togo	France	Distribution
6	Scoa	France	Distribution
7	Societe Sica Togo	France	Imports
8	Ciment Du Togo	France	Construction materials
9	Satelit	France	Public works
10	Sototoles	France	Construction materials
11	Sotedi	France	Commerce
12	Satal		Agro/Industry
13	Ste de Produits Alimentaires	France	Food trade
14	L'Air Liquide SA	France	Industrial games

Source:

UNESC, Commission for Africa, 'List of Major Transnational Corporations and Foreign Companies in Selected African Countries', October, 1983. John M Stopford, *The World Directory of Multinational Enterprises 1982–83,* Bath: The Pitman Press, 1982.

ZAIRE

The inflow of foreign direct investment in Zaire has fluctuated annually, falling considerably during the years 1975–78, and again in 1980. In the years 1981–83 there was a marked increase in the inflow.

The main sources of investment in Zaire are Japan and the EEC, notably Belgium, West Germany, the UK, and France. The US also has significant interests in Zaire. Investment is mainly concentrated in mining and plantation agriculture; at the same time, in 1974, it was estimated that between 30 and 35% of employment in the manufacturing industry was accounted for by foreign affiliates.

The Government of Zaire is anxious to attract foreign investments, and during the 1980s policy has become increasingly favourable towards private enterprise. With the exception of the mineral extractions industry, Zaire neither requires nor generally seeks participation in foreign investments. Foreign owned companies are subject to the same tax and labour laws as domestic firms. In 1984 new regulations were enacted allowing the repatriation of dividends.

MAIN SOURCES OF DATA:

A Official

1. Zaire Ministry of Planning: compiles data about the investment position of Zaire.
2. US Department of Commerce International Trade Administration, *Investment Climate in Foreign Countries,* Washington, 1983 and 1985, vol II.
3. UNESC, Economic Commission for Africa, 'List of Major Transnational Corporations and Foreign Companies in Selected African Countries', October 1983.
4. UNCTC, *Transnational Corporations in World Development: Third Survey,* New York: UN, 1983.

Note:

Data do not allow us to complete Tables A4, A6, A9, A10 or A11 for Zaire.

Table A1

SUMMARY OF THE COUNTRY'S INTERNATIONAL INVESTMENT POSITION

		Inward Investment	Outward Investment
1	Number of foreign affiliates in host country, and of foreign affiliates of home country firms at the end of 1980	192[1]	*N.A.*
2	Number of foreign firms with direct investments in host country, and home country firms with direct foreign affiliates	*N.A.*	*N.A.*
3	Total foreign direct capital stock at book value as a percentage of GNP at factor cost in 1980	22.84	*N.A.*
4	Flow of foreign direct investment in the five year period, 1979-83 (US $ m)	686.67	*N.A.*
5	Employment in foreign affiliates or abroad	*N.A.*	*N.A.*
6	Output of foreign affiliates or abroad	*N.A.*	*N.A.*

Source:

UNCTC, *Transnational Corporations in World Development: Third Survey,* New York: UN, 1983; IMF, *Balance of Payments Statistics Yearbook,* various issues; IMF, *International Financial Statistics Yearbook, 1984.*

NOTES TO TABLE A1

1 Represents number of foreign affiliates of MNEs from selected home countries, as identified by UNCTC, 1983.

Table A2

PRIVATE FOREIGN CAPITAL STOCK, 1978 - 83 (US $ m)

	Inward Investment			Outward Investment		
	Portfolio	*Direct*[1]	*Total*	*Portfolio*	*Direct*	*Total*
Book value of capital stock						
1978	*Not Available*	1,250.0	*Not Available*	*Not Available*		
1981		1,621.9				
1983		1,936.7				

Source:

UNCTC, *Transnational Corporations in World Development: Third Survey,* New York: UN, 1983; IMF, *Balance of Payments Statistics Yearbook, 1984.*

NOTES TO TABLE A2

1 Foreign direct capital stock figures for 1981 and 1983 have been estimated by adding cumulative investment flows to the UNCTC stock figure of 1978.

Table A3

FLOW OF FOREIGN DIRECT INVESTMENT, 1970 - 83 (US $ m)

	Inward Investment				Outward Investment		
	Reinvested Profits	*Other*	*Total*		*Reinvested Profits*	*Other*	*Total*
1970	*Not Separately Available*		42.0		*Not Available*		
1971			52.2				
1972			104.2				
1973			75.1				
1974			125.1				
1975			37.6				
1976			79.8				
1977			59.2				
1978			114.9				
1979			60.1				
1980			56.0				
1981			255.9				
1982			176.5				
1983			138.2				

Source:

IMF, *Balance of Payments Statistics Yearbook,* various issues.

NOTES TO TABLE A3

1 *Excluding reinvested earnings.*

Table A5

GEOGRAPHICAL DISTRIBUTION OF FOREIGN DIRECT CAPITAL STOCK, 1980 (US $ m)

	Inward Investment			Outward Investment		
	Developed Countries	*Other Countries*	*Total*	*Developed Countries*	*Developing Countries*	*Total*
1980	1,065.9[1]	277.3	1,343.2[2]	*Not Available*		

Source:

US Department of Commerce, *Investment Climate in Foreign Countries,* Washington, 1983; Japanese Ministry of Finance, data as cited in F Marsh, *Japanese Overseas Investment,* EIU, 1983.

NOTES TO TABLE A5

1 Including only those countries as specified in Table A7. Estimate obtained by applying the geographical distribution of sources of foreign investment for the period 1969 - 76 to the FDI stock figure of 1980 (Table A2).

2 Total includes 'unspecified' figure.

Table A7

LEADING SOURCE AND RECIPIENT COUNTRIES, 1980 (US $ m)[1]

	Inward Investment	Outward Investment
	1980	
DEVELOPED AREAS	1,065.9	*Not Available*
Europe	745.0	
EEC of which:	745.0	
Belgium	212.8	
France	133.0	
W. Germany	172.6	
Italy	84.8	
UK	141.8[2]	
North America of which:	77.9	
USA	77.9[3]	
Other developed countries of which:	243.0	
Japan	243.0[4]	
UNSPECIFIED	277.3	
TOTAL	1,343.2	

Source:

US Department of Commerce, *Investment Climate in Foreign Countries,* Washington, 1983; Ministry of Finance, Japan, data as cited in F Marsh, *Japanese Overseas Investment,* EIU, 1983.

ZAIRE NOTES TO TABLE A7

1 Estimates obtained by applying the percentage geographical distribution of sources of foreign investment for the period 1969 - 76, to the FDI stock figure of 1980 (Table A2).

2 UK Department of Trade and Industry estimate for 1981 is US S 18.7.

3 US Department of Commerce estimate for 1980 is US S 164m.

4 Japan was omitted from the above mentioned geographical distribution; this estimate was obtained from the Japanese Ministry of Finance.

Table A8

INDICATORS OF THE SIGNIFICANCE OF INWARD FOREIGN DIRECT INVESTMENT OR THE ACTIVITIES OF FOREIGN-BASED COMPANIES TO THE NATIONAL ECONOMY, 1980

1	Direct capital stock of foreign affiliates at book value in 1980 as a proportion of:		
	a	GNP at factor cost	22.84
	b	population (in US $ per head)	50.92
2	Employment in foreign affiliates in 1974 as a percentage of all employment in manufacturing		30.35

Source:
UNCTC, *Transnational Corporations in World Development: Third Survey,* New York: UN, 1983; IMF, *Balance of Payments Statistics Yearbook, 1984;* IMF, *International Financial Statistics Yearbook, 1984.*

Table A12

LEADING FOREIGN MULTINATIONAL COMPANIES, 1983

	Name	*Home Country*	*Sector*
1	ABAY	Belgium	Oil
2	Cometra Oil Co.	Belgium	Oil
3	Ishikawajima Harima Heavy Industries	Japan	Construction
4	Mitsui Mining and Smelting	Japan	Mining
5	Teikoku Oil Co	Japan	Oil
6	Astaldi Estero	Italy	Construction
7	Gulf Oil	US	Oil

Source:
UNESC, Economic Commission for Africa, 'List of Major Transnational Corporations and Foreign Companies in Selected African Countries', October, 1983.

Table A12 (Continued)

LEADING FOREIGN MULTINATIONAL COMPANIES, 1983

	Name	*Home Country*	*Sector*
8	Gulf Oil	USA	Petroleum
9	Royal Dutch/Shell Group of Companies	Netherlands/UK	Petroleum
10	British American Tobacco	UK	Tobacco
11	Peugeot	France	Motor vehicles
12	Hoechst	W. Germany	Pharmaceuticals
13	British Leyland PLC	UK	Motor vehicles
14	Ciba-Geigy AG	Switzerland	Chemicals
15	Crown Cork and Seal Company Inc	USA	Metal cans and closures
16	ENI	Italy	Petroleum
17	Fiat SpA	Italy	Motor vehicles
18	General Motors Corp	USA	Motor vehicles
19	Goodyear Tyre and Rubber Co	USA	Rubber tyres
20	The Heineken Group	Netherlands	Beer
21	Petrofina SA	Belgium	Petroleum
22	NV Philips Gloeilampenfabrieken	Netherlands	Electrotechnical equipment
23	The Singer Company	USA	Sewing machines
24	Texaco Incorporated	USA	Petroleum
25	Unilever	UK/Netherlands	Consumer products
26	Warner - Lambert Company	USA	Pharmaceuticals

Source:

UNESC, Economic Commission for Africa, 'List of Major Transnational Corporations and Foreign Companies in Selected African Countries', October 1983; John M Stopford, *The World Directory of Multinational Enterprises 1982–83*,, Bath: The Pitman Press, 1982.

ZAMBIA

There is little official information available on the investment position of Zambia. The inflow of foreign direct investment into Zambia has not changed much throughout the 1970s and early 1980s, and the bulk of such investment has been reinvested earnings. There has been very little new foreign direct investment during this period.

The main investor countries are the UK and the USA, which together accounted for nearly 90% of total FDI in Zambia in 1981. There is no disaggregation by industrial sector; Table A6, however, indicates the sectoral distribution of UK investment in 1981, which accounts for around 56% of total FDI. Such investment is concentrated in the manufacturing sector, particularly chemicals, tobacco and textiles. UK investment in the distributive trade is also significant.

Foreign direct investment in Zambia is subject to several major laws, including the Industrial Development Act of 1977, which sets out the kind of sectors the Zambian Government wishes to develop. Officially, there is no distinction between the treatment of foreign and domestic investment, but all applications by foreign multinational enterprises, particularly in the manufacturing sector, are carefully screened; and often applicants are required to prepare feasibility studies demonstrating the economic viability of the proposed enterprise. Approved remittance of profits, as with other payments are placed in a queue of accounts awaiting foreign exchange cover. The use of foreign personnel in Zambian affiliates is discouraged. More positively the Zambian government offers several incentives to both foreign and domestic investors.

MAIN SOURCES OF DATA:

A Official

1. Central Bank of Zambia: provides data on investment flows for balance of payments purposes.
2. US Department of Commerce International Trade Administration, *Investment Climate in Foreign Countries,* Washington, 1983 and 1985, vol II.
3. UNESC, Economic Commission for Africa. 'List of Major Transnational Corporations and Foreign Companies in Selected African Countries', October, 1983.

Note:
Data do not allow us to complete Tables A9, A10 or A11 for Zambia.

Table A1

SUMMARY OF THE COUNTRY'S INTERNATIONAL INVESTMENT POSITION

		Inward Investment	Outward Investment
1	Number of foreign affiliates in host country, and of foreign affiliates of home country firms at the end of 1980	269[1]	*N.A.*
2	Number of foreign firms with direct investments in host country, and home country firms with direct foreign affiliates	*N.A.*	*N.A.*
3	Total foreign direct capital stock at book value as a percentage of GNP at factor cost in 1981	11.31	*N.A.*
4	Flow of foreign direct investment in the five year period, 1977-81 (US $m)	182.70	*N.A.*
5	Employment in foreign affiliates or abroad	*N.A.*	*N.A.*
6	Output of foreign affiliates or abroad	*N.A.*	*N.A.*

Source:

UNCTC, *Transnational Corporations in World Development: Third Survey,* New York: UN, 1983; IMF, *Balance of Payments Statistics Yearbook, 1984;* IMF, *International Financial Statistics Yearbook, 1984.*

NOTES TO TABLE A1

1 Represents number of affiliates of foreign MNEs from selected home countries identified by UNCTC, 1983.

Table A2

PRIVATE FOREIGN CAPITAL STOCK, 1975 - 81 (US $m)

	Inward Investment			Outward Investment		
	Portfolio	*Direct*	*Total*	*Portfolio*	*Direct*	*Total*
Book value of capital stock						
1975	*Not Available*	200.0	*Not Available*	*Not Available*		
1978		330.0				
1981		456.4 [1]				

Source:

UNCTC, *Transnational Corporations in World Development: Third Survey,* New York: UN, 1983; IMF, *Balance of Payments Statistics Yearbook, 1984.*

NOTES TO TABLE A2

1 Estimated by adding cumulative investment flows, 1979-81 to the UNCTC stock figure of 1978.

Table A3

FLOW OF FOREIGN DIRECT INVESTMENT, 1970 - 81 (US $m)

	Inward Investment			Outward Investment		
	Reinvested Profits	*Other*	*Total*	*Reinvested Profits*	*Other*	*Total*
1970	*N.A.*	*N.A.*	-297.0	*Not Available*		
1971	*N.A.*	*N.A.*	*N.A.*			
1972	16.3	13.0	29.3			
1973	22.7	5.9	28.6			
1974	36.1	2.4	38.5			
1975	38.9	-1.3	37.6			
1976	30.0	1.2	31.2			
1977	17.5	0.0	17.5			
1978	38.8	0.0	38.8			
1979	34.9	0.0	34.9			
1980	57.3	0.0	57.3			
1981	34.2	0.0	34.2			

Source:

IMF, *Balance of Payments Statistics Yearbook,* various issues.

Table A4

SECTORAL DISTRIBUTION OF FOREIGN DIRECT CAPITAL STOCK, 1981 (US $ m)[1]

	Inward Investment			Outward Investment		
	Primary	*Secondary*	*Tertiary*	*Primary*	*Secondary*	*Tertiary*
1981	*N.A.*	134.5	50.0	*Not Available*		

Source:

UK Department of Trade and Industry, 'Census of Overseas Assets, 1981', *Business Monitor,* Supplement, 1981.

NOTES TO TABLE A4

1 Figures refer to UK investment only, which in 1981 accounts for around 56% of total foreign direct investment in Zambia.

Table A5

GEOGRAPHICAL DISTRIBUTION OF FOREIGN DIRECT CAPITAL STOCK, 1981 (US $ m)

	Inward Investment			Outward Investment		
	Developed Countries	*Other Countries*	*Total*	*Developed Countries*	*Developing Countries*	*Total*
1981	399[1]	57	456[2]	*Not Available*		

Source:

UK Department of Trade & Industry, *Business Monitor,* Supplement, 1981; US Department of Commerce, *Survey of Current Business,* November, 1984.

NOTES TO TABLE A5

1 Includes US and UK investment only.

2 Total estimated by adding cumulative investment flow 1979-81, to the UNCTC stock figure for 1978.

Table A6

INDUSTRIAL DISTRIBUTION OF FOREIGN DIRECT CAPITAL STOCK, 1981 (US $ m)[1]

	Inward Investment		Outward Investment
	1981		
Primary	*N.A.*		*Not Available*
Secondary	134.5		
Food & drink	17.0		
Chemicals & allied	24.2		
Electrical equipment	17.4		
Textiles & clothing	16.4		
Other manufacturing	12.8		
Tertiary	50.0		
Distributive trade	50.0		
TOTAL	257.0[1]		

Source:

UK Department of Trade and Industry, 'Census of Overseas Assets, 1981', *Business Monitor,* Supplement, 1981.

NOTES TO TABLE A6

1 Figures refer to UK investment only, which in 1981 accounts for around 56% of total foreign direct investment in Zambia. Total therefore does not match Table A2.

Table A7

LEADING SOURCE AND RECIPIENT COUNTRIES, 1981 (US $ m)

	Inward Investment		Outward Investment
	1981		
DEVELOPED AREAS[1]	399		*Not Available*
Europe			
UK	257		
North America			
USA	142		
UNSPECIFIED	57		
TOTAL	465[2]		

Source:

UK Department of Trade and Industry, 'Census of Overseas Assets, 1981', *Business Monitor,* Supplement, 1981; US Department of Commerce, *Survey of Current Business,* November 1984.

NOTES TO TABLE A7

1 Including only those countries shown below.

2 Estimated by adding cumulative investment flows, 1979-81, to the UNCTC stock figure of 1978.

Table A8

INDICATORS OF THE SIGNIFICANCE OF INWARD FOREIGN DIRECT INVESTMENT OR THE ACTIVITIES OF FOREIGN-BASED COMPANIES TO THE NATIONAL ECONOMY, 1978–81

1	Direct capital stock of foreign affiliates at book value in 1981 as a proportion of:	
	a GNP at factor cost	11.31
	b population (in US $ per head)	76.58
2	Foreign investment as a percentage of domestic investment in all industry, 1978-80	5.2

Source:
UNCTC, *Transnational Corporations in World Development: Third Survey,* New York: UN, 1983; IMF, *Balance of Payments Statistics Yearbook, 1984;* IMF, *International Financial Statistics Yearbook, 1984.*

Table A12

LEADING FOREIGN MULTINATIONAL COMPANIES, 1983

	Name	*Home Country*	*Sector*
1	British American Tobacco	UK	Tobacco
2	Turner & Newall	UK	Non-metallic mineral products
3	International Development & Construction Co	Saudi Arabia	Mining
4	Mobil Oil	USA	Petroleum
5	IBM	USA	Office equipment
6	Johnson & Johnson	USA	Pharmaceuticals
7	Coca Cola	USA	Drink
8	Searle	USA	Pharmaceuticals
9	Citicorp	USA	Banking & finance
10	British Petroleum	UK	Petroleum
11	Babcock International PLC	UK	Engineering
12	British Leyland PLC	UK	Motor vehicles
13	Cadbury Schweppes PLC	UK	Food
14	The Colgate - Palmolive Company	USA	Consumer products
15	Compagnie Francaise des Petroles SA	France	Petroleum
16	Crown Cork and Seal Company Inc	USA	Metal cans and closures
17	Daimler - Benz AG	W. Germany	Motor vehicles
18	Dunlop Holdings PLC	UK	Rubber products
19	ENI	Italy	Petroleum
20	The General Electric Company PLC	UK	Electrical equipment
21	ICL PLC	UK	Computers
22	NV Philips Gloeilampenfabrieken	Netherlands	Electrotechnical products
23	Royal Dutch/Shell Group of Companies	Netherlands/UK	Petroleum
24	Unilever	UK/Netherlands	Consumer products
25	The Wellcome Foundation Ltd	UK	Pharmaceuticals

Source:

John M Stopford, *The World Directory of Multinational Enterprises 1982–83,* Bath: The Pitman Press, 1982

ZIMBABWE

Foreign investment in Zimbabwe has always played a major role in the economy, and indeed, a large foreign corporate presence is now identifiable there. The pace of inflow of foreign capital has varied substantially during different periods, and since UDI in 1965 little new investment has flowed into the country. This is despite the fact that since Independence in 1980, government policy has recognised the need to encourage FDI. Inward investment in Zimbabwe has continued mainly through the reinvested earnings of foreign companies with long standing investments in the country.

Official policy on foreign investment is laid down in the Government's publication, *Foreign Investment: Policy, Guidelines and Procedures*, issued in September 1982. While welcoming inward investment, the Government offers few incentives to attract it. There is a Foreign Investment Committee, the task of which is to review all foreign investment applications, and to ensure that they meet a set of guidelines stipulated by the Ministry of Finance. Zimbabwe operates a policy of stringent control on outward investment, which it strongly discourages.

The main investor countries in Zimbabwe are the UK, South Africa and to a lesser extent, North America and other European countries.

MAIN SOURCES OF DATA:

A **Official**

1 US Department of Commerce International Trade Administration, *Investment Climate in Foreign Countries,* Washington, 1985, vol II.

B **Private**

1 D C Clarke, *Foreign Companies and International Investment in Zimbabwe,* Mambo Press, 1980.

2 R C Riddell, 'Zimbabwe's experience of Foreign Investment Policy', paper prepared for the Commonwealth Secretariat, 1984.

3 C F Stoneman, *Foreign Capital in Zimbabwe,* UNCTAD, Geneva, 1979.

Note:

Data do not allow us to complete Table A10 for Zimbabwe.

Table A1

SUMMARY OF THE COUNTRY'S INTERNATIONAL INVESTMENT POSITION

		Inward Investment	Outward Investment
1	Number of foreign affiliates in host country, and of foreign affiliates of home country firms at the end of 1980	293	*N.A.*
2	Number of foreign firms with direct investments in host country, and home country firms with direct foreign affiliates	*N.A.*	*N.A.*
3	Total foreign direct capital stock at book value as a percentage of GNP at factor cost in 1982	40.65	0.87
4	Flow of foreign direct investment in the five year period, 1980-84 (Z $m)	46.89	51.18
5	Employment in foreign affiliates or abroad	*N.A.*	*N.A.*
6	Output of foreign affiliates or abroad	*N.A.*	*N.A.*

Source:

D C Clarke, *Foreign Companies and International Investment in Zimbabwe,* Mambo Press, 1980; IMF, *Balance of Payments Statistics Yearbook,* various issues; IMF, *International Financial Statistics Yearbook, 1984.*

Table A2

PRIVATE FOREIGN CAPITAL STOCK, 1978 - 84 (Z $m)

	Inward Investment			Outward Investment		
	Portfolio	*Direct*	*Total*	*Portfolio*	*Direct*	*Total*
Book value of capital stock						
1978	*Not Available*	1,750.0[1]	*Not Available*	*Not Available*	*N.A.*	*Not Available*
1981		1,787.8[2]			42.1	
1984		1,813.6[2]			73.2[3]	

Source:

D C Clarke, *Foreign Companies and International Investment in Zimbabwe,* Mambo Press, 1980; IMF, *Balance of Payments Statistics Yearbook,* various issues; C F Stoneman, *Foreign Capital in Zimbabwe,* UNCTAD, Geneva, 1979.

NOTES TO TABLE A2

1 Estimate (Stoneman).

2 Estimate obtained by adding cumulative investment flows to the 1978 stock figure.

3 Estimate obtained by adding cumulative investment flow of 1984 to the 1981 stock figure.

Table A3

FLOW OF FOREIGN DIRECT INVESTMENT, 1977 - 84 (Z $m)

	Inward Investment			Outward Investment		
	Reinvested Profits	*Other*	*Total*	*Reinvested Profits*	*Other*	*Total*
1977	*Not Separately Available*		2.93	*Not Separately Available*		5.28
1978			3.98			2.29
1979			5.79			5.71
1980			15.13			14.13
1981			5.94			5.94
1982			11.14			11.14
1983			4.76			6.82
1984			9.92			13.15

Source:

IMF, *Balance of Payments Statistics Yearbook,* various issues.

NOTES TO TABLE A3

1 Excluding reinvested profits.

Table A4

SECTORAL DISTRIBUTION OF FOREIGN DIRECT CAPITAL STOCK, 1981 (Z $ m)

	Inward Investment[1]				Outward Investment		
	Primary	Secondary	Tertiary		Primary	Secondary	Tertiary
1981	561.7	616.8	598.4		*Not Available*		

Source:

R C Riddell, 'Zimbabwe's Experience of Foreign Investment Policy', *Commonwealth Secretariat paper, 1984.*

NOTES TO TABLE A4

1 Estimates obtained by applying percentage of foreign share of total capital stock to the private foreign capital stock estimate of 1981.

Table A5

GEOGRAPHICAL DISTRIBUTION OF FOREIGN DIRECT CAPITAL STOCK, 1978 (Z $ m)

	Inward Investment				Outward Investment		
	Developed Countries	Developing Countries	Total		Developed Countries	Developing Countries	Total
1978	1,698[1]	N.S.A.	1,787.8		*Not Available*		

Source:

D C Clarke, *Foreign Companies and International Investment in Zimbabwe,* Mambo Press, 1980.

NOTES TO TABLE A5

1 Includes estimates of UK, US and South African investment only.

Table A6

INDUSTRIAL DISTRIBUTION OF FOREIGN DIRECT CAPITAL STOCK, 1981 (Z $ m)

	Inward Investment	Outward Investment
	1981	
Primary	561.7[1]	Not Available
Agriculture	165.3[1]	
Mining & quarrying	396.4[1]	
Oil	*N.A.*	
Secondary	616.8[1]	
Food & drink	43.4[2]	
Chemicals & allied	25.7[2]	
Metals	*N.S.A.*	
Mechanical engineering	17.5[2]	
Electrical equipment	27.0[2]	
Motor vehicles	*N.S.A.* (Motor vehicles and Other transportation equipment together)	
Other transportation equipment		
Textiles & clothing	37.2[2]	
Paper & allied	31.3[2]	
Rubber	*Not Separately Available* (Rubber to Other manufacturing)	
Stone, clay & glass		
Coal & petroleum products		
Other manufacturing		
Tertiary	598.4[1]	
Construction	7.5[2]	
Transport & communications	*N.S.A.*	
Distributive trade	58.3[2]	
Property	0.8[2]	
Banking & finance	*N.S.A.*	
Other services	6.8[2]	
TOTAL	1,776.9	

Source:
R C Riddell, 'Zimbabwe's Experience of Foreign Investment Policy', *Commonwealth Secretariat paper,* 1984; HMSO, 'Census of Overseas Assets 1981', *Business Monitor,* Supplement, 1981.

NOTES TO TABLE A6

1 Estimates obtained by applying percentage of foreign share of total capital stock to the private foreign capital stock estimate of 1981.

2 UK investment only.

Table A7

LEADING SOURCE AND RECIPIENT COUNTRIES, 1978 (Z $ m)

	Inward Investment	Outward Investment
	1978	
DEVELOPED AREAS	1,698[1]	*Not Available*
Europe	815	
EEC of which:	815	
UK	815	
North America of which:	300	
USA	300	
Other developed countries of which:	583	
South Africa	583	
TOTAL	1,750	

Source:
D C Clarke, *Foreign Companies and International Investment in Zimbabwe,* Mambo Press, 1980; HMSO, 'Census of Overseas Assets 1981', *Business Monitor,* Supplement, 1981.

NOTES TO TABLE A7

1 Includes estimates of UK, US and South African investment only.

Table A8

INDICATORS OF THE SIGNIFICANCE OF INWARD FOREIGN DIRECT INVESTMENT OR THE ACTIVITIES OF FOREIGN-BASED COMPANIES TO THE NATIONAL ECONOMY, 1978 - 82

1	Direct capital stock of foreign affiliates at book value in 1982 as a proportion of:		
	a	GNP at factor cost	37.15
	b	population (in Z $ per head)	237.10
2	Foreign investment as a percentage of domestic investment 1978-80		8.6
3	Assets of foreign affiliates in 1982 as a percentage of all assets		
	a	in agriculture	30
	b	in mining	90
	c	in secondary (ie manufacturing) industry	70

Source:
D C Clarke, *Foreign Companies and International Investment in Zimbabwe,* Mambo Press, 1980; IMF, *Balance of Payments Statistics Yearbook,* various issues; IMF, *International Financial Statistics Yearbook, 1984.*

Table A9

INDICATORS OF THE SIGNIFICANCE OF OUTWARD FOREIGN DIRECT INVESTMENT OR THE ACTIVITIES OF HOME-BASED COMPANIES ABROAD FOR THE NATIONAL ECONOMY, 1982

1	Foreign capital stock of home-based firms at book value in 1982 as a proportion of:		
	a	GNP at factor cost	0.87
	b	population (in Z $ per head)	5.6

Source:
As for Table 8.

Table A11

ROYALTY RECEIPTS AND PAYMENTS, 1977 - 84 (Z $ m)

	Payments			Receipts		
	To Affiliates	*To Non-affiliates*	*Total*	*From Affiliates*	*From Non-affiliates*	*Total*
1977	*Not Separately Available*		5.57	*Not Separately Available*		0.51
1978			4.92			1.19
1979			7.03			0.70
1980			8.78			1.84
1981			9.52			1.38
1982			12.90			1.09
1983			14.19			0.97
1984			9.28			0.77

Source:
IMF, *Balance of Payments Statistics Yearbook,* various issues.

Table A12

LEADING FOREIGN MULTINATIONAL COMPANIES, 1980

	Name	*Home Country*	*Sector*
1	BOC International Ltd	UK	Chemicals
2	Beecham Group Ltd	UK	Pharmaceuticals
3	British Steel	UK	Iron & steel
4	Brooke-Bond Liebig Ltd	UK	Food
5	Cadbury-Schweppes Ltd	UK	Food
6	Delta Metal Co Ltd	UK	Metals
7	The General Electric Co Ltd	UK	Electrical
8	Glaxo Holdings Ltd	UK	Pharmaceuticals
9	ICL Ltd	UK	Computer Services
10	Imperial Group Ltd	UK	Tobacco
11	Incas Industries Ltd	UK	Motor vehicles
12	Metal Box Ltd	UK	Metals
13	Pilkington Bros Ltd	UK	Glass
14	Tate & Lyle Ltd	UK	Food
15	Thorn Electrical Industries Ltd	UK	Electrical
16	Unilever	UK/Netherlands	Food
17	Ford Motor Co	USA	Motor vehicles
18	Pfizer International Ltd	USA	Chemicals
19	Massey-Ferguson	Canada	Machinery
20	Aberdare Cables Ltd	South Africa	Electrical equipment
21	Charter Consolidated Ltd	South Africa	Mining
22	Dermacult Ltd	South Africa	Chemicals
23	Johannesburg Consolidated Investment Co	South Africa	Mining
24	South African Pulp & Paper Industries	South Africa	Paper
25	United Tobacco Companies	South Africa	Tobacco

Source:
D C Clarke, *Foreign Companies and International Investment in Zimbabwe,* Mambo Press, 1980.

ASIA & PACIFIC

(except Japan)

BANGLADESH

There are no regular published data or estimates of foreign direct investment in Bangladesh. Existing US investment consists of three pharmaceutical factories, a sewing machine factory, a plastic pipe plant, a commercial bank, a life insurance company, and storage and processing facilities for edible oil. There is also investment in office and transport equipment of about 10 American service sector firms. Investment from the UK exceeds that from other countries with Dutch investment roughly equal to American, and Japanese and Korean following closely. There is also some inward investment from Thailand, India and Singapore.

The Government of Bangladesh states that it will encourage foreign participation in joint ventures on mutually beneficial terms and conditions. Special emphasis is being placed on foreign investments in (a) new enterprises, particularly those which require foreign technology and will make a net contribution to the economy, (b) ventures that make more intensive use of local natural resources, (c) export oriented industries, (d) capital intensive industries whose output is designed for export or input substitution and (e) existing public or private sector enterprises where an injection of foreign capital or technology would increase productivity and improve product quality.

The Investment Board of the Ministry of Industries & Commerce screens all investment proposals involving foreign participation, and negotiates such matters as equity arrangements, special incentives and managerial structure.

Bangladesh does not encourage outward direct investment.

MAIN SOURCES OF DATA:

A **Official:**

1 Ministry of Industries, unpublished data.

2 OECD, *Geographical Distribution of Financial Flows to Developing Countries,* Paris, various issues.

3 UNCTC, *Transnational Corporations in World Development: Third Survey,* New York: UN, 1983.

4 US Department of Commerce International Trade Administration, *Investment Climate in Foreign Countries,* Washington, 1985, vol III.

Note:
Data do not allow us to complete Tables A4, A6, A9, A10, A11 or A12 for Bangladesh.

Table A1

SUMMARY OF THE COUNTRY'S INTERNATIONAL INVESTMENT POSITION

		Inward Investment	Outward Investment
1	Number of foreign affiliates in host country, and of foreign affiliates of home country firms at the end of 1980	71[1]	*N.A.*
2	Number of foreign firms with direct investments in host country, and home country firms with direct foreign affiliates	*N.A.*	*N.A.*
3	Total foreign direct capital stock at book value as a percentage of GNP at factor cost in 1981	0.97	*N.A.*
4	Flow of foreign direct investment in the five year period, 1980-84 (US $ m)	14.3	*N.A.*
5	Employment in foreign affiliates or abroad	*N.A.*	*N.A.*
6	Output of foreign affiliates or abroad	*N.A.*	*N.A.*

Source:
Ministry of Industries, Unpublished data; OECD, *Geographical Distribution of Financial Flows to Developing Countries,* Paris, various issues.

NOTES TO TABLE A1

1 Represents number of foreign affiliates of multinational enterprises from selected home countries as identified by UNCTC, 1983.

Table A2

PRIVATE FOREIGN CAPITAL STOCK, 1972 - 84 (US $ m)

	Inward Investment			Outward Investment		
	Portfolio	*Direct*	*Total*	*Portfolio*	*Direct*	*Total*
Book value of capital stock						
1972	*Not Available*	55.0	*Not Available*	*Not Available*		
1978		80.0				
1981		85.9				
1983		87.3				
1984		85.7				

Source:

UNCTC, 1983, *op cit.* for 1972 and 1978. Cumulative flow figures have been added to 1978 stock figure to get an estimate of foreign direct capital stock for other years.

Table A3

FLOW OF FOREIGN DIRECT INVESTMENT, 1972 - 84 (US $ m)

	Inward Investment[1]			Outward Investment		
	Reinvested Profits	*Other*	*Total*	*Reinvested Profits*	*Other*	*Total*
1972	*Not Separately Available*		0.1	*Not Available*		
1973			2.3			
1974			2.2			
1975			*N.A.*			
1976			4.7			
1977			7.0			
1978			7.7			
1979			–8.0			
1980			8.5			
1981			5.4			
1982			1.0			
1983			0.4			
1984			–1.6			

Source:

OECD, *Geographical Distribution of Financial Flows to Developing Countries,* Paris, various issues; IMF, *Balance of Payments Statistics,* various issues.

NOTES TO TABLE A3

1 Flow from OECD countries only.

Table A5

GEOGRAPHICAL DISTRIBUTION OF FOREIGN DIRECT CAPITAL STOCK, 1981 (US $ m)[1]

	Inward Investment			Outward Investment		
	Developed Countries	*Developing Countries*	*Total*	*Developed Countries*	*Developing Countries*	*Total*
1981	59.14	14.57	73.71	*Not Available*		

Source:
Ministry of Industries, unpublished data.

NOTES TO TABLE A5
1 Cumulative investment flows, 1972-81.

Table A7

LEADING SOURCE AND RECIPIENT COUNTRIES, 1981 (US $ m)[1]

	Inward Investment	Outward Investment
	1981	
DEVELOPED AREAS	59.14	*Not Available*
Europe	41.07	
EEC of which:	14.27	
W. Germany	1.96	
Italy	0.18	
Netherlands	1.13	
UK	11.00	
Other Europe of which:	26.80	
Austria	0.05	
Bulgaria	0.02	
Sweden	0.29	
Switzerland	26.44	
North America of which:	1.58	
Canada	0.15	
USA	1.43	
Other developed countries of which:	16.49	
Japan	16.49	
DEVELOPING AREAS	14.57	
Asia & Pacific of which:	10.44	
Hong Kong	0.06	
India	1.33	
S. Korea	4.34	
Singapore	1.97	
Thailand	2.74	
Middle East of which:	4.13	
Kuwait	4.13	
TOTAL	73.71	

Source:
Ministry of Industries, unpublished data.

NOTES TO TABLE A7
1 Calculations based on cumulative investment flows, 1972-81.

Table A8

INDICATORS OF THE SIGNIFICANCE OF INWARD FOREIGN DIRECT INVESTMENT OR THE ACTIVITIES OF FOREIGN-BASED COMPANIES TO THE NATIONAL ECONOMY, 1978 - 84

1	Direct capital stock of foreign affiliates at book value in 1984 as a proportion of:	
	a GNP at factor cost	0.97
	b population (in US $ per head)	0.90
2	Foreign investment as a percentage of domestic investment, 1978-80	0.20

Source:

Ministry of Industries, unpublished data; OECD, *Geographical Distribution of Financial Flows to Developing Countries,* Paris, various issues.

CHINA

There are no official statistics available on the investment position of China, and we are unable to compile a comprehensive set of tables using the limited data available from other sources.

Prior to the mid-1970s foreign investment in China occurred on a very limited scale, but the situation is now changing. Since 1978, the Chinese government has encouraged foreign investment and indeed, Table A3 indicates the rapid rise of the inflow of investment from OECD countries. Between 1978 and 1983, US $ 1.8 billion was invested in China, and according to Chinese reports, a further US $ 1.1 billion was invested during 1984.

To attract foreign direct investment into China, 'Special Economic Zones' have been set up in Shekou, Shenzhen, Zhuhai, and Xiamen, whereby investors in these zones are subject to a lower tax rate than investors in other regions. Reports indicate that the realised foreign investment in the Special Economic zones at the end of 1981 was US $ 250 million, much of which originated from Hong Kong.

The major forms of foreign investment as specified by Chinese law and tax are the 'equity Joint-Venture' and the 'Co-operative Venture' (or 'contractual joint-venture'). The former involves the formation of a limited liability corporation with joint investment, ownership and management, and sharing of risk, profits and losses. (A Chinese-foreign ratio of 51 : 49 is favoured.) However, despite the significant legislative and tax developments which have occurred, including laws relating specifically to the formation and regulations of joint-ventures, the number of such ventures which have come into operation is still only moderate.

The Chinese government has recently emphasised the second form of foreign investment, whereby control over production, share of profits and so on, are pre-determined by contracts, rather than by the relative share of capital invested. About 300 such co-operative ventures were in operation by the end of 1980, the majority of which were taken up by investors from Hong Kong.

Singapore's investments in China are becoming increasingly important, althought the main source of investment in the country remains Hong Kong, due to its familiarity with China and its close geographical proximity. Again there are no official statistics on the amount of Hong Kong's investment in China, but an estimated 500 Hong Kong-based firms have interests in various activities. (Chen 1983.) The amount of investment for each of these projects is usually less than US $ 1 m, although there are a few notable exceptions.

Hong Kong's investors in the Chinese manufacturing sector are generally involved in smaller projects, primarily in textiles, electronics, metals and plastics. Many of these projects are really joint production agreements, as mentioned above. Within the services sector, the emphasis lies on construction and tourism, and Hong-Kong interests are mainly in the form of equity joint-ventures. The flow of investment into the oil industry has increase significantly. China has been undergoing a period of economic readjustment whereby the country's pattern of resource allocations and its use of foreign resources are to be adjusted so shifting its emphasis from heavy industries to light industries and transportation. This will undoubtedly affect the position of foreign investors and the pattern of FDI in China to some degree.

MAIN SOURCES OF DATA:

A Official

1 Dr T B Lin, 'China' in *Patterns and Impact of Foreign Investment in the ESCAP Region,* Thailand: UN, 1985.

MAIN SOURCES OF DATA (cont'd):

B Private

1 E K Y Chen, 'Multinationals from Hong Kong', in S Lall (Ed), *The New Multinationals,* John Wiley: Chichester, 1983.

2 Susan Ware, 'China — The Foreign Investment Framework', EIU, *Multinational Business,* no 1, 1985.

3 Mah Hui Lim, 'Survey of Activities of Transnational Corporations from Asian Developing Countries', paper submitted to ESCAP/UNCTC Joint Unit on Transnational Corporations, Bangkok, March 1984.

4 N T Wang, 'China's Modernization and Transnational Corporations', Aldershot: Gower, 1984.

Note:
Data do not allow us to complete Tables A4, A5, A9, A10 or A11 for China.

Table A1

SUMMARY OF THE COUNTRY'S INTERNATIONAL INVESTMENT POSITION

		Inward Investment	Outward Investment
1	Number of foreign affiliates in host country, and of foreign affiliates of home country firms	*N.A.*	*N.A.*
2	Number of foreign firms with direct investments in host country, and home country firms with direct foreign affiliates	*N.A.*	*N.A.*
3	Total foreign direct capital stock at book value as a percentage of GNP at factor cost in 1983	0.70[1]	*N.A.*
4	Flow of foreign direct investment in the four year period, 1979-82 (US $ m)	91.2	*N.A.*
5	Employment in foreign affiliates or abroad	*N.A.*	*N.A.*
6	Output of foreign affiliates or abroad	*N.A.*	*N.A.*

Source:
Susan Ware, 'China – The Foreign Investment Framework', EIU, *Multinational Business,* no 1, 1985; OECD, *Geographical Distribution of Financial Flows to Developing Countries,* Paris, 1984.

NOTES TO TABLE A1

1 Represents stock of FDI, 1978-83, as a percentage of GNP in 1982.

Table A2

PRIVATE FOREIGN CAPITAL STOCK, 1983 (US $ bn)

	Inward Investment			Outward Investment		
	Portfolio	*Direct*	*Total*	*Portfolio*	*Direct*	*Total*
Book value of capital stock 1983	*N.S.A.*	1.8[1]	*N.A.*	*Not Available*		

Source:
Susan Ware, 'China – The Foreign Investment Framework', EIU, *Multinational Business,* No. 1, 1985.

NOTES TO TABLE A2

1 Represents foreign investment in China between 1978 and end 1983.

Table A3

FLOW OF FOREIGN DIRECT INVESTMENT, 1979 - 82 (US $ m)[1]

	Inward Investment				Outward Investment		
	Reinvested Profits	*Other*	*Total*		*Reinvested Profits*	*Other*	*Total*
1979	*Not Separately Available*		0.1		*Not Available*		
1980			23.5				
1981			26.0				
1982			41.6				

Source:
OECD, *Geographical Distribution of Financial Flows to Developing Countries,* Paris, 1984.

CHINA NOTES TO TABLE A3

1 Represents flow from OECD countries.

Table A6

INDUSTRIAL DISTRIBUTION OF FOREIGN DIRECT CAPITAL STOCK, 1983 (US $ m)[1]

	Inward Investment		Outward Investment
	1983		
Primary			*Not Available*
Agriculture	5.6		
Mining & quarrying	2.5		
Oil	2.0		
Secondary			
Food & drink	11.7		
Chemicals & allied	26.1		
Mechanical engineering	86.5		
Electrical equipment	68.0		
Motor vehicles	51.0		
Textiles & clothing	24.9		
Paper & allied	3.7		
Stone, clay & glass	15.1		
Other manufacturing	18.4		
Tertiary			
Hotels	251.5		
Banking, finance & insurance	25.0		
Other services	17.6		
TOTAL	715.4		

Source:
Dr T B Lin, *op cit.*

NOTES TO TABLE A6

1 Represents total value of investment in 89 joint equity ventures, involving a foreign capital share of US $ 305.2 million as at September 1983. The sectoral distribution listed are only those with a total investment of US $ 0.5 million or more.

Table A7

LEADING SOURCE AND RECIPIENT COUNTRIES, 1983, (US $ m)[1]

	Inward Investment	Outward Investment
	1983	
DEVELOPED AREAS	495.3	
Europe	214.2	
EEC of which:	143.7	
Belgium & Luxembourg	20.0	
France	1.0	
W. Germany	0.7	
UK	122.0	
Other Europe of which:	70.5	
Norway	42.5	
Sweden	12.0	*Not*
Switzerland	16.0	*Available*
North America	226.2	
USA	226.2	
Other developed countries of which:	54.9	
Australia	0.5	
Japan	54.4	
DEVELOPING AREAS	219.9	
Asia & Pacific (except Japan or Middle East) of which:	219.9	
Hong Kong	152.3	
Philippines	66.8	
Thailand	0.8	
UNSPECIFIED	0.2	
TOTAL	715.4	

Source:
Dr T B Lin, *op cit.*

NOTES TO TABLE A7

1 Represents total value of investment in 89 joint equity ventures, involving a foreign capital share of US $ 305.2 million as at September 1983.

Table A8

INDICATORS OF THE SIGNIFICANCE OF INWARD FOREIGN DIRECT INVESTMENT OR THE ACTIVITIES OF FOREIGN-BASED COMPANIES TO THE NATIONAL ECONOMY, 1983

1	Direct capital stock of foreign affiliates at book value in 1983 as a proportion of:		
	a	GNP at factor cost	0.70[1]
	b	population (in US $ per head)	1.79[2]

Source:

S Ware, 'China – The Foreign Investment Framework', EIU, *Multinational Business,* no 1, 1985; OECD, *Geographical Distribution of Financial Flows to Developing Countries,* Paris, 1984.

CHINA NOTES TO TABLE A8

1 Represents stock of FDI, 1978-83, as a percentage of GNP in 1982.

2 Represents stock of FDI, 1978-83, as a proportion of the population in 1982.

Table A12

LEADING FOREIGN MULTINATIONAL COMPANIES, 1984[1]

	Name	*Home Country*	*Sector*
1	Schindler Holding	Switzerland	Machinery
2	Hitachi Co	Japan	Electrical
3	Otis Elevator Co	USA	Electrical
4	Gillette Co	USA	Metals
5	Beatrice Co	USA	Food
6	Remy Martin	France	Beverages
7	American Motors	USA	Motor vehicles
8	Racal Survey	UK	Oil
9	R J Reynolds	USA	Tobacco
10	Cable & Wireless	UK	Electrical
11	Gladhover	Hong Kong	Oil
12	Hewlett-Packard	USA	Electronics/office equipment
13	Occidental	USA	Mining/oil
14	Paulaner-Salvator Thomasbrau	W. Germany	Beverages
15	Otenz Export Co	New Zealand	Machinery
16	Pilkington Bros	UK	Building materials
17	Trinity Development Co	Hong Kong	Steel
18	Foxboro Co	USA	Electronics
19	Henry James	Australia	Agriculture
20	Asia International Electronics	Hong Kong	Electronics
21	Stelux	Hong Kong	Electronics

Source:
Susan Ware, 'China – The Foreign Investment Framework', EIU, *Multinational Business,* no 1, 1985.

CHINA NOTES TO TABLE A12

1 Represents Chinese/Foreign Joint-Ventures in China.

HONG KONG

Hong Kong is both an important source and recipient of investment among the Asian developing countries. Indeed, in terms of foreign direct investment, Hong Kong is the largest Asian foreign investor, excluding Japan. The flow of foreign direct investment into Hong Kong from OECD countries experienced a steadily rising trend to 1981.

Indonesia is the major destination of Hong Kong's outward investments; other significant recipients include Taiwan, Singapore and Malaysia. There is also some Hong Kong investment in the USA, Japan and Canada. The traditional sources of foreign direct investment into Hong Kong are the UK, USA and Japan: of the developing countries the Philippines and Singapore are the leading investors.

Hong Kong's outward investments occur in all sectors but are largely concentrated in service sectors such as property, tourism and construction, and in the labour intensive and lower technology manufacturing sectors, such as textiles and electrical goods. Data on the sectoral distribution of foreign direct investment into Hong Kong are limited to the manufacturing sector, within which the bulk of investment is concentrated in electrical equipment, textiles and construction industries. However, most of the remaining inward foreign direct capital stock outside manufacturing (about two-thirds of the total) is thought to be in banking and services, which have been the major areas of expansion in the 1970s and early 1980s.

MAIN SOURCES OF DATA:

A **Official**

1 Industry Department, Government of Territory of Hong Kong: *Report on the survey of Overseas Investment in Hong Kong's manufacturing industry* provides data on the stock of foreign investment in Hong Kong, by geographical and sectoral distribution for manufacturing.

2 OECD, *Investing in Developing Countries,* (5th Ed.), Paris, 1983.

B **Private**

1 Mah Hui Lim, 'Survey of Activities of Transnational Corporations from Asian Developing Countries', paper submitted to the ESCAP/UNCTC Joint Unit on Transnational Corporations, Bangkok, March 1984.

2 E K Y Chen, 'Multinationals from Hong Kong', in S Lall (Ed), *The New Multinationals,* Chichester: John Wiley, 1983.

3 T B Lin, 'Foreign Investment in the Economy of Hong Kong' in Economic Bulletin for Asia and the Pacific, Vol. XXXV, no 2, Dec 1984.

4 T B Lin, 'Hong Kong' in ESCAP *Patterns and Impact of Foreign Direct Investment in the ESCAP Region,* Bangkok, 1985.

Note:
Data do not allow us to complete Table A11 for Hong Kong.

Table A1

SUMMARY OF THE COUNTRY'S INTERNATIONAL INVESTMENT POSITION

		Inward Investment	Outward Investment
1	Number of foreign affiliates in host country, and of foreign affiliates of home country firms at the end of 1984	442[2]	*N.A.*
2	Number of foreign firms with direct in investments in host country, and home country firms with direct foreign affiliates	*N.A.*	*N.A.*
3	Total foreign direct capital stock at book value as a percentage of GNP at factor cost in 1981	15.17	7.26
4	Flow of foreign direct investment in the five year period, 1978-82 (US $ m)	2,448.7[1]	*N.A.*
5	Employment in foreign affiliates or abroad, 1984	89033[2]	*N.A.*
6	Output of foreign affiliates or abroad	*N.A.*	*N.A.*

Source:
OECD, Investing in Developing Countries (5th ed), Paris, 1983; OECD, *Geographical Distribution of Financial Flows to Developing Countries,* various issues; E K Y Chen, 'Multinationals from Hong Kong', in S Lall (Ed), *The New Multinationals,* Chichester: John Wiley, 1983; Hong Kong Government Industry Department, *Overseas Investment in Hong Kong's Manufacturing Industry,* 1984.

NOTES TO TABLE A1

1 Represents flow from OECD countries.

2 Data are available for the manufacturing sector only.

Table A2

PRIVATE FOREIGN CAPITAL STOCK, 1975 - 84 (US $ bn)

	Inward Investment			Outward Investment		
	Portfolio	*Direct*	*Total*	*Portfolio*	*Direct*	*Total*
Book value of capital stock						
1975	*Not Available*	1.3	*Not Available*	*Not Available*	*N.A.*	*Not Available*
1978		2.1			*N.A.*	
1981		3.8			1.8	
1984		*N.A.*			3.0[1]	

Source:
OECD, *Investing in Developing Countries,* (5th ed.), Paris, 1983; E K Y Chen, 'Multinationals from Hong Kong', in S Lall (Ed), *The New Multinationals,* Chichester: John Wiley, 1983; Hong Kong Government Industry Department, *Report on the survey of Overseas Investment in Hong Kong's Manufacturing Industry,* 1984.
manufacturing industry 1984.

NOTES TO TABLE A2

1 This represents the author's best guess, which is partly based on data provided by recipient countries to direct investment from Hong Kong. In 1984, for example, the Hong Kong investment stake in the USA, Canada and Japan amounted to US $ 840 million.

Table A3

FLOW OF FOREIGN DIRECT INVESTMENT, 1970 - 82 (US $m)

	Inward Investment[1]			Outward Investment		
	Reinvested Profits	*Other*	*Total*	*Reinvested Profits*	*Other*	*Total*
1970	*Not Separately Available*		26.3	*Not Available*		
1971			31.4			
1972			58.3			
1973			143.2			
1974			81.0			
1975			214.7			
1976			154.3			
1977			144.5			
1978			252.0			
1979			342.1			
1980			373.9			
1981			952.9			
1982			527.8			

Source:

UNCTC, *Transnational Corporations in World Development: Third Survey,* New York, 1983; OECD, *Geographical Distribution of Financial Flows to Developing Countries,* various issues.

NOTES TO TABLE A3

1 Represents flow from OECD countries.

Table A4

SECTORAL DISTRIBUTION OF FOREIGN DIRECT CAPITAL STOCK, 1981 - 84 (US $m)

	Inward Investment[1]			Outward Investment[2]		
	Primary	*Secondary*	*Tertiary*	*Primary*	*Secondary*	*Tertiary*
1981	100.0	1,260.4[3]	2,440.0	268.6	756.0	404.1
1984	*N.A.*	1,463.4	*N.A.*		*Not Available*	

Source:

Industry Department, Government of Territory of Hong Kong, *op cit;* Various National Sources regarding Incoming Foreign Investment of each country, data as cited in Mah Hui Lim, 'Survey of Activities of Transnational Corporations from Asian Developing Countries', paper submitted to the ESCAP/UNCTC Joint Unit on Transnational Corporations, Bangkok, March 1984; OECD, *Investing in Developing Countries,* (5th ed), Paris, 1983.

NOTES TO TABLE A4

1 The stock of foreign investment includes fixed assets plus working capital. Detailed data is available for the manufacturing sector only; the bulk of the remaining investment in Hong Kong is thought to be concentrated in the services sector (primarily banking), hence we have estimated a figure accordingly.

2 Includes outward investment to Indonesia, Malaysia (1982), Thailand, Taiwan and Sri Lanka (1982) only. Total therefore does not match Table A2.

3 1982.

Table A5

GEOGRAPHICAL DISTRIBUTION OF FOREIGN DIRECT CAPITAL STOCK, 1978 - 82 (US $m)

	Inward Investment[1]			Outward Investment		
	Developed Countries	*Developing Countries*	*Total*	*Developed Countries*	*Developing Countries*	*Total*
1978	348.0	36.5	440.0[3]	*N.A.*	*N.A.*	*N.A.*
1981	*N.S.A.*	*N.S.A.*	1,235.9	*N.S.A.*	1,482.4[2]	1,820.0[3]
1982	1,093.7	51.6	1,260.4[3]	*N.A.*	*N.A.*	*N.A.*
1984	*N.S.A.*	*N.S.A.*	1,463.4	1,000[4]	2,000[4]	3,000[4]

Source:

Industry Department, Government of Territory of Hong Kong, *op cit;* and Various National Sources referring to Incoming Foreign Investment of each country; data as cited in Mah Hui Lim, 'Survey of Activities of Transnational Corporations from Asian Developing Countries', paper submitted to the ESCAP/UNCTC Joint Unit on Transnational Corporations, Bangkok, March 1984; E K Y Chen, 'Multinationals from Hong Kong', in S Lall (Ed), *The New Multinationals,* Chichester: John Wiley, 1983.

NOTES TO TABLE A5

1 The stock of foreign investment consists of fixed assets plus working capital. Data is available for the manufacturing sector only and thus the total does not match Table A2.

2 Includes outward investment to Asia and the Pacific only (except Japan or the Middle East).

3 Total includes unspecified figure.

4 Authors' estimates

Table A6

INDUSTRIAL DISTRIBUTION OF FOREIGN DIRECT CAPITAL STOCK, 1981 - 84 (US $m)

	Inward Investment[1]		Outward Investment[2]
	1981	*1984*	*1981*
Primary	100.0	*N.A.*	268.6
Agriculture	*N.S.A.*	*N.A.*	249.2[3]
Mining & quarrying			19.4[4]
Secondary	1,260.4[13]	1,463.4	756.0
Food & drink	64.5	105.7	24.5[5]
Chemicals & allied	80.6	102.8	65.3[6]
Metals	41.7	69.8	16.0[7]
Mechanical engineering	30.6	*N.A.*	
Electrical equipment	540.0	635.9	28.7[8]
Transportation equipment	25.8	15.2	9.3[7]
Textiles & clothing	146.1	142.5	115.4[6]
Paper & allied	30.7	86.6	22.5[5]
Stone, clay & glass	131.7	110.8	11.0[8]
Coal & petroleum products			
Other manufacturing	168.7	193.7	2.2[9]
Tertiary	2,440.0		404.1
Construction	*Not Separately Available*	*Not Available*	96.8[10]
Transport & communications			*N.A.*
Distributive trade			95.1[10]
Property			130.1[4]
Banking & finance			6.8[11]
Other services			75.3[12]
TOTAL	3,800.0[1]	*N.A.*	1,428.7[2]

Source:

Industry Department, Government of Territory of Hong Kong *op cit;* data as cited in Mah Hui Lim, 'Survey of Activities of Transnational Corporations from Asian Developing Countries', paper presented to the ESCAP/UNCTC Joint Unit on Transnational Corporations, Bangkok, March 1984; Various National Sources regarding Incoming Foreign Investment of each country in *Indonesian Financial Statistics,* December 1983; Malaysian Industrial Development Authority; Board of Investment, Thailand, December 1978 and 1981; Ministry of Finance and Planning, Sri Lanka; OECD, *Investing in Developing Countries,* (5th ed), Paris, 1983.

NOTES TO TABLE A6

1 The stock of foreign investment consists of fixed assets plus working capital. Detailed data is available for the manufacturing sector only; the bulk of the remaining investment is thought to be concentrated in the services sector, hence we have estimated a figure accordingly.
2 Includes Indonesia, Malaysia (1982), Thailand, Taiwan and Sri Lanka (1982) only, thus total does not match Table A2.
3 Includes Indonesia, Thailand & Taiwan only.
4 Includes Indonesia & Sri Lanka only.
5 Includes Malaysia & Taiwan only.
6 Includes Malaysia, Thailand, Taiwan and Sri Lanka only. (Including petroleum products.)
7 Includes Malaysia, Taiwan & Sri Lanka only.
8 Includes Malaysia, Taiwan & Thailand only.
9 Includes Malaysia only.
10 Includes Indonesia & Taiwan only.
11 Includes Taiwan only.
12 Includes Indonesia, Taiwan, Thailand and Sri Lanka only.
13 1982.

Table A7

LEADING SOURCE AND RECIPIENT COUNTRIES, 1978 - 84 (US $m)

	Inward Investment[1]			Outward Investment
	1978	*1984*		*1981*
DEVELOPED AREAS	348.0	1,262.4		
EEC	68.0	168.2		*Not Separately Available*[3]
North America				
United States	197.0	786.3		
Other developed countries				
Japan	83.0	307.9		
DEVELOPING AREAS	36.5	92.5		1,482.4
Asia & Pacific of which:	36.5	92.5		1,482.4
Bangladesh	*Not Available*	*Not Available*		0.1
China				280.0
India				0.2
Indonesia		3.1		400.0
S. Korea		*N.A.*		45.1[2]
Malaysia		2.8		130.0
Philippines		38.1		97.3
Singapore		30.2		230.0
Sri Lanka		*N.A.*		7.8[2]
Taiwan		12.9		*N.A.*
Thailand		5.4		*N.A.*
UNSPECIFIED	55.5	108.6		337.6
TOTAL	440.0[1]	1,463.4		1,820.0

Source:

Industry Department, Government of Territory of Hong Kong *op cit;* Various National Sources Referring to Incoming Foreign Investment of each country; data as cited in Mah Hui Lim, 'Survey of Activities of Transnational Corporations from Asian Developing Countries', paper submitted to the ESCAP/UNCTC Joint Unit on Transnational Corporations, Bangkok, March 1984; E K Y Chen, 'Multinationals from Hong Kong', in S Lall (Ed), *The New Multinationals,* Chichester: John Wiley, 1983.

NOTES TO TABLE A7

1 The stock of foreign investment consists of fixed assets plus working capital. Data is available for the manufacturing sector only and this the total does not match Table A2.

2 1982.

3 According to recipient country data there was some US $ 553 million Hong Kong direct investment in the USA in 1984, US $ 172 million in Japan and Canadian $ 147 million in Canada.

Table A8

INDICATORS OF THE SIGNIFICANCE OF INWARD FOREIGN DIRECT INVESTMENT OR THE ACTIVITIES OF FOREIGN-BASED COMPANIES TO THE NATIONAL ECONOMY, 1981 - 84

1	Direct capital stock of foreign affiliates at book values in 1981 as a proportion of:	
	a GNP at factor cost	15.2
	b population (in US $ per head)	730.8
2	Employment in foreign affiliates in 1984 as a percentage of all employment in manufacturing	9.8
3	Output of foreign affiliates in 1981 as a percentage of all companies' output in secondary (ie, manufacturing) industry	13.9
4	Exports of foreign affiliates in 1984 as a percentage of profits of all companies in the host country	
	a in all sectors	10.0
	b in manufacturing	16.5
5	Percentage share of assets[2] accounted for by foreign affiliates in the manufacturing sector, 1984	
	Food and Drink	7.2
	Chemicals and allied	7.0
	Electrical equipment[3]	8.0
	Textiles and clothing	9.8
	Stone, glass & clay	7.6
	Other manufacturing	24.9

Source:
OECD, *Investing in Developing Countries,* (5th ed), Paris, 1983; OECD, *Geographical Distribution of Financial Flows to Developing Countries,* Paris, 1984; Industry Department, Government of Territory of Hong Kong, *op cit.*

NOTES TO TABLE A8

1 Since only sales data is available, this figure represents the sales value of foreign affiliates as a percentage of total manufacturing sales.

2 Represents sum of fixed assets of companies surveyed at original cost before depreciation and their working capital as at end of accounting periods adopted by the companies included in the survey.

3 For electronics, share of assets accounted for by foreign affiliates is 35.5%.

Table A9

INDICATORS OF THE SIGNIFICANCE OF OUTWARD FOREIGN DIRECT INVESTMENT OR THE ACTIVITIES OF HOME-BASED COMPANIES ABROAD FOR THE NATIONAL ECONOMY, 1971 - 81

1	Foreign capital stock of home-based firms at book value in 1981 as a proportion of:	
	a GNP at factor cost	7.26
	b population (in US $ per head)	350.00
2	Employment in foreign affiliates in 1971 as a percentage of domestic employment in manufacturing	11.0

Source:
E K Y Chen, 'Multinationals from Hong Kong', in S Lall (Ed), *The New Multinationals,* Chichester: John Wiley, 1983; OECD, *Geographical Distribution of Financial Flows to Developing Countries,* Paris, 1984; UNCTC, 1983.

Table A10

DISTRIBUTION OF FOREIGN SUBSIDIARIES AND ASSOCIATES AND FOREIGN CAPITAL STOCK BY PERCENTAGE OWNERSHIP OF PARENT COMPANIES, 1984

	Inward Investment		**Outward Investment**	
	Number of Affiliates	*Value of Capital Stock HK $*	*Number of Affiliates*	*Value of Capital Stock*
100% owned subsidiaries	229	8,445.7	*Not Available*	
50–99.9% owned subsidiaries and associates Less than 50% owned subsidiaries and associates	213	3,002.6		
TOTAL	442	11,448.3		

Source:
Report on the Survey of Overseas Investment in Hong Kong's Manufacturing Industry, 1984

Table A12

LEADING FOREIGN AND DOMESTIC MULTINATIONAL COMPANIES

A Leading Foreign Multinational Companies in the country, 1984

	Name[1]	*Home Country*	*Sector*	*HK Turnover (HK $m)*
1	Lee Tai Textile Co	Indonesia	Textiles	100
2	D J Limited	USA	Textiles	250
3	Kian Dai Wools Co Ltd	Japan	Textiles	120
4	G F Mark Five Knitting Fty Ltd	China (PRC)	Textiles	60
5	Famous Horse Garment Fty Ltd	USA	Garments	*N.A.*
6	Texwood Ltd	USA	Garments	*N.A.*
7	Digital Equipment Int Ltd	USA	Electronics	1151
8	National Semiconductor (HK) Ltd	USA	Electronics	*N.A.*
9	Philips (HK) Ltd •	Netherlands	Electronics	1000

NOTES TO TABLE A12(A)

1 These multinational corporations have an employment of 1000–2000 workers

Table A12 (cont'd)

LEADING FOREIGN AND DOMESTIC MULTINATIONAL COMPANIES

B Leading Domestic Companies with Multinational Interests, 1983

	Name	*Sector*	*No. of overseas subsidiaries*
1	The Hong Kong & Shanghai Banking Corporation	Banking and finance, insurance	344
2	Orient Overseas (Holdings) Ltd	Investment, transportation equipment, shipping	242
3	Jardine Matheson & Co Ltd	Insurance, investment	181
4	Wheelock Marden & Co Ltd	Electronics, engineering, shipping	96
5	Swire Pacific Ltd	Air transport, transportation equipment, properties	87
6	Wah Kwong Shipping & Investment Co (Hong Kong) Ltd	Shipping & investment	47
7	Jack Chia Holdings (Hong Kong) Ltd	Insurance, motor vehicles, property	31
8	Faber Merlin Ltd	Hotels, mining	24
9	The Hong Kong Land Co Ltd	Food	24
10	Public International Investments Ltd	Investments	20
11	Continental Mariner Investment Co Ltd	Mechanical engineering	20
12	Hang Chong Investment Co Ltd	Motor vehicles, investment	19
13	International Maritime Carriers (Holdings)	Shipping	17
14	Pioneer Industries (Holdings) Ltd	Investments, shipping	17
15	Yangtzekiang Garment Mftg Co	Textiles	15
16	World International (Holdings) Ltd	Shipping & finance	14
17	Patt Manfield & Co Ltd	Shipping	12
18	Goodyear Investors Ltd	Investment	11
19	Jardine Fleming Holdings Ltd	Investment	11
20	John Manners & Co Ltd	Shipping	11
21	Sun Hung Kai Securities Ltd	Investment	11
22	Hsin Chong Holdings (HK) Ltd	Investment & shipping	10
23	Hong Kong Carpet Manufacturers Ltd	Textiles	9
24	Hutchison Whampoa Ltd	Shipping & investment	9
25	Ling Kee Group of Companies Ltd	Publishing	9
26	Mendez International Ltd	Insurance	9

INDIA

Historically, India was one of the major recipient countries of foreign direct investment, especially from the UK. However, since the 1960s a greater proportion of such investment has been directed towards other developed countries, and since 1974 the activities of foreign affiliates which are more than 40% owned have been constrained by the Foreign Exchange Regulations Act. The new government of Rajiv Gandhi has suggested a more open approach, although as yet no amendments have been made to FERA, nor have any proposals been initiated to that effect. No estimates of the total stock of direct investment in India have been made since 1974, though it seems certain to have fallen. On the other hand, outward investment has recently grown rapidly through a proliferation of Indian joint ventures abroad. These affiliates have made use of the capability of Indian firms to adapt technology to their own developing country framework, and they have therefore been mainly established in other developing countries, notably Kenya, Nigeria and Senegal in Africa, and Indonesia and Malaysia in Asia.

MAIN SOURCES OF DATA:

A Official

1. Indian Investment Centre: issue regular statements on Indian joint ventures abroad showing their equity capital stock and the Indian share of it; also provide information on approved gross inward investment flows, and royalties.
2. Reserve Bank of India: published the last available estimates of the stock of inward investment, and regularly provide details of capital flows and exchange transactions (excluding reinvested earnings, etc).
3. UNCTC, *Transnational Corporations in World Development: Third Survey,* New York: UN, 1983.

B Private

1. S Lall, 'The export of capital from developing countries: the Indian case', in J Black and J H Dunning (Eds), *International Capital Movements,* London: Macmillan, 1982.
2. S Lall, *The New Multinationals: the spread of third world enterprises*, Chichester: John Wiley & Sons, 1984.
3. S Lall, 'India', in J H Dunning (Ed), *Multinational Enterprises, Economic Structure and International Competitiveness,* Chichester: John Wiley & Sons, 1985.
4. J P Agarwal, *Pros and Cons of Third World Multinationals: A case study of India,* Tubingen: Mohn, 1985.
5. S Lall and S Mohammad, 'Multinationals in Indian business: industrial characteristics of foreign investment in a heavily regulated economy, *Journal of Development Economics, 13,* 1983, 143-157.

Table A1

SUMMARY OF THE COUNTRY'S INTERNATIONAL INVESTMENT POSITION

		Inward Investment	Outward Investment
1	Number of foreign affiliates in host country, and of foreign affiliates of home country firms at the end of June 1981	800[1]	207[2]
2	Number of foreign firms with direct investments in host country, and home country firms with direct foreign affiliates at the end of 1981	*N.A.*	120[3]
3	Total foreign direct capital stock at book value as a percentage of GNP at factor cost in 1980	3.1[4]	0.07
4	Flow of foreign direct investment in the five year period 1976-80 (I Rup m)	352.4[5]	407[6]
5	Employment in foreign affiliates or abroad	*N.A.*	*N.A.*
6	Output of foreign affiliates or abroad, 1977-78 (I Rup m)	11,500[7]	*N.A.*

Source:

S Lall 'India', in J H Dunning (Ed, 1985), *op cit;* Indian Investment Centre, unpublished statements on *Indian Joint Ventures Abroad;* Reserve Bank of India, *Bulletin,* March 1978; UN *Statistical Yearbook for Asia and the Pacific, 1978;* OECD, *Geographical Distribution of Financial Flows to Developing Countries, 1978-81;* Indian Investment Centre, unpublished statements on *Foreign Investment involved in Collaboration Agreements, approved 1969-82.*

NOTES TO TABLE A1

1 Approximate figure for 1974; Lall estimates that since then 61 of these have been dissolved and no new affiliates have been established.

2 Of the 205 initiated by the end of 1980, 118 were in production and 87 under construction.

3 Author's estimate. The largest 18 Indian investors were responsible for 76 ventures which account for over two-thirds of total outward investment, at the end of June 1981; and most of the remaining parent firms have only one foreign venture.

4 Inward capital stock at the end of March 1974 as a percentage of GNP in 1974; since that time the ratio has declined.

5 This is a gross investment inflow not allowing for repatriations, and covers approved foreign collaborations. Lall estimates that 60% of these proposed collaborations did not materialise in the period 1975-81. Net inward investment flows reported to the IMF for 1972-76 amount to a net disinvestment of I Rup 289.4 m.

6 Estimated assuming that the growth rate of outward investment stake between January 1980 and June 1981 (from I Rup 794.5 m to I Rup 945 m) was a continuation of the same growth rate from 1976-80.

7 Estimated value added of a sample of 276 foreign controlled firms in manufacturing, which Lall says account for the bulk of inward investment stock.

Table A2

PRIVATE FOREIGN CAPITAL STOCK, 1963 - 82 (I Rup m)

	Inward Investment				Outward Investment		
	Portfolio	*Direct*	*Total*		*Portfolio*	*Direct*	*Total*
Book value of capital stock							
1971	*Not Available*	12,010	*Not Available*		*Not Available*		
1974		19,430					
1978		20,470					
1980		*N.S.A.*			*N.A.*	926.5	*N.A.*
1982		*N.S.A.*			*N.A.*	1,214.1	*N.A.*

Source:

Reserve Bank of India, *Foreign Collaboration in Indian Industry, Survey Report, 1968,* Reserve Bank of India, *Bulletin, March 1978;* Indian Investment Centre, unpublished statements on *Indian Joint Ventures Abroad;* UNCTC, 1983, *op cit.*

Table A3

FLOW OF FOREIGN DIRECT INVESTMENT, 1970 - 80 (I Rup m)

	Inward Investment				Outward Investment		
	Reinvested Profits	*Other*[1]	*Total*		*Reinvested Profits*	*Other*	*Total*
1970	*Not Separately Available*	24.5	45.4		*Not Available*		
1971		58.4	-7.5				
1972		62.3	24.7				
1973		28.2	-101.5				
1974		67.1	-48.7				
1975		32.1	-91.5				
1976		72.7	-72.4				
1977		40.0	*N.S.A.*				
1978		94.1	*N.S.A.*				
1979		56.4	*N.S.A.*				
1980		89.2	*N.S.A.*		*N.S.A.*	*N.S.A.*	102.5[2]

Source:

Indian Investment Centre, unpublished statements on *Foreign Investment involved in Collaboration Agreements, approved 1969-82;* IMF, *Balance of Payments Yearbook, 1977;* IMF, *International Financial Statistics, 1981;* Indian Investment Centre, unpublished statements on *Indian Joint Ventures Abroad.*

NOTES TO TABLE A3

1 Gross capital inflow, consisting of equity capital, loans and advances; excluding reinvested earnings and disinvestment.

2 Authors' estimate from outward capital stock figures for January 1980 and June 1981 (see footnote 6, Table A1).

Table A4

SECTORAL DISTRIBUTION OF FOREIGN DIRECT CAPITAL STOCK, 1974 - 82 (I Rup m)

	Inward Investment			Outward Investment		
	Primary	*Secondary*	*Tertiary*	*Primary*	*Secondary*	*Tertiary*
1974	3,063	10,732	5,635		*Not Available*	
1980		*Not Available*		*N.S.A.*	757	170
1982				23	994	197

Source:

Reserve Bank of India, *Bulletin, March 1978,* Indian Investment Centre, unpublished statements on *Indian Joint Ventures Abroad* S Lall, 'The export of capital from developing countries: the Indian case' in J Black and J H Dunning (Eds, 1982), *International Capital Movements.*

Table A5

GEOGRAPHICAL DISTRIBUTION OF FOREIGN DIRECT CAPITAL STOCK, 1974 - 82 (I Rup m)

	Inward Investment			Outward Investment		
	Developed Countries[1]	*Developing Countries*[2]	*Total*	*Developed Countries*	*Developing Countries*	*Total*
1974	16,871	2,559[3]	19,430		*Not Available*	
1982		*Not Available*		30.3	1,183.3	1,214.1

Source:

Reserve Bank of India, *Bulletin, March 1978;* Indian Investment Centre, unpublished statement on *Indian Joint Ventures Abroad as on 30/9/1982.*

NOTES TO TABLE A5

1 UK, USA, West Germany, Italy, France, Switzerland, Japan, Sweden and Canada.

2 Other countries and international institutions.

3 Of which I Rup 1,347 m from 'other countries' and I Rup 1,212 m from international institutions.

Table A6

INDUSTRIAL DISTRIBUTION OF FOREIGN DIRECT CAPITAL STOCK, 1974 - 82 (I Rup m)

	Inward Investment		Outward Investment
	1974	*1978*[1]	*1982*
Primary	3,063	*N.A.*	22.9
Agriculture	1,136	946[2]	0.9
Mining & quarrying	169	*N.A.*	22.0
Oil	1,758	*N.A.*	0.0
Secondary	10,732	6,321	994.1
Food & drink	647	751[3]	99.6
Chemicals & allied	4,105	2,217	225.9
Metals	1,535	756	85.2
Mechanical engineering	620	*N.A.*	106.3
Electrical equipment	967	748	17.4
Motor vehicles	608	574 (Motor vehicles and Other transportation equipment)	22.6
Other transportation equipment	125		0.0
Textiles & clothing	675	*Not Available* (Textiles & clothing to Coal & petroleum products)	236.5
Paper & allied	*N.S.A.*		131.6
Rubber	507		9.4
Stone, clay & glass	*N.S.A.*		48.4
Coal & petroleum products	*N.S.A.*		
Other manufacturing	943	1,275	11.2[4]
Tertiary	5,635	*N.A.*	197.1
Construction	3,298 (Construction and Transport & communications)	*N.A.*	40.8
Transport & communications			3.4
Distributive trade	354	411	5.7
Property	100	*N.A.*	1.0
Banking & finance	1,810	194[5]	70.7
Other services	73	*N.A.*	75.3[6]
TOTAL	19,430	8,427[7]	1,214.1

Source:

Reserve Bank of India, *Bulletin, March 1978;* Indian Investment Centre, unpublished statement on *Indian Joint Ventures Abroad as on 30/9/82;* UK Department of Industry, *Census of Overseas Assets, 1978;* US Department of Commerce, Bureau of Economic Analysis, International Investment Division unpublished data.

NOTES TO TABLE A6

1 Source country estimates of UK and US direct investment stock in India only; total inward investment is greater than that shown.

2 UK only; but note that the Indian estimate of UK inward investment stock in this sector in 1974 was I Rup 1,120 m, ie, virtually all capital invested in this area.

3 UK only.

4 Bottle capping.

5 For the UK, non-insurance financial institutions only, and for the USA, banking only.

6 Of which hotels and restaurants I Rup 68,859 m.

7 I Rup 9,085 m including West Germany's outward capital stock in India in 1978. The Indian estimate of total UK and US inward investment stock in 1974 was I Rup 12,200 m, and of UK, US and German investment I Rup 14,008 m (ie, 63% and 72% of total capital respectively). It seems quite possible that the UK and USA accounted for a lower proportion of the total in 1978 than in 1974, but if they held the same share then total inward investment stock in 1978 would have fallen to I Rup 13,420 m.

Table A7 **LEADING SOURCE AND RECIPIENT COUNTRIES, 1974 - 82 (I Rup m)**

	Inward Investment		Outward Investment
	1974	*1978*[1]	*1982*
DEVELOPED AREAS	16,871[2]	9,085[2]	30.31
Europe	10,822[2]	6,432[2]	22.37
EEC of which:	10,080[2]	6,432[2]	19.39
France	497	*N.A.*	0.26
W. Germany	1,808	658	4.08
Greece	*N.A.*	*Not Available*	11.51
Italy	834		*Neg.*
Netherlands	*N.A.*		0.48
UK	6,891	5,774	3.06
Other Europe of which:	792[2]		2.98[2]
Cyprus	*N.A.*	*Not Available*	2.93
Sweden	343		*Neg.*
Switzerland	449		0.05
North America	5,633	2,653	7.25
Canada	324	*N.A.*	*Neg.*
USA	5.309	2,653	7.25
Other developed countries	416[2]		0.69
Australia	*N.A.*	*Not Available*	0.69
Japan	416		*Neg.*
DEVELOPING AREAS	2,559[3]		1,183.75
Africa of which:	*Not Available*		524.21
Kenya			126.44
Nigeria			165.34
Senegal			169.60
Sudan			36.00
Asia & Pacific of which:			575.33
Indonesia			161.72
Malaysia			132.13
Singapore			77.01
Sri Lanka			62.96
Thailand			93.91
Middle East of which:			65.02
Saudi Arabia			19.95
United Arab Emirates			14.02
Other developing countries			19.20[5]
TOTAL	19,430		1,214.05

Source:
Reserve Bank of India, *Bulletin, March 1978;* Deutsche Bundesbank, *Monthly Report, October 1981;* UK Department of Trade and Industry, *Census of Overseas Assets, 1978;* US Department of Commerce, Bureau of Economic Analysis, International Investment Division unpublished data; Indian Investment Centre, unpublished statement on *Indian Joint Ventures Abroad as on 30/9/82.*

NOTES TO TABLE A7

1 Source country estimates.
2 Including only those countries listed separately.
3 Including international institutions.
4 Investment of international institutions.
5 Investment in Yugoslavia.

Table A8

INDICATORS OF THE SIGNIFICANCE OF INWARD FOREIGN DIRECT INVESTMENT OR THE ACTIVITIES OF FOREIGN-BASED COMPANIES TO THE NATIONAL ECONOMY, 1974 - 79

1	Direct capital stock of foreign affiliates at book value in 1974 as a proportion of:	
	a GNP at factor cost	3.1
	b population (in I Rup per head)	3,312.0
2	Output of foreign affiliates in 1979 as a percentage of all companies' output	
	a in primary (ie, extractive) industry	*N.A.*
	b in secondary (ie, manufacturing) industry	7.0[1]
	c in tertiary industry (ie, services, etc)	*N.A.*

3 Percentage share of (a) output of foreign affiliates and (b) dividends paid abroad by firms in selected manufacturing sectors

Manufacturing Sector	*Output (1974)*	*Dividends (1977-78)*[2]
Food & drink[3]	*N.A.*	18.0
Chemicals & allied[4]	33	32.8
Metals	41	25.5
Mechanical engineering[5]	25	13.7
Electrical equipment	33	26.0
Motor vehicles	10 (Motor vehicles and Other transportation equipment)	21.6
Other transportation equipment		18.3
Textiles & clothing[6]	*N.A.*	6.0
Paper & allied[7]	*N.A.*	4.3
Rubber	52	42.5
Stone, glass & clay[8]	*N.A.*	6.8
Other manufacturing[9]	*N.A.*	28.7

Source:

Reserve Bank of India, *Bulletin, March 1978;* UN *Statistical Yearbook for Asia and the Pasific, 1978;* S Lall, *India,* in J H Dunning (Ed), 1985, *op cit;* S Lall and S Mohammad, 1983, *op cit.*

NOTES TO TABLE A8

1 Value added of 276 foreign controlled firms in manufacturing as a percentage of all value added in manufacturing.

2 Percentage share of total dividends of 1,180 large private sector companies paid abroad, 1977-78.

3 A weighted average of the share of dividends sent abroad in sugar, other food products, and tobacco (weighted by the number of firms in each sub-sector).

4 A weighted average of chemical fertilisers, dyes and dye stuffs, manmade fibres, plastic raw materials, other basic industrial chemicals, medicines and pharmaceuticals, paints and varnishes, and other chemicals.

5 Non-electrical machinery and foundries and engineering workshops.

6 Cotton, silk and rayon and woollen textiles.

7 Paper and products and printing and publishing.

8 Cement, glass and glassware.

9 Industries and medical gases.

Table A9

INDICATORS OF THE SIGNIFICANCE OF OUTWARD FOREIGN DIRECT INVESTMENT OR THE ACTIVITIES OF HOME-BASED COMPANIES ABROAD FOR THE NATIONAL ECONOMY, 1980

1	Foreign capital stock of home-based firms at book value in 1980 as a proportion of:		
	a	GNP at factor cost	0.07
	b	population (in I Rup per head)	1.38

Source:
Indian Investment Centre, unpublished statement on *Indian Joint Ventures Abroad as on 31/8/1980;* OECD, *Geographical Distribution of Financial Flows to Developing Countries, 1978-81.*

Table A10

DISTRIBUTION OF FOREIGN SUBSIDIARIES AND ASSOCIATES AND FOREIGN CAPITAL STOCK BY PERCENTAGE OWNERSHIP OF PARENT COMPANIES, 1978 - 82

	Inward Investment[1] (1978)		Outward Investment (1982)	
	Number of Affiliates	*Value of Capital Stock (I Rup m)*	*Number of Affiliates*	*Value of Capital Stock (I Rup m)*
100% owned subsidiaries	13.	246.5	0	0.0
50-99.9% owned subsidiaries and associates	71	3,271.8	54	196.4
Less than 50% owned subsidiaries and associates	112[2]	2,085.6[2]	171	1,017.7
TOTAL	196	5,603.9	225	1,214.1

Source:
UK Department of Industry, *Census of Overseas Assets, 1978;* Indian Investment Centre, unpublished statement on *Indian Joint Ventures Abroad as on 30/9/1982.*

NOTES TO TABLE A10

1 UK-owned subsidiaries and associates only.

2 Associates only.

Table A11

ROYALTY RECEIPTS AND PAYMENTS, 1970 - 80 (I Rup m)

	Payments			Receipts		
	To Affiliates	*To Non-affiliates*	*Total*	*From Affiliates*	*From Non-affiliates*	*Total*
1970-75[1]						1.9
1975-76			361.0			13.0
1976-77	*Not*		536.8	16.4[2]	*Not*	13.0
1977-78	*Available*		476.4		*separately*	19.6
1978-79			448.8		*available*	21.8
1979-80			*N.A.*			27.1

Source:

Indian Investment Centre, unpublished statement on *Royalties and Technical Know-How Payments Abroad by Private Sector during 1975-76 to 1978-79,* S Lall, *India,* in J H Dunning (Ed), 1985, *op cit.*

NOTES TO TABLE A11

1 Annual average.

2 Receipts of 276 foreign controlled firms, all of which were earned by 134 UK firms who presumably receive royalties primarily from other affiliates. The 1,077 Indian firms in the RBI *Bulletin, July 1981,* survey received I Rup 10.5 m, but it is not possible to apportion this between affiliate and non-affiliate receipts.

Table A12

LEADING FOREIGN AND DOMESTIC MULTINATIONAL COMPANIES, 1981 - 85

A Indian Affiliates of Multinational Companies in the country, 1985

	Name	*Home Country*	*Sector*	*Foreign Equity Stake (in %)*
1	Alkali & Chemical Corp of India	UK	General Chemicals	51
2	Ashok Leyland	UK	Motor vehicles	51
3	Brooke Bond (India) Ltd	UK	Tea products	40
4	Cadbury India	UK	Confectionery	40
5	Chemicals & Fibres of India Ltd	UK	Plastics & fibres	51
6	Dunlop India Ltd	UK	Rubber tyres	51
7	Ericsson (India) Ltd	Sweden	Telecommunications equip.	40
8	Fiberglass Pilkington Ltd	UK	Glass fibres	50
9	Firestone Tyre & Rubber Co of India Private Ltd	USA	Rubber tyres	74
10	Guest Keen Williams	UK	Motor vehicle components	59
11	Godfrey Philips India Ltd	USA	Tobacco products	40
12	Hindustan Ferado Ltd	UK	Motor vehicle components	71
13	Hindustan Lever Ltd	UK/Netherlands	Soap products, fats, etc	51
14	Hoechst Pharmaceuticals Ltd	W. Germany	Chemicals	50
15	Lucas-TVS Ltd	UK	Motor vehicle components	51
16	Metal Boc India Ltd	UK	Containers & equipment	60
17	Motor Industries Ltd	W. Germany	Motor vehicle components	51
18	National Organic Chemical Industries	UK/Netherlands	Oil products	33
19	Pfizer Ltd	USA	Pharmaceuticals	75
20	Philips India Ltd	Netherlands	Electrical products	60
21	Reckett & Colman of India Ltd	UK	Household products	40
22	Siemens India Ltd	W. Germany	Electrical products	51
23	Tractor Engineers Ltd	USA	Tractors	50
24	Tribeni Tissues Ltd	UK	Paper products	51
25	Tube Investments of India	UK	Metal products	46

Table A12 (cont'd)

LEADING FOREIGN AND DOMESTIC MULTINATIONAL COMPANIES

B Leading Domestic Companies with Multinational Interests, June 1981

	Name	*Sector*	*Equity held in foreign ventures (I Rup m)*
1	Birla Group	Paper, textiles, rayon, palm oil	142.76
2	Thapar Group	Paper, trading	126.91
3	Tata Group	Oil mills, trucks, tools, metal production	99.71
4	JK Group	Textiles, metal products	42.97
5	Modi Group	Textiles, metal products	40.87
6	HMT (Hindustan Machine Tools)	Machine tools	37.69
7	Usha Martin Black	Metals	33.90
8	Oberoi Hotels	Hotels	26.75
9	Shahibag Enterprises	Textiles	21.13
10	Larsen & Toubro	Project engineering & construction services	18.70
11	Godrej Group	Metals	13.73
12	Kirloskar Group	Engines, machinery	11.79
13	Sarabhai Chemicals	Chemicals & pharmaceuticals	7.21
14	Indian Tobacco Company	Tobacco	4.59
15	Chemical Construction Co	Chemicals	3.84
16	Mahindra & Mahindra Group	Transport	3.35
17	ITDC (Indian Tourism Development Corp)	Tourism	2.93
18	Mafatlal Group	Mechanical engineering	0.58

Source:
Sanjaya Lall, *The New Multinationals: The Spread of Third World Enterprises,* Chichester: John Wiley, 1983.

INDONESIA

Foreign investment increased rapidly from 1967 to reach a peak in 1974. A total number of 92 projects valued at US $ 1, 500 million were approved in 1974. From 1974, foreign investment declined, but recovered in 1979 when foreign investments valued at about US $ 1,700 million were approved. The decline in foreign investment approvals between 1974 and 1978 resulted from a combination of factors which included the world-wide economic recession of 1974-75, a fall in investor confidence following the Pertamina financial crisis of 1975 and subsequent renegotiations of investment contracts with the oil companies and the imposition of new investment regulations in 1974.

By March 1984, the government had approved a total of 794 foreign investment projects with an intended investment of US $ 13.0 billion. While investment approvals for the agriculture and mining sectors decreased, those for manufacturing, construction and fishery sectors increased. A total of 48.5% of the intended foreign capital investment approved by March 1983 were sourced from Japan, Hong Kong and the USA.

Outward foreign direct investment is small and mainly confined to the ASEAN region and the USA. There are however a few large Indonesian firms such as the First Pacific Group which have investments in several overseas countries.

MAIN SOURCES OF DATA:

A Official

1 Bank of Indonesia annual publications:

a *Report for the Financial Year*

b *Statistik Ekonomi — Keuangan Indonesia* (Indonesian Financial Statistics)

2 D Kuntjoro-Jakti 'Indonesia' in Economic and Social Commission for Asia and the Pacific, *Patterns and Impact of Foreign Investment in the ESCAP Region,* Bangkok: UN, 1985.

B Private

1 V N Balasubramanyam, 'Factor Proportions and Productive Efficiency of Foreign-Owned Firms in the Indonesian Manufacturing Sector', *Bulletin of Indonesian Economic Studies,* vol XX, no 3, December 1984.

2 Friedrich von Kirchbach, 'TNCs in the ASEAN region: A Survey of the Major Issues', *Economic Bulletin for Asia & Pacific,* vol XXXIII, no 1.

3 Mah Hui Lim, "Survey of Activities of Transnational Corporations from Asian Developing Countries," paper submitted to the ESCAP/UNCTC Joint Unit on Transnational Corporations, Bangkok, March 1984.

Note:
Data do not allow us to complete Table A9, A10 or A11 for Indonesia.

Table A1

SUMMARY OF THE COUNTRY'S INTERNATIONAL INVESTMENT POSITION

		Inward Investment	Outward Investment
1	Number of foreign affiliates in host country, and of foreign affiliates of home country firms at the end of 1980	684	*N.A.*
2	Number of foreign firms with direct investments in host country, and home country firms with direct foriegn affiliates	*N.A.*	*N.A.*
3	Total foreign direct capital stock at book value as a percentage of GNP at factor cost in 1982	10.92	*N.A.*
4	Flow of foreign direct investment in the five year period, 1980-84 (US $ m)	1,058.10	*N.A.*
5	Employment in foreign affiliates or abroad, 1977	380,000	*N.A.*
6	Output of foreign affiliates or abroad	*N.A.*	*N.A.*

Source:

Bank of Indonesia, *Report for the Financial Year 1981/82;* IMF, *Balance of Payments Statistics Yearbook 1984;* Mah Hui Lim, *op cit.;* IMF, *International Financial Statistics Yearbook 1984;* F von Kirchbach, *op cit.*

NOTES TO TABLE A1

1 Represents number of affiliates of foreign MNEs from selected countries as identified in UNCTC, 1983,

Table A2

PRIVATE FOREIGN CAPITAL STOCK, 1967 - 83 (US $ m)[1]

	Inward Investment			Outward Investment		
	Portfolio	*Direct*	*Total*	*Portfolio*	*Direct*	*Total*
Book value of capital stock						
1974	*Not Available*	1,738.1	*Not Available*	*Not Available*		
1975		2,285.2				
1976		2,710.7				
1977		2,969.5				
1978		3,374.7				
1979		3,693.3				
1980		4,039.9				
1981		4,418.9				
1983		4,990.6				

Source:

Bank of Indonesia, *Report for the Financial Year 1981/82.*

NOTES TO TABLE A2

1 Figures represent implemented foreign capital investment projects cumulated as from June 1967 after taking into account the cancellation and shifting of projects from the foreign investment scheme (PMA) into the domestic investment scheme (PMDN). The data excludes investment in petroleum, banking and insurance.

Table A3

FLOW OF FOREIGN DIRECT INVESTMENT, 1970 - 84 (US $ m)

	Inward Investment			Outward Investment		
	Reinvested Profits	*Other*	*Total*	*Reinvested Profits*	*Other*	*Total*
1970	*Not Separately Available*		83.0	*Not Available*		
1971			139.4			
1972			207.4			
1973			15.5			
1974			49.3			
1975			547.1			
1976			425.5			
1977			234.7			
1978			279.2			
1979			226.1			
1980			183.5			
1981			133.2			
1982			226.3			
1983			288.6			
1984			226.5			

Source:

Bank of Indonesia, *Report for the Financial Year 1981/82;* IMF, *Balance of Payments Statistics Yearbook,* various issues.

Table A4

SECTORAL DISTRIBUTION OF FOREIGN DIRECT CAPITAL STOCK, 1967 - 83 (US $ m)[1]

	Inward Investment				Outward Investment		
	Primary	*Secondary*	*Tertiary*		*Primary*	*Secondary*	*Tertiary*
1974	496.6	1,033.0	208.5		*Not Available*		
1975	585.9	1,425.4	273.9				
1976	667.5	1,726.6	316.6				
1977	725.0	1,912.8	331.7				
1978	820.9	2,179.8	374.0				
1979	902.4	2,371.8	419.1				
1980	1,000.4	2,607.2	432.3				
1981	1,118.7	2,850.7	449.5				
1983	1,561.0	3,144.5	284.1				

Source:
Bank of Indonesia, *Report for the Financial Year 1981/83.*

NOTES TO TABLE A4

1 Figures represent implemented foreign capital investment projects cumulated as from June 1967 after taking into account the cancellation and shifting of projects from the foreign investment scheme (PMA) into the domestic investment scheme (PMDN). These data exclude investment in petroleum, banking and insurance.

Table A5

GEOGRAPHICAL DISTRIBUTION OF FOREIGN DIRECT CAPITAL STOCK, 1967 - 81 (US $ m)[1]

	Inward Investment				Outward Investment		
	Developed Countries[2]	*Other Countries*	*Total*		*Developed Countries*	*Developing Countries*	*Total*
1975	2,945.7	1,886.6	4,832.3		*Not Available*		
1976	3,108.1	2,163.0	5,271.1				
1977	3,300.4	2,617.8	5,918.2				
1978	3,545.1	2,775.8	6,320.9				
1979	4,738.3	3,421.5	8,159.8				
1980	5,185.7	3,880.8	9,066.5				
1981	5,591.5	4,654.3	10,245.8				

Source:
Bank of Indonesia, *Report for the Financial Year 1981/82.*

NOTES TO TABLE A5

1 Figures represent approved foreign capital investment projects cumulated as from 1967 after taking into account the cancellation and shifting of projects from the foreign investment scheme (PMA) into the domestic investment scheme (PMDN). These data exclude investment in petroleum, banking and insurance.

2 Represents approved foreign capital investment by European countries, Northern American countries, Japan and Australia.

Table A6

INDUSTRIAL DISTRIBUTION OF FOREIGN DIRECT CAPITAL STOCK, 1967 - 81 (US $ m)[1]

	Inward Investment		Outward Investment
	1967-74	*1981*	
Primary	496.6	1,118.7	
Agriculture[2]	280.2	575.2	
Mining & quarrying	216.4	543.5	
Oil	*N.S.A.*	*N.S.A.*	
Secondary	1,033.0	2,850.7	
Food & drink	111.7	193.5	
Chemicals & allied[3]	146.3	456.9	
Metals[4]	217.7	768.7	*Not Available*
Textiles & clothing[5]	443.3	999.1	
Paper & allied	13.9	49.3	
Rubber[3]	*N.S.A.*	*N.S.A.*	
Stone, clay & glass	85.3	326.8	
Other manufacturing	14.8	54.4	
Tertiary	208.5	449.5	
Construction	22.1	52.3	
Transport & communications	9.7	51.0	
Distributive trade[6]	54.0	110.8	
Other services	122.7	235.4	
TOTAL	1,738.1	4,418.9	

Source:

Bank of Indonesia, *Report for the Financial Year 1981/82.*

NOTES TO TABLE A6

1 Figures represent implemented foreign capital investment projects cumulated as from June 1967 after taking into account the cancellation and shifting of projects from the foreign investment scheme (PMA) into the domestic investment scheme (PMDN). The data excludes investment in petroleum, banking and insurance.

2 Includes fishery and forestry.

3 Includes rubber.

4 Represents basic metals and metal products.

5 Represents textiles and leather.

6 Represents trade and hotels.

Table A7

LEADING SOURCE AND RECIPIENT COUNTRIES, 1967 - 81 (US $ m)[1]

	Inward Investment		Outward Investment
	1976-75	*1981*	
DEVELOPED AREAS	2,932.1	5,562.4	
Europe	469.3	1,080.6	
EEC of which:	420.7	936.6	
Belgium	35.7	140.2	
France	13.2	26.6	
W. Germany	175.0	234.1	
Netherlands	156.8	411.3	
UK	40.0	124.4	
Other Europe	48.6	144.0	
North America of which:	195.6	468.1	
Canada	2.4	9.4	
USA	193.2	458.7	
Other developed countries of which:	2,267.2	4,013.7	*Not Available*
Australia	227.0	269.6	
Japan	2,040.2	3,744.1	
DEVELOPING AREAS	613.2	1,902.6	
Africa (except S. Africa) of which:	11.4	20.2	
Liberia	11.4	20.2	
Asia & Pacific (except Japan or Middle East) of which:	588.2	1,853.3	
Hong Kong	413.7	1,225.2	
South Korea		121.9	
Malaysia	21.8	28.8	
Philippines	19.8	38.3	
Singapore	46.9	142.7	
Taiwan		135.9	
Thailand	2.4	7.7	
Latin America	13.6	29.1	
UNSPECIFIED	1,287.0	2,780.8	
TOTAL	4,832.3	10,245.8	

Source:

Bank of Indonesia, *Report for the Financial Year 1981/82;* Mah Hui Lim, *op. cit.*

NOTES TO TABLE A7

1 Figures represent approved foreign capital investment projects cumulated as from June 1967 after taking into account cancellation and shifting of projects from the foreign investment scheme (PMDN). The data excludes investment in petroleum, banking and insurance. The total therefore does not match Table A2.

Table A8

INDICATORS OF THE SIGNIFICANCE OF INWARD FOREIGN DIRECT INVESTMENT OR THE ACTIVITIES OF FOREIGN-BASED COMPANIES TO THE NATIONAL ECONOMY, 1974 - 82

1	Direct capital stock of foreign affiliates at book value in 1982 as a proportion of:	
	a GNP at factor cost	10.92
	b population (in US $ per head)	62.23
2	Employment in foreign affiliates in 1977 as a percentage of all employment in all industry	0.75
3	Output of foreign affiliates in 1974 as a percentage of all companies' output in secondary (ie manufacturing) industry	27.0[1]
4	Foreign investment as a percentage of domestic investment, 1978-80	0.9
5	Percentage share of value added accounted for by foreign affiliates in selected sectors, 1974	
		Value Added
	Manufacturing Sector	
	Food & drink[2]	11.0
	Chemicals & allied	40.0
	Metals[3]	81.0
	Mechanical engineering	14.0
	Electrical equipment	59.0
	Motor vehicles	34.0
	Textiles & clothing[4]	24.0
	Paper & allied	28.0
	Rubber	21.0
	Stone, glass & clay[5]	71.0
	Timber & furniture	2.0
	Other manufacturing	57.0

Source:

Kirchbach, *op cit.;* V N Balasubramanyam, 'Factor Proportions and Productive Efficiency of Foreign Owned Firms in the Indonesian Manufacturing Sector', *Bulletin of Indonesian Economic Studies,* vol XX, no 3, December 1984; Bank of Indonesia, *op cit.*; IMF, *International Financial Statistics Yearbook 1984.*

NOTES TO TABLE A8

1 Represents share of value added accounted for by foreign firms in the manufacturing industry.
2 Represents food alone. For beverages, foreign share of value-added is 58%.
3 Represents non-ferrous metals. For metal products, foreign share of value added is 24%.
4 Represents textiles alone. For clothing, foreign share of value added is 8%.
5 Represents glass and glass products. For cement, foreign share of value added is 7%.

Table A12

LEADING FOREIGN MULTINATIONAL COMPANIES, 1983

Name	*Home Country*	*Sector*
AEG - Telefunken AG	W. Germany	Electrical engineering
Allied - Lyons PLC	UK	Food and drink
B A T Industries PLC	UK	Tobacco
BICC PLC	UK	Electrical energy
Bristol - Myers Company	USA	Pharmaceuticals
Ciba-Geigy AG	Switzerland	Chemicals
Compagnie Francaise des Petroles SA	France	Petroleum
Daimler - Benz AG	W. Germany	Motor vehicles
The Dow Chemical Co	USA	Chemicals
Union Carbide Corporation	USA	Chemicals
E I Du Pont de Nemours and Company	USA	Chemicals and fibres
Goodyear Tire and Rubber Co	USA	Rubber Tyres
The Heineken Group	Netherlands	Beer
Johnson & Johnson	USA	Health care products
Nestle SA	Switzerland	Food products
Petrofina SA	Belgium	Petroleum/petrochemicals
Pfizer Incorporated	USA	Pharmaceuticals
NV Philips Gloeilampenfabricken	Netherlands	Electrotechnical equipment
Philips Petroleum Company	USA	Petroleum
Roche/Sapae Group	Switzerland	Pharmaceuticals
Royal Dutch/Shell Group of Companies	Netherlands/UK	Petroleum
Sanduik AB	Sweden	Engineering
Texaco Incorporated	USA	Petroleum
Unilever	UK/Netherlands	Consumer products
Union Oil Company	USA	Petroleum

Source:
John M Stopford, *The World Directory of Multinational Enterprises 1982-83,* Bath: The Pitman Press, 1982

INDONESIA: DEFINITIONS

Official data on the level of foreign direct investment in Indonesia are available only for approved foreign investment. Foreign investment approvals exclude investment undertaken prior to the introduction of the investment promotion programme as well as investments by non-promoted direct foreign investment firms. Moreover, since some approved foreign investment projects are never actually implemented, approved investment figures overstate the actual investment. Foreign capital investment actually implemented as at March 1983 represented only 38.4% of total approved foreign capital investment since 1967.

Moreover, official data on foreign investment in Indonesia refer only to those sectors which are covered by the 1967 Law on Foreign Investment, thus omitting direct investment in the energy sector and in banking and insurance. Foreign investment in the energy sector accounts for as much as 62% of the total foreign direct investment in Indonesia. The inclusion of foreign investment in energy would greatly increase the recorded capital inflows by about two-thirds, as well as alter the relative importance of individual investors. With the exclusion of oil, Japan appears to be twice as important as the USA but in reality, total US investment in Indonesia is nearly six times that of Japan.

Furthermore, official data hides the fact that a majority of the investment projects from newly industrialising economies in the ESCAP region and developing East Asian economies come from economies with a Chinese majority or a large Chinese population: Hong Kong, Singapore, Taiwan and Malaysia. There has been some suspicion that a significant part of investment from these countries comes from Indonesian Chinese capital; such capital is chanelled via these countries to take advantage of the facilities and incentives available to foreign but not domestic private investment in Indonesia.

Source:
'Indonesia', by Dr Dorodjatun Kuntjoro-Jakti in Patterns and Impact of Foreign Investment in the ESCAP Region, Thailand: UN, 1985.

SOUTH KOREA

Prospects for increased foreign direct investment are of particular interest in the context of South Korea's efforts to reduce its foreign borrowing. In the past, foreign direct investment in Korea has not been very significant, averaging only 5% of total long-term capital inflows over the last 20 years. In recent years, with the share increase in Korea's borrowing abroad and inward direct investment stable at about US $ 100 million a year, this proportion has been even lower — about 3.5% in 1978-82. A major reason for this low level of FDI has been the many constraints imposed by the Korean government. Realising the need to encourage the inflow of advanced technology, Korean authorities began to relax some restrictions in 1981 and 1982. On a government approvals basis, FDI increased by 30% in 1982 and 43% in 1983 to reach US $ 268 million. This growth however was not reflected in actual investment, which remained essentially unchanged in 1981-83. Furthermore, a large part of this recent surge in approvals represented investment in the tourism sector (primarily hotels) rather than the high-technology industries the authorities would like to attract.

In September 1983, the Korean government announced a series of significant revisions of FDI regulations. A new Foreign Capital Inducement Act was passed by the National Assembly in December to take effect 1 July 1984. The *positive list* system that specifies industries in which FDI is permitted is to be replaced by a *negative list* which should greatly simplify approval procedures in many instances. Restrictions on withdrawal of original equity and the reinvestment of retained earnings are also being eased. Even with these changes, however, the investment climate in South Korea does not compare with that of the open economies of its chief competitors, namely Hong Kong and Taiwan.

Data on the geographical distribution of investment show that inward investment is substantially accounted for by the developed countries, particularly Japan and North America, while for outward investment, Asia and the Pacific is a major growth area.

Most inward investment is concentrated upon manufacturing, although, whereas a decade ago the textile industry was the most significant, particular emphasis now lies on the chemical and electrical equipment industries (including electronics), with textiles having a less important role. Although a generally rising trend is apparent, outward foreign investment by Korea began on a small scale in the late 1960s and did not substantially increase until 1974 when significant investment was made in manufacturing industries. Two further important areas of outward foreign investment have been construction and trade (particularly in banking and finance).

MAIN SOURCES OF DATA:

A Official

1 Ministry of Finance: provides data on investment flows and their geographical and industrial distribution.

B Private

1 Bohn-Young Koo, 'Industrial Structure and Foreign Investment: A case study of their Interelationship for Korea', Korea Development Institute, 1983.

2 Bohn-Young Koo, 'Outward Investment by Korean Firms: Their Forms and Characteristics', paper presented at OECD meeting, Paris, June 1984.

3 Bohn-Young Koo, 'Role of Foreign Direct Investment in Korea's Recent Economic Growth', Korea Development Institute, 1983.

4 Bohn-Young Koo, 'Korea', in J H Dunning (Ed), *Multinational Enterprises, Economic Structure & International Competitiveness,* Chichester: John Wiley & Sons, 1985.

Table A1

SUMMARY OF THE COUNTRY'S INTERNATIONAL INVESTMENT POSITION

		Inward Investment	Outward Investment
1	Number of foreign affiliates in host country, and of foreign affiliates of home country firms at the end of 1982	881	343
2	Number of foreign firms with direct investments in host country, and home country firms with direct foreign affiliates	*N.A.*	*N.A.*
3	Total foreign direct capital stock at book value as a percentage of GNP at factor cost in 1983	1.87	0.51
4	Flow of foreign direct investment in the five year period, 1978-82 (US $m)	530.1	256.8
5	Employment in foreign affiliates or abroad, 1982	315,000	10,475
6	Output of foreign affiliates or abroad	*N.A.*	*N.A.*

Source:
Bohn-Young Koo, *op cit*

Table A2

PRIVATE FOREIGN CAPITAL STOCK, 1962 - 83 (US $ m)[1]

	Inward Investment			Outward Investment		
	Portfolio	*Direct*	*Total*	*Portfolio*	*Direct*	*Total*
Book value of capital stock						
1962	*Not Available*	0.6	*Not Available*	*Not Available*	*N.A.*	*Not Available*
1965		16.5			*N.A.*	
1970		81.0			25.0	
1975		569.1			49.6	
1976		674.7			56.5	
1977		768.1			68.9	
1978		851.0			107.6	
1979		887.2			126.4	
1980		895.0			141.9	
1981		996.4			173.6	
1982		1,143.2			289.6	
1983		1,269.3			386.4	
1984		1,381.0			423.3	

Source:

Bohn-Young Koo, *op cit.*

NOTES TO TABLE A2

1 Based on cumulative investment flows.

Table A3

FLOW OF FOREIGN DIRECT INVESTMENT, 1970 - 83 (US $m)

	Inward Investment			Outward Investment		
	Reinvested Profits	*Other*	*Total*	*Reinvested Profits*	*Other*	*Total* [1]
1970	0.6 (1970–71)	61.4 (1970–71)	25.3			7.5
1971			36.7			6.9
1972	0.3	60.9	61.2			5.1
1973	1.1	157.3	158.4			3.9
1974	3.4	159.2	162.6			23.1
1975	0.6	68.6	69.2			9.2
1976	0.9	104.7	105.6	*Not Separately Available*		8.2
1977			93.4			21.0
1978			82.9			27.5
1979			36.2			19.4
1980	*Not Separately Available*		7.8			13.0
1981			101.4			42.4
1982			146.8			68.4
1983			126.1			126.1
1984			111.7			36.9

Source:

Bohn-Young Koo, *op cit;* Bohn-Young Koo, in J H Dunning (Ed), *Multinational Enterprises, Economic Structure and International Competitiveness,* Chichester: John Wiley, 1985.

NOTES TO TABLE A3

1 Excluding reinvested profits.

Table A4

SECTORAL DISTRIBUTION OF FOREIGN DIRECT CAPITAL STOCK, 1963 - 83 (US $m)[1]

	Inward Investment			Outward Investment		
	Primary	*Secondary*	*Tertiary*	*Primary*	*Secondary*	*Tertiary*
1963	*N.A.*	7.50	*N.A.*		*Not Available*	
1968	0.40	44.58	5.22			
1973	1.70	311.20	26.10	10.3	0.2	11.3
1977	12.32	626.02	136.67	21.1	13.4	34.4
1978	13.10	693.93	168.39	25.4	19.4	62.8
1980	14.51	827.11	257.10	31.6	25.0	85.3
1982	15.81	1,004.31	284.15	149.4	33.5	106.7
1983	16.13	1,072.73	316.62	210.5	59.0	116.9

Source:

Bohn-Young Koo, *op cit*

NOTES TO TABLE A4

1 Figures for sectoral distribution of investment, except for 1983, do not match table A2 due to an unallocated component. They represent cumulative investment flows.

Table A5

GEOGRAPHICAL DISTRIBUTION OF FOREIGN DIRECT CAPITAL STOCK, 1962 - 83 (US $m)[1]

	Inward Investment			Outward Investment		
	Developed Countries	*Developing Countries*	*Total*	*Developed Countries*	*Developing Countries*	*Total*
1962-76	604.24	70.42	674.66		*Not Available*	
1977	696.70	80.25	776.95	36.96	46.45	83.41
1979	894.30	110.08	1,004.38	108.56	71.10	180.66
1980	990.02	110.99	1,101.01	122.93	80.90	203.83
1982	1,187.66	119.40	1,307.06	226.97	133.03	360.00
1983	1,273.33	135.16	1,408.49	239.12	147.26	386.38

Source:

Ministry of Finance, *Annual Report,* various years; Bohn-Young Koo, 'Outward Investments by Korean Firms', *op cit.*

NOTES TO TABLE A5

1 Based on cumulative investment flows.

Table A6

INDUSTRIAL DISTRIBUTION OF FOREIGN DIRECT CAPITAL STOCK, 1968 - 83 (US $ m)[1]

	Inward Investment		Outward Investment	
	1973	*1983*	*1968-77*	*1968-82*
Primary	1.70	19.14	25.41	150.27
Agriculture[2]	1.70	16.13	25.41	47.26
Mining & quarrying		3.01	*N.S.A.*	103.01
Oil	*N.S.A.*	*N.S.A.*	*N.S.A.*	*N.S.A.*
Secondary	311.20	1,072.73	7.58	33.45
Food & drink	5.76	29.79	1.60	1.60
Chemicals & allied[3]	40.34	342.86	*N.S.A.*	9.21
Metals	16.61	66.84	1.22	3.72
Mechanical engineering	11.87	107.30	*Not Separately Available*	0.55
Electrical equipment[4]	43.73	207.72		1.10
Motor vehicles	25.09	55.64		*N.S.A.*
Other transportation equipment	1.02			*N.S.A.*
Textiles & clothing	83.39	136.31		1.55
Paper & allied	4.07	*N.S.A.*	1.41	1.41
Rubber	17.97	*N.S.A.*	0.54	*N.S.A.*
Stone, clay & glass[5]	14.92	20.09	1.76	5.87
Coal & petroleum products	35.26	63.28	*N.S.A.*	*N.S.A.*
Other manufacturing	11.19	42.92	1.05	8.45
Tertiary	26.10	316.62	41.40	85.74
Construction	*N.S.A.*	79.87	4.45	30.43
Transport & communications[6]	2.03	26.22	1.70	2.74
Distributive trade	*N.S.A.*	*N.S.A.*	*N.S.A.*	*N.S.A.*
Property	*N.S.A.*	*N.S.A.*	*N.S.A.*	*N.S.A.*
Banking & finance	11.87	49.01	21.61	36.66
Other services	12.20	161.53	13.64	15.91
TOTAL	339.00	1,408.49	74.39	269.46

Source:

Bohn-Young Koo, 'Industrial Structure and Foreign Investment, *op cit;* Ministry of Finance, *Annual Report,* various years.

NOTES TO TABLE A6

1 Calculations based on cumulative foreign direct investment, and do not match Tables A2 and A5 (except for 1983) due to an unallocated component.

2 Including fishery & forestry.

3 Represents synthetic resins, rubber products and other chemical products.

4 Including electronic and communication equipment.

5 Represents non-metallic mineral products.

6 Including warehousing.

Table A7

LEADING SOURCE AND RECIPIENT COUNTRIES, 1962 - 83 (US $ m)[1]

	Inward Investment		Outward Investment	
	1962-76	*1962-82*	*1977*	*1983*
DEVELOPED AREAS	604.24	1,187.66	36.96	239.12
Europe	30.41	140.30		9.30
EEC of which:	29.79	123.91		8.77
Belgium & Luxembourg	*N.S.A.*	9.79		0.05
France	5.73	13.99		2.00
W. Germany	4.71	19.67		4.08
Italy	1.25	1.25		
Netherlands	14.93	56.39		0.36
UK	3.17	22.82	*Not*	2.28
Other Europe of which:	0.63	16.39	*Separately*	0.53
Lichtenstein	0.47	0.59	*Available*	
Portugal	*N.S.A.*	*N.S.A.*		0.28
Spain	*N.S.A.*	*N.S.A.*		0.25
Switzerland	0.16	15.80		
North America of which:	132.32	374.37		164.08
Canada	0.13	0.18		60.64
USA	136.19	374.19		103.44
Other developed countries of which:	437.51	672.99		65.74
Australia	*N.S.A.*	*N.S.A.*		45.14
Japan	437.51	672.99		19.18
New Zealand	*N.S.A.*	*N.S.A.*		1.42
DEVELOPING COUNTRIES	70.42	119.40	46.45	147.26
Africa of which:				17.79
Egypt				0.26
Gabon				2.87
Moritanio	*Not*	*Not*		5.00
Morocco	*Separately*	*Separately*		0.34
Nigeria	*Available*	*Available*		1.37
Senegal			*Not*	0.08
Sudan			*Separately*	7.88
Asia & Pacific of which:	3.95	20.92	*Available*	95.16
Bangladesh	*Not*	*Not*		0.14
Brunei	*Separately*	*Separately*		0.01
Guani	*Available*	*Available*		2.68
Hong Kong	3.86	20.48		4.82
India	*N.S.A.*	*N.S.A.*		0.12

Table A7 (cont'd)

LEADING SOURCE AND RECIPIENT COUNTRIES, 1962 - 83 (US $ m)[1]

	Inward Investment		Outward Investment	
	1962-76	*1962-82*	*1977*	*1983*
DEVELOPING AREAS (cont'd)				
Indonesia	*Not Available*	*Not Available*		39.72
Malaysia				14.67
Pakistan				19.50
Papua New Guinea				2.07
Philippines				3.96
Samoa	0.09	0.44		0.46
Singapore	*Not Available*	*Not Available*		3.18
Solomon Islands				0.72
Thailand				3.12
Latin America of which:	46.49	53.83		6.54
Argentina	*N.S.A.*	*N.S.A.*		0.01
Bahamas	13.33	13.33		*Not Available*
Barbados	*N.S.A.*	*N.S.A.*		
Bermuda	10.25	15.01		
Chile	*Not Available*	*Not Available*	*Not Separately Available*	2.50
Dominico				0.45
Equador				0.16
Honduras				0.06
Mexico				0.05
Panama	22.90	25.49		2.99
Puerto Rico	*Not Available*	*Not Available*		0.20
Surinam				0.06
Trinidad & Tobago				0.07
Middle East of which:	4.12	21.20		27.77
Iran	4.12	12.40		0.26
Kuwait	*Not Available*	6.21		0.36
Qatar		*N.S.A.*		0.20
Saudi Arabia		2.59		26.85
United Arab Emirates		*N.S.A.*		0.10
UNSPECIFIED	15.87	23.45		*N.S.A.*
TOTAL	674.66	1,307.06	83.41	386.38

Source:
Ministry of Finance, *Annual Reports,* various years.

NOTES TO TABLE A7

1 Based on cumulative investment flows.

Table A8

INDICATORS OF THE SIGNIFICANCE OF INWARD FOREIGN DIRECT INVESTMENT OR THE ACTIVITIES OF FOREIGN-BASED COMPANIES TO THE NATIONAL ECONOMY, 1978 - 83

1	Direct capital stock of foreign affiliates at book value in 1983 as a proportion of:	
	a GNP at factor cost	1.87
	b population (in US $ per head)	35.26
2	Investment in foreign affiliates by OECD countries as a percentage of domestic investment 1978 - 80	–0.2
3	Employment in foreign affiliates in 1978 as a percentage of all employment	
	a in all industry	2.3
	b in manufacturing	9.5
4	Output of foreign affiliates in 1978 as a percentage of all companies' output in secondary (ie, manufacturing) industry	19.3
5	Exports of foreign affiliates in 1978 as a percentage of all manufacturing exports	24.6

Source:
Bohn-Young Koo, *Role of Foreign Direct Investment in Recent Korean Economic Growth,* Korean Development Institute, 1983.

NOTES TO TABLE A8

There are no up to date data on foreign participation in particular sectors of Korean industry. However, a survey conducted by the *Economic Planning Board* of Korea in 1974 revealed that foreign owned firms accounted for 22% of the employment in the chemical industry, 37% of the output in the iron and steel industry and 19% of the output of the non-electrical machinery industry in 1970.

Table A9

INDICATORS OF THE SIGNIFICANCE OF OUTWARD FOREIGN DIRECT INVESTMENT OR THE ACTIVITIES OF HOME-BASED COMPANIES ABROAD FOR THE NATIONAL ECONOMY, 1978 - 83

1	Foreign capital stock of home-based firms at book value in 1983 as a proportion of:		
	a	GNP at factor cost	0.51
	b	population (in $ per head)	9.67
2	Employment in foreign affiliates in 1978 as a percentage of domestic employment		
	a	in all industry	0.08
	b	in manufacturing	0.32

Source:
Bohn-Young Koo, *op. cit.*

Table A10

DISTRIBUTION OF FOREIGN SUBSIDIARIES AND ASSOCIATES AND FOREIGN CAPITAL STOCK BY PERCENTAGE OWNERSHIP OF PARENT COMPANIES, 1983

	Inward Investment[1]		Outward Investment	
	Number of Affiliates	*Value of Capital Stock (US $ m)*	*Number of Affiliates*	*Value of Capital Stock (US $ m)*
100% owned subsidiaries	123	369.5	250	272.0
50-99.9% owned subsidiaries and associates	334	568.1	72	73.7
Less than 50% owned subsidiaries and associates	365	284.2	79	40.7
TOTAL	822	1,221.8	401	386.4

Source:
Eul Y Park, *Pattern of Foreign Direct Investment, Foreign Ownership and Industrial Performance;* Ministry of Finance, *Annual Report,* various issues.

NOTES TO TABLE A10

1 Represents 1962-80.

Table A11

ROYALTY RECEIPTS AND PAYMENTS, 1972 - 82 (US $ m)

	Payments			Receipts		
	To Affiliates	*To Non-affiliates*	*Total*	*From Affiliates*	*From Non-affiliates*	*Total*
1972			7.51			
1973			13.65			
1974			17.89			
1975			25.26			
1976	*Not*		39.86			
1977	*Separately*		66.86		*Not Available*	
1978	*Available*		77.55			
1979			93.93			
1980			107.23			
1981			107.10			
1982			115.69			

Source:
Bohn-Young Koo, *Industrial Structure and Foreign Investment,* 1983.

Table A12

LEADING FOREIGN AND DOMESTIC MULTINATIONAL COMPANIES

A Leading Foreign Multinational Companies in the Country, 1982

	Name	*Home Country*	*Sector*	*S. Korean Turnover (US $m)*
1	Hotel Lotte	Japan	Hotel	149.67
2	Honam Oil Refinery	Bahamas	Oil refining	59.83
3	Daewoo Motor	USA	Motor vehicles	43.19
4	Honam Petrochemical	Japan	Petrochemicals	41.41
5	Poongsan Metal	Japan	Metal	39.84
6	Korea Long-term Credit Bank	World Bank, etc	Banking	22.06
7	Korea Petrochemical	Japan	Petrochemicals	21.59
8	Lotte Construction	Japan	Construction	19.79
9	Namhae Chemical	Panama	Fertilizers	17.50
10	Fairchild Semiconductor (Korea)	Hong Kong	Semiconductors	17.48
11	Union Gas	USA	Gas	16.70
12	IBM Korea	USA	Computer services	15.97
13	Samsung Petrochemicals	USA	Petrochemicals	15.72
14	Lotte Ham & Milk	Japan	Food	14.71
15	Facom Korea	Japan	Computer services	14.63
16	Yongnam Chemical	USA	Fertilizers	13.00
17	Hansea Food	Switzerland	Food	12.38
18	Motorola Korea	USA	Semiconductors	12.10
19	Samsung Corning	USA	Electrical equipment	11.52
20	Taesung Methanol	Japan	Methanol	10.53
21	Chinhae Chemical	USA	Fertilizers	10.50
22	Korea Merchant Banking	UK	Banking	10.41
23	Kyung In Energy	USA	Oil refining	10.25
24	Hanjin Container Lines	Bermuda	Shipping	10.03
25	Korean French Banking	France	Banking	9.65

Table A12 (cont'd)

LEADING FOREIGN AND DOMESTIC MULTINATIONAL COMPANIES

B Leading Domestic Companies with Multinational Interests, 1982

	Name	*Sector*	*Global Turnover (US $m)*
1	Pohang Iron & Steel	Mining	136.26
2	Halla Resources	Forestry	20.10
3	Korea Heavy Industries & Construction	Cement	13.11
4	Korean Air	Real Estate	10.27
5	Daewoo Corporation	Tyres, trade	10.26
6	Korea Development Company	Forestry, plywood	9.84
7	Samsung Company	Trade	8.01
8	Dongwha Enterprises	Forestry	7.53
9	You One Construction	Forestry	6.96
10	YMCA	Real Estate	6.54
11	Keang Nam Enterprises	Construction	6.20
12	Korea Trade Association	Real Estate	6.14
13	Hyundai Corporation	Mining, trade	6.08
14	Ahju Forestry	Forestry	5.26
15	Hyundai Wood Industry	Forestry, furniture	5.23
16	Hyundai Electronics	Electronics	5.00
17	Atlantic Industrial	Fishery	5.00
18	Daesung Consolidated Coal Mining	Mining	4.93
19	Hyundai Engineering & Construction	Construction	3.38
20	Hanni Industrial	Forestry	3.28
21	Ssangyong Corporation	Trade	3.09
22	Kukje Corporation	Trade	3.02
23	Samsung Semiconductor & Telecommunication	Electronics	3.00
24	Ssangyong Cement Industrial	Cement	2.98
25	Namkwang Engineering & Construction	Construction	2.98

Source:
Korea Development Institute, unpublished data.

KOREA: DEFINITIONS

The Economic Planning Board of Korea gives cumulative data on the annual distribution of foreign investors by ownership patterns as from 1962. The data indicate the number and amount of foreign investment. The amount refers to the initial amount of investment approved. An industrial and geographical distribution of such foreign investment by ownership pattern is also provided.

The Economic Planning Board also gives data on the amount of investment arrived which may differ from approved data because of cancellations before arrival and the different timing of arrival from approval. The amount of investments that are withdrawn are also provided as well as reinvestments. Reinvestments here refer to reinvestments from both dividends and reassessment of assets. The total remaining amount of investment refers tothe cumulative total equity capital operating in Korea, subtracting withdrawn investments and adding reinvestments to the arrived investments.

The *Ministry of Finance* gives data on cumulative arrived and approved foreign equity investments as well as number of projects by country and industry as from 1962. The Ministry also gives distribution of FDI inflow by industries based on total approved amount.

The *Bank of Korea* gives data on the trend of outward investment by Korean firms by number of projects approved and by amount as from 1968. These investment data include both equity and loans. Moreover, investments in pure real estate is excluded from the data. The Bank also gives industrial distribution of outward investments both by number and by amount.

Source:

The Economic Planning Board, Korea; Ministry of Finance of Korea; Bank of Korea.

MALAYSIA

Statistics on foreign direct investment in Malaysia are restricted to inflows of foreign investment and approved foreign investment in manufacturing. Figures for approved foreign investment in manufacturing overstate actual investments because not all projects approved are implemented.

Between 1978 and 1982, a total number of 3,855 domestic and foreign manufacturing projects were approved, of which 79% were implemented and 7% were in production at the end of 1979. Applications for investment projects rose from 392 in 1976 to 614 in 1980. In 1980, approvals were granted to 460 projects.

The major sources of foreign investment at the end of 1979 were Japan, Singapore, the UK, the USA, and Hong Kong. Singapore, Japan and the UK accounted for about 62% of total foreign investment in Malaysian manufacturing in 1979. By the end of 1983, these three countries contributed about 66% of the stock of foreign investment. Data on the industrial distribution of foreign direct investment in Malaysia show that the electrical and electronic as well as textile industries figured prominently in the late 1970s as recipients of foreign investment, accounting for 35% of foreign investment flows into pioneer industries in 1979. However, at the end of 1983, these two industries accounted for only 22% of total foreign capital investment, both paid-up capital and loans. In terms of fixed assets, textiles and electronics contributed 29% of foreign fixed assets in Malaysia. Other industries of importance to foreign investors include food manufacturing, non-metallic mineral products, chemicals and chemical products, beverages and tobacco and basic metal products which together account for 48% of total foreign capital investments.

The industrial distribution of foreign direct investment reflects the general pattern of private investment in manufacturing in Malaysia. Over the years, the sectoral distribution has changed in line with the emphasis given by the government to industrial development. In the initial phase of industrialisation, private investment in manufacturing mainly occurred in import-substituting consumer goods industries. With the shift in emphasis in the early 1970s towards the promotion of export-oriented industries, private investment in labour-intensive and resource-based industries increased both in magnitude and share in of the total manufacturing investment. The major industries in this category were textiles, electrical and electronic goods, rubber and wood products. There were also significant increases in private investment in import substituting industries which include ferrous and non-ferrous metals, non-metallic mineral products, machinery and transport equipment. However, the relative importance of foreign investment in all sectors has declined markedly over the last 10 years.

It was not until the mid-1970s that Malaysia began to have its own MNEs. This internationalization process came about through a nationalization program in which the Malaysian government through its state corporations began to acquire foreign companies operating in Malaysia particularly those in the tin and rubber industries. This process was soon followed by Malaysian private companies. Thus, Malaysian capital, both state and private, increasingly in partnership, began to own some of the largest TNCs in Southeast Asia. Twenty-four Malaysian MNEs have 153 overseas ventures with more than two thirds located in Asia, notably Singapore and Hong Kong. The UK is also a significant recipient, and is host to 21 overseas affiliates. There are also 17 overseas ventures in other ASEAN countries and only 14 in Australia. Malaysian MNEs are mostly concentrated in non-manufacturing activities, with only 15% of their foreign ventures engaged in manufacturing. The largest number of Malaysian overseas ventures are concentrated in the trading sector, followed by investment companies. There has also been significant investments in the mining sector.

MAIN SOURCES OF DATA:

A **Official**

1 Malaysian Industrial Development Authority (MIDA) unpublished statistics on foreign investment.

2 ESCAP/UNCTC *Transnational Corporation from Developing Asian Regions,* Bangkok: UN, 1985.

B **Private**

1 Mohamed Ariff and Chee Peng Lim, 'Foreign Investment in Malaysia', paper submitted to the Commonwealth Secretariat, London, October 1984.

2 Friedrich von Kirchback, 'Economic Policies towards TNCs: The Experience of ASEAN countries', PhD theses, University of Regensburg, July 1981, and 'TNCs in the ASEAN region: A Survey of the Major Issues' in Economic Bulletin for Asia and Pacific, vol 33, no 1.

3 Mah Hui Lim, 'Survey of Activities of Transnational Corporations from Asian Developing Countries', paper submitted to the ESCAP/UNCTC Joint Unit on Transnational Corporations, Bangkok: UN, March 1984.

4 Tan Siew Ee and M Kulasingan, *New Forms of International Investment; the Malaysian Experience,* Paris: OECD, 1984.

5 J K Sundavam and Tan Boon Kean, 'Malaysia', in Economic and Social Commission for Asia and the Pacific, *Patterns and Impact of Foreign Investment in the ESCAP Region,* Bangkok, 1985.

Note:
Data do not allow us to complete Table A9 for Malaysia.

Table A1

SUMMARY OF THE COUNTRY'S INTERNATIONAL INVESTMENT POSITION

		Inward Investment	Outward Investment
1	Number of foreign affiliates in host country, and of foreign affiliates of home country firms at the end of 1981	537	153[1]
2	Number of foreign firms with direct investments in host country, and home country firms with direct foreign affiliates at the end of 1982	898[2]	24[1]
3	Total foreign direct capital stock at book value as a percentage of GNP at at factor cost in 1984	29.59	0.07[3]
4	Flow of foreign direct investment in the five year period, 1980-84 (M $ m)	13,574.6	*N.A.*
5	Employment in foreign affiliates or abroad, 1975	236.580[4]	*N.A.*
6	Output of foreign affiliates or abroad, 1975 (M $ m)	14,451.6	*N.A.*

Source:
Friedrich von Kirchbach, *Economic Policies towards TNCs: The Experience of ASEAN countries,* PhD theses, University of Regensburg, July 1981, and *TNCs in the ASEAN region: A Survey of the Major Issues,* in Economic Bulletin for Asia and Pacific, vol 33, no 1: Stopford and Dunning, *Multinationals: Company Performance and Global Trends,* London: Macmillan, 1983; Sundavam and Tan Boong Kean *op cit.;* Ee and Kulasingan, *op cit.;* Mah Hui Lim, *op cit.;* IMF, *International Financial Statistics Yearbook 1985* and *Balance of Payments Statistics Yearbook*, various issues.

NOTES TO TABLE A1

1 Of 24 Malaysian MNEs in 1982 identified by ESCAP/UNCTC, 1985.
2 Represents 1977.
3 Represents 1982.
4 Represents employment in foreign-controlled limited companies.

Table A2

PRIVATE FOREIGN CAPITAL STOCK, 1971 - 84 (M $ m)

	Inward Investment				Outward Investment		
	Portfolio	*Direct*	*Total*		*Portfolio*	*Direct*	*Total*
Book value of capital stock							
1971		2539.7					
1975		5953.1				*Not*	
1978	*Not*	6353.3	*Not*			*Available*	
1981	*Available*	12558.2	*Available*				
1982		*N.A.*			*N.A.*	41.1[1]	*N.A.*
1984		21183.3				*N.A.*	

Source:

IMF, *Balance of Payments Statistics Yearbook*, various issues; Mah Hui Lim, "Survey of Activities of Transnational Corporations from Asian Developing Countries", paper submitted to the ESCAP/UNCTC Joint Unit on Transnational Corporations, Bangkok, March, 1984.

NOTES TO TABLE A2

1 Represents stock of direct overseas investment to Indonesia, Thailand, Sri Lanka and the Philippines only.

Table A3

FLOW OF FOREIGN DIRECT INVESTMENT, 1970 - 84 (M $ m)

	Inward Investment				Outward Investment		
	Reinvested Profits	*Other*	*Total*		*Reinvested Profits*	*Other*	*Total*
1970			287.8				
1971			395.3				
1972			402.7				
1973			487.8				
1974			604.2				
1975			748,3				
1976	*Not*		890.3				
1977	*Separately*		1,000.0			*Not*	
1978	*Available*		1,157.0			*Available*	
1979			1,255.4				
1980			2,034.3				
1981			2,915.2				
1982			3,264.1				
1983			3,059.6				
1984			2,301.4				

Source:

IMF, *Balance of Payments Statistics Yearbook*, various issues; Ali and Osman-Rani, data as cited in Mohamed Ariff and Chee Peng Lim, "Foreign Investment in Malaysia", paper submitted to the Commonwealth Secretariat, London, October 1984.

Table A4

SECTORAL DISTRIBUTION OF FOREIGN DIRECT CAPITAL STOCK, 1982 - 83 (M $ m)

	Inward Investment				Outward Investment[1]		
	Primary	*Secondary*	*Tertiary*		*Primary*	*Secondary*	*Tertiary*
1982	*Not Available*				9	22	121
1983	*N.A.*	3,848.1[2]	212.6[2]		*Not Available*		

Source:
Arift and Lim, *op cit;* data taken from Anuwar Ali and Osman-Rani (1984); Mah Hui Lim, *op cit.*

NOTES TO TABLE A4

1 Represents number of affiliates.

2 Refers to foreign investment into "Pioneer" industries as classified under the Investment Incentive Scheme of Malaysia. This represents only a limited component of total FDI in Malaysia, thus the total does not match Table A2.

Table A5

GEOGRAPHICAL DISTRIBUTION OF FOREIGN DIRECT CAPITAL STOCK, 1982 - 83 (M $ m)

	Inward Investment[1]				Outward Investment[4]		
	Developed Countries	*Developing Countries*	*Total*		*Developed Countries*	*Developing Countries*	*Total*
1982	*Not Available*				43	109	152
1983	1,824.0[2]	1,781.5[2]	18,540.8[3]		*Not Available*		

Source:
Ariff and Lim, *op cit;* data provided by Malaysian Industrial Development Authority; Mah Hui Lim, *op cit.*

NOTES TO TABLE A5

1 Figures represent stock of foreign capital investment in companies in production as from 31 December 1983 calculated from unpublished data provided by MIDA.

2 Represents only foreign investment into "Pioneer" industries as classified under the Investment Incentive Scheme of Malaysia. This represents only a limited component of total FDI in Malaysia.

3 Cumulative investment flow, 1968-83.

4 Number of affiliates in 1982.

Table A6

INDUSTRIAL DISTRIBUTION OF FOREIGN DIRECT CAPITAL STOCK, 1982 - 83 (M $ m)

	Inward Investment	Outward Investment
	1983[1]	*No. of affiliates 1982*
Primary		9
Agriculture & forestry	*Not*	3
Mining & quarrying	*Available*	6
Oil		–
Secondary	3,484.1	22
Food & drink	983.9	
Chemicals & allied	327.3	
Metals	388.3	
Mechanical engineering	63.7	
Electrical equipment	394.1	*Not*
Other transportation equipment	194.2	*Separately*
Textiles & clothing	507.7[2]	*Available*
Paper & allied	29.0	
Rubber	129.7[3]	
Stone, clay & glass	401.6	
Coal & petroleum products	124.5	
Other manufacturing	304.1	
Tertiary	212.6	121
Construction		3
Transport & communications	*Not*	4
Distributive trade	*Separately*	42
Property	*Available*	14
Banking & finance		35
Other services	212.6[4]	23
TOTAL	4,060.7	152

Source:
Ariff and Lim, *op cit;* from Anuwar Ali and Osman-Rani, 1984; Mah Hui Lim, *op cit.*

NOTES TO TABLE A6

1 Figures represent foreign investment in "Pioneer" industries of Malaysia in those years. Pioneer industries are those industries which enjoy pioneer status under the investment incentives scheme. This represents only a limited component of total FDI in Malaysia, thus the total does not match Table A2.

2 Including leather.

3 Including plastics.

4 Represents tourism.

Table A7

LEADING SOURCE AND RECIPIENT COUNTRIES, 1982 - 83 (M $ m)

	Inward Investment[1]	Outward Investment
	1983	*No. of affiliates 1982*
DEVELOPED AREAS	1,824.0	43[2]
Europe	806.1	*N.S.A.*
EEC of which:		21
W. Germany	109.3	*Not*
Netherlands	52.0	*Separately*
UK	644.8	*Available*
North America of which:	227.3	4
USA	227.3	*N.S.A.*
Other developed countries of which:	790.6	18
Australia	86.9	13
Japan	703.7	2
DEVELOPING AREAS	1,781.5	109
Asia & Pacific of which:	1,781.5	21
Hong Kong	372.7	16
India	57.4	
Indonesia	*N.A.*	*Not*
S. Korea	1.5	*Separately*
Philippines	*N.A.*	*Available*
Singapore	1,336.6	58
Sri Lanka	*N.A.*	*Not*
Taiwan	13.3	*Separately*
Thailand	*N.A.*	*Available*
UNSPECIFIED	455.2	
TOTAL	4,060.7	152

Source:
Ariff and Lim, *op cit;* based on calculations from unpublished data from MIDA; Mah Hui Lim, *op cit.*

NOTES TO TABLE A7

1 Figures represent foreign investment into "Pioneer" industries as classified under the Investment Incentive Scheme of Malaysia. This represents only a limited component of total FDI in Malaysia, thus the total does not match Table A2.

2 Including those not identified.

Table A8

INDICATORS OF THE SIGNIFICANCE OF INWARD FOREIGN DIRECT INVESTMENT OR THE ACTIVITIES OF FOREIGN-BASED COMPANIES TO THE NATIONAL ECONOMY, 1971 - 84

1	Direct capital stock of foreign affiliates at book value in 1984 as a proportion of:		
	a	GNP at factor cost	29.59
	b	population (in M $ per head)	1,394.55
2	Employmnet in foreign affiliates in 1975 as a percentage of all employment		
	a	in all industry	5.90
	b	in manufacturing	19.70
3	Output of foreign affiliates in 1975 as a percentage of all companies' output		
	a	in primary (ie, extractive) industry	8.50
	b	in secondary (ie. manufacturing) industry	39.80
	c	in tertiary industry (ie. services, etc)	28.70

4 Percentage share of output accounted for by foreign affiliates in selected sectors, 1971 and 1980.

	Output	
	1971	*1980*
Primary Goods Sector		
Mining & quarrying	40	7
Manufacturing Sector	50	40
Services Sector		
Wholesale trade	35	27
Retail trade	*N.A.*	10

Source:
Kirchbach, PhD Theses, *op cit;* Kirchbach, TNCs in the ASEAN region, *op cit;* Ariff and Lim, *op cit;* data taken from Anuwar Ali and Osman-Rani, 1984; Ee and Kulasingan.

Table A9

INDICATORS OF THE SIGNIFICANCE OF OUTWARD FOREIGN DIRECT INVESTMENT OR THE ACTIVITIES OF HOME-BASED COMPANIES ABROAD FOR THE NATIONAL ECONOMY, 1982

1	Foreign capital stock of home-based firms at book value in 1982 as a proportion of:	
	a GNP at factor cost	0.07
	b population (in M $ per head)	2.83

Source:
Mah Hui Lim, "Survey of Activities of Transnational Corporations from Asian Developing Countries", paper submitted to the ESCAP/UNCTC Joint Unit on Transnational Corporations, Bangkok, March 1984; IMF, *International Financial Statistics Yearbook*, various issues.

Table A10

DISTRIBUTION OF FOREIGN SUBSIDIARIES AND ASSOCIATES AND FOREIGN CAPITAL STOCK BY PERCENTAGE OWNERSHIP OF PARENT COMPANIES, 1981 (M $ m)

	Inward Investment		Outward Investment	
	Number of Affiliates	*Value of Capital Stock*	*Number of Affiliates*	*Value of Capital Stock*[1]
100% owned subsidiaires	*Not Available*		101	8,391.83
50–99.9% owned subsidiaries and associates			21	4,162.63
Less than 50% owned subsidiaries and associates			31	30.18
TOTAL			153	12584.64

Source:
Kirchbach; PhD theses, *op cit;* Stopford and Dunning, *op cit.*

NOTES TO TABLE A10

1 Converted from US dollars at the average exchange rate in 1981 of 2.3041 Malaysian dollars per US dollar.

Table A11

ROYALTY RECEIPTS AND PAYMENTS, 1979 - 81 (M $ m)

	Payments			Receipts		
	To Affiliates	*To Non-affiliates*	*Total*	*From Affiliates*	*From Non-affiliates*	*Total*
1979	*Not Separately Available*		48.07	*Not Available*		
1980			82.16			
1981			95.09			

Source:
IMF, *Balance of Payments Yearbook*, various issues.

Table A12

LEADING DOMESTIC MULTINATIONAL COMPANIES, 1980/81[1]

	Name	*Sector*	*Global Turnover (US $m)*
1	Assoc Plastics Industries Bhd	Plastics	12.8
2	Genting Bhd	Tourism/Property	77.0
3	Hume Industries	Building Materials	100.8
4	Tractors Malaysia	Transportation equipment	292.6
5	Kuala Lumpar Kepong Bhd	Rubber	149.9
6	Island and Peninsula Development Bhd	Palm oil/mining	19.2
7	Palmco Holdings Bhd	Palm oil	225.3
8	Tan Chong Motor Holdings Bhd	Motor vehicles (distributors)	266.9
9	Pegi Malaysia	Submarine & offshore contract	4.4
10	Faber Merlin Malaysia Bhd	Tourism/Property	21.9
11	Kulim Malaysia Bhd	Palm oil/property/shipping	38.4
12	Malaysian Mining	Mining	171.7
13	Boustead Holdings Bhd	Investment holding company interest in engineering, plantations, marketing, shipping and insurance	77.4
14	Ganda Holdings Bhd	Investment holding company with interest in plantation, manufactuirng, trading, property and hotels	10.0
15	United Motor Works Holdings Bhd	Holding company in investment and trading, distribution of Toyota vehicles, finance, manufacturing.	144.1
16	Multi-Purpose Holding Bhd	Investment holding (conglomerate)	137.0
17	Malayan United Industries	Investment holding (conglomerate)	N.A.
18	Malaysian Mining Bhd	Mining	171.7
19	Sime Darby Holding Bhd	Investment holding, (conglomerate)	1,147.8

Source:
Mah Hui Lim, *op cit;* data taken from Kuala Lumpur Stock Exchange Handbook, 1982.

NOTES TO TABLE A12
1 Represents public corporations in Malaysia with overseas subsidiaries/associated companies.

MALAYSIA : DEFINITIONS

Foreign direct investment in Malaysia is defined as an acquisition of ownership interest in an overseas enterprise, accompanied by some degree of control over its operations. Foreign capital investments comprise both paid-up capital and loans. The loan component forms less than 20% of total foreign capital investments on average.

Source:
Malaysian Industrial Development Authority (MIDA).

PAKISTAN

There is little information available on the international investment position of Pakistan. The inflow of foreign direct investment in Pakistan has fluctuated annually since the late 1960s, while the level of re-invested profits has been low, although on a rising trend.

A broad geographical distribution provided by the State Bank of Pakistan referring to the sources of foreign investment in Pakistan, indicates that the main investor countries are the USA, the UK and other EEC countries.

UK investment in Pakistan is mainly concentrated in manufacturing, particularly chemicals and goods. Within the services sector, the emphasis lies on distributive trades.

The Government of Pakistan welcomes foreign investment, and particularly encourages joint ventures with local investors. Ideally ventures are sought which (1) serve overall national objectives, (2) contribute to the development of capital, technology and managerial knowhow, (3) lead to the discovery, mobilization or better utilization of natural resources, (4) strengthen the balance of payments and (5) generate domestic employment. There are no prohibitions either on the reinvestment or repatriation of earnings and capital.

MAIN SOURCES OF DATA:

A Official

1 State Bank of Pakistan: provides data on foreign investment in Pakistan, by broad geographical distribution.

2 US Department of Commerce International Trade Administration, *Investment Climate in Foreign Countries,* Washington, 1985, vol III.

B Private

1 Mah Hui Lim, 'Survey of Activities of Transnational Corporations from Asian Developing Countries', paper submitted to the ESCAP/UNCTC Joint Unit on Transnational Corporations, Bangkok, March 1984.

Note:
Data do not allow us to complete Tables A9, A10, A11 or A12 for Pakistan.

Table A1

SUMMARY OF THE COUNTRY'S INTERNATIONAL INVESTMENT POSITION

		Inward Investment	Outward Investment
1	Number of foreign affiliates in host country, and of foreign affiliates of home country firms at the end of 1980	211	*N.A.*
2	Number of foreign firms with direct investments in host country, and home country firms with direct foreign affiliates	*N.A.*	*N.A.*
3	Total foreign direct capital stock at book value as a percentage of GNP at factor cost in 1982	3.10	*N.A.*
4	Flow of foreign direct investment in the five year period, 1979-83 (US $m)	324.00	*N.A.*
5	Employment in foreign affiliates or abroad	*N.A.*	*N.A.*
6	Output of foreign affiliates or abroad	*N.A.*	*N.A.*

Source:

State Bank of Pakistan, data as cited in US Department of Commerce, *Investment Climate in Foreign Countries,* Washington, 1983; IMF, *International Financial Statistics Yearbook, 1984;* IMF, *Balance of Payments Statistics Yearbook, 1984;* UNCTC, *Transnational Corporations in World Development: Third Survey,* New York: UN, 1983.

NOTES TO TABLE A1

1 Represents affiliates of MNEs from selected home countries as identified by UNCTC, 1983.

Table A2

PRIVATE FOREIGN CAPITAL STOCK, 1975 - 82 (US $ m)

	Inward Investment			Outward Investment		
	Portfolio	*Direct*	*Total*	*Portfolio*	*Direct*	*Total*
Book value of capital stock						
1975	*Not Available*	750.0	*Not Available*	*Not Available*		
1978		790.0				
1982		837.8				

Source:
State Bank of Pakistan, data as cited in US Department of Commerce, *Investment Climate in Foreign Countries,* Washington, 1983. UNCTC, *op. cit.*

Table A3

FLOW OF FOREIGN DIRECT INVESTMENT, 1970 - 83 (US $ m)

	Inward Investment			Outward Investment		
	Reinvested Profits	*Other*	*Total*	*Reinvested Profits*	*Other*	*Total*
1970	6.0	17.0	23.0	*Not Available*		
1971	3.0	-2.0	1.0			
1972	3.3	14.1	17.4			
1973	*N.S.A.*	*N.S.A.*	-3.6			
1974	1.2	2.4	3.6			
1975	1.2	24.3	25.5			
1976	1.2	6.9	8.1			
1977	3.5	11.7	15.2			
1978	2.5	26.3	28.8			
1979	7.8	54.2	62.0			
1980	6.5	52.1	58.6			
1981	7.1	100.2	107.3			
1982	8.8	56.3	65.1			
1983	7.5	23.5	31.0			

Source:
IMF, *Balance of Payments Statistics Yearbook,* various issues.

Table A4

SECTORAL DISTRIBUTION OF FOREIGN DIRECT CAPITAL STOCK, 1981 (US $ m)[1]

	Inward Investment			Outward Investment		
	Primary	*Secondary*	*Tertiary*	*Primary*	*Secondary*	*Tertiary*
1981	*N.A.*	89.9	23.5	*Not Available*		

Source:

UK Department of Trade and Industry, 'Census of Overseas Assets, 1981', *Business Monitor,* Supplement, 1981.

NOTES TO TABLE A4

1 Refers to UK investment in Pakistan only. In 1981 this accounted for 18% of total foreign investment in Pakistan.

Table A5

GEOGRAPHICAL DISTRIBUTION OF FOREIGN DIRECT CAPITAL STOCK, 1978 - 82 (US $ m)

	Inward Investment			Outward Investment		
	Developed Countries	*Developing Countries*	*Total*	*Developed Countries*	*Developing Countries*	*Total*
1978	43.0	*N.A.*	121.5[1]	*Not Available*		
1982	509.0[2]	57.1	837.8[1]			

Source:

State Bank of Pakistan, Statistics Department, 'Foreign Liabilities and Assets and Foreign Investment in Pakistan, 1978'; State Bank of Pakistan, data as cited in US Department of Commerce, *Investment Climate in Foreign Countries,* Washington, 1983.

NOTES TO TABLE A5

1 Total includes 'unspecified' figure.

2 Including International Financial Institutions ($249.7 m).

Table A6

INDUSTRIAL DISTRIBUTION OF FOREIGN DIRECT CAPITAL STOCK, 1981 (US $m)[1]

	Inward Investment	Outward Investment
	1981	
Primary	*N.A.*	*Not Available*
Secondary	89.9	
Food & drink	25.4	
Chemicals & allied	55.5	
Electrical equipment	6.7	
Other manufacturing	2.3	
Tertiary	23.5	
Distributive trade	21.0	
Other services	2.5	
TOTAL	113.4	

Source:

UK Department of Trade and Industry, 'Census of Overseas Assets, 1981', *Business Monitor,* Supplement, 1981.

NOTES TO TABLE A6

1 UK investment in Pakistan only. In 1981 this accounted for 18% of total foreign investment in Pakistan. It excludes investment by oil companies, banks and insurance companies.

Table A7

LEADING SOURCE AND RECIPIENT COUNTRIES, 1978 - 82 (US $m)

	Inward Investment		Outward Investment
	1978	*1982*	
DEVELOPED AREAS[1]	43.0	509.0[2]	*Not Available*
Europe	26.5	142.3	
EEC of which:	26.5	142.3	
UK	26.5	142.3	
North America	15.5	117.0	
USA	15.5	117.0	
Other developed countries	1.0	*N.A.*	
Japan	1.0	*N.A.*	
DEVELOPING AREAS	*N.A.*	57.1	
Middle East	*N.A.*	57.1	
UNSPECIFIED	78.5	271.7	
TOTAL	121.5	837.8	

Source:

State Bank of Pakistan, Statistics Department, 'Foreign Liabilities and Assets and Foreign Investment in Pakistan, 1978'; State Bank of Pakistan, data as cited in US Department of Commerce, *Investment Climate in Foreign Countries,* Washington, 1983.

NOTES TO TABLE A7

1 Including only those countries shown below.

2 Including International Financial Institutions, $249.7 m.

Table 8

INDICATORS OF THE SIGNIFICANCE OF INWARD FOREIGN DIRECT INVESTMENT OR THE ACTIVITIES OF FOREIGN-BASED COMPANIES TO THE NATIONAL ECONOMY, 1982

1	Direct capital stock of foreign affiliates at book value in 1982 as a proportion of		
	a	GNP at factor cost	2.86
	b	population (in $ per head)	9.62
2	Foreign direct investment as a percentage of domestic investment 1978-80		
		in all industry	0.3

Source:
State Bank of Pakistan, data as cited in US Department of Commerce, *Investment Climate in Foreign Countries,* Washington, 1983; IMF, *International Financial Statistics Yearbook, 1985.*

PHILIPPINES

At the end of 1984, direct foreign equity investments in the Philippines accounted for about 45% of total equity investments in projects approved by the Board of Investments. The annual additions to the stock of foreign equity investments, as indicated by the actual inward remittance net of cancellations and adjustments as monitored by the Central Bank of Philippines starting from February 21, 1970, grew at an annual average rate of 27.4% during the period 1970 to 1982.

The major source of foreign direct investment in the Philippines is the USA which in 1983 accounted for 53.3% of total actual inward remittances of direct foreign equity investment. The share of Japanese investors was 14.9% and EEC investors 13.4%. Most notable among the EEC investors was the Netherlands and the United Kingdom with a 4.7% and 4.1% share respectively.

Prior to the 1970s, the sectoral distribution of foreign investment had a similar pattern to that of indigenous investment, except in agriculture and public utilities where it assumed a less important role owing to regulatory restrictions; and in some branches of manufacturing and commercial financial services where its share was slightly more. The broad correspondence between investment patterns can be explained *inter alia* by the fact that both local and foreign investments were undertaken within the same incentive structure. However, with the introduction of restrictions to foreign participation in certain areas in the 1970s, the investment patterns began to diverge.

Of the total actual inward remittances of direct foreign equity, investments as at 31 March 1983, 47% were in manufacturing, 25% in mining and 14% in banking and other financial institutions. Within the manufacturing sector, the largest investments are in the chemical and chemical products, food, basic metals and transport equipment sectors. These investments have been made in accordance with the government policy to encourage foreign investment in new capital intensive manufacturing activities which involve the processing of Philippine raw materials. Permanently closed to any foreign equity participation are rural banking, retail trade, trading in rice and maize, mass media including advertising and production of certain military goods. There is also a list of 'overcrowded industries' which are temporarily closed to MNCs. In banking, no more than 30% foreign ownership is allowed with the exception of offshore banking units. Up to 100% foreign ownership is permitted in the pioneer and 'liberalised areas' of the various priorities plans, in export processing zones and in cases of export-oriented enterprises.

It is difficult to give any quantitative picture of the role of Philippine companies abroad. In part, this difficulty is due to the fragmentary nature of official statistics and the confidentiality attached to such information. Almost certainly, the officially published data set out in this entry grossly underestimate the true involvement of Philippine firms abroad. For example, data from the US Department of Commerce places Philippine foreign direct investment in the USA at US S 72 million as at 1980, half of which represented investments in the banking sector. Data from other Asian countries reveal that Philippine foreign direct investments in Asia amounted to about US S 69.7 million in 1982 with 96% of this amount representing investments in Indonesia. Another indication of the importance of Philippine MNCs is that 36 of the top 500 corporations in the Philippines had foreign operations and had a combined gross revenue of US S 4.6 billion in 1981.

MAIN SOURCES OF DATA:

A Official

1 Central Bank of the Philippines Management of External Debt, Investment and Aid Department (MEDIAD) publishes quarterly statistics on Central Bank approved and actual remittances of both inward and outward investments.

MAIN SOURCES OF DATA (cont'd)

2 Board of Investments furnishes annual data on BOI-approved investments, both local and foreign.

3 Securities and Exchange Commission publishes annual information on flows of paid-up capital or equity investments of foreign corporations and regional headquarters of multinational companies that are approved by the Securities and Exchange Commission as well as a list of the Top 1000 Corporations in the Philippines.

4 UNCTC, *Transnational Corporations in World Development: A Re-examination,* New York: UN, 1978.

5 Chita Tantaco-Scbiolo, *Employment Effects of Multinational Enterprises in the Philippines,* Geneva: International Labour Office, 1979.

B Private

1 Falih Alsaaty, 'The Impact of Foreign Private Direct Investment on the Economic Development of the Philippines', PhD dissertation, New York University, 1973.

2 Augusto Cesar Espiritu, A Filipino Looks at Multinational Corporations' in *Philippine Perspectives on Multinational Corporations,* Quezon City: University of the Philippines Law Centre, 1977.

3 Maj Hui Lim, *Survey of Activities of Transnational Corporations from Asian developing countries,* Bangkok: ESCAP/UNCTC Joint Unit on Transnational Corporations, March 1984.

4 Paz Estrella E Tolentino, 'The Contribution of Multinational Corporations to Philippine Development: A study of the growth, determinants and the impact of foreign direct investment on the provision of capital funds and the transfer of technology', MA dissertation, University of Reading, 1984.

Note:
Data do not allow us to complete Table A10 for the Philippines.

Table A1

SUMMARY OF THE COUNTRY'S INTERNATIONAL INVESTMENT POSITION

		Inward Investment	Outward Investment
1	Number of foreign affiliates in host country, and of foreign affiliates of home country firms at the end of 1980	675[1]	*N.A.*
2	Number of foreign firms with direct investments in host country, and home country firms with direct foreign affiliates at the end of 1974	93	*N.A.*
3	Total foreign direct capital stock at book value as a percentage of GNP at factor cost in 1983	7.71	0.04[2]
4	Flow of foreign direct investment in the five year period, 1978-82 (US $ m)[3]	1,187.92	12.61
5	Employment in foreign affiliates or abroad, 1976	130,965[4]	*N.A.*
6	Output of foreign affiliates or abroad, 1981 (US $ bn)[5]	1,703[6]	4,605

Source:

Mah Hui Lim, *Survey of Activities of Transnational Corporations from Asian Developing Countries,* ESCAP/UNCTC Joint Unit on Transnational Corporations, Bangkok, March 1984; Central Bank of the Philippines Management of External Debt, Investment and Aid Department (MEDIAD), *CB Approved Direct Foreign Equity Investments by Year of Approval,* various issues; Friedrich von Kirchbach, 'Economic Policies towards TNCs: The Experience of ASEAN Countries', PhD theses, University of Regensburg, July 1981; IMF, *International Financial Statistics, 1984;* A C Espiritu. 'A Filipino Looks at MNCs' in *Philippine Perspectives in MNC,* Quezon City: University of the Philippines Law Center, 1977; Chita-Tantaco-Subidu, *Employment effects of multinational enterprises in the Philippines,* Geneva: 'International Labour Office, 1979.

NOTES TO TABLE A1

1 Represents number of affiliates of MNEs from selected home countries, as identified by UN Centre on Transnational Corporations

2 Represents year 1981. This figure may be underestimated due to the fragmentary nature of official statistics on outward investment.

3 Inward investment flows represent actual inward remittances of direct foreign equity investments net of cancellation and adjustments. Outward investment flows represent actual outward-remittances of Philippine direct equity investments in 1980 and 1981 as the Central Bank of the Philippines only began to collect data on the outflow of investment on a systematic basis only after 1979.

4 Represents employment in 138 TNCs.

5 Represents gross revenues of 36 Philippine TNCs in the top 500 corporations in the Philippines.

6 Represents combined sales volume of 93 MNCs in production identified by the Business Day in 1974 of 11.557 billion Philippine pesos converted at the average exchange rate in 1974 of 6.7879 Philippine pesos per US dollar.

Table A2

PRIVATE FOREIGN CAPITAL STOCK, 1970-83 (US $ m)[1]

	Inward Investment			Outward Investment		
	Portfolio	*Direct*	*Total*	*Portfolio*	*Direct*	*Total*
Book value of capital stock						
1970		121.96				
1975		485.21				
1976		601.76				
1977		746.81				
1978	*Not Available*	897.03	*Not Available*			
1979		1,100.08				
1980		1,331.23		*N.A.*	141.8[3]	*N.A.*
1981		1,671.37				
1982		1,934.73				
1983[2]		1,985.67				

Source:

Central Bank of the Philippines, MEDIAD, *CB Approved Direct Foreign Equity Investments by Year of Approval,* various issues.

NOTES TO TABLE A2

1 For inward investment, figures represent stock of actual inward-remittances of direct foreign equity investments net of cancellation and adjustments starting from February 21, 1970 when the outstanding level of accumulated foreign equity investments were first monitored. For outward investment, figures represent stock of actual outward-remittances of Philippines foreign equity investments. The Central Bank of the Philippines only began to collect data on the outflow of investment on a systematic basis only after 1979.

2 As of first quarter.

3 Author's estimate based on value of Philippine FDI in the United States of US $ 72 million in 1980 and in Indonesia, Malaysia, Thailand and Hong Kong of US $ 69.8 in the years 1980 to 1982.

Table A3

FLOW OF FOREIGN DIRECT INVESTMENT, 1970-83 (US $ m)[1]

	Inward Investment			Outward Investment		
	Reinvested Profits	*Other*	*Total*	*Reinvested Profits*	*Other*	*Total*
1970	*Not Separately Available*		–25.00	*Not Separately Available*		4.00
1971			–1.00			5.01
1972			–11.94			8.68
1973			54.84			1.19
1974			3.61			*N.A.*
1975			98.35			1.21
1976	66.96	64.65	131.62			5.77
1977	78.22	131.93	208.99	*Not Available*		
1978	61.35	38.81	101.41			
1979	58.14	–50.39	7.75			
1980	39.04	–145.77	–106.72			
1981	62.50	110.84	173.34			
1982	43.06	27.60	15.46			
1983	25.66	78.04	104.76			
1984	15.38	–21.53	–6.15			

Source:

Central Bank of the Philippines, MEDIAD, *op cit.*

NOTES TO TABLE A3

1 For inward investment, figures represent flows of actual inward-remittances of direct foreign equity investments net of cancellations and adjustments starting from February 21, 1970 when the outstanding level of accumulated foreign equity investments were first monitored. For outward investment, figures represent flows of actual outward-remittances of Philippine direct equity investments.

Table A4

SECTORAL DISTRIBUTION OF FOREIGN DIRECT CAPITAL STOCK, 1980-83 (US $ m)[1]

	Inward Investment			Outward Investment		
	Primary	*Secondary*	*Tertiary*	*Primary*	*Secondary*	*Tertiary*
1973	12.1	57.2	51.1	*N.A.*	*N.A.*	*N.A.*
1976	88.7	249.8	174.4	*N.A.*	*N.A.*	
1983[2]	530.19	935.64	519.84	20.3	44.7	40.8

Source:
1983 figures, Central Bank of the Philippines, MEDIAD, *op cit.* 1973 & 76 figures: UNCTC, *Transnational Corporations in World Development; A Re-examination,* New York: UN, 1978.

NOTES TO TABLE A4

1 For inward investment, figures represent stock of actual inward-remittances of direct foreign equity investments net of cancellations and adjustments starting from February 21, 1970 when the outstanding level of accumulated foreign equity investments were first monitored. For outward investment, figures represent stock of actual outward-remittances of Philippine foreign equity investments. The Central Bank of the Philippines only began to collect data on the outflow of investment on a systematic basis after 1979.

2 As of first quarter.

3 Figures presented are author's estimate for 1980 and excludes S 36 million of unspecified foreign direct investments in the USA.

Table A5

GEOGRAPHICAL DISTRIBUTION OF FOREIGN DIRECT CAPITAL STOCK, 1980-83 (US $ m)[1]

	Inward Investment			Outward Investment		
	Developed Countries	*Developing Countries*	*Total*	*Developed Countries*	*Developing Countries*	*Total*
1980		*Not Available*		72.0	69.8	141.8
1981					*Not Available*	
1983[2]	1,792.78[3]	192.89	1,985.67			

Source:
Central Bank of the Philippines, MEDIAD, *op cit*; Mah Hui Lim, *op cit.*

NOTES TO TABLE A5

1 For inward investment, figures represent stock of actual inward-remittances of direct foreign equity investments net of cancellation and adjustments starting from February 21, 1970 when the outstanding level of accumulated foreign equity investments were first monitored. For outward investment, figures represent stock of actual outward-remittances of Philippine foreign equity investments after 1979 when the Central Bank of the Philippines began to collect data on the outflow of investment on a systematic basis.

2 Up to first quarter.

3 Including direct foreign equity investments of Agency for International Development and International Finance Corporation.

4 Figures presented for developed countries reflect direct investments in the USA only and those for developing countries reflect direct investments in Indonesia, Malaysia, Thailand and Hong Kong only.

Table A6 **INDUSTRIAL DISTRIBUTION OF FOREIGN DIRECT CAPITAL STOCK, 1981 and 1983 (US $ m)**[1]

	Inward Investment	Outward Investment
	1983[2]	
Primary	530.19	20.3
Agriculture	25.04[3]	20.3
Mining & quarrying	505.15	*N.A.*
Secondary	935.64	44.66
Food & drink[4]	158.45	
Chemicals & allied	269.93	*N.A.*
Metals	153.49[5]	*N.A.*
Mechanical engineering	11.17	*N.A.*
Electrical equipment	50.46	0.40
Motor vehicles	67.57	*N.A.*
Other transportation equipment		*N.A.*
Textiles & clothing	50.03	0.21[6]
Paper & allied	19.66	*N.A.*
Rubber	36.49	*N.A.*
Stone, clay & glass	25.42	0.20
Coal & petroleum products	36.00	*N.A.*
Other manufacturing	30.11	1.20
Tertiary	519.84	40.80
Construction	21.06	0.80
Transport & communications	31.48	*N.A.*
Distributive trade	103.63	*N.A.*
Property		0.5
Banking & finance	286.02	36.0
Other services	77.65[7]	3.5
TOTAL	1,985.67	105.8[8]

Source:
Central Bank of the Philippines, MEDIAD, *op cit.*

NOTES TO TABLE A6

1 For inward investment, figures represent stock of actual inward-remittances of direct foreign equity investments net of cancellation and adjustments starting from February 21, 1970 when the outstanding level of accumulated foreign equity investments were first monitored. For outward investment, figures represent stock of actual outward-remittances of Philippine foreign equity investments. The Central Bank of the Philippines only began to collect data on the outflow of investment on a systematic basis after 1979.

2 Up to first quarter, 1983.

3 Including fishery and forestry.

4 Represents food only.

5 Represents basic metal products, 121.66, and metal products except machinery and transport equipment, 31.83.

6 Includes leather.

7 Represents 77.15 and others unclassified 0.50.

8 Excludes US S 36 million to unspecified investment in the USA.

Table A7

LEADING SOURCE AND RECIPIENT COUNTRIES, 1976-83 (US $ m)[1]

	Inward Investment		Outward Investment
	1976	*1983*[2]	*1980*[6]
DEVELOPED AREAS		1,792.89[3]	
Europe		344.11	
EEC of which	*Not Available*	267.17	
Belgium & Luxembourg		14.07	
Denmark		13.63	
France		41.23	
W. Germany	1.54	21.82	
Ireland	*Not Available*	1.62	*Not Available*
Italy		0.80	
Netherlands		93.04	
UK	29.75	80.96	
Other Europe of which:		76.94	
Austria	*Not Available*	10.78	
Liechtenstein		0.19	
Norway		0.70	
Spain		3.73	
Sweden		13.73	
Switzerland	9.23	47.70	
USSR	*N.A.*	0.11	
North America of which:		1,105.05	
Canada	40.01	45.82	
USA	245.73	1,059.23	72.0
Other developed countries of which:		339.64	
Australia	12.82	40.66	
Japan	124.15	295.85	*Not Available*
New Zealand	*N.A.*	3.13	
DEVELOPING AREAS		192.78	
Africa of which:	*N.A.*	1.47[4]	
Liberia	*N.A.*	1.47	
Asia & Pacific of which:	*N.A.*	158.16[5]	
Hong Kong	9.23	107.23	8.40
India	*Not Available*	1.74	*N.A.*
Indonesia		0.23	60.30
S. Korea		6.44	*N.A.*
Malaysia		0.84	0.06
Singapore		12.37	*N.A.*

Table A7 (cont'd)

LEADING SOURCE AND RECIPIENT COUNTRIES, 1976-83 (US $ m)[1]

	Inward Investment		Outward Investment
	1976	*1983*[2]	*1980*
DEVELOPING AREAS (cont'd)			
Taiwan		2.73	
Thailand		0.14	1.0
Latin America of which:	*Not Available*	29.72	
Argentina		0.04	
Bahamas		0.20	
Bermuda		6.55	
British West Indies		0.36	*Not Available*
El Salvador		0.53	
Panama	2.05	19.23	
Uruguay		2.81	
Middle East of which:	*Not Available*	3.43	
Bahrain		0.68	
Israel		0.57	
Saudi Arabia		2.13	
United Arab Emirates		0.05	
UNSPECIFIED	38.48		
TOTAL	513.00	1,985.67	141.76

Source:

Central Bank of the Philippines, MEDIAD, *op cit;* Mah Hui Lim, *op cit.*

NOTES TO TABLE A7

1 For inward investment, figures represent stock of actual inward-remittances of direct foreign equity investments net of cancellation and adjustments starting from February 21, 1970 when the outstanding level of accumulated foreign equity investments were first monitored. For outward investment, figures represent stock of actual outward-remittances of Philippine foreign equity investments after 1979 when the Central Bank of the Philippines began to collect data on the outflow of investment on a systematic basis.

2 As of first quarter 1983.

3 Including direct foreign equity investments of Agency for International Development of US $ 3.15 million and International Finance Corporation of US $ 0.94 million.

4 Represents Liberia only.

5 Including Republic of Nauru US'$ 10.07 million and New Hebrides US $ 16.37 million.

6 Figures for Thailand are for 1981 and that for Indonesia and Hong Kong for 1982.

Table A9

INDICATORS OF THE SIGNIFICANCE OF OUTWARD FOREIGN DIRECT INVESTMENT OR THE ACTIVITIES OF HOME-BASED COMPANIES ABROAD FOR THE NATIONAL ECONOMY, 1981

1	Foreign capital stock of home-based firms at book value in 1981 as a proportion of:	
	a GNP at factor cost	0.03[1]
	b population (in US $ per head)	0.25[1]

Source:
IMF, *International Financial Statistics, 1984;* Central Bank of the Philippines, MEDIAD, *op cit.*

NOTES TO TABLE A9

1 May be underestimated because of sparcity of official statistics on outward investment.

Table A11

ROYALTY AND RECEIPTS AND PAYMENTS, 1970-77 (US $ m)[1]

	Payments			Receipts		
	To Affiliates	*To Non-affiliates*	*Total*	*From Affiliates*	*To Non-affiliates*	*Total*
1970	*Not Separately Available*		3.1	*Not Available*		
1975			11.5			
1976			11.3			
1977			16.1			

Source:
Central Bank of the Philippines Foreign Exchange Department, *Annual Reports,* various issues.

NOTES TO TABLE A11

1 Denotes receipt and payment of patents, royalties and copyrights.

Table A8

INDICATORS OF THE SIGNIFICANCE OF INWARD FOREIGN DIRECT INVESTMENT OR THE ACTIVITIES OF FOREIGN-BASED COMPANIES TO THE NATIONAL ECONOMY, 1974-82

1	Directo capital stock of foreign affiliates at book value in 1982 as a proportion of:		
	a GNP at factor cost		4.90
	b population (in US $ per head)		38.1
2	Employment in foreign affiliates in 1976 as a percentage of all employment[1]		
	a in all industry		1.57
	b in manufacturing		8.60
3	Output of foreign affiliates in 1974 as a percentage of all companies' output[2] in secondary (ie manufacturing) industry		78%
4	Investment in foreign affiliates by OECD countries as a percentage of domestic investment 1978-80		2.2
5	Percentage share of assets and employment accounted for by foreign affiliates in selected sectors.[4]		
		Assets[3]	*Employment*[5]
	Primary Goods Sector		
	Agriculture	27.7	0.2[6]
	Mining & quarrying	22.6	64.9
	Oil	42.1[7]	*N.A.*
	Manufacturing Sector	64.4[8]	8.7[8]
	Services Sector	33.6	*N.A.*
	Construction	33.6	5.0
	Transport & communications	*N.A.*	1.2[9]
	Distributive trade	12.0[10]	0.3
	Property	29.3	*N.A.*
	Banking & finance	28.0	0.1
	Other services	93.9	*N.A.*

Source:

Board of Investments, *Annual Report,* various issues; Merlin Magallona, 'Transnational Corporations – Problem and its Resolution', in *Philippine Perspectives on Multinational Corporations;* Kirchbach, "Economic Policies towards TNCs: The Experience of ASEAN countries" PhD thesis, University of Regensburg, 1981; Falih Alsaaty, "The Impact of Foreign Private Direct Investment on the Economic Development of the Philippines", PhD thesis, New York University, 1973; A C Espiritu, *op cit.*

NOTES TO TABLE A8

1 Represents employment in 175 TNCs with more than 1% foreign equity.

2 The total sales of multinationals engaged in production as a proportion of total output of goods and services in 1974 was 11.68%.

3 Represents share of foreign equity investments in total equity investments in projects approved by the Board of Investments from January to December 1983.

4 In 1974-75, 69 TNCs dominated strategic industry lines. Its penetration is most active in the manufacturing sector. Out of 15 industry lines in the manufacturing sector where the TNCs are strong, they enjoy virtual monopoly in four, dominate four others, and are prominent in all other lines. They have near monopoly in the manufacture of motor vehicles in 1975. While there are 17 corporations in the manufacture of motor vehicles, nine TNCs have virtually appropriated the whole industry to themselves. The rubber industry is in the hands of 3 corporations, all US transnational firms, which virtually cover the entire market. In batteries and accessories, Union Carbide, a US TNC, enjoys near monopoly with sales in 1974 three times more than combined sales of two other companies in the industry line. The dominance of 11 TNCs is clear in food manufacturing. Of 4 companies that control petroleum refining in 1974, 3 are TNCs. TNCs enjoy near monopoly in soap and other washing compounds. 3 out of 5 giant firms in soap industry are TNCs. Their 1974 total sales of over 1.150 billion Philippine pesos account for about 90% of total sales volume of the soap industry. The pharmaceutical industry is a TNC domain, controlling 70% of sales volume. In electrical equipment, TNCs also easily crowd-out competition, also in paper and paper products, chemical and chemical products and office equipment.

5 Based on 175 TNCs with more than 1% foreign equity in 1976.

6 Including fishery and forestry.

7 Represents energy-related projects.

8 Figure represents total manufacturing.

9 Including storage.

10 Represents exporters of merchandise and services.

Table A12

LEADING FOREIGN AND DOMESTIC MULTINATIONAL COMPANIES

A Leading Foreign Affiliates in the country, 1983

	Name	*Home Country*	*Sector*	*Philippine Sales (P₱ m)*
1	Caltex (Phils) Inc	USA	Petroleum & petroleum products, wholesaling	10,424.3
2	Mobil Oil (Phils) Inc	USA	Petroleum & petroleum products, wholesaling	3,143.4
3	Citibank NA	USA	Deposit money bank	2,708.2
4	Advanced Micro Devices (Phils)	USA	Manufacture of electrical machinery, apparatus, appliances, & supplies	1,463.3
5	Pepsico Inc	USA	Beverage manufacturing	1,361.1
6	Phil Refining Co Inc	Netherlands	Food manufacturing	1,071.1
7	Phil American Life Insurance	USA	Life insurance	1,068.9
8	Colgate-Palmolive Phils Inc	USA	Manufacture of other chemical products	1,062.3
9	Procter & Gamble Phils Manufacturing Corp	USA	Manufacture of other chemical products	1,036.4
10	Texas Instruments (Phils) Inc	USA	Manufacture of electrical machinery, apparatus, appliances, & supplies	969.7
11	Phil Packing Corp	USA	Food manufacturing	944.5
12	Dole Phils Inc	USA	Fruit & nut (excl. coconut production)	826.1
13	Bank of America NT & SA	USA	Deposit money bank	755.4
14	Ford Philippines, Inc	USA	Manufacture of transport equipment	753.3
15	Banque Nationale de Paris	France	Deposit money bank	692.7
16	General Motors Phils Inc	USA	Manufacture of transport equipment	682.2
17	Carnation Phils Inc	USA	Food manufacturing	609.3
18	Union Carbide Phils Inc	USA	Manufacture of electrical machinery, apparatus, appliances, & supplies	600.3
19	Manufacturer Hanover Trust Co	USA	Deposit money bank	576.4
20	Philippine Sinter Corp	Japan	Basic iron & steel industries	569.8
21	California Manufacturing Corp	USA	Food manufacturing	520.5
22	Chemical Bank	USA	Deposit money bank	484.5
23	Goodyear Tyre & Rubber Co	USA	Manufacture of rubber products	483.2
24	Firestone Tyre & Rubber Co	USA	Manufacture of rubber products	444.2
25	Philippine Geothermal Inc	USA	Steam heat & power plant	443.8

Table A12 (cont'd)

LEADING FOREIGN AND DOMESTIC MULTINATIONAL COMPANIES

B Leading Domestic Companies with Multinational Interests, 1983

	Name	*Sector*	*Global Sales (P₱ m)*
1	Philippine National Bank	Deposit money bank	7,738.3
2	San Miguel Corp	Food & beverage manufacture	6,522.9
3	Philippine Airlines, Inc	Transport	5,723.9
4	Atlantic, Gulf & Pacific Co of Manila Inc	Construction	1,640.6
5	Bank of the Philippine Islands	Deposit money bank	1,361.4
6	Metropolitan Bank & Trust Co	Deposit money banks	1,336.1
7	International Copra Export Corp	Food products	1,237.1
8	Universal Robina Corp	Food manufacturing	1,220.2
9	Rustan Commercial Corp	Food manufacturing	1,124.7
10	Engineering Equipment, Inc	Contracting & engineering, steel fabrication, industrial equipment	1,112.1
11	United Coconut Planters Bank	Deposit money bank	1,049.9
12	Manila Banking Corp	Deposit money bank	1,048.1
13	Allied Banking Corp	Deposit money bank	1,021.0
14	Philippine Commercial International Bank	Deposit money bank	982.5
15	United Laboratories Inc	Pharmaceuticals	885.7
16	China Banking Corp	Deposit money bank	661.9
17	Ayala Corp	Food & beverage manufacture, banking, other manufacturing	657.9
18	La Tondena, Inc	Beverage manufacture	615.6
19	Pacific Banking Corp	Deposit money bank	590.6
20	Insular Bank of Asia & America	Deposit money bank	577.6
21	Consolidated Bank & Trust Co	Deposit money bank	559.5
22	Security Bank & Trust Co	Deposit money bank	531.1
23	Rubberworld (Phil) Inc	Manufacture of rubber products	518.7
24	The Philippine Banking Corp	Deposit money bank	426.3
25	Equitable Banking Corp	Deposit money bank	408.6

Source:
Investments and Research Dept., Securities and Exchange Commission, *Top 1000 Corporations in the Philippines, 1983.*

PHILIPPINES : DEFINITIONS

Foreign direct investment data as given by the Central Bank of the Philippines reflect only Central Bank-approved direct foreign equity investments net of cancellations and adjustments by year of approval as from 21 February 1970. A breakdown can be obtained between committed and inwardly remitted foreign direct investments.

Foreign direct investments can also be obtained from the Board of Investments. These refer to BOI-approved foreign investments as from 1968. Foreign investments refer to equity investments owned by a non-Philippine national made in the form of foreign exchange or other assets actually transferred to the Philippines and registered with the Central Bank and the BOI, that contribute greater than 30% of total equity.

Source:

Central Bank of the Philippines, Management of External Debt and Investment Accounts Department, *CB-Approved Direct Foreign Equity Investment;* Board of Investments, *BOI-Approved Foreign Investments.*

SINGAPORE

Inward direct investment has played a critical role in the economic development of Singapore. From 1960 to 1980, foreign capital financed over a third of total investment in Singapore, and comprised about 90% of investment in the manufacturing sector and 20% of investment in the service sector. In 1981 the foreign direct investment stake in Singapore amounted to S $ 15,603.7 million, representing 34.1% of total equity investment in Singapore. There were 7,065 foreign affiliates in that year, of which 2,967 were wholly foreign-owned, 1,336 majority foreign-owned and 2,762 minority foreign-owned. Almost 50% of foreign funds were directed into the manufacturing sector, and in particular, petroleum (15.6%), electronics (9.7%) and machinery (6.1%). The share of foreign equity directed into low value-added industries as food, tobacco, textile and wood products have decreased in the 1970s and by 1981, these industries accounted for only 7% of total foreign equity compared with 14 in 1970.

The UK, the USA, Hong Kong, Malaysia and Japan account for 80% of foreign equity investments in Singapore. The UK is Singapore's largest investor, with over half of its investments directed towards manufacturing, particularly petroleum refining. The USA is the second largest source; its investments are mostly directed towards petroleum refining and high value-added industries such as electronics, computer peripherals, machine tools and oilfield equipment. Hong Kong is the third largest investor whose investments are most noted in the non-manufacturing sector, including commercial banking, property development, wholesale trade and hotels.

Singapore has adopted a very liberal policy stance towards foreign direct investment. The government makes no distinction between foreign-owned and locally-owned firms. In the late 1970s, the government placed considerable emphasis on encouraging foreign investors, especially those from high income countries to form joint ventures with local entrepreneurs, increase the local value added-output ratio and to depackage their investments, especially in capital and knowledge-intensive industries. The various investment incentives that have been offered have been in the form of low taxes, few controls over operations, no local ownership requirements and a substantial investment in infrastructure development. Singapore has also attracted FDI through its political stability and disciplined labour force.

Data on outward foreign direct investment from Singapore is scarce as the government does not publish statistics. The only available data are those that exist in the various host countries and particularly in neighbouring Asian countries. It is estimated that Singaporean direct investment abroad amounted to about S $ 1 billion in 1980. Singapore is the second largest foreign direct investor among low- and middle-income, non-oil exporting countries, second only to Hong Kong.

MAIN SOURCES OF DATA:

A Official

1 Department of Statistics, Government of Singapore publications:

a *Reports on Census of Industrial Production*

b *Survey of Services*

c *Survey of Wholesale and Retail Trades, Restaurants and Hotels*

d *Foreign Investment Survey*

2 Ministry of Trade and Industry publication entitled *Economic Survey of Singapore.*

3 ESCAP/UNCTC *Transnational Corporations from Developing Asian Economies,* Bangkok, 1985.

B Private

1 Don Lecraw, 'Singapore' in J H Dunning (ed.) *Multinational Enterprises, Economic Structure and International Competitiveness,* London: John Wiley, 1985.

2 Pang Eng Fong, 'Foreign Investment and the State in Singapore' , revised version of paper prepared for the Commonwealth Secretariat, September 1984.

3 Chia Siow Yue, 'Singapore' in ESCAP *Patterns and Impact of Foreign Investment in the ESCAP Region,* Bangkok, 1985.

Note:

Data do not allow us to complete Table A11 for Singapore.

Table A1

SUMMARY OF THE COUNTRY'S INTERNATIONAL INVESTMENT POSITION

		Inward Investment		Outward Investment
1	Number of foreign affiliates in host country, and of foreign affiliates of home country firms at the end of 1981	7,065		*N.A.*
2	Number of foreign firms with direct investments in host country, and home country firms with direct foreign affiliates	*N.A.*		*N.A.*
3	Total foreign direct capital stock at book value as a percentage of GNP at factor cost in 1983	65.29		10.79
4	Flow of foreign direct investment in the five year period 1980-84 (S $ m)	17,642.1		*N.A.*
5	Employment in foreign affiliates or abroad, 1982	190,945		*N.A.*
6	Output of foreign affiliates or abroad, 1982 (S $ m)	30,152		*N.A.*

Source:
Pang Eng Fong, 'Foreign Investment and the State in Singapore', Revised paper prepared for the Commonwealth Secretariat, September 1984, data taken from Ministry of Trade and Industry, *Economic Survey of Singapore* and Department of Statistics, *Report on the Census of Industrial Production.*

NOTES TO TABLE A1

1 Figure is for 1980.

Table A2

PRIVATE FOREIGN CAPITAL STOCK, 1970-84 (S $ m)[1]

	Inward Investment			Outward Investment		
	Portfolio	*Direct*	*Total*	*Portfolio*	*Direct*	*Total*
Book value of capital stock						
1970	281.0	1,462.5	1,743.5			
1973	471.8	3,296.1	3,767.9		*Not*	
1975	*N.S.A.*	*N.S.A.*	5,514.9		*Available*	
1976	670.3	6,255.3	6,925.6			
1979	771.6	9,376.2	10,147.8			
1980				*N.A.*	2,516.6	*N.A.*
1981	1,181.5	15,603.7	16,785.2			
1982	*Not*	19,461.8	*Not*		*Not*	
1983	*Available*	22,515.8	*Available*		*Available*	
1984		25,624.9				

Source:
Pang Eng Fong, *op cit.*

NOTES TO TABLE A2

1 Figures refer only to foreign equity investment. Cumulative inward direct investment flows have been added on to foreign direct capital stock of 1981 to estimate fdi stock for subsequent years.

2 Represents stock of outward direct investment in selected Asian countries, the USA and Australia.

Table A3

FLOW OF FOREIGN DIRECT INVESTMENT, 1970-84 (S $ m)

	Inward Investment				Outward Investment		
	Reinvested Profits	*Other*	*Total*		*Reinvested Profits*	*Other*	*Total*
1970	*Not Separately Available*		284.7		*Not Available*		
1971			354.6				
1972			536.8				
1973			949.7				
1974			1,453.6				
1975			1,448.2				
1976			1,608.9				
1977			817.4				
1978			1,679.8				
1979			2,045.3				
1980			3,572.7				
1981			4,048.2				
1982			3,858.1				
1983			3,054.0				
1984			3,109.1				

Source:
IMF, *Balance of Payments Yearbook,* various issues.

Table A4

SECTORAL DISTRIBUTION OF FOREIGN DIRECT CAPITAL STOCK, 1970-81 (S $ m)[1]

	Inward Investment			Outward Investment		
	Primary	*Secondary*	*Tertiary*	*Primary*	*Secondary*	*Tertiary*
1970	*Not Available*	777.6	965.9	*Not Available*		
1973		1,808.6	1,959.3			
1976		3,663.6	3,262.0			
1979		5,713.2	4,434.6			
1981		8,208.0	8,577.2			

Source:
Pang Eng Fong, *op cit,* data taken from Ministry of Trade and Industry, *Economic Survey of Singapore.*

NOTES TO TABLE A4

1 Represents total foreign equity investment, both direct and portfolio. Portfolio investment accounts for 16.1% of total foreign equity investment in 1970, 12.5% in 1973, 9.7% in 1976, 7.6% in 1979 and 7.0% in 1981.

Table A5

GEOGRAPHCAL DISTRIBUTION OF FOREIGN DIRECT CAPITAL STOCK, 1970-81 (S $ m)[1]

	Inward Investment			Outward Investment		
	Developed Countries[2]	*Developing Countries*[3]	*Total*	*Developed Countries*[4]	*Developing Countries*[5]	*Total*
1970	997.7	684.2	1,743.5	*Not Available*		
1975	3,578.0	1,686.6	5,514.9			
1978	6,177.4	2,151.9	8,329.3			
1981	11,499.3	4,557.1	16,785.2	1,526.3	990.3	2,516.6

Source:
Pang Eng Fong, *op cit,* data taken from Ministry of Trade and Industry, *Economic Survey of Singapore.*

NOTES TO TABLE A5

1 Represents total foreign equity investment, both direct and portfolio. Portfolio investment accounts for 16.1% of total foreign equity investment in 1970, 12.5% in 1973, 9.7% in 1976, 7.6% in 1979 and 7.0% in 1981.

2 Developed countries include the USA, Australia, European countries and Japan.

3 Developing countries include Hong Kong, Taiwan, Malaysia and other Asian countries.

4 Australia and the USA only.

5 Asean developing countries only.

Table A6

INDUSTRIAL DISTRIBUTION OF FOREIGN DIRECT CAPITAL STOCK, 1970-81 (S$ m)[1]

	Inward Investment		Outward Investment
	1970	*1981*	
Primary	8.5	100.9	Not Avalable
Agriculture	2.8	82.2	
Mining & quarrying	5.7	18.7	
Secondary	777.9	8,203.1	
Food, drink & tobacco	173.9	282.5	
Chemicals & allied	17.6	842.9	
Metal products	26.0	354.9	
Mechanical engineering	30.9	1,024.6	
Electrical equipment	43.7	1,635.3	
Motor vehicles Other transportation equipment	41.8	560.9	
Textiles & clothing	20.1	156.2	
Paper & allied	22.3	74.5	
Wood & wood products	13.4	105.7	
Coal & petroleum products	400.4	2,620.0	
Other manufacturing	23.6	545.6	
Tertiary	966.1	8,481.2	
Construction	71.3	224.3	
Transport & communications	16.9	564.3	
Distributive trade	347.7	2,726.5	
Banking & finance	508.8	4,904.2	
Other services	12.4	61.9	
TOTAL	1,743.5	16,785.2	

Source:
Ministry of Trade and Industry, *Economic Survey of Singapore,* 1984.

NOTES TO TABLE A6

1 Represents total foreign equity investment, both direct and portfolio. Portfolio investment accounts for 16.1% of total foreign equity investment in 1970.

2 Includes textiles and wood.

Table A7

LEADING SOURCE AND RECIPIENT COUNTRIES, 1970-81 (S $ m)

	Inward Investment[1]		Outward Investment[2]
	1970	*1981*	*1980/2*
DEVELOPED AREAS	997.7	11,499.3	
Europe	547.9	6,096.9	
EEC of which:	511.6	5,395.5	*Not*
W. Germany	2.8	412.9	*Available*
Netherlands	26.8	382.3	
UK	472.4	4,438.9	
Other Europe of which	36.3	701.4	
Switzerland	33.9	583.8	
North America of which:	259.4	3,255.5	
USA	259.4	3,255.5	481.3
Other developed countries of which:	190.4	2,146.9	*N.A.*
Australia	65.4	412.2	1,045.0
Japan	125.0	1,734.7	*N.A.*
DEVELOPING AREAS	684.2	4,557.1	990.1
Asia & Pacific of which:	684.2	4,557.1	990.1
Hong Kong	181.9	2,223.6	43.3
Indonesia	*N.A.*	*N.A.*	235.2[1]
Malaysia	436.1	1,836.8	651.7
Philippines	*N.A.*	*N.A.*	24.9
Sri Lanka	*N.A.*	*N.A.*	24.7
Taiwan	17.3	56.4	*N.A.*
Thailand	*N.A.*	*N.A.*	10.3
UNSPECIFIED	61.6	728.8	*N.A.*
TOTAL	1,743.5	16,785.2	*N.A.*

Source:

Pang Eng Fong, *op cit,* data taken from Ministry of Trade and Industry, *Economic Survey of Singapore.*

NOTES TO TABLE A7

1 Figures represent foreign equity investment, both direct and portfolio. Portfolio investment accounts for 16.1% of total foreign equity investment in 1970.

2 Outward investment represents stock of FDI in selected Asian countries gathered through interviews in Singapore and FDI statistics of the host countries. The year of information ranges from 1980-82.

Table A8

INDICATORS OF THE SIGNIFICANCE OF INWARD FOREIGN DIRECT INVESTMENT OR THE ACTIVITIES OF FOREIGN-BASED COMPANIES TO THE NATIONAL ECONOMY, 1975-83

1	Direct capital stock of foreign affiliates at book value in 1983 as a proportion of:			
	a GNP at factor cost			65.29
	b population (in S $ per head)			9,006.32
2	Employment in foreign affiliates in 1982 as a percentage of all employment in manufacturing			54.6
3	Output of foreign affiliates in 1982 as a percentage of all companies' output in secondary (ie, manufacturing) industry			62.9
4	Exports of foreign affiliates in 1982 as a percentage of all manufacturing exports			72.1
5	Percentage share of assets, value added and employment accounted for by foreign affiliates in selected sectors, 1975			
		Assets	*Value Added*	*Employment*
	Manufacturing Sector			
	Food & drink[1]	67.3	64.8	48.9
	Chemicals & allied[2]	97.2	88.0	88.6
	Metals[3]	96.7	90.5	73.3
	Mechanical engineering Electrical equipment[4] Motor vehicles	88.7	93.1	90.4
	Other transportation equipment[5]	73.7	57.1	59.6
	Textiles & clothing[6]	98.0	93.1	92.3
	Paper and allied	45.4	61.2	45.4
	Rubber	70.5	80.9	71.0
	Stone, glass & clay[7]	98.0	93.2	
	Coal & petroleum products	100.0	100.0	100.0
	Timber & furniture	72.5	54.6	51.4
	Other manufacturing	78.2	*N.A.*	*N.A.*

Source:

Pang Eng Fong, *op cit,* data taken from Dept. of Statistics, *Report on the Census of Industrial Production.* Don Lecrow, 'Singapore' in S H Dunning, *Multinational Enterprises, Economic Structure and International Competitiveness,* 1985, data taken from S Y Chia, 'Foreign Investment in Singapore', Dept. of Economics and Statistics, University of Singapore.

NOTES TO TABLE A8

1 Figures represent food sector along. The percentage share of assets, value added and employment accounted for by foreign affiliates in the beverage sector are 6.1%, 4.9% and 9.1% respectively.

2 Figures represent industrial chemicals. The percentage share of assets, value added and employment accounted for by foreign affiliates in other chemicals are 82.9%, 87.0% and 61.6% respectively.

3 Figures represent iron and steel. For non-ferrous metals, the corresponding figures for assets, value added and employment are 99.5%, 97.0% and 94.6% respectively. For fabricated metal products, the corresponding figures for assets, value added and employment are 64.8%, 61.7% and 53.1% respectively.

4 Figures represent radios, TVs, semiconductors and other electrical machinery. For calculators, refrigerators, air conditioners and industrial machinery, the corresponding figures for assets, value added and employment are 76.4%, 76.0% and 63.5%.

5 Figures include oil rigs.

6 Figures represent textiles alone. For garments, the corresponding figures for assets, value added and employment are 81.6%, 64.6% and 65.6%.

Table A9

INDICATORS OF THE SIGNIFICANCE OF OUTWARD FOREIGN DIRECT INVESTMENT OR THE ACTIVITIES OF HOME-BASED COMPANIES ABROAD FOR THE NATIONAL ECONOMY, 1975-80

1	Foreign capital stock of home-based firms at book value in 1980 as a proportion of		
	a	GNP at factor cost	10.79
	b	population (in S $ per head)	1,044.23
2	Employment in foreign affiliates in 1975 as a percentage of domestic employment in all industry		67.2

Source:
Lecrow, *op cit.*

Table A10

DISTRIBUTION OF FOREIGN SUBSIDIARIES AND ASSOCIATES AND FOREIGN CAPITAL STOCK BY PERCENTAGE OWNERSHIP OF PARENT COMPANIES, 1981 (S $ m)[1]

	Inward Investment		Outward Investment	
	Number of Affiliates	*Value of Capital Stock*	*Number of Affiliates*	*Value of Capital Stock*
100% owned subsidiaries	2,967	*Not Separately Available*	*Not Available*	
50-99.9% owned subsidiaries and associates	1,336			
Less than 50% owned subsidiaries and associates	2,762			
TOTAL	7,065	15,603.7		

Source:
Pang Eng Fong, *op cit.*

NOTES TO TABLE A10

1 As a percentage of value of output in 1978, wholly owned subsidiaries accounted for 71.5% and joint ventures 28.5%; and in terms of exports 77.5% and 22.5%.

Table A12

LEADING DOMESTIC MULTINATIONAL COMPANIES

Name		*Sector*	*Sales (US $ m)*
1	Wah Chang International Corp Pte Ltd	Conglomerate – food, electronic equipment, engineering, construction, trading, oil rigs, real estate	200.0 (1982)
2	Gold Coin Ltd	Food & pharmaceutical distributor	144.5 (1982)
3	Haw Par Brothers International	Conglomerate – textiles, pharmaceuticals, financial and travel services	142.3 (1981)
4	YEOH Hiap Seng Ltd	Food	105.0 (1981)
5	Jack Chia MPH Ltd	Conglomerate – pharmaceuticals, textiles, food, publishing, hotels, services	90.0 (1982)
6	Intraco	Conglomerate – trading, textiles, furniture, mining, shipping, property & services	60.0
7	ACMA Electrical Industries Ltd	Electrical equipment	52.7 (1981)
8	Prima Ltd Flour Mills	Food, shipping, finance, real estate, services	22.7
9	Lam Soon Soap & Oil Manufacturing	Manufacturer of oil, soap, detergent, canned food	18-23 (1981)
10	Lamipack Industries Pte Ltd	Plastic products	13.6 (1978)
11	Amoy Canning Corp	Food canning	*N.A.*
12	Joo Seng	Conglomerate – trading, manufacturing, hotel, property	*N.A.*
13	Keck Seng & Co Ltd	Conglomerate – trading in agriculturural products & plantations, property development	*N.A.*
14	Keppel Shipyard Ltd	Marine conglomerate	*N.A.*
15	Malayan Breweries	Beer manufacturer	*N.A.*
16	Pan Electric Industries Ltd	Electrical equipment, engineering equipment & supply of marine products	*N.A.*
17	Times Publishing Bld	Printing & distribution of newspapers and books	*N.A.*

Source:
ESCAP/UNCTC, *Transnational Corporations from Developing Asian Economies,* Publication Series B, No 7.

SRI LANKA

During the period 1970-77 the climate was not favourable for foreign investment in Sri Lanka mainly due to the somewhat restrictive policies of the government. However, after the 1977 General Election, policy changes occurred which have had a major impact on private investment, particularly on foreign investment. In 1978 the Investment Promotion Zone (IPZ) was established, an area of about 200 square miles near Colombia, one of the main objectives of which is the encouragement of inflow of foreign capital. Foreign investments in the IPZ have indeed promoted a rapid increase in the stock of foreign capital in Sri Lanka. The flow of inward investment continued to rise until 1982, but fell significantly in 1983 and 1984.

The sources of foreign investment were largely determined by the nature of the industrial activity of the businesses established at the outset of the IPZ. Far Eastern sources predominate, followed at a considerable distance by the USA, West Germany and the UK. Nevertheless, for businesses still in the process of establishment, much of the investment is from Western Europe and the USA, with Japan involved to a limited extent.

In the IPZ, new investments have been concentrated in the textiles and ready-made garments, and non-metallic mineral sectors, although since 1981 there has been a slight shift to basic metals and engineering products sectors. The major area, however, for inward investment, particularly outside the IPZ, is in the tertiary sector, with main emphasis on construction, tourist hotels and recreational industries.

MAIN SOURCES OF DATA:

A Official

1. Ministry of Finance and Planning, 'Field Survey of Projects Approved by the Foreign Investment Advisory Committee, 1977-84'.
2. Central Bank of Sri Lanka, *Annual Reports,* various issues.
3. UNCTC, *Transnational Corporations in World Development: Third Survey,* New York: UN, 1983.
4. UN, *Transnational Corporations from Developing Asian Economies* ESCAP/UNCTC Publication Series B, no 7, Bangkok, Thailand, 1985.

B Private

1. Dr P Nugawela, 'Policies to Attract Export Oriented Industries: The Role of Free Export Processing Zones, The Investment Promotion Zone in Sri Lanka', Ceylon Institute of Scientific and Industrial Research, May 1981.

Note:
Data do not allow us to complete Tables A9, or A11 for Sri Lanka.

Table A1

SUMMARY OF THE COUNTRY'S INTERNATIONAL INVESTMENT POSITION

		Inward Investment	Outward Investment
1	Number of foreign affiliates in host country, and of foreign affiliates of home country firms at the end of 1980[1]	100	*N.A.*
2	Number of foreign firms with direct investments in host country, and home country firms with direct foreign affiliates	*N.A.*	*N.A.*
3	Total foreign direct capital stock at book value as a percentage of GNP at factor cost in 1983	4.11	*N.A.*
4	Flow of foreign direct investment in the five year period, 1980-84 (S Rup m)	4,699.3	*N.A.*
5	Employment in foreign affiliates or abroad	*N.A.*	*N.A.*
6	Output of foreign affiliates or abroad	*N.A.*	*N.A.*

Source:

Central Bank of Sri Lanka, *Annual Report,* various issues; IMF, *International Financial Statistics, 1984.*

NOTES TO TABLE A1

1 Represents number of foreign affiliates of MNEs from selected home countries as estimated by UNCTC, 1983.

Table A2

PRIVATE FOREIGN CAPITAL STOCK, 1975 - 84 (S Rup m)[1]

	Inward Investment			Outward Investment		
	Portfolio	*Direct*	*Total*	*Portfolio*	*Direct*	*Total*
Book value of capital stock						
1975		462.8				
1978	*Not Available*	1,085,4	*Not Available*	*Not Available*		
1981		3,472.4				
1984		6,512.9				

Source:
Central Bank of Sri Lanka, *Annual Report,* various years, UNCTC, 1983, *op cit*

NOTES TO TABLE A2

1 Stock figures for 1981 and 1984 have been estimated by adding cumulative investment flows to the stock figure of 1978.

Table A3

FLOW OF FOREIGN DIRECT INVESTMENT, 1970 - 84 (S Rup m)[1]

	Inward Investment			Outward Investment		
	Reinvested Profits	*Other*	*Total*	*Reinvested Profits*	*Other*	*Total*
1970			−1.8			
1971			1.8			
1972			2.6			
1973			3.1			
1974			8.8			
1975			0.9			
1976	*Not Separately Available*		*N.A.*	*Not Available*		
1977			−10.4			
1978			23.5			
1979			728.3			
1980			710.2			
1981			948.6			
1982			1,323.5			
1983			887.9			
1984			829,15			

Source:
Central Bank of Sri Lanka, *Annual Report,* various years.

NOTES TO TABLE A3

1 Excluding reinvested profits.

Table A4

SECTORAL DISTRIBUTION OF FOREIGN DIRECT CAPITAL STOCK, 1984 (S Rup m)[1]

	Inward Investment				Outward Investment		
	Primary	*Secondary*	*Tertiary*		*Primary*	*Secondary*	*Tertiary*
1977-84	52.47	1,419.04	2,081.42		*Not Available*		

Source:

Ministry of Finance and Planning, 'Field Survey of Projects Approved by the Foreign Investment Advisory Committee, 1977-84', International Economic Co-operation Division.

NOTES TO TABLE A4

1 Calculations based on cumulative flows, 1977-84, which are smaller than the figures shown in Table A3 due to an unallocated component.

Table A5

GEOGRAPHICAL DISTRIBUTION OF FOREIGN DIRECT CAPITAL STOCK, 1981 (S Rup m)[1]

	Inward Investment				Outward Investment		
	Developed Countries	*Developing Countries*	*Total*		*Developed Countries*	*Developing Countries*	*Total*
1978-81	934.75	711.79	1,646.54		*Not Available*		

Source:

Dr P Nugawela, 'Policies to Attract Export Oriented Industries: The Role of Free Export Processing Zones. The Investment Promotion Zone in Sri Lanka', Ceylon Institute of Scientific and Industrial Research, May 1981.

NOTES TO TABLE A5

1 Calculations based on cumulative flows, 1978-81, and refer only to projects for which agreements are in force in the IPZ.

Table A6

INDUSTRIAL DISTRIBUTION OF FOREIGN DIRECT CAPITAL STOCK, 1984 (S Rup m)[1]

	Inward Investment	Outward Investment
	1977-84	
Primary	52.47	Not Available
Agriculture[2]	52.47	
Mining & quarrying	*neg.*	
Oil	*neg.*	
Secondary	1,419.04	
Food & drink	635.05	
Chemicals & allied	78.81[3]	
Metals Mechanical engineering Electrical equipment Motor vehicles Other transportation equipment	48.81[4]	
Textiles & clothing	351.73	
Paper & allied	9.91[5]	
Rubber	*N.S.A.*[3]	
Stone, clay & glass	269.59[6]	
Other manufacturing	25.14	
Tertiary	2,081.42	
Construction[7]	320.61	
Banking & finance[8]	164.51	
Other services[9]	1,596.30	
TOTAL	3,552.93	

Source:

Ministry of Finance and Planning, 'Field Survey of Projects Approved by the Foreign Investment Advisory Committee, 1977-84', International Economic Co-operation Division.

NOTES TO TABLE A6

1 Calculations based on cumulative flows, 1977-84.
2 Including animal husbandry and fishing.
3 Plastics and rubber based industries are included under chemicals.
4 Represents basic metal and engineering industries.
5 Represents wood and paper products, printing and publishing.
6 Represents non-metallic mineral products.
7 Represents civil engineering, construction and property development.
8 Specialised services.
9 Represents tourist hotels and recreation.

Table A7

LEADING SOURCE AND RECIPIENT COUNTRIES, 1978 - 82 (S Rup m)

	Inward Investment		Outward Investment
	1978-81[1]	*1982*[2]	
DEVELOPED AREAS	934.75	1,264.24	
Europe	476.54	918.89	
EEC of which:	363.58		
Belgium & Luxembourg	57.80		
Denmark	13.13		
France	28.39		
W. Germany	190.90		
Netherlands	3.78	*Not Separately Available*	
UK	69.58		
Other Europe of which:	112.96		
Leichtenstein	60.06		
Norway	10.10		
Switzerland	33.80		
North America of which:	397.15	102.34	
USA	397.15		
Other developed countries of which:	61.06	243.01	
Australia	35.06	*N.S.A.*	
Japan	26.00	243.01	
DEVELOPING AREAS	711.79	*N.S.A.*	*Not Available*
Africa of which:	42.76	*N.S.A.*	
Asia & Pacific of which:	645.92	948.86	
Fiji	1.97	*N.S.A.*	
Hong Kong	252.90	*N.S.A.*	
India	195.90	228.12	
S. Korea	33.38	*N.S.A.*	
Malaysia	*N.S.A.*	13.01	
Singapore	121.66	249.44	
Taiwan	15.01	*N.S.A.*	
Thailand	25.10	*N.S.A.*	
UNSPECIFIED	23.11	315.38	
TOTAL	1,646.54	2,213.10	

Source:
Dr P Nugawela, 'Policies to Attract Export Orientated Industries: The Role of Free Export Processing Zones. The Investment Promotion Zone in Sri Lanka', Ceylon Institute of Scientific and Industrial Research, May 1981; Ministry of Finance and Planning, Sri Lanka, 1982.

NOTES TO TABLE A7

1 Calculations based on cumulative flows, 1978-81 and refer only to projects for which agreements are signed in the IPZ.

2 Stock of incoming foreign investment as of 1982. Total does not match Table A2 due to an unallocated component whereby recent investment flows (including those into the IPZ) have not been fully incorporated into this stock figure. Hence, these figures are not comparable with those for 1978-81 which show inflows into the IPZ.

Table A8

INDICATORS OF THE SIGNIFICANCE OF INWARD FOREIGN DIRECT INVESTMENT OR THE ACTIVITIES OF FOREIGN-BASED COMPANIES TO THE NATIONAL ECONOMY, 1978 - 83

1	Direct capital stock of foreign affiliates at book value in 1983 as a proportion of:		
	a	GNP at factor cost	4.11
	b	population (in Rs per head)[1]	261.45
2	Investment in foreign affiliates as a percentage of domestic investment, 1978/80		0.7

NOTES TO TABLE A8

1 1982.

Table A10

There are few data on the distribution of foreign affiliates by percentage of ownership of the parent companies. However, in 1978, 58.2% of the UK capital stake in Sri Lanka took the form of joint ventures.

Table A12

LEADING FOREIGN MULTINATIONAL COMPANIES, 1983

Name	*Home Country*	*Sector*
BAT Industries PLC	UK	Tobacco
Glaxo Holdings PLC	UK	Pharmaceuticals
Royal Dutch/Shell Group of Companies	Netherlands/UK	Petroleum
The Singer Company	USA	Sewing machines
Union Carbide Corporation	USA	Chemicals
Warner-Lambert Company	USA	Pharmaceuticals

Source:
John M Stopford, *The World Directory of Multinational Enterprises 1982-83,* Bath: The Pitman Press, 1982.

TAIWAN

The data on foreign direct investment in Taiwan do not distinguish between direct and portfolio investment. Moreover, there is often significant deviation between approved and actual FDI which vary among different periods and different sectors. In any case, foreign investments account for only a small share in the capital of domestic companies. In the five-year period 1977-81 foreign direct investment flows to Taiwan amounted to only US $ 714.15 million, of which 95% represents investment in the manufacturing sector. Most of these foreign investments are sourced from Japan, the USA and Europe.

Taiwan is also a growing outward investor. In the five year period 1977-81, the flows of outward investment amounted to US $ 51.256 million, 80% of which represented investments in the manufacturing sector. These direct investments were directed towards the USA, Europe and Asia.

MAIN SOURCES OF DATA:

A **Official**

1 Central Bank of China, *Balance of Payments.*

2 Ministry of Economic Affairs Investment Commission, *A Survey Report of Business Operations and Economic Impact of Foreign and Overseas Chinese Enterprises in Taiwan, Republic of China, 1981* and *A Survey of Private Outward Investment in Taiwan, Republic of China.*

3 Republic of China Directorate General of Budget, Accounting and Statistics, *Statistical Yearbook 1982.*

B **Private**

1 Chi Schive, "Direct Foreign Investment, Technology Transfer and Industrialization in Taiwan," *Industrialization in Taiwan Proceedings*, Taipei: Academia Sinica 1983.

Table A1

SUMMARY OF THE COUNTRY'S INTERNATIONAL INVESTMENT POSITION

		Inward Investment	Outward Investment[1]
1	Number of foreign affiliates in host country, and of foreign affiliates of home country firms at the end of 1981	948	83
2	Number of foreign firms with direct investments in host country, and home country firms with direct foreign affiliates at the end of 1981	*N.A.*	54
3	Total foreign direct capital stock at book value as a percentage of GNP at factor cost in 1981	2.04	0.17
4	Flow of foreign direct investment in the five year period, 1976-80 (US $ m)	182.82	*N.A.*
5	Employment in foreign affiliates or abroad, 1981	322,473	*N.A.*
6	Output of foreign affiliates or abroad, US $ m	10,517	*N.A.*

Source:

Central Bank of China, *Balance of Payments*, various issues; Ministry of Economic Affairs Investment Commission, *A Survey Report of Business Operations* and *Economic Impact of Foreign and Overseas Chinese Enterprises in Taiwan, Republic of China 1981* and *A Survey of Private Outward Investment in Taiwan, Republic of China.*

NOTES TO TABLE A1

1 Outward investment refers to private outward investment only.

Table A2

PRIVATE FOREIGN CAPITAL STOCK, 1981 (US $ m)

	Inward Investment			Outward Investment		
	Portfolio	*Direct*	*Total*	*Portfolio*	*Direct*	*Total*
Book value of capital stock 1981	*N.A.*	911.063	*N.A.*	*N.A.*	59.883	*N.A.*

Source:
Ministry of Economic Affairs Investment Commission, *A Survey Report of Business Operations and Economic Impact of Foreign and Overseas Chinese Enterprises in Taiwan, Republic of China 1981* and *A Survey Report of Private Outward Investment in Taiwan, Republic of China.*

Table A3

FLOW OF FOREIGN DIRECT INVESTMENT, 1970 - 80 (US $ m)

	Inward Investment			Outward Investment		
	Reinvested Profits	*Other*	*Total*	*Reinvested Profits*	*Other*	*Total*
1970	*Not Separately Available*		3.60	*Not Available*		
1971			3.71			
1972			5.49			
1973			12.26			
1974			17.63			
1975			21.09			
1976			19.10			
1977			28.00			
1978			22.70			
1979			51.37			
1980			61.65			

Source:
Central Bank of China, *Balance of Payments,* various issues.

Table A4

SECTORAL DISTRIBUTION OF FOREIGN DIRECT CAPITAL STOCK, 1981 (US $ m)

	Inward Investment				Outward Investment		
	Primary	*Secondary*	*Tertiary*		*Primary*	*Secondary*	*Tertiary*
1981[1]	*N.A.*	849.693	61.362		*N.A.*	40.815	10.441

Source:
Ministry of Economic Affairs Investment Commission, *A Survey Report of Business Operations and Economic Impact of Foreign and Overseas Chinese Enterprises in Taiwan, Republic of China 1981* and *A Survey Report of Private Outward Investment in Taiwan, Republic of China.*

NOTES TO TABLE A4

1 Figures presented were converted to US dollars at the exchange rate 38 New Taiwan dollars to 1 US dollar. The total for both inward and outward investment excludes an unallocated component.

Table A5

GEOGRAPHICAL DISTRIBUTION OF FOREIGN DIRECT CAPITAL STOCK, 1981 (US $ m)

	Inward Investment				Outward Investment		
	Developed Countries[2]	*Developing Countries*	*Total*		*Developed Countries*	*Developing Countries*	*Total*
1981[1]	576.851	334.213	911.063		32.812	27.071	59.883

Source:
Ministry of Economic Affairs Investment Commission, *A Survey Report of Business Operations and Economic Impact of Foreign and Overseas Chinese Enterprises in Taiwan, Republic of China 1981* and *A Survey Report of Private Outward Investment in Taiwan, Republic of China.*

NOTES TO TABLE A5

1 Figures presented were converted to US dollars at the exchange rate 38 New Taiwan dollars to 1 US dollar.

2 Developed countries' investment include overseas Chinese direct investment in Taiwan, notably from Japan, as well as Western MNEs registered in LDCs.

Table A6

INDUSTRIAL DISTRIBUTION OF FOREIGN DIRECT CAPITAL STOCK, 1981 (US $ m)

	Inward Investment	Outward Investment
	1981	*1981*
Primary	*N.A.*	*N.A.*
Secondary	849.693	40.815
Food & drink	23.500	933
Chemicals & allied	204.344	8.343
Metals	48.478	1.013
Mechanical engineering	53.698	.050
Electrical equipment Motor vehicles Other transportation equipment	311.871	12.339
Textiles & clothing	104.623	.593
Paper & allied	4.529	1.960
Rubber	37.768	6.566
Stone, clay & glass	16.659	.977
Coal & petroleum products	*N.A.*	*N.A.*
Other manufacturing	44.226	*N.A.*
Tertiary	61.362	10.441
Construction	3.239	1.784
Transport & communications	13.414	*N.A.*
Distributive trade	5.971	7.383
Property	*N.A.*	*N.A.*
Banking & finance	*N.A.*	*N.A.*
Other services	38.738	1.274
TOTAL[1]	911.063	59.883

Source:
As for Table A4.

Table A7

LEADING SOURCE AND RECIPIENT COUNTRIES, 1981 (US $ m)

	Inward Investment	Outward Investment
	1981	*1981*
DEVELOPED AREAS	576.851	32.812
Europe	54.134	3.359
North America of which	228.306	27.071
United States	228.306	27.071
Other developed countries of which	294.409	2.382
Japan	294.409	.810
DEVELOPING AREAS	334.213	27.071
Asia & Pacific (except Japan or Middle East) of which	*Not Available*	16.311
Hong Kong		5.987
Indonesia		2.530
Malaysia		1.971
Philippines		.344
Singapore		5.479
Latin America		.938
TOTAL	911.063	59.883

Source:
As for Table A5.

Table A8

INDICATORS OF THE SIGNIFICANCE OF INWARD FOREIGN DIRECT INVESTMENT OR THE ACTIVITIES OF FOREIGN-BASED COMPANIES TO THE NATIONAL ECONOMY, 1981

1	Direct capital stock of foreign affiliates at book value in 1981 as a proportion of	
	a GNP at factor cost	2.04
	b population (in US $ per head)	50.23
2	Employment in foreign affiliates in 1981 as a percentage of all employment	
	a in all industry	4.83
	b in manufacturing	16.65
3	Exports of foreign affiliates in 1981 as a percentage of all manufacturing exports	25.60

4 Percentage share of sales and employment accounted for by foreign affiliates in selected sectors.

	Sales	*Employment*
Primary Goods Sector	*N.A.*	*N.A.*
Manufacturing Sector		
Food & drink	6.86	5.91
Chemicals & allied	28.79	27.94
Metals	4.40	8.03
Mechanical engineering	24.52	20.06
Electrical equipment	48.58	48.11
Motor vehicles	*N.A.*	*N.A.*
Other transportation equipment	*N.A.*	*N.A.*
Textiles & clothing	6.52	12.65
Paper & allied	7.90	4.47
Rubber[1]	5.46	7.84
Stone, glass & clay	26.75	11.33
Coal & petroleum products	*N.A.*	*N.A.*
Timber & furniture	2.12	3.30
Other manufacturing	*N.A.*	19.47
Services Sector		
Construction		0
Transport & communications	*Not*	0.57
Trade & distribution	*Available*	0
Banking & finance		*N.A.*
Other services		0.84

Source:
Ministry of Economic Affairs, *op cit;* Republic of China Directorate General of Budget, Accounting and Statistics, *Statistical Yearbook 1982.*

NOTES TO TABLE A8

1 Including plastic products.

Table A9

INDICATORS OF THE SIGNIFICANCE OF OUTWARD FOREIGN DIRECT INVESTMENT OR THE ACTIVITIES OF HOME-BASED COMPANIES ABROAD FOR THE NATIONAL ECONOMY, 1981

1	Foreign capital stock of home-based firms at book value in 1981 as a proportion of	
	a GNP at factor cost	0.17
	b population (in US $ per head)	4.19

Table A10

DISTRIBUTION OF FOREIGN SUBSIDIARIES AND ASSOCIATES AND FOREIGN CAPITAL STOCK BY PERCENTAGE OWNERSHIP OF PARENT COMPANIES, 1981

	Inward Investment		**Outward Investment**	
	Number of Affiliates	*Value of Capital Stock*	*Number of Affiliates*	*Value of Capital Stock*
100% owned subsidiaries	208		25	
50-99.9% owned subsidiaries and associates	318	*Not Available*	24	*Not Available*
Less than 50% owned subsidiaries and associates	269		35	
TOTAL	795		84	

Source:
As in Table A8.

Table A11

ROYALTY RECEIPTS AND PAYMENTS, 1976 - 81 (US $ th)

	Payments			Receipts		
	To Affiliates	*To Non-affiliates*	*Total*	*From Affiliates*	*From Non-affiliates*	*Total*
1976			38,569	*Not*		
1977			42,040	*Separately*		
1978	*Not*		51,868	*Available*		
1979	*Available*		69,120			1,394
1980			85,400			1,750
1981			95,130			3,029

Source:
As for Table A4.

Table A12

LEADING FOREIGN AND DOMESTIC MULTINATIONAL COMPANIES, 1983

A Leading Foreign Affiliates in the Country

	Name	*Home Country*	*Sector*	*Taiwanese Sales (NT $ million)*
1	RCA (Taiwan) Ltd	USA	Electrical equipment	7,241
2	Atari Taiwan Manufacturing Corp	USA	Electronic equipment	5,041
3	Texas Instruments Taiwan Ltd	USA	Data processing equipment	4,976
4	Uniden Corp of Taiwan			3,663
5	Philips Electronics Industries (Taiwan) Ltd	Netherlands	Electrotechnical equipment	3,590
6	The Flying Tiger Line			3,486
7 7	Philips Electronics Building Elements	Netherlands	Electrotechnical equipment	3,380
8	AOC International			3,040
9	Capetronic (Taiwan) Ltd	UK	Electrical equipment	2,750
10	Canon Inc Taiwan	Japan	Office equipment	2,539
11	Zenith Taiwan Corp	USA	Consumer electronic products	2,400
12	TMX Taiwan Ltd			2,236
13	General Instrument of Taiwan Ltd	USA	Electronic equipment	2,144
14	Orion Electric (Taiwan) Co Ltd		Electrical equipment	2,088
15	Philips Video Products (Taiwan) Ltd	Netherlands	Electrotechnical equipment	1,950
16	Digital Equipment Taiwan Ltd	USA	Computers and associated peripheral equipment, related software & supplies	1,899
17	Taiwan Yazaki Corp	Japan		1,886
18	Wang Laboratories (Taiwan) Ltd	USA	Office equipment	1,852
19	Funai Electronics Co Ltd	Japan	Electronic equipment	1,779
20	Oak East Industries Ltd			1,748
21	Getz Bros & Co Inc			1,712
22	TC Electronics (Taiwan) Corp	USA	Electronic equipment	1,619
23	Mattel Ltd (Taiwan)	USA	Toys	1,592
24	Funai Electric Co of Taiwan	Japan	Electrical equipment	1,443
25	Casa Liebermann Taiwan Ltd			1,378

Table A12 (cont'd)

LEADING FOREIGN AND DOMESTIC MULTINATIONAL COMPANIES, 1983

B	Leading Domestic Companies with Multinational Interests		
Name		*Sector*	*Global Sales (NT $ million)*
1	Tatung Co	Electronics	13,431
2	Taiwan Glass Industry Corp	Glass	2,503
			No. of subsidiaries overseas
3	Dyecharm Trading & Engineering Co Ltd	Trade & engineering	4
4	Hotel New Asia	Hotels	2
5	The Tai Ping Insurance Co, Ltd	Insurance	2
6	Paul C T Chen & Co	Distributive trade	1
7	Formosa Furniture & Wood Industry Co Ltd	Furniture & wood manufacture	1
8	Houseware Taiwan Industries Ltd	Houseware	1
9	Jumbo Specialities Ltd	Distributive trade	1
10	Lynnbros Industrial Co Ltd	Chemicals, trading	1
11	Million International Corp	Banking & finance	1
12	Zimmerman Scientific Co Ltd	Laboratory supplies	1

Source:
Who Owns Whom 1984.

TAIWAN: DEFINITIONS

Foreign direct investment statistics as provided by the Ministry of Economic Affairs Investment Commission do not include investments made by foreigners in the banking sector and outward direct investments undertaken by public enterprises in Taiwan. Moreover, there is a significant deviation between approved and actual FDI. These deviations vary among different period and among different sectors.

Source:
Ministry of Economic Affairs, *A Survey Report of Operations and Economic Effects of Foreign and Overseas Chinese Enterprises in Taiwan, Republic of China* and *A Survey of Private Outward Investment of Taiwan, Republic of China.*

THAILAND

Thailand has adopted a favourable attitude toward foreign investment and MNEs. The official envouragement of private investment was started in the late 1950s and there has been a rapid increase in the inflow of foreign direct investment in Thailand over the last 25 years. Such inflow of foreign direct investment has contributed to the diversification of the country's industrial structure and has helped to accelerate the pace of industrialization. MNEs are among the largest companies in the various economic sectors of Thailand, accounting for a large proportion of the sales of Thailand's top 1000 companies.

The major sources of foreign investment in Thailand are the USA and Japan, but in recent years, there has been the rapid growth of direct investment from the Third World, notably from Hong Kong and Taiwan. The pattern of foreign direct investment has shifted from resource-based activities such as agriculture and mining towards other sectors, particularly manufacturing, trade and construction. The combined share of these industries in the total net inflow of foreign direct investment has increased from 57% in the period 1970 to 1974 to 77% in the period 1975 to 1979. Indeed, MNEs are predominant in various manufacturing activities, namely: chemicals, iron, steel and basic metals, machinery and fabricated metal products and textiles. Moreover, MNEs have also been present in the mining, trade and finance sectors. Textiles, electrical appliances, chemicals and food accounted for 82% of the total value of foreign direct investment inflows into the manufacturing sector between 1970 and 1979. This pattern of sectoral distribution of foreign direct investment reflects the emphasis given by the government to the promotion of investment in labour-intensive and resource-based export industries during the 1970s.

There is a limited amount of Thai foreign direct investment: mainly in other Asian countries. in 1982, for example, there was US S 13 million of Thai investment in Indonesian manufacturing industry.

MAIN SOURCES OF DATA:

A **Official**

1. Bank of Thailand, *Monthly Bulletin,* provides data on the flows of foreign direct investment, by geographical and sectoral distribution.
2. Board of Investments: provides statistics on BOI-promoted investments.
3. UN, *Costs and Conditions of Technology Transfer through Transnational Corporations,* ESCAP/UNCTC Joint Unit on Transnational Corporations, Bangkok, Thailand, April 1984.
4. UN Economic and Social Commission for Asia and the Pacific, *Patterns and Impact of Foreign Investment in the ESCAP Region,* Thailand: UN, 1985.

B **Private**

1. Somsak Tambunlertchai and Ian McGovern, 'An Overview of the Role of MNEs in the Economic Development of Thailand', paper prepared for Conference on the Role of MNEs in Thailand organized by Thammasat University, 7-9 July 1984.
2. Friedrich von Kirchback, 'Economic Policies towards TNCs: The Experience of ASEAN countries', PhD thesis, University of Regensburg, 1981.

Note
Data do not allow us to complete Table A9 for Thailand.

Table A1

SUMMARY OF THE COUNTRY'S INTERNATIONAL INVESTMENT POSITION

		Inward Investment	Outward Investment
1	Number of foreign affiliates in host country, and of foreign affiliates of home country firms at the end of 1980[1]	564	*N.A.*
2	Number of foreign firms with direct Investments in host country, and home country firms with direct for foreign affiliates at the end of 1983	698	*N.A.*
3	Total foreign direct capital stock at book value as a percentage of GNP at factor cost in 1984	4.87	0.10[2]
4	Flow of foreign direct investment in the five year period, 1980-84 (Baht m)	32,294.0	204.3
5	Employment in foreign affiliates or abroad, 1976[3]	50,882	*N.A.*
6	Output of foreign affiliates or abroad, 1980 (Baht m)	215,019[4]	*N.A.*

Source:

Board of Investments, Thailand, *Annual Report;* Bank of Thailand, *Monthly Bulletin,* various issues; Friedrich von Kirchback, 'Economic Policies towards TNCs: The Experience of ASEAN countries', PhD thesis, University of Regensburg, 1981; Somsak Tambunlertchai and Ian McGovern, 'An Overview of the Role of MNEs in the Economic Development of Thailand', paper prepared for Conference on the Role of MNEs in Thailand organized by Thammasat University, 7-9 July 1984; IMF, *Balance of Payments Yearbook 1985.*

NOTES TO TABLE A1

1 Represents affiliates of MNEs from selected home countries as identified by the UNCTC, 1983.

2 Estimated by authors.

3 Employment figure based on 103 Thai-Japanese joint ventures in the manufacturing sector corresponding to 0.27% of total labour force and 1.1% of non-agricultural labour force in 1976.

4 Represents total sales of the top 214 foreign companies in the manufacturing sector and 64 foreign companies in services that are included in the list of Thailand's top 1,000 companies tanked by sales. The sales of foreign owned manufacturing companies are 150,461 million baht and sales of foreign owned service companies are 64,558 million baht.

Table A2

PRIVATE FOREIGN CAPITAL STOCK, 1970 - 84 (Baht m)

	Inward Investment			Outward Investment		
	Portfolio	*Direct*[1]	*Total*	*Portfolio*	*Direct*	*Total*
Book value of capital stock						
1970	237.0	890.5	1,127.5			
1975	1,048.4	10,312.1	11,360.5		*Not Available*	
1978	1,152.8	15,100.8	16,253.5			
1981	4,336.5	26,327.7	30,664.2			
1982	4,946.3	30,666.3	35,612.6	*N.A.*	2,012.5	*N.A.*
1984	5,199.6	48,442.5	53,642.1	*N.A.*	2,061.3	*N.A.*

Source:
Bank of Thailand, *Monthly Bulletin,* various issues; Tambunlertchai and McGovern, *op cit.*

NOTES TO TABLE A2

1 Represents cumulative flows of foreign direct investment from 1970.

2 Estimated by adding cumulative investment flows of 1983 and 1984 to stock figure of 1982.

Table A3

FLOW OF FOREIGN DIRECT INVESTMENT, 1970 - 84 (Baht m)[1]

	Inward Investment			Outward Investment		
	Reinvested Profits	*Other*	*Total*	*Reinvested Profits*	*Other*	*Total*
1970			890.5			
1971			808.4			
1972			1,427.1	*Not Available*		
1973			1,604.9			
1974			3,836.4			
1975			1,744.8			
1976	*Not Separately Available*		1,614.1	*Not Separately Available*		70.7
1977			2,163.9			*N.A.*
1978			1,010.7			127.3
1979			1,047.7			79.1
1980			3,816.0			53.3
1981			6,363.2			51.4
1982			4,338.6			50.8
1983			8,008.4			24.6
1984			9,767.8			24.2

Source:
Bank of Thailand, *Monthly Bulletin,* various issues; IMF, *Balance of Payments Yearbook,* various issues.

NOTES TO TABLE A3

1 Excludes reinvested profits.

Table A4

SECTORAL DISTRIBUTION OF FOREIGN DIRECT CAPITAL STOCK, 1970 - 84 (Baht m)[1]

	Inward Investment			Outward Investment		
	Primary	*Secondary*	*Tertiary*	*Primary*	*Secondary*	*Tertiary*
1970	18.7	446.9	424.9	*Not Available*		
1972	247.0	866.0	2,013.0			
1973	295.1	1,474.6	2,961.2			
1975	1,554.3	3,087.5	5,670.3			
1977	1,733.9	4,205.4	8,150.8			
1979	1,941.3	5,392.2	8,815.0			
1982	5,214.8	10,139.3	15,312.2			
1984	9,531.9	15,865.0	23,045.6			

Source:
Bank of Thailand, *Monthly Bulletin,* various issues.

NOTES TO TABLE A4

1 Represents cumulative flows of foreign direct investment as from 1974.

Table A5

GEOGRAPHICAL DISTRIBUTION OF FOREIGN DIRECT CAPITAL STOCK, 1970 - 84 (Baht m)[1]

	Inward Investment			Outward Investment		
	Developed Countries[2]	*Developing Countries*[3]	*Total*	*Developed Countries*	*Developing Countries*	*Total*
1970	758.7	62.8	890.5	*Not Available*		
1972	2,628.5	266.7	3,126.0			
1973	3,972.6	587.0	4,730.9			
1975	8,430.0	1,610.0	10,312.1			
1977	11,526.6	2,291.6	14,090.1			
1979	13,627.2	2,278.9	16,148.5			
1982	23,860.7	5,359.8	30,666.3			
1984	36,643.4	8,501.6	48,442.5			

Source:
Bank of Thailand, *Monthly Bulletin,* various issues.

NOTES TO TABLE A5

1 Represents cumulative flows of foreign direct investment as from 1970.

2 Developed countries refer to Japan, USA, UK, West Germany, France, Netherlands, Italy, Switzerland, and Canada. For 1982, developed countries refer only to Japan, USA, UK and West Germany.

3 Developing countries refer to Hong Kong, Singapore, Malaysia and Taiwan. For 1982, developing countries refer only to Hong Kong and Singapore.

Table A6

INDUSTRIAL DISTRIBUTION OF FOREIGN DIRECT CAPITAL STOCK, 1970 - 84 (Baht m)[1]

	Inward Investment		Outward Investment
	1970-75	*1970-84*	
Primary	1,554.3	9,531.9	Not Available
Agriculture	27.2	362.7	
Mining & quarrying	1,527.1	9,169.2[2]	
Oil	*N.A.*	*N.A.*	
Secondary	3,087.5	15,865.0	
Food & drink	410.0	876.1	
Chemicals & allied	373.8	1,778.9[3]	
Metals[4]	174.2	1,667.0	
Mechanical engineering[5]	75.0	1,318.8	
Electrical equipment	351.3	4,326.8	
Motor vehicles / Other transportation equipment	*N.A.*	*N.A.*	
Textiles & clothing	1,355.1	2,874.1	
Paper & allied	*N.A.*	*N.A.*	
Rubber	*N.A.*	*N.A.*	
Stone, clay & glass	57.7	–20.2	
Coal & petroleum products	161.2	2,269.9	
Other manufacturing	129.2	773.6	
Tertiary	5,670.3	23,045.6	
Construction	1,029.6	6,489.3	
Transport & communications[6]	226.4	2,057.5	
Distributive trade	2,088.3	8,986.7	
Property	91.3	491.4	
Banking & finance	2,067.8	3,220.7	
Other services	166.9	1,800.0	
TOTAL	10,312.1	48,442.5	

Source:
Bank of Thailand, *Monthly Bulletin,* various issues.

NOTES TO TABLE A6

1 Represents cumulative flows of foreign direct investment as from 1970.
2 Includes oil exploration.
3 Including paper.
4 Including non-metallic minerals.
5 Including transportation equipment.
6 Including travel.

Table A7

LEADING SOURCE AND RECIPIENT COUNTRIES, 1970 - 84 (Baht m)[1]

	Inward Investment			Outward Investment
	1970-75	*1970-84*		
DEVELOPED AREAS	8,430.0	34,551.7		Not Available
Europe	1,459.1	6.499.4		
EEC of which:	1,261.1	5,774.5		
France	255.9	422.4		
W. Germany	82.5	1,295.4		
Italy	91.0	839.9		
Netherlands	259.2	465.6		
UK	572.5	2,751.2		
Other Europe of which:	198.0	724.9		
Switzerland	198.0	724.9		
North America of which:	4,163.5	14,740.3		
Canada	49.1	119.5		
USA	4,114.4	14,620.8		
Other developed countries of which:	2,807.4	13,312.0		
Japan	2,807.4	13,312.0		
DEVELOPING AREAS	1,610.0	8,501.6		
Asia & Pacific (except Japan or Middle East) of which:	1,610.0	8,501.6		
Hong Kong	1,001.8	4,477.2		
Malaysia	94.5	452.4		
Singapore	496.0	3,466.8		
Taiwan	17.7	105.2		
Other unspecified countries	272.1	5,389.2		
TOTAL	10,312.1	48,442.5		

Source:

Bank of Thailand, *Monthly Bulletin,* various issues.

NOTES TO TABLE A7

1 Represents cumulative flows of foreign direct investment as from 1970.

Table A8

INDICATORS OF THE SIGNIFICANCE OF INWARD FOREIGN DIRECT INVESTMENT OR THE ACTIVITIES OF FOREIGN-BASED COMPANIES TO THE NATIONAL ECONOMY, 1971 - 84

1	Direct capital stock of foreign affiliates at book value in 1984 as a proportion of:	
	a GNP at factor cost	4.87
	b population (in Baht per head)	957.74
2	Output of foreign affiliates in 1971 as a percentage of all companies' output in secondary (ie, manufacturing) industry	18.17
3	Exports of foreign affiliates in 1971 as a percentage of all manufacturing exports[2]	22.73
4	Profits of foreign affiliates in 1971 as a percentage of profits of all companies in the host country	17.38
5	Percentage share of sales accounted for by foreign affiliates in selected sectors, 1980	
		Sales[3]
	Primary Goods Sector	
	Mining and quarrying	50.3
	Manufacturing Sector	
	Food and drink	32.1[4]
	Chemicals and allied	95.0[5]
	Metals	84.1
	Mechanical engineering	82.2[6]
	Textiles and clothing	71.6
	Paper and allied	52.8
	Rubber	*N.S.A.*
	Stone, glass & clay	28.6
	Coal & petroleum products	*N.S.A.*
	Timber and furniture	11.6
	Other manufacturing	5.7
	Services Sector	
	Trade and distribution	70.1[7]

Source:

Kirchbach, *op cit.*; Tambunlertchai, *op cit.*

NOTES TO TABLE A8

1 Employment figures are derived from 103 Thai-Japanese joint ventures in the manufacturing sector.

2 Figure refers to a sample of 18,340 firms including 131 foreign firms (25 subsidiaries of foreign firms and 106 firms with more than 25% foreign capital participation.

3 Represents share of foreign companies in the sales of the top 1,066 companies.

4 Including tobacco.

5 Including petroleum, rubber and plastic.

6 Including fabricated metal products.

7 Represents general trading. For agricultural wholesaling, 4.6%, food wholesaling, 9.7%, other wholesaling, 32.0%.

Table A10

DISTRIBUTION OF FOREIGN SUBSIDIARIES AND ASSOCIATES AND FOREIGN CAPITAL STOCK BY PERCENTAGE OWNERSHIP OF PARENT COMPANIES, 1983 (Baht m)

	Inward Investment		Outward Investment	
	Number of Affiliates	*Value of Capital Stock*	*Number of Affiliates*	*Value of Capital Stock*
100% owned subsidiaries	33	689,822	*Not Available*	
50-99.9% owned subsidiaries and associates Less than 50% owned subsidiaries and associates	665[2]	6,446,193		
TOTAL	698	7,136,015		

Source:
Tambunlertchai, *op cit.;* Data taken from Board of Investments

NOTES TO TABLE A10

1 Figures represent registered capital of foreign firms with promotion certifications from the Board of Investments.

2 Represents total number of firms that are joint ventures between Thai and foreign investors.

Table A11

ROYALTY RECEIPTS AND PAYMENTS, 1970 - 84 (Baht m)

	Payments			Receipts		
	To Affiliates	*To Non-affiliates*	*Total*	*From Affiliates*	*From Non-affiliates*	*Total*
1970	*Not Separately Available*		66.2	*Not Available*		
1973			164.2			
1976			256.9			
1977			337.9			
1978			401.7			
1979			456.9			
1980			610.4			
1981			816.2			
1982			872.7			
1983			933.6			
1984			1,161.3			

Source:
Bank of Thailand, *Monthly Bulletin,* various issues.

Table A12

LEADING FOREIGN MULTINATIONAL COMPANIES, 1983

	Name	*Home Country*	*Sector*
1	ASEA AB	Sweden	Electrical equipment
2	BBC – Brown Boveri & Company	Switzerland	Electrical engineering
3	Ciba-Geigy	Switzerland	Chemicals
4	Carnation Company	USA	Food products
5	Castle and Cooke Incorporated	USA	Food products
6	Citicorp Development Finance Corporation	USA	Finance
7	The Colgate Palmolive Company	USA	Consumer products
8	Diamond Shamrock Corp	USA	Energy and chemicals
9	The Dow Chemical Company	USA	Chemicals
10	Exxon Corporation	USA	Petroleum
11	Goodyear Tyre and Rubber Company	USA	Rubber tyres
12	The Upjohn Company	USA	Pharmaceuticals
13	Hoechst AG	W. Germany	Chemicals
14	AB Volvo	Sweden	Motor vehicles
15	Honda Motor Company Limited	Japan	Motorcycles
16	International Business Machines Corp	USA	Computers
17	Nestle SA	Switzerland	Food products
18	Phelps Dodge Corporation	USA	Metals
19	NV Philips Gloeilampenfabrieken	Netherlands	Electrotechnical equipment
20	Royal Dutch/Shell Group of Companies	Netherlands/UK	Petroleum
21	The Wellcome Foundation	UK	Pharmaceuticals
22	Thorn EMI PLC	UK	Electric consumer products
23	Unilever	UK/Netherlands	Consumer products
24	AB Electrolux	Sweden	Electrical equipment
25	Sanyo Electric Company Limited	Japan	Electrical and Electronic equipment

Source:

John M Stopford, *The World Directory of Multinational Enterprises 1982–83,* Bath: The Pitman Press, 1982.

THAILAND TABLES : DEFINITIONS

The Bank of Thailand provides annual data on the inflows of foreign direct capital. It includes equity and loans from parent or related companies, including capital funds of foreign commercial banks.

Official data on foreign direct investment in Thailand are available only for the registered capital of firms granted promotion certificates (firms granted investment incentives). Registered capital is the intended equity capital that the firm registers with the Ministry of Commerce prior to commencing operations. However, it is the proposed and not the actual capital of promoted firms that is indicated by these data. Moreover, details on the capital investment of non-promoted direct foreign investment firms are also excluded.

Source:

Bank of Thailand; Board of Investments, Thailand.

AUSTRALASIA

(except Australia or New Zealand)

FIJI

Fiji is a modern host country for foreign direct investment, with effectively no outward investment. The penetration by foreign companies has slightly declined in recent years due to a slow down of new foreign investment and a trend of 'buy-outs' by European nationals. The main foreign investor is Australia, with New Zealand, the UK, the USA and Japan also being of importance. Nearly 70% of all inward investment is in the tertiary sector but there are also substantial foreign interests in fishing, mining and forestry. There is some anxiety about dependence on Australia, and a wish not to become as reliant on foreign owned firms as Canada, but generally foreign investment has been well received and considered beneficial. Joint ventures between foreign and local investors are encouraged; only in the sugar industry is no foreign participation allowed.

Policy towards inward investment is implemented by Economic Development Board, created in 1980; such investment is especially welcomed in the secondary processing of primary products and in other areas likely to benefit Fijian employment and regional development objectives.

MAIN SOURCES OF DATA:

A Official

1 Fiji Bureau of Statistics, *Survey of Overseas Investment in Fiji, 1969-70,* Suva, 1973.

B Private

1 R T Carstairs and R D Prasad, *Impact of Foreign Direct Private Investment on the Fiji Economy,* University of the South Pacific Centre for Applied Studies in Development, Suva, Fiji, November, 1981.

2 H M Gunasekeva, 'Fiji' in ESCAP, *Patterns and Impact of Foreign Investment in the ESCAP Region,* Bangkok, 1985.

Note:

Data do not allow us to complete Table A9.

Table A1

SUMMARY OF THE COUNTRY'S INTERNATIONAL INVESTMENT POSITION

		Inward Investment	Outward Investment
1	Number of foreign affiliates in host country, and of foreign affiliates of home country firms at the end of 1979	736[1]	*N.A.*
2	Number of foreign firms with direct investments in host country, and home country firms with direct foreign affiliates at the end of 1983	297	*N.A.*
3	Total foreign direct capital stock at book value as a percentage of GNP at at factor cost in 1984	37.4	*N.A.*
4	Flow of foreign direct investment in in the five year period, 1980-84 (F $ m)	152.9	2.0
5	Employment in foreign affiliates or abroad, 1980	14,800	*N.A.*
6	Output of foreign affiliates or abroad, 1980 (F $ m)	483.2	*N.A.*

Source:

R Carstairs and R Prasad, *Impact of Foreign Direct Private Investment on the Fiji Economy,* Centre for Applied Studies in Development, Suva, Fiji, November, 1981.

NOTES TO TABLE A1

1 Including 218 branches (companies not incorporated in Fiji); 31 of the affiliates are less than 20% foreign owned.

Table A2

PRIVATE FOREIGN CAPITAL STOCK, 1977 - 84 (F $ m)

	Inward Investment			Outward Investment		
	Portfolio	*Direct*[1]	*Total*	*Portfolio*	*Direct*[2]	*Total*
Book value of capital stock						
1977	*Not Available*	235	*Not Available*	*Not Available*	2.4	*Not Available*
1978		245			2.4	
1981		315			3.0	
1982		348			3.7	
1983		382			3.8	
1984		407			4.4	

Source:
R Carstairs and R Prasad, *Impact of Foreign Direct Private Investment on the Fiji Economy,* Centre for Applied Studies in Development, Suva, Fiji, 1981

NOTES TO TABLE A2

1 Figures after 1977 represent author's estimates based on cumulative investment flows.

2 Figures represent cumulative investment flows from 1970.

Table A3

FLOW OF FOREIGN DIRECT INVESTMENT, 1970 - 84 (F $ m)

	Inward Investment			Outward Investment		
	Reinvested Profits	*Other*	*Total*	*Reinvested Profits*	*Other*	*Total*
1970	*Not Separately Available*	*Not Separately Available*	7	*Not Separately Available*		*Not Available*
1971			8			
1972			9			
1973			13			–2.0
1974			12			1.8
1975			12			2.6
1976			*Not Available*			*Not Available*
1977						
1978						
1979	8.7	*N.A.*	8.7			
1980	10.3	20.5	30.8			1.9
1981	9.9	20.8	30.7			–1.3
1982	9.7	23.6	33.3			0.7
1983	10.1	22.8	33.0			0.1
1984	9.9	15.2	25.1			0.6

Source:
IMF, *Balance of Payments Statistics Yearbook,* various issues.

Table A4

SECTORAL DISTRIBUTION OF FOREIGN DIRECT CAPITAL STOCK, 1980 (F $ m)[1]

	Inward Investment				Outward Investment		
	Primary	*Secondary*	*Tertiary*		*Primary*	*Secondary*	*Tertiary*
1980	8.73	49.04	212.68		*Not Available*		

Source:

R Carstairs and R Prasad, *Impact of Foreign Direct Private Investment on the Fiji Economy,* Centre for Applied Studies in Development, Suva, Fiji, November, 1981.

NOTES TO TABLE A4

1 Figures estimated by applying the percentage shares of gross turnover of (20% or more) foreign-owned companies to the relevant years private foreign capital stock figure from Table A2.

Table A5

GEOGRAPHICAL DISTRIBUTION OF FOREIGN DIRECT CAPITAL STOCK, 1979 (numbers of affiliates)

	Inward Investment[1]				Outward Investment		
	Developed[2] Countries	*Developing[3] Countries*	*Total*		*Developed Countries*	*Developing Countries*	*Total*
1979	589	116	705		*Not Available*		

Source:

R Carstairs and R Prasad, *Impact of Foreign Direct Private Investment on the Fiji Economy,* Centre for Applied Studies in Development, Suva, Fiji, November, 1981.

NOTES TO TABLE A5

1 Number of affiliates with 20% or more foreign participation.

2 Australia, New Zealand, USA, UK and Japan, including 56 affiliates with more than one foreign parent.

3 Other countries.

Table A6

INDUSTRIAL DISTRIBUTION OF FOREIGN DIRECT CAPITAL STOCK, 1980 (F $ m)[1]

	Inward Investment	Outward Investment
	1980	
Primary	8.73	Not Available
Agriculture	2.36	
Mining & quarrying	6.37	
Oil	*N.S.A.*	
Secondary	49.04	
Food & drink	Not Separately Available	
Chemicals & allied		
Metals		
Mechanical engineering		
Electrical equipment		
Motor vehicles		
Other transportation equipment		
Textiles & clothing		
Paper & allied		
Rubber		
Stone, clay & glass		
Coal & petroleum products		
Other manufacturing		
Tertiary	212.68	
Construction	2.95	
Transport & communications	17.38	
Distributive trade	156.85	
Property	3.11	
Banking & finance	29.22	
Other services[2]	3.17	
TOTAL	270.45	

Source:

R Carstairs and R Prasad, *Impact of Foreign Direct Private Investment on the Fiji Economy,* Centre for Applied Studies in Development, Suva, Fiji, November, 1981.

NOTES TO TABLE A6

1 Figures estimated by applying the percentage share of gross turnover of (20% or more) foreign-owned companies to the relevant years private foreign capital stock figure of Table A2.

2 Including unspecified.

Table A7

LEADING SOURCE AND RECIPIENT COUNTRIES, 1979 (numbers of affiliates)

	Inward Investment[1]	Outward Investment
	1979	
DEVELOPED AREAS	565	
Europe		
EEC of which:		
Belgium & Luxembourg	1	
France	15	
W. Germany	2	
Italy	4	
Netherlands	1	
UK	50	
Other Europe of which:		
Switzerland	1	
North America of which:	69	
Canada	8	
USA	61	*Not*
Other developed countries of which:	422	*Available*
Australia	257	
Japan	11	
New Zealand	154	
DEVELOPING AREAS	38	
Asia & Pacific (except Japan or Middle East) of which:	22	
Hong Kong	14	
India	4	
Malaysia	2	
Singapore	2	
Middle East of which:	2	
Kuwait	2	
Other developing countries	14	
TOTAL	705[2]	

Source:

R Carstairs and R Prasad, *Impact of Foreign Direct Private Investment on the Fiji Economy,* Centre for Applied Studies in Development, Suva, Fiji, November, 1981.

NOTES TO TABLE A7

1 Number of affiliates with 20% or more foreign participation.

2 Includes 56 affiliates with more than one foreign parent, and 46 which are unallocated.

Table A8

INDICATORS OF THE SIGNIFICANCE OF INWARD FOREIGN DIRECT INVESTMENT OR THE ACTIVITIES OF FOREIGN-BASED COMPANIES TO THE NATIONAL ECONOMY

1	Direct capital stock of foreign affiliates at book value in 1984 as a proportion of:[1]		
	a	GNP at factor cost	37.36
	b	population (in F $ per head)[1]	598.53
2	Employment in foreign affiliates in 1980 as a percentage of all employment[2]		
	a	in all industry	18.3
	b	in manufacturing	29.0[3]
3	Output of foreign affiliates in 1980 as a percentage of all companies'[2] output		
	a	in primary (ie, extractive) industry	82.27
	b	in secondary (ie, manufacturing) industry	31.83
	c	in tertiary industry (ie, services, etc)	62.56
4	Private foreign investment as a percentage of all investment 1980/2		10.72

5 Percentage share of sales and value added accounted for by foreign affiliates in selected sectors[2], 1980

	Sales	*Value Added*
Primary Goods Sector	82.3	*N.A.*
Agriculture	56.2	60.0
Mining & quarrying	99.6	99.7
Manufacturing Sector	31.8	24.8
Services Sector	62.6	*N.A.*
Construction	28.4	33.5
Transport & communications	45.9	42.7
Trade & distribution	64.0	70.3
Banking & finance	93.2	93.0
Other services	27.4	16.5

Source:
R Carstairs and R Prasad, *Impact of Foreign Direct Private Investment on the Fiji Economy,* Centre for Applied Studies in Development, Suva, Fiji, November, 1981.

NOTES TO TABLE A8

1 1982.

2 Affiliates which are 20% or above foreign owned.

3 1977.

Table A10

DISTRIBUTION OF FOREIGN SUBSIDIARIES AND ASSOCIATES AND FOREIGN CAPITAL STOCK BY PERCENTAGE OWNERSHIP OF PARENT COMPANIES, 1979

	Inward Investment		Outward Investment	
	Number of Affiliates	*Value of Capital Stock*	*Number of Affiliates*	*Value of Capital Stock*
100% owned subsidiaries				
50-99.9% owned subsidiaries and associates	660	*Not Available*	*Not Available*	
Less than 50% owned subsidiaries and associates	76			
TOTAL	736			

Source:

R Carstairs and R Prasad, *Impact of Foreign Direct Private Investment on the Fiji Economy,* Centre for Applied Studies in Development, Suva, Fiji, November, 1981.

Table A11

ROYALTY RECEIPTS AND PAYMENTS, 1979 - 80 (F $ th)

	Payments			Receipts		
	To Affiliates	*To Non-affiliates*	*Total*	*From Affiliates*	*From Non-affiliates*	*Total*
1979	*Not Separately Available*		1,200	*Not Available*		
1980			1,276			

Sources:

R Carstairs and R Prasad, *Impact of Foreign Direct Private Investment on the Fiji Economy,* Centre for Applied Studies in Development, Suva, Fiji, November, 1981.

Table A12

LEADING FOREIGN MULTINATIONAL COMPANIES, 1985

Name	Home Country	Sector
Burns Phelp	Australia	Wholesale & retail trade general manufacturing
W R Carpenters	Australia	Wholesale & retail trade general manufacturing
Cable & Wireless	UK	Telecommunications
Price Waterhouse	UK	Accounting
Coopers and Lybrand	UK	Accounting
Emperor Gold Mining	Australia	Mining
Pacific Fishing Company	Japan	Fishing & canning activities
Toya Seikar	Japan	Fishing & canning activities
Australian Forest Industries	Australia	Forestry & timber
Travelodge Hotel	Hong Kong	Hotels
Regent Hotel	Hong Kong	Hotels

Source:
John M Stopford, *The World Directory of Multinational Enterprises 1982-83,* Bath: The Pitman Press, 1982

PAPUA NEW GUINEA

Investment by overseas residents in Papua New Guinea is defined by the National Statistical Office as comprising net increases in all financial liabilities of Papua New Guinean enterprises to non-residents, *including* shares, debentures, loans, advances, indebtedness on current account between related companies, and in undistributed income (before appropriation, if any, to reserves). Such investment flows remained at very low levels to 1980, although retained earnings continued to be an important source of investment finance. From 1980/81 onwards, however, there has been a substantial increase in inflows, particularly in mining and, to a lesser extent, in agriculture and forestry.

Australia has continued to be the single-most important source — and recipient — of investment during the 1970s and early 1980s, with the USA, then Japan and the UK following at considerable distance, although in 1983 the total direct investment inflow from the USA was greater.

Papua New Guinea has long held a deliberate policy of explicitly defining activities in which foreign investment is encouraged, and those in which it is not, a practice which was formalised in the National Investment and Development Act of 1974. Data on the sectoral distribution of foreign investment indeed indicate that the bulk of overseas capital inflows have been directed towards mining and large-scale deep-sea fisheries, the so-called 'priority' activities, with substantial investment in distributive trade, restaurants and hotels.

MAIN SOURCES OF DATA:

A Official

1 Bank of Papua New Guinea, *Balance of Payments Data,* May 1984.

2 Papua New Guinea, National Statistical Office, *Statistical Bulletin,* August 1978.

3 UNCTC, *Transnational Corporations in World Development: Third Survey*, New York: UN, 1983.

B Private

1 P Daniel & R Sims, 'Comparative private foreign direct investment policies and performance: a Papua New Guinea case study', Commonwealth Secretariat Paper, 1984.

Note:
Data do not allow us to complete Table A10 for Papua New Guinea.

Table A1

SUMMARY OF THE COUNTRY'S INTERNATIONAL INVESTMENT POSITION

		Inward Investment	Outward Investment
1	Number of foreign affiliates in host country, and of foreign affiliates of home country firms at the end of 1980	281[1]	*N.A.*
2	Number of foreign firms with direct investments in host country, and home country firms with direct foreign affiliates	*N.A.*	*N.A.*
3	Total foreign direct capital stock at book value as a percentage of GNP at factor cost in 1982	60.74	3.21
4	Flow of foreign direct investment in the five year period, (K m)	388.97	15.36
5	Employment in foreign affiliates or abroad	*N.A.*	*N.A.*
6	Output of foreign affiliates or abroad	*N.A.*	*N.A.*

Source:

Bank of Papua New Guinea, *Balance of Payments Data,* May 1984; Papua New Guinea, National Statistical Office, *Statistical Bulletin,* August 1978; IMF, *International Financial Statistics Yearbook,* 1984.

NOTES TO TABLE A1

1 Represents number of foreign affiliates of MNEs from selected home countries as identified by UNCTC, 1983.

Table A2

PRIVATE FOREIGN CAPITAL STOCK, 1975 - 85 (K m)

	Inward Investment				Outward Investment[1]		
	Portfolio	*Direct*	*Total*		*Portfolio*	*Direct*	*Total*
Book value of capital stock							
1975	*Not Available*	482.0	*Not Available*		*Not Available*	*N.A.*	*Not Available*
1978		592.0				*N.A.*	
1982		1,213.5[2]				22.5	
1983		1,328.0				23.5	
1984		1,432.2				25.5	

Source:

Bank of Papua New Guinea, *Balance of Payments Data,* May 1984; Papua New Guinea, National Statistical Office, *Statistical Bulletin,* August 1978.

NOTES TO TABLE A2

1 Estimates based on cumulative flows as from 1976.

2 Estimate calculated by deducting a change in stock figure proportional to the investment flow for 1983 from the 1983 stock.

Table A3

FLOW OF FOREIGN DIRECT INVESTMENT, 1971 - 84 (K m)

	Inward Investment				Outward Investment		
	Reinvested Profits	*Other*	*Total*		*Reinvested Profits*	*Other*	*Total*[1]
1971	4.40	51.10	55.50		*Not Separately Available*		*Not Available*
1972	25.65	34.65	60.30				
1973	68.20	8.75	76.95				
1974	37.80	28.25	66.05				
1975	2.20	34.35	36.55				
1976	16.85	4.35	21.20				3.00
1977	22.10	-6.50	15.60				1.38
1978	28.50	-0.90	27.60				3.46
1979	38.00	-6.60	31.40				2.30
1980	44.00	6.50	50.50				10.57
1981	44.00	12.00	56.00				0.48
1982	30.00	33.80	63.80				1.30
1983	30.00	84.50	114.50				0.98
1984	32.05	72.12	104.17				2.03

Source:

Bank of Papua New Guinea, *Balance of Payments Data,* May 1984; Papua New Guinea, National Statistical Office, *Statistical Bulletin,* August 1978.

NOTES TO TABLE A3

1 Excluding reinvested profits.

Table A4

SECTORAL DISTRIBUTION OF FOREIGN DIRECT CAPITAL STOCK, 1970 - 77 (K m)[1]

	Inward Investment				Outward Investment		
	Primary	*Secondary*	*Tertiary*		*Primary*	*Secondary*	*Tertiary*
1970-77	453.7	30.6	56.4		*Not Available*		

Source:

Papua New Guinea, National Statistical Office, *Statistical Bulletin,* August 1978.

NOTES TO TABLE A4

1 Estimates based on cumulative total net flows of equity and loans, 1970-71 to 1976-77. Total does not match Table A2 due to an unallocated component.

Table A5

GEOGRAPHICAL DISTRIBUTION OF FOREIGN DIRECT CAPITAL STOCK, 1970 - 83 (K m)

	Inward Investment				Outward Investment		
	Developed Countries	*Developing Countries*	*Total*[1]		*Developed Countries*	*Developing Countries*	*Total*[1]
1970-77[2]	508.1	*N.S.A.*	540.7		*Not Available*		
1970-83[3]	677.5	6.2	722.7				
1976-83[4]	*Not Available*				50.8	8.3	60.5

Source:

Bank of Papua New Guinea, *Balance of Payments Data,* May 1984; Papua New Guinea, National Statistical Office, *Statistical Bulletin,* August 1978.

NOTES TO TABLE A5

1 Total includes 'unspecified' figure.

2 Estimates based on cumulative total net flows of equity and loans, 1970-71 to 1976-77. Total does not match Table A2 due to an unallocated component.

3 Excluding loans as from 1977.

4 Estimated from cumulative flows, 1976-83.

Table A6

INDUSTRIAL DISTRIBUTION OF FOREIGN DIRECT CAPITAL STOCK, 1970 - 77 (K m)[1]

	Inward Investment	Outward Investment
	1970-77	
Primary	453.70	Not Available
Agriculture[2]	26.00	
Mining and quarrying	427.70	
Secondary	30.60	
Tertiary	56.40	
Construction	0.30	
Transport & communications	−1.50	
Distributive trade[3]	48.00	
Property	*N.S.A.*	
Banking & finance	9.60	
Other services	*N.S.A.*	
TOTAL	540.70	

Source:
Papua New Guinea, National Statistical Office, *Statistical Bulletin,* August 1978.

NOTES TO TABLE A6

1 Estimates based on cumulative total net flows of equity and loans, 1970-71 to 1976-77. Total does not match Table A2 due to an unallocated component.

2 Including forestry and fishing.

3 Represents wholesale and retail trade, restaurants and hotels.

Table A7

LEADING SOURCE AND RECIPIENT COUNTRIES, 1970 - 83 (K m)

	Inward Investment		Outward Investment
	1970-77[1]	*1970-83*[2]	*1976-83*[3]
DEVELOPED AREAS[4]	508.1	677.5	50.8
Europe[4]	41.7	80.1	1.9
EEC of which:			
W. Germany	*N.A.*	28.4	0.7
UK	41.7	51.7	1.2
North America of which:[4]	95.4	157.9	6.0
USA	95.4	157.9	6.0
Other developed countries of which:[4]	371.0	439.5	42.9
Australia	306.5	370.7	42.6
Japan	64.5	68.2	*N.A.*
New Zealand	*N.A.*	0.6	0.3
DEVELOPING AREAS[4]	32.6	6.2	8.3
Asia & Pacific of which:[4]	*N.A.*	6.2	8.3
Hong Kong	*N.A.*	6.2	8.3
UNSPECIFIED[5]	32.6	39.0	1.4
TOTAL	540.7	722.7	60.5

Source:

Papua New Guinea, National Statistical Office, *Statistical Bulletin,* August 1978; Bank of Papua New Guinea, May 1984.

NOTES TO TABLE A7

1 Estimates based on cumulative total net flows of equity and loans, 1970-71 to 1976-77. Total does not match Table A2 to an unallocated component.

2 Excluding loans as from 1977.

3 Estimated from cumulative flows, 1976-83.

4 Including only these countries shown below.

5 Known to include Singapore, South Korea, The Netherlands and Belgium.

Table A8

INDICATORS OF THE SIGNIFICANCE OF INWARD FOREIGN DIRECT INVESTMENT OR THE ACTIVITIES OF FOREIGN-BASED COMPANIES TO THE NATIONAL ECONOMY, 1982

1	Direct capital stock of foreign affiliates at book value in 1982 as a proportion of:		
	a	GNP at factor cost	60.74
	b	population (in K per head)	338.48
2	Investment in foreign affiliates by OECD countries as a percentage of domestic investment, 1978-80		5.6

Source:

Bank of Papua New Guinea, *Balance of Payments Data,* May 1984; Papua New Guinea, National Statistical Office, *Statistical Bulletin*, August 1978; IMF, *International Financial Statistics Yearbook,* 1984; UNCTC, 1983, *op cit.*

Table A9

INDICATORS OF THE SIGNIFICANCE OF OUTWARD FOREIGN DIRECT INVESTMENT OR THE ACTIVITIES OF HOME-BASED COMPANIES ABROAD FOR THE NATIONAL ECONOMY, 1982

1	Foreign capital stock of home-based firms at book value in 1982 as a proportion of:		
	a	GNP at factor cost	3.21
	b	population (in K per head)	17.86

Source:

Bank of Papua New Guinea, *Balance of Payments Data,* May 1984; IMF, *International Financial Statistics Yearbook,* 1984.

Table A11

ROYALTY RECEIPTS AND PAYMENTS, 1970 - 83 (K m)

	Payments			Receipts		
	To Affiliates	*To Non-affiliates*	*Total*	*From Affiliates*	*From Non-affiliates*	*Total*
1976	*Not Separately Available*		0.3	*Not Available*		
1977			0.2			
1978			0.2			
1979			0.1			
1980			0.1			
1981			0.4			
1982			0.1			
1983			0.4			

Source:

Bank of Papua New Guinea, *Balance of Payments Data,* May 1984.

Table A12

LEADING FOREIGN MULTINATIONAL COMPANIES, 1983

Name	*Home Country*	*Sector*
Commonwealth Development Corporation	UK	Palm Oil
Societe Internationale de Plantations et de Finance, SA	Belgium	Palm Oil
Harrisons and Crosfield Ltd	UK	Palm Oil
Burns Philip & Co Ltd	Australia	Forestry
Star-Kist Inc	USA	Fishing
New Britain Fishing Industries	Japan	Fishing
Nippon Suisan Kaisha Ltd	Japan	Fishing
Hokoku Suisan Kaisha Ltd	Japan	Fishing
C Itoh	Japan	Fishing
The Rio Tinto-Zinc Corporation PLC	UK	Mining
Broken Hill Pty Ltd	Australia	Mining
Hurieda Mining	Japan	Mining
Heineken Company	Netherlands	Brewing
ICI	UK	Chemicals
W R Carpenter Holdings Ltd	Australia	Chemicals
Hoechst AG	W. Germany	Chemicals
Wilkinson	Australia	Other manufacturing
Rothmans of Pall Mall	Australia	Tobacco
Kinmore Investment Pty Ltd	Hong Kong	Steel
Australia and New Zealand Banking Group Ltd	Australia	Banking
National Commercial Banking Corp of Australia	Australia	Banking
GRE Insurance Ltd	Australia	Insurance

Source:
John M Stopford, *The World Directory of Multinational Enterprises 1982-83,* Bath: The Pitman Press, 1982.

PAPUA NEW GUINEA : DEFINITIONS

"Investment by overseas residents in Papua New Guinea comprises net increases in all financial viabilities of Papua New Guinean enterprises to non-residents, *including* shares, debentures, loans, advances, indebtedness on current account between related companies, and in undistributed income (before appropriation, if any, to reserves)."

Source:
Papua New Guinea, National Statistical Office, 1978.

LATIN AMERICA & CARIBBEAN

ARGENTINA

Although there appears to be no official policy towards inward direct investment, Argentina's foreign investment laws are very liberal. However, despite this attraction, recent economic and political uncertainties have resulted in a significant decline in new inflows of foreign capital. Reinvested earnings retain an important role in foreign investment in Argentina.

FDI in Argentina is dispersed over a wide range of industries. The major recipient areas are gas and oil, chemicals, transportation equipment and finance and banking.

The main source of investment is the USA. Other investor countries are largely European.

Argentina outward investment is mainly directed toward the other developing countries of Latin America and is industrially diversified. The figures quoted in Government authorised investment (see eg Tables A4 to A7) grossly underestimated the actual value of the stock of outward investment, which some observers (eg Katz and Kosacoft in Lall 1983) put as high as US $ 1 billion. Both foreign affiliates and indigenous Argentinian firms record foreign direct investments.

MAIN SOURCES OF DATA:

A Official

1 Central Bank of Argentina: provides information on royalty payments.

B Private

1 W Lohr, "Foreign Direct Investment in Argentina", paper prepared for the International Trade Administration, US Department of Commerce, 1984.

2 J Sourrouille, F Gatto and B Kosacoff, *Inversiones Extranjeras en America Latina,* BIO/INTAI, Buenos Aires, 1984.

3 A J Lucio, "The East, the South and the Transnational Corporations", *CEPAL Review,* August 1981.

4 *CEPAL Document LC/R 369,* "Las Empresas Transnacionales y America Latina, situacion actuel y perspectivos fente a las crisis", 1984.

5 J Katz and B Kosacoff, "Multinationals from Argentina" in S Lall (ed), *The New Multinationals,* Chichester: John Wiley, 1983.

6 R Jenkins, *Transnational Corporations and Industrial Transformation in Latin America,* London: Macmillan, 1984.

7 E White, "The Forms of Foreign Involvement by Argentine Firms", paper prepared for the OECD, May, 1985.

8 J Sourrouille et al, *Transnacionalization y Politica Economics en la Argentina*, Buenos Aires, 1985.

9 E Basueldo, "La structure de propiedod du capital extranjero en la Argentina, 1979", Centro de Economics Transnacional, 1984.

10 J Sourrouille, "El impacto de las empresas transnacionales sobre el empleo y los ingresos: el cas de Argentina", International Labour Office working papers on the employment effects of MNES, Geneva, 1976.

11 "Ranking de las 1000 enterpresas inderes de la Argentina", *Prensa Economica*, October 1984.

12 Estudios e Informes de la CEPAL, LC/G 1377, "Las Empresas Transnacionales en La Argentina", January 1986.

Table A1

SUMMARY OF THE COUNTRY'S INTERNATIONAL INVESTMENT POSITION

		Inward Investment	Outward Investment
1	Number of foreign affiliates in host country, and of foreign affiliates of home country firms at the end of 1974	1,753[1]	361
2	Number of foreign firms with direct investments in host country, and home country firms with direct foreign affiliates at the end of 1978	634[1]	63
3	Total foreign direct capital stock at book value as a percentage of GNP at factor cost in 1983[2]	23.90	206
4	Flow of foreign direct investment in the five year period, 1980-84 (US $ m)	2,182	245
5	Employment in foreign affiliates or abroad, 1963 (US $ m)	158,588	*N.A.*
6	Output of foreign affiliates or abroad, 1963 (US $ m)	991.77[3]	*N.A.*

Source:
W Lohr, "Foreign Direct Investment in Argentina", paper prepared for the International Trade Administration, US Department of Commerce, 1984; IMF, *Balance of Payments Statistics Yearbook*, various issues; E White, "The Forms of Foreign Involvement by Argentine Firms", paper prepared for the OECD, May 1985; E Besueldo, "La structura de propiedod du capital extranjero en la Argentina 1979", Centro de Economics Transnacional, 1984; J Sourrouille et al, "Transnacionalizations y Politica Economics en la Argentina", Buenos Aires, 1985; IMF, *International Financial Statistics Yearbook, 1984*; UNCTC, 1983, *op cit;* CEPAL, 1986, *op cit.*

NOTES TO TABLE A1

1 Represents 1973.

2 Estimate of outward stock figure obtained from cumulative investment flows 1965-83. Figure for inward investment refer to year 1982.

3 Represents value added in manufacturing, by foreign affiliates.

Table A2

PRIVATE FOREIGN CAPITAL STOCK, 1977-84 (US $ m)

	Inward Investment			Outward Investment		
	Portfolio	*Direct*[1]	*Total*	*Portfolio*	*Direct*[2]	*Total*
Book value of capital stock						
1973		2,274				
1977		4,657				
1978		4,801			21.6	
1981	*Not Available*	6,555	*Not Available*	*Not Available*	87.1	*Not Available*
1982		6,780				
1983		6,964			142.0	
1984		7,233				

Source:

E White, "The Forms of Foreign Involvement by Argentine Firms", paper prepared for the OECD, May 1985; J Katz and B Kosacoff, "Multinationals from Argentina" in S Lall (ed), *The New Multinationals,* Chichester, John Wiley, 1983; UNCTC, 1983, *op cit.*

NOTES TO TABLE A2

1 Estimates for 1982, 1983 and 1984 obtained by adding investment flows to the stock figure of 1982.

2 Non financial direct investments registered by the Argentine government as from 1965.

Table A3

FLOW OF FOREIGN DIRECT INVESTMENT, 1970-84 (US $ m)

	Inward Investment			Outward Investment		
	Reinvested Profits	*Other*	*Total*	*Reinvested Profits*	*Other*	*Total*
1970	*Not Separately Available*		11	*Not Available*		
1971			11			
1972			10			
1973			10			
1974			10			
1977	122	22		*Not Separately Available*		1
1978	119	131	250			23
1979	195	9	204			59
1980	347	334	681			111
1981	351	472	823			107
1982	120	105	225			29
1983	146	38	184			–2
1984	248	21	269			*N.A.*

Source:
IMF, *Balance of Payments Statistics Yearbook,* various issues.

Table A4

SECTORAL DISTRIBUTION OF FOREIGN DIRECT CAPITAL STOCK, 1978-83 (US $ m)

	Inward Investment			Outward Investment		
	Primary	*Secondary*	*Tertiary*	*Primary*	*Secondary*	*Tertiary*
1973	127	1,478.8	557		*Not*	
1978	*N.A.*	983	*N.A.*		*Available*	
1981 [1]				29	45	12
1983	793[2]	1,399[2]	754[2]		*Not Available*	

Source:
J Katz and B Kosacoff, "Multinationals from Argentina" in S Lall (ed), *The New Multinationals,* Chichester: John Wiley, 1983; J Sourrouille et al, *Inversiones extranjera en America Latina*, BID/INTAI, Buenos Aires, 1981.

NOTES TO TABLE A4

1 Based on cumulative authorised investment flows, 1965-81.

2 Based on cumulative investment applications, 1977-83.

Table A5

GEOGRAPHICAL DISTRIBUTION OF FOREIGN DIRECT CAPITAL STOCK, 1977-83 (US $ m)

	Inward Investment			Outward Investment		
	Developed Countries	*Developing Countries*	*Total*	*Developed Countries*	*Developing Countries*	*Total*
1977	2,721[1]	1,936[2]	4,657		*Not Available*	
1981 [3]				10[4]	77[2]	87
1982	6,220	98	6,780[5]		*Not Available*	

Source:
W Lohr, "Foreign Investment in Argentina", paper prepared for the International Trade Administration, US Department of Commerce, 1984; J Katz and B Kosacoff, "Multinationals from Argentina" in S Lall (ed), *The New Multinationals,* Chichester; John Wiley, 1983; A J de Lucio, "The East, the South and the Transnational Corporations", *CEPAL Review,* August 1981.

NOTES TO TABLE A5

1 USA, Switzerland, UK, France, Italy, West Germany and Netherlands only.

2 Rest of world.

3 Based on cumulative authorised investment flows, 1965-81, recorded by the Argentine Ministry for the Economy.

4 USA, West Germany, France, Belgium, Italy and Spain only.

5 Total includes unspecified figure.

Table A6

INDUSTRIAL DISTRIBUTION OF FOREIGN DIRECT CAPITAL STOCK, 1978-83 (US $ m)

	Inward Investment		Outward Investment
	1978	*1977-83*[1]	*1965-81*[1]
Primary		793	29.37
Agriculture	*Not Available*	67[2]	3.34
Mining & quarrying		24	
Oil		702	26.03
Secondary	983	1,399	45.44
Food & drink	59	146[3]	*Not Separately Available*
Chemicals & allied	235	366[4]	
Metals	24	72	
Mechanical engineering	174	106	
Electrical equipment		22	
Motor vehicles	241	530	
Other transportation equipment		8	
Textiles & clothing		5	
Paper & allied		5	
Rubber		18	
Stone, clay & glass		32	
Coal & petroleum products			
Other manufacturing		89	
Tertiary		754	12.33
Construction		50	6.98
Transport & communications		17	1.07
Distributive trade	*Not*	*N.A.*	3.05
Banking & finance	*Available*	488	*N.S.A.*
Other services		199	1.23
TOTAL		2,854	87.14

Source:

W Lohr, "Foreign Investment in Argentina", paper prepared for the International Trade Administration, US Department of Commerce, 1984; J Sourrouille, F Gatto and B Kosacoff, *Inversiones extranjeras en America Latina*, BIO/INTAI, Buenos Aires, 1981: J Katz and B Kosacoff, "Multinationals from Argentina" in S Lall (ed), *The Ne New Multinationals,* Chichester: John Wiley, 1983; CEPAL, 1986, *op cit.*

NOTES TO TABLE A6

1 Estimates based on cumulative investment flows reported by the Argentine Central Bank and the Registry of Foreign Investment at the Argentine Ministry for the Economy.

2 Including fishing (US $ 44 m).

3 Including tobacco.

4 Including petrochemicals (US $ 173 m) and pharmaceuticals (US $ 81 m).

Table A7

LEADING SOURCE AND RECIPIENT COUNTRIES
1977-83 (US $ m)

	Inward Investment		Outward Investment[1]	
	1977	*1982*	*1965-81*	*1965-78*
DEVELOPED AREAS[2]	2,721	6,220	10.39	0.30
Europe[2]	1,459	3,139	1.94	0.20
EEC of which[2]	1,030	2,278	0.95	0.20
Belgium	*N.A.*	5[3]	0.10	0.10
France	206	493	0.02	0.02
W. Germany	204	417	0.48	0.08
Italy	128	572	0.35	
Netherlands	219	389	*N.A.*	*Not Available*
UK	273	396	*N.A.*	
Other Europe of which[2]	429	861	0.99	
Portugal		*N.A.*	0.07	
Spain	*Not Available*	102[3]	0.92	*Not Available*
Sweden		46[3]	*N.A.*	
Switzerland	429	711	*N.A.*	
North America of which:	1,262	3,035	8.35	0.1
Canada	*N.A.*	56[3]	*N.A.*	*N.A.*
USA	1,262	2,979	8.35	0.1
Other developed countries of which[2]		46[3]	0.10	
Japan	*Not Available*	42[3]	*N.A.*	*Not Available*
New Zealand			*N.A.*	
DEVELOPING AREAS[2]		98	76.72	21.35
Africa of which:		20[3]	*N.A.*	*N.A.*
Liberia		20[3]	*N.A.*	*N.A.*
Asia & Pacific of which[2]		3[3]	*N.A.*	
Hong Kong		3[3]	*N.A.*	
Latin America of which[2]		75[3]	76.72	21.35
Bolivia		*N.A.*	2.79	1.72
Brazil		36[3]	14.26	6.56
Chile		2[3]	8.30	0.07
Colombia			1.13	0.49
Ecuador		*Not Available*	1.57	0.35
Honduras			0.30	
Mexico			6.85	*Not Available*
Panama		37[3]	0.81	
Paraguay		*Not Available*	2.75	1.18
Peru			21.54	3.45
Trinidad & Tobago[4]			1.00	
Uruguay		6[3]	11.39	6.87
Venezuela		*N.A.*	3.90	0.66
TOTAL	4.657	6,821	87.11	21.64

Table A7 (cont'd)

Source:
W Lohr, "Foreign Investment in Argentina", paper prepared for the International Trade Administration, US Department of Commerce, 1984; J Katz and B Kosacoff, "Multinationals from Argentina" in S Lall (ed), *The New Multinationals,* Chichester: John Wiley, 1983; A J de Lucio; "The East, the South and the Transnational Corporations", *CEPAL Review*, August 1981; UNCTC, 1983, *op cit.*

NOTES TO TABLE A7

1 Based on cumulative authorised investment flows, from 1965 as recorded by the Argentine Ministry for the Economy.

2 Including only those countries shown below.

3 Refers to cumulative investment applications, 1977-83.

4 West Indies as a whole.

Table A8

INDICATORS OF THE SIGNIFICANCE OF INWARD FOREIGN DIRECT INVESTMENT OR THE ACTIVITIES OF FOREIGN-BASED COMPANIES TO THE NATIONAL ECONOMY, 1981

1	Direct capital stock of foreign affiliates at book value in 1982 as a proportion of:	
	a GNP at factor cost	23.90
	b population (in US $ per head)	232.51
2	Employment in foreign affiliates in 1977 as a percentage of all employment in all industry	1.2[1]
3	Output of foreign affiliates in 1983 as a percentage of all companies' output in secondary (ie, manufacturing) industry	29.4
4	Exports of foreign affiliates in 1977 as a percentage of all manufacturing exports	24.9
5	Percentage share of sales accounted for by foreign affiliates in selected sectors, 1963	
		Sales
	Manufacturing Sector	23.8
	Food & drink	15.3
	Chemicals & allied	34.9
	Metals	21.1
	Mechanical engineering	35.6
	Electrical equipment	27.6
	Motor vehicles Other transportation equipment	} 44.4
	Textiles & clothing	14.2
	Paper & allied	25.7
	Rubber	72.1
	Coal & petroleum products	31.2
	Timber & furniture	0.5
	Other manufacturing	2.4

Source:

IMF, *International Financial Statistics Yearbook 1984;* E White, "The Forms of Foreign Involvement by Argentine Firms", paper prepared for the OECD, May 1985; J Sourrouille et al, *Inversiones extranjeras en America Latina,* BIO/INTAI, Buenos Aires 1984; *CEPAL* document, "Las Empresas Transacionales y America Latina, situacion actual y perspectivos fente a las crisis", LC/R 369, 1984; R Jenkins, *Transnational Corporations and Industrial Transformation in Latin America,* London: Macmillan, 1984; *CEPAL,* 1986, *op cit.*

NOTES TO TABLE A8

1 US affiliates only.

Table A9

INDICATORS OF THE SIGNIFICANCE OF OUTWARD FOREIGN DIRECT INVESTMENT OR THE ACTIVITIES OF HOME-BASED COMPANIES ABROAD FOR THE NATIONAL ECONOMY, 1983

1	Foreign capital stock[1] of home based firms at book value in 1983 as a proportion of:	
	a GNP at factor cost	2.06
	b population (in US $ per head)	4.79

Source:
IMF, *Balance of Payments Statistics Yearbook*, various issues; IMF, *International Financial Statistics Yearbook 1984.*

NOTES TO TABLE A9

1 Estimate of stock obtained from cumulative investment flows, 1965-83.

Table A10

DISTRIBUTION OF FOREIGN SUBSIDIARIES AND ASSOCIATES AND FOREIGN CAPITAL STOCK BY PERCENTAGE OWNERSHIP OF PARENT COMPANIES, 1984

	Inward Investment		Outward Investment	
	Number of Affiliates	*Value of Capital Stock*	*Number of Affiliates*	*Value of Capital Stock*
100% owned subsidiaries	*Not Available*		42	*Not Available*
50-99.9% owned subsidiaries and associates			34	
Less than 50% owned subsidiaries and associates			51	
TOTAL			135	

Source:
E White, "The Forms of Foreign Investment by Argentine Firms", paper prepared for the OECD, May 1985.

NOTES TO TABLE A10

1 Includes only subsidiaries of manufacturing firms.

2 Total includes joint ventures where shares are not identified.

Table A11

ROYALTY RECEIPTS AND PAYMENTS, 1977-83 (US $ m)

	Payments				Receipts		
	To Affiliates	*To Non-affiliates*	*Total*		*From Affiliates*	*From Non-affiliates*	*Total*
1977	*Not Separately Available*		51.4		*Not Available*		
1978			148.2				
1979			156.7				
1980			239.2				
1981			246.9				
1982			361.1				
1983			483.9				

Source:
Banco Central de la Republica Argentina.

Table A12

LEADING FOREIGN AND DOMESTIC MULTINATIONAL COMPANIES

A Leading Foreign Multinational Companies in the country, 1983

Name	*Home Country*	*Sector*	*Turnover (US $ th)*
1 Exxon Corp	USA	Petroleum refining	1,678,210
2 Royal Dutch Shell	Netherlands/ UK	Petroleum refining	1,460,300
3 British American Tobacco	UK	Tobacco	1,086,950
4 Ford Motor Co	USA	Motor vehicles	957,500
5 IRI Techint	Italy	Metallurgy	869,634
6 Philip Morris Inc.	USA	Tobacco	806,872
7 Regie Nationale des Usines Renaul	France	Motor vehicles	792,874
8 IBM	USA	Electronic and electrical equipment	593,744
9 Sevel		Motor vehicles	513,085
10 Imperial Chemical Industries	UK	Chemical products	367,101
11 Astra AB	Sweden	Petroleum	348,072
12 Indo			334,629
13 E I Dupont de Nemours	USA	Textiles	326,449
14 Goodyear	USA	Rubber	308,963
15 Dunlop Holdings	UK	Rubber products	270,590
16 Muller's Muhle Muller & Co	Germany	Food	269,956
17 Saiff Armour	USA	Food	254,689
18 Continental Oil Co	USA	Petrochemicals	254,177
19 Mercedes Benz	Germany	Motor vehicles	243,175
20 Volkswagen	Germany	Motor vehicles	220,211
21 CPC	USA	Food	214,425
22 Rio Colorado		Petroleum	209,838
23 Nestlé	Switzerland	Food	186,398
24 Firestone	USA	Rubber	180,515
25 Ciba Geigy	Switzerland	Chemicals	175,788

Source:
CEPAL, *Las Empresas Transnacionales En La Argentine,* UN: Chile, Jan 1986.

Table A12 (cont'd)

LEADING FOREIGN AND DOMESTIC MULTINATIONAL COMPANIES

B Leading Domestic Companies with Multinational Interests, 1983

Name		*Sector*	*Global (US $ m)*[1] *Turnover*
1	YPF	Oil	5,747.39
2	Dalmine	Steel	869.90
3	Molinos Rio de la Plata	Food	698.96
4	Alpargatas	Textiles	477.68
5	Celulosa	Paper	272.55
6	Perez Companc	Oil	247.86
7	Arcor	Food	182.34
8	Bridas	Oil	181.39
9	Massuh	Paper	133.90
10	Minelti Y Cia	Food	113.96
11	Siam Di Tella	Mechanical engineering	101.61
12	Laboratorios Bago	Chemicals	86.42

Source:
W Lohr, "Foreign Direct Investment in Argentina", paper prepared for the International Trade Administration, US Department of Commerce, 1984; J Sourrouille, "El impacao de las empresas transnacionales sobre el empleo y los ingre sus: el caso de Argentina", *ILO*, Geneva, 1976; *Prensa Economica*, "Ranking de las 1000 enterpresas lideres de la Argentina", October 1984.

NOTES TO TABLE A12

1 Converted into US dollars ar the average exchange rate in 1983 of .01053 Argentinian Australs per US dollar.

BARBADOS

In an attempt to encourage inward direct investment – particularly in manufacturing, Barbados has adopted increasingly liberal incentive schemes since the early 1960s, culminating in the Incentives Act of 1974. Joint ventures may be freely entered into without the approval of the Government. There are no performance requirements expected of foreign firms and no barriers to technology agreements.

The UK and the USA accounted for about 41% of the total stock of foreign investment in 1981 (Table A7). Other investor countries include Canada and West Germany.

There are no detailed statistics on the sectoral distribution of foreign direct investment in Barbados until 1977, although it was largely concentrated in the services sector, particularly tourism and banking and finance. Since then, the bulk of foreign investment has been directed towards the manufacturing and services sectors. Within manufacturing, 64% of FDI has been in metals, mechanical engineering and electrical engineering. Chemicals and textiles are also significant recipients of foreign investment.

MAIN SOURCES OF DATA:

A Official

1 Central Bank of Barbados: provides data on inflows of foreign investment in Barbados, with a broad sectoral distribution.

2 UNCTC, *Transnational Corporations in World Development: Third Survey*, New York: UN, 1983.

B Private

1 H Codrington, Z Khan, L Nurse, D Worrell, "Private Foreign Investment in Barbados", paper presented at the Commonwealth Secretariat Conference on New Opportunities for Foreign Direct Investment in Developing Countries, March/April, 1985.

Note:
Data do not allow us to complete Tables A9 or A10 for Barbados.

Table A1

SUMMARY OF THE COUNTRY'S INTERNATIONAL INVESTMENT POSITION

		Inward Investment	Outward Investment
1	Number of foreign affiliates in host country, and of foreign affiliates of home country firms at the end of 1983	53[1]	*N.A.*
2	Number of foreign firms with direct investments in host country, and home country firms with direct foreign affiliates	*N.A.*	*N.A.*
3	Total foreign direct capital stock at book value as a percentage of GNP at factor cost in 1982	13.92	*N.A.*
4	Flow of foreign direct investment in the five year period, 1979-83 (B $ m)	75.0	7.4
5	Employment in foreign affiliates or abroad	*N.A.*	*N.A.*
6	Output of foreign affiliates or abroad	*N.A.*	*N.A.*

Source:
Central Bank of Barbados, data as cited in H Codrington et al, "Private Foreign Investment in Barbados," paper presented at the Commonwealth Secretariat Conference on New Opportunities for FDI in Developing Countries, March/April, 1985; IMF, *International Financial Statistics Yearbook, 1984;* Barbados Industrial Development Corporation List of Manufacturing Establishments, 1983, data as cited in H Codrington et al, *op cit.*

NOTES TO TABLE A1

1 Based on a survey of 183 manufacturing firms.

Table A2

PRIVATE FOREIGN CAPITAL STOCK, 1971 - 83 (B $ m)[1]

	Inward Investment			Outward Investment		
	Portfolio	*Direct*	*Total*	*Portfolio*	*Direct*	*Total*
Book value of capital stock						
1971	*Not Available*	282.08	*Not Available*	*Not Available*		
1975		320.61				
1978		362.03				
1981		392.42				
1983		437.00				

Source:
UNCTC, *op cit.*

NOTES TO TABLE A2

1 Foreign direct capital stock for 1981 and 1984 have been estimated by adding cumulative investment flows to the stock figure of 1978.

Table A3

FLOW OF FOREIGN DIRECT INVESTMENT, 1970 - 83 (B $ m)

	Inward Investment			Outward Investment		
	Reinvested Profits	*Other*	*Total*	*Reinvested Profits*	*Other*	*Total*
1970	*N.S.A.*	*N.S.A.*	16.9	*Not Separately Available*		*N.A.*
1971	2.0	27.2	29.2			2.0
1972	4.2	29.2	33.4			*N.A.*
1973	2.4	2.7	5.1			2.3
1974	7.4	5.0	12.4			*N.A.*
1975	9.9	34.8	44.7			2.5
1976	3.0	10.9	13.9			1.4
1977	3.0	6.8	9.8			0.5
1978	3.8	14.1	17.9			0.8
1979	2.6	8.1	10.7			0.5
1980	0.5	2.6	3.1			1.3
1981	1.2	15.4	16.6			2.4
1982	0.7	8.4	9.1			0.4
1983	1.1	34.4	35.5			2.8

Source:
Central Bank of Barbados, data as cited in H Codrington et al, *op cit;* IMF, *Balance of Payments Statistics,* various issues.

Table A4

SECTORAL DISTRIBUTION OF FOREIGN DIRECT CAPITAL STOCK, 1983 (B $ th)

	Inward Investment				Outward Investment		
	Primary	*Secondary*	*Tertiary*		*Primary*	*Secondary*	*Tertiary*
1977-83[1]	*N.A.*	25,100	18,118		*Not Available*		

Source:
Central Bank of Barbados, Balance of Payments Survey, data as cited in H Codrington et al, *op cit.*

NOTES TO TABLE A4

1 Cumulative gross foreign direct investment flows, 1977-83, recorded for Balance of Payments purposes.

Table A5

GEOGRAPHICAL DISTRIBUTION OF FOREIGN DIRECT CAPITAL STOCK, 1981 (B $ m)

	Inward Investment				Outward Investment		
	Developed Countries	*Other Countries*	*Total*		*Developed Countries*	*Developing Countries*	*Total*
1981	108.7[1]	157.7	266.4[2]		*Not Available*		

Source:
HMSO, *Business Monitor*, Supplement 1981; US Department of Commerce, *Survey of Current Business*, November 1984.

NOTES TO TABLE A5

1 Includes UK and US investment only

2 Cumulative investment flow, 1965-81.

Table A6

INDUSTRIAL DISTRIBUTION OF FOREIGN DIRECT CAPITAL STOCK, 1983 (B $ th)[1]

	Inward Investment	Outward Investment
	1977-83[1]	
Primary	*N.S.A.*	*Not Available*
Secondary	25,100	
Food & drink	909	
Chemicals & allied	5,261	
Metals } Mechanical engineering } Electrical equipment }	16,000	
Textiles & clothing	1,076	
Stone, clay & glass	4	
Other manufacturing	1,850	
Tertiary	18,118	
Distributive trade[2]	12,935	
Other services[3]	5,183	
TOTAL	43,218	

Source:
Central Bank of Barbados, Balance of Payments Survey, data as cited in H Codrington et al, *op cit.*

NOTES TO TABLE A6

1 Cumulative gross foreign direct investment flows, 1977-83, recorded for Balance of Payments purposes.

2 Of which oil companies, B $ 11,258.

3 Represents public utilities & tourism.

Table A7

LEADING SOURCE AND RECIPIENT COUNTRIES, 1981 (B $ m)

	Inward Investment	Outward Investment
	1981	
DEVELOPED AREAS[1]	108.72	*Not Available*
UK	24.25	
USA	84.47	
TOTAL	266.4[2]	

Source:
HMSO, "Census of Overseas Assets 1981", *Business Monitor*, Supplement, 1981; US Department of Commerce, *Survey of Current Business,* November, 1984.

NOTES TO TABLE A7

1 Including only those countries shown below.

2 Cumulative investment flow, 1965-81.

Table A8

INDICATORS OF THE SIGNIFICANCE OF INWARD FOREIGN DIRECT INVESTMENT OR THE ACTIVITIES OF FOREIGN-BASED COMPANIES TO THE NATIONAL ECONOMY, 1978-82

1	Direct capital stock of foreign affiliates at book value in 1982 as a proportion of	
	a GNP at factor cost	13.92
	b population (in B $ per head)	1,058.46
2	Foreign investment as a percentage of domestic investment 1978-80	4.2

Source:
Central Bank of Barbados, data as cited in H Codrington et al, *op cit;* IMF, *International Financial Statistics Yearbook, 1984.*

Table A11

ROYALTY RECEIPTS AND PAYMENTS, 1976-83 (B $ m)

	Payments			Receipts		
	To Affiliates	*To Non-affiliates*	*Total*	*From Affiliates*	*From Non-affiliates*	*Total*
1976	*Not Separately Available*		1.2	*Not Separately Available*		*N.A.*
1977			1.9			*N.A.*
1978			4.3			*N.A.*
1979			5.2			0.5
1980			4.2			0.8
1981			4.5			0.7
1982			4.2			0.9
1983			9.5			1.3

Source:
IMF, *Balance of Payments Statistics Yearbook,* various issues.

Table A12

LEADING FOREIGN MULTINATIONAL COMPANIES, 1985

Name	*Home Country*	*Sector*
Intel	USA	Electrical
Bayer	W. Germany	Chemicals
Marriotts	USA	Hotels
Trusthouse Forte	UK	Hotels
Cable & Wireless	UK	Electrical
Royal Dutch/Shell	UK/Netherlands	Oil
Exxon	USA	Oil
Mobil	USA	Oil
Texaco	USA	Oil
Chase Manhattan	USA	Banking
BAT	UK	Tobacco
Manufacturers Life Insurance	USA	Insurance
Confederation Life Insurance	USA	Insurance
British-American Insurance	UK	Insurance
Barclays Bank	UK	Banking
Bank of Nova Scotia	Canada	Banking
Canadian Imperial Bank of Commerce	Canada	Banking
Royal Bank of Canada	Canada	Banking
Hertz	USA	Car Rentals
Coca Cola	USA	Drinks

Source:
H Codrington, Central Bank of Barbados, 1985.

BRAZIL

In general, Brazil has offered a favourable climate for foreign investment, with a range of tariff and fiscal incentives. This is reflected in the rising trend of inward foreign direct investment. The Brazilian government consistently states that it wishes to encourage FDI in certain sectors; at the same time, there are also sectors in which FDI is prohibited (for example, petroleum), or restricted (including petro-chemicals, mining, and telecommunications).

Data on outward investment is limited; foreign investment by Brazilian firms is not very significant although the flow of outward investment has increased in recent years. Most outward investment is directed towards the developed countries or other Latin American countries, and is mainly concentrated in the engineering, construction, oil exploration and banking sectors. Several of Brazilian MNEs are state owned.

The leading source of investment in Brazil is the USA; other investor countries include West Germany, Switzerland and Japan.

The bulk of FDI is concentrated in the manufacturing sector, particularly chemicals, transportation equipment and mechanical engineering. Investment in the services sector is also significant.

MAIN SOURCES OF DATA:

A **Official**

1 Central Bank of Brazil: publishes comprehensive data on investment flows into Brazil, by sectoral and geographical distribution.

2 *Diario Official:* provides information on outward investment flows by sectoral and geographical distribution.

B **Private**

1 M Possas, 'Employment Effects of MNEs in Brazil', *International Labour Office,* Working Papers on the Employment Effects of MNEs, no 7, Geneva, 1979.

2 US Department of Commerce, 'Brazil's Foreign Debt Crisis: Origin and Implication' and 'Foreign Direct Investment in Brazil', paper prepared for the Undersecretary for International Trade, April 1984.

3 F Albavera, 'Dos Estudios Sobre Empresas Transnacionales en Brasil', prepared for CEPAL, Santiago de Chile: UN, 1983.

4 A Villela, 'Multinationals from Brazil', in S Lall (Ed), *The New Multinationals,* Chichester: John Wiley, 1983.

5 R Jenkins, *Transnational Corporations and Industrial Transformation in Latin America,* London: Macmillan, 1984.

6 *Conjunctura Economica,* vol 38 no 9, Sept 1984.

7 'Quem e Quem na Economica Brasileira', *Visao,* various issues.

8 E Guimares, 'The Activities of Brazilian Firms Abroad', prepared for the OECD project on New Forms of Investment in Developing Countries, June, 1984.

Note:
Data do not allow us to complete Table A10 for Brazil.

Table A1

SUMMARY OF THE COUNTRY'S INTERNATIONAL INVESTMENT POSITION

		Inward Investment	Outward Investment
1	Number of foreign affiliates in host country, and of foreign affiliates of home country firms at the end of 1980	2,889[1]	*N.A.*
2	Number of foreign firms with direct investments in host country, and home country firms with direct foreign affiliates	*N.A.*	*N.A.*
3	Total foreign direct capital stock at book value as a percentage of GNP at factor cost in 1982	11.09	0.96
4	Flow of foreign direct investment in the five year period, 1980-84 (US $ m)	10,515	1,176
5	Employment in foreign affiliates or abroad	*N.A.*	*N.A.*
6	Output of foreign affiliates or abroad	*N.A.*	*N.A.*

Source:
Central Bank of Brazil, *Bulletin,* various issues; IMF, *Balance of Payments Statistics Yearbook,* various issues; IMF, *International Financial Statistics Yearbook, 1984.*

NOTES TO TABLE A1

1 Represents number of affiliates of foreign MNEs from selected home countries, as identified by UNCTC, 1983.

Table A2

PRIVATE FOREIGN CAPITAL STOCK, 1970 - 84 (US $ bn)

	Inward Investment[1]			Outward Investment		
	Portfolio	*Direct*	*Total*	*Portfolio*	*Direct*[2]	*Total*
Book value of capital stock						
1970		2.35				
1971		2.91				
1975		6.89				
1976		8.04				
1977	*Not Available*	9.87	*Not Available*		*Not Available*	
1978		11.87				
1979		14.28				
1980		16.19				
1981		18.72				
1982		21.64			1.83	
1983		23.20		*Not Available*	2.01	*Not Available*
1984		24.80			2.06	

Source:
Central Bank of Brazil, *Bulletin,* October 1978 and March 1984; IMF, *Balance of Payments Statistics Yearbook,* various issues.

NOTES TO TABLE A2

1 Estimates based on cumulative investment flows.

2 Estimated from cumulative investment flows as from 1970.

Table A3

FLOW OF FOREIGN DIRECT INVESTMENT, 1970 - 84 (US $ m)

	Inward Investment			Outward Investment[1]		
	Reinvested Profits	*Other*	*Total*	*Reinvested Profits*	*Other*	*Total*
1970	22	146	168			14
1971	395	169	564			1
1972	201	337	538			27
1973	512	977	1,489			37
1974	*N.S.A.*	*N.S.A.*	945			59
1975	298	710	1,008			142
1976	410	734	1,144	*Not Separately Available*		135
1977	873	956	1,829			146
1978	975	1,024	1,999			125
1979	718	1,696	2,414			195
1980	411	1,502	1,913			370
1981	745	1,781	2,526			209
1982	1,572	1,350	2,922			371
1983	691	865	1,556			183
1984	474	1,124	1,598			43

Source:
Central Bank of Brazil, *Bulletin,* various issues; IMF, *Balance of Payments Statistics Yearbook,* various issues.

NOTES TO TABLE A3

1 Outward investment excludes reinvested profits.

Table A4

SECTORAL DISTRIBUTION OF FOREIGN DIRECT CAPITAL STOCK, 1971 - 83 (US $ m)

	Inward Investment[1]			Outward Investment		
	Primary	*Secondary*	*Tertiary*	*Primary*	*Secondary*	*Tertiary*
1971	47	2,380	434		*Not Available*	
1976	225	6,889	1,675			
1977-82[2]		*Not Available*		238	170	454
1983[3]	759	16,007	2,215		*Not Available*	

Source:
Central Bank of Brazil, *Bulletin,* various issues; *Diario Official,* various issues.

NOTES TO TABLE A4

1 Based on cumulative investment flows.

2 Refers to cumulative authorised investment flows, 1977-82.

3 Figures as for June 1983.

Table A5

GEOGRAPHICAL DISTRIBUTION OF FOREIGN DIRECT CAPITAL STOCK, 1971 - 83 (US $ m)

	Inward Investment[1]			Outward Investment		
	Developed Countries	*Developing Countries*	*Total*	*Developed Countries*	*Developing Countries*	*Total*
1971	2,441[2]	466	2,907[3]		*Not Available*	
1965-76[4]		*Not Available*		21	27	260[3]
1965-82[5]				712	221	1,113[3]
1983[6]	19,269	2,562	21,831		*Not Available*	

Source:
Central Bank of Brazil, *Bulletin,* various issues; *Diario Official,* various issues.

NOTES TO TABLE A5

1 Based on cumulative investment flows.

2 Including only those countries as specified in Table A7.

3 Total includes 'unspecified' figure.

4 Cumulative direct investment abroad, 1965-76, according to the authorisation certificates issued by the Central Bank.

5 Cumulative direct investment abroad, 1965-82, according to the authorisation certificates issued by the Central Bank.

6 Estimates as of June, 1983.

Table A6

INDUSTRIAL DISTRIBUTION OF FOREIGN DIRECT CAPITAL STOCK, 1971 - 83 (US $ m)

	Inward Investment[1]		Outward Investment
	1971	*1983*[2]	*1977-82*[3]
Primary	46.8	758.6	238.0
Agriculture	20.7	134.2	*N.A.*
Mining & quarrying	26.1	624.4	*N.A.*
Oil	*N.A.*	*N.A.*	238.0
Secondary	2,379.7	16,007.1	170.2
Food & drink	247.5	1,312.7	
Chemicals & allied	737.9	3,882.3	*Not Available*
Metals	213.6	1,634.4	
Mechanical engineering	123.7	2,083.5	31.9
Electrical equipment	261.6	1,625.3	
Motor vehicles	309.8	2,149.0	
Other transportation equipment	95.7	694.1	*Not Available*
Textiles & clothing	69.7	527.6	
Paper & allied	67.9	511.5	
Rubber	103.4	543.7	
Stone, clay & glass	61.6	384.1	
Other manufacturing	87.3	658.9	138.3
Tertiary	433.7	2,215.0	454.3
Transport & communications	*N.A.*	44.1	30.2
Banking & finance	89.8	993.8	390.2
Other services	343.9	1,177.1	33.9
TOTAL	2,911.5[4]	21,831.4[4]	862.5

Source:
Central Bank of Brazil, *Bulletin,* various issues; *Diario Official*, various issues.

NOTES TO TABLE A6

1 Based on cumulative investment flows.
2 Figures as of June 1983.
3 Cumulative authorised investment flows, 1977-82. Total actual investment flows for the same period if US $ 1,416 million.
4 Total includes 'unspecified' figure.

Table A7

LEADING SOURCE AND RECIPIENT COUNTRIES, 1971 - 83 (US $ m)

	Inward Investment[1]		Outward Investment	
	1971	*1983*[2]	*1965-76*[4]	*1965-82*[5]
DEVELOPED AREAS	2,441[3]	19,269.1	213.7	712.1
Europe	926[3]	9,288.5	*Not Available*	
EEC of which	734[3]	6,586.1		
Belgium & Luxembourg	*N.A.*	668.4		
Denmark	*N.A.*	41.1		
France	130	724.0		
W. Germany	*N.A.*	2,894.0		
Greece	331	*N.A.*		
Italy	*N.A.*	660.9		
Netherlands	*N.A.*	521.0		
UK	273	1,076.7		
Other Europe of which	192[3]	2,702.4		
Austria	*Not Available*	15.8		
Finland		40.5		
Liechtenstein		141.5		
Norway		31.7		
Portugal		51.0		
Spain		86.1		
Sweden		373.6		
Switzerland	192	1,962.2		
North America of which	1,390	7,969.8		
Canada	294	1,020.2		
USA	1,096	6,949.6		
Other developed countries of which	125[3]	2,010.8		
Australia	*N.A.*	11.5		
Japan	125	1,991.3		
DEVELOPING AREAS		2,562.2	27.3	221.4
Africa	*Not Available*	475.0	*Not Available*	
Liberia		475.0		
Asia & Pacific of which		89.4		
Hong Kong		73.0		
Singapore		16.3		
Latin America of which		1,648.3	27.3	221.4
Argentina		35.2	*Not Available*	
Bahamas		68.4		
Bermuda		238.7		
Colombia		1.6		
Costa Rica		1.2		
Mexico		13.6		
Netherlands Antilles		444.9		
Panama		802.7		

Table A7 (cont'd)

LEADING SOURCE AND RECIPIENT COUNTRIES, 1971 - 83 (US $ m)

	Inward Investment[1]			Outward Investment	
	1971	*1983*[2]		*1965-76*[4]	*1965-82*[5]
Uruguay	*Not Available*	23.4		*Not Available*	
Venezuela		16.5			
Middle East of which		87.6			
Iran		55.1			
Iraq		8.9			
Saudi Arabia		23.3			
OTHER DEVELOPING COUNTRIES	466[6]	261.9		18.7[6]	179.1[6]
TOTAL	2,907	21,831.1		259.7	1,112.6

Source:
Central Bank of Brazil, Bulletin, various issues; *Diario Official,* various issues.

NOTES TO TABLE A7

1 Based on cumulative investment flows.
2 Estimate as of June 1983.
3 Including only those countries shown below.
4 Cumulative direct investment abroad, 1965-76, according to authorisation certificates issued by the Central Bank.
5 Cumulative direct investment abroad, 1965-82, according to authorisation certificates issued by the Central Bank.
6 Unspecified.

Table A8

INDICATORS OF THE SIGNIFICANCE OF INWARD FOREIGN DIRECT INVESTMENT OR THE ACTIVITIES OF FOREIGN-BASED COMPANIES TO THE NATIONAL ECONOMY, 1977 - 82

1	Direct capital stock of foreign affiliates at book value in 1982 as a proportion of	
	a GNP at factor cost	11.09
	b population (in US $ per head)	167.02
2	Employment in foreign affiliates[1] in 1977 as a percentage of all employment in manufacturing	23
3	Output[2] of foreign affiliates[1] in 1977 as a percentage of all companies' output in secondary (ie manufacturing) industry	32
4	Exports of foreign affiliates[1] in 1978 as a percentage of all manufacturing exports	37.2

5 Percentage share of assets, sales and employment as accounted for by foreign affiliates[1] in selected sectors, 1977

	Assets	*Sales*[2]	*Employment*
Manufacturing Sector			
Food products	36	52	41
Beverages	23	24	17
Tobacco	99	89	96
Chemicals	57	57	61
Pharmaceutical products	82	84	79
Metal products	29	32	33
Mechanical engineering	51	59	54
Electrical products	86	79	83
Motor vehicles	100	100	100
Textiles	37	34	26
Paper	20	24	24
Rubber	62	81	70
Petroleum products	9	36	14
Timber and furniture	24	13	33

Source:

J Mooney and R Newfarmer, *State Enterprise* and *Private Sector Development in Brazil* as quoted by UNCTC, 1983, *op cit.*

NOTES TO TABLE A8

1 Foreign affiliates represent MNEs (manufacturing activities only).

2 Represents total value of production (manufacturing sector only).

Table A9

INDICATORS OF THE SIGNIFICANCE OF OUTWARD FOREIGN DIRECT INVESTMENT OR THE ACTIVITIES OF HOME-BASED COMPANIES ABROAD FOR THE NATIONAL ECONOMY, 1982

1	Foreign capital stock of home-based firms at book value in 1982 as a proportion of	
	a GNP at factor cost	0.96
	b population (in US $ per head)	14.4

Table A10

There are no detailed data on the structure of ownership of foreign affiliates in Brazil. However, it is known that in 1978, 59.8% of the investment made by UK firms was in other than wholly owned affiliates.

Table A11

ROYALTY RECEIPTS AND PAYMENTS, 1975 - 82 (US $ m)

	Payments			Receipts		
	To Affiliates	*To Non-affiliates*	*Total*	*From Affiliates*	*From Non-affiliates*	*Total*
1975	*Not Separately Available*		223.4	*Not Separately Available*		134.8
1976			263.2			131.6
1977			169.3			126.1
1978			210.3			159.0
1979			36.2			11.6
1980			37.7			11.7
1981			29.5			18.9
1982			30.9			15.5

Source:
IMF, *Balance of Payments Statistics Yearbook, 1983.*

Table A12

LEADING FOREIGN AND DOMESTIC MULTINATIONAL COMPANIES

A Leading Foreign Multinational Companies in the country, 1983

	Name	*Home Country*	*Sector*	*Brazilian Turnover (Cr m)*
1	BAT Industries PLC	UK	Tobacco	1,317.7
2	Esso	USA	Petroleum	1,263.9
3	Volkswagen	W. Germany	Motor vehicles	950.1
4	General Motors	USA	Motor vehicles	819.7
5	Texaco	USA	Petroleum	793.3
6	Atlantic	USA	Petroleum	781.1
7	Ford	USA	Motor vehicles	778.3
8	Pirelli	Italy	Rubber	471.4
9	Nestlé	Switzerland	Food	450.6
10	Fiat	Italy	Motor vehicles	414.1
11	Sanbra		Food	393.2
12	Rhodia	France	Chemicals	334.2
13	Mercedes Benz	W. Germany	Motor vehicles	322.1
14	Goodyear	USA	Rubber	288.6
15	Anderson Clayton	USA	Food	210.8
16	Cargill		Food	197.0
17	Alcan	Canada	Metals	186.3
18	Dow	USA	Chemicals	183.6
19	Verolme		Motor vehicles	181.1
20	Firestone	USA	Rubber	179.4
21	Bayer	W. Germany	Chemicals	168.3
22	Xerox	USA	Office equipment	150.4
23	Philip Morris	USA	Tobacco	149.7
24	Hoechst	W. Germany	Chemicals	141.2
25	Ciba-Geigy	Switzerland	Chemicals	139.2

Table A12 (cont'd)

LEADING FOREIGN AND DOMESTIC MULTINATIONAL COMPANIES

B Leading Domestic Companies with Multinational Interests, 1983

	Name	*Sector*	*Global Turnover (Cr m)*	*Sales of overseas subsidiaries as % of worldwide sales (1983)*
1	Petrobras	Oil	7,818,851	132.1
2	Constr Mendes Junior	Construction	279,234	208.1
3	Constr Norberto Odebrecht	Construction	241,516	208.5
4	Cica-Cia	Food	135,460	180.3
5	Cotia Com Exp	Foreign trade	86,602	290.8
6	Gradiente Amazonia	Home appliances	66,816	94.2
7	Engevix	Engineering	33,775	222.3
8	Promon Engenharia	Engineering	33,754	222.2
9	Themag Engenharia	Engineering	26,893	222.4
10	Caloi SA	Transportation equipment	22,250	105.5
11	Iesa-Internacional de Engenharia SA	Engineering	17,952	222.7
12	Ifema	Electrical equipment	4,503	92.6
13	Cicasui-Ind Cons	Food	2,801	182.9
14	Braspetro	Oil	2,552	54.1
15	Constr Rabello	Construction	1,303	212.1
16	Securit	Furniture	*Not Available*	
17	Bergamo	Furniture		
18	Sisal	Construction		
19	Esusa	Construction		
20	Transcon	Engineering		

Source:
Conjuntura Economica, vol 38, no 9, Sept 1984; Quem e Quem na Economia Brasileira, *Visao,* August 1978, 1979, 1980, 1981, 1984.

CHILE

The Chilean government has pursued liberal and non-discriminatory policies towards foreign direct investment since the mid 1970s, and the inflow of foreign investment has fluctuated annually during this period. Chilean foreign investment policy is embodied in its Foreign Investment Statute Decree Law 600 which was issued in 1974 and then amended in 1977 under Decree Law 1978.

Mining activity continues to attract substantial inward investment, particularly in non-ferrous metals. There is also some foreign investment in fishing, agri-business and forestry where Chile enjoys a comparative advantage. The share of foreign investment in manufacturing has increased in significance, where chemicals and mechanical engineering are the major recipient industries. Within the services sector, the emphasis lies on distributive trades.

The main source of investment continues to be the USA, while Western European countries and other Latin American countries — notably Panama — are also significant investors in Chile.

There is some outward investment by Chilean firms mainly in trading and financial activities. The bulk of this investment is concentrated in other parts of Latin America.

MAIN SOURCES OF DATA:

A **Official**

1 Central Bank of Chile: provides data on foreign direct investment flows in and from Chile.

2 Committee on Foreign Investment: gives information on accumulated foreign direct investment in Chile by sectoral distribution.

3 US Department of Commerce International Trade Administration, *Investment Climate in Foreign Countries,* Washington, 1985.

B **Private**

1 F Albavera, *Las Empresas Transnacionales en la Economia de Chile 1974 - 1980,* prepared for CEPAL, Santiago, Chile: UN, 1983.

2 School of Administration, Department of Systems Engineering and Computer Sciences Centre, *Chile: Sociedades Anonimas,* Santiago, Chile: Catholic University (SISSA), 1980.

3 E Lahera, "The Transnational Corporations in the Chilean Economy", *CEPAL Review,* UN, August 1981.

Note:
Data do not allow us to complete Table A10 for Chile.

Table A1

SUMMARY OF THE COUNTRY'S INTERNATIONAL INVESTMENT POSITION

		Inward Investment	Outward Investment
1	Number of foreign affiliates in host country, and of foreign affiliates of home country firms at the end of 1980	244[1]	*N.A.*
2	Number of foreign firms with direct investments in host country, and home country firms with direct foreign affiliates	*N.A.*	*N.A.*
3	Total foreign direct capital stock at book value as a percentage of GNP at factor cost in 1980	3.74	0.45[2]
4	Flow of foreign direct investment in the five year period 1980 - 84 (US $m)	1,263.4	131.7
5	Employment in foreign affiliates[3] or abroad, 1979	39,894	*N.A.*
6	Output of foreign affiliates[3] or abroad, 1979 (US $m)	2,756.3	*N.A.*

Source:

Committee on Foreign Investment, data as cited in Albavera, *op cit;* Central Bank of Chile, data as cited in US Department of Commerce, *Investment Climate in Foreign Countries,* Washington, 1983; IMF, *Balance of Payments Statistics Yearbook,* various issues; IMF, *International Financial Statistics Yearbook, 1984;* National Institute of Statistics, *Compendio Estadistico, 1980.*

NOTES TO TABLE A1

1 Represents foreign affiliates of MNEs from selected home countries as identified by UNCTC, 1983.

2 Represents cumulative investment flow, 1977-82 as a percentage of GNP in 1982.

Table A2

PRIVATE FOREIGN CAPITAL STOCK, 1973 - 84 (US $ m)

	Inward Investment			Outward Investment		
	Portfolio	*Direct*	*Total*	*Portfolio*	*Direct*	*Total*
Book value of capital stock						
1973	*Not Available*	357	*Not Available*	*Not Available*	*Not Available*	*Not Available*
1977		426				
1979		892				
1982		1,863			100.9[1]	
1983		2,045			140.5[1]	
1984		2,123[2]			151.8[1]	

Source:

Committee on Foreign Investments, data as cited in Albavera, *Las Empresas Transnacionales en la Economia de Chile, 1974-1980,* prepared for CEPAL, Santiago, Chile: UN, 1983.

NOTES TO TABLE A2

1 Cumulative investment flows, as from 1977.

2 Estimated using 1983 stock figure plus cumulative investment flows in 1984.

Table A3

FLOW OF FOREIGN DIRECT INVESTMENT, 1974 - 84 (US $ m)

	Inward Investment			Outward Investment		
	Reinvested Profits	*Other*	*Total*	*Reinvested Profits*	*Other*	*Total*
1974	*N.S.A.*	-14.2	-14.2	*Not Separately Available*		*Not Available*
1975	32.2	46.4	78.6			
1976	13.4	-40.4	-27.0			
1977	15.0	9.3	24.3			4.7
1978	7.6	213.2	220.8			3.8
1979	6.9	240.3	247.2			11.6
1980	*Not Separately Available*	*Not Separately Available*	213.4			43.0
1981			383.2			21.2
1982			400.8			16.6
1983			188.1			39.6
1984			77.9			11.3

Source:

Committee for Foreign Investment (for inward investment, 1974-80), data as cited in Albavera, *op cit;* Central Bank of Chile (for inward investment, 1981-83), data as cited in US Department of Commerce *Investment Climate in Foreign Countries,* Washington, 1983; IMF, *Balance of Payments Statistics Yearbook;* various issues (for outward investment).

Table A4

SECTORAL DISTRIBUTION OF FOREIGN DIRECT CAPITAL STOCK, 1973 - 79 (US $ m)

	Inward Investment				Outward Investment[3]		
	Primary	*Secondary*	*Tertiary*		*Primary*	*Secondary*	*Tertiary*
1973[1]	60.03	197.41	97.61				
1979[2]	83.18	586.35	222.44		*neg.*	0.88	9.22
1983[4]	824.10	502.50	667.10				

Source:

Committee on Foreign Investment and SISSA, data as cited in Albavera, *Las Empresas Transnacionales en la Economia de Chile, 1974-1980,* prepared for CEPAL, Santiago, Chile: UN, 1983.

NOTES TO TABLE A4

1 Figures as for June 1973.

2 Based on the percentage sectoral distribution of FDI companies organised as joint stock companies.

3 1976-9 Registered investment approved by Central Bank of Chile.

4 1974-83 Realised Foreign Investment in Chile.

Table A5

GEOGRAPHICAL DISTRIBUTION OF FOREIGN DIRECT CAPITAL STOCK, 1979 (US $ m)

	Inward Investment				Outward Investment[2]		
	Developed Countries[1]	*Developing Countries*	*Total*		*Developed Countries*[3]	*Developing Countries*	*Total*
1979	764.0	54.0	892.0[1]		0.53	9.57	10.1
1983[4]	1,718.5	275.1	1,993.6			*Not Available*	

Source:

SISSA, data as cited in Albavera, *Las Empresas Transnacionales en la Economia de Chile, 1974-1980,* prepared for CEPAL, Santiago, Chile: UN, 1983.

NOTES TO TABLE A5

1 Total includes unspecified figure.

2 1976-9 Registered investment approved by Central Bank of Chile.

3 In USA only.

4 1974-83 Realised foreign investment in Chile.

Table A6

INDUSTRIAL DISTRIBUTION OF FOREIGN DIRECT CAPITAL STOCK, 1973 - 83 (US $m)

	Inward Investment		Outward Investment
	1973[1]	*1974-83*	*1976-9*
Primary	60.03	824.1	
Agriculture[2]	0.68	53.2	
Mining & quarrying	59.35	769.2	*neg.*
Oil	*N.A.*	1.7	
Secondary	197.41	502.5	0.88
Food & drink	27.09		
Chemicals & allied[3]	82.52		
Metals	5.19		
Mechanical engineering	49.80		
Textiles & clothing	23.10	*Not*	*Not*
Paper & allied	4.26	*Separately*	*Separately*
Rubber[3]	*N.A.*	*Available*	*Available*
Stone, clay & glass	3.66		
Coal & petroleum products[3]	*N.A.*		
Other manufacturing	1.79		
Tertiary	97.61	667.1	9.22
Construction		97.5	0.01
Transport & communications	*Not*	9.4	*N.A.*
Distributive trade	*Separately*	*N.A.*	1.54
Banking & finance	*Available*	*N.A.*	6.00
Other services		560.2	1.95
TOTAL	357.27[4]	1,993.6	10.10

Source:

Committee on Foreign Investment, and SISSA, data as cited in Albavera, *Las Empresas Transnacionales en la Economia de Chile 1974-1980,*prepared for CEPAL, Santiago, Chile: UN, 1983; Central Bank of Chile.

NOTES TO TABLE A6

1 Figures as for June 1973.

2 Including fishing & forestry.

3 Rubber, plastics, coal and petroleum products included under 'chemicals and allied'.

4 Total includes unspecified figure.

Table A7

LEADING SOURCE AND RECIPIENT COUNTRIES, 1979 (US $ m)

	Inward Investment		Outward Investment
	1979	*1974-83*	*1976-79*
DEVELOPED AREAS	745.71		
Europe	362.15	*Not*	
EEC of which:	248.86	*Available*	
Belgium & Luxembourg	34.79		
France	37.46	60.5	
W. Germany	26.76	47.1	
Italy	24.08	*N.A.*	*neg.*
Netherlands	14.27	91.6	
UK	111.50	145.5	
Other Europe of which:	113.29	*N.A.*	
Spain	11.60	191.4	
Sweden	16.06	*N.A.*	
Switzerland	85.63	37.3	
North America of which:	383.56	1,000.6	
Canada	24.98	27.8	
USA	358.58	972.8	0.53
Japan	*N.A.*	45.2	*N.A.*
DEVELOPING AREAS	54.41	*N.A.*	9.57
Latin America of which:	54.41	275.1	9.57
Argentina	*N.A.*	22.1	*N.A.*
Brazil	*N.A.*	57.6	*N.A.*
Panama	49.06	124.3	3.37
Peru	*N.A.*	*N.A.*	3.34
UNSPECIFIED	91.88	88.9	
TOTAL	892.00	1,993.6	10.10

Source:
SISSA, data as cited in Albavera, *op cit;* Central Bank of Chile.

Table A8

INDICATORS OF THE SIGNIFICANCE OF INWARD FOREIGN DIRECT INVESTMENT OR THE ACTIVITIES OF FOREIGN-BASED COMPANIES TO THE NATIONAL ECONOMY, 1979 - 80

1	Direct capital stock of foreign affiliates at book value in 1980 as a proportion of:	
	a GNP at factor cost	3.74
	b population (in US $ per head)	89.73
2	Employment in foreign affiliates in 1979 as a percentage of all employment in all industry	15.40
3	Output of foreign affiliates in 1979 as a percentage of all companies' output	
	a in primary (ie, extractive) industry b in secondary (ie, manufacturing) industry c in tertiary industry (ie, services, etc) }	23.20
4	Investment by foreign affiliates as a percentage of domestic investment, 1978-80	2.6
5	Profits of foreign affiliates in 1979 as a percentage of profits of all companies in the host country in all sectors	23.10

6 Percentage share of assets, sales and employment accounted for by foreign affiliates in selected sectors, 1979[1]

	Assets	*Sales*	*Employment*
Primary Goods Sector			
Agriculture[2]	30.0	31.7	38.7
Mining & quarrying	64.1	79.2	62.3
Oil	16.9	00.0	85.7
Manufacturing Sector			
Food & drink	17.2	25.5	24.1
Chemicals & allied[3]	40.4	46.6	30.9
Non-Ferrous Metals	*N.A.*	46.7	*N.A.*
Mechanical engineering	41.8	55.0	32.1
Textiles & clothing	7.1	14.6	9.9
Paper & allied	16.7	16.2	12.4
Rubber[3]	*N.A.*	*N.A.*	*N.A.*
Stone, glass & clay	41.7	54.1	40.0
Coal & petroleum products[3]	*N.A.*	*N.A.*	*N.A.*
Timber & furniture	5.6	6.0	4.8
Other manufacturing	64.3	64.3	55.9

Table A8 (cont'd)

INDICATORS OF THE SIGNIFICANCE OF INWARD FOREIGN DIRECT INVESTMENT OR THE ACTIVITIES OF FOREIGN-BASED COMPANIES TO THE NATIONAL ECONOMY, 1979 - 80

6 (cont'd)	*Assets*	*Sales*	*Employment*
Services Sector			
Construction	0.5	2.0	1.4
Transport & communications[4]	13.8	12.9	15.4
Trade & distribution[5]	27.0	42.7	16.5
Banking & finance[6]	27.8	47.4	29.8
Other services	2.1	2.8	5.4

Source:

Chile: Sociedades Anonimas, data as cited in Albavera, *op cit;* Committee on Foreign Investment, data as cited in Albavera, *op cit;* IMF, *International Financial Statistics Yearbook, 1984.*

NOTES TO TABLE A8

1 Represents percentage share of foreign participation in joint stock companies relative to total participation in joint stock companies.

2 Represents fishing.

3 Rubber, plastics, coal and petroleum products included under 'chemicals & allied'.

4 Represents transport & storage. The percentage share of assets, sales and employment in communications are 1.6, 3.6 and 4.5 respectively.

5 Represents wholesale trade only. The percentage share of assets, sales and employment in retail trade are 7.7, 8.8 and 9.6 respectively.

6 Represents real estate.

Table A9

INDICATORS OF THE SIGNIFICANCE OF OUTWARD FOREIGN DIRECT INVESTMENT OR THE ACTIVITIES OF HOME-BASED COMPANIES ABROAD FOR THE NATIONAL ECONOMY, 1982

1	Foreign capital stock[1] of home-based firms at book value in 1982 as a proportion of:	
	a GNP at factor cost	0.45
	b population (in US $ per head)	8.78

Source:
IMF, *Balance of Payments Statistics Yearbook,* various issues; IMF, *International Financial Statistics Yearbook, 1984.*

NOTES TO TABLE A9

[1] Cumulative investment flows, 1977-82.

Table A11

ROYALTY RECEIPTS AND PAYMENTS

	Payments				Receipts		
	To Affiliates	*To Non-affiliates*	*Total*		*From Affiliates*	*From Non-affiliates*	*Total*
1975	*Not Separately Available*		6.1		*Not Available*		
1976			8.1				
1977			14.0				
1978			16.3				
1979			20.7				
1980			28.6				
1981			38.9				
1982			32.1				

Source:
IMF, *Balance of Payments Statistics Yearbook, 1983.*

Table A12

LEADING FOREIGN MULTINATIONAL COMPANIES

Name	*Home Country*	*Sector*
Atlas Copco	Sweden	Machinery
Bayer	W. Germany	Chemicals
Black & Decker	USA	Electrical
Brown Boveri & Co	Switzerland	Electrical
Dow Chemicals	USA	Chemicals
Exxon	USA	Oil
Fiat	Italy	Motor vehicles
Firestone	USA	Rubber
Glaxo Holdings	UK	Pharmaceuticals
Goodyear	USA	Rubber
Hoechst	W. Germany	Chemicals
IBM	USA	Office equipment
ITT	USA	Electrical
Johnson & Johnson	USA	Pharmaceuticals
Levi Strauss	USA	Textiles
Massey-Ferguson Ltd	Canada	Machinery
Mitsui	Japan	Chemicals
Mobil Corp	USA	Oil
Pepsi Co	USA	Beverages
Renault	France	Motor vehicles
Royal Dutch/Shell	Netherlands/UK	Oil
SKF	Sweden	Machinery
Texaco	USA	Oil
Thorn-EMI	UK	Electrical
Xerox	USA	Office equipment

Source:
Albavera, *op cit*.

CHILE. DEFINITIONS

Foreign direct investments are those investments from outside the national boundary with the pursued end of establishing or promoting some type of permanent participation in a firm situated within the national boundary. Such participation has to be sufficient for the foreign investor to exercise effective influence or control over the administration of the firm. Such control or influence is conveniently defined as ownership of not less than 10% of the share capital of the firm without considering foreign investment by naturalised persons and others which represent a minority of the investments.

There are three important exceptions to the above definition. First, the realized investments in foreign firms controlled by residents in Chile. Second, the investments that result in participation in the share capital in the recipient firm in sectors not financed in part by foreign financial entities. Third, those firms where state participation predominate.

Foreign direct investment companies are those firms where foreign direct investment is equivalent to 10% or more of the capital. These firms are FDI firms by definition. Eighty percent of these firms are in the industrial sector, where the participation of such firms are equal to or superior to 50%. The participation is over 80% in half of these firms and local participation constitute only a minority.

The accumulated value of foreign direct investment includes ownership capital of foreign investors in FDI firms and their obligations. In general, these values are as at the end of the calendar year and determines the sum of reserved capital and reinvested profits.

The flows of foreign direct investment include inflows and outflows of foreign direct investment with the difference defined as net flows. Inflows include payments from abroad, capital raised by debt, local credit and others. Outflows are repatriation of capital, remittance of profits and dividends, amortization of debt and payment of interest.

Source:
F Albavera, *op cit.*

COLOMBIA

Over the past three years, the Colombian government has shown a more favourable attitude towards inward investment. However, the basic concept is that foreign investment should complement domestic capital; and there are comprehensive rules and regulations governing the sectoral and ownership patterns of foreign participation.

While the inflow of foreign direct investment has been steadily rising since the early 1970s, Colombia's outward investment has fluctuated annually throughout the same period.

The largest foreign investor in Colombia is the USA, which accounts for 56% of total inward investment to the country. Switzerland, the UK and Panama follow at a considerable distance.

Within the manufacturing sector, the major growth areas have been in chemicals, mechanical engineering, electrical equipment and transportation equipment. However, the main recipient of the rise in inward investment has been the extractive sector, and particularly oil, nickel and coal.

Colombia is quite an important outward direct investor; at the end of 1983, the value of her overseas assets were over US $ 400 million. The greater part of the activities of Colombian MNEs is in finance, insurance and real estate.

MAIN SOURCES OF DATA:

A. Official

1 Oficina de Cambios, Banco de la Republica: provides information on registered foreign direct investment by sectoral distribution.

2 US Department of Commerce International Trade Administration, *Investment Climate in Foreign Countries,* Washington, 1985, vol IV.

3 UNCTC, *Joint Ventures Among Firms in Latin America,* New York: UN, 1983.

4 UNCTC, *Transnational Corporations and World Development: A Reexamination,* New York: UN, 1978.

5 UNCTC, *Transnational Corporations in World Development: Third Survey,* New York: UN, 1983.

B. Private

1 CEPAL/CET, 'Informe Sobre la Encuesta de las Principales Empresas con Participacion Extranjera del Sector Manufacturero Colombiano', UNCES, LC/L.323, December 1984.

2 A J de Lucio, 'The East, the South and the Transnational Corporations', *CEPAL Review,* no 14, Santiago, Chile: UN, August 1981.

3 Michael Mortimore, ''Foreign Participation in Colombian Development: The Role of Transnational Corporations'', Economic Commission for Latin America, Joint CEPAL/ CTC Unit Working Paper no 14, June 1979.

Note:
Data do not allow us to complete Table A10 for Colombia.

Table A1

SUMMARY OF THE COUNTRY'S INTERNATIONAL INVESTMENT POSITION

		Inward Investment	Outward Investment
1	Number of foreign affiliates in host country, and of foreign affiliates of home country firms at the end of 1980	557[1]	*N.A.*
2	Number of foreign firms with direct investments in host country, and home country firms with direct foreign affiliates at the end of 1978	*N.A.*	71
3	Total foreign direct capital stock at book value as a percentage of GNP at factor cost in 1984	15.83	1.94
4	Flow of foreign direct investment in the five year period, 1980-84 (US $m)	1,838.7	295.9
5	Employment in foreign affiliates or abroad	*N.A.*	*N.A.*
6	Output of foreign affiliates or abroad	*N.A.*	*N.A.*

Source:

IMF, *Balance of Payments Statistics Yearbook,* various issues; IMF, *International Financial Statistics Yearbook, 1984*; UNCTC, *Joint Ventures among Firms in Latin America, op cit.*

NOTES TO TABLE A1

1 Represents number of foreign affiliates of MNEs from selected home countries identified by UNCTC, *Transnational Corporation in World Development: Third Survey, op cit.*

Table A2

PRIVATE FOREIGN CAPITAL STOCK, 1971 - 84 (US $ m)[1]

	Inward Investment			Outward Investment		
	Portfolio	*Direct*	*Total*	*Portfolio*	*Direct*	*Total*
Book value of capital stock						
1971	*Not Available*	692.0	*Not Available*	*Not Available*	25.5	*Not Available*
1975		965.0			38.1	
1978		1,195.7			90.1	
1981		1,745.1			256.5	
1984		3,161.0			410.5	

Source:
US Department of Commerce, unpublished data; UNCTC, -*TNCs in World Development,* 1983, *op cit.* for inward direct investment from 1971 to 1978; UNCTC, *Joint Ventures among Firms in Latin America,* 1983, *op. cit.* for outward direct investment 1971 to 1978.

NOTES TO TABLE A2

1 Cumulative investment flows have been added to 1978 stock figures to estimate direct investment stock for subsequent years.

Table A3

FLOW OF FOREIGN DIRECT INVESTMENT, 1970 - 84 (US $ m)

	Inward Investment			Outward Investment		
	Reinvested Profits	*Other*	*Total*	*Reinvested Profits*	*Other*	*Total*
1970	*Not Separately Available*		43.0	*Not Separately Available*		4.0
1971			43.1			3.0
1972			18.5			1.1
1973			23.8			1.2
1974			40.9			6.0
1975			40.1			4.9
1976			58.9			10.4
1977	19.8	45.5	65.4	2.3	19.8	22.2
1978	50.1	56.3	106.4	3.8	37.6	41.3
1979	45.2	81.4	126.6	3.9	20.7	24.5
1980	40.3	117.2	157.5	7.8	97.6	105.4
1981	47.2	218.1	265.3	5.9	30.7	36.5
1982	46.4	320.1	366.5	5.5	23.2	28.7
1983	53.4	564.5	617.9	7.5	97.3	104.8
1984	57.4	374.1	431.5	0.0	20.5	20.5

Source:
IMF, *Balance of Payments Statistics Yearbook,* various issues.

Table A4

SECTORAL DISTRIBUTION OF FOREIGN DIRECT CAPITAL STOCK, 1974–81 (US $ m)[1]

	Inward Investment			Outward Investment		
	Primary	*Secondary*	*Tertiary*[2]	*Primary*	*Secondary*	*Tertiary*
1974		*Not Available*		*N.A.*	10.2	25.3
1975	347.4	426.5	191.1		*Not Available*	
1978		*Not Available*		2.8	8.6	78.8
1981	*N.A.*	868.6	*N.A.*		*Not Available*	

Source:
Oficiana de Cambios, Banco de la Republica, data as cited in CEPAL/CET, LC/L. 323, *op cit.;* UNCTC, 1978 and 1983, *op cit.*

NOTES TO TABLE A4
1 Registered FDI.
2 Including 'others'.

Table A5

GEOGRAPHICAL DISTRIBUTION OF FOREIGN DIRECT CAPITAL STOCK, 1975–84 (US $ m)

	Inward Investment			Outward Investment		
	Developed Countries	*Developing Countries*	*Total*[3]	*Developed Countries*	*Developing Countries*	*Total*
1975[1]	480.0	79.0	632.0		*Not Available*	
1976		*Not Available*		10.3	32.8	43.1
1984	1,237.7[2]	151.3	1,731		*Not Available*	

Source:
US Department of Commerce, unpublished data; Foreign Exchange Office, Banco de la Republica, data as cited in de Lucio, CEPAL Review, August 1981, *op cit.;* UNCTC, 1978 and 1983, *op cit.*

NOTES TO TABLE A5
1 Excluding investment in petroleum sector
2 USA, UK and Switzerland only.
3 Total includes unspecified figure. It does not match Table A2 due to an unallocated component.

Tabel A6

INDUSTRIAL DISTRIBUTION OF FOREIGN DIRECT CAPITAL STOCK, 1974–81 (US $m)[1]

	Inward Investment		Outward Investment	
	1974	*1981*	*1974*	*1978*
Primary	*Not Available*		*Not Available*	2.8
Agriculture				1.4
Mining & quarrying				1.4
Oil				0.0
Secondary	395.4	868.6	10.2	8.6
Food & drink	35.7	99.1	*Not Separately Available*	
Chemicals & allied[2]	182.5	347.3		
Metals	8.7	14.6		
Mechanical engineering				
Electrical equipment	64.8	209.7		
Motor vehicles				
Other transportation equipment				
Textiles & clothing	21.9	45.3		
Paper & allied	44.5	92.2		
Rubber[2]				
Stone, clay & glass	28.7	42.6		
Coal & petroleum products[2]				
Other manufacturing	8.6	17.8		
Tertiary			25.3	78.8
Construction	*Not Available*		*N.A.*	*N.A.*
Transport & communications			*N.A.*	0.5
Distributive trade			0.3	2.3
Property[3]			*N.A.*	21.0
Banking, finance & insurance			20.3	52.9
Other services			4.7	2.1
TOTAL	*N.A.*	*N.A.*	35.5	90.2

Source:
Oficiana de Cambios, Banco de la Republica, data as cited in CEPAL/CET, LC/L. 323, *op cit.*

NOTES TO TABLE A6

1 Registered FDI.
2 Rubber, coal & petroleum products included under 'chemicals & allied'.
3 Including social and personal services.

Table A7

LEADING SOURCE AND RECIPIENT COUNTRIES, 1976 - 84 (US $ m)

	Inward Investment	Outward Investment
	1984	*1976*
DEVELOPED AREAS[1]	1,237.67	10.3
Europe of which:		4.9
UK	115.98	*N.A.*
Switzerland	152.33	*N.A.*
North America of which:		5.4
USA	969.36	*N.A.*
DEVELOPING AREAS[1]	151.31	32.8
Latin America of which:	151.31	32.8
Argentina	1.06[2]	*Not Available*
Brazil	2.40[2]	
Chile	0.20[2]	
Ecuador	17.62[2]	2.3
Mexico	4.14[2]	*N.A.*
Panama	96.94	13.7
Peru	1.72[2]	0.1
Uruguay	1.11[2]	*N.A.*
Venezuela	26.12[2]	7.9
UNSPECIFIED	342.02	0.0
TOTAL	1,731.00[3]	43.1

Source:
US Department of Commerce, unpublished data; Foreign Exchange Office, Banco de la Republica, data as cited in de Lucio, CEPAL Review, August 1981, *op cit;* UNCTC, 1983, *op cit.*

NOTES TO TABLE A7

1 Including only those countries shown below.

2 Accumulated FDI up to end 1978. Does not include investments in the oil industry.

3. Total does not match Table A2 due to an unallocated component.

Table A8

INDICATORS OF THE SIGNIFICANCE OF INWARD FOREIGN DIRECT INVESTMENT OR THE ACTIVITIES OF FOREIGN-BASED COMPANIES TO THE NATIONAL ECONOMY, 1974–84

1	Direct capital stock of foreign affiliates at book value in 1984 as a proportion of:	
	a. GNP at factor cost	15.83
	b. population (in US $ per head)	123.15
2	Output of foreign affiliates in 1974 as a percentage of all companies' output in secondary (ie, manufacturing) industry	43.4
3	Exports of foreign affiliates in 1978 as a percentage of all manufacturing exports	14.4
4	Percentage share of sales accounted for by foreign affiliates in selected sectors, 1974	*Sales*[1]
	Oil	
	Food & Drink	16.4
	Chemicals & allied	62.4
	Metals	54.7
	Textiles & clothing	50.2
	Paper & allied	55.8
	Stone, glass & clay	58.4
	Furniture	23.2
	Other manufacturing	23.4

Source:
IMF, *Balance of Payments Statistics Yearbook,* various issues, IMF, *International Financial Statistics Yearbook,* 1985; Mortimore, *op cit;* UNCTC, 1983, *op cit.*

NOTES TO TABLE A8

1 Represents share of production accounted for by firms with foreign production in the manufacturing sector.

Table A9

INDICATORS OF THE SIGNIFICANCE OF OUTWARD FOREIGN DIRECT INVESTMENT OR THE ACTIVITIES OF FOREIGN-BASED COMPANIES TO THE NATIONAL ECONOMY, 1978–84

1	Foreign capital stock of home-based firms at book value in 1984 as a proportion of:		
	a	GNP at factor cost	1.94
	b	population (in US $ per head)	15.13
2	Investment by affiliates from OECD countries as a percentage of domestic investment, 1978-80.		1.5

Source:
IMF, *Balance of Payments Statistics Yearbook,* various issues; IMF, *International Financial Statistics Yearbook, 1984;* UNCTC, 1983, *op cit.*

Table A11

ROYALTY RECEIPTS AND PAYMENTS, 1975–78 (US $ m)

	Payments			Receipts		
	To Affiliates	*To Non-Affiliates*	*Total*	*From Affiliates*	*From Non-affiliates*	*Total*
1975	*Not Separately Available*		4.9	*Not Separately Available*		2.4
1976			8.1			2.3
1977			7.0			*Not Available*
1978			5.0			
1979			*N.A.*			
1980			10.4			
1981			10.6			
1982			11.0			
1983			11.8			
1984			11.3			32.8

Source:
IMF, *Balance of Payments Statistics Yearbook,* various issues.

Table A12

LEADING FOREIGN MULTINATIONAL COMPANIES, 1982

	Name	*Home Country*	*Sector*	*Turnover (C P m)*
1	General Motors	USA	Motor vehicles	11,931
2	Mobil Oil	USA	Oil	10,678
3	DSM	Netherlands	Chemicals	8,255
4	Colgate Palmolive Inc	USA	Chemicals	7,022
5	International Paper Co	USA	Paper	6,348
6	Nestle	Switzerland	Food	5,601
7	Goodyear	USA	Rubber	5,388
8	Akzo	Netherlands	Chemicals	5,256
9	Owens Illinois Inc	USA	Miscellaneous	5,089
10	B F Goodrich Co	USA	Rubber	4,940
11	Fiat	Italy	Motor vehicles	3,830
12	Dow Chemical Co	USA	Chemicals	3,160
13	N V Philips	Netherlands	Electrical	2,967
14	Union Carbide Corp	USA	Chemicals	2,771
15	Siemens	W. Germany	Electrical	2,665
16	Uniroyal	USA	Rubber	2,604
17	Boise Cascade Inc.	USA	Paper	2,594
18	Ceat International General Cable Corp	USA	Electrical	*N.A.*
19	Celanese Corp	USA	Chemicals	2,489
20	Eternit Co		Non-metallic products	2,268
21	Crillette	USA	Metals	2,000
22	J & P Coats Ltd	UK	Textiles	1,940
23	Holderbank Financiere Glaris	Switzerland	Building materials	1,479
24	El Dupont de Nemours & Co	USA	Chemicals	*N.A.*
25	Millmaster Onix (Gulf Oil)	USA	Oil	931

Source:
CEPAL/CET, 'Informa Sobre la Encuesta de las Principales Empresas con Participation Extranjera del Sector Manufacturero Colombiano', UNCES, LC/L.323, December 1984.

DOMINICAN REPUBLIC

The inflows of direct foreign investment have fluctuated annually since the early 1970s, while the level of reinvested profits steadily increased during the period 1972-76.

Foreign direct investment has been mainly concentrated on the manufacturing sector, particularly food and drink and in the tertiary sector, largely in distributive trade.

The USA has been the main source of investment, accounting for 53% of total foreign direct capital stock in 1982.

The Government supports and encourages inward investment. A Commission has been set up to promote foreign investment in four targeted areas, namely: agro-industry, mining, tourism and free zone operations. Applications for investment incentives are considered on an individual basis. Foreign firms are not usually allowed to acquire Dominican companies.

MAIN SOURCES OF DATA:

A Official

1. Central Bank of the Dominican Republic: issues monthly statistical bulletins providing data on foreign direct investment by sectoral distribution.
2. UNCTC, *Transnational Corporations in World Development: Third Survey,* New York: UN, 1983.
3. US Department of Commerce International Trade Administration, *Investment Climate in Foreign Countries,* Washington, 1985, Vol IV.

Note:
Data do not allow us to complete Tables A7, A9, A10 or A11 for the Dominican Republic.

Table A1

SUMMARY OF THE COUNTRY'S INTERNATIONAL INVESTMENT POSITION

		Inward Investment	Outward Investment
1	Number of foreign affiliates in host country, and of foreign affiliates of home country firms at the end of 1980	104[1]	*N.A.*
2	Number of foreign firms with direct investments in host country, and home country firms with direct foreign affiliates	*N.A.*	*N.A.*
3	Total foreign direct capital stock at book value as a percentage of GNP at factor cost in 1981	11.20	*N.A.*
4	Flow of foreign direct investment in the five year period, 1979-83 (US $ m)	236.2	*N.A.*
5	Employment in foreign affiliates or abroad	*N.A.*	*N.A.*
6	Output of foreign affiliates or abroad	*N.A.*	*N.A.*

Source:

IMF, *Balance of Payments Statistics Yearbook,* various issues; IMF, *International Financial Statistics Yearbook, 1984.*

NOTES TO TABLE A1

1 Representing number of affiliates of foreign MNEs from selection home countries, as identified by UNCTC, 1983.

Table A2

PRIVATE FOREIGN CAPITAL STOCK, 1975 - 83 (US $ m)

	Inward Investment			Outward Investment		
	Portfolio	*Direct*[1]	*Total*	*Portfolio*	*Direct*	*Total*
Book value of capital stock						
1975	*Not Available*	391.3	*Not Available*	*Not Available*		
1978		586.3				
1982		775.7				

Source:
IMF, *Balance of Payments Statistics Yearbook,* various issues.

NOTES TO TABLE A2

1 Represents cumulative investment flows as from 1968.

Table A3

FLOW OF FOREIGN DIRECT INVESTMENT, 1970 - 83 (US $ m)

	Inward Investment			Outward Investment		
	Reinvested Profits	*Other*	*Total*	*Reinvested Profits*	*Other*	*Total*
1970	*Not Separately Available*		72.0	*Not Available*		
1971			65.2			
1972	16.3	52.1	68.4			
1973	27.4	7.2	34.6			
1974	32.5	21.6	54.1			
1975	51.0	0.0	51.0			
1976	53.1	6.9	60.0			
1977	*Not Separately Available*		71.4			
1978			63.6			
1979			17.1			
1980			92.6			
1981			79.7			
1982			*N.A.*			
1983			48.2			

Source:
IMF, *Balance of Payments Statistics Yearbook,* various issues.

Table A4

SECTORAL DISTRIBUTION OF FOREIGN DIRECT CAPITAL STOCK, 1984 (US $ m)[1]

	Inward Investment				Outward Investment		
	Primary	*Secondary*	*Tertiary*		*Primary*	*Secondary*	*Tertiary*
1984[1]	20.1	115.8	116.5		*Not Available*		

Source:
Central Bank of the Dominican Republic, *Monthly Statistical Bulletin,* February 1984.

NOTES TO TABLE A5

1 Registered foreign investment, February 1984. Total does not match Table A2 due to an unallocated component.

Table A5

GEOGRAPHICAL DISTRIBUTION OF FOREIGN DIRECT CAPITAL STOCK, 1982 (US $ m)

	Inward Investment				Outward Investment		
	Developed Countries	*Other Countries*	*Total*		*Developed Countries*	*Developing Countries*	*Total*
1982	408.0[1]	367.7	775.7[2]		*Not Available*		

Source:
US Department of Commerce, *Survey of Current Business,* November 1984.

NOTES TO TABLE A5

1 US investment only.

2 Cumulative investment flow, 1968-82.

Table A6

INDUSTRIAL DISTRIBUTION OF FOREIGN DIRECT CAPITAL STOCK, 1984 (US $ m)[1]

	Inward Investment	Outward Investment
	1984[1]	
Primary	20.1	Not Available
Agriculture	0.3	
Mining & quarrying	19,8	
Secondary	115.8	
Food & drink	83.0	
Chemicals & allied	22.2	
Metals Mechanical engineering	6.0	
Textiles & clothing	4.0	
Other manufacturing[2]	0.6	
Tertiary	116.5	
Transport & communications[3]	16.5	
Distributive trade	40.2	
Property[4] Banking & finance	59.8	
TOTAL	252.4[5]	

Source:
Central Bank of the Dominican Republic, *Monthly Statistical Bulletin,* February 1984.

NOTES TO TABLE A6

1 Registered foreign investment, February 1984.
2 Represents wood and wood products.
3 Including storage.
4 Including tourism.
5 Total does not match Table A2 due to an unallocated component.

Table A8

INDICATORS OF THE SIGNIFICANCE OF INWARD FOREIGN DIRECT INVESTMENT OR THE ACTIVITIES OF FOREIGN-BASED COMPANIES TO THE NATIONAL ECONOMY, 1981

1	Direct capital stock of foreign affiliates at book value in 1981 as a proportion of		
	a	GNP at factor cost	11.20
	b	population (in US $ per head)	135.14[1]

Source:
IMF, *Balance of Payments Statistics Yearbook,* various issues; IMF, *International Financial Statistics Yearbook, 1984.*

NOTES TO TABLE A8

[1] 1982.

Table A12

LEADING FOREIGN MULTINATIONAL COMPANIES, 1985

Name	*Home Country*	*Sector*
Abbott Laboratories Incorporated	USA	Pharmaceuticals
American Can Company	USA	Packaging products
Johnson & Johnson	USA	Health care products
Nabisco Brands Incorporated	USA	Food products
Nestle SA	Switzerland	Food products
Noranda Mines Ltd	Canada	Non-ferrous metals
Philip Morris Incorporated	USA	Cigarettes
Squibb Corporation	USA	Pharmaceuticals
Warner-Lambert Company	USA	Pharmaceuticals
Xerox Corporation	USA	Copiers

Source:
Dun & Bradstreet, *Who Owns Whom 1985,* London: Business Marketing Division (Publications), 1985.

ECUADOR

The inflow of foreign direct investment in Ecuador has fluctuated widely since the mid-1960s, reaching a peak in the early 1970s. There is no available data on outward investments by Ecuador.

The main source of foreign direct investment in Ecuador is the USA, followed by Western European countries and other Latin American countries.

Foreign investment is largely concentrated in the manufacturing sector, particularly food and drink, chemicals and metals. Investment in the services sector is also significant.

The Government of Ecuador welcomes foreign investment, especially in the industrial and export-orientated sectors. There are numerous tax incentives to foreign investors; investment terms and benefits are negotiated on a case by case basis. All investments have to be registered with the Central Bank of Ecuador's Foreign Exchange Department.

Ecuador maintains no exchange controls on outward investment. In the mid-1970s Ecuador had US S 18.7 million invested in other Latin American countries, of which US S 17.6 million was in Brazil.

MAIN SOURCES OF DATA:

A **Official**

1 Superintendent for Companies: gives information on FDI by sectoral distribution.

2 Ministry of Industry, Commerce & Integration (MICE): provides data on FDI by sectoral & geographical distribution.

3 US Department of Commerce International Trade Administration, *Investment Climate in Foreign Countries,* Washington, 1975, vol IV and 1983.

4 UNCTC, *Transnational Corporations in World Development, Third Survey,* New York: UN, 1983.

B **Private**

1 F Albavera, *La Presencia de las Empresas Transnactionales en la Economia Ecuatoriana,* prepared for CEPAL, Santiago, Chile: UN, 1984.

Note:

Data do not allow us to complete Tables A9 or A10 for Ecuador.

Table A1

SUMMARY OF THE COUNTRY'S INTERNATIONAL INVESTMENT POSITION

		Inward Investment	Outward Investment
1	Number of foreign affiliates in host country, and of foreign affiliates of home country firms at the end of 1982	223[1]	*N.A.*
2	Number of foreign firms with direct investments in host country, and home country firms with direct foreign affiliates	*N.A.*	*N.A.*
3	Total foreign direct capital stock at book value as a percentage of GNP at factor cost in 1983.	10.33	*N.A.*
4	Flow of foreign direct investment in the five year period 1980-84 (Sucre bn)	9.79	*N.A.*
5	Employment in foreign affiliates or abroad	*N.A.*	*N.A.*
6	Output of foreign affiliates or abroad	*N.A.*	*N.A.*

Source:

US Department of Commerce, *Investment Climate in Foreign Countries,* Washington, 1983; IMF, *Balance of Payments Payments Statistics Yearbook,* various issues; IMF, *International Financial Statistics Yearbook, 1984*; Superintendent of Companies, data as cited in Albavera, *op cit.*

NOTES TO TABLE A1

1 Represents only those new firms established in 1982, which accounted for 1.1% of the foreign direct capital stock in the country at the end of that year.

Table A2

PRIVATE FOREIGN CAPITAL STOCK, 1975 - 84 (Sucre bn)

	Inward Investment			Outward Investment		
	Portfolio	*Direct*	*Total*	*Portfolio*	*Direct*	*Total*
Book value of capital stock						
1975	*Not Available*	12.50	*Not Available*	*Not Available*		
1978		16.50				
1981		21.34				
1984		27.87				

Source:
UNCTC, 1983, *op cit.*

Table A3

FLOW OF FOREIGN DIRECT INVESTMENT, 1970 - 84 (Sucre bn)

	Inward Investment			Outward Investment		
	Reinvested Profits	*Other*	*Total*	*Reinvested Profits*	*Other*	*Total*
1970	0.17	1.69	1.86	*Not Available*		
1971	0.28	3.78	4.06			
1972	0.92	1.09	2.01			
1973	0.45	0.86	1.31			
1974	0.63	1.29	1.92			
1975	1.06	1.34	2.40			
1976	1.36	-1.85	-0.49			
1977	2.16	-1.30	0.86			
1978	1.78	-0.56	1.22			
1979	*Not Separately Available*		1.58			
1980			1.76			
1981			1.50			
1982			1.19			
1983			2.21			
1984			3.13			

Source:
IMF, *Balance of Payments Statistics Yearbook,* various issues; US Department of Commerce, *Investment Climate in Foreign Countries,* Washington, 1983.

Table A4

SECTORAL DISTRIBUTION OF FOREIGN DIRECT CAPITAL STOCK, 1980 (Sucre m)[1]

	Inward Investment				Outward Investment		
	Primary	*Secondary*	*Tertiary*		*Primary*	*Secondary*	*Tertiary*
1972-80[1]	859	7,161	3,843		*Not Available*		

Source:

MICEI, Direccion de Inversiones Extranjeras, data as cited in Albavera, *op cit.*

NOTES TO TABLE A4

1 Cumulative authorised investment flows, 1972-80, excluding an unallocated component of 786 million sucres.

Table A5

GEOGRAPHICAL DISTRIBUTION OF FOREIGN DIRECT CAPITAL STOCK, 1980 (Sucre m)

	Inward Investment				Outward Investment		
	Developed Countries	*Developing Countries*	*Total*		*Developed Countries*	*Developing Countries*	*Total*
1972-80[1]	9,883	1,979	12,649[2]		*Not Available*		

Source:

MICEI, Direccion de Inversiones Extranjeras, data as cited in F. Albavera, *Las Presencia de las Empresas Transnacionales en la Economia Ecuatoriana,* prepared for CEPAL, Santiago, Chile: UN, 1984.

NOTES TO TABLE A5

1 Cumulative authorised investment flows, 1972-80.

2 Total includes unspecified figure.

Table A6

INDUSTRIAL DISTRIBUTION OF FOREIGN DIRECT CAPITAL STOCK, 1980 (Sucre m)[1]

	Inward Investment		Outward Investment
	1972-80[1]		
Primary	858.8		Not Available
Agriculture	658.6		
Mining & quarrying	200.2		
Oil			
Secondary	7,161.4		
Food & drink	2,203.6		
Chemicals & allied	1,254.0		
Metals	877.6		
Mechanical engineering	51.9		
Electrical equipment	468.0		
Motor vehicles / Other transportation equipment	348.9		
Paper & allied	248.6		
Rubber	39.7		
Stone, clay & glass	688.2		
Coal & petroleum products	219.8		
Other manufacturing	661.6		
Tertiary	3,843.0		
Construction	198.8		
Transportation & communications	61.7		
Distributive trade	1,241.4		
Property	*N.A.*		
Banking & finance	2,050.1		
Other services	291.0		
TOTAL	12,648.6[2]		

Source:

Superintendent of Companies & MICEI, Direccion de Inversiones Extranjeras, data as cited in F. Albavera, *Las Presencia de las Empresas Transnacionales en la Economia Ecuatoriana,* prepared for CEPAL, Santiago, Chile: UN, 1984.

NOTES TO TABLE A6

1 Cumulative authorised investment flows, 1972-80.

2 Total includes 'unspecified' figure.

Table A7

LEADING SOURCE AND RECIPIENT COUNTRIES, 1980 (Sucre m)[1]

	Inward Investment	Outward Investment
	1972-80[1]	
DEVELOPED AREAS	9,882.8	Not Available
Europe	3,811.7	
EEC	1,876.1	
Other Europe of which	1,935.6	
North America	6,061.5	
Other developed countries of which	9.6	
Australia / New Zealand	9.6	
DEVELOPING AREAS	1,979.3	
Africa	0.3	
Asia & Pacific	105.1	
Latin America	1,755.3	
Middle East	118.6	
UNSPECIFIED	786.5	
TOTAL	12,648.6	

Source:

MICEI, Direccion de Inversiones Extranjeras, data as cited in Albavera, *La Presencia de las Empresas Transnacionales en la Economia Ecuatoriana,* prepared for CEPAL, Santiago, Chile: UN, 1984.

NOTES TO TABLE A7

1 Cumulative authorised investment flows, 1972-80.

Table A8

INDICATORS OF THE SIGNIFICANCE OF INWARD FOREIGN DIRECT INVESTMENT OR THE ACTIVITIES OF FOREIGN-BASED COMPANIES TO THE NATIONAL ECONOMY, 1978 - 84

1	Direct capital stock of foreign affiliates at book value in 1984 as a proportion of	
	a GNP at factor cost	3.92
	b population (in Sucre per head)	3,070.25
2	Foreign investment as a percentage of domestic investment, 1978-80	0.40

Source:
US Department of Commerce, *Investment Climate in Foreign Countries,* Washington, 1983; IMF, *International Financial Statistics Yearbook, 1984.*

Table A11

ROYALTY RECEIPTS AND PAYMENTS, 1976 - 84 (Sucre m)

	Payments			Receipts		
	To Affiliates	*To Non-affiliates*	*Total*	*From Affiliates*	*From Non-affiliates*	*Total*
1976	*Not Separately Available*		106.8	*Not Available*		
1977			294.8			
1978			303.6			
1979			326.2			
1980			549.9			
1981			698.7			
1982			1,200.0			
1983			1,721.3			
1984			1,878.1			

Source:
IMF, *Balance of Payments Statistics Yearbook,* various issues.

Table A12

LEADING FOREIGN MULTINATIONAL COMPANIES, 1980

	Name	*Home Country*	*Sector*	*Turnover (Sucre m)*
1	Latin American Corp	USA	Beverages	1,766.8
2	Core Investment	USA	Distributive trade	1,735.7
3	Philips Morris Inc	USA	Tobacco	1,379.3
4	Scopar International	USA	Electrical	1,224.6
5	Nestle	Switzerland	Food	1,108.1
6	Impregilo SpA	Italy	Services	1,706.4
7	Standard Fruit Company	USA	Distributive trade	1,025.6
8	General Tire International	USA	Rubber	1,001.0
9	Core Investments	UK	Food	991.9
10	Rodora Holding	USA	Miscellaneous services	899.4
11	Philips	Netherlands	Electrical	898.7
12	Pacific Fruits	USA	Paper	873.4
13	Dublin Trade Co	USA	Steel	870.0
14	Entrecanales y Tabara	Spain	Services	738.6
15	Heartland Investments CA	Panama	Finance	705.5
16	Noblefort Trading	Netherlands Antilles	Food	702.8

Source:

Various publications: Memorias de las Empresas; Superintendencia de Bancos; Superintendencia de Companias; Moody's Industrial Manual; Japan Company Handbook; US Securities & Exchange Commission: data as cited in Albavera, *op cit.*

GUYANA

There is little statistical information available on the investment position of Guyana, although the decline of foreign direct investment in the country since 1971 is apparent from Table A3.

Until 1970, the government pursued a favourable policy towards foreign direct investment. However, during the early 1970s, extensive nationalisation of foreign affiliates occurred (including those of Alcan, Reynolds and Booker McConnells). Not surprisingly in the following years, direct investment inflows have been reduced substantially. In consequence, the "Guyana Investment Code" was produced in 1979 in which it was stated that the government recognises and encourages both local private investment and foreign private investment in certain areas. Nevertheless, despite this code, there does not appear to have been much noticeable effect on the investment climate of Guyana.

All outflows of capital are strictly controlled by the Guyanese Government.

MAIN SOURCES OF DATA:

A Official

1 Bank of Guyana: publishes *Annual Reports* indicating the investment position of Guyana.

2 US Department of Commerce International Trade Administration, *Investment Climate in Foreign Countries,* Washington, 1985, vol IV.

B Private

1 Ramesh F Ramsaran, *US Investment in Latin America and the Caribbean,* London: Hodder & Stoughton, 1985.

Note:
Data do not allow us to complete Tables A4, A5, A6, A7, A9, A10 or A11 for Guyana.

Table A1

SUMMARY OF THE COUNTRY'S INTERNATIONAL INVESTMENT POSITION

		Inward Investment	Outward Investment
1	Number of foreign affiliates in host country, and of foreign affiliates of home country firms at the end of 1980	23[1]	*N.A.*
2	Number of foreign firms with direct investment in host country, and home country firms with direct foreign affiliates	*N.A.*	*N.A.*
3	Total foreign direct capital stock at book value as a percentage of GNP at factor cost in 1983	47.31	*N.A.*
4	Flow of foreign direct investment in the five year period 1979-83 (G $ m)	25.6	*N.A.*
5	Employment in foreign affiliates or abroad	*N.A.*	*N.A.*
6	Output of foreign affiliates or abroad	*N.A.*	*N.A.*

Source:

UNCTC, *Transnational Corporations in World Development: Third Survey,* New York: UN, 1983; IMF, *Balance of Payments Statistics Yearbook, 1984;* IMF, *International Financial Statistics Yearbook, 1984.*

NOTES TO TABLE A1

1 Represents number of affiliates of foreign MNEs from selected home countries, as identified by UNCTC, 1983.

Table A2

PRIVATE FOREIGN CAPITAL STOCK, 1975 - 83 (G $ m)

	Inward Investment			Outward Investment		
	Portfolio	*Direct*[1]	*Total*	*Portfolio*	*Direct*	*Total*
Book value of capital stock						
1975		459.0				
1978	*Not Available*	586.5	*Not Available*	*Not Available*		
1981		584.8				
1983		612.1				

Source:

UNCTC, *Transnational Corporations in World Development: Third Survey,* New York: UN, 1983;
IMF, *Balance of Payments Statistics Yearbook, 1984.*

NOTES TO TABLE A2

1 Foreign direct capital stock for 1981 and 1983 have been estimated by adding cumulative investment flows to the UNCTC stock figure of 1978.

Table A3

FLOW OF FOREIGN DIRECT INVESTMENT, 1970 - 83 (G $ m)

	Inward Investment			Outward Investment		
	Reinvested Profits	*Other*	*Total*	*Reinvested Profits*	*Other*	*Total*
1970	26.0	−8.0	18.0	*Not Available*		
1971	31.8	−143.0	111.2			
1972	27.2	−22.7	4.5			
1973	32.6	−15.0	17.6			
1974	34.8	−32.1	2.7			
1975	48.6	−45.7	2.9			
1976	5.9	−73.6	67.7			
1977	*Not Separately Available*		−4.5			
1978			*N.A.*			
1979			1.6			
1980			1.7			
1981			−5.0			
1982			13.2			
1983			14.1			

Source:
IMF, *Balance of Payments Statistics Yearbook,* various issues.

Table A8

INDICATORS OF THE SIGNIFICANCE OF INWARD FOREIGN DIRECT INVESTMENT OR THE ACTIVITIES OF FOREIGN-BASED COMPANIES TO THE NATIONAL ECONOMY, 1978 - 83

1	Direct capital stock of foreign affiliates at book value in 1983 as a proportion of		
	a	GNP at factor cost	47.31
	b	population (in G$ per head)	637.85
2	Foreign investment as a percentage of domestic investment 1978-80		0.4

Source:
UNCTC, *Transnational Corporations in World Development: Third Survey,* New York: UN, 1983;
IMF, *Balance of Payments Statistics Yearbook, 1984;* IMF, *International Financial Statistics Yearbook, 1984.*

Table A12

LEADING FOREIGN MULTINATIONAL COMPANIES, 1985

Name	*Home Country*	*Sector*
1 L'Air Liquide SA	France	Industrial gases
2 B A T Industries PLC	UK	Tobacco
3 Tate & Lyle PLC	UK	Sugar refining

Source:
Dun and Bradstreet, *Who Owns Whom 1985,* London: Business Marketing Division (Publications), 1985.

JAMAICA

The inflow of foreign direct investment to Jamaica fell steadily in 1979, although since then, has made some recovery. The importance of reinvested earnings, especially in recent years, is indicated by Table A3. The Government's action in liberalizing the economy and creating an attractive package of incentives brought in J $ 454.8 million in new investment between 1981 and 1984.

While in 1960s and 70s there was a good deal of foreign investment in the mining (mainly bauxite) sector, since 1981, new investment has been largely concentrated in the tertiary sector, particularly in construction and tourism. The main source of such investment is the USA. Other investor countries include Canada, Hong Kong and Latin American countries, notably Venezuela.

MAIN SOURCE OF DATA:

A Official

1 UNCTC, *Transnational Corporations in World Development: Third Survey,* New York: UN, 1983.

B Private

1 US Department of Commerce International Trade Administration, *Investment Climate in Foreign Countries,* Washington, August 1985, PB86-100104.

Note:
Data do not allow us to complete Tables A9 or A10 for Jamaica.

Table A1

SUMMARY OF THE COUNTRY'S INTERNATIONAL INVESTMENT POSITION

		Inward Investment	Outward Investment
1	Number of foreign affiliates in host country, and of foreign affiliates of home country firms at the end of 1980[1]	278	*N.A.*
2	Number of foreign firms with direct investments in host country, and home country firms with direct foreign affiliates	*N.A.*	*N.A.*
3	Total foreign direct capital stock at book value as a percentage of GNP at factor cost in 1984	26.32	*N.A.*
4	Flow of foreign direct investment in the five year period, 1980-84 (J $m)	211.9	*N.A.*
5	Employment in foreign affiliates or abroad	*N.A.*	*N.A.*
6	Output of foreign affiliates or abroad	*N.A.*	*N.A.*

Source:

IMF, *Balance of Payments Statistics Yearbook,* various issues; IMF, *International Financial Statistics Yearbook, 1984;* US Department of Commerce, *Investment Climate in Foreign Countries,* Washington, 1985.

NOTES TO TABLE A1

1 From selected home countries as identified by UNCTC, 1983.

Table A2

PRIVATE FOREIGN CAPITAL STOCK, 1974 - 84 (J $m)[1]

	Inward Investment			Outward Investment		
	Portfolio	*Direct*	*Total*	*Portfolio*	*Direct*	*Total*
Book value of capital stock						
1974	*Not Available*	1,200.0	*Not Available*	*Not Available*		
1975		881.8				
1978		1,525.5				
1981		1,549.6				
1984		1,691.8				

Source:

UNCTC, 1983, *op cit.*

NOTES TO TABLE A2

1 The stock figures for 1981 and 1984 have been calculated on the basis of 1978 stock figures plus cumulative flows for the relevant years.

Table A3

FLOW OF FOREIGN DIRECT INVESTMENT, 1970 - 84 (J $m)

	Inward Investment			Outward Investment		
	Reinvested Profits	*Other*	*Total*	*Reinvested Profits*	*Other*	*Total*
1970	6.7	128.3	135.0	*Not Separately Available*		0.8
1971	5.8	138.5	144.3			- 0.8
1972	0.9	77.5	78.4			*N.A.*
1973	6.5	60.7	67.2			-2.2
1974	4.4	22.9	27.3			6.6
1975	3.3	- 5.5	- 2.2	*Not Available*		
1976	7.3	- 8.3	- 1.0			
1977	7.4	-15.9	- 8.5			
1978	16.3	-54.4	-38.1			
1979	22.8	-68.4	-45.6			
1980	115.9	-67.2	48.7			
1981	48.3	-27.3	21.0			
1982	43.3	-15.8	27.5			
1983	*Not Separately Available*		21.0			
1984			93.7			

Source:

IMF, *Balance of Payments Statistics Yearbook,* various issues; US Department of Commerce, *Investment Climate in Foreign Countries,* Washington, 1983.

Table A4

SECTORAL DISTRIBUTION OF FOREIGN DIRECT CAPITAL STOCK, 1984 (J $m)[1]

	Inward Investment			Outward Investment		
	Primary	*Secondary*	*Tertiary*	*Primary*	*Secondary*	*Tertiary*
1981-84[1]	32.52	43.47	87.00	*Not Available*		

Source:
US Department of Commerce, *Investment Climate in Foreign Countries,* Washington, 1983.

NOTES TO TABLE A4

1 Refers to foreign investment projects implemented from July 1981 to September 1984, including joint ventures.

Table A5

GEOGRAPHICAL DISTRIBUTION OF FOREIGN DIRECT CAPITAL STOCK, 1984 (J $m)[1]

	Inward Investment			Outward Investment		
	Developed Countries	*Developing Countries*	*Total*	*Developed Countries*	*Developing Countries*	*Total*
1981-84[1]	86.62	76.37	162.99	*Not Available*		

Source:
US Department of Commerce, *Investment Climate in Foreign Countries,* Washington, 1983.

NOTES TO TABLE A5

1 Refers to foreign investment projects implemented from July 1981 to September 1984, including joint ventures.

Table A6

INDUSTRIAL DISTRIBUTION OF FOREIGN DIRECT CAPITAL STOCK, 1984 (J $ m)[1]

	Inward Investment	Outward Investment
	1981-84[1]	
Primary	32.52	Not Available
Agriculture	32.52	
Secondary	43.47	
Stone, clay & glass	0.06	
Other manufacturing	43.41	
Tertiary	87.00	
Construction	50.77	
Banking & finance	5.30	
Other services	30.93[2]	
TOTAL	162.99	

Source:
US Department of Commerce, *Investment Climate in Foreign Countries,* Washington, 1983.

NOTES TO TABLE A6

1 Refers to Foreign Investment Projects implemented from July 1981 to September 1984, including joint ventures.

2 Including tourism (J $ 28.53 million).

Table A7

LEADING SOURCE AND RECIPIENT COUNTRIES
1984 (J $ m)[1]

	Inward Investment	Outward Investment
	1981-84[1]	
DEVELOPED AREAS	86.62	
Europe	11.93	
EEC of which:	3.80	
Greece	0.16	
UK	3.64	
Other Europe of which:	8.13	
Norway	8.13	
North America of which:	73.10	
Canada	10.72	
USA	62.38	
Other developed countries of which:	1.59	
Japan	1.59	*Not Available*
DEVELOPING AREAS	76.37	
Asia & other Pacific of which:	22.38	
Hong Kong	22.38	
Latin America of which:	49.19	
Barbados	0.04	
Colombia	0.85	
Puerto Rico	5.30	
Suriname	3.00	
Venezuela	40.00	
Middle East of which:	4.80	
Israel	4.80	
TOTAL	162.99	

Source:
US Department of Commerce, *Investment Climate in Foreign Countries,* Washington, 1983.

NOTES TO TABLE A7

1 Refers to foreign investment projects implemented from July 1981 to September 1984, including joint ventures.

Table A8

INDICATORS OF THE SIGNIFICANCE OF INWARD FOREIGN DIRECT INVESTMENT OR THE ACTIVITIES OF FOREIGN-BASED COMPANIES TO THE NATIONAL ECONOMY, 1982

1	Direct capital stock of foreign affiliates at book value in 1984 as a proportion of:	
	a GNP at factor cost	26.32
	b population (in J $ per head)	748.58
2	Inward investment as a percentage of domestic investment in 1978-80[1]	–5.0

Source:
IMF, *Balance of Payments Statistics Yearbook,* various issues; IMF, *International Financial Statistics Yearbook, 1984;* UNCTC, 1983, *op cit.*

NOTES TO TABLE A8
[1] From OECD countries.

Table A11

ROYALTY RECEIPTS AND PAYMENTS, 1975 - 82 (J$ m)

	Payments			Receipts		
	To Affiliates	*To Non-affiliates*	*Total*	*From Affiliates*	*From Non-affiliates*	*Total*
1975	*Not Separately Available*		4.4	*Not Available*		
1976			4.1			
1977			1.3			
1978			4.4			
1979			8.7			
1980			1.6			
1981			1.7			
1982			13.4			

Source:
IMF, *Balance of Payments Statistics Yearbook, 1983.*

Table A12

LEADING FOREIGN MULTINATIONAL COMPANIES, 1984

	Name	*Home Country*	*Sector*
1	Alcan	Canada	Metals
2	Henkel	W. Germany	Pharmaceuticals
3	Mitsubishi Heavy Ind	Japan	Motor vehicles
4	Beecham	UK	Pharmaceuticals
5	BICC	UK	Electrical
6	ICL	UK	Office equipment
7	Metal Box	UK	Metal
8	Reckitt & Colman	UK	Pharmaceuticals
9	Rothmans	UK	Tobacco
10	Royal Dutch/Shell	UK	Oil
11	Beatrice	USA	Food
12	Bristol Myers	USA	Pharmaceuticals
13	Colgate-Palmolive	USA	Pharmaceuticals
14	Control Data	USA	Office equipment
15	Exxon	USA	Oil
16	Goodyear	USA	Rubber
17	Grace, W R	USA	Chemicals
18	IBM	USA	Office equipment
19	ITT	USA	Electrical
20	Johnson & Johnson	USA	Pharmaceuticals
21	Nabisco Brands	USA	Food
22	Pillsbury	USA	Food
23	Reynolds Metals	USA	Metals
24	Sherwin-Williams	USA	Chemicals
25	Singer	USA	Electrical

Source:
Paul Chen-Young & Associates, Economic & Financial Consultants.

MEXICO

In the late 1970s there was a considerable increase of foreign direct investment in Mexico. Such investment has been largely concentrated in the manufacturing sector, particularly in chemicals and transportation equipment. FDI in the services sector is also gaining in significance. By far the most important investing country is the USA. Other sources of investment include West Germany, the UK, Japan and Switzerland.

According to source country data, Mexico has some outward direct investment estimated at between US $ 350 and US $ 400 million in 1982. The USA is the leading recipient country.

Since the beginning of 1983 the Mexican authorities have professed an open attitude towards inward investment; and in October 1983 created the Undersecretariat for Regulation of Foreign Investment and Transfer of Technology to strengthen the work of the National Commission on Foreign Investment. In 1984 the Government identified six sectors in which inward investment would be especially welcomed; there are also priority development zones. Fiscal incentives are complex; normally companies with a minority of foreign ownership are the main beneficiaries. Industrial and foreign investment policies are closely interlinked. Though there are no legal restrictions to outward investment, Mexican banks limit the amount of foreign exchange which can be purchased at favourable rates.

MAIN SOURCES OF DATA:

A Official

1 National Commission of Foreign Investment: provides data on foreign investment in Mexico.

2 Banco Nacional de Comercio Exterior: published an article by Miguel Wionezek in the May 1968 issue showing the stock of FDI in Mexico in the early 1960s.

3 US Department of Commerce International Trade Administration, *Investment Climate in Foreign Countries,* Washington, 1985.

4 UNCTC, *Transnational Corporations in World Development: A Reexamination,* New York, UN: 1978.

B Private

1 Council of the Americas, Inc., *Impact of Foreign Investment in Mexico*, New York, 1970.

2 Fajnzylber, F and Martinez Tarrago, T, *Las Empresas Transnacionales Expansíon a Nive Mundial y Proyeccion en la Industria Mexicana,* Mexico City: CIDE/CONACYC.

Note:

Data do not allow us to complete Table A9 or A10 for Mexico.

Table A1

SUMMARY OF THE COUNTRY'S INTERNATIONAL INVESTMENT POSITION

		Inward Investment	Outward Investment
1	Number of foreign affiliates in host country, and of foreign affiliates of home country firms at the end of 1983	6,390	*N.A.*
2	Number of foreign firms with direct investments in host country, and home country firms with direct foreign affiliates	*N.A.*	*N.A.*
3	Total foreign direct capital stock at book value as a percentage of GNP at factor cost in 1982	6.97	2.20
4	Flow of foreign direct investment in the five year period, 1979-83 (US $ m)	7,912.2	*N.A.*
5	Employment in foreign affiliates or abroad	*N.A.*	*N.A.*
6	Output of foreign affiliates or abroad	*N.A.*	*N.A.*

Source:

US Department of Commerce, *Investment Climate in Foreign Countries,* Washington, 1983; IMF, *International Financial Statistics Yearbook, 1984;* IMF, *Balance of Payments Statistics Yearbook,* various issues. The estimate of the stock of outward direct investment per capita is by the authors, based on source country data.

Table A2

PRIVATE FOREIGN CAPITAL STOCK, 1971 - 84 (US $m)

	Inward Investment			Outward Investment		
	Portfolio	*Direct*	*Total*	*Portfolio*	*Direct*	*Total*
Book value of capital stock						
1971	*Not Available*	2.5	*Not Available*	*Not Available*		
1975		4.8				
1978[1]		6.8				
1981		12.8				
1984		15.3			0.38[2]	

Source:

US Department of Commerce, *Investment Climate in Foreign Countries,* Washington, 1983; UNCTC, *Transnational Corporations in World Development, Third Survey,* New York: UN, 1983.

NOTES TO TABLE A2

1 Based on OECD data plus an allowance for intra Latin American capital investment from UNCTC, 1983.

2 Estimate by authors.

Table A3

FLOW OF FOREIGN DIRECT INVESTMENT, 1970 - 84 (US $m)

	Inward Investment			Outward Investment		
	Reinvested Profits	*Other*	*Total*	*Reinvested Profits*	*Other*	*Total*
1970	122.0	201.0	323.0	*Not Available*		
1971	110.3	196.6	306.9			
1972	120.5	180.2	300.7			
1973	191.9	268.7	460.6			
1974	317.5	360.8	678.3			
1975	348.5	261.0	609.5			
1976	339.4	233.2	572.6			
1977	230.0	325.7	555.7			
1978	465.7	363.1	828.8			
1979	590.4	744.2	1,334.6			
1980	939.7	1,244.3	2,184.0			
1981	1,345.4	1,168.7	2,514.1			
1982	761.8	882.1	1,643.9			
1983	195.6	258.7	454.3			
1984	214.2	177.3	391.5			

Source:

IMF, *Balance of Payments Statistics Yearbook,* various issues.

Table A4

SECTORAL DISTRIBUTION OF FOREIGN DIRECT CAPITAL STOCK, 1957 - 83 (US $m)

	Inward Investment				Outward Investment		
	Primary	*Secondary*	*Tertiary*		*Primary*	*Secondary*	*Tertiary*
1957	250	413	537				
1975	194	3,670	867			*Not Available*	
1981	269[1]	5,812[2]	1,112[3]				
1983	253	9,004	2,243				

Source:

Banco de Mexico, *Informes Anuales,* 1958; Deutschen Bundesbank, *Monthly Report,* Supplement, June 1983; US Department of Commerce, *Survey of Current Business,* August 1983; UK Department of Trade & Industry, *Business Monitor,* Supplement, 1981; US Department of Commerce, *Investment Climate in Foreign Countries,* Washington, 1983.

NOTES TO TABLE A4

1 US and West German investment only.

2 US, UK and West German investment only.

3 US, UK & West German investment only.

Table A5

GEOGRAPHICAL DISTRIBUTION OF FOREIGN DIRECT CAPITAL STOCK, 1962 - 83 (US $m)

	Inward Investment				Outward Investment		
	Developed Countries	*Other Countries*	*Total*		*Developed Countries*	*Developing Countries*	*Total*
1962	1,176[1]	110	1,286[4]				
1975	4,177	559	4,739			*Not Available*	
1981	9,117[2]	503	9,620[4]				
1983	9,936[3]	1,564	11,500[4]				

Source:

Deutschen Bundesbank, *Monthly Report,* Supplement, June 1983; US Department of Commerce, *Survey of Current Business,* August, 1983; UK Department of Trade & Industry, *Business Monitor,* Supplement, 1981; F Marsh, *Japanese Overseas Investment,* EIU, 1983; US Department of Commerce, *Investment Climate in Foreign Countries,* Washington, 1983.

NOTES TO TABLE A5

1 USA, Canada, Sweden and UK only.

2 Includes US, UK, West German and Japanese investment only.

3 Includes US, West German, Swiss and Japanese investment only.

4 Total includes 'unspecified' figure.

Table A6

INDUSTRIAL DISTRIBUTION OF FOREIGN DIRECT CAPITAL STOCK, 1981 - 83 (US $m)

	Inward Investment		Outward Investment
	1981	*1983*	*1983*
Primary	269[1]	253	
Mining & quarrying	77[1]	253	
Oil	192[1]		
Secondary	5,812[2]	9,004	
Food & drink	436[1]	*N.S.A.*	
Chemicals & allied	1,380[3]	*N.S.A.*	
Metals	593[2]	*N.S.A.*	*Not Separately Available*
Mechanical engineering	425[3]	*N.S.A.*	
Electrical equipment	572[3]	*N.S.A.*	
Motor vehicles / Other transportation equipment	846[1]	*N.S.A.*	
Other manufacturing	1,248[1]	*N.S.A.*	
Tertiary	1,112[3]	2,243	
Distributive trade	902[3]	978	
Finance	178[1]	*N.S.A.*	
Other services	82[4]	1,265	
TOTAL	8,218[3]	11,500	375

Source:
Deutschen Bundesbank, 'Die Kapitalverflechtung der Unternehmen mit dem Ausland nach Landern und Wirtschaftszweigen 1976 bis 1981', *Monthly Report,* Supplement, June 1983; US Department of Commerce, *Survey of Current Business,* August 1983; UK Department of Trade & Industry, 'Census of Overseas Assets 1981', *Business Monitor,* Supplement 1981; US Department of Commerce, *Investment Climate in Foreign Countries,* Washington, 1983.

NOTES TO TABLE A6

1 US investment only.
2 US and West German investment only.
3 US, UK and West German investment only.
4 West German investment only.

Table A7

LEADING SOURCE AND RECIPIENT COUNTRIES, 1975 - 83 (US $m)

	Inward Investment		Outward Investment
	1975	*1983*	*1983*
DEVELOPED AREAS	4,178	9,936[1]	*Not Separately Available*
Europe	753		
W. Germany	109	978	
UK	265		
Switzerland	142	586	
North America	3,363		
USA	3,254	7,590	0.30[2]
Other developed countries			*N.S.A.*
Japan	62	782	*N.S.A.*
UNSPECIFIED	558	1,564	*N.S.A.*
TOTAL	4,736	11,500	0.38

Source:

Deutschen Bundesbank, 'Die Kapitalverflechtung der Unternehmen mit dem Ausland nach Landern und Wirtechaftszweigen 1976 bis 1981', *Monthly Report,* Supplement, June 1983; US Department of Commerce, *Survey of Current Business,* August 1983; UK Department of Trade & Industry, 'Census of Overseas Assets 1981', *Business Monitor,* Supplement, 1981; F Marsh, *Japanese Overseas Investment,* EIU, 1983; US Department of Commerce, *Investment Climate in Foreign Countries,* Washington, 1983.

NOTES TO TABLE A7

1 Includes US, West German, Japanese and Swiss investment only.

2 Estimated from US data.

Table A8

INDICATORS OF THE SIGNIFICANCE OF INWARD FOREIGN DIRECT INVESTMENT OR THE ACTIVITIES OF FOREIGN-BASED COMPANIES TO THE NATIONAL ECONOMY 1970 - 82

1	Direct capital stock of foreign affiliates at book value in 1982 as a proportion of:	
	a GNP at factor cost	6.97
	b population (in US $ per head)	150.81
2	Employment in foreign affiliates in 1970 as a percentage of all employment in manufacturing	21
3	Sales of foreign affiliates in 1972 as a percentage of all companies' sales in secondary (ie, manufacturing) industry	27
4	Investment by foreign affiliates as a percentage of all domestic investment 1978-80	3.3
5	Percentage share of output accounted for by foreign affiliates in selected sectors	
		Output
	Manufacturing Sector	
	Food	21.5
	Drink	30.0
	Tobacco	96.8
	Chemicals and allied	50.7
	Metals	20.6
	Mechanical engineering	52.1
	Electrical equipment	50.1
	Transport equipment	64.0
	Textiles	15.3
	Clothing and footwear	6.2
	Paper	32.9
	Rubber	63.9
	Petroleum products	48.7

Source:
US Department of Commerce, *Investment Climate in Foreign Countries,* Washington, 1983; IMF, *International Financial Statistics Yearbook 1984;* UNCTC, 1978, *op cit.* Fajnzylber and Tarrago, 1975, *op cit.*

Table A11

ROYALTY RECEIPTS AND PAYMENTS, 1975 - 82 (US $ m)

	Payments				Receipts		
	To Affiliates	*To Non-affiliates*	*Total*		*From Affiliates*	*From Non-affiliates*	*Total*
1975	*Not Separately Available*		140.8		*Not Available*		
1976			137.4				
1977			190.3				
1978			200.3				
1979			328.2				
1980			518.0				
1981			818.3				
1982			585.1				

Source:
IMF, *Balance of Payments Statistics Yearbook, 1983.*

Table A12

LEADING FOREIGN MULTINATIONAL COMPANIES, 1983

Name	*Home Country*	*Sector*
AEG - Telefunken AG	W. Germany	Electrical engineering
Alfa - Laval AB	Sweden	Mechanical engineering
Babcock International PLC	UK	Engineering
BASF AG	W. Germany	Chemicals
Beecham Group PLC	UK	Pharmaceuticals
B F Goodrich Co	USA	Rubber tyres
Celanese Corporation	USA	Chemicals, fibres
Ciba-Geigy AG	Switzerland	Chemicals
The Colgate - Palmolive Co	USA	Consumer products
Diamond Shamrock Corp	USA	Energy and chemicals
The Dow Chemical Co	USA	Chemicals
Emhart Corporation	USA	Chemicals
Firestone Tire and Rubber Co	USA	Rubber tyres
Ford Motor Company	USA	Motor vehicles
General Motors Corp	USA	Motor vehicles
Goodyear Tire and Rubber Co	USA	Rubber tyres
Hoechst AG	W. Germany	Chemicals
International Business Machines Corp	USA	Computers
Minnesota Mining & Manufacturing Co	USA	Diversified manufacturing
Procter & Gamble Company	USA	Consumer products
Siemens AG	W. Germany	Electrical and engineering equipment
Unilever	UK/Netherlands	Consumer products
The Wellcome Foundation	UK	Pharmaceuticals
The Xerox Corporation	USA	Copiers
Chrysler Corporation	USA	Motor vehicles

Source :
John M Stopford, *The World Directory of Multinational Enterprises 1982-83,* Bath: The Pitman Press, 1982.

PANAMA

Among the Latin American countries, Panama is an important recipient of foreign direct investment, although there is little information available about its international investment position. The inflows of foreign direct investment into Panama have fluctuated annually, with the level of reinvested earnings on a rising trend since the mid-1970s. One major difficulty with the official statistics is that there are major discrepancies between the amounts reported by home and recipient countries.

The USA is the most important source of investment in Panama, with Japan also having substantial interests in the country.

Table A6 indicates the sectoral distribution of US and UK investment in Panama. The bulk of such investment is concentrated in the services sector, particularly banking and finance, wholesale trade and regional distribution. However, investment is also significant in the oil industry and to a lesser extent in manufacturing, primarily chemicals. The Colon Free Trade Zone, set up in 1948, is the second largest free trade zone in the world after Hong Kong.

The Government of Panama actively promotes inward investment through the provision of tax and other incentives for export industries, and through the establishment in 1982 of an investment promotion agency – the Investment Council of Panama. There are few restrictions on foreign investors and there is no formal investment screening mechanism. A survey conducted in 1984 by the Chamber of Commerce and Industry of Panama showed that Panama rated very well as an investment centre.

There is a considerable amount of outward direct investment from Panama, mainly in the USA and Brazil. This however mainly reflects the fact that several foreign companies (including shipping companies) have their headquarters registered in Panama or recycle investment via their Panamanian affiliates.

MAIN SOURCES OF DATA:

A Official

1. Bank of Panama: provides data on FDI flows for balance of payments purposes.
2. US Department of Commerce International Trade Administration, *Investment Climate in Foreign Countries,* Washington, 1985, Vol IV.
3. UNCTC, *Transnational Corporations in World Development: Third Survey,* New York: UN, 1983.

Note:
Data do not allow us to complete Tables A5, A9 or A10 for Panama.

Table A1

SUMMARY OF THE COUNTRY'S INTERNATIONAL INVESTMENT POSITION

		Inward Investment	Outward Investment
1	Number of foreign affiliates in host country, and of foreign affiliates of home country firms at the end of 1980	800[1]	*N.A.*
2	Number of foreign firms with direct investments in host country, and home country firms with direct foreign affiliates	*N.A.*	*N.A.*
3	Total foreign direct capital stock at book value as a percentage of GNP at factor cost in 1981	135.20[2]	*N.A.*
4	Flow of foreign direct investment in the five year period, 1979-83 (US $ m)	336.4	*N.A.*
5	Employment in foreign affiliates or abroad	*N.A.*	*N.A.*
6	Output of foreign affiliates or abroad	*N.A.*	*N.A.*

Source:
US Department of Commerce, *Survey of Current Business,* August 1983; UK Department of Trade and Industry, *Business Monitor,* Supplement, 1981; Japanese Ministry of Finance, data as cited in F Marsh, *Japanese Investment Overseas,* EIU, 1983; IMF, *Balance of Payments Statistics Yearbook, 1984;* IMF, *International Financial Statistics Yearbook, 1984.*

NOTES TO TABLE A1

1 Represents number of affiliates of foreign MNEs from selected home countries identified by UNCTC, 1983.

2 Represents stock of US, UK and Japanese investment in Panama as a percentage of GNP in 1981.

Table A2

PRIVATE FOREIGN CAPITAL STOCK, 1981 (US $ m)

	Inward Investment			Outward Investment		
	Portfolio	*Direct*	*Total*	*Portfolio*	*Direct*	*Total*
Book value of capital stock 1981	*N.A.*	5,136.7[1]	*N.A.*	*Not Available*		

Source:

US Department of Commerce, *Survey of Current Business,* August 1983; UK Department of Trade and Industry, 'Census of Overseas Assets 1981', *Business Monitor,* Supplement, 1981; Japanese Ministry of Finance, data as cited in F Marsh, *Japanese Overseas Investment*, EIU, 1983.

NOTES TO TABLE A2

1 Includes US, UK and Japanese investment in Panama only.

Table A3

FLOW OF FOREIGN DIRECT INVESTMENT, 1970 - 83 (US $ m)[1]

	Inward Investment			Outward Investment		
	Reinvested Profits	*Other*	*Total*	*Reinvested Profits*	*Other*	*Total*
1970	6.0	27.0	33.0	*Not Available*		
1971	10.0	12.1	22.1			
1972	5.4	7.6	13.0			
1973	3.6	32.2	35.8			
1974	−14.4	49.3	34.9			
1975	−15.8	25.5	9.7			
1976	−4.6	11.5	6.9			
1977	5.8	4.7	10.5			
1978	3.8	−6.3	−2.5			
1979	25.8	24.6	50.4			
1980	49.5	−96.4	−46.9			
1981	27.1	9.5	36.6			
1982	30.9	246.2	277.1			
1983	49.2	0.0	49.2			

Source:

IMF, *Balance of Payments Statistics Yearbook,* various issues.

NOTES TO TABLE A3

1 These data represent those reported by the Panamanian Government; they are considerably below those reported by the major investing countries (notably the USA).

Table A4

SECTORAL DISTRIBUTION OF FOREIGN DIRECT CAPITAL STOCK, 1981 (US $ m)

	Inward Investment				Outward Investment		
	Primary	*Secondary*	*Tertiary*		*Primary*	*Secondary*	*Tertiary*
1981	702.0[1]	320.7[2]	2,405.2[2]		*Not Available*		

Source:

US Department of Commerce, *Survey of Current Business,* August 1983; UK Department of Trade and Industry, *Business Monitor,* Supplement, 1981.

NOTES TO TABLE A4

1 US investment only.

2 UK & US investment only.

Table A6

INDUSTRIAL DISTRIBUTION OF FOREIGN DIRECT CAPITAL STOCK, 1981 (US $ m)

	Inward Investment		Outward Investment
	1981		
Primary	702.0[1]		*Not Available*
Oil	702.0[1]		
Secondary	320.7[2]		
Food & drink	90.0[1]		
Chemicals & allied	176.0[1]		
Electrical equipment	1.0[1]		
Other manufacturing	37.0[1]		
Tertiary	2,405.2[2]		
Transport & communications	0.6[3]		
Distributive trade	666.0[1]		
Banking & finance	1,738.0[1]		
Other activities	0.6[3]		
TOTAL	3,835.7[2]		

Source:

US Department of Commerce, *Survey of Current Business,* August 1983; UK Department of Trade & Industry, 'Census of Overseas Assets 1981', *Business Monitor,* Supplement, 1981.

NOTES TO TABLE A6

1 US investment only.

2 US & UK investment only.

3 UK investment only.

Table A7

LEADING SOURCE AND RECEIPIENT COUNTRIES
1981 (US $ m)

	Inward Investment	Outward Investment
	1981	
DEVELOPED AREAS[1]	5,136.7	*Not Available*
UK	51.7	
USA	3,784.0	
Japan	1,301.0	
TOTAL	5,136.7[1]	

Source:

US Department of Commerce, *Survey of Current Business,* August 1983; UK Department of Trade and Industry, 'Census of Overseas Assets 1981', *Business Monitor,* Supplement, 1981; Japanese Ministry of Finance, data as cited in F Marsh, *Japanese Overseas Investment,* EIU, 1983.

NOTES TO TABLE A7

1 Including UK, US and Japanese investment only.

Table A8

INDICATORS OF THE SIGNIFICANCE OF INWARD FOREIGN DIRECT INVESTMENT OR THE ACTIVITIES OF FOREIGN-BASED COMPANIES TO THE NATIONAL ECONOMY, 1981

1	Direct capital stock of foreign affiliates[1] at book value in 1981 as a proportion of	
	a GNP at factor cost	135.20
	b population (in US $ per head)	2,647.78
2	Foreign investment as a percentage of domestic investment 1978-80.	44.0

Source:
US Department of Commerce, *Survey of Current Business,* August 1983; UK Department of Trade and Industry, 'Census of Overseas Assets 1981', *Business Monitor,* Supplement, 1981; Japanese Ministry of Finance, data as cited in F Marsh, *Japanese Overseas Investment,* EIU, 1983; IMF, *International Financial Statistics Yearbook, 1984.*

NOTES TO TABLE A8

1 Includes US, UK and Japanese investment in Panama only.

Table A11

ROYALTY RECEIPTS AND PAYMENTS, 1977 - 82 (US $ m)

	Payments			Receipts		
	To Affiliates	*To Non-affiliates*	*Total*	*From Affiliates*	*From Non-affiliates*	*Total*
1977	*Not Separately Available*		4.1	*Not Available*		
1978			5.8			
1979			7.4			
1980			8.7			
1981			7.5			
1982			9.1			

Source:
IMF, *Balance of Payments Statistics Yearbook,* various issues.

Table A12

LEADING FOREIGN MULTINATIONAL COMPANIES, 1982 - 83

Name	*Home Country*	*Sector*
Babcock International PLC	UK	Engineering
B A T Industries PLC	UK	Tobacco
The Black and Decker Manufacturing Co	USA	Power tools
Bristol-Myers Company	USA	Pharmaceuticals
Carnation Company	USA	Food
Diamond Shamrock Corporation	USA	Energy and chemicals
The Dow Chemical Company	USA	Chemicals
Exxon Corporation	USA	Petroleum
Goodyear Tire and Rubber Company	USA	Rubber tyres
Gulf Oil Corporation	USA	Petroleum
International Business Machines Corporation	USA	Computers
Johnson & Johnson	USA	Health care products
Kimberly-Clark Corporation	USA	Paper products
Nestle SA	Switzerland	Food products
Ing C Olivetti and C SpA	Italy	Office equipment
Pepsico Incorporated	USA	Beverage
Phizer Incorporated	USA	Pharmaceuticals
Philip Morris Incorporated	USA	Cigarettes
Revlon Incorporated	USA	Cosmetics
Roche/Sapre Group	Switzerland	Pharmaceuticals
Sony Corporation	Japan	Electrical equipment
Squibb Corporation	USA	Pharmaceuticals
Tenneco Incorporated	USA	Petroleum
Texaco Incorporated	USA	Petroleum
Xerox Corporation	USA	Copiers

Source:
John M Stopford, *The World Directory of Multinational Enterprises 1982-83,* Bath: The Pitman Press, 1982.

PARAGUAY

There is little information available about foreign direct investment in Paraguay. The inflows of foreign investment have been on a rising trend to the early 1980s, and originate largely from Argentina and Brazil. The USA is also a significant investor in Paraguay, while other sources of investment include West Germany, Japan and Spain. There is some outward direct investment from Paraguay, mainly in real estate in Argentina, Brazil and Uruguay.

Policy toward inward investment is welcoming; and there is requirement for local participation in foreign investment projects. Often, however, investment proposals are debated in the local press. The standard law governing foreign investment in Paraguay is Law 550 for the Promotion of Investment for Economic and Social Development of December 19, 1975. This sets out certain performance requirements for foreign operation in Paraguay.

MAIN SOURCES OF DATA:

A **Official**

1 Central Bank of Paraguay: issues data on FDI flows into the country.

2 US Department of Commerce International Trade Administration, *Investment Climate in Foreign Countries,* Washington: 1985, vol IV.

B **Private**

1 Parquet, Reinerio: *Las Empresas Transnacionales en la Economia del Paraguay,* CEPAL September, 1985.

Note:
Data do not allow us to complete Table A9 for Paraguay.

Table A1

SUMMARY OF THE COUNTRY'S INTERNATIONAL INVESTMENT POSITION

		Inward Investment	Outward Investment
1	Number of foreign affiliates in host country, and of foreign affiliates of home country firms at the end of 1980	409	*N.A.*
2	Number of foreign firms with direct investments in host country, and home country firms with direct foreign affiliates	*N.A.*	*N.A.*
3	Total foreign direct capital stock at book value as a percentage of GNP at factor cost in 1983	4.73	*N.A.*
4	Flow of foreign direct investment in the five year period, 1980-84 (US dollars m)	110.0	*N.A.*
5	Employment in foreign affiliates or abroad	*N.A.*	*N.A.*
6	Output of foreign affiliates or abroad	*N.A.*	*N.A.*

Source:

IMF, *Balance of Payments Statistics Yearbook,* various issues; IMF, *International Financial Statistics Yearbook, 1984;* Parquet, Reinerio *Las Empresas Transnacionales en la Economia del Paraguay,* CEPAL, September 1985.

Table A2

PRIVATE FOREIGN CAPITAL STOCK, 1975-84 (US $m)

	Inward Investment				Outward Investment		
	Portfolio	*Direct*	*Total*		*Portfolio*	*Direct*	*Total*
Book value of capital stock							
1975	*Not Available*	70.0[1]	*Not Available*		*Not Available*		
1978		110.0[1]					
1981		223.6[2]					
1984		270.4[2]					

Source

IMF, *Balance of Payments Statistics Yearbook,* various issues

NOTES TO TABLE A2

1 Investment by OECD countries

2 1978 stock plus investment flows since that date

Table A3

FLOW OF FOREIGN DIRECT INVESTMENT, 1970 - 84 (US $m)

	Inward Investment				Outward Investment		
	Reinvested Profits	*Other*	*Total*		*Reinvested Profits*	*Other*	*Total*
1970	*Not Separately Available*		4.0		*Not Separately Available*		*Not Available*
1971			7.0				
1972			3.3				
1973			9.5				
1974			20.4				
1975			14.6				
1976			18.5				25.4
1977			22.2				*N.A.*
1978			25.0				5.0
1979			50.4				*Not Available*
1980			31.2				
1981			32.0				
1982			36.7				
1983			4.9				
1984			5.2				

Source:

IMF, *Balance of Payments Statistics Yearbook,* various issues.

Table A4

SECTORAL DISTRIBUTION OF FOREIGN DIRECT CAPITAL STOCK, 1984 (US $ m)

	Inward Investment				Outward Investment		
	Primary	*Secondary*	*Tertiary*		*Primary*	*Secondary*	*Tertiary*
1984 [1]	35.2	107.6	97.6		*Not Available*		

Source

Parquet Reinerio, *Las Empresas Transnacionales en la Economia del Paraguay,* CEPAL, September 1985.

NOTES TO TABLE A4

1 Cumulative investment flows from 1970 to June 1984.

Table A5

GEOGRAPHICAL DISTRIBUTION OF FOREIGN DIRECT CAPITAL STOCK, 1984 (US $ m)

	Inward Investment				Outward Investment		
	Developed Countries	*Developing Countries*	*Total*		*Developed Countries*	*Developing Countries*	*Total*
1984 [1]	140.2	50.6	310.4 [2]		*Not Available*		

Source

Inter-American Development Bank, Washington; IMF, *Balance of Payments Statistics Yearbook,* various issues; Parquet, Reinerio *Las Empresas Transnacionales en la Economia del Paraguay,* CEPAL, September 1985.

NOTES TO TABLE A5

1 Cumulative investment flows from 1970 to June 1984.

2 Total includes an 'unspecified' figure.

Table A6

INDUSTRIAL DISTRIBUTION OF FOREIGN DIRECT CAPITAL STOCK, 1984 (US $ m)

	Inward Investment	Outward Investment
	1984 [1]	
Primary	35.2	*Not Available*
Agriculture	35.2	
Secondary	107.6	
Tertiary	97.6	
Transport & communications	2.5	
Banking & finance	87.3	
Other services	7.8	
TOTAL	310.4 [2]	

Table A7

LEADING SOURCE AND RECIPIENT COUNTRIES, 1984 (US $ m)[1]

	Inward Investment	Outward Investment
	1984[1]	
DEVELOPED AREAS	140.2	Not Available
Europe	65.8	
EEC of which:[2]	14.1	
W. Germany	9.7	
Italy	4.4	
Other Europe of which:[2]	20.0	
Spain	20.0	
North America of which:[2]	63.7	
USA	63.7	
Other developed countries of which:[2]	10.7	
Japan	10.7	
DEVELOPING AREAS	58.2	
Latin America of which:	58.2	
Argentina	8.7	
Brazil	40.0	
Chile	2.1[3]	
Uruguay	0.9[3]	
Venezuela	4.6[3]	
UNSPECIFIED	112.0	
TOTAL	310.4	

Source

Unpublished data from INTEL, as cited in *Economic and Social Progress in Latin America, 1984 Report,* Inter-American Development Bank, Washington; Banco Central del Paraguay; *Balanze de Pagos,* Boletines Anuales, 1970 to June 1984; Parquet, Reinerio, *Las Empresas Transnacionales en la Economia del Paraguay,* CEPAL, September 1985.

NOTES TO TABLE A7

1 Cumulative investment flows from 1970 to June 1984.

2 Including only those countries shown below.

3 Stock of direct foreign investment as at December 1982.

Table A8

INDICATORS OF THE SIGNIFICANCE OF INWARD FOREIGN DIRECT INVESTMENT OR THE ACTIVITIES OF FOREIGN-BASED COMPANIES TO THE NATIONAL ECONOMY, 1978 - 83

1	Direct capital stock of foreign affiliates at book value in 1983 as a proportion of:	
	a GNP at factor cost	4.73
	b population (in US $ per head)	88.41
2	Investment in foreign affiliates from OECD countries as a percentage of domestic investment, 1978 - 80	0.4

Source
IMF, *Balance of Payments Statistics Yearbook,* various issues; IMF, *International Financial Statistics Yearbook, 1984.*

Table A10

DISTRIBUTION OF FOREIGN SUBSIDIARIES AND ASSOCIATES AND FOREIGN CAPITAL STOCK BY PERCENTAGE OWNERSHIP OF PARENT COMPANIES, 1984

	Inward Investment		Outward Investment	
	Number of Affiliates	*Value of Capital Stock*	*Number of Affiliates*	*Value of Capital Stock*
100% owned subsidiaries	109	*Not Available*	*Not Available*	
50–99.9% owned subsidiaries and associates	59			
Less than 50% owned subsidiaries and associates	85			
TOTAL	437[1]			

Source

Parquet, Reinerio, *Las Empresas Transnacionales en la Economia del Paraguay,* CEPAL, September 1985.

NOTES TO TABLE A10

1 Total includes 184 affiliates not specified to any category.

Table A11

ROYALTY RECEIPTS AND PAYMENTS, 1976 - 83 (US $ m)

	Payments			Receipts		
	To Affiliates	*To Non-affiliates*	*Total*	*From Affiliates*	*From Non-affiliates*	*Total*
1976	*Not Separately Available*		1.1	*Not Available*		
1977			1.7			
1978			5.1			
1979			5.5			
1980			6.5			
1981			6.5			
1982			6.4			
1983			7.5			

Source

Banco Central del Paraguay, *Balanza de Pagos;* Parquet, Reinerio, *Las Empresas Transnacionales en la Economia del Paraguay,* CEPAL, September 1985.

Table A12

LEADING FOREIGN MULTINATIONAL COMPANIES, 1983

Name	*Home Country*	*Sector*
L'Air Liquide SA	France	Industrial gases
Brooke Bond Group PLC	UK	Tea
Firestone Tire and Rubber Company	USA	Rubber tyres
NV Philips Gloeilampenfabricken	Netherlands	Electrotechnical equipment
Texaco Incorporated	USA	Petroleum
The Wellcome Foundation	UK	Pharmaceuticals
Xerox Corporation	USA	Copiers

Source:
John M Stopford, *The World Directory of Multinational Enterprises 1982-83,* Bath: The Pitman Press, 1982.

PERU

Since the appointment of a democratically elected Government in 1979, Peru has adopted a more positive attitude towards inward direct investment. Nevertheless certain sectors remained prohibited to foreign investors and there are strict regulations governing new investments, take-overs, capital repatriation and the transfer of technology. Incentives for investment apply equally to foreign and domestic enterprises, although foreign firms may not own property within fifty kilometres of the Peruvian border.

Over the past fourteen years the inflow of new foreign investment has fluctuated markedly. By far the largest inward investor is the USA; FDI from European countries and Japan follows at a considerable distance.

The bulk of FDI is concentrated in the primary sector, predominantly in the mining and petroleum industries. Within the manufacturing sector, the main recipient industries of investment are food and drink, chemicals, textiles and clothing, and electrical equipment.

Although Peru practices a liberal trade and foreign exchange policy, the government does not actively encourage outward direct investment. What there is, is mainly concentrated in other Latin American countries, notably Bolivia.

MAIN SOURCES OF DATA:

A **Official**

1 Central Reserve Bank of Peru: publishes data on FDI flows and stocks, by sectoral distribution.

2 Comite de Inversion Nacional de Inversion Extranjera y Tecnologia (CONITE): provides information on foreign investments in Peru.

3 Junta del Acuerdo de Cartagena: gives data on royalty payments, and the distribution of foreign capital.

4 UNCTC, *Transnational Corporations in World Development: Third Survey,* New York: UN, 1983.

5 UNCTC, *Joint Ventures Among Firms in Latin America,* New York: UN, 1983.

B **Private**

1 F Portocarrero, 'Anatomia de la Exportacion No Tradicional', prepared for DESCO, 1983.

2 F Albavera, 'El Capital Extranjero en la Economia Peruana', prepared for CEPAL, Santiago, Chile: UN, 1984.

3 *Peru Portafolio,* Andean Report, December 1982.

Note:
Data do not allow us to complete Tables A9 or A10 for Peru.

Table A1

SUMMARY OF THE COUNTRY'S INTERNATIONAL INVESTMENT POSITION

		Inward Investment	Outward Investment
1	Number of foreign affiliates in host country, and of foreign affiliates of home country firms at the end of 1980	406[1]	*N.A.*
2	Number of foreign firms with direct investments in host country, and home country firms with direct foreign affiliates	*N.A.*	*N.A.*
3	Total foreign direct capital stock at book value as a percentage of GNP at factor cost in 1983	24.21	*N.A.*
4	Flow of foreign direct investment in the five year period, 1980-84 (US $ m)	150	*N.A.*
5	Employment in foreign affiliates or abroad 1979	15,620[2]	*N.A.*
6	Output of foreign affiliates or abroad, 1979 (US $ m)	890.9[3]	*N.A.*

Source:
Central Reserve Bank of Peru, CONITE, as cited in Albavera, *op cit.;* IMF, *Balance of Payments Statistics Yearbook,* various issues; IMF, *International Financial Statistics Yearbook, 1984;* Junta del Acuerdo de Cartagena, data as cited in Albavera, *op. cit.*

NOTES TO TABLE A1

1 Represents number of affiliates of MNEs from selected home countries, as identified by UNCTC, 1983.

2 Refers to employment in manufacturing sector by wholly-owned foreign firms only. A further 18,090 are employed in joint-ventures with minority foreign ownership.

3 Refers to the gross value of production in manufacturing sector of wholly-owned foreign firms. Joint ventures with minority foreign ownership are responsible for a further US $ 717.7 m.

Table A2

PRIVATE FOREIGN CAPITAL STOCK, 1971 - 84 (US $ m)

	Inward Investment			Outward Investment		
	Portfolio	*Direct*	*Total*	*Portfolio*	*Direct*	*Total*
Book value of capital stock						
1971		820				
1975		1,700				
1978		2,150				
1979		2,300				
1980[1]	*Not Available*	2,400	*Not Available*		*Not Available*	
1981[1]		2,650				
1982		2,696				
1983		2,733				
1984		2,645				

Source:

Albavera, 'El Capital Extranjero en la Economia Peruana' prepared for CEPAL, Santiago, Chile: UN, 1984; Central Reserve Bank of Peru, Comité de Inversion Nacional de Inversion Extranjera y Tecnologia (CONITE), data as cited in Albavera, *op cit.*

NOTES TO TABLE A2

1 CEPAL estimates for 1980 and 1981 based on information from CONITE. FDI stock for 1982, 1983 and 1984 have been estimated by adding cumulative investment flows to FDI stock of 1981.

Table A3

FLOW OF FOREIGN DIRECT INVESTMENT, 1970 - 84 (US $ m)

	Inward Investment			Outward Investment		
	Reinvested Profits	*Other*	*Total*	*Reinvested Profits*	*Other*	*Total*
1970	5	–75	–70			
1971	5	–63	–58			
1972	11	13	24			
1973	*Not Separately Available*		49			
1974			144			
1975			316			
1976	15	156	171			
1977	15	39	54		*Not Available*	
1978	18	7	25			
1979	25	46	71			
1980	29	–2	27			
1981	37	91	128			
1982	35	11	46			
1983	40	–3	37			
1984	20	–108	–88			

Source:

Central Reserve Bank of Peru, *Memoria,* 1981; IMF, *Balance of Payments Statistics Yearbook,* various issues.

Table A4

SECTORAL DISTRIBUTION OF FOREIGN DIRECT CAPITAL STOCK, 1975 - 81 (US $ m)

	Inward Investment			Outward Investment		
	Primary	*Secondary*	*Tertiary*	*Primary*	*Secondary*	*Tertiary*
1975	1,348	240	112			
1977	1,410	350	170			
1978	1,518	373	259		*Not Available*	
1979	1,591	451	258			
1980	1,599	483	318			
1981	1,846	486	318			

Source:
CEPAL estimates based on information from the Central Reserve Bank of Peru, CONITE, as cited in Albavera, *op cit.*

Table A5

GEOGRAPHICAL DISTRIBUTION OF FOREIGN DIRECT CAPITAL STOCK, 1984 (US $ m)[1]

	Inward Investment			Outward Investment		
	Developed Countries	*Developing Countries*	*Total*	*Developed Countries*	*Developing Countries*	*Total*
1 1984[1]	1,129.2[2]	122.5[2]	1,399.2[3]		*Not Available*	

Source:
Central Reserve Bank of Peru, CONITE, as cited in Albavera, *op cit.*

NOTES TO TABLE A5

1 Figures as for June 1984 refer to accumulated authorised foreign investment.
2 Including only those countries as specified in Table A7.
3 Total includes 'unspecified' figure.

Table A6

INDUSTRIAL DISTRIBUTION OF FOREIGN CAPITAL STOCK, 1975 - 81 (US $ m)

	Inward Investment			Outward Investment
	1975	*1981*		
Primary	1,348.0	1,846.0		*Not Available*
Agriculture[1]	11.0	16.0		
Mining & quarrying } Oil	1,337.0	1,830.0		
Secondary	240.0[2]	486.0		
Food & drink	63.1	*Not Separately Available*		
Chemicals & allied	55.0			
Metals	15.4			
Mechanical engineering	7.9			
Electrical equipment	25.4			
Motor vehicles } Other transportation equipment	9.6			
Textiles & clothing[3]	33.1			
Paper & allied	3.1			
Stone, clay & glass	5.3			
Coal & petroleum products	0.7			
Other manufacturing	21.4			
Tertiary	112.0	318.0		
Banking & finance	75.0	212.0		
Other services	37.0	106.0		
TOTAL	1,700.0	2,650.0		

Source:
Albavera, *op cit.*

NOTES TO TABLE A6

1 Including fishing and forestry.

2 Estimates for manufacturing sector distribution obtained by applying percentages given by the Junta del Acuerdo de Cartagena to the total stock figure for the manufacturing sector, 1975.

3 Including leather.

Table A7

LEADING SOURCE AND RECIPIENT COUNTRIES, 1984[1] (US $ m)

	Inward Investment		Outward Investment
	1984[1]		
DEVELOPED AREAS[2]	1,129.2		
Europe[2]	416.4		
EEC of which[2]	180.0		
Luxembourg	32.2		
France	25.5		
Italy	55.7		
Netherlands	18.9		
UK	47.7		
Other Europe of which[2]	236.4		
Austria, Cyprus, Finland, Norway, Portugal, Spain, Sweden	71.3		*Not Available*
Switzerland	165.1		
North America of which	671.0		
Canada	36.5		
USA	634.5		
Other developed countries of which[2]	41.8		
Japan	41.8		
DEVELOPING AREAS[2]	122.5		
Latin America of which[2]	122.5		
Panama	122.5		
UNSPECIFIED	87.5		
TOTAL	1,339.2		

Source:

Central Reserve Bank of Peru, CONITE, as cited in Albavera, *op cit.*

NOTES TO TABLE A7

1 Figures as for June 1984, and refer to accumulated authorised foreign investment, 1972 - 84.

2 Including only those countries shown below.

Table A8

INDICATORS OF THE SIGNIFICANCE OF INWARD FOREIGN DIRECT INVESTMENT OR THE ACTIVITIES OF FOREIGN-BASED COMPANIES TO THE NATIONAL ECONOMY, 1975 - 83

1	Direct capital stock of foreign affiliates at book value in 1983 as a proportion of	
	a GNP at factor cost	24.21
	b population (in US $ per head)	146.07
2	Employment in foreign affiliates[1] in 1975 as a percentage of all employment in manufacturing	13.5
3	Output of foreign affiliates[1] in 1975 as a percentage of all companies' output in secondary (ie, manufacturing) industry	21.2
4	Exports of foreign affiliates in 1978 as a percentage of all manufacturing exports	8[2]

5 Percentage share of sales and employment accounted for by foreign affiliates in selected sectors[3], 1979.

	Sales	*Employment*
Manufacturing Sector		
Food & drink	25.38	17.47
Chemicals & allied	23.20	26.90
Metals	4.17	2.83
Mechanical engineering, Electrical equipment, Motor vehicles, Other transportation equipment	39.53	31.92
Textiles & clothing	5.61	15.97
Paper & allied	0.23	0.11
Stone, glass & clay	1.35	0.80
Timber & furniture	0.53	4.00

Source:
Central Reserve Bank of Peru, CONITE, data as cited in Albavera, *op cit.;* Junta del Acuerdo de Cartagena, data as cited in Albavera, *op cit.;* F Portocarrero, 'Anatomia de la Exportacion No Tradicional' prepared for DESCO, 1983.

NOTES TO TABLE A8

1 Manufacturing sector only.

2 Refers to the share of foreign firms, out of the 20 most important exporting firms, in the total value of non-traditional exports.

3 Refers to the distribution of the gross value of production, and employment of the major foreign firms in manufacturing industries. This does not include joint ventures, with minority foreign-ownership.

Table A11

ROYALTY RECEIPTS AND PAYMENTS, 1975 - 80 (US $ m)

	Payments			Receipts		
	To Affiliates	*To Non-affiliates*	*Total*	*From Affiliates*	*From Non-affiliates*	*Total*
1975	*Not Separately Available*		10,903	*Not Available*		
1976			5,677			
1977			6,000			
1978			6,700			
1979			5,100			
1980			7,400			

Source:
Junta del Acuerdo de Cartagena; as cited in Albavera, *op cit.*; CONITE, *Memorias*, 1978-80.

Table A12

LEADING FOREIGN MULTINATIONAL COMPANIES, 1980

Name	*Home Country*	*Sector*	*Peruvian (US $m)*
1 Occidental	USA	Oil	803
2 AB Volvo	Sweden	Motor vehicles	71
3 NV Philips Gloeilampenfabricken	Netherlands	Electrical equipment	66
4 Goodyear Tire & Rubber Co	USA	Rubber tyres	61
5 Bayer	W. Germany	Chemicals	60
6 Nissan Motor	Japan	Motor vehicles	54
7 IBM	USA	Office equipment	54
8 Toyota	Japan	Motor vehicles	53
9 Alfa-Laval AB	Sweden	Mechanical engineering	
10 ASEA AB	Sweden	Electrical equipment	
11 Bristol-Myers Company	USA	Pharmaceuticals	
12 BBC - Brown Boveri and Co	Switzerland	Electrical engineering	
13 Celanese Corporation	USA	Chemicals/fibres	
14 Ciba-Geigy AG	Switzerland	Chemicals	
15 Chrysler Corporation	USA	Motor vehicles	
16 Compagnie Francaise des Petroles SA	France	Petroleum exploration	*Not*
17 The Dow Chemical Company	USA	Chemicals	*Available*
18 Johnson & Johnson	USA	Health care products	
19 Nestle SA	Switzerland	Food products	
20 Ing C Olivetti and C SpA	Italy	Office equipment	
21 Phelps Dodge Corporation	USA	Metals	
22 Procter and Gamble Company	USA	Consumer products	
23 Roche/Sapac Group	Switzerland	Pharmaceuticals	
24 Saab-Scania AB	Sweden	Motor vehicles	
25 Xerox Corporation	USA	Copiers	

Source:
John M Stopford, *The World Directory of Multinational Enterprises 1982-83,* Bath: The Pitman Press, 1982.

TRINIDAD AND TOBAGO

There has been little regulation of foreign direct investment in Trinidad and Tobago since Independence in 1962. This 'Open Door' policy largely continues, offering a favourable climate for foreign investment. The government has consistently held a positive attitude towards foreign investment, encouraging it by means of the standard package of tax and tariff incentives. More recently, joint-ventures between MNEs and both local private and government enterprises have been favoured, with some sectors — notably energy-based projects — being closed to wholly- or majority-owned foreign investors.

The main source of foreign investment in Trinidad and Tobago is now the USA, having overtaken the UK. Other investor countries include Canada, Switzerland, Sweden and Japan.

Foreign ownership is spread throughout most sectors, but the bulk of foreign direct investment is concentrated in petroleum and oil-based activities. Within the manufacturing sector, the emphasis lies on food and drink, textiles, rubber and chemicals and allied, while the banking and finance sector was at one time dominated by foreign ownership — notably British, Canadian and US financial institutions. There is also a significant foreign presence in the construction industry.

MAIN SOURCES OF DATA:

A **Official**

1 Trinidad and Tobago Central Statistical Office: provides data on inflows of foreign direct investment, by sectoral distribution.

2 UNCTC, *Transnational Corporations in World Development: Third Survey*, New York: UN, 1983.

B **Private**

1 T Farrell, 'Foreign Direct Investment, The Transnational Corporation and the Prospects for L.D.C. Transformation in Today's World — Lessons from the Trinidad-Tobago Experience', paper presented at the Commonwealth Secretariat Conference on New Opportunities for Foreign Direct Investments in Developing Countries, March/April, 1985.

2 T Turner, 'Multinational Enterprises and Employment in the Caribbean with special reference to Trinidad and Tobago', no 20 in the series of working papers on the employment effects of MNEs, *International Labour Office,* Geneva, 1982.

Note:
Data do not allow us to complete Tables A9 or A10 for Trinidad and Tobago.

Table A1

SUMMARY OF THE COUNTRY'S INTERNATIONAL INVESTMENT POSITION

		Inward Investment	Outward Investment
1	Number of foreign affiliates in host country, and of foreign affiliates of home country firms at the end of 1980	174[1]	*N.A.*
2	Number of foreign firms with direct investments in host country, and home country firms with direct foreign affiliates	*N.A.*	*N.A.*
3	Total foreign direct capital stock at book value as a percentage of GNP at factor cost in 1979	29.09	*N.A.*
4	Flow of foreign direct investment in the five year period 1980-84 (TT $ m)	3,293.32	*N.A.*
5	Employment in foreign affiliates or abroad, 1977	31,025[2]	*N.A.*
6	Output of foreign affiliates or abroad	*N.A.*	*N.A.*

Source:
Trinidad and Tobago, Central Statistical Office, *Balance of Payments of Trinidad and Tobago, 1980-81*; IMF, *Balance of Payments Statistics Yearbook*, various issues; IMF, *International Financial Statistics Yearbook, 1984.*

NOTES TO TABLE A1

1 Represents number of affiliates of foreign MNEs from selected countries identified in UNCTC, 1983.

2 Represents employment in foreign affiliates in selected sectors, excluding banking and tourism.

Table A4

SECTORAL DISTRIBUTION OF FOREIGN DIRECT CAPITAL STOCK, 1981 (TT $ m)[1]

	Inward Investment				Outward Investment		
	Primary	*Secondary*	*Tertiary*		*Primary*	*Secondary*	*Tertiary*
1974-81[1]	2,735.5	162.0	60.5		*Not Available*		

Source:
Trinidad and Tobago, Central Statistical Office, *Balance of Payments of Trinidad and Tobago, 1980-81.*

NOTES TO TABLE A4

1 Cumulative flows of net direct investment 1974-81, dervied from the Flow of Funds data compiled by Trinidad and Tobago Central Statistical Office in its Survey of Direct Investment Enterprises.

Table A5

GEOGRAPHICAL DISTRIBUTION OF FOREIGN DIRECT CAPITAL STOCK, 1981 (TT $ m)

	Inward Investment				Outward Investment		
	Developed Countries	*Other Countries*	*Total*		*Developed Countries*	*Developing Countries*	*Total*
1981	2,464.8[1]	1,401.1	3,865.9[2]		*Not Available*		

Source:
HMSO, *Business Monitor,* Supplement, 1981; US Department of Commerce, *Survey of Current Business,* August 1983; Trinidad and Tobago, Central Statistical Office, *Balance of Payments of Trinidad and Tobago 1980-81.*

NOTES TO TABLE A5

1 Includes US and UK investment only.

2 Cumulative investment flow, 1968-81.

Table A6

INDUSTRIAL DISTRIBUTION OF FOREIGN DIRECT CAPITAL STOCK, 1981 (TT $ m)[1]

	Inward Investment	Outward Investment
	1974-81[1]	
Primary	2,735.5	*Not Available*
Secondary	162.0	
Food & drink	63.0	
Chemicals & allied[2]	35.8	
Rubber	63.2	
Tertiary	60.5	
Transport & communications	60.5	
TOTAL	3,034.5[3]	

Source:
Trinidad and Tobago Central Statistical Office, *Balance of Payments of Trinidad and Tobago, 1980-81.*

NOTES TO TABLE A6

1 Cumulative flows of net direct investment, 1974-81, derived from Flow of Funds data compiled by Trinidad and Tobago's Central Statistical Office in its Survey of Direct Investment Enterprises.

2 Non-metallic minerals are included under 'chemicals and allied'.

3 Total includes an unallocated amount of TT $ 76.5 m.

Table A7

LEADING SOURCE AND RECIPIENT COUNTRIES 1981 (TT $ m)

	Inward Investment	Outward Investment
	1981	
DEVELOPED AREAS[1]	2,464.8	*Not Available*
UK	81.6	
USA	2,383.2	
TOTAL	3,865.9[2]	

Source:
HMSO, 'Census of Overseas Assets 1981', *Business Monitor*, Supplement, 1981; US Department of Commerce, *Survey of Current Business,* August 1983; Trinidad and Tobago Central Statistical Office, *Balance of Payments of Trinidad and Tobago 1980-81.*

NOTES TO TABLE A7

1 Including only those countries shown below.

2 Cumulative investment flow, 1968-81.

Table A8

INDICATORS OF THE SIGNIFICANCE OF INWARD FOREIGN DIRECT INVESTMENT OR THE ACTIVITIES OF FOREIGN-BASED COMPANIES TO THE NATIONAL ECONOMY, 1977 - 80

1	Direct capital stock of foreign affiliates at book value in 1979 as a proportion of		
	a GNP at factor cost		29.09
	b population (in TT $ per head)		3,248.66[1]
2	Employment in foreign affiliates in 1977 as a percentage of all employment		
	a in all industry		10[2]
	b in manufacturing		44[3]
3	Foreign investment as a percentage of domestic investment 1978-80		1.8
4	Percentage share of assets and employment accounted for by foreign affiliates in selected sectors, 1977		
		Assets[4]	*Employment*
	Primary Goods Sector		
	Oil	73	70
	Manufacturing Sector		
	Food & drink	35	28
	Chemicals & allied[5]	42	34
	Textiles & clothing	32	26
	Paper & allied	47	26
	Rubber	57	47
	Stone, glass & clay[5]	*N.S.A.*	*N.S.A.*
	Timber & furniture	6	5
	Services Sector		
	Construction	3	9
	Transport & communications[6]	4	3
	Trade & distribution	9	9

Source:

Trinidad and Tobago Central Statistical Office, *Balance of Payments of Trinidad and Tobago, 1980-81;* Central Statistical Office, data as cited T Turner, *op cit.*; IMF, *Balance of Payments Statistics Yearbook,* various issues; IMF, *International Financial Statistics Yearbook, 1984.*

NOTES TO TABLE A8

1 1981.

2 Including government services and education.

3 Including petroleum. Employment in foreign affiliates in oil is 70%.

4 1976

5 Non-metallic minerals included under 'chemicals and allied'.

6 Including storage.

Table A11

ROYALTY RECEIPTS AND PAYMENTS, 1974 - 84 (TT $ m)

	Payments			Receipts		
	To Affiliates	*To Non-affiliates*	*Total*	*From Affiliates*	*From Non-affiliates*	*Total*
1974	*Not Separately Available*		2.7	*Not Available*		
1975			3.7			
1976			4.9			
1977			9.8			
1978			8.1			
1979			11.8			
1980			13.4			
1981			13.6			
1982			20.7			
1983			25.9			
1984			24.6			

Source:
IMF, *Balance of Payments Statistics Yearbook,* various issues.

Table A12

LEADING FOREIGN MULTINATIONAL COMPANIES, 1985

Name	*Home Country*	*Sector*
Amoco (Standard Oil)	USA	Oil
Tesoro	USA	Oil
W R Grace	USA	Chemicals
Cable & Wireless	UK	Electrical
Unilever	UK/ Netherlands	Food
BAT	UK	Tobacco
Nestlé	Switzerland	Food
Texaco	USA	Oil
Heineken Beer Ltd	Netherlands	Brewing

Source:
T Farrell, University of West Indies, St Augustine, Trinidad and Tobago, 1985.

URUGUAY

There is very little detailed information available on the international investment position of Uruguay. US investment in the country is largely concentrated in the manufacturing sector, primarily in textiles, motor vehicles and other transportation equipment, and cement production. Other sources of investment include West Germany and the UK, where again the bulk of such investment is in manufacturing, particularly chemicals.

The Uruguayan Government encourages inward investment. Policy is laid down in the Foreign Investment Act 1974. A declaration of an investment project by the Government as being in the national interests yields important tax benefits. The 1974 Act also guarantees the remittance abroad of company profits corresponding to the contribution made by foreign capital. Local content and export requirements are imposed on producers of cars, trucks and farm equipment.

In the mid 1970s, Uruguay had some £32 million invested in other Latin American countries, mostly in Brazil and Argentina.

MAIN SOURCES OF DATA:

A **Official**

1 Bank of Uruguay: provides some data on investment flows for balance of payments purposes.

2 US Department of Commerce International Trade Administration, *Investment Climate in Foreign Countries,* Washington, 1983 and 1985, vol IV.

3 Dun and Bradstreet, *Who Owns Whom 1984,* London: Business Marketing Division (Publications), 1984.

Note:

Data do not allow us to complete Tables A4, A6, A9, A10 or A11 for Uruguay.

Table A1

SUMMARY OF THE COUNTRY'S INTERNATIONAL INVESTMENT POSITION

		Inward Investment	Outward Investment
1	Number of foreign affiliates in host country, and of foreign affiliates of home country firms at the end of 1980	133[1]	*N.A.*
2	Number of foreign firms with direct investments in host country, and home country firms with direct foreign affiliates	*N.A.*	*N.A.*
3	Total foreign direct capital stock at book value as a percentage of GNP at factor cost in 1981	8.54	*N.A.*
4	Flow of foreign direct investment in the five year period, 1977-81 (US $ m)	754.0	11.5[2]
5	Employment in foreign affiliates or abroad	*N.A.*	*N.A.*
6	Output of foreign affiliates or abroad	*N.A.*	*N.A.*

Source:

UNCTC, *Transnational Corporations in World Development: Third Survey,* New York: UN, 1983; IMF, *Balance of Payments Statistics Yearbook, 1984;* IMF, *International Financial Statistics Yearbook, 1984.*

NOTES TO TABLE A1

1 Represents number of affiliates of MNES from selected home countries as identified by UNCTC, 1983.

2 Three years 1982/84.

Table A2

PRIVATE FOREIGN CAPITAL STOCK, 1978 - 1981 (US $ m)

	Inward Investment[1]			Outward Investment		
	Portfolio	*Direct*	*Total*	*Portfolio*	*Direct*	*Total*
Book value of capital stock	*Not Available*		*Not Available*	*Not Available*		*Not Available*
1978		330.0			32[2]	
1981		881.4[1]			*N.S.A.*	

Source:

UNCTC, *Transnational Corporations in World Development: Third Survey,* New York: UN, 1983; IMF, *Balance of Payments Statistics Yearbook, 1984.*

NOTES TO TABLE A2

1 Estimated by adding cumulative investment flow 1979-81 to the UNCTC stock figure for 1978.

2 Latin America only.

Table A3

FLOW OF FOREIGN DIRECT INVESTMENT, 1977 - 83 (US $ m)

	Inward Investment			Outward Investment		
	Reinvested Profits	*Other*	*Total*[1]	*Reinvested Profits*	*Other*	*Total*[1]
1977	*Not Separately Available*		68.6	*Not Available*		
1978			134.0			
1979			219.7			
1980			283.7			
1981			48.0			
1982			*N.A.*	*Not Separately Available*		13.7
1983			*N.A.*			–5.4
1984			*N.A.*			3.2

Source:

IMF, *Balance of Payments Stastics Yearbook,* various issues.

NOTES TO TABLE A3

1 Excluding reinvested profits.

Table A5

GEOGRAPHICAL DISTRIBUTION OF FOREIGN DIRECT CAPITAL STOCK, 1981 (US $ m)

	Inward Investment				Outward Investment		
	Developed Countries	*Other Countries*	*Total*		*Developed Countries*	*Developing Countries*	*Total*
1981	204[1]	679	883[2]		*Not Available*		

Source:

US Department of Commerce, *Investment Climate in Foreign Countries,* Washington, 1983.

NOTES TO TABLE A5

1 Including UK, US and West Germany investment only.

2 Estimated by adding cumulative investment flow 1979-81 to the UNCTC stock figure for 1978.

Table A7

LEADING SOURCE AND RECIPIENT COUNTRIES, 1981 (US $ m)

	Inward Investment		Outward Investment
	1981		
DEVELOPED AREAS[1]	204		*Not Available*
Europe			
W. Germany	20		
UK	25[2]		
North America			
USA	159		
UNSPECIFIED	679		
TOTAL	883[3]		32[4]

Source:

US Department of Commerce, *Investment Climate in Foreign Countries,* Washington, 1983.

NOTES TO TABLE A7

1 Including only those countries shown below.

2 UK Department of Trade and Industry estimate is $9.9m,

3 Estimated by adding cumulative investment flows 1979-81 to the UNCTC stock figure for 1978.

4 Investment in other Latin American countries in the mid 1970s.

Table A8

INDICATORS OF THE SIGNIFICANCE OF INWARD FOREIGN DIRECT INVESTMENT OR THE ACTIVITIES OF FOREIGN-BASED COMPANIES TO THE NATIONAL ECONOMY, 1981

1	Direct capital stock of foreign affiliates at book value in 1981 as a proportion of:		
	a	GNP at factor cost	8.54
	b	population (in US $ per head)	301.37
2	Foreign investment as a percentage of domestic investment 1978-80		0.3

Source:

UNCTC, *Transnational Corporations in World Development: Third Survey,* New York: UN, 1983; IMF, *Balance of Payments Statistics Yearbook,* 1984; IMF, *International Financial Statistics Yearbook,* 1984.

Table A12

LEADING FOREIGN MULTINATIONAL COMPANIES, 1983

	Name	*Home Country*	*Sector*
1	Abbott Laboratories Inc	USA	Pharmaceuticals
2	Avon Products Inc	USA	Cosmetics
3	Alcan Aluminium Ltd	Canada	Aluminium
4	Bank of Boston Corporation	USA	Banking and finance
5	Borden Inc	USA	Chemicals
6	Ford Motor Company	USA	Motor vehicles
7	International Business Machines Corp	USA	Computers
8	Merrill Lynch & Co Inc	USA	Finance
9	Philips Morris Inc	USA	Tobacco
10	Xerox Corp	USA	Copiers
11	Ciba-Geigy	Switzerland	Chemicals
12	Glaxo Holdings PLC	UK	Pharmaceuticals
13	Honeywell Incorporated	USA	Electronic information
14	Johnson and Johnson	USA	Health Care products
15	L'Oreal SA	France	Cosmetics
16	Nabisco Brands Inc	USA	Food products
17	Ing C Olivetti & Co SpA	Italy	Office equipment
18	Pepsico Incorporated	USA	Beverage
19	Philip Morris Incorporated	USA	Cigarettes
20	NV Philips Gloeilampenfabrieken	Netherlands	Electrotechnical equipment
21	Revlon Incorporated	USA	Cosmetics
22	Roche / Sapac Group	Switzerland	Pharmaceuticals
23	Sandoz AG	Switzerland	Chemicals
24	Texaco Incorporated	USA	Petroleum
25	Xerox Corporation	USA	Copiers

Source:
John M Stopford, *The World Directory of Multinational Enterprises 1982–83,* Bath: The Pitman Press, 1982.

VENEZUELA

Prior to the establishment of the *Superintendencia de Inversiones Extranjeras (SIEX)* in 1974, the Central Bank of Venezuela recorded foreign direct investment statistics. Between 1974 and 1984, as a result of Venezuela joining the Andean Pact in 1976 – and more specifically, the implementation in Venezuela of *Decision 24* of this Pact – there was strict control over foreign direct investment in the country. This restrictive stance is now undergoing some reappraisal; *inter alia* the Government is interpreting Andean Pact registrations rather more flexibly.

Foreign investment in Venezuela is largely concentrated in the primary sector (oil) and the manufacturing sector, particularly chemicals, metal products and machinery, and food, drinks and tobacco.

The USA and Panama are the dominant sources of foreign investment. Switzerland is increasing its share, while the UK, although still a significant investor in Venezuela, has a declining share.

The Government pursues a neutral policy towards outward foreign investment.

MAIN SOURCES OF DATA:

A **Official**

1 Central Bureau of Venezuela: provides data on foreign direct investment, by sectoral and geographical distribution, from 1950–74.

2 Superintendent for Foreign Investments (SIEX): gives data on foreign direct investment registered by the SIEX, by sectoral and geographical distribution, from 1975 onwards.

3 Dun and Bradstreet, *Who Owns Whom 1984,* London: Business Marketing Division (Publications) 1984.

B **Private**

1 P Nell, 'Direct Foreign Investment in Venezuela, 1950–1982: A Focus on the Industrial Sector', paper prepared for the Inter-American Development Bank.

Note:
Data do not allow us to complete Tables A9, A10 or A11 for Venezuela.

Table A1

SUMMARY OF THE COUNTRY'S INTERNATIONAL INVESTMENT POSITION

		Inward Investment	Outward Investment
1	Number of foreign affiliates in host country, and of foreign affiliates of home country firms at the end of 1984	16,848[1]	*N.A.*
2	Number of foreign firms with direct investments in host country, and home country firms with direct foreign affiliates	*N.A.*	*N.A.*
3	Total foreign direct capital stock at book value as a percentage of GNP at factor cost in 1982	10.01	*N.A.*
4	Flow of foreign direct investment in the five year period 1980-84 (Bol m)	2905.9	*N.A.*
5	Employment in foreign affiliates or abroad, 1975-84	80,438[2]	*N.A.*
6	Output of foreign affiliates or abroad	*N.A.*	*N.A.*

Source:

IMF, *Balance of Payments Statistics Yearbook, 1984;* IMF, *International Financial Statistics Yearbook, 1984;* Superintendent for Foreign Investments (SIEX).

NOTES TO TABLE A1

1 Represents the number of firms classified by the SIEX. Within these firms, foreign capital stock is 8,610.8 million bolivares, which is about 26% of the total.

2 Represents the number of posts generated by FDI in the period 1975-84.

Table A2

PRIVATE FOREIGN CAPITAL STOCK, 1966 - 84 (Bol m)

	Inward Investment			Outward Investment		
	Portfolio	*Direct*	*Total*	*Portfolio*	*Direct*	*Total*
Book value of capital stock						
1966	833	11,713	12,546	*Not Available*		
1970	1,153	12,713	13,866			
1974	1,505	16,169	17,674			
1976[1]	*Not Available*	19,161	*Not Available*			
1978		20,315				
1981		24,915				
1984		33,246				

Source:
Central Bank of Venezuela, *Economic Report,* (1966-74 data); Superintendent for Foreign Investments (SIEX), (1976-84 data).

NOTES TO TABLE A2

1 From 1976 onwards, stocks have been estimated from SIEX data assuming that it reflects 30.5% of the total foreign capital stock. (See Definitions.)

Table A3

FLOW OF FOREIGN DIRECT INVESTMENT, 1970 - 83 (Bol m)

	Inward Investment			Outward Investment		
	Reinvested Profits	*Other*	*Total*[1]	*Reinvested Profits*	*Other*	*Total*[1]
1970	*Not Separately Available*		-103.5	*Not Available*		
1971			948.0			
1972			-1,652.9			
1973			-364.3			
1974			-1,468.7			
1975			1,519.2			
1976			-3,551.2			
1977			-15.0			
1978			290.2			
1979			377.1			
1980			234.6			
1981			789.6			
1982			1,104.2	*N.S.A.*	*N.S.A.*	19.0
1983			367.5	*Not Available*		
1984			410.0			

Source:
IMF, *Balance of Payments Statistics Yearbook,* various issues.

NOTES TO TABLE A3

1 Excluding reinvested earnings.

Table A4

SECTORAL DISTRIBUTION OF FOREIGN DIRECT CAPITAL STOCK, 1966 - 84 (Bol m)

	Inward Investment			Outward Investment		
	Primary	*Secondary*	*Tertiary*	*Primary*	*Secondary*	*Tertiary*
1966	8,138	2,209	1,366	*Not Available*		
1974	8,189	5,272	2,708			
1984[1]	15,903	12,275	5,068			

Source:

Central Bank of Venezuela, *Economic Report,* (1966-74 data); Superintendent for Foreign Investments (SIEX), (1984 data).

NOTES TO TABLE A4

1 Estimated by applying percentage sectoral distribution according to the SIEX data, to the stock figure of 1984

Table A5

GEOGRAPHICAL DISTRIBUTION OF FOREIGN DIRECT CAPITAL STOCK, 1966 - 84 (Bol m)

	Inward Investment			Outward Investment		
	Developed Countries	*Developing Countries*	*Total*[1]	*Developed Countries*	*Developing Countries*	*Total*
1966	11,133	296	11,713	*Not Available*		
1974	13,950	842	16,169			
1984[2]	28,090	4,129	33,246			

Source:

Central Bank of Venezuela, *Economic Report,* (1966-74 data); Superintendent for Foreign Investments, (SIEX), (1984 data).

NOTES TO TABLE A5

1 Total includes 'unspecified' figure.

2 Estimated by applying percentage geographical distribution according to the SIEX data, to the stock figure of 1984.

Table A6

INDUSTRIAL DISTRIBUTION OF FOREIGN DIRECT CAPITAL STOCK, 1974 - 84 (Bol m)

	Inward Investment		Outward Investment
	1974	*1984*[1]	
Primary	8,189	15,903	Not Available
Agriculture[2]	47	454	
Mining & quarrying	649	42	
Oil	7,493	15,407	
Secondary	5,272	12,275	
Food & drink	816	3,509	
Chemicals & allied[3]	914	3,319	
Metals	399	1,052	
Mechanical engineering	1,047	2,744	
Electrical equipment / Motor vehicles / Other transportation equipment	645	N.S.A.	
Textiles & clothing	197	299	
Paper & allied	125	475	
Rubber[3]	N.S.A.	N.S.A.	
Stone, clay & glass	215	742	
Coal & petroleum products[3]	N.S.A.	N.S.A.	
Other manufacturing	914	135	
Tertiary	2,708	5,068	
Construction	106	673	
Transport & communications	108	179	
Distributive trade	1,433	846	
Property	N.S.A.	N.S.A.	
Banking & finance	522	2,387	
Other services	539	987	
TOTAL	16,169	33,246	

Source:
Central Bank of Venezuela, *Economic Report,* (1974 data); Superintendent for Foreign Investment (SIEX), (1984 data).

NOTES TO TABLE A6

1 Figures estimated by applying percentage sectoral distribution according to the SIEX data, to the stock figure of 1984 (Table A2).

2 Including fishing.

3 Rubber, plastics, coal and petroleum products are included under 'chemicals and allied'.

Table A7

LEADING SOURCE AND RECIPIENT COUNTRIES, 1974 - 84 (Bol m)

	Inward Investment		Outward Investment
	1974	*1984*[1]	
DEVELOPED AREAS	13,950	28,089.5	
Europe	3,343	6,793.0	
EEC of which:	3,212	4,018.2	
Belgium	4	493.1	
Denmark	2	171.4	
France	183	531.5	
W. Germany		268.3	
Italy	43	319.8	
Netherlands	1,794	522.9	
UK	1,286	1,711.2	
Other Europe of which:	131	2,774.8	
Austria		62.2	
Czechoslavakia		3.3	
Lichtenstein	*Not Separately Available*	0.2	
Malta		25.7	
Norway		0.9	
Portugal		30.1	
Spain		387.3	*Not Available*
Sweden	80	416.5	
Switzerland	51	1,848.1	
Turkey		0.5	
North America of which:	10,607	20,281.9	
Canada	420	1,906.5	
USA	10,187	18,375.4	
Other developed countries of which:		1,014.6	
Japan		1,011.0	
South Africa	*N.S.A.*	3.6	
DEVELOPING AREAS	842	4,129.1	
Africa of which:	26	22.1	
Liberia	26	22.1	
Asia & Pacific of which:	*N.S.A.*	3.4	
Hong Kong	*N.S.A.*	3.4	
Latin America of which:	816	3,987.5	
Argentina	7	110.8	
Bahamas	*N.S.A.*	239.0	
Bermuda	*N.S.A.*	143.9	

Table A7 (cont'd)

LEADING SOURCE AND RECIPIENT COUNTRIES, 1974 - 84 (Bol m)

	Inward Investment			Outward Investment
	1974	*1984*[1]		
DEVELOPING AREAS (cont'd)				
Brazil	*Not Separately Available*	9.6		*Not Available*
Chile		3.0		
Colombia		210.2		
Costa Rica		7.9		
Guatemala		1.7		
Mexico		49.7		
Netherlands Antilles	36			
Panama	747	2,330.9		
Paraguay	*Not Separately Available*	1.1		
Peru		53.0		
Puerto Rico		10.3		
Trinidad & Tobago		4.5		
Uruguay	26	44.4		
Venezuela		797.5[2]		
Middle East of which:	*Not Separately Available*	86.1		
Israel		14.4		
Lebanon		71.7		
UNSPECIFIED	1,377	1,027.4		
TOTAL	16,169	33,246.0		

Source:

Central Bank of Venezuela, *Economic Report,* (1974 data); Superintendent for Foreign Investments (SIEX), (1984 data).

NOTES TO TABLE A7

1 Estimated by applying percentage geographical distribution according to the SIEX data, to the stock figure of 1984.

2 FDI from foreign residents in Venezuela.

Table A8

INDICATORS OF THE SIGNIFICANCE OF INWARD FOREIGN DIRECT INVESTMENT OR THE ACTIVITIES OF FOREIGN-BASED COMPANIES TO THE NATIONAL ECONOMY, 1974 - 82

1	Direct capital stock of foreign affiliates at book value in 1982 as a proportion of:	
	a GNP at factor cost	10.01
	b population (in BoI per head)	1,787.45
2	Foreign investment as a percentage of domestic investment 1978 - 80	0.9
3	Output of foreign affiliates in 1975 as a percentage of all companies' output in secondary (ie, manufacturing) industry	35.90
4	Percentage share of assets accounted for by foreign affiliates in selected sectors, 1974	
		Assets[1]
	Manufacturing Sector	
	Food & drink	25.23
	Chemicals & allied[2]	19.21
	Metals	2.73
	Mechanical engineering	33.09
	Electrical equipment	53.00
	Motor vehicles	39.06
	Other transportation equipment	0.38
	Textiles and clothing	25.15
	Paper & allied	27.16
	Rubber	71.10
	Stone, glass & clay	1.60
	Coal & petroleum products[3]	9.37
	Timber & furniture	13.04
	Other manufacturing	25.29

Source:

R Jenkins, *Transnational Corporations and Industrial Transformation in Latin America,* London: Macmillan, 1984; IMF, *International Financial Statistics Yearbook, 1984;* Superintendent for Foreign Investment (SIEX); OCIE, *Encuesta Industrial, 1974.*

NOTES TO TABLE A8

1 Represents share of FDI in each industry to total subscribed capital in the sector. FDI is defined as subscribed capital by foreigners.

2 Industrial chemicals.

3 Represents refining of petroleum. The manufacture of miscellaneous products of petroleum and coal is nil.

Table A12

LEADING FOREIGN MULTINATIONAL COMPANIES, 1983

	Name	*Home Country*	*Sector*
1	Alfa Laval AB	Sweden	Mechanical engineering
2	BAT Industries PLC	UK	Tobacco
3	Colgate-Palmolive Company	USA	Consumer products
4	Beecham Group PLC	UK	Pharmaceuticals
5	BF Goodrich Company	USA	Rubber tyres
6	BBC - Brown Boveri and Company	Switzerland	Electrical engineering
7	Ciba-Geigy AG	Switzerland	Chemicals
8	The Colgate-Palmolive Company	USA	Consumer productss
9	Ford Motor Company	USA	Motor vehicles and parts
10	General Motors Corp	USA	Motor vehicles
11	Goodyear Tyre and Rubber Company	USA	Rubber tyres
12	International Business Machines Corp	USA	Manufacture of office equipment and data processing equipment
13	Nabisco Brands Inc	USA	Food products
14	Procter and Gamble Company	USA	Consumer products
15	Minnesota Mining & Manufacturing Company	USA	Diversified manufacturing
16	Ing C Olivetti & C SpA	Italy	Office equipment
17	Pepsico Incorporated	USA	Beverage
18	The Wellcome Foundation	UK	Pharmaceuticals
19	Philips Petroleum Company	USA	Petroleum
20	Regie Nationale des Usines Renault	France	Motor vehicles
21	Roche / Sapac Group	Switzerland	Pharmaceuticals
22	Wang Laboratories Inc	USA	Office and data processing equipment
23	Warner - Lambert Co	USA	Pharmaceuticals
24	Unilever	UK/Netherlands	Consumer products
25	Xerox Corporation	USA	Copiers

Source:

John M Stopford, *The World Directory of Multinational Enterprises 1982–83,* Bath: The Pitman Press, 1982.

VENEZUELA : DEFINITIONS

The two main sources of data which have been used in compiling these tables are the Central Bank of Venezuela (giving data on accumulated FDI, 1950 - 1974) and the Superintendent for Foreign Investment – SIEX – (providing data on FDI as registered by the SIEX from 1975 onwards).

The Central Bank statistics refer to long term private foreign investment, whereby FDI are defined as investments made in Venezuela, but controlled abroad.

The SIEX statistics refer only to FDI registered by the SIEX, according to a more broad definition whereby FDI include paid capital, profit or loss, legal reserve, reserve for reinvestments, and reinvestments and increases of capital previously authorised and registered. In compiling these tables we have estimated that the SIEX data reflects 30.5% of the total FDI stock, by means of applying the average growth trend of the SIEX stock series to calculate a stock for 1974 which was thus expressed as a proportion of the Central Bank stock figure of that year.

MIDDLE EAST

SAUDI ARABIA

There is little information about the investment position of Saudi Arabia; official foreign investment statistics are unavailable. The flows of inward investment to Saudi Arabia fluctuated widely until 1981; since then there has been a sustained and substantial inflow of new investment.

The 1983 Annual Report of the Saudi Arabian Monetary Agency indicated that 51% out of the 2700 industrial projects in production or planned as of the end of 1982, were organised as Saudi/foreign joint ventures, and had foreign equity participation averaging 48%. Table A6 indicates that within the manufacturing sector, the emphasis lies on metals and machinery, construction materials and petro-chemicals. Foreign interests are also significant in oil and the services sector, notably construction and finance.

The main source of foreign direct investment to Saudi Arabia is other Arab countries and the USA. Japan and the UK follow at considerable distance. The great majority of the investments take the form of joint ventures, and often (particularly in the case of Arab investment) there is some public sector involvement.

MAIN SOURCES OF DATA:

A **Official**

1 Ministry of Industry and Electricity: provides data on the cumulative authorised capital in Saudi/foreign joint-ventures by sectoral distribution.

2 US Department of Commerce International Trade Administration, *Investment Climate in Foreign Countries,* Washington, 1985.

B **Private**

1 Jeffrey B Nugent, *Arab Multinationals: Problems, Potential and Policies,* paper presented to Conference in 'Third World Multinationals as New Actors in the World Economy', Hamburg, Nov 1985.

Note:
Data do not allow us to complete Tables A9, A10 and A11 for Saudi Arabia.

Table A1

SUMMARY OF THE COUNTRY'S INTERNATIONAL INVESTMENT POSITION

		Inward Investment	Outward Investment
1	Number of foreign affiliates in host country, and of foreign affiliates of home country firms at the end of 1980	137[1]	*N.A.*
2	Number of foreign firms with direct investments in host country, and home country firms with direct foreign affiliates	*N.A.*	*N.A.*
3	Total foreign direct capital stock at book value as a percentage of GNP at factor cost in 1983	15.24	*N.A.*
4	Flow of foreign direct investment in the five year period, 1979-83 (Riyal bn)	57.40	*N.A.*
5	Employment in foreign affiliates or abroad	*N.A.*	*N.A.*
6	Output of foreign affiliates or abroad	*N.A.*	*N.A.*

Source:

UNCTC, *Transnational Corporations in World Development: Third Survey,* New York, 1983; IMF, *International Financial Statistics Yearbook, 1984;* IMF, *Balance of Payments Statistics Yearbook, 1984.*

NOTES TO TABLE A1

1 Represents affiliates of MNEs from selected home countries as identified by UNCTC, 1983.

Table A2

PRIVATE FOREIGN CAPITAL STOCK, 1975 - 84 (Riyal bn)

	Inward Investment			Outward Investment		
	Portfolio	*Direct*	*Total*	*Portfolio*	*Direct*	*Total*
Book value of capital stock[1]						
1975		2.29				
1978	*Not*	0.83	*Not*		*Not Available*	
1981	*Available*	7.53	*Available*			
1984		81.53				

Source:
UNCTC, *Transnational Corporation in World Development: Third Survey,* New York, 1983; IMF, *Balance of Payments Statistics Yearbook, 1984.*

NOTES TO TABLE A2

1 Stock figures for 1981 and 1984 have been estimated by adding cumulative investment flows to UNCTC stock figure of 1978.

Table A3

FLOW OF FOREIGN DIRECT INVESTMENT, 1970 - 84 (Riyal bn)

	Inward Investment			Outward Investment		
	Reinvested Profits	*Other*	*Total*[1]	*Reinvested Profits*	*Other*	*Total*
1970			0.1			
1971			-0.5			
1972			0.1			
1973			-2.5			
1974			-16.2			
1975			6.0			
1976	*Not*		-1.4		*Not*	
1977	*Separately*		2.9		*Available*	
1978	*Available*		1.9			
1979			-4.6			
1980			-10.4			
1981			21.7			
1982			38.2			
1983			17.4			
1984			18.4			

Source:
IMF, *Balance of Payments Statistics Yearbook,* various issues.

NOTES TO TABLE A3

1 Excluding re-invested earnings.

Table A4

SECTORAL DISTRIBUTION OF FOREIGN DIRECT CAPITAL STOCK, 1982 (Riyal m)[1]

	Inward Investment[1]			Outward Investment		
	Primary	*Secondary*	*Tertiary*	*Primary*	*Secondary*	*Tertiary*
1982	*N.A.*	32,264	*N.A.*	*Not Available*		

Source:

Ministry of Industry and Electricity, Saudi Arabia, data as cited in the US Department of Commerce, *Investment Climate in Foreign Countries,* Washington, 1983.

NOTES TO TABLE A4

1 Refers to cumulative authorised capital in Saudi/foreign joint-ventures in production within the manufacturing sector. Total does not therefore match Table A2; the remainder is concentrated in oil & services, particularly construction.

Table A5

GEOGRAPHICAL DISTRIBUTION OF FOREIGN DIRECT CAPITAL STOCK, 1981 (Riyal m)

	Inward Investment			Outward Investment		
	Developed Countries	*Other Countries*	*Total*	*Developed Countries*	*Developing Countries*	*Total*
1981	2,876.2[1]	4,640.0[2]	7,516.2[3]	*Not Available*		

Source:

UK Department of Trade and Industry, 'Census of Overseas Assets, 1981', *Business Monitor,* Supplement, 1981; US Department of Commerce, *Survey of Current Business,* November, 1984; Ministry of Finance, Japan, data as cited in F Marsh, *Japanese Overseas Investment,* EIU, 1983

NOTES TO TABLE A5

1 Including UK, US & Japanese investment only.
2 Thought to be mainly from other Arab countries.
3 Estimated by adding cumulative investment flow, 1979-81, to the UNCTC stock figure for 1978.

Table A6

INDUSTRIAL DISTRIBUTION OF FOREIGN DIRECT CAPITAL STOCK, 1982 (Riyal m)[1]

	Inward Investment[1]	Outward Investment
	1982	
Primary	*N.S.A.*	
Secondary	32,264	
Food & drink	3,763	
Chemicals & allied[2]	6,543	
Metals } Mechanical engineering }	7,060	*Not Available*
Textiles & clothing	265	
Paper & allied	897	
Stone, clay & glass	12,928	
Other manufacturing	808	
Tertiary	*N.A.*	
TOTAL	45,700	

Source:
Ministry of Industry and Electricity, Saudi Arabia, data as cited in the US Department of Commerce, *Investment Climate in Foreign Countries,* Washington, 1983.

NOTES TO TABLE A6

1 Refers to cumulative authorised capital in Saudi/foreign joint-ventures in production within the manufacturing sector. Total is estimated from cumulative investment flows; the remainder is concentrated in oil and services, particularly construction.

2 Rubber and plastics are included under 'chemicals and allied'.

Table A7

LEADING SOURCE AND RECIPIENT COUNTRIES, 1981 (Riyal m)

	Inward Investment	Outward Investment
	1981	
DEVELOPED AREAS[1]	2,876.2	
Europe:		
UK	168.1	
North America:		*Not Available*
USA	2,134.4	
Other developed countries		
Japan	573.7	
UNSPECIFIED	4,640.0[2]	
TOTAL	7,516.2[3]	

Source:
UK Department of Trade and Industry, 'Census of Overseas Assets, 1981', *Business Monitor,* Supplement, 1981; US Department of Commerce, *Survey of Current Business,* November 1984; Ministry of Finance, Japan, data as cited in F Marsh, *Japanese Overseas Investment,* EIU, 1983.

NOTES TO TABLE A7

1 Including only those countries shown below.
2 Thought to be mainly from other Arab countries.
3 Estimated by adding cumulative investment flow, 1979-81, to the UNCTC stock figure for 1978.

Table A8

INDICATORS OF THE SIGNIFICANCE OF INWARD FOREIGN DIRECT INVESTMENT OR THE ACTIVITIES OF FOREIGN-BASED COMPANIES TO THE NATIONAL ECONOMY, 1983

1	Direct capital stock of foreign affiliates at book value in 1983 as a proportion of:	
	a GNP at factor cost	15.24
	b population (in Riyal per head)	5,585.41

Source:
UNCTC, *Transnational Corporations in World Development: Third Survey,* New York: UN, 1983; IMF, *Balance of Payments Statistics Yearbook, 1984;* IMF, *International Financial Statistics Yearbook, 1984.*

Table A12

LEADING FOREIGN MULTINATIONAL COMPANIES, 1983

Name	*Home Country*	*Sector*
Asea AB	Sweden	Electrical equipment
BICC PLC	UK	Electrical energy
BOC Group PLC	UK	Industrial gases
Ciba-Geigy AG	Switzerland	Chemicals
Dresser Industries Inc	USA	High technology products
AB Electrolux	Sweden	Electrical equipment
Granges AB	Sweden	Metals
Norton Company	USA	Industrial consumables
Owens-Corning Fiberglas Corporation	USA	Manufacture of glass fibre
Procter and Gamble Company	USA	Consumer products
Royal Dutch/Shell Group of Companies	UK	Petroleum
Texaco Incorporated	USA	Petroleum
Westinghouse Electric Corporation	USA	Electrical equipment
Wheelabrator-Frye Inc	USA	Engineering

Source:
John M Stopford, *The World Directory of Multinational Enterprises 1982-83* Bath: The Pitman Press, 1983.

Part B
Comparative Tables

INTRODUCTION TO THE COMPARATIVE TABLES

From the wealth of data set out in the individual country tables, we have chosen to make a limited number of cross country comparisons. In later editions of this Directory, we hope to expand this part of our work.

Table B1 sets out a comparison of the foreign direct capital stock of the 80 countries for three years viz. 1975, 1982 and 1983; and Tables B2 and B3 the distribution of this capital stock by main economic sector for 1975 and 1982. The following two tables provide data on the geographical distribution of the foreign capital stake for the same years. Table B6 then presents a couple of indicators of the importance of inward and outward capital stock viz. their relationship to gross national product (GNP) and population. The data suggest the great variability of the role played by foreign and domestic MNEs in the economies of the countries considered: they also show that inward investment plays a relatively more significant role in the case of the developing countries and outward investment in the case of developed countries.

Table B7 and B9 then give details of the annual flow of outward and inward investment over the past decade or so. *Inter alia*, the Tables reveal the fall in the value of international direct investment since 1981. This is mainly due to the decline of the US as a major outward investor and the debt crisis, particularly as faced by the major Latin American economies.

The last group of Tables (B10–18) set out some comparative data in a rather different way. Table B10, for example, lists the countries which are the largest outward direct investors in 1975 and 1983; Table B11 the largest inward direct investors; and Table B12 for the largest *net* debtor countries. The countries most dependent on outward and inward direct investment are set out in Tables B13 and 14; while the following two Tables present the distribution of the world stock of outward and inward foreign direct investment by major region and countries. Tables B17 and 18 complete this section of the Directory by setting out the annual average flows of outward and inward direct investment by region.

Most of the data presented in these Tables relate to years up to 1984, and in some cases only to 1982. While in the case of some countries, there are data available beyond these dates, in others there are not; because of this the comparative Tables are inevitably a little dated. In subsequent editions, however, we hope to reduce the time lag between the receipt of these data and the publication of the Directory.

Table B1

TOTAL FOREIGN DIRECT CAPITAL STOCK, 1975 - 83 (US $ m)

	Inward Investment			Outward Investment		
	1975	*1982*	*1983*	*1975*	*1982*	*1983*
DEVELOPED AREAS	183,399.4	384,039.9	401,084.8	268,817.3	564,875.2	575,599.9
Europe	98,710.6	165,038.1	159,696.0	117,361.3	252,954.1	249,466.4
EEC	85,555.3	142,933.3	138,308.1	88,680.4	200,334.8	197,518.3
Belgium	4,176.8	9,850.8	9,085.2	3,038.4	4,603.6	4,211.0
Denmark	1,396.7	1,713.4	1,514.1	458.0	1,035.3	971.0
France	9,497.3	14,805.9	13,426.1	10,607.5	19,307.1	17,242.3
W. Germany	23,075.2	32,131.3	29,587.3	14,353.8	40,143.1	38,934.6
Greece	1,039.2	4,401.1	4,840.5	*Not Available*		
Ireland	2,953.3	3,392.8	2,909.8			
Italy	9,113.5	7,376.6	7,320.3	3,298.7	8,115.3	8,495.3
Netherlands	9,812.9	17,975.2	16,924.5	19,922.3	39,737.5	39,120.9
United Kingdom	24,490.4	51,286.2	52,700.3	37,001.7	87,392.9	88,543.2
Other Europe	13,155.3	22,104.8	21,387.9	28,680.9	52,619.3	51,948.1
Austria	1,811.0	2,969.1	2,745.5	*N.A.*	675.9	755.9
Finland	347.5	421.9	399.3	307.0	891.9	1,062.0
Norway	1,541.6	3,491.6	3,436.8	728.7	1,348.2	1,565.6
Portugal	302.8	389.8	292.5	91.6	59.6	55.7
Spain	2,909.3	4,538.4	4,789.2	440.5	1,176.7	1,215.3
Sweden	1,426.6	1,530.5	1,423.6	4,670.4	6,331.1	6,761.4
Switzerland	4,084.0	8,373.0	8,029.4	22,442.7	42,135.9	40,532.2
Turkey	564.9	179.8	155.3	*Not Available*		
Yugoslavia	167.6	210.7	116.3			
North America	64,447.7	180,964.6	196,985.5	134,406.2	249,389.0	255,757.4
Canada	36,785.7	56,287.6	59,924.5	10,356.2	27,546.0	28,795.4
United States	27,662.0	124,677.0	137,061.0	124,050.0	221,843.0	226,962.0
Other Developed Countries	20,241.1	38,037.2	44,403.3	17,049.8	62,532.1	70,376.1
Australia	8,846.2	15,647.4	16,138.2	1,108.8	2,741.8	2,997.9
Japan	1,497.0	4,157.0	4,974.0	15,941.0	53,131.0	61,276.0
New Zealand	1,353.4	2,308.0	2,250.0	*N.A.*	387.9	422.5
S. Africa	8,544.5	15,924.8	21,041.1	*N.A.*	6,271.4	5,679.7
DEVELOPING AREAS	59,439.5	129,466.7	139,460.0	120.3	6,774.8	6,162.9
Africa (except S. Africa)	15,445.2	19,296.7	19,271.1	11.8	296.3	332.9
Botswana	59.6	335.2	330.4	*Not Available*		
Cameroon	300.0	805.6	1,017.6			
Central African Republic	60.0	138.8	141.0			
Congo	345.6	330.7	317.7			
Egypt	*N.A.*	3,444.6	4,308.4			
Gabon	620.0	1,052.9	1,164.7			
Ghana	300.0	294.0	27.1			
Ivory Coast	491.8	1,023.3	923.6			

Table B1 (cont'd)

TOTAL FOREIGN DIRECT CAPITAL STOCK, 1975 - 83 (US $ m)

	Inward Investment			Outward Investment		
	1975	*1982*	*1983*	*1975*	*1982*	*1983*
Kenya	332.8	499.4	512.2	*N.A.*	10.7	18.4
Liberia	*N.A.*	874.3	888.6		*Not Available*	
Libya	704.6	606.0	279.0	*N.A.*	203.0	230.8
Malawi	*N.A.*	375.0	375.0			
Mauritius	22.0	64.5	66.1			
Morocco	202.2	715.7	629.4		*Not Available*	
Nigeria	7,384.1	3,546.5	3,517.4			
Senegal	300.0	355.5	367.5			
Seychelles	10.0	52.2	58.6	*N.A.*	24.7	29.4
Sierra Leone	99.9	79.5	40.3		*Not Available*	
Tanzania	140.0	215.8	227.2			
Togo	90.0	240.2	276.6	2.6	*N.A.*	*N.A.*
Zaire	996.1	1,798.4	1,936.7		*Not Available*	
Zambia	200.0	492.1	527.7			
Zimbabwe	2,786.5	1,956.5	1,631.6	9.2	57.9	54.3
Asia & Pacific (except Japan or M. East)	13,039.0	26,280.3	28,120.8	49.6	4,033.3	3,066.4
Bangladesh	59.5	86.9	87.3			
China	*N.A.*	1,770.0	1,800.0		*Not Available*	
Hong Kong	1,300.0	4,327.8	4,720.3	*N.A.*	2,150.0	2,540.0
India	2,163.9	*N.A.*	*N.A.*	*N.A.*	126.0	140.0
Indonesia	2,285.2	4,645.2	4,990.6		*Not Available*	
S. Korea	569.1	1,143.2	1,269.3	49.6	289.6	386.4
Malaysia	2,300.0	6,816.1	8,075.1	*N.A.*	17.7	*N.A.*
Pakistan	750.0	837.8	868.8		*Not Available*	
Philippines	485.2	1,934.7	1,985.7	*Not Available*	150.0	*Not Available*
Singapore	1,866.4	2,215.3	1,435.8		1,235.0	
Sri Lanka	60.0	224.9	227.3		*N.A.*	
Taiwan	694.2	945.1	979.1		65.0	
Thailand	505.5	1,333.3	1,681.5		*Not Available*	
Latin America & Caribbean	29,386.6	68,836.7	73,246.2	56.1	2,367.5	2,690.9
Argentina	2,284.0	6,780.0	7,233.0	18.0	144.0	142.0
Barbados	160.0	199.6	217.3	*Not Available*	7.0	8.4
Brazil	6,890.0	21,640.0	23,200.0		1,830.0	2,010.0
Chile	421.4	1,863.0	2,045.0		100.9	140.5
Colombia	965.0	2,111.6	2,729.5	38.1	285.2	390.0
Dominican Republic	391.3	775.7	823.9			
Ecuador	500.0	679.6	935.2		*Not Available*	
Guyana	180.0	199.3	204.0			
Jamaica	969.9	885.3	487.5			

Table B1 (cont'd)

TOTAL FOREIGN DIRECT CAPITAL STOCK, 1975 - 83 (US $ m)

	Inward Investment			Outward Investment		
	1975	*1982*	*1983*	*1975*	*1982*	*1983*
Mexico	4,800.0	14,443.9	14,898.2	*N.A.*	0.4	*N.A.*
Panama	5,081.7	5,413.8	5,463.0			
Paraguay	70.0	260.3	265.2			
Peru	1,700.0	2,696.0	2,733.0		*Not Available*	
Trinidad & Tobago	1,199.9	3,368.0	3,653.0			
Uruguay	*N.A.*	883.0	1,066.8			
Venezuela	3,773.4	6,637.6	7,291.6			
Middle East:						
Saudi Arabia	650.0	13.287.2	16,940.0			
Australasia	918.7	1,765.8	1,881.9	2.8	77.7	72.7
Fiji	272.3	367.3	365.1	2.8	3.9	3.6
Papua New Guinea	646.4	1,398.5	1,516.8	*N.A.*	73.8	69.1
TOTAL	242,838.9	513,544.8	540,544.8	268,937.6	571,320.0	579,228.8[1]

NOTE TO TABLE B1

1 Excluding from the 1983 totals, the foreign direct capital stock of 5 developing countries included in the equivalent 1982 totals due to the non-availability of data. The combined stock of these countries in 1982 was US $ 1,468.1 million.

Table B2

SECTORAL DISTRIBUTION OF FOREIGN DIRECT CAPITAL STOCK, 1975 (US $ m)

	Inward Investment			Outward Investment		
	Primary	*Secondary*	*Tertiary*	*Primary*	*Secondary*	*Tertiary*
DEVELOPED AREAS	34,824.0	79,943.9	48,672.1	60,696.5	108,715.8	67,668.2
Europe	12,636.4	48,066.0	26,593.3	21,110.8	41,853.1	22,660.6
EEC	12,539.1	43,488.6	24,138.4	21,053.0	41,688.3	22,442.7
Belgium[1]	625.2	3,126.2	425.4		*Not Available*	
France	244.2	3,393.2	5,859.9	2,219.1	4,088.2	4,300.2
W. Germany	87.7	15,252.7	7,734.8	575.6	8,676.9	5,101.3
Italy	1,073.0	5,206.7	2,833.8	878.6	1,177.2	1,242.9
Netherlands[2]	2,742.1	4,380.5	2,690.3	6,212.8	10,790.8	2,918.7
United Kingdom	7,766.9	12,129.3	4,594.2	11,166.9	16,955.2	8,879.6
Other Europe	97.3	4,577.4	2,454.9	57.8	164.8	217.9
Austria	*neg.*	884.7	926.3			
Norway	25.8	822.6	693.2		*Not Available*	
Portugal	11.8	171.0	120.0			
Spain	54.1	2,218.9	636.3	57.8	164.8	217.9
Turkey	5.6	480.2	79.1		*Not Available*	
North America	19,953.7	27,126.8	17,367.2	34,704.2	61,115.3	38,586.7
Canada	12,030.7	15,740.8	9,014.2	2,184.2	5,229.3	2,942.7
United States	7,923.0	11,386.0	8,353.0	32,520.0	55,586.0	35,644.0
Other Developed Countries	2,233.9	4,751.1	4,711.6	4,881.5	5,747.4	6,420.9
Australia	1,968.6	3,038.4	3,839.2	202.5	385.4	520.9
Japan	234.0	986.0	277.0	4,679.0	5,362.0	5,900.0
New Zealand	31.3	726.7	595.4		*Not Available*	
DEVELOPING AREAS	10,014.7	19,907.4	7,469.7	*N.A.*	10.9	27.2
Africa (except S. Africa)	4,191.2	2,598.7	1,246.4			
Morocco	26.8	78.8	96.6			
Nigeria	4,164.4	2,519.9	1,149.8			
Asia & Pacific (except Japan or Middle East)	1,096.1	4,455.2	2,324.0		*Not Available*	
India	341.1	1,195.2	627.6			
Indonesia	585.9	1,425.4	273.9			
South Korea	9.0	459.7	100.4			
Philippines	83.9	236.3	165.0			
Singapore	*neg.*	987.3	879.1			
Thailand	76.2	151.3	278.0			

Table B2 (cont'd)

SECTORAL DISTRIBUTION OF FOREIGN DIRECT CAPITAL STOCK, 1975 (US $ m)

	Inward Investment			Outward Investment		
	Primary	*Secondary*	*Tertiary*	*Primary*	*Secondary*	*Tertiary*
Latin America & Caribbean	4,185.0	12,816.9	3,831.9	*N.A.*	10.9	27.2
Argentina	134.1	1,561.7	588.2			
Brazil	176.4	5,400.5	1,313.1		*Not Available*	
Chile	71.2	234.3	115.9			
Colombia	347.4	426.5	191.1	*neg.*	10.9	27.2
Mexico	196.8	3,723.6	879.6			
Peru	1,348.0	240.0	112.0			
Venezuela	1,911.1	1,230.3	632.0		*Not Available*	
Australasia	542.4	36.6	67.4			
Papua New Guinea	542.4	36.6	67.4			
TOTAL	44,838.7	99,851.3	56,141.8	60,696.5	108,726.7	67,695.4

NOTES TO TABLE B2

1 Figures for primary investment are authors' estimate based on US sources.

2 Netherlands industrial distribution represent authors' estimate.

Table B3

SECTORAL DISTRIBUTION OF FOREIGN DIRECT CAPITAL STOCK, 1982 (US $ m)

	Inward Investment			Outward Investment		
	Primary	*Secondary*	*Tertiary*	*Primary*	*Secondary*	*Tertiary*
DEVELOPED AREAS	70,165.3	164,374.0	141,127.5	132,332.1	214,163.3	163,886.2
Europe	25,898.8	78,346.5	52,419.7	50,678.7	92,877.0	61,564.1
EEC	25,292.0	70,759.7	46,881.6	49,574.3	88,427.0	56,694.6
Belgium	1,398.4	6,991.9	1,460.5		*Not Available*	
Denmark	60.2	1,027.3	625.9			
France	236.9	5,478.2	9,090.8	5,270.8	6,718.9	7,317.4
W. Germany	96.4	17,816.8	14,218.1	1,754.3	23,295.0	15,093.8
Greece	126.6	3,109.2	1,165.3		*Not Available*	
Ireland	117.0	2,538.4	737.4			
Italy	690.5	3,842.3	2,843.8	1,803.6	3,694.2	2,617.5
Netherlands[1]	4,092.1	6,378.0	7,505.1	13,900.5	17,187.8	8,649.2
United Kingdom	18,473.9	23,577.6	9,234.7	26,845.1	37,531.1	23,016.7
Other Europe	606.8	7,586.8	5,538.1	1,104.4	4,450.0	4,869.5
Austria	*neg.*	1,648.7	1,320.4	*neg.*	320.4	355.5
Finland	0.3	104.0	317.6	11.7	405.6	474.6
Norway[2]	271.9	1,339.5	1,880.2	*neg.*	533.3	815.0
Portugal	17.5	206.1	166.2		*Not Available*	
Spain	101.8	3,213.9	1,222.6	136.1	365.8	674.8
Sweden[1]	186.5	803.0	541.0	956.6	2,824.9	2,549.6
Turkey	4.5	109.5	65.8		*Not Available*	
Yugoslavia	24.3	162,1	24.3			
North America	38,985.0	65,902.7	76,076.9	70,848.9	103,449.9	75,090.2
Canada	18,400.0	21,837.7	16,049.9	7,716.9	12,840.9	6,988.2
United States	20,585.0	44,065.0	60,027.0	63,132.0	90,609.0	68,102.0
Other Developed Countries	5,281.5	20,124.8	12,630.9	10,804.5	17,836.4	27,231.9
Australia	3,675.3	4,684.3	7,287.8	581.5	892.4	1,267.9
Japan	492.0	2,640.0	1,025.0	10,223.0	16,944.0	25,964.0
New Zealand	35.7	1,074.4	1,197.9		*Not Available*	
South Africa	1,078.5	11,726.1	3,120.2			
DEVELOPING AREAS	26,664.9	63,936.7	27,544.5	571.4	1,247.2	811.9
Africa (except S. Africa)	6,697.0	3,619.7	2,549.2			
Botswana[1]	310.2	12.5	12.5			
Cameroon	85.4	718.6	1.6			
Central African Republic	47.0	56.6	35.2		*Not Available*	
Congo	70.6	94.8	165.3			
Egypt	2,983.9	105.3	355.4			
Gabon	736.6	299.2	17.1			
Ivory Coast	192.6	481.6	349.1			
Kenya	71.4	252.2	175.8			
Liberia	633.5	120.4	120.4			

Table B3 (cont'd)

SECTORAL DISTRIBUTION OF FOREIGN DIRECT CAPITAL STOCK, 1982 (US $ m)

	Inward Investment			Outward Investment		
	Primary	*Secondary*	*Tertiary*	*Primary*	*Secondary*	*Tertiary*
Libya	573.6	17.3	15.1			
Malawi	206.0	123.0	46.0			
Morocco	80.4	244.7	310.6		*Not Available*	
Tanzania[1]	17.9	156.9	41.0			
Zambia[1]	69.4	257.5	165.2			
Zimbabwe	618.5	679.1	658.9			
Asia & Pacific (except Japan or Middle East)	2,889.9	11,751.3	9,230.1	522.8	1,163.1	699.7
China	29.3	886.8	853.9		*Not Available*	
Hong Kong	113.9	1,435.3	2,778.6	342.2	963.0	514.8
India		*Not Available*		2.4	103.2	20.4
Indonesia	1,176.0	2,996.7	472.5		*Not Available*	
S. Korea	13.8	880.3	249.1	149.4	33.5	106.7
Malaysia[1]	797.5	4,133.3	1,885.3		*Not Available*	
Pakistan	12.7	334.5	490.6			
Philippines	516.6	911.2	506.9	28.8	63.4	57.8
Singapore	*neg.*	1,083.3	1,132.0			
Sri Lanka	3.4	89.8	131.7		*Not Available*	
Taiwan	*neg.*	881.4	63.7			
Thailand	226.7	440.8	665.8			
Latin America & Caribbean	13,950.6	39,106.4	14,697.4	48.6	84.1	112.2
Argentina	1,825.0	3,219.7	1,735.3	48.6	75.3	20.1
Barbados[1]	39.8	53.3	106.5		*Not Available*	
Brazil	865.3	18,249.3	2,525.4			
Chile	770.1	469.5	623.4	*neg.*	8.8	92.1
Colombia[1]	530.3	1,051.0	530.3			
Dominican Republic	61.8	355.9	358.0			
Ecuador	49.2	410.2	220.2			
Jamaica	176.6	236.2	472.5			
Mexico	317.8	11,308.9	2,817.2		*Not Available*	
Panama	1,108.7	506.4	3,798.7			
Paraguay	38.1	116.5	105.7			
Peru	1,878.1	494.4	323.5			
Trinidad & Tobago	3,114.7	184.4	68.9			
Venezuela	3,175.1	2,450.7	1,011.8			
Middle East	3,115.6	9,392.7	778.9			
Saudi Arabia	3,115.6	9,392.7	778.9			
Australasia	11.8	66.6	288.9			
Fiji	11.8	66.6	288.9			
TOTAL	96,830.2	228,310.7	168,672.0	132,903.5	215,410.5	164,698.1

NOTES TO TABLE B3

1 The industrial distribution represent authors' estimate.

2 The industrial distribution of outward investment represent authors' estimate.

Table B4

GEOGRAPHICAL DISTRIBUTION OF FOREIGN DIRECT CAPITAL STOCK, 1975 (US $ m)

	Inward Investment			Outward Investment		
	Developed Countries	*Developing Countries*	*Total*	*Developed Countries*	*Developing Countries*	*Total*
DEVELOPED AREAS	147,549.0	8,656.2	156,205.2	176,748.8	57,033.0	233,781.8
Europe	75,778.1	4,282.8	80,060.9	65,072.1	17,253.7	82,325.8
EEC	70,871.2	4,173.9	75,045.1	64,828.1	17,057.2	81,885.3
Belgium[1]	3,819.3	357.5	4,176.8		*Not Available*	
France	8,400.7	1,096.6	9,497.3	7,848.0	2,759.5	10,607.5
W. Germany	22,610.0	465.2	23,075.2	11,490.9	2,862.9	14,353.8
Greece	883.3	155.9	1,039.2		*Not Available*	
Ireland	2,953.3	*neg.*	2,953.3			
Netherlands	8,878.5	934.4	9,812.9	16,144.0	3,778.3	19,922.3
United Kingdom	23,326.1	1,164.3	24,490.4	29,345.2	7,656.5	37,001.7
Other Europe	4,906.9	108.9	5,015.8	244.0	196.5	440.5
Norway	1,539.3	2.3	1,541.6		*Not Available*	
Spain	2,836.4	72.9	2,909.3	244.0	196.5	440.5
Turkey	531.2	33.7	564.9		*Not Available*	
North America	60,754.4	3,693.3	64,447.7	103,994.7	30,411.5	134,406.2
Canada	36,191.4	594.3	36,785.7	7,822.7	2,533.5	10,356.2
United States	24,563.0	3,099.0	27,662.0	96,172.0	27,878.0	124,050.0
Other Developed Countries	11,016.5	680.1	11,696.6	7,682.0	9,367.8	17,049.8
Australia	8,242.3	630.9	8,846.2	606.0	502.8	1,108.8
Japan	1,468.0	29.0	1,497.0	7,076.0	8,865.0	15,941.0
New Zealand	1,306.2	47.2	1,353.4		*Not Available*	
DEVELOPING AREAS	34,836.5	3,837.6	38,674.1	22.0	27.6	49.6
Africa (except S. Africa)	7,147.8	258.3	7,406.1			
Mauritius	22.0	*neg.*	22.0		*Not Available*	
Nigeria	7,125.8	258.3	7,384.1			
Asia & Pacific (except Japan or Middle East)	7,199.9	1,490.2	8,690.1	22.0	27.6	49.6
Hong Kong	1,176.6	123.4	1,300.0			
India	1,878.9	285.0	2,163.9		*Not Available*	
Indonesia	1,941.2	344.0	2,285.2			
S. Korea	510.3	58.8	569.1	22.0	27.6	49.6
Singapore	1,268.5	597.9	1,866.4		*Not Available*	
Thailand	424.4	81.1	505.5			

Table B4 (cont'd)

GEOGRAPHICAL DISTRIBUTION OF FOREIGN DIRECT CAPITAL STOCK, 1975 (US $ m)

	Inward Investment			Outward Investment		
	Developed Countries	*Developing Countries*	*Total*	*Developed Countries*	*Developing Countries*	*Total*
Latin America & Caribbean	19,881.4	2,050.1	21,931.5			
Brazil	5,785.5	1,104.5	6,890.0			
Chile	393.6	27.8	421.4			
Colombia	828.6	136.4	965.0		*Not Available*	
Mexico	4,233.4	566.6	4,800.0			
Panama	5,081.7	*neg.*	5,081.7			
Venezuela	3,558.6	214.8	3,773.4			
Australasia	607.4	39.0	646.4			
Papua New Guinea	607.4	39.0	646.4			
TOTAL	182,385.5	12,493.8	194,879.3	176,770.8	57,060.6	233,831.4

NOTES TO TABLE B4

1 Authors' estimate based on the average share of developed and developing countries in the total stock of foreign direct investment in EEC countries.

Table B5

GEOGRAPHICAL DISTRIBUTION OF FOREIGN DIRECT CAPITAL STOCK, 1982 (US $ m)

	Inward Investment			Outward Investment		
	Developed Countries	*Developing Countries*	*Total*	*Developed Countries*	*Developing Countries*	*Total*
DEVELOPED AREAS	338,454.0	32,811.8	371,265.8	420,720.3	139,103.8	559,824.1
Europe	142,958.3	9,305.7	152,264.0	198,349.1	49,941.8	248,290.9
EEC	129,716.8	8,815.4	138,532.2	153,992.6	41,738.6	195,731.2
Belgium[1]	9,253.8	597.0	9,850.8		*Not Available*	
Denmark	1,638.0	75.4	1,713.4	730.5	304.8	1,035.3
France	13,088.4	1,717.5	14,805.9	14,499.6	4,807.5	19,307.1
W. Germany	31,267.4	863.9	32,131.3	33,602.7	6,540.4	40,143.1
Ireland	3,392.8	*neg.*	3,392.8		*Not Available*	
Italy	7,299.2	77.4	7,376.6	4,259.7	3,855.6	8,115.3
Netherlands	15,003.6	2,971.6	17,975.2	32,567.0	7,170.5	39,737.5
United Kingdom	48,773.6	2,512.6	51,286.2	68,333.1	19,059.8	87,392.9
Other Europe	13,241.5	490.3	13,731.8	44,356.5	8,203.2	52,559.7
Austria	2,959.0	10.1	2,969.1	636.3	39.6	675.9
Finland	382.0	39.9	421.9	821.0	70.9	891.9
Norway	3,405.0	86.6	3,491.6	1,145.9	202.3	1,348.2
Portugal	371.9	17.9	389.8		*Not Available*	
Spain	4,282.5	255.9	4,538.4	471.1	705.6	1,176.7
Sweden	1,492.0	38.5	1,530.5	5,350.4	980.7	6,331.1
Switzerland		*Not Available*		35,931.8	6,204.1	42,135.9
Turkey	139.5	40.3	179.8		*Not Available*	
Yugoslavia	209.6	1.1	210.7			
North America	160,492.1	20,472.5	180,964.6	191,589.7	57,799.3	249,389.0
Canada	55,078.1	1,209.5	56,287.6	23,558.7	3,987.3	27,546.0
United States	105,414.0	19,263.0	124,677.0	168,031.0	53,812.0	221,843.0
Other Developed Countries	35,003.6	3,033.6	38,037.2	30,781.5	31,362.7	62,144.2
Australia	14,035.3	1,612.1	15,647.4	1,551.3	1,190.5	2,741.8
Japan	3,900.6	256.4	4,157.0	24,817.0	28,314.0	53,131.0
New Zealand	2,225.5	82.5	2,308.0		*Not Available*	
S. Africa	14,842.2	1,082.6	15,924.8	4,413.2	1,858.2	6,271.4
DEVELOPING AREAS	105,530.2	23,369.9	128,900.1	1,091.0	927.4	2,018.4
Africa (except S. Africa)	16,640.5	2,656.2	19,296.7			
Botswana[1]	323.5	11.7	335.2			
Cameroon	788.3	17.3	805.6			
Central African Republic[1]	123.9	14.9	138.8		*Not Available*	
Congo	179.0	151.7	330.7			
Egypt	2,532.5	912.1	3,444.6			
Gabon	1,031.2	21.7	1,052.9			
Ghana[1]	280.9	13.1	294.0			
Ivory Coast	910.3	113.0	1,023.3			
Kenya[1]	485.5	13.9	499.4			

Table B5 (cont'd)

GEOGRAPHICAL DISTRIBUTION OF FOREIGN DIRECT CAPITAL STOCK, 1982 (US$ m)

	Inward Investment			Outward Investment		
	Developed Countries	*Developing Countries*	*Total*	*Developed Countries*	*Developing Countries*	*Total*
Liberia	839.9	34.4	874.3			
Libya[1]	606.0	*neg.*	606.0			
Malawi	351.0	24.0	375.0			
Mauritius	64.5	*neg.*	64.5			
Morocco[1]	622.3	93.4	715.7		*Not*	
Nigeria[1]	2,649.0	897.5	3,546.5		*Available*	
Senegal[1]	339.3	16.2	355.5			
Seychelles[1]	39.2	13.0	52.2			
Sierra Leone[1]	58.0	21.5	79.5			
Tanzania[1]	215.8	*neg.*	215.8			
Togo[1]	227.9	12.3	240.2			
Zaire[1]	1,612.8	185.6	1,798.4			
Zambia[1]	461.3	30.8	492.1			
Zimbabwe[1]	1,898.4	58.1	1,956.5			
Asia & Pacific (except Japan or Middle East)	21,312.0	4,968.3	26,280.3	1,011.0	789.6	1,800.6
Bangladesh	69.7	17.2	86.9			
China	1,225.8	544.2	1,770.0		*Not Available*	
Hong Kong	4,132,8	195.0	4,327.8			
India		*Not Available*		3.2	122.8	126.0
Indonesia[1]	3,590.1	1,055.1	4,645.2		*Not Available*	
S. Korea	1,038.8	104.4	1,143.2	182.6	107.0	289.6
Malaysia[1]	5,353.0	1,463.1	6,816.1		*Not Available*	
Pakistan[1]	753.3	84.5	837.8			
Philippines	1,747.0	187.7	1,934.7	76.2	73.8	150.0
Singapore	1,586.6	628.7	2,215.3	749.0	486.0	1,235.0
Sri Lanka	127.7	97.2	224.9			
Taiwan	598.4	346.7	945.1		*Not Available*	
Thailand	1,088.8	244.5	1,333.3			
Latin America & Caribbean	60,989.7	7,647.7	68,637.4	16.6	127.4	144.0
Argentina[1]	6,715.0	65.0	6,780.0	16.6	127.4	144.0
Barbados[1]	140.5	59.1	199.6			
Brazil	19,100.4	2,539.6	21,640.0			
Chile	1,605.9	257.1	1,863.0			
Colombia[1]	1,996.6	115.0	2,111.6		*Not*	
Dominican Republic[1]	591.9	183.8	775.7		*Available*	
Ecuador	566.2	113.4	679.6			
Jamaica	470.5	414.8	885.3			
Mexico	12,479.5	1,964.4	14,443.9			
Panama	5,413.8	*neg.*	5,413.8			
Paraguay	191.2	69.1	260.3			

Table B5 (cont'd)

GEOGRAPHICAL DISTRIBUTION OF FOREIGN DIRECT CAPITAL STOCK, 1982 (US $ m)

	Inward Investment			Outward Investment		
	Developed Countries	*Developing Countries*	*Total*	*Developed Countries*	*Developing Countries*	*Total*
Peru	2,432.2	263.8	2,696.0	*Not Available*		
Trinidad & Tobago[1]	2,757.7	610.3	3,368.0			
Uruguay	741.3	141.7	883.0			
Venezuela	5,787.0	850.6	6,637.6			
Middle East:						
Saudi Arabia	5,202.2	8,085.0	13,287.2			
Australasia	1,385.8	12.7	1,398.5	63.4	10.4	73.8
Papua New Guinea	1,385.8	12.7	1,398.5	63.4	10.4	73.8
TOTAL	443,984.2	56,181.7	500,165.9	421,811.3	140,031.2	561,842.5

NOTE TO TABLE B5

1 The geographical distribution represent authors' estimate.

Table B6

INDICATORS OF THE SIGNIFICANCE OF INWARD AND OUTWARD FOREIGN DIRECT CAPITAL STOCK TO VARIOUS NATIONAL ECONOMIES, 1982

	Inward Investment		Outward Investment	
	Capital Stock as % of GNP	*Capital Stock Per Head (US $)*	*Capital Stock as % of GNP*	*Capital Stock Per Head (US $)*
DEVELOPED AREAS	5.0	483.8	7.6	792.8
Europe	5.4	445.4	9.1	874.4
EEC	5.8	639.6	8.9	953.1
Belgium	11.8	999.7	5.5	467.4
Denmark	3.2	334.6	1.9	202.2
France	2.8	273.1	3.6	356.1
W. Germany	4.8	521.3	6.0	651.3
Greece	10.0	449.6	*Not Available*	
Ireland	20.1	974.9		
Italy	2.2	130.2	2.4	143.3
Netherlands	12.9	1,256.1	28.5	2,776.9
United Kingdom	11.4	910.3	19.5	1,551.2
Other Europe	3.9	150.3	10.0	665.3
Austria	4.4	392.2	1.0	89.3
Finland	0.9	87.5	2.0	185.0
Norway	7.1	849.5	2.7	328.0
Portugal	2.2	39.6	0.3	6.0
Spain	2.9	119.6	0.8	31.0
Sweden	1.8	183.7	7.5	760.0
Switzerland	8.1	1,294.1	41.0	6,512.5
Turkey	0.4	4.0	*Not Available*	
Yugoslavia	8.3	9.3		
North America	5.4	705.0	7.5	971.6
Canada	19.3	2,285.3	9.6	1,118.4
United States	4.1	537.3	7.2	956.0
Other Developed Countries	3.0	228.4	4.9	375.5
Australia	10.2	1,051.2	1.8	184.2
Japan	0.4	35.1	4.7	448.6
New Zealand	10.0	730.4	1.7	122.8
South Africa	22.5	530.1	8.9	208.8
DEVELOPING AREAS	8.5	87.2	0.7	5.5
Africa (except S. Africa)	17.2	69.9	1.1	10.2
Botswana	42.5	342.0	*Not Available*	
Cameroon	12.2	90.7		
Central African Republic	21.5	57.8		
Congo	18.9	204.1		
Egypt	11.3	77.1		
Gabon	36.9	948.1		
Ghana	1.0	23.9		
Ivory Coast	10.2	115.5		

Table B6 (cont'd)

INDICATORS OF THE SIGNIFICANCE OF INWARD AND OUTWARD FOREIGN DIRECT CAPITAL STOCK TO VARIOUS NATIONAL ECONOMIES, 1982

	Inward Investment		Outward Investment	
	Capital Stock as % of GNP	*Capital Stock Per Head (US $)*	*Capital Stock as % of GNP*	*Capital Stock Per Head (US $)*
Kenya	9.8	27.7	0.4	1.0
Liberia	113.5	453.0	*Not Available*	
Libya	3.5	182.0	1.0	61.0
Malawi	39.6	59.8	*Not Available*	
Mauritius	12.3	67.9		
Morocco	5.0	33.5		
Nigeria	6.4	51.3		
Senegal	14.7	58.9		
Seychelles	35.9	815.6	17.2	385.9
Sierra Leone	6.3	22.9	*Not Available*	
Tanzania	4.3	10.9		
Togo	35.9	87.3		
Zaire	35.1	59.4		
Zambia	14.6	87.8		
Zimbabwe	40.7	259.1	1.2	7.7
Asia & Pacific (except Japan or Middle East)	4.1	16.8	0.9	3.7
Bangladesh	0.8	0.9	*Not Available*	
China	0.7	1.7		
Hong Kong	16.5	832.3	6.9	350.0
India	*Not Available*		0.1	0.2
Indonesia	5.6	30.4	*Not Available*	
S. Korea	1.9	33.2	0.5	9.2
Malaysia	27.0	469.1	0.1	1.2
Pakistan	2.9	9.6	*Not Available*	
Philippines	4.9	38.1	0.4	3.0
Singapore	7.1	869.9	4.0	484.3
Sri Lanka	4.9	14.8	*Not Available*	
Taiwan	2.0	51.6	0.1	3.6
Thailand	3.7	27.5	*Not Available*	
Latin America & Caribbean	11.5	195.6	0.5	8.1
Argentina	23.9	232.5	0.5	4.9
Barbados	20.1	767.7	0.7	26.9
Brazil	11.3	170.6	1.0	14.4
Chile	12.0	162.1	0.7	8.8
Colombia	6.0	77.7	0.8	10.5
Dominican Republic	10.1	135.1	*Not Available*	
Ecuador	10.3	78.1		
Guyana	47.3	212.6		
Jamaica	28.9	396.9		
Mexico	7.0	150.8		

Table B6 (cont'd)

INDICATORS OF THE SIGNIFICANCE OF INWARD AND OUTWARD FOREIGN DIRECT CAPITAL STOCK TO VARIOUS NATIONAL ECONOMIES, 1982

	Inward Investment		Outward Investment	
	Capital Stock as % of GNP	*Capital Stock Per Head (US $)*	*Capital Stock as % of GNP*	*Capital Stock Per Head (US $)*
Mexico	7.0	150.8	*neg.*	*neg.*
Panama	144.4	2,653.8		
Paraguay	4.0	77.2		
Peru	19.4	147.8	*Not Available*	
Trinidad & Tobago	80.8	2,980.5		
Uruguay	8.4	301.3		
Venezuela	10.0	416.4		
Middle East: Saudi Arabia	8.7	1,328.7		
Australasia	0.6	514.8	2.4	22.7
Fiji	41.5	556.5	0.5	5.9
Papua New Guinea	60.7	415.0	3.2	21.9

Table B7

AVERAGE ANNUAL FLOW OF FOREIGN DIRECT INVESTMENT, 1974 - 83 (US $ m)

	Inward Investment		Outward Investment	
	Average 1974-78	*Average 1978-83*	*Average 1974-78*	*Average 1978-83*
DEVELOPED AREAS	15,875.9	31,682.2	31,855.6	50,562.6
Europe	9,497.0	14,012.4	11,787.0	24,644.5
EEC	7,747.9	11,490.2	9,601.5	20,140.6
Belgium	1,039.8	1,433.4	306.2	298.2
Denmark	99.3	101.6	89.2	148.3
France	1,536.6	2,337.5	1,422.9	2,934.2
W. Germany	1,284.6	974.7	2,439.4	3,621.8
Greece	242.2	536.4	*Not Available*	
Ireland	179.3	247.4		
Italy	593.7	735.6	282.9	1,110.0
Netherlands	864.0	1,755.7	1,330.4	5,156.9
United Kingdom	1,908.4	3,367.9	3,730.5	6,871.2
Other Europe	1,749.1	2,522.2	2,185.5	4,503.9
Austria	129.5	264.1	57.4	193.3
Finland	49.6	14.9	42.7	178.3
Norway	437.4	368.9	139.2	227.8
Portugal	65.3	139.5	10.7	10.7
Spain	535.8	887.5	100.8	251.7
Sweden	78.3	159.6	523.0	846.5
Switzerland	335.1	558.1	1,311.7	2,795.6
Turkey	65.8	57.8	*Not Available*	
Yugoslavia	52.3	71.8		
North America	5,034.3	15,204.1	17,779.8	21,402.3
Canada	367.5	–582.5	5,141.0	10,394.7
United States	4,666.8	15,786.6	12,638.8	11,007.6
Other Developed Countries	1,344.6	2,465.7	2,288.8	4,515.8
Australia	985.8	1,841.7	246.1	548.6
Japan	114.8	311.2	1,947.8	3,641.2
New Zealand	196.5	272.9	15.0	93.1
South Africa	47.5	39.9	79.9	232.9
DEVELOPING AREAS	5,043.2	15,816.2	229.1	548.5
Africa (except S. Africa)	859.8	1,410.1	41.9	63.5
Botswana	25.9	77.3	0.1	0.1
Cameroon	22.8	129.5	2.7	–0.3
Central African Republic	4.8	9.1	0.7	*N.A.*
Congo	30.2	34.0	*Not Available*	
Egypt	136.3	807.6	–12.5	9.1
Gabon	75.4	76.9	15.4	6.2
Ghana	23.5	2.9	*Not Available*	
Ivory Coast	100.9	239.5		

Table B7

AVERAGE ANNUAL FLOW OF FOREIGN DIRECT INVESTMENT, 1974 - 83 (US $ m)

	Inward Investment		Outward Investment	
	Average 1974-78	*Average 1978-83*	*Average 1974-78*	*Average 1978-83*
Kenya	45.8	69.0	3.0	4.0
Liberia	54.8	42.0	*Not Available*	
Libya	−256.6	−628.0	18.4	27.8
Malawi	13.0	6.9	*Not Available*	
Mauritius	3.3	1.4	0.4	*N.A.*
Morocco	70.8	110.4	*Not Available*	
Nigeria	342.7	180.0		
Senegal	20.5	3.9	5.5	*N.A.*
Seychelles	5.5	7.6	2.3	4.5
Sierra Leone	11.7	2.3		
Tanzania	*N.A.*	11.5	*Not Available*	
Togo	15.0	34.6		
Zaire	83.3	137.3		
Zambia	25.0	42.1		
Zimbabwe	5.2	12.3	5.9	12.1
Asia & Pacific (except Japan or Middle East)	1,764.5	3,887.2	21.3	56.2
Bangladesh	6.5	3.0		
China	*N.A.*	22.8	*Not Available*	
Hong Kong	169.3	549.2		
India	−8,3	*N.A.*		
Indonesia	307.2	211.5		
S. Korea	90.5	83.7	17.8	53.8
Malaysia	364.0	1,097.8	*Not Available*	
Pakistan	16.2	64.8		
Philippines	108.8	38.9	3.5	*N.A.*
Singapore	586.4	1,554.6		
Sri Lanka	0.4	48.1	*Not Available*	
Taiwan	21.7	*N.A.*		
Thailand	101.8	212.8	*N.A.*	2.4
Latin America & Caribbean	2,733.3	5,738.6	155.1	416.7
Argentina	197.0	390.6	12.0	64.0
Barbados	9.8	7.5	0.4	0.7
Brazil	1,385.0	2,266.2	121.4	205.6
Chile	56.5	286.5	4.3	26.4
Colombia	62.3	306.8	17.0	60.0
Dominican Republic	60.0	63.1		
Ecuador	47.3	64.4		
Guyana	6.8	2.2	*Not Available*	
Jamaica	8.8	7.9		
Mexico	649.0	1,626.2		

Table B7

AVERAGE ANNUAL FLOW OF FOREIGN DIRECT INVESTMENT, 1974 - 83 (US $ m)

	Inward Investment		Outward Investment	
	Average 1974-78	*Average 1978-83*	*Average 1974-78*	*Average 1978-83*
Panama	11.9	73.3	*Not Available*	
Paraguay	20.1	31.0		
Peru	142.0	61.8		
Trinidad & Tobago	125.9	233.4		
Uruguay	101.3	183.8		
Venezuela	–150.4	133.9		
Middle East: Saudi Arabia	–374.5	4,664.8		
Australasia	60.1	115.5	10.8	12.1
Fiji	14.4	30.2	2.6	0.4
Papua New Guinea	45.7	85.3	8.2	11.7
TOTAL	20,919.1	47,498.4	32,084.7	51,111.1

Table B8

ANNUAL FLOW OF INWARD FOREIGN DIRECT INVESTMENT, 1979 - 84 (US $ m)

	INWARD INVESTMENT					
	1979	*1980*	*1981*	*1982*	*1983*	*1984*
DEVELOPED AREAS	29,466.5	38,698.8	37,251.2	26,353.3	26,426.9	37,949.7
Europe	15,265.4	18,756.4	13,190.8	9,855.0	12,780.2	11,585.5
EEC	12,874.3	16,148.5	9,886.9	7,727.2	10,815.4	9,791.9
Belgium	1,006.2	2,572.1	1,352.0	1,389.8	847.8	400.8
Denmark	103.4	105.4	100.2	134.7	64.2	9.3
France	2,745.4	3,294.2	2,432.9	1,573.8	1,641.3	2,408.8
W. Germany	1,718.0	416.5	318.6	827.9	1,592.8	1,166.8
Greece	612.4	672.9	520.0	437.2	439.4	485.8
Ireland	336.8	286.9	204.0	241.8	167.5	119.3
Italy	374.4	540.6	1,085.8	588.3	1,088.9	1,171.0
Netherlands	2,284.2	2,349.0	1,849.6	653.1	1,642.9	436.3
United Kingdom	3,693.5	5,910.9	2,023.8	1,880.6	3,330.6	3,593.8
Other Europe	2,391.1	2,607.9	3,303.9	2,127.8	1,964.8	1,793.6
Austria	187.3	238.1	332.5	272.7	289.7	145.5
Finland	27.2	27.9	17.4	−13.9	15.8	53.9
Norway	400.5	59.9	681.6	441.6	260.8	−163.0
Portugal	78.8	157.6	174.5	145.6	141.1	195.8
Spain	810.1	926.1	917.2	969.0	814.9	918.5
Sweden	110.8	254.4	195.9	207.6	29.5	143.5
Switzerland	632.9	850.6	889.6	50.1	367.1	386.9
Turkey	75.0	18.2	95.2	55.1	45.9	112.5
Yugoslavia	68.5	75.1	*Not Available*			
North America	12,517.3	17,602.2	20,731.0	13,062.5	12,107.3	24,351.7
Canada	640.3	684.2	−3,670.0	−729.5	162.3	1,837.7
United States	11,877.0	16,918.0	24,401.0	13,792.0	11,945.0	22,514.0
Other Developed Countries	1,683.8	2,340.2	3,329.4	3,435.8	1,539.4	2,012.5
Australia	1,513.7	1,738.2	2,734.0	2,367.1	855.3	1,819.5
Japan	245.0	274.0	189.0	445.0	403.0	−10.0
New Zealand	269.9	333.9	346.4	223.1	191.5	160.9
South Africa	−344.8	−5.9	60.0	400.6	89.6	39.1
DEVELOPING AREAS	7,860.0	5,588.0	20,413.5	23,793.3	14,165.1	12,373.8
Africa (except S. Africa)	1,886.3	−812.5	1,500.9	1,464.8	1,623.4	505.6
Botswana	127.9	124.8	88.8	21.2	23.8	47.5
Cameroon	62.1	129.8	135.0	108.7	212.0	*Not Available*
Central African Republic	23.3	5.2	5.9	8.8	2.1	
Congo	17.4	37.6	29.2	34.5	51.3	
Egypt	1,215.7	548.0	752.3	658.0	863.7	
Gabon	55.0	31.5	54.6	131.8	111.8	
Ghana	−0.8	4.4	5.0	5.4	0.8	0.6
Ivory Coast	272.1	344.1	102.3	*Not Available*		

Table B8 (cont'd)

ANNUAL FLOW OF INWARD FOREIGN DIRECT INVESTMENT, 1979 - 84 (US $ m)

	Inward Investment					
	1979	*1980*	*1981*	*1982*	*1983*	*1984*
Kenya	84.0	79.4	62.2	65.1	54.5	56.9
Liberia		*Not Available*		34.8	49.1	39.0
Libya	–587.7	–1,689.3	–744.1	–391.8	–326.9	*N.A.*
Malawi	12.9	6.5	1.2		*Not Available*	
Mauritius	1.8	1.2	0.7	1.8	1.6	4.9
Morocco	100.7	129.8	114.7	133.7	72.9	47.2
Nigeria	310.1	–739.4	545.9	429.4	353.9	294.2
Senegal	3.9	1.9	5.2	4.5	*N.A.*	*N.A.*
Seychelles	6.5	7.8	8.3	8.8	6.4	5.5
Sierra Leone	16.0	–18.6	7.6	4.6	1.9	*N.A.*
Tanzania	8.0	4.6	18.9	14.3	*N.A.*	*N.A.*
Togo	53.9	41.4	8.5		*Not Available*	
Zaire	60.1	56.0	255.9	176.5	138.2	*N.A.*
Zambia	34.9	57.3	34.2		*Not Available*	
Zimbabwe	8.5	23.5	8.6	14.7	6.3	9.8
Asia & Pacific (except Japan or Middle East)	2,330.0	3,443.1	5,021.7	4,476.8	3,698.2	3,215.8
Bangladesh	–8.0	8.5	5.4	1.0	0.4	–1.6
China	0.1	23.5	26.0	41.6	*N.A.*	*N.A.*
Hong Kong	342.1	373.9	952.9	527.8	*N.A.*	*N.A.*
Indonesia	226.1	183.5	133.2	226.3	288.6	226.5
S. Korea	36.2	7.8	101.4	146.8	126.1	111.7
Malaysia	573.7	934.5	1,265.2	1,397.7	1,318.1	982.0
Pakistan	62.0	58.6	107.3	65.1	31.0	*N.A.*
Philippines	7.8	–106.7	173.3	15.5	104.8	–6.1
Singapore	940.5	1,668.5	1,916.1	1,802.8	1,445.3	1,457.5
Sri Lanka	46.8	42.9	49.3	63.6	37.7	32.6
Taiwan	51.4	61.7		*Not Available*		
Thailand	51.3	186.4	291.6	188.6	346.2	413.2
Latin America & Caribbean	4,958.0	5,969.4	7,357.4	6,584.6	3,638.1	3,292.4
Argentina	204.0	681.0	823.0	225.0	184.0	269.0
Barbados	5.3	1.5	8.3	4.5	17.7	*N.A.*
Brazil	2,411.0	1,913.0	2,526.0	2,922.0	1,556.0	1,598.0
Chile	247.2	213.4	383.2	400.8	188.1	77.9
Colombia	126.6	157.5	265.3	366.5	617.9	431.5
Dominican Republic	17.1	92.6	79.7	*N.A.*	48.2	*N.A.*
Ecuador	63.2	70.4	60.0	39.6	88.8	50.1
Guyana	1.6	0.7	–0.6	4.4	4.2	*N.A.*
Jamaica	–25.8	27.3	11.8	15.4	10.9	23.8
Mexico	1,334.6	2,184.0	2,514.1	1,643.9	454.3	391.5
Panama	50.4	46.9	36.6	277.1	49.2	*N.A.*
Paraguay	50.4	31.2	32.0	36.7	4.9	5.2
Peru	71.0	27.0	128.0	46.0	37.0	88.0

Table B8 (cont'd)

ANNUAL FLOW OF INWARD FOREIGN DIRECT INVESTMENT, 1979 - 84 (US $ m)

	Inward Investment					
	1979	*1980*	*1981*	*1982*	*1983*	*1984*
Trinidad & Tobago	93.8	184.5	258.1	345.5	285.0	299.0
Uruguay	219.7	283.7	48.0		*Not Available*	
Venezuela	87.9	54.7	183.9	257.2	91.9	58.4
Middle East:						
Saudi Arabia	−1,368.7	−3.126.2	6,415.2	11,145.5	5,036.6	5,221.6
Australasia	54.4	114.2	118.3	121.6	168.8	138.4
Fiji	10.3	38.9	35.0	35.1	31.5	21.9
Papua New Guinea	44.1	75.3	83.3	86.5	137.3	116.5
TOTAL	37,326.5	44,286.8	57,664.7	50,146.6	40,592.0	50,323.5

Table B9

ANNUAL FLOW OF OUTWARD FOREIGN DIRECT INVESTMENT, 1979 - 84 (US $ m)

	Outward Investment					
	1979	*1980*	*1981*	*1982*	*1983*	*1984*
DEVELOPED AREAS	61.947.3	65,786.6	55,671.1	20,308.5	36,756.0	36,248.4
Europe	24,994.1	33,521.4	26,942.2	15,285.6	22,252.9	20,434.3
EEC	20,278.7	24,804.7	24,355.1	12,791.8	18,246.2	13,973.4
Belgium	1,118.7	61.6	29.6	−76.6	357.9	295.2
Denmark	*N.A.*	195.2	140.4	79.5	99.4	95.3
France	1,977.7	3,149.1	4,623.5	3,072.8	1,848.1	2,134.1
W. Germany	4,492.9	4,080.4	3,883.2	2,485.0	3,167.3	3,074.9
Italy	567.2	694.3	1,330.0	1,012.4	1,946.4	1,810.5
Netherlands	5,684.0	8,908.5	3,936.8	1,791.3	5,464.1	2,555.6
United Kingdom	6,438.2	7,715.6	10,411.6	4,427.4	5,363.0	4,007.8
Other Europe	4,715.4	8,716.7	2,587.1	2,493.8	4,006.7	6,460.9
Austria	85.3	339.7	209.9	147.9	183.9	77.9
Finland	125.0	130.6	141.8	233.4	260.5	412.5
Norway	43.9	253.8	182.8	304.7	353.8	539.2
Portugal	−7.7	14.3	18.9	9.9	18.2	10.2
Spain	189.0	257.2	181.8	445.6	184.9	243.7
Sweden	609.0	632.9	906.7	1,051.5	1,032.5	998.4
Switzerland	3,670.9	7,088.2	945.2	300.8	1,972.9	4,178.0
North America	33,638.4	28,863.6	22,750.2	−299.0	9,940.5	8,713.7
Canada	8,416.4	9,641.6	13,126.2	4,125.0	4,546.5	4,210.7
United States	25,222.0	19,222.0	9,624.0	−4,424.0	5,394.0	4,503.0
Other Developed Countries	3,314.8	3,401.6	5,978.7	5,321.9	4,562.6	7,100.4
Australia	254.5	516.9	509.3	718.3	744.0	1,353.5
Japan	2,956.0	2,340.0	4,850.0	4,528.0	3,532.0	5,685.0
New Zealand	97.0	115.0	89.5	87.2	77.0	64.6
South Africa	7.3	429.7	529.9	−11.6	209.6	−2.7
DEVELOPING AREAS	389.4	1,046.8	481.4	596.0	502.6	127.7
Africa (except S. Africa)	55.9	82.6	55.0	62.3	43.3	14.5
Botswana	*N.A.*	2.3	−0.1	*N.A.*	−1.3	
Cameroon	−2.1	−8.3	−0.5	4.4	5.2	*Not Available*
Egypt	5.1	6.6	5.9	8.9	19.3	
Gabon	6.7	7.9	7.1	4.9	5.8	
Kenya	6.5	1.3	2.3	5.5	4.3	
Libya	20.6	46.9	24.6	18.9	*N.A.*	
Mauritius	2.5			*Not Available*		
Nigeria	5.1					
Seychelles	3.1	3.9	7.1	5.0	3.2	3.9
Zimbabwe	8.4	22.0	8.6	14.7	6.8	10.6

Table B9 (cont'd)

ANNUAL FLOW OF OUTWARD FOREIGN DIRECT INVESTMENT, 1979 - 84 (US $ m)

	Outward Investment					
	1979	*1980*	*1981*	*1982*	*1983*	*1984*
Asia & Pacific (except Japan or Middle East)	23.3	28.6	44.7	70.6	127.2	37.9
India	*N.A.*	13.0	*Not Available*			
S. Korea	19.4	13.0	42.4	68.4	126.1	36.9
Thailand	3.9	2.6	2.3	2.2	1.1	1.0
Latin America & Caribbean	290.4	920.5	374.9	449.9	326.8	74.8
Argentina	59.0	111.0	107.0	29.0	−2.0	*N.A.*
Barbados	0.3	0.7	1.2	0.2	1.4	*N.A.*
Brazil	195.0	370.0	209.0	371.0	183.0	43.0
Chile	11.6	43.0	21.2	16.6	39.6	11.3
Colombia	24.5	105.4	36.5	28.7	104.8	20.5
Venezuela	*Not Available*			4.4	*Not Available*	
Australisia	19.8	15.1	6.8	13.2	5.3	0.5
Fiji	*N.A.*	2.4	−1.5	0.7	0.1	0.5
Papua New Guinea	19.8	12.7	8.3	12.5	5.2	*N.A.*
TOTAL	62,336.7	66,833.4	56,152.5	20,904.5	37,258.6	36,376.1

Table B10

15 LARGEST OUTWARD INVESTORS, BY SIZE OF FOREIGN DIRECT CAPITAL STOCK 1975 AND 1983 (US $ m)

		1975	*% Distribution*	*1983*	*% Distribution*
1	USA	124,050,0	44.2	226,962.0	38.4
2	UK	37,001.7	13.2	88,543.2	15.0
3	Japan	15,941.0	5.7	61,276.0	10.4
4	Switzerland	22,442.7	8.0	40,532.2	6.9
5	Netherlands	19,922.3	7.1	39,120.9	6.6
6	W. Germany	14,353.8	5.1	38,934.6	6.6
7	Canada	10,356.2	3.7	28,795.4	4.9
8	France	10,607.5	3.8	17,242.3	2.9
9	Italy	3,298.7	1.2	8,495.3	1.4
10	Sweden	4,670.4	1.7	6,761.4	1.1
11	South Africa	2,867.3	1.0	5,679.7	1.0
12	Belgium	3,038.4	0.4	4,211.0	0.7
13	Australia	1,108.8	1.1	2,997.9	0.5
14	Hong Kong	*N.S.A.*	—	2,540.0	0.4
15	Brazil	279.0	0.1	2,010.0	0.3
	Other Countries	10,197.8[1]	3.6	591,572.4[2]	2.9
	TOTAL	280,135.6[1]	100.0	591,572.4[2]	100.0

NOTES TO TABLE B10

1 Authors' estimate. The total diverges from that in Tables B1 to B9 due to the lack of data for 1975 on South Africa, Austria, and New Zealand which we have approximated for inclusion here. It is also due to the underestimation of developing country outward investment in the official sources that have been used in Tables B1 to B9 which we have revised accordingly here.

2 Authors' estimate. The total diverges from that in Tables B1 to B9 due to the lack of data for 1983 on 5 developing countries which we have approximated for inclusion here. The authors estimate that 2.7% of total world outward investment is from developing countries.

Table B11

15 LARGEST INWARD INVESTORS, BY SIZE OF FOREIGN DIRECT CAPITAL STOCK 1975 AND 1983 (US $ m)

		1975	*% Distribution*	*1983*	*% Distribution*
1	USA	27,662.0	11.2	137,061.0	25.4
2	Canada	36,785.7	14.9	59,924.5	11.1
3	UK	24,490.4	9.9	52,700.3	9.7
4	W. Germany	23,075.2	9.4	29,587.3	5.5
5	Brazil	6,890.0	2.8	23,200.0	4.3
6	South Africa	8,544.5	3.5	21,041.1	3.9
7	Saudi Arabia	650.0	0.3	16,940.0	3.1
8	Netherlands	9,812.9	4.0	16,924.5	3.1
9	Australia	8,846.2	3.6	16,138.2	3.0
10	Mexico	4,800.0	1.9	14,898.2	2.8
11	France	9,497.3	3.9	13,426.1	2.5
12	Belgium	4,176.8	1.7	9,085.2	1.7
13	Malaysia	2,300.0	0.9	8,075.1	1.5
14	Switzerland	4,084.0	1.7	8,029.4	1.5
15	Italy	9,113.5	3.7	7,320.3	1.4
	Other Countries	65,938.8[1]	26.7	106,193.6	19.6
	TOTAL	246,667.3[1]	100.0	540,544.8	100.0

NOTES TO TABLE B11

1 Authors' estimate. The total diverges from that in Tables B1 to B9 due to the lack of data for 1975 on Egypt, Liberia, Malawi, China and Uruguay, which we have approximated for inclusion here.

Table B12

A. 15 LARGEST NET DEBTOR NATIONS, BY THE SIZE OF NET INWARD FOREIGN DIRECT CAPITAL STOCK, 1975 AND 1983 (US $ m)

i. 1975				*ii. 1983*		
1	Canada	26,429.5		1	Canada	31,129.1
2	W. Germany	8,721.4		2	Brazil	21,190.0
3	Australia	7,737.4		3	S. Africa	15,361.4
4	Nigeria	7,384.1		4	Mexico	14,895.0
5	Brazil	6,890.0		5	Australia	13,140.3
6	Italy	5,814.8		6	Venezuela	7,291.6
7	Panama	5,081.7		7	Argentina	7,091.0
8	Mexico	4,800.0		8	Panama	5,463.0
9	Venezuela	3,773.4		9	Indonesia	4,990.6
10	Zimbabwe	2,786.5		10	Belgium	4,874.2
11	Spain	2,468.8		11	Greece	4,840.5
12	Malaysia	2,300.0		12	Egypt	4,308.4
13	Indonesia	2,285.2		13	Trinidad & Tobago	3,653.0
14	Argentina	2,266.0		14	Spain	3,573.9
15	India	2,163.9		15	Nigeria	3,517.4

B. LARGEST NET CREDITOR NATIONS, BY THE SIZE OF NET OUTWARD FOREIGN DIRECT CAPITAL STOCK, 1975 AND 1983 (US $ m)

i. 1975				*ii. 1983*		
1	USA	96,388.0		1	USA	89,901.0
2	Switzerland	18,358.7		2	Japan	56,302.0
3	Japan	14,444.0		3	UK	35,842.9
4	UK	12,511.3		4	Switzerland	32,502.8
5	Netherlands	10,109.4		5	Netherlands	22,196.4
6	Sweden	3,243.8		6	W. Germany	9,347.3
7	France	1,110.2		7	Sweden	5,337.8
				8	France	3,816.2
				9	Italy	1,175.0
				10	Finland	662.7

Table B13

COUNTRIES MOST DEPENDENT ON OUTWARD INVESTMENT IN 1982 AS INDICATED BY FOREIGN DIRECT CAPITAL STOCK AS A PROPORTION OF GNP

	Country	%
1	Switzerland	41.0
2	Netherlands	28.5
3	UK	19.5
4	Seychelles	17.2
5	Canada	9.6
6	S. Africa	8.9
7	Sweden	7.5
8	USA	7.2
9	Hong Kong	6.9
10	W. Germany	6.0

Table B14

COUNTRIES MOST DEPENDENT ON INWARD INVESTMENT IN 1982 AS INDICATED BY FOREIGN DIRECT CAPITAL STOCK AS A PROPORTION OF GNP

	Country	%
1	Panama	144.4
2	Liberia	113.5
3	Trinidad & Tobago	80.8
4	Papua New Guinea	60.7
5	Guyana	47.3
6	Botswana	42.5
7	Fiji	41.5
8	Zimbabwe	40.7
9	Malawi	39.6
10	Gabon	36.9

Table B15

WORLD STOCK OF OUTWARD DIRECT INVESTMENT BY REGION (US $ m)

	Amount		*Percentage Distribution*		*Annual Average Growth Rate*
	1975	*1983*	*1975*	*1983*	*1975-83*
All Countries	280,135.6	591,572.4[1]	100.0	100.0	9.7
DEVELOPED AREAS	272,035.6	575,599.9	97.1	97.3	9.8
Europe	117,687.3	249,466.4	42.0	42.2	9.8
EEC	88,680.4	197.518.3	31.7	33.4	10.5
UK	37,001.7	88,543.2	13.2	15.0	19.1
Netherlands	19,922.3	39,120.9	7.1	6.6	8.8
W. Germany	14,353.8	38,934.6	5.1	6.6	13.3
France	10,607.5	17,242.3	3.8	2.9	10.2
Other Europe	29,006.9	51,948.1	10.4	8.8	7.6
Switzerland	22,442.7	40,532.2	8.0	6.9	7.7
Sweden	4,670.4	6,761.4	1.7	1.1	4.7
Norway	728.7	1,565.6	0.3	0.3	1.0
North America	134,406.2	255,757.4	48.0	43.2	8.4
USA	124,050.0	226,962.0	44.3	38.4	7.8
Canada	10,356.2	28,795.4	3.7	4.9	13.6
Other Developed Countries	19,942.1	70,376.1	7.1	11.9	17.1
Japan	15,941.0	61,276.0	5.7	10.4	18.3
S. Africa	2,867.3	5,679.7	1.0	1.0	8.9
DEVELOPING AREAS	8,100.0	15,972.5[1]	2.9	2.7	6.0
Africa		698.6[1]		0.1	
Asia & Pacific		9,509.0[1]		1.6	
Hong Kong		2,540.0		0.4	
Latin America & Caribbean	*Not Available*	5,581,7[1]	*Not Available*	0.9	*Not Available*
Brazil		2,010.0		0.3	
Australasia		183.2[1]		0.03	

1 Total diverges from that in Table B1 owing to the estimation by the authors of total developing area investment, which has been divided between regions in the same proportions as in Table B1. This is due to the underestimation of developing country outward investment in the official sources used in Table B1.

Table B16

WORLD STOCK OF INWARD DIRECT INVESTMENT BY REGION (US $ m)

	Amount		*Percentage Distribution*		*Annual Average Growth Rate*
	1975	*1983*	*1975*	*1983*	*1975-83*
All Countries	246,667.3	540,544.8	100.0	100.0	10.3
DEVELOPED AREAS	183,399.4	401,084.8	74.4	74.2	10.3
Europe	98,710.6	159,696.0	40.0	29.5	6.2
EEC	85,555.3	138,308.1	34.7	25.5	6.2
UK	24,490.4	52,700.3	9.9	9.7	10.1
W. Germany	23,075.2	29,587.3	9.4	5.5	3.2
Netherlands	9,812.9	16,924.5	4.0	3.1	7.1
France	9,497.3	13,426.1	3.8	2.5	4.4
Belgium	4,176.8	9,085.2	1.7	1.7	10.2
Other Europe	13,155.3	21,387.9	5.3	4.0	6.3
Switzerland	4,084.0	8,029.4	1.6	1.5	8.8
Spain	2,909.3	4,789.2	1.2	0.9	6.4
Norway	1,541.6	3,436.8	0.6	0.6	10.5
North America	64,447.7	196,985.5	26.1	36.4	15.0
USA	27,662.0	137,061.0	11.2	25.3	22.1
Canada	36,785.7	59,924.5	14.9	11.1	6.3
Other Developed Countries	20,241.1	44,403.3	8.2	8.2	10.3
South Africa	8,544.5	21,041.1	3.5	3.9	11.9
Australia	8,846.2	16,138.2	3.6	3.0	7.8
DEVELOPING AREAS	63,267.9	139,460.0	25.6	25.8	10.4
Africa	19,273.6	19,271.1	7.8	3.6	−1.0
Egypt	3,828.4	4,308.4	1.6	0.8	1.5
Nigeria	7,384.1	3,517.4	3.0	0.7	−9.7
Zaire	996.1	1,936.7	0.4	0.4	8.7
Zimbabwe	2,786.5	1,631.6	1.1	0.3	6.9
Asia & Pacific	13,039.0	28,120.8	5.3	5.2	10.1
Malaysia	2,300.0	8,075.1	0.9	1.5	17.0
Indonesia	2,285.2	4,990.6	0.9	0.9	10.2
Hong Kong	1,300.0	4,720.3	0.5	0.9	17.5
Philippines	485.2	1,985.7	0.2	0.4	19.3
Latin America & Caribbean	29,386.6	73,246.2	11.9	13.6	12.1
Brazil	6,890.0	23,200.0	2.8	4.3	16.4
Mexico	4,800.0	14,898.2	1.9	2.8	15.2
Venezuela	3,773.4	7,291.6	1.5	1.3	8.6
Argentina	2,284.0	7,233.0	0.9	1.3	15.5
Panama	5,081.7	5,463.0	2.1	1.0	0.9
Middle East	650.0	16,940.0	0.3	3.1	50.3
Saudi Arabia	650.0	16,940.0	0.3	3.1	50.3
Australasia	918.7	1,881.9	0.4	0.3	9.4
Papua New Guinea	646.4	1,516.8	0.3	0.3	11.3

Table B17

AVERAGE ANNUAL FLOWS OF OUTWARD DIRECT INVESTMENT 1974 - 78 AND 1979 - 83 (US $ m)

	1974-78	*1979-83*
All Countries	32,084.7	51,111.1
DEVELOPED AREAS	31,855.6	50,562.6
Europe	11,787.0	24,644.5
EEC	9,601.5	20,140.6
UK	3,730.5	6,871.2
Netherlands	1,330.4	5,156.9
W. Germany	2,439.4	3,621.8
France	1,422.9	2,934.2
Italy	282.9	1,110.0
Other Europe	2,185.5	4,503.9
Switzerland	1,311.7	2,795.6
Sweden	523.0	846.0
Spain	100.8	251.7
North America	17,779.8	21,402.3
Canada	5,141.0	10,394.7
USA	12,638.8	11,007.6
Other Developed Countries	2,288.8	4,515.8
Japan	1,947.8	3,641.2
Australia	246.1	548.6
DEVELOPING AREAS	229.1	548.5
Africa	41.9	63.5
Libya	18.4	27.8
Zimbabwe	5.9	12.1
Asia & Pacific	21.3	56.2
S. Korea	17.8	53.8
Latin America & Caribbean	155.1	416.7
Brazil	121.4	265.6
Argentina	12.0	64.0
Colombia	17.0	60.0
Australasia	10.8	12.1

Table B18

AVERAGE ANNUAL FLOWS OF INWARD DIRECT INVESTMENT 1974 - 78 AND 1979 - 83 (US $ m)

	1974-78	*1979-83*
All Countries	20,919.1	47,498.4
DEVELOPED AREAS	15,875.9	31,682.2
Europe	9,497.0	14,012.4
EEC	7,747.9	11,490.2
UK	1,908.4	3,367.9
France	1,536.6	2,337.5
Netherlands	864.0	1,755.7
Belgium	1,039.8	1,433.4
W. Germany	1,284.6	974.7
Other Europe	1,749.1	2,522.2
Spain	535.8	887.5
Switzerland	335.1	558.1
Norway	437.4	368.9
North America	5,034.3	15,204.1
Canada	367.5	–582.5
USA	4,666.8	15,786.6
Other Developed Countries	1,344.6	2,465.7
Australia	985.8	1,841.7
Japan	114.8	311.2
DEVELOPING AREAS	5,043.2	15,816.2
Africa	859.8	1,410.1
Egypt	136.3	807.6
Ivory Coast	100.9	239.5
Nigeria	342.7	180.0
Asia & Pacific	1,764.5	3,887.2
Singapore	586.4	1,554.6
Malaysia	364.0	1,097.8
Hong Kong	169.3	549.2
Latin America & Caribbean	2,733.3	5,738.6
Brazil	1,385.0	2,266.2
Mexico	649.0	1,626.2
Middle East	–374.5	4,664.8
Saudi Arabia	–374.5	4,664.8
Australasia	60.1	115.5
Papua New Guinea	45.7	85.3